NetBSD system operation and maintenance manuals

NetBSD System Manager's Manual
Volume 1 of 2
ac(8) - multiboot(8)

Title: NetBSD System Manager's Manual (Volume 1 of 2)
Subtitle: NetBSD system operation and maintenance manuals
Editor: Jeremy C. Reed
Publisher: Reed Media Services
Website: http://www.reedmedia.net/

Set ISBN 978-0-9790342-4-4
Volume 1 ISBN 978-0-9790342-5-1
Volume 2 ISBN 978-0-9790342-6-8

Contents

Preface

This is volume 1 of the NetBSD System Manager's Manual.

This two volume set contains a permuted index (in volume 1) and the definitive and official NetBSD system operation and maintenance manual from **ac** through **zpool**.

While this book is not officially published by NetBSD, it does contain the definitive documentation as maintained and distributed with the open source NetBSD operating system. It was compiled by Jeremy C. Reed, an active member of The NetBSD Foundation. Many documentation improvements from this book were *committed* into the official NetBSD source.

This set includes the section 8 manuals and a selection of section 1 manuals that also cover system maintenance procedures and commands. This book was published in May 2010 and reflects both NetBSD 5 and many features in the upcoming NetBSD 6.

This documentation was provided by a wide range of developers and projects. The many copyrights and licenses are included at the end of volume 2.

Historically, the System Manager's Manual (SMM) also included other system installation and administration documentation. Much of the original SMM and the Programmer's Supplementary Documents (PSD) and User's Supplementary Documents (USD), since published in print in 1994, have become stagnant and out-of-date or cover software or features no longer included with NetBSD. This printing does not include that unmaintained documentation. If you are interested in helping update this aged documentation, see the `src/share/doc/{smm,usd,psd}/` source files and contact the `netbsd-docs@NetBSD.org` mailing list. NetBSD also provides other open source books: *The NetBSD Guide*, *The pkgsrc Guide*, and *NetBSD Internals* (for developers).

Donations to NetBSD

The NetBSD Foundation is a non-profit organization that produces widely-used open source software. The Foundation has no regular source of income and relies on generous donations. The Foundation has U.S. Internal Revenue Code 501(c)(3) status. Please donate by visiting `http://www.NetBSD.org/donations/` or by emailing `finance-exec@NetBSD.org`.

A portion of the profits from this printed book will also be donated to The NetBSD Foundation.

License acknowledgements

Several of the documents require acknowledgements. For further details, please see the copyrights and licenses at the end of Volume 2.

- This product includes software developed by Berkeley Software Design, Inc.
- This product includes software developed by Bill Paul.

- This product includes software developed by Christian E. Hopps.
- This product includes software developed by Christopher G. Demetriou.
- This product includes software developed by Jonathan Stone.
- This product includes software developed by Marshall M. Midden.
- This product includes software developed by Matthew Fredette.
- This product includes software developed by Mike Pritchard.
- This product includes software developed by Minoura Makoto.
- This product includes software developed by TooLs GmbH.
- This product includes software developed by Winning Strategies, Inc.
- This product includes software developed by Zembu Labs, Inc.
- This product includes software developed by the Computer Systems Engineering Group at Lawrence Berkeley Laboratory.
- This product includes software developed by the NetBSD Foundation, Inc. and its contributors.
- This product includes software developed by the University of California, Berkeley and its contributors.
- This product includes software developed by the University of California, Berkeley.
- This product includes software developed by the University of California, Lawrence Berkeley Laboratory and its contributors.
- This product includes software developed by the University of Southern California, Information Sciences Institute.
- This product includes software developed by the WIDE Project, Japan.
- This product includes software developed for the NetBSD Project by Emmanuel Dreyfus.
- This product includes software developed for the NetBSD Project by Frank van der Linden
- This product includes software developed for the NetBSD Project by John M. Vinopal.
- This product includes software developed for the NetBSD Project by Perry E. Metzger.
- This product includes software developed for the NetBSD Project by Scott Bartram and Frank van der Linden
- This product includes software developed for the NetBSD Project by Wasabi Systems, Inc.
- This product includes software developed for the NetBSD Project. See `http://www.NetBSD.org/` for information about NetBSD.

Permuted Index

pcnfsd, rpc.pcnfsd: (PC)NFS authentication and	print request server.	rpc.pcnfsd(8)
bootptest: send BOOTP queries and	print responses.	bootptest(8)
sa:	print system accounting statistics.	sa(8)
traceroute6:	print the route IPv6 packets will take to the destination.	traceroute6(8)
traceroute:	print the route packets take to network host.	traceroute(8)
lpc: line	printer control program.	lpc(8)
lpd: line	printer spooler daemon.	lpd(8)
pac:	printer/plotter accounting information.	pac(8)
renice: alter	priority of running processes.	renice(8)
pam_ssh: authentication and session management with SSH	private keys.	pam_ssh(8)
tlsmgr: Postfix TLS session cache and	PRNG manager.	tlsmgr(8)
mopprobe: MOP	Probe Utility.	mopprobe(1)
kcm: is a	process based credential cache for Kerberos tickets..	kcm(8)
init:	process control initialization.	init(8)
mount_procfs: mount the	process file system.	mount_procfs(8)
master: Postfix master	process.	master(8)
ypset: tell ypbind(8) which NIS server	process to use.	ypset(8)
schedctl: control scheduling of	processes and threads.	schedctl(8)
renice: alter priority of running	processes.	renice(8)
supfilesrv, supscan: sup server	processes.	supservers(8)
psrset: control	processor sets.	psrset(8)
kgmon: generate a dump of the operating system's	profile buffers.	kgmon(8)
pam_permit:	Promiscuous PAM module.	pam_permit(8)
iprop, ipropd-master, ipropd-slave:	propagate changes to a Heimdal Kerberos master KDC to slave KDCs.	iprop(8)
hprop:	propagate the KDC database.	hprop(8)
hpropd: receive a	propagated database.	hpropd(8)
pppd: Point-to-Point	Protocol Daemon.	pppd(8)
sdpd: Bluetooth Service Discovery	Protocol daemon.	sdpd(8)
dhclient: Dynamic Host Configuration	Protocol (DHCP) Client.	dhclient(8)
mount_9p: mount a file server using the 9P resource sharing	protocol.	mount_9p(8)
ndp: control/diagnose IPv6 neighbor discovery	protocol.	ndp(8)
sup: software upgrade	protocol.	sup(1)
rmt: remote magtape	protocol module.	rmt(8)
mopd: Maintenance Operations	Protocol (MOP) Loader Daemon.	mopd(8)
ftp-proxy: Internet File Transfer	Protocol proxy daemon.	ftp-proxy(8)
tftp-proxy: Internet Trivial File Transfer	Protocol proxy.	tftp-proxy(8)
dhcrelay: Dynamic Host Configuration	Protocol Relay Agent.	dhcrelay(8)
dhcpd: Dynamic Host Configuration	Protocol Server.	dhcpd(8)
ftpd: Internet File Transfer	Protocol server.	ftpd(8)
identd: TCP/IP Ident	protocol server.	identd(8)
ndbootd: Sun Network Disk (ND)	Protocol server.	ndbootd(8)
telnetd: DARPA TELNET	protocol server.	telnetd(8)
tftpd: DARPA Internet Trivial File Transfer	Protocol server.	tftpd(8)
bootpd, bootpgw: Internet Boot	Protocol server/gateway.	bootpd(8)
trpt: transliterate	protocol trace.	trpt(8)
isdntrace: isdn4bsd ISDN	protocol trace utility.	isdntrace(8)
httpd: hyper text transfer	protocol version 1.1 daemon.	httpd(8)
ipwctl: configure Intel	PRO/Wireless 2100 network adapter.	ipwctl(8)

Manuals

ac(8) – multiboot(8)

NAME

     `intro` — introduction to system maintenance procedures and commands

DESCRIPTION

     This section contains information related to system operation and maintenance.

     It describes commands used to create new file systems (`newfs`(8)), verify the integrity of the file systems (`fsck`(8)), control disk usage (`edquota`(8)), maintain system backups (`dump`(8)), and recover files when disks die an untimely death (`restore`(8)). The `format`(8) manual for the specific architecture the system is running on should be consulted when formatting disks and tapes. Network related services like `inetd`(8) and `ftpd`(8) are also described.

     A number of pages in this section describe general system management topics. For example, the `diskless`(8) page describes how to boot a system over a network, and the `compat_linux`(8) page describes how to run Linux binaries on NetBSD architectures that support it. Other system management topics are covered in `afterboot`(8), `kerberos`(8), `i386/multiboot`(8), `nis`(8), `pam`(8), `security`(8), and `veriexec`(8).

HISTORY

     The **intro** section manual page appeared in 4.2 BSD.

NAME

ac — display connect time accounting

SYNOPSIS

ac [-d | -p] [-t *tty*] [-w *file*] [*users* ...]

DESCRIPTION

If the file /var/log/wtmp exists, a record of individual login and logout times are written to it by login(1) and init(8), respectively. The program **ac** examines these records and writes the accumulated connect time for all logins to the standard output.

Options available:

-d   Display the connect times in 24 hour chunks.

-p   Display individual user totals.

-t *tty*   Only do accounting logins on certain ttys. The *tty* specification can start with '!' to indicate not this *tty* and end with '*' to indicate all similarly named ttys. Multiple -t flags may be specified.

-w *file*   Read raw connect time data from *file* instead of the default file /var/log/wtmp.

users ...
            Display totals for the given individuals only.

If no arguments are given, **ac** displays the total amount of login time for all active accounts on the system.

The default wtmp file is an infinitely increasing file unless frequently truncated. This is normally done by the daily daemon scripts scheduled by cron(8), which rename and rotate the wtmp files before truncating them (and keep about a week's worth on hand). No login times are collected, however, if the file does not exist.

For example,

```
ac -p -t "ttyd*" > modems
ac -p -t "!ttyd*" > other
```

allows times recorded in modems to be charged out at a different rate than other.

The **ac** utility exits 0 on success, and >0 if a fatal error occurs.

FILES

/var/log/wtmp   connect time accounting file
/var/log/wtmp.[0-7]   rotated files

SEE ALSO

login(1), utmp(5), init(8), sa(8)

HISTORY

An **ac** command appeared in Version 6 AT&T UNIX. This version of **ac** was written for NetBSD 1.0 from the specification provided by various systems' manual pages.

NAME
accton — enable/disable system accounting

SYNOPSIS
accton [*file*]

DESCRIPTION
With an argument naming an existing *file*, **accton** causes system accounting information for every process executed to be placed at the end of the file. If no argument is given, accounting is turned off.

The default accounting file is /var/account/acct. Typically, accounting is enabled by rc scripts during the boot process. In NetBSD, one may enable accounting by setting the variable "accounting" to "YES" in /etc/rc.conf.

Note that, traditionally, the system accounting log file can not be rotated cleanly by newsyslog(8). Instead, a default installation of NetBSD rotates /var/account/acct using the /etc/daily script.

FILES
/var/account/acct Default accounting file.

SEE ALSO
lastcomm(1), acct(5), sa(8)

NAME
     `acpidump` — dump ACPI tables and ASL

SYNOPSIS
     `acpidump` [`-d`] [`-t`] [`-h`] [`-v`] [`-f` *dsdt_input*] [`-o` *dsdt_output*]

DESCRIPTION
     The `acpidump` utility analyzes ACPI tables in physical memory and can dump them to a file. In addition, `acpidump` can call `iasl`(8) to disassemble AML (ACPI Machine Language) found in these tables and dump them as ASL (ACPI Source Language) to stdout.

     ACPI tables have an essential data block (the DSDT, Differentiated System Description Table) that includes information used on the kernel side such as detailed information about PnP hardware, procedures for controlling power management support, and so on. The `acpidump` utility can extract the DSDT data block from physical memory and store it into an output file and optionally also disassemble it. If any Secondary System Description Table (SSDT) entries exist, they will also be included in the output file and disassembly.

     When `acpidump` is invoked without the `-f` option, it will read ACPI tables from physical memory via `/dev/mem`. First it searches for the RSDP (Root System Description Pointer), which has the signature "RSD PTR ", and then gets the RSDT (Root System Description Table), which includes a list of pointers to physical memory addresses for other tables. The RSDT itself and all other tables linked from RSDT are generically called SDTs (System Description Tables) and their header has a common format which consists of items such as Signature, Length, Revision, Checksum, OEMID, OEM Table ID, OEM Revision, Creator ID and Creator Revision. When invoked with the `-t` flag, the `acpidump` utility dumps contents of the following tables:

         APIC
         BERT
         BOOT
         CPEP
         DBGP
         DSDT
         ECDT
         EINJ
         ERST
         FACS
         FADT
         HEST
         HPET
         MADT
         MCFG
         MSCT
         RSD PTR
         RSDT
         SBST
         SLIT
         SPCR
         SRAT
         TCPA
         WAET
         WDAT

WDRT

The RSDT contains a pointer to the physical memory address of the FACP (Fixed ACPI Description Table). The FACP defines static system information about power management support (ACPI Hardware Register Implementation) such as interrupt mode (INT_MODEL), SCI interrupt number, SMI command port (SMI_CMD) and the location of ACPI registers. The FACP also has a pointer to a physical memory address for the DSDT. While the other tables are fixed format, the DSDT consists of free-formatted AML data.

OPTIONS

The following options are supported by **acpidump**:

-d   Disassemble the DSDT into ASL using `iasl`(8) and print the results to stdout.

-t   Dump the contents of the various fixed tables listed above.

-h   Displays usage and exit.

-v   Enable verbose messages.

-f *dsdt_input*
        Load the DSDT from the specified file instead of physical memory. Since only the DSDT is stored in the file, the **-t** flag may not be used with this option.

-o *dsdt_output*
        Store the DSDT data block from physical memory into the specified file.

FILES

`/dev/mem`

EXAMPLES

If a developer requests a copy of your ASL, please use the following command to dump all tables and compress the result.

```
# acpidump -dt | gzip -c9 > my_computer.asl.gz
```

This example dumps the DSDT from physical memory to foo.dsdt. It also prints the contents of various system tables and disassembles the AML contained in the DSDT to stdout, redirecting the output to foo.asl.

```
# acpidump -t -d -o foo.dsdt > foo.asl
```

This example reads a DSDT file and disassembles it to stdout. Verbose messages are enabled.

```
# acpidump -v -d -f foo.dsdt
```

SEE ALSO

`acpi`(4), `amldb`(8), `iasl`(8)

HISTORY

The **acpidump** utility first appeared in FreeBSD 5.0 and was rewritten to use `iasl`(8) for FreeBSD 5.2.

AUTHORS
Doug Rabson ⟨dfr@FreeBSD.org⟩
Mitsuru IWASAKI ⟨iwasaki@FreeBSD.org⟩
Yasuo YOKOYAMA ⟨yokoyama@jp.FreeBSD.org⟩
Nate Lawson ⟨njl@FreeBSD.org⟩

Some contributions made by Chitoshi Ohsawa ⟨ohsawa@catv1.ccn-net.ne.jp⟩, Takayasu IWANASHI ⟨takayasu@wendy.a.perfect-liberty.or.jp⟩, Yoshihiko SARUMARU ⟨mistral@imasy.or.jp⟩, Hiroki Sato

⟨hrs@FreeBSD.org⟩, Michael Lucas ⟨mwlucas@blackhelicopters.org⟩ and Michael Smith ⟨msmith@FreeBSD.org⟩.

BUGS

The current implementation does not dump some miscellaneous tables.

NAME

afterboot — things to check after the first complete boot

DESCRIPTION

Starting Out

This document attempts to list items for the system administrator to check and set up after the installation and first complete boot of the system. The idea is to create a list of items that can be checked off so that you have a warm fuzzy feeling that something obvious has not been missed. A basic knowledge of UNIX is assumed.

Complete instructions for correcting and fixing items is not provided. There are manual pages and other methodologies available for doing that. For example, to view the man page for the ls(1) command, type:

```
man 1 ls
```

Administrators will rapidly become more familiar with NetBSD if they get used to using the manual pages.

Security alerts

By the time that you have installed your system, it is quite likely that bugs in the release have been found. All significant and easily fixed problems will be reported at http://www.NetBSD.org/support/security/. It is recommended that you check this page regularly.

Additionally, you should set "fetch_pkg_vulnerabilities=YES" in /etc/daily.conf to allow your system to automatically update the local database of known vulnerable packages to the latest version available on-line. The system will later check, on a daily basis, if any of your installed packages are vulnerable based on the contents of this database. See daily.conf(5) and security.conf(5) for more details.

Login

Login as "**root**". You can do so on the console, or over the network using ssh(1). If you have enabled the SSH daemon (see sshd(8)) and wish to allow root logins over the network, edit the /etc/ssh/sshd_config file and set "PermitRootLogin" to "yes" (see sshd_config(5)). The default is to not permit root logins over the network after fresh install in NetBSD.

Upon successful login on the console, you may see the message "We recommend creating a non-root account...". For security reasons, it is bad practice to login as root during regular use and maintenance of the system. In fact, the system will only let you login as root on a secure terminal. By default, only the console is considered to be a secure terminal. Instead, administrators are encouraged to add a "regular" user, add said user to the "wheel" group, then use the su(1) command when root privileges are required. This process is described in more detail later.

Root password

Change the password for the root user. (Note that throughout the documentation, the term "superuser" is a synonym for the root user.) Choose a password that has numbers, digits, and special characters (not space) as well as from the upper and lower case alphabet. Do not choose any word in any language. It is common for an intruder to use dictionary attacks. Type the command **/usr/bin/passwd** to change it.

It is a good idea to always specify the full path name for both the passwd(1) and su(1) commands as this inhibits the possibility of files placed in your execution PATH for most shells. Furthermore, the superuser's PATH should never contain the current directory (".").

System date

Check the system date with the date(1) command. If needed, change the date, and/or change the symbolic link of /etc/localtime to the correct time zone in the /usr/share/zoneinfo directory.

Examples:

date 200205101820
> Set the current date to May 10th, 2002 6:20pm.

ln -fs /usr/share/zoneinfo/Europe/Helsinki /etc/localtime
> Set the time zone to Eastern Europe Summer Time.

Console settings
One of the first things you will likely need to do is to set up your keyboard map (and maybe some other aspects about the system console). To change your keyboard encoding, edit the "*encoding*" variable found in `/etc/wscons.conf`.

`wscons.conf`(5) contains more information about this file.

Check hostname
Use the **hostname** command to verify that the name of your machine is correct. See the man page for hostname(1) if it needs to be changed. You will also need to change the contents of the "*hostname*" variable in `/etc/rc.conf` or edit the `/etc/myname` file to have it stick around for the next reboot. Note that "*hostname*" is supposed include a domainname, and that this should not be confused with YP (NIS) domainname(1). If you are using dhclient(8) to configure network interfaces, it might override these local hostname settings if your DHCP server specifies client's hostname with other network configurations.

Verify network interface configuration
The first thing to do is an **ifconfig -a** to see if the network interfaces are properly configured. Correct by editing `/etc/ifconfig.`*interface* or the corresponding "*ifconfig_interface*" variable in `rc.conf`(5) (where *interface* is the interface name, e.g., "le0") and then using ifconfig(8) to manually configure it if you do not wish to reboot.

Alternatively, you can configure interfaces automatically via DHCP with dhclient(8) if you have a DHCP server running somewhere on your network. To get dhclient(8) to start automatically on boot, you will need to have this line in `/etc/rc.conf`:

> dhclient=YES

See dhclient(8) and dhclient.conf(5) for more information on setting up a DHCP client.

You can add new "virtual interfaces" by adding the required entries to `/etc/ifconfig.`*interface*. Read the ifconfig.if(5) man page for more information on the format of `/etc/ifconfig.`*interface* files. The loopback interface will look something like:

```
lo0: flags=8009<UP,LOOPBACK,MULTICAST> mtu 32972
        inet 127.0.0.1 netmask 0xff000000
        inet6 fe80::1%lo0 prefixlen 64 scopeid 0x3
        inet6 ::1 prefixlen 128
```

an Ethernet interface something like:

```
le0: flags=9863<UP,BROADCAST,NOTRAILERS,RUNNING,SIMPLEX,MULTICAST>
        inet 192.168.4.52 netmask 0xffffff00 broadcast 192.168.4.255
        inet6 fe80::5ef0:f0f0%le0 prefixlen 64 scopeid 0x1
```

and a PPP interface something like:

```
ppp0: flags=8051<UP,POINTOPOINT,RUNNING,MULTICAST>
        inet 203.3.131.108 --> 198.181.0.253 netmask 0xffff0000
```

See mrouted(8) for instructions on configuring multicast routing.

Check routing tables

Issue a **netstat -rn** command. The output will look something like:

```
Routing tables

Internet:
Destination      Gateway            Flags  Refs      Use  Mtu  Interface
default          192.168.4.254      UGS       0 11098028    -  le0
127              127.0.0.1          UGRS      0        0    -  lo0
127.0.0.1        127.0.0.1          UH        3       24    -  lo0
192.168.4        link#1             UC        0        0    -  le0
192.168.4.52     8:0:20:73:b8:4a    UHL       1     6707    -  le0
192.168.4.254    0:60:3e:99:67:ea   UHL       1        0    -  le0

Internet6:
Destination      Gateway            Flags  Refs  Use    Mtu  Interface
::/96            ::1                UGRS      0    0   32972  lo0 =>
::1              ::1                UH        4    0   32972  lo0
::ffff:0.0.0.0/96 ::1               UGRS      0    0   32972  lo0
fc80::/10        ::1                UGRS      0    0   32972  lo0
fe80::/10        ::1                UGRS      0    0   32972  lo0
fe80::%le0/64    link#1             UC        0    0    1500  le0
fe80::%lo0/64    fe80::1%lo0        U         0    0   32972  lo0
ff01::/32        ::1                U         0    0   32972  lo0
ff02::%le0/32    link#1             UC        0    0    1500  le0
ff02::%lo0/32    fe80::1%lo0        UC        0    0   32972  lo0
```

The default gateway address is stored in the "*defaultroute*" variable in /etc/rc.conf, or in the file /etc/mygate. If you need to edit this file, a painless way to reconfigure the network afterwards is to issue

/etc/rc.d/network restart

Or, you may prefer to manually configure using a series of **route add** and **route delete** commands (see route(8)). If you run dhclient(8) you will have to kill it by running

/etc/rc.d/dhclient stop

after you flush the routes.

If you wish to route packets between interfaces, add one or both of the following directives (depending on whether IPv4 or IPv6 routing is required) to /etc/sysctl.conf:

```
net.inet.ip.forwarding=1
net.inet6.ip6.forwarding=1
```

As an alternative, compile a new kernel with the "GATEWAY" option. Packets are not forwarded by default, due to RFC requirements.

Secure Shell (SSH)

By default, all services are disabled in a fresh NetBSD installation, and SSH is no exception. You may wish to enable it so you can remotely control your system. Set "*sshd=YES*" in /etc/rc.conf and then starting the server with the command

```
/etc/rc.d/sshd start
```

The first time the server is started, it will generate a new keypair, which will be stored inside the directory `/etc/ssh`.

BIND Name Server (DNS)

If you are using the BIND Name Server, check the `/etc/resolv.conf` file. It may look something like:

```
domain some.thing.dom
nameserver 192.168.0.1
nameserver 192.168.4.55
search some.thing.dom. thing.dom.
```

For further details, see `resolv.conf(5)`. Note the name service lookup order is set via `nsswitch.conf(5)` mechanism.

If using a caching name server add the line "nameserver 127.0.0.1" first. To get a local caching name server to run you will need to set "named=YES" in `/etc/rc.conf` and create the `named.conf` file in the appropriate place for `named(8)`, usually in `/etc/namedb`. The same holds true if the machine is going to be a name server for your domain. In both these cases, make sure that `named(8)` is running (otherwise there are long waits for resolver timeouts).

RPC-based network services

Several services depend on the RPC portmapper `rpcbind(8)` - formerly known as **portmap** - being running for proper operation. This includes YP (NIS) and NFS exports, among other services. To get the RPC portmapper to start automatically on boot, you will need to have this line in `/etc/rc.conf`:

```
rpcbind=YES
```

YP (NIS) Setup

Check the YP domain name with the `domainname(1)` command. If necessary, correct it by editing the `/etc/defaultdomain` file or by setting the "*domainname*" variable in `/etc/rc.conf`. The `/etc/rc.d/network` script reads this file on bootup to determine and set the domain name. You may also set the running system's domain name with the `domainname(1)` command. To start YP client services, simply run **ypbind**, then perform the remaining YP activation as described in `passwd(5)` and `group(5)`.

In particular, to enable YP passwd support, you'll need to update `/etc/nsswitch.conf` to include "nis" for the "passwd" and "group" entries. A traditional way to accomplish the same thing is to add following entry to local passwd database via `vipw(8)`:

```
+:*:::::::::
```

Note this entry has to be the very last one. This traditional way works with the default `nsswitch.conf(5)` setting of "passwd", which is "compat".

There are many more YP man pages available to help you. You can find more information by starting with `nis(8)`.

Check disk mounts

Check that the disks are mounted correctly by comparing the `/etc/fstab` file against the output of the `mount(8)` and `df(1)` commands. Example:

```
# cat /etc/fstab
/dev/sd0a / ffs      rw          1 1
/dev/sd0b none swap sw
/dev/sd0e /usr ffs   rw          1 2
/dev/sd0f /var ffs   rw          1 3
```

```
/dev/sd0g /tmp ffs   rw                      1 4
/dev/sd0h /home ffs rw                       1 5

# mount
/dev/sd0a on / type ffs (local)
/dev/sd0e on /usr type ffs (local)
/dev/sd0f on /var type ffs (local)
/dev/sd0g on /tmp type ffs (local)
/dev/sd0h on /home type ffs (local)

# df
Filesystem  1024-blocks     Used    Avail Capacity  Mounted on
/dev/sd0a        22311     14589     6606     69%    /
/dev/sd0e       203399    150221    43008     78%    /usr
/dev/sd0f        10447       682     9242      7%    /var
/dev/sd0g        18823         2    17879      0%    /tmp
/dev/sd0h         7519      5255     1888     74%    /home

# pstat -s
Device       512-blocks     Used    Avail Capacity  Priority
/dev/sd0b       131072     84656    46416     65%    0
```

Edit /etc/fstab and use the mount(8) and umount(8) commands as appropriate. Refer to the above example and fstab(5) for information on the format of this file.

You may wish to do NFS mounts now too, or you can do them later.

Concatenated disks (ccd)

If you are using ccd(4) concatenated disks, edit /etc/ccd.conf. You may wish to take a look to ccdconfig(8) for more information about this file. Use the **ccdconfig -U** command to unload and the **ccdconfig -C** command to create tables internal to the kernel for the concatenated disks. You then mount(8), umount(8), and edit /etc/fstab as needed.

Automounter daemon (AMD)

To use the amd(8) automounter, create the /etc/amd directory, copy example config files from /usr/share/examples/amd to /etc/amd and customize them as needed. Alternatively, you can get your maps with YP.

Clock synchronization

In order to make sure the system clock is synchronized to that of a publicly accessible NTP server, make sure that /etc/rc.conf contains the following:

```
ntpdate=YES
ntpd=YES
```

See date(1), ntpdate(8), ntpd(8), rdate(8), and timed(8) for more information on setting the system's date.

CHANGING /etc FILES

The system should be usable now, but you may wish to do more customizing, such as adding users, etc. Many of the following sections may be skipped if you are not using that package (for example, skip the **Kerberos** section if you won't be using Kerberos). We suggest that you **cd /etc** and edit most of the files in that directory.

Note that the `/etc/motd` file is modified by `/etc/rc.d/motd` whenever the system is booted. To keep any custom message intact, ensure that you leave two blank lines at the top, or your message will be overwritten.

Add new users

To add new users and groups, there are `useradd`(8) and `groupadd`(8); see also `user`(8) for further programs for user and group manipulation. You may use `vipw`(8) to add users to the `/etc/passwd` file and edit `/etc/group` by hand to add new groups. The manual page for `su`(1), tells you to make sure to put people in the 'wheel' group if they need root access (non-Kerberos). For example:

```
wheel:*:0:root,myself
```

Follow instructions for `kerberos`(8) if using Kerberos for authentication.

System boot scripts and /etc/rc.local

`/etc/rc` and the `/etc/rc.d/*` scripts are invoked at boot time after single user mode has exited, and at shutdown. The whole process is controlled by the master script `/etc/rc`. This script should not be changed by administrators.

The directory `/etc/rc.d` contains a series of scripts used at startup/shutdown, called by `/etc/rc`. `/etc/rc` is in turn influenced by the configuration variables present in `/etc/rc.conf`.

The script `/etc/rc.local` is run as the last thing during multiuser boot, and is provided to allow any other local hooks necessary for the system.

rc.conf

To enable or disable various services on system startup, corresponding entries can be made in `/etc/rc.conf`. You can take a look at `/etc/defaults/rc.conf` to see a list of default system variables, which you can override in `/etc/rc.conf`. Note you are *not* supposed to change `/etc/defaults/rc.conf` directly, edit only `/etc/rc.conf`. See `rc.conf`(5) for further information.

X Display Manager

If you've installed X, you may want to turn on `xdm`(1), the X Display Manager. To do this, set "xdm=YES" in `/etc/rc.conf`.

Printers

Edit `/etc/printcap` and `/etc/hosts.lpd` to get any printers set up. Consult `lpd`(8) and `printcap`(5) if needed.

Tighten up security

In `/etc/inetd.conf` comment out any extra entries you do not need, and only add things that are really needed. Note that by default all services are disabled for security reasons.

Kerberos

If you are going to use Kerberos for authentication, see `kerberos`(8) and "info heimdal" for more information. If you already have a Kerberos master, change directory to `/etc/kerberosV` and configure. Remember to get a `srvtab` from the master so that the remote commands work.

Mail Aliases

Check `/etc/mail/aliases` and update appropriately if you want e-mail to be routed to non-local addresses or to different users.

Run newaliases(1) after changes.

Postfix

NetBSD uses Postfix as its MTA. Postfix is started by default, but its initial configuration does not cause it to listen on the network for incoming connections. To configure Postfix, see /etc/postfix/main.cf and /etc/postfix/master.cf. If you wish to use a different MTA (e.g., sendmail), install your MTA of choice and edit /etc/mailer.conf to point to the proper binaries.

DHCP server

If this is a DHCP server, edit /etc/dhcpd.conf and /etc/dhcpd.interfaces as needed. You will have to make sure /etc/rc.conf has "dhcpd=YES" or run dhcpd(8) manually.

Bootparam server

If this is a Bootparam server, edit /etc/bootparams as needed. You will have to turn it on in /etc/rc.conf by adding "bootparamd=YES".

NFS server

If this is an NFS server, make sure /etc/rc.conf has:

```
nfs_server=YES
mountd=YES
rpcbind=YES
```

Edit /etc/exports and get it correct. After this, you can start the server by issuing:

/etc/rc.d/rpcbind start
/etc/rc.d/mountd start
/etc/rc.d/nfsd start

which will also start dependencies.

HP remote boot server

Edit /etc/rbootd.conf if needed for remote booting. If you do not have HP computers doing remote booting, do not enable this.

Daily, weekly, monthly scripts

Look at and possibly edit the /etc/daily.conf, /etc/weekly.conf, and /etc/monthly.conf configuration files. You can check which values you can set by looking to their matching files in /etc/defaults. Your site specific things should go into /etc/daily.local, /etc/weekly.local, and /etc/monthly.local.

These scripts have been limited so as to keep the system running without filling up disk space from normal running processes and database updates. (You probably do not need to understand them.)

Other files in /etc

Look at the other files in /etc and edit them as needed. (Do not edit files ending in .db — like pwd.db, spwd.db, nor localtime, nor rmt, nor any directories.)

Crontab (background running processes)

Check what is running by typing **crontab -l** as root and see if anything unexpected is present. Do you need anything else? Do you wish to change things? For example, if you do not like root getting standard output of the daily scripts, and want only the security scripts that are mailed internally, you can type **crontab -e** and change some of the lines to read:

```
30  1  *  *  *    /bin/sh /etc/daily 2>&1 > /var/log/daily.out
30  3  *  *  6    /bin/sh /etc/weekly 2>&1 > /var/log/weekly.out
30  5  1  *  *    /bin/sh /etc/monthly 2>&1 > /var/log/monthly.out
```

See crontab(5).

Next day cleanup

After the first night's security run, change ownerships and permissions on files, directories, and devices; root should have received mail with subject: "<hostname> daily insecurity output.". This mail contains a set of security recommendations, presented as a list looking like this:

```
var/mail:
        permissions (0755, 0775)
etc/daily:
        user (0, 3)
```

The best bet is to follow the advice in that list. The recommended setting is the first item in parentheses, while the current setting is the second one. This list is generated by mtree(8) using /etc/mtree/special. Use chmod(1), chgrp(1), and chown(8) as needed.

Packages

Install your own packages. The NetBSD packages collection, pkgsrc, includes a large set of third-party software. A lot of it is available as binary packages that you can download from ftp://ftp.NetBSD.org/pub/NetBSD/packages/ or a mirror, and install using pkg_add(1). See http://www.NetBSD.org/docs/pkgsrc/ and pkgsrc/doc/pkgsrc.txt for more details.

Copy vendor binaries and install them. You will need to install any shared libraries, etc. (Hint: **man -k compat** to find out how to install and use compatibility mode.)

There is also other third-party software that is available in source form only, either because it has not been ported to NetBSD yet, because licensing restrictions make binary redistribution impossible, or simply because you want to build your own binaries. Sometimes checking the mailing lists for past problems that people have encountered will result in a fix posted.

Check the running system

You can use ps(1), netstat(1), and fstat(1) to check on running processes, network connections, and opened files, respectively. Other tools you may find useful are systat(1) and top(1).

COMPILING A KERNEL

Note: The standard NetBSD kernel configuration (GENERIC) is suitable for most purposes.

First, review the system message buffer in /var/run/dmesg.boot and by using the dmesg(8) command to find out information on your system's devices as probed by the kernel at boot. In particular, note which devices were not configured. This information will prove useful when editing kernel configuration files.

To compile a kernel inside a writable source tree, do the following:

```
$ cd /usr/src/sys/arch/SOMEARCH/conf
$ cp GENERIC SOMEFILE (only the first time)
$ vi SOMEFILE (adapt to your needs)
$ config SOMEFILE
$ cd ../compile/SOMEFILE
$ make depend
$ make
```

where *SOMEARCH* is the architecture (e.g., i386), and *SOMEFILE* should be a name indicative of a particular configuration (often that of the hostname).

If you are building your kernel again, before you do a **make** you should do a **make clean** after making changes to your kernel options.

After either of these two methods, you can place the new kernel (called `netbsd`) in / (i.e., /netbsd) by issuing **make install** and the system will boot it next time. The old kernel is stored as /onetbsd so you can boot it in case of failure.

If you are using toolchain to build your kernel, you will also need to build a new set of toolchain binaries. You can do it by changing into /usr/src and issuing:

```
$ cd /usr/src
$ K=sys/arch/'uname -m'/conf
$ cp $K/GENERIC $K/SOMEFILE
$ vi $K/SOMEFILE (adapt to your needs)
$ ./build.sh tools
$ ./build.sh kernel=SOMEFILE
```

SYSTEM TESTING

At this point, the system should be fully configured to your liking. It is now a good time to ensure that the system behaves according to its specifications and that it is stable on your hardware. You can easily do so by running the test suites available at /usr/tests/, assuming that you installed the tests.tgz set. If not, you can install it now by running:

```
# cd /
# tar xzpf /path/to/tests.tgz
```

Once done, edit the /etc/atf/NetBSD.conf file to tune the configuration of the test suite, go to /usr/tests/ hierarchy and use the atf-run(1) and atf-report(1) utilities to run all the tests in an automated way:

```
# cd /usr/tests/
# atf-run | atf-report
```

Should any problems appear when running the test suite, please let the NetBSD developers know by sending a message to the appropriate mailing list or by sending a problem report. For more details see:

- http://www.netbsd.org/mailinglists/
- http://www.netbsd.org/support/send-pr.html

SEE ALSO

atf-report(1), atf-run(1), chgrp(1), chmod(1), config(1), crontab(1), date(1), df(1), domainname(1), fstat(1), hostname(1), make(1), man(1), netstat(1), newaliases(1), passwd(1), pkg_add(1), ps(1), ssh(1), su(1), systat(1), top(1), xdm(1), ccd(4), aliases(5), crontab(5), dhclient.conf(5), exports(5), fstab(5), group(5), ifconfig.if(5), mailer.conf(5), nsswitch.conf(5), passwd(5), printcap(5), rc.conf(5), resolv.conf(5), sshd_config(5), wscons.conf(5), hier(7), hostname(7), pkgsrc(7), amd(8), ccdconfig(8), chown(8), dhclient(8), dhcpd(8), dmesg(8), groupadd(8), ifconfig(8), inetd(8), kerberos(8), lpd(8), mount(8), mrouted(8), mtree(8), named(8), nis(8), ntpd(8), ntpdate(8), rbootd(8), rc(8), rdate(8), rmt(8), route(8), rpc.bootparamd(8), rpcbind(8), sshd(8), timed(8), umount(8), useradd(8), vipw(8), yp(8), ypbind(8)

AFTERBOOT (8)   NetBSD   AFTERBOOT (8)

HISTORY

This document first appeared in OpenBSD 2.2. It has been adapted to NetBSD and first appeared in NetBSD 2.0.

NAME

    ahdilabel — modify AHDI partitions

SYNOPSIS

    ahdilabel *disk*

DESCRIPTION

    ahdilabel allows you to modify the AHDI partition table on a disk partitioned with AHDI or an AHDI compatible formatter. The AHDI partition format is usually only present on disks shared between NetBSD and some other OS. The partition identifiers are used by NetBSD as a guideline to emulate a disklabel on such a disk.

    ahdilabel supports the following options:

    disk The name of the disk you want to edit. **ahdilabel** will first try to open a disk of this name. If this cannot be opened, it will attempt to open *r*<disk>*c*. Finally, if this also cannot be opened, it will attempt to open */dev/r*<disk>*c*.

    ahdilabel will display information about the number of sectors, tracks and sectors on the disk, as well as the current AHDI partition information. It will then prompt for input. The input choices are:

    a–p Modify a partition. You will be prompted for a partition id, root, start and size. NetBSD recognises the following partition id's:

        NBD   Partition is reserved for NetBSD. This can be either a root or an user partition. The first NBD partition on a disk will be mapped to NetBSD partition letter *a*. The following NBD partitions will be mapped from letter *d* up. The filesystem type is ffs by default.

        SWP   The first SWP partition is mapped to partition *b*.

        GEM or BGM These partitions are mapped from *d* up. The filesystem type is msdos.

    The root, start and size parameters can be entered using sector, cylinder/track/sector or megabyte notations. Whole numbers of cylinders can be entered using the shorthand <cylinder>/. Likewise, whole numbers of tracks can be entered using the shorthand <cylinder>/<track>/. Megabytes are entered using the suffix *M*.

    The following can also be used to enter partition parameters:

        –N (root)   Position the root sector for this partition immediately after partition N.

        –N (start)   Make this partition start after partition N (leaving a gap of 1 sector for a root sector, if necessary).

        –N (size)   Make this partition end immediately before partition N.

        -1 (size)   Make this partition extend to the end of the disk.

    The sector holding the primary AHDI partition table only has space for four partitions. Thus, if a disk has more than four partitions, the extra partition information is held in auxiliary root sectors. There is one auxiliary root for each additional partition (and also for the fourth partition, if the disk has more than four partitions).

    r Recalculate the root sectors. This will automatically assign auxiliary root sectors if the disk has more than 4 partitions. The auxiliary root sectors will be positioned in a default location preceding the relevant partition.

    s Show the current partition information.

    u Toggle the unit display between sector and cylinder/track/sector notation.

w   Write the AHDI partition table to the disk.

z   Options for zero'ing the boot sector and bad sector lists. The default is to preserve them both.

q   Quit

EXAMPLES
```
ahdilabel sd0
```
Edit the AHDI label for disk sd0.

SEE ALSO
bootpref(8), disklabel(8), installboot(8)

HISTORY
The **ahdilabel** command first appeared in NetBSD 1.5.

BUGS
The changes made to the AHDI partitions will become active on the next *first open* of the disk. You are advised to use **ahdilabel** only on a disk without any mounted or otherwise active partitions. This is not enforced by **ahdilabel**.

Because of way NetBSD interprets AHDI partition tables to create the NetBSD disklabel, the NetBSD partition ordering may change if partitions labelled NBD are created or removed.

Creating an AHDI partition table on a disk that previously did not have one will almost certainly overwrite any existing partition information and/or data on that disk. This is especially the case if auxiliary root sectors are needed for the AHDI partition table.

As soon as a disk contains at least one NBD partition, you are allowed to write NetBSD disklabels and install bootstraps.

NAME
   altqd — ALTQ daemon

SYNOPSIS
   altqd [**-dv**] [**-f** *conf_file*]

DESCRIPTION
   altqd is a daemon program that reads a configuration file and then sets up the ALTQ state of network interfaces. After configuring the ALTQ state, **altqd** will detach and become a daemon.

   The signals SIGINT or SIGTERM will shutdown **altqd**, and the signal SIGHUP will restart **altqd**.

   The following options are available:

   -d   Debug mode. **altqd** does not detach and goes into the command mode.

   -f *conf_file*
                   Specify a configuration file to read instead of the default. The default file is /etc/altq.conf.

   -v   Print debugging information. This option implies **-d**.

COMMANDS
   When **-d** option is provided, **altqd** goes into the command mode after reading the configuration file and setting up the ALTQ state. Each command is a single line, starting with the command verb.

   The basic commands are as follows:

   help | ?
                   Display a complete list of commands and their syntax.

   quit Exit.

   altq *reload*
                   Reload the configuration file and reinitialize ALTQ.

   altq *interface* [enable|disable]
                   Enables or disables ALTQ on the interface named *interface*. When **altqd** enters the command mode, ALTQ is enabled on all the interfaces listed in the configuration file.

FILES
   /etc/altq.conf   configuration file
   /var/run/altqd.pid   pid of the running **altqd**
   /var/run/altq_quip   Unix domain socket for communicating with altqstat(1)

SEE ALSO
   altqstat(1), altq.conf(5), altq(9)

NAME
altqstat — show altq status

SYNOPSIS
altqstat [**-enrs**] [**-c** *count*] [**-w** *wait*] [**-i** *interface*] [**-I** *input_interface*]

DESCRIPTION
The **altqstat** command displays the status of a queueing discipline. The contents displayed by **altqstat** is specific to each queueing discipline.

The options are as follows:

-e   Echo communication with altqd(8) to standard output. This option is for debugging.

-n   Disable communication with altqd(8). The interface should be explicitly specified.

-r   Enter the raw console mode to talk to altqd(8). This option is for debugging queue information exchange between **altqstat** and altqd(8).

-s   List all interfaces, classes and filters currently installed.

-c *count* **altqstat** exits after displaying *count* times. If no repeat *count* is specified, the default is infinity.

-w *wait*   Pause *wait* seconds between each display. If no repeat *wait* interval is specified, the default is 5 seconds.

-i *interface*
                Show information about the specified interface. If no *interface* is specified, the default interface is the first interface returned from altqd(8).

-I *input_interface*
                Show information about the specified input interface. This option is used to specify *traffic conditioner* at an input interface.

FILES
/var/run/altq_quip Unix domain socket for communicating with altqd(8)

SEE ALSO
altq.conf(5), altqd(8), altq(9)

NAME
    amd – automatically mount file systems

SYNOPSIS
    amd –H
    amd [**–F** *conf_file*]
    amd [**–nprvHS**] [**–a** *mount_point*] [**–c** *duration*] [**–d** *domain*] [**–k** *kernel-arch*] [**–l** *logfile*] [**–o**
    op_sys_ver] [**–t** *interval.interval*] [**–w** *interval*] [**–x** *log-option*] [**–y** *YP-domain*] [**–A** *arch*] [**–C**
    cluster-name] [**–D** *option*] [**–F** *conf_file*] [**–O** *op_sys_name*] [**–T** *tag*] [*directory mapname* [*–map-
    options*]] . . .

DESCRIPTION
    Amd is a daemon that automatically mounts filesystems whenever a file or directory within that filesystem
    is accessed. Filesystems are automatically unmounted when they appear to have become quiescent.

    Amd operates by attaching itself as an NFS server to each of the specified *directories*. Lookups within the
    specified directories are handled by **amd**, which uses the map defined by *mapname* to determine how to
    resolve the lookup. Generally, this will be a host name, some filesystem information and some mount
    options for the given filesystem.

    In the first form depicted above, **amd** will print a short help string. In the second form, if no options are
    specified, or the -**F** is used, **amd** will read configuration parameters from the file *conf_file* which defaults to
    /etc/amd.conf. The last form is described below.

OPTIONS
    –a *temporary-directory*
            Specify an alternative location for the real mount points. The default is **/a**.

    –c *duration*
            Specify a *duration*, in seconds, that a looked up name remains cached when not in use. The
            default is 5 minutes.

    –d *domain*
            Specify the local domain name. If this option is not given the domain name is determined from
            the hostname.

    –k *kernel-arch*
            Specifies the kernel architecture. This is used solely to set the ${karch} selector.

    –l *logfile*
            Specify a logfile in which to record mount and unmount events. If *logfile* is the string **syslog** then
            the log messages will be sent to the system log daemon by *syslog*(3). The default syslog facility
            used is LOG_DAEMON. If you wish to change it, append its name to the log file name, delimited
            by a single colon. For example, if *logfile* is the string **syslog:local7** then **Amd** will log messages
            via *syslog*(3) using the LOG_LOCAL7 facility (if it exists on the system).

    –n   Normalize hostnames. The name refereed to by ${rhost} is normalized relative to the host data-
            base before being used. The effect is to translate aliases into "official" names.

    –o *op_sys_ver*
            Override the compiled-in version number of the operating system. Useful when the built in ver-
            sion is not desired for backward compatibility reasons. For example, if the build in version is
            "2.5.1", you can override it to "5.5.1", and use older maps that were written with the latter in
            mind.

−p Print PID. Outputs the process-id of **amd** to standard output where it can be saved into a file.

−r Restart existing mounts. **Amd** will scan the mount file table to determine which filesystems are currently mounted. Whenever one of these would have been auto-mounted, **amd** *inherits* it.

−t *timeout.retransmit*
  Specify the NFS timeout *interval*, in tenths of a second, between NFS/RPC retries (for UDP only). The default is 0.8 seconds. The second value alters the retransmit counter, which defaults to 11 retransmissions. Both of these values are used by the kernel to communicate with amd. Useful defaults are supplied if either or both values are missing.

  Amd relies on the kernel RPC retransmit mechanism to trigger mount retries. The values of these parameters change the overall retry interval. Too long an interval gives poor interactive response; too short an interval causes excessive retries.

−v Version. Displays version and configuration information on standard error.

−w *interval*
  Specify an *interval*, in seconds, between attempts to dismount filesystems that have exceeded their cached times. The default is 2 minutes.

−x *options*
  Specify run-time logging options. The options are a comma separated list chosen from: fatal, error, user, warn, info, map, stats, defaults, and all. Note that "fatal" and "error" are mandatory and cannot be turned off.

−y *domain*
  Specify an alternative NIS domain from which to fetch the NIS maps. The default is the system domain name. This option is ignored if NIS support is not available.

−A *arch*
  Specifies the OS architecture. This is used solely to set the ${arch} selector.

−C *cluster-name*
  Specify an alternative HP-UX cluster name to use.

−D *option*
  Select from a variety of debug options. Prefixing an option with the strings **no** reverses the effect of that option. Options are cumulative. The most useful option is **all**. Since −D is only used for debugging other options are not documented here: the current supported set of options is listed by the −v option and a fuller description is available in the program source.

−F *conf_file*
  Specify an amd configuration file to use. See **amd.conf**(5) for description of this file's format. This configuration file is used to specify any options in lieu of typing many of them on the command line. The *amd.conf* file includes directives for every command line option amd has, and many more that are only available via the configuration file facility. The configuration file specified by this option is processed after all other options had been processed, regardless of the actual location of this option on the command line.

–H   Print help and usage string.

–O *op_sys_name*
Override the compiled-in name of the operating system. Useful when the built in name is not desired for backward compatibility reasons. For example, if the build in name is "sunos5", you can override it to "sos5", and use older maps which were written with the latter in mind.

–S   Do not lock the running executable pages of amd into memory. To improve amd's performance, systems that support the **plock**(3) call, could lock the amd process into memory. This way there is less chance the operating system will schedule, page out, and swap the amd process as needed. This tends improves amd's performance, at the cost of reserving the memory used by the amd process (making it unavailable for other processes). If this behavior is not desired, use the **–S** option.

–T *tag*   Specify a tag to use with **amd.conf**(5). All map entries tagged with *tag* will be processed. Map entries that are not tagged are always processed. Map entries that are tagged with a tag other than *tag* will not be processed.

FILES
/a   directory under which filesystems are dynamically mounted

/etc/amd.conf
default configuration file

CAVEATS
Some care may be required when creating a mount map.

Symbolic links on an NFS filesystem can be incredibly inefficient. In most implementations of NFS, their interpolations are not cached by the kernel and each time a symlink is encountered during a *lookuppn* translation it costs an RPC call to the NFS server. It would appear that a large improvement in real-time performance could be gained by adding a cache somewhere. Replacing symlinks with a suitable incarnation of the auto-mounter results in a large real-time speedup, but also causes a large number of process context switches.

A weird imagination is most useful to gain full advantage of all the features.

SEE ALSO
domainname(1), **hostname**(1), **syslog**(3). **amd.conf**(5), **mtab**(5), **amq**(8), **mount**(8), **umount**(8),

"am-utils" **info**(1) entry.

Linux NFS and Automounter Administration by Erez Zadok, ISBN 0-7821-2739-8, (Sybex, 2001).

http://www.am-utils.org

Amd − The 4.4 BSD Automounter

AUTHORS
Jan-Simon Pendry <jsp@doc.ic.ac.uk>, Department of Computing, Imperial College, London, UK.

Erez Zadok <ezk@cs.sunysb.edu>, Computer Science Department, Stony Brook University, Stony Brook, New York, USA.

Other authors and contributors to am-utils are listed in the **AUTHORS** file distributed with am-utils.

NAME

    amldb — executing and debugging AML interpreter (with DSDT files)

SYNOPSIS

    amldb [**-dhst**] *dsdt_file* . . .

DESCRIPTION

    The **amldb** utility parses the DSDT (Differentiated System Description Table) files, which usually are acquired from ACPI BIOS, and executes the sequence of ACPI Control Methods described in AML (ACPI Machine Language) with its AML interpreter. The **amldb** utility also has a simple ACPI virtual machine. During execution of the Control Methods each access to the region, such as SystemMemory, SystemIO, PCI_Config, does not affect the real hardware but only the virtual machine. Because the sequence of virtual accesses is maintained in user space, AML interpreter developers need not worry about any effect on hardware when they analyze DSDT data files. They can develop and debug the interpreter, even if the machine has no ACPI BIOS.

    The developer will need to acquire a DSDT data file from any machine with ACPI BIOS through acpidump(8). The DSDT is a table, a part of the whole ACPI memory table located in somewhere in the BIOS area (0xa0000 – 0x100000). It includes such information as the detailed hardware information for PnP, and the set of procedures which perform power management from the OS. The information is stored in AML format.

    The AML interpreter can execute any of the Control Methods specified by users. When executed, it interprets the byte sequence in the Control Method of DSDT, and disassembles the opcodes that it recognizes into ASL (ACPI Source Language) format to be displayed.

    If it encounters one of more accesses to the region such as SystemMemory in executing the Control Methods, its ACPI Virtual Machine simulates the input/output operations to the resources in the region. In writing to a certain region, the ACPI Virtual Machine prepares a piece of memory corresponding to its address, if necessary, and holds the specified value in the memory as the *region contents*. In reading from a certain region, it fetches the value in the memory (*region contents*), prompts with it as the following:

```
DEBUG[read(0, 0x100b6813)&mask:0x1](default: 0x1 / 1) >>
```

for users to have the opportunity to modify it, and hands it to the AML interpreter. In case that there is no corresponding region in the AML Virtual Machine, the value zero is handed.

    The interpreter continues to maintain all of the *region contents* until **amldb** terminates. You can specify their initial values with the file region.ini in the current directory. If it is executed with **-d** option, it dumps the final status of all of its *region contents* to the file region.dmp when it terminates. Each line of there files consists of the following fields, separated by tabs; region type, address, and value. Region types are specified as follows;

Value	Region type
0	SystemMemory
1	SystemIO
2	PCI_Config
3	EmbeddedControl
4	SMBus

Interactive commands are described below:

s   *Single step*: Performs single-step execution of the current Control Method. If the next instruction is an invocation of another Control Method, the step execution will continue in the following Control Method.

n   *Step program*: Performs single-step execution of the current Control Method. Even if the next instruction is an invocation of another Control Method, the step execution will not continue.

c   *Continue program being debugged*: Resumes execution of the AML interpreter. Because the current **amldb** has no way of breakpoint, this command might not so much useful.

q   *Quit method execution*: Terminates execution of the current Control Method. If **amldb** is not in execution, this command causes to input the next DSDT data file. If there are no next DSDT data files, it terminates **amldb** itself.

t   *Show local name space tree and variables*: Displays the structure of the ACPI namespace tree. If **amldb** is in execution, this command displays the structure that relates to the objects, arguments, and local variables below the scope of the current Control Method.

i   *Toggle region input prompt*: Switches whether the prompt for modifying the value read from the *region contents* be showed or not. Default is On.

o   *Toggle region output prompt*: Switches whether the prompt for modifying the value to be written to the region contents will be shown or not. The default is Off.

m   *Show memory management statistics*: Displays the current statistics of the memory management system on the AML interpreter.

r *method*

     Run specified method: Executes the specified Control Method. If it requires one or more arguments, a prompt such as the following appears;

```
Method: Arg 1 From 0x280626ce To 0x28062775
  Enter argument values (ex. number 1 / string foo). 'q' to quit.
  Arg0 ?
```

     For each argument, a pair of type string and value delimited by one or more spaces can be entered. Now only **number** and **string** can be specified as the type string. In the current implementation, only the first character of the type string, such as **n** or **s**, is identified. For example, we can enter as follows:

```
  Arg0 ? n 1
```

f *string*

     Find named objects from namespace: Lists the named objects that includes the specified string as the terminate elements searching from the ACPI namespace. For the namespace is expressed as the sequence of four-character elements, appropriate number of additional underscore ('_') characters are necessary for specifying objects which have less than four character string. Unless additional underscores specified, matching occurs as the beginning of word with the specified number of characters.

h   *Show help messsage*: Displays the command summary of **amldb**.

OPTIONS

     Exactly one of the following options must be specified. Otherwise, **amldb** shows its usage and terminates.

−d   Dump the final status of all of the *region contents* in the ACPI Virtual Machine to the file `region.dmp`.

−h   Terminate with the usage of this command.

−s   Display the statistics of the memory management system on the AML interpreter when **amldb** terminates.

     −t   Display the tree structure of ACPI namespace after the DSDT data file is read.

FILES

    region.ini
    region.dmp

EXAMPLES

The following is an example including, invoking the **amldb**, searching _PRS (Possible Resource Settings) objects, and executing the _PTS (Prepare To Sleep) Control Method by the AML interpreter.

```
% amldb p2b.dsdt.dat
Loading p2b.dsdt.dat...done
AML>f _PRS
\_SB_.PCI0.ISA_.PS2M._PRS.
\_SB_.PCI0.ISA_.IRDA._PRS.
\_SB_.PCI0.ISA_.UAR2._PRS.
\_SB_.PCI0.ISA_.UAR1._PRS.
\_SB_.PCI0.ISA_.ECP_._PRS.
\_SB_.PCI0.ISA_.LPT_._PRS.
\_SB_.PCI0.ISA_.FDC0._PRS.
\_SB_.LNKD._PRS.
\_SB_.LNKC._PRS.
\_SB_.LNKB._PRS.
\_SB_.LNKA._PRS.
AML>r _PTS
Method: Arg 1 From 0x2805f0a3 To 0x2805f0db
  Enter argument values (ex. number 1 / string foo). 'q' to quit.
  Arg0 ? n 5
==== Running _PTS. ====
AML>s
[\_PTS. START]
If(LNot(LEqual(Arg0, 0x5)))
AML>
If(LEqual(Arg0, 0x1))
AML>
If(LEqual(Arg0, 0x2))
AML>
Store(One, TO12)
[aml_region_write(1, 1, 0x1, 0xe42c, 0x18, 0x1)]
amldb: region.ini: No such file or directory
        [1:0x00@0xe42f]->[1:0x01@0xe42f]
[write(1, 0x1, 0xe42f)]
[aml_region_read(1, 1, 0xe42c, 0x18, 0x1)]
        [1:0x01@0xe42f]
DEBUG[read(1, 0xe42f)&mask:0x1](default: 0x1 / 1) >>
[read(1, 0xe42f)->0x1]
AML>
Or(Arg0, 0xf0, Local2)[Copy number 0xf5]
AML>t
_PTS  Method: Arg 1 From 0x2805f0a3 To 0x2805f0db
  Arg0    Num:0x5
  Local2  Num:0xf5
```

```
AML>s
Store(Local2, DBG1)
[aml_region_write(1, 1, 0xf5, 0x80, 0x0, 0x8)]
        [1:0x00@0x80]->[1:0xf5@0x80]
[write(1, 0xf5, 0x80)]
[aml_region_read(1, 1, 0x80, 0x0, 0x8)]
        [1:0xf5@0x80]
DEBUG[read(1, 0x80)&mask:0xf5](default: 0xf5 / 245) >>
[read(1, 0x80)->0xf5]
AML>
[\_PTS. END]
_PTS  Method: Arg 1 From 0x2805f0a3 To 0x2805f0db
NO object
==== _PTS finished. ====
AML>q
%
```

SEE ALSO
acpi(4), acpidump(8)

HISTORY
The **amldb** utility appeared in FreeBSD 5.0.

AUTHORS
Takanori Watanabe ⟨takawata@FreeBSD.org⟩
Mitsuru IWASAKI ⟨iwasaki@FreeBSD.org⟩
Yasuo YOKOYAMA ⟨yokoyama@jp.FreeBSD.org⟩

Some contributions made by
Chitoshi Ohsawa ⟨ohsawa@catv1.ccn-net.ne.jp⟩,
Takayasu IWANASHI ⟨takayasu@wendy.a.perfect-liberty.or.jp⟩,
Norihiro KUMAGAI ⟨kumagai@home.com⟩,
Kenneth Ingham ⟨ingham@I-pi.com⟩, and
Michael Lucas ⟨mwlucas@blackhelicopters.org⟩.

BUGS
The ACPI virtual machine does not completely simulate the behavior of a machine with an ACPI BIOS. In the current implementation, the ACPI virtual machine only reads or writes the stored values by emulating access to regions such as SystemMemory.

Because the AML interpreter interprets and disassembles simultaneously, it is impossible to implement such features as setting breakpoints with the specified line number in ASL. Setting breakpoints at certain Control Methods, which is not very difficult, has not yet implemented because nobody has ever needed it.

NAME

amq – automounter query tool

SYNOPSIS

amq [**−fmpqsvwHTU**] [**−h** *hostname*] [**−l** *log_file*] [**−x** *log_options*] [**−D** *debug_options*] [**−P** *program_number*] [[**−u**] *directory* . . .]

DESCRIPTION

Amq provides a simple way of determining the current state of **amd** program. Communication is by RPC. Three modes of operation are supported by the current protocol. By default a list of mount points and automounted filesystems is output. An alternative host can be specified using the *−h* option.

If *directory* names are given, as output by default, then per-filesystem information is displayed.

OPTIONS

−f   Ask the automounter to flush the internal caches and reload all the maps.

−h *hostname*
   Specify an alternate host to query. By default the local host is used. In an HP-UX cluster, the root server is queried by default, since that is the system on which the automounter is normally run.

−l *log_file*
   Tell amd to use *log_file* as the log file name. For security reasons, this must be the same log file which amd used when started. This option is therefore only useful to refresh amd's open file handle on the log file, so that it can be rotated and compressed via daily cron jobs.

−m   Ask the automounter to provide a list of mounted filesystems, including the number of references to each filesystem and any error which occurred while mounting.

−p   Return the process ID of the remote or locally running amd. Useful when you need to send a signal to the local amd process, and would rather not have to search through the process table. This option is used in the *ctl-amd* script.

−q   Suppress error messages produced when attempting synchronous unmounts with the **−u** option.

−s   Ask the automounter to provide system-wide mount statistics.

−u   Ask the automounter to unmount the filesystems named in *directory* instead of providing information about them. Unmounts are requested, not forced. They merely cause the mounted filesystem to timeout, which will be picked up by **amd**'s main scheduler thus causing the normal timeout action to be taken. If the **−u** option is repeated, **amq** will attempt to unmount the file system synchronously by waiting until the timeout action is taken and returning an error if the unmount fails. Any error messages produced may be suppressed with the **−q** option.

−v   Ask the automounter for its version information. This is a subset of the information output by **amd**'s *-v* option.

−w   Translate a full pathname as returned by *getcwd*(3) into a short **Amd** pathname that goes through its mount points. This option requires that **Amd** is running.

−x *log_options*
   Ask the automounter to use the logging options specified in *log_options* from now on. Note that the "fatal" and "error" options cannot be turned off.

–D *debug_options*
> Ask the automounter to use the debugging options specified in *debug_options* from now on.

–H   Display short usage message.

–P *program_number*
> Contact an alternate running amd that had registered itself on a different RPC *program_number* and apply all other operations to that instance of the automounter. This is useful when you run multiple copies of amd, and need to manage each one separately. If not specified, amq will use the default program number for amd, 300019. For security reasons, the only alternate program numbers amd can use range from 300019 to 300029, inclusive.

–T   Contact **amd** using the TCP transport only. Normally **amq** will try TCP, and if that failed, will try UDP.

–U   Contact **amd** using UDP (connectionless) transport only. Normally **amq** will try TCP, and if that failed, will try UDP.

FILES
> **amq.x**   RPC protocol description.

CAVEATS
> **Amq** uses a Sun registered RPC program number (300019 decimal) which may not be in the /etc/rpc database.
>
> If the TCP wrappers library is available, and the **use_tcpwrappers** global **amd.conf** option is set to "yes", then **amd** will verify that the host running **amq** is authorized to connect. The *amd* service name must used in the **/etc/hosts.allow** and **/etc/hosts.deny** files. For example, to allow only localhost to connect to **amd,** add this line to **/etc/hosts.allow:**
>
> > amd: localhost
>
> and this line to **/etc/hosts.deny:**
>
> > amd: ALL

SEE ALSO
> **amd**(8), **amd.conf**(5), **hosts_access**(5).
>
> "am-utils" **info**(1) entry.
>
> *Linux NFS and Automounter Administration* by Erez Zadok, ISBN 0-7821-2739-8, (Sybex, 2001).
>
> *http://www.am-utils.org*
>
> *Amd – The 4.4 BSD Automounter*

AUTHORS
> Jan-Simon Pendry <jsp@doc.ic.ac.uk>, Department of Computing, Imperial College, London, UK.
>
> Erez Zadok <ezk@cs.sunysb.edu>, Computer Science Department, Stony Brook University, Stony Brook, New York, USA.
>
> Other authors and contributors to am-utils are listed in the **AUTHORS** file distributed with am-utils.

NAME
   amrctl — Control utility for AMI MegaRaid controllers

SYNOPSIS
   amrctl *stat* [**-bgv**] [**-a** *attempts*] [**-f** *device*] [**-l** *volno*] [**-p** *driveno*]
        [**-s** *busno*] [**-s** *busno:driveno*] [**-t** *microseconds*]

DESCRIPTION
   The **amrctl** queries or controls AMI MegaRaid controllers supported by the amr(4) driver.

   Only the *stat* subcommand is currently implemented, and reports status of the controller. The options for the *stat* subcommand are as follows:

   -a *attempts*
   > Number of retries for a command before giving up. Default 5.

   -b   Report battery status.

   -f *device*   Device to use. Default to /dev/amr0.

   -g   Report global paramters for the controller.

   -l *volno*   Report status of a logical drive.

   -p *driveno* Report status of a physical drive.

   -s *busno*   Report status of all physical drives on the specified bus.

   -s *busno:driveno*
   > Report status of the specified physical drive on the specified bus.

   -t *microseconds*
   > Delay between retries for a command.

   -v   Increase verbosity level by one.

SEE ALSO
   amr(4)

HISTORY
   The **amrctl** command first appeared in NetBSD 4.0.

AUTHORS
   The **amrctl** command was written by Pierre David ⟨Pierre.David@crc.u-strasbg.fr⟩ and Jung-uk Kim ⟨jkim@FreeBSD.org⟩ for FreeBSD.

NAME

anvil – Postfix session count and request rate control

SYNOPSIS

anvil [generic Postfix daemon options]

DESCRIPTION

The Postfix **anvil**(8) server maintains statistics about client connection counts or client request rates. This information can be used to defend against clients that hammer a server with either too many simultaneous sessions, or with too many successive requests within a configurable time interval. This server is designed to run under control by the Postfix **master**(8) server.

In the following text, **ident** specifies a (service, client) combination. The exact syntax of that information is application-dependent; the **anvil**(8) server does not care.

CONNECTION COUNT/RATE CONTROL

To register a new connection send the following request to the **anvil**(8) server:

request=connect
ident=_string_

The **anvil**(8) server answers with the number of simultaneous connections and the number of connections per unit time for the (service, client) combination specified with **ident**:

status=0
count=_number_
rate=_number_

To register a disconnect event send the following request to the **anvil**(8) server:

request=disconnect
ident=_string_

The **anvil**(8) server replies with:

status=0

MESSAGE RATE CONTROL

To register a message delivery request send the following request to the **anvil**(8) server:

request=message
ident=_string_

The **anvil**(8) server answers with the number of message delivery requests per unit time for the (service, client) combination specified with **ident**:

status=0
rate=_number_

RECIPIENT RATE CONTROL

To register a recipient request send the following request to the **anvil**(8) server:

request=recipient
ident=_string_

The **anvil**(8) server answers with the number of recipient addresses per unit time for the (service, client) combination specified with **ident**:

> **status=0**
> **rate=**_number_

TLS SESSION NEGOTIATION RATE CONTROL

The features described in this section are available with Postfix 2.3 and later.

To register a request for a new (i.e. not cached) TLS session send the following request to the **anvil**(8) server:

> **request=newtls**
> **ident=**_string_

The **anvil**(8) server answers with the number of new TLS session requests per unit time for the (service, client) combination specified with **ident**:

> **status=0**
> **rate=**_number_

To retrieve new TLS session request rate information without updating the counter information, send:

> **request=newtls_report**
> **ident=**_string_

The **anvil**(8) server answers with the number of new TLS session requests per unit time for the (service, client) combination specified with **ident**:

> **status=0**
> **rate=**_number_

SECURITY

The **anvil**(8) server does not talk to the network or to local users, and can run chrooted at fixed low privilege.

The **anvil**(8) server maintains an in-memory table with information about recent clients requests. No persistent state is kept because standard system library routines are not sufficiently robust for update-intensive applications.

Although the in-memory state is kept only temporarily, this may require a lot of memory on systems that handle connections from many remote clients. To reduce memory usage, reduce the time unit over which state is kept.

DIAGNOSTICS

Problems and transactions are logged to **syslogd**(8).

Upon exit, and every **anvil_status_update_time** seconds, the server logs the maximal count and rate values measured, together with (service, client) information and the time of day associated with those events. In order to avoid unnecessary overhead, no measurements are done for activity that isn't concurrency limited or rate limited.

BUGS

Systems behind network address translating routers or proxies appear to have the same client address and can run into connection count and/or rate limits falsely.

In this preliminary implementation, a count (or rate) limited server process can have only one remote client at a time. If a server process reports multiple simultaneous clients, state is kept only for the last reported client.

The **anvil**(8) server automatically discards client request information after it expires. To prevent the **anvil**(8) server from discarding client request rate information too early or too late, a rate limited service should always register connect/disconnect events even when it does not explicitly limit them.

CONFIGURATION PARAMETERS

On low-traffic mail systems, changes to **main.cf** are picked up automatically as **anvil**(8) processes run for only a limited amount of time. On other mail systems, use the command "**postfix reload**" to speed up a change.

The text below provides only a parameter summary. See **postconf**(5) for more details including examples.

anvil_rate_time_unit (60s)
> The time unit over which client connection rates and other rates are calculated.

anvil_status_update_time (600s)
> How frequently the **anvil**(8) connection and rate limiting server logs peak usage information.

config_directory (see 'postconf -d' output)
> The default location of the Postfix main.cf and master.cf configuration files.

daemon_timeout (18000s)
> How much time a Postfix daemon process may take to handle a request before it is terminated by a built-in watchdog timer.

ipc_timeout (3600s)
> The time limit for sending or receiving information over an internal communication channel.

max_idle (100s)
> The maximum amount of time that an idle Postfix daemon process waits for an incoming connection before terminating voluntarily.

max_use (100)
> The maximal number of incoming connections that a Postfix daemon process will service before terminating voluntarily.

process_id (read-only)
> The process ID of a Postfix command or daemon process.

process_name (read-only)
> The process name of a Postfix command or daemon process.

syslog_facility (mail)
> The syslog facility of Postfix logging.

syslog_name (see 'postconf -d' output)
> The mail system name that is prepended to the process name in syslog records, so that "smtpd" becomes, for example, "postfix/smtpd".

SEE ALSO

> smtpd(8), Postfix SMTP server
> postconf(5), configuration parameters
> master(5), generic daemon options

README FILES

> Use "**postconf readme_directory**" or "**postconf html_directory**" to locate this information.
> TUNING_README, performance tuning

LICENSE

> The Secure Mailer license must be distributed with this software.

HISTORY

> The anvil service is available in Postfix 2.2 and later.

AUTHOR(S)
Wietse Venema
IBM T.J. Watson Research
P.O. Box 704
Yorktown Heights, NY 10598, USA

NAME

apm, **zzz** — Advanced Power Management control program

SYNOPSIS

apm [**-abdlmsSvz**] [**-f** *sockname*]
zzz [**-Sz**] [**-f** *sockname*]

DESCRIPTION

The **apm** program communicates with the Advanced Power Management (APM) daemon, apmd(8), making requests of the current power status or placing the system either into suspend or stand-by state. The **apm** tool is only installed on supported platforms.

With no flags, **apm** displays the current power management state in verbose form.

Available command-line flags are:

-z	Put the system into suspend (deep sleep) mode.
-s	Put the system into stand-by (light sleep) mode.
-l	Display the estimated battery lifetime in percent.
-m	Display the estimated battery lifetime in minutes.
-b	Display the battery status: 0 means high, 1 means low, 2 means critical, 3 means charging, 4 means absent, and 255 means unknown.
-a	Display the external charger (A/C status): 0 means disconnected, 1 means connected, 2 means backup power source, and 255 means unknown.
-s	Display if power management is enabled.
-v	Request more verbose description of the displayed states.
-f *sockname*	Set the name of the socket via which to contact apmd(8) to sockname.
-d	Do not communicate with the APM daemon; attempt instead to manipulate the APM control device directly.

The **zzz** variant of this command is an alternative for suspending the system. With no arguments, **zzz** places the system into suspend mode. The command line flags serve the same purpose as for the **apm** variant of this command.

This command does not wait for positive confirmation that the requested mode has been entered; to do so would mean the command does not return until the system resumes from its sleep state.

FILES

/var/run/apmdev is the default UNIX-domain socket used for communication with apmd(8). The **-f** flag may be used to specify an alternate socket name. The protection modes on this socket govern which users may access the APM functions.

/dev/apmctl is the control device which is used when the **-d** flag is specified; it must be writable for the **-d** flag to work successfully. /dev/apm is the status device used when the socket is not accessible; it must be readable to provide current APM status.

SEE ALSO

acpi(4), apm(4), apmd(8)

Intel Corporation and Microsoft Corporation, *Advanced Power Management (APM) BIOS Interface Specification*, Revision 1.2, February 1996.

HISTORY

The **apm** command appeared in NetBSD 1.3.

The APM specification first appeared in 1992. The last update to the standard was made in 1996 - the same year when it was superceded by the ACPI 1.0 standard. Thereafter power management on IBM-compatible personal computers has relied on ACPI, implemented in NetBSD by the acpi(4) subsystem. The acpi(4) provides an emulation layer for the legacy **apm**.

NAME

apmd — Advanced Power Management monitor daemon

SYNOPSIS

apmd [**-adlqsv**] [**-t** *rate*] [**-S** *sockname*] [**-m** *sockmode*]
    [**-o** *sockowner:sockgroup*] [**-f** *devname*]

DESCRIPTION

The **apmd** daemon monitors the Advanced Power Management (APM) pseudo-device, acting on signaled events and upon user requests as sent by the apm(8) utility. The **apmd** daemon is only installed on supported platforms.

*The **apmd** is largely deprecated.* Modern systems supporting ACPI should rely on acpi(4), powerd(8), and the envsys(4) framework instead.

For suspend and standby request events delivered by the BIOS, or via apm(8), **apmd** runs the appropriate configuration program (if one exists), syncs the buffer cache to disk and initiates the requested mode. When resuming after suspend or standby, **apmd** runs the appropriate configuration utility (if one exists). For power status change events, **apmd** fetches the current status and reports it via syslog(3) with logging facility LOG_DAEMON.

apmd announces the transition to standby mode with a single high tone on the speaker (using the /dev/speaker device). Suspends are announced with two high tones.

apmd periodically polls the APM driver for the current power state. If the battery charge level changes substantially or the external power status changes, the new status is logged. The polling rate defaults to once per 10 minutes, but this may be altered by using the **-t** command-line flag.

apmd supports the following options:

-a   Any BIOS-initiated suspend or standby requests are ignored if the system is connected to line current and not running from batteries (user requests are still honored).

-d   Enter debug mode, log to facility LOG_LOCAL1 and stay in the foreground on the controlling terminal.

-f *devname*
         Specify an alternate device file name.

-l   A low-battery event causes a suspend request to occur.

-m *sockmode*
         Use *sockmode* instead of '0660' for the mode of /var/run/apmdev.

-o *sockowner:sockgroup*
         Use *sockowner:sockgroup* instead of "0:0" for the owner/group of /var/run/apmdev.

-q   Do not announce suspend and standby requests on the speaker.

-s   The current battery statistics are reported via syslog(3) and exit without monitoring the APM status.

-S *sockname*
         Specify an alternate socket name (used by apm(8) to communicate with **apmd**).

-t *rate*   Change the polling rate from 600 seconds to *rate* seconds.

-v   Periodically log the power status via syslog(3).

When a client requests a suspend or stand-by mode, **apmd** does not wait for positive confirmation that the requested mode has been entered before replying to the client; to do so would mean the client does not get a reply until the system resumes from its sleep state. Rather, **apmd** replies with the intended state to the client and then places the system in the requested mode after running the configuration script and flushing the buffer cache.

Actions can be configured for the five transitions: **suspend**, **standby**, **resume**, **line** or **battery**. The suspend and standby actions are run prior to **apmd** performing any other actions (such as disk syncs) and entering the new mode. The resume program is run after resuming from a stand-by or suspended state.

The line and battery actions are run after switching power sources to AC (line) or battery, respectively. The appropriate line or battery action is also run upon the startup of apmd based on the current power source.

FILES
```
/etc/apm/suspend
/etc/apm/standby
/etc/apm/resume
/etc/apm/line
/etc/apm/battery
```
                        Contain the host's customized actions. Each file must be an executable binary or shell script suitable for execution by the execve(2) function. If you wish to have the same program or script control all transitions, it may determine which transition is in progress by examining its *argv[0]* which is set to one of *suspend*, *standby*, *resume*, *line* or *battery*. See /usr/share/examples/apm/script for such an example script.

/var/run/apmdev   The default UNIX-domain socket used for communication with apm(8). The socket is protected by default to mode 0660, UID 0, GID 0.

/dev/apmctl   The default device used to control the APM kernel driver.

SEE ALSO
execve(2), syslog(3), apm(4), speaker(4), apm(8), syslogd(8)

HISTORY
The **apmd** daemon appeared in NetBSD 1.3.

NAME

apmlabel — update disk label from Apple Partition Map

SYNOPSIS

apmlabel [**-fqrw**] *device*

DESCRIPTION

apmlabel is used to update a NetBSD disk label from the Apple Partition Map found on disks that were previously used on Mac OS systems (or other APM using systems).

apmlabel scans the APM contained in the first blocks of the disk and generates additional partition entries for the disk from the entries found. Driver and patches partitions are ignored.

Each APM entry which does not have an equivalent partition in the disk label (equivalent in having the same size and offset) is added to the first free partition slot in the disk label. A free partition slot is defined as one with an fstype of 'unused' and a size of zero ('0'). If there are not enough free slots in the disk label, a warning will be issued.

The raw partition (typically partition *c*, but *d* on i386 and some other platforms) is left alone during this process.

By default, the proposed changed disk label will be displayed and no disk label update will occur.

Available options:

-f

   Force an update, even if there has been no change.

-q

   Performs operations in a quiet fashion.

-r

   In conjunction with **-w**, also update the on-disk label.

-w

   Update the in-core label if it has been changed.

SEE ALSO

disklabel(8), dkctl(8), pdisk(8)

HISTORY

The **apmlabel** command appeared in NetBSD 5.0.

NAME
arp — address resolution display and control

SYNOPSIS
arp [**−n**] *hostname*
arp [**−nv**] **−a**
arp [**−v**] **−d −a**
arp [**−v**] **−d** *hostname* [*proxy*]
arp −s *hostname ether_addr* [*temp*] [*pub* [*proxy*]]
arp −f *filename*

DESCRIPTION
The **arp** program displays and modifies the Internet-to-Ethernet address translation tables used by the address resolution protocol (arp(4)). With no flags, the program displays the current ARP entry for *hostname*. The host may be specified by name or by number, using Internet dot notation.

Available options:

−a   The program displays all of the current ARP entries.

−d   A super-user may delete an entry for the host called *hostname* with the **−d** flag. If the **proxy** keyword is specified, only the published "proxy only" ARP entry for this host will be deleted. If used with **−a** instead of a *hostname*, it will delete all arp entries.

−f   Causes the file *filename* to be read and multiple entries to be set in the ARP tables. Entries in the file should be of the form

             hostname ether_addr [*temp*] [*pub*]

       with argument meanings as described below.

−n   Show network addresses as numbers (normally **arp** attempts to display addresses symbolically).

−s *hostname ether_addr*
       Create an ARP entry for the host called *hostname* with the Ethernet address *ether_addr*. The Ethernet address is given as six hex bytes separated by colons. The entry will be permanent unless the word *temp* is given in the command. If the word *pub* is given, the entry will be "published"; i.e., this system will act as an ARP server, responding to requests for *hostname* even though the host address is not its own. If the word *proxy* is also given, the published entry will be a "proxy only" entry.

−v   Display verbose information when adding or deleting ARP entries.

SEE ALSO
inet(3), arp(4), ifconfig(8)

HISTORY
The **arp** command appeared in 4.3BSD.

NAME

atactl — a program to manipulate ATA (IDE) devices and busses

SYNOPSIS

atactl *device command* [*arg* [...]]

DESCRIPTION

atactl allows a user or system administrator to issue commands to and otherwise control devices which reside on standard IDE and ATA controllers, or the ATA bus itself. It is used by specifying a device or bus to manipulate, the command to perform, and any arguments the command may require.

DEVICE COMMANDS

The following commands may be used on IDE and ATA devices. Note that not all devices support all commands.

identify   Identify the specified device, displaying the device's vendor, product, revision strings, and the device's capabilities.

idle   Place the specified device into Idle mode. This mode may consume less power than Active mode.

standby   Place the specified device into Standby mode. This mode will consume less power than Idle mode.

sleep   Place the specified device into Sleep mode. This mode will consume less power than Standby mode, but requires a device reset to resume operation. Typically the wd(4) driver performs this reset automatically, but this should still be used with caution.

setidle *idle-timer*
Places the specified device into Idle mode, and sets the Idle timer to *idle-timer* seconds. A value of 0 will disable the Idle timer.

setstandby *standby-timer*
Places the specified device into Standby mode, and sets the Standby timer to *standby-timer* seconds. A value of 0 will disable the Standby timer.

checkpower
Will print out if the device is in Active, Idle, or Standby power management mode.

apm [*disable* | *set #*]
Controls the Advanced Power Management feature of the specified device. Advanced Power Management is an optional feature used to specify a power management level to balance between device performance and power consumption.

disable   Disable the Advanced Power Management.

set #   Enable the Advanced Power Management feature and set its level to the value #, where # is an integer within the scale 0-253; being 0 the mode with the lowest power consumption (and thus the worse performance) and 253 the mode which provides the better performance at a cost of more power consumption.

It should be noted that the effect of the value need not be continous. For example, a device might provide only two modes: one from 0 to 126 and other from 127 to 253. Per the specification, values of 127 and higher do not permit the device to spin down to save power.

smart [*enable* | *disable* | *status* | *offline #* | *error-log* | *selftest-log*]

>   Controls SMART feature set of the specified device. SMART stands for Self-Monitoring, Analysis, and Reporting Technology. It provides an early warning system by comparing subtle operation characteristics to those determined in vendor testing to precede device failures.

>   *enable*   Enables access to SMART capabilities within the device. Prior to being enabled, a SMART capable device neither monitors nor saves SMART attribute values. The state of SMART, either enabled or disabled, will be preserved by the device across power cycles.

>   *disable*   Disables access to SMART capabilities within the device. Attribute values will be saved, and will no longer be monitored.

>   *status*   Reports whether SMART is supported by the device, and whether SMART is enabled on the device (can only be determined on ATA6 or better devices). If SMART is enabled, then a table of attribute information is printed. Attributes are the specific performance or calibration parameters that are used in analyzing the status of the device. The specific set of attributes being used and the identity of these attributes is vendor specific and proprietary.

>   Attribute values are used to represent the relative reliability of individual performance or calibration parameters. The valid range of attribute values is from 1 to 253 decimal. Lower values indicate that the analysis algorithms being used by the device are predicting a higher probability of a degrading or faulty condition.

>   Each attribute value has a corresponding threshold limit which is used for direct comparison to the attribute value to indicate the existence of a degrading or faulty condition. The numerical value of the attribute thresholds are determined by the device manufacturer through design and reliability testing and analysis. Each attribute threshold represents the lowest limit to which its corresponding attribute value can equal while still retaining a positive reliability status.

>   If the crit field is "yes" then negative reliability of this attribute predicts imminent data loss. Otherwise it merely indicates that the intended design life period of usage or age has been exceeded. The collect field indicates whether this attribute is updated while the device is online. The reliability field indicates whether the attribute value is within the acceptable threshold.

>   *offline #*   Runs the numbered offline self-test on the drive.

>   *error-log*   Prints the error log.

>   *selftest-log* Prints the self-test log.

security [*freeze* | *status*]

>   Controls "security" (password protection) features of modern ATA drives. The security commands are intended to be issued by low-level software (firmware / BIOS) only. Generally, the security status should be "frozen" before the operating system is started so that misbehaving or malicious software cannot set or change a password. Older and buggy BIOSes neglect to do so; in these cases it might make sense to issue the "freeze" command early in the boot process.

freeze   freezes the drive's security status

status   displays the drive's security status

BUS COMMANDS

The following commands may be used on IDE and ATA busses. Note that not all devices support all commands.

reset   Reset the bus. This will reset all ATA devices present on the bus. Any ATAPI device with pending commands will also be reset.

SEE ALSO

ioctl(2), wd(4), dkctl(8), scsictl(8)

HISTORY

The **atactl** command first appeared in NetBSD 1.4.

AUTHORS

The **atactl** command was written by Ken Hornstein. It was based heavily on the scsictl(8) command written by Jason R. Thorpe.

BUGS

The output from the **identify** command is rather ugly.

NAME
     atf-cleanup — safe removal of directory hierarchies

SYNOPSIS
     atf-cleanup *path1* [*.. pathN*]
     atf-cleanup -h

DESCRIPTION
     atf-cleanup is a utility that removes files and directories recursively, but doing it in a safe manner to
     avoid crossing mount point boundaries. Before the removal of a given tree, **atf-cleanup** will look for file
     systems mounted anywhere inside it and try to unmount them. If all mount points were properly unmounted,
     it later proceeds to do the real removal. This tool is used internally by test programs to clean up the test
     cases' work directories, as they may have left other file systems mounted inside them.

     In the first synopsis form, **atf-cleanup** proceeds to scan and remove all the given files or directories.

     In the second synopsis form, **atf-cleanup** will print information about all supported options and their
     purpose.

     The following options are available:

     -h   Shows a short summary of all available options and their purpose.

SEE ALSO
     atf(7)

NAME
   atf-format — formats a text paragraph to fit nicely on screen

SYNOPSIS
   atf-format [*str1* [*.. strN*]]
   atf-format -t *tag* [**-l** *length*] [**-r**] [*str1* [*.. strN*]]
   atf-format -h

DESCRIPTION
   atf-format formats text messages to not overflow the terminal's width, and optionally adds a prefix string
   to them. Messages can be fed through the standard input or through multiple arguments; in the latter case, all
   of them are concatenated as if they were separated by a single space. Different lines (those separated by a
   new-line character) are treated as different paragraphs and thus formatted accordingly.

   In the first synopsis form, **atf-format** formats the message to not overflow the terminal's width. The
   message is supposed to start at column 0.

   In the second synopsis form, **atf-format** also formats the message to not overflow the terminal's width,
   but it appends a tag to the beginning of the string. This tag may or may be not repeated on each line of the
   text; if it is not repeated, the text is simply indented. This synopsis form is useful to easily format two-col-
   umn tables, being the first one much shorter than the second one. The message is supposed to start at column
   0.

   In the third synopsis form, **atf-format** will print information about all supported options and their purpose.

   The following options are available:

   -h   Shows a short summary of all available options and their purpose.

   -l *length*   Specifies the length in characters of the tag. Useful if the tag is shorter than the desired
                       length, which happens when formatting two-column tables.

   -r   Repeat the tag on each line. Otherwise it is only shown on the first one, and all others are
                       indented appropriately using whitespace.

   -t *tag*   Specifies the tag to use

SEE ALSO
   atf(7)

NAME
    atrun — run jobs queued for later execution

SYNOPSIS
    atrun [**-l** *load_avg*] [**-d**]

DESCRIPTION
    atrun runs jobs queued by `at`(1). Root's `crontab`(5) must contain the line:

```
*/10      *        *        *        *        root      /usr/libexec/atrun
```

    so that `atrun`(8) gets called every ten minutes.

    At every invocation, every job in lowercase queues whose starting time has passed is started. A maximum of one batch job (denoted by uppercase queues) is started each time **atrun** is invoked.

OPTIONS
    -l *load_avg*

        Specifies a limiting load factor, over which batch jobs should not be run, instead of the compiled-in value of 1.5.

    -d   Debug; print error messages to standard error instead of using `syslog`(3).

WARNINGS
    For **atrun** to work, you have to start up a `cron`(8) daemon.

FILES
    `/var/at/spool` Directory containing output spool files
    `/var/at/jobs`   Directory containing job files

SEE ALSO
    `at`(1), `crontab`(1), `syslog`(3), `crontab`(5), `cron`(8)

AUTHORS
    Thomas Koenig ⟨ig25@rz.uni-karlsruhe.de⟩

BUGS
    The functionality of **atrun** should be merged into `cron`(8).

NAME
authpf — authenticating gateway user shell

SYNOPSIS
authpf

DESCRIPTION
authpf is a user shell for authenticating gateways. It is used to change pf(4) rules when a user authenticates and starts a session with sshd(8) and to undo these changes when the user's session exits. It is designed for changing filter and translation rules for an individual source IP address as long as a user maintains an active ssh(1) session. Typical use would be for a gateway that authenticates users before allowing them Internet use, or a gateway that allows different users into different places. **authpf** logs the successful start and end of a session to syslogd(8). This, combined with properly set up filter rules and secure switches, can be used to ensure users are held accountable for their network traffic.

authpf can add filter and translation rules using the syntax described in pf.conf(5). **authpf** requires that the pf(4) system be enabled before use. **authpf** can also maintain the list of IP address of connected users in the "authpf_users" table.

authpf is meant to be used with users who can connect via ssh(1) only. On startup, **authpf** retrieves the client's connecting IP address via the SSH_CLIENT environment variable and, after performing additional access checks, reads a template file to determine what filter and translation rules (if any) to add. On session exit the same rules that were added at startup are removed.

Each **authpf** process stores its rules in a separate ruleset inside a pf(4) anchor shared by all **authpf** processes. By default, the anchor name "authpf" is used, and the ruleset names equal the username and PID of the **authpf** processes as "username(pid)". The following rules need to be added to the main ruleset /etc/pf.conf in order to cause evaluation of any **authpf** rules:

```
nat-anchor "authpf/*"
rdr-anchor "authpf/*"
binat-anchor "authpf/*"
anchor "authpf/*"
```

The "/*" at the end of the anchor name is required for pf(4) to process the rulesets attached to the anchor by **authpf**.

FILTER AND TRANSLATION RULES
Filter and translation rules for **authpf** use the same format described in pf.conf(5). The only difference is that these rules may (and probably should) use the macro *user_ip*, which is assigned the connecting IP address whenever **authpf** is run. Additionally, the macro *user_id* is assigned the user name.

Filter and translation rules are stored in a file called authpf.rules. This file will first be searched for in /etc/authpf/users/$USER/ and then in /etc/authpf/. Only one of these files will be used if both are present.

Per-user rules from the /etc/authpf/users/$USER/ directory are intended to be used when non-default rules are needed on an individual user basis. It is important to ensure that a user can not write or change these configuration files.

The authpf.rules file must exist in one of the above locations for **authpf** to run.

CONFIGURATION
Options are controlled by the /etc/authpf/authpf.conf file. If the file is empty, defaults are used for all configuration options. The file consists of pairs of the form name=value, one per line. Currently, the allowed values are as follows:

anchor=name
> Use the specified `anchor` name instead of "authpf".

table=name
> Use the specified `table` name instead of "authpf_users".

USER MESSAGES

On successful invocation, **authpf** displays a message telling the user he or she has been authenticated. It will additionally display the contents of the file `/etc/authpf/authpf.message` if the file exists and is readable.

There exist two methods for providing additional granularity to the control offered by **authpf** - it is possible to set the gateway to explicitly allow users who have authenticated to ssh(1) and deny access to only a few troublesome individuals. This is done by creating a file with the banned user's login name as the filename in `/etc/authpf/banned/`. The contents of this file will be displayed to a banned user, thus providing a method for informing the user that they have been banned, and where they can go and how to get there if they want to have their service restored. This is the default behaviour.

It is also possible to configure **authpf** to only allow specific users access. This is done by listing their login names, one per line, in `/etc/authpf/authpf.allow`. If "*" is found on a line, then all usernames match. If **authpf** is unable to verify the user's permission to use the gateway, it will print a brief message and die. It should be noted that a ban takes precedence over an allow.

On failure, messages will be logged to syslogd(8) for the system administrator. The user does not see these, but will be told the system is unavailable due to technical difficulties. The contents of the file `/etc/authpf/authpf.problem` will also be displayed if the file exists and is readable.

CONFIGURATION ISSUES

authpf maintains the changed filter rules as long as the user maintains an active session. It is important to remember however, that the existence of this session means the user is authenticated. Because of this, it is important to configure sshd(8) to ensure the security of the session, and to ensure that the network through which users connect is secure. sshd(8) should be configured to use the *ClientAliveInterval* and *ClientAliveCountMax* parameters to ensure that a ssh session is terminated quickly if it becomes unresponsive, or if arp or address spoofing is used to hijack the session. Note that TCP keepalives are not sufficient for this, since they are not secure. Also note that the various SSH tunnelling mechanisms, such as *AllowTcpForwarding* and *PermitTunnel*, should be disabled for **authpf** users to prevent them from circumventing restrictions imposed by the packet filter ruleset.

authpf will remove state table entries that were created during a user's session. This ensures that there will be no unauthenticated traffic allowed to pass after the controlling ssh(1) session has been closed.

authpf is designed for gateway machines which typically do not have regular (non-administrative) users using the machine. An administrator must remember that **authpf** can be used to modify the filter rules through the environment in which it is run, and as such could be used to modify the filter rules (based on the contents of the configuration files) by regular users. In the case where a machine has regular users using it, as well as users with **authpf** as their shell, the regular users should be prevented from running **authpf** by using the `/etc/authpf/authpf.allow` or `/etc/authpf/banned/` facilities.

authpf modifies the packet filter and address translation rules, and because of this it needs to be configured carefully. **authpf** will not run and will exit silently if the `/etc/authpf/authpf.conf` file does not exist. After considering the effect **authpf** may have on the main packet filter rules, the system administrator may enable **authpf** by creating an appropriate `/etc/authpf/authpf.conf` file.

FILES
```
/etc/authpf/authpf.conf
/etc/authpf/authpf.allow
/etc/authpf/authpf.rules
/etc/authpf/authpf.message
/etc/authpf/authpf.problem
```

EXAMPLES

Control Files – To illustrate the user-specific access control mechanisms, let us consider a typical user named bob. Normally, as long as bob can authenticate himself, the **authpf** program will load the appropriate rules. Enter the `/etc/authpf/banned/` directory. If bob has somehow fallen from grace in the eyes of the powers-that-be, they can prohibit him from using the gateway by creating the file `/etc/authpf/banned/bob` containing a message about why he has been banned from using the network. Once bob has done suitable penance, his access may be restored by moving or removing the file `/etc/authpf/banned/bob`.

Now consider a workgroup containing alice, bob, carol and dave. They have a wireless network which they would like to protect from unauthorized use. To accomplish this, they create the file `/etc/authpf/authpf.allow` which lists their login ids, one per line. At this point, even if eve could authenticate to `sshd`(8), she would not be allowed to use the gateway. Adding and removing users from the work group is a simple matter of maintaining a list of allowed userids. If bob once again manages to annoy the powers-that-be, they can ban him from using the gateway by creating the familiar `/etc/authpf/banned/bob` file. Though bob is listed in the allow file, he is prevented from using this gateway due to the existence of a ban file.

Distributed Authentication – It is often desirable to interface with a distributed password system rather than forcing the sysadmins to keep a large number of local password files in sync. The `login.conf`(5) mechanism in OpenBSD can be used to fork the right shell. To make that happen, `login.conf`(5) should have entries that look something like this:

```
shell-default:shell=/bin/csh

default:\
        ...
        :shell=/usr/sbin/authpf

daemon:\
        ...
        :shell=/bin/csh:\
        :tc=default:

staff:\
        ...
        :shell=/bin/csh:\
        :tc=default:
```

Using a default password file, all users will get **authpf** as their shell except for root who will get `/bin/csh`.

SSH Configuration – As stated earlier, `sshd`(8) must be properly configured to detect and defeat network attacks. To that end, the following options should be added to `sshd_config`(5):

```
Protocol 2
ClientAliveInterval 15
ClientAliveCountMax 3
```

This ensures that unresponsive or spoofed sessions are terminated within a minute, since a hijacker should not be able to spoof ssh keepalive messages.

Banners – Once authenticated, the user is shown the contents of `/etc/authpf/authpf.message`. This message may be a screen-full of the appropriate use policy, the contents of `/etc/motd` or something as simple as the following:

```
This means you will be held accountable by the powers that be
for traffic originating from your machine, so please play nice.
```

To tell the user where to go when the system is broken, `/etc/authpf/authpf.problem` could contain something like this:

```
Sorry, there appears to be some system problem. To report this
problem so we can fix it, please phone 1-900-314-1597 or send
an email to remove@bulkmailerz.net.
```

Packet Filter Rules – In areas where this gateway is used to protect a wireless network (a hub with several hundred ports), the default rule set as well as the per-user rules should probably allow very few things beyond encrypted protocols like ssh(1) or ipsec(4). On a securely switched network, with plug-in jacks for visitors who are given authentication accounts, you might want to allow out everything. In this context, a secure switch is one that tries to prevent address table overflow attacks.

Example `/etc/pf.conf`:

```
# by default we allow internal clients to talk to us using
# ssh and use us as a dns server.
internal_if="fxp1"
gateway_addr="10.0.1.1"
nat-anchor "authpf/*"
rdr-anchor "authpf/*"
binat-anchor "authpf/*"
block in on $internal_if from any to any
pass in quick on $internal_if proto tcp from any to $gateway_addr \
      port = ssh
pass in quick on $internal_if proto udp from any to $gateway_addr \
      port = domain
anchor "authpf/*"
```

For a switched, wired net – This example `/etc/authpf/authpf.rules` makes no real restrictions; it turns the IP address on and off, logging TCP connections.

```
external_if = "xl0"
internal_if = "fxp0"

pass in log quick on $internal_if proto tcp from $user_ip to any
pass in quick on $internal_if from $user_ip to any
```

For a wireless or shared net – This example `/etc/authpf/authpf.rules` could be used for an insecure network (such as a public wireless network) where we might need to be a bit more restrictive.

```
internal_if="fxp1"
ipsec_gw="10.2.3.4"

# rdr ftp for proxying by ftp-proxy(8)
rdr on $internal_if proto tcp from $user_ip to any port 21 \
      -> 127.0.0.1 port 8021
```

```
# allow out ftp, ssh, www and https only, and allow user to negotiate
# ipsec with the ipsec server.
pass in log quick on $internal_if proto tcp from $user_ip to any \
      port { 21, 22, 80, 443 }
pass in quick on $internal_if proto tcp from $user_ip to any \
      port { 21, 22, 80, 443 }
pass in quick proto udp from $user_ip to $ipsec_gw port = isakmp
pass in quick proto esp from $user_ip to $ipsec_gw
```

Dealing with NAT – The following /etc/authpf/authpf.rules shows how to deal with NAT, using tags:

```
ext_if = "fxp1"
ext_addr = 129.128.11.10
int_if = "fxp0"
# nat and tag connections...
nat on $ext_if from $user_ip to any tag $user_ip -> $ext_addr
pass in quick on $int_if from $user_ip to any
pass out log quick on $ext_if tagged $user_ip
```

With the above rules added by **authpf**, outbound connections corresponding to each users NAT'ed connections will be logged as in the example below, where the user may be identified from the ruleset name.

```
# tcpdump -n -e -ttt -i pflog0
Oct 31 19:42:30.296553 rule 0.bbeck(20267).1/0(match): pass out on fxp1: \
129.128.11.10.60539 > 198.137.240.92.22: S 2131494121:2131494121(0) win \
16384 <mss 1460,nop,nop,sackOK> (DF)
```

Using the authpf_users table – Simple **authpf** settings can be implemented without an anchor by just using the "authpf_users" table. For example, the following pf.conf(5) lines will give SMTP and IMAP access to logged in users:

```
table <authpf_users> persist
pass in on $ext_if proto tcp from <authpf_users> \
        to port { smtp imap }
```

It is also possible to use the "authpf_users" table in combination with anchors. For example, pf(4) processing can be sped up by looking up the anchor only for packets coming from logged in users:

```
table <authpf_users> persist
anchor "authpf/*" from <authpf_users>
rdr-anchor "authpf/*" from <authpf_users>
```

SEE ALSO
pf(4), pf.conf(5), ftp-proxy(8)

HISTORY
The **authpf** program first appeared in OpenBSD 3.1 and later in NetBSD 3.0.

BUGS
Configuration issues are tricky. The authenticating ssh(1) connection may be secured, but if the network is not secured the user may expose insecure protocols to attackers on the same network, or enable other attackers on the network to pretend to be the user by spoofing their IP address.

authpf is not designed to prevent users from denying service to other users.

NAME

bad144 — read/write DEC standard 144 bad sector information

SYNOPSIS

bad144 [**-c**] [**-f**] [**-v**] *disk* [*sno* [*bad* . . .]]
bad144 **-a** [**-c**] [**-f**] [**-v**] *disk* [*bad* . . .]

DESCRIPTION

bad144 can be used to inspect the information stored on a disk that is used by the disk drivers to implement
bad sector forwarding. The **bad144** tool is only installed on supported platforms.

Available options:

-a   The argument list consists of new bad sectors to be added to an existing list. The new sectors are
           sorted into the list, which must have been in order. Replacement sectors are moved to accommodate
           the additions; the new replacement sectors are cleared.

-c   Forces an attempt to copy the old sector to the replacement, and may be useful when replacing an
           unreliable sector.

-f   (vax only) For a RP06, RM03, RM05, Fujitsu Eagle, or SMD disk on a MASSBUS, the **-f** option
           may be used to mark the new bad sectors as "bad" by reformatting them as unusable sectors. This
           option is *required unless* the sectors have already been marked bad, or the system will not be noti-
           fied that it should use the replacement sector. This option may be used while running multiuser; it is
           no longer necessary to perform format operations while running single-user.

-v   The entire process is described as it happens in gory detail if **-v** (verbose) is given.

The format of the information is specified by DEC standard 144, as follows. The bad sector information is
located in the first 5 even numbered sectors of the last track of the disk pack. There are five identical copies
of the information, described by the *dkbad* structure.

Replacement sectors are allocated starting with the first sector before the bad sector information and working
backwards towards the beginning of the disk. A maximum of 126 bad sectors are supported. The position of
the bad sector in the bad sector table determines the replacement sector to which it corresponds. The bad
sectors must be listed in ascending order.

The bad sector information and replacement sectors are conventionally only accessible through the "c" file
system partition of the disk. If that partition is used for a file system, the user is responsible for making sure
that it does not overlap the bad sector information or any replacement sectors. Thus, one track plus 126 sectors must be reserved to allow use of all of the possible bad sector replacements.

The bad sector structure is as follows:

```
struct dkbad {
        int32_t   bt_csn;           /* cartridge serial number */
        u_int16_t bt_mbz;           /* unused; should be 0 */
        u_int16_t bt_flag;          /* -1 => alignment cartridge */
        struct bt_bad {
                u_int16_t bt_cyl;       /* cylinder number of bad sector */
                u_int16_t bt_trksec;    /* track and sector number */
        } bt_bad[126];
};
```

Unused slots in the *bt_bad* array are filled with all bits set, a putatively illegal value.

bad144 is invoked by giving a device name (e.g. wd0, hk0, hp1, etc.). With no optional arguments it reads the first sector of the last track of the corresponding disk and prints out the bad sector information. It issues a warning if the bad sectors are out of order. **bad144** may also be invoked with a serial number for the pack and a list of bad sectors. It will write the supplied information into all copies of the bad-sector file, replacing any previous information. Note, however, that **bad144** does not arrange for the specified sectors to be marked bad in this case. This procedure should only be used to restore known bad sector information which was destroyed.

It is no longer necessary to reboot to allow the kernel to reread the bad-sector table from the drive.

SEE ALSO
    badsect(8)

HISTORY
    The **bad144** command appeared in 4.1 BSD.

BUGS
    It should be possible to format disks on-line under 4 BSD.

    It should be possible to mark bad sectors on drives of all type.

    On an 11/750, the standard bootstrap drivers used to boot the system do not understand bad sectors, handle ECC errors, or the special SSE (skip sector) errors of RM80-type disks. This means that none of these errors can occur when reading the file /netbsd to boot. Sectors 0-15 of the disk drive must also not have any of these errors.

    The drivers which write a system core image on disk after a crash do not handle errors; thus the crash dump area must be free of errors and bad sectors.

NAME

badsect — create files to contain bad sectors

SYNOPSIS

badsect *bbdir sector ...*

DESCRIPTION

badsect makes a file to contain a bad sector. Normally, bad sectors are made inaccessible by the standard formatter, which provides a forwarding table for bad sectors to the driver; see bad144(8) for details. If a driver supports the bad blocking standard it is much preferable to use that method to isolate bad blocks, since the bad block forwarding makes the pack appear perfect, and such packs can then be copied with dd(1). The technique used by this program is also less general than bad block forwarding, as **badsect** can't make amends for bad blocks in the i-list of file systems or in swap areas.

On some disks, adding a sector which is suddenly bad to the bad sector table currently requires the running of the standard DEC formatter. Thus to deal with a newly bad block or on disks where the drivers do not support the bad-blocking standard **badsect** may be used to good effect.

badsect is used on a quiet file system in the following way: First mount the file system, and change to its root directory. Make a directory BAD there. Run **badsect** giving as argument the *BAD* directory followed by all the bad sectors you wish to add. The sector numbers must be relative to the beginning of the file system, but this is not hard as the system reports relative sector numbers in its console error messages. Then change back to the root directory, unmount the file system and run fsck(8) on the file system. The bad sectors should show up in two files or in the bad sector files and the free list. Have fsck(8) remove files containing the offending bad sectors, but *do not* have it remove the BAD/*nnnnn* files. This will leave the bad sectors in only the BAD files.

badsect works by giving the specified sector numbers in a mknod(2) system call, creating an illegal file whose first block address is the block containing bad sector and whose name is the bad sector number. When it is discovered by fsck(8) it will ask "HOLD BAD BLOCK ?" A positive response will cause fsck(8) to convert the inode to a regular file containing the bad block.

DIAGNOSTICS

badsect refuses to attach a block that resides in a critical area or is out of range of the file system. A warning is issued if the block is already in use.

SEE ALSO

bad144(8), fsck(8)

HISTORY

The **badsect** command appeared in 4.1BSD.

BUGS

If more than one of the sectors in a file system fragment are bad, you should specify only one of them to **badsect**, as the blocks in the bad sector files actually cover all the sectors in a file system fragment.

NAME

binpatch — examine and or modify initialized data in a binary file

SYNOPSIS

binpatch [-b | -w | -l] [-o *offset*] -s *symname* [-r *value*] *binfile*
binpatch [-b | -w | -l] [-o *offset*] -a *addr* [-r *value*] *binfile*

DESCRIPTION

binpatch is used to modify or examine the data associated with a symbol in a binary file *binfile*. The flags **-b**, **-w** and **-l** specify the size of the data to be modified or examined (byte, word and long respectively.) The *binfile* is scanned in search of the symbol *symname* (specified with the **-s** flag) If the symbol is found the current data and address are printed. Next if the **-r** flag has been given, the current data is replaced with that of *value*.

If the second form is used the address *addr* specified with the **-a** flag is used as a direct address into the data section of the binary and no symbol search is performed.

The **-o** flag specifies an offset in byte, word or long (**-b**, **-w**, or **-l**) units from the given locator (**-s** or **-a**) for binpatch to perform its described actions.

NAME

   binpatch — examine and or modify initialized data in an executable binary

SYNOPSIS

   binpatch [**-b** | **-w** | **-l** | **-d**] [**-o** *offset*] [**-T** *saddr*] **-s** *symname* [**-r** *value*]
           binfile
   binpatch [**-b** | **-w** | **-l** | **-d**] [**-o** *offset*] [**-T** *saddr*] **-a** *addr* [**-r** *value*] *binfile*

DESCRIPTION

   binpatch is used to modify or examine the data associated with a symbol in a binary file *binfile*.

   The flags **-b**, **-w**, **-l**, and **-d** specify the size of the data to be modified or examined. **-b** is for 8bit
   (int8_t), **-w** is for 16bit (int16_t), **-l** is for 32bit (int32_t), and **-d** is for 64bit (int64_t)
   variables.

   The *binfile* is scanned in search of the symbol *symname* (specified with the **-s** flag). If the symbol is
   found the current data and address are printed.

   Next if the **-r** flag has been given, the current data is replaced with that of *value*.

   If the second form is used the address *addr* specified with the **-a** flag is used as a direct address into the
   data section of the binary and no symbol search is performed.

   The **-o** flag specifies an offset in int8_t, int16_t, int32_t, and int64_t (**-b**, **-w**, **-l**, or **-d**)
   units from the given locator (**-s** or **-a**) for **binpatch** to perform its described actions. This might be useful to patch a member of array or structure.

   The **-T** flag is used to specify the starting address of a.out binary text segment. Ignored for other binary
   executable formats.

SEE ALSO

   gdb(1), mdsetimage(8)

BUGS

   The **binpatch** command doesn't check if size of specified symbol is the same as the specified size by **-b**,
   -w, **-l**, or **-d** flag.

   The **binpatch** command doesn't check if specified address or symbol is a patchable variable and it might
   corrupt the specified executable binary.

NAME
/usr/mdec/binstall — install sparc and sparc64 boot blocks

SYNOPSIS
/usr/mdec/binstall [−htUuv] [−b *bootprog*] [−f *filesystem*] [−m *mdec*]
            [−i *installbootprog*] ["net" | "ffs"] [directory]

DESCRIPTION
The **/usr/mdec/binstall** program prepares a sparc or sparc64 system for booting, either from local disk from a "ffs" partition or over the network. The default type of boot block installed is derived from the host system. If it is an UltraSPARC, the sparc64 boot blocks will be used, otherwise the SPARC boot blocks will be used. **/usr/mdec/binstall** can be forced to prepare a disk for either.

OPTIONS
The following options are available:

−b   Set the second stage boot program to *bootprog*. This will typically be boot.net for sparc systems and ofwboot.net for sparc64 systems.

−f   Set the path to the filesystem being installed for to *filesystem*. This is otherwise derived from the [directory].

−h   Display help.

−i   Set the path to the installboot(8) program to *installbootprog*. This is useful for using **/usr/mdec/binstall** on non-sparc or sparc64 systems.

−m   Sets the path to the machine dependent directory to *mdec*. This is the directory that both the boot blocks and the installboot(8) program live.

−t   Test mode; does not run any program. Implies the −v option.

−U   Install sparc (SPARC) boot blocks.

−u   Install sparc64 (UltraSPARC) boot blocks.

−v   Be verbose.

SEE ALSO
disklabel(8), installboot(8)

NAME
bioctl — RAID management interface

SYNOPSIS
bioctl *device command* [*arg* [...]]

DESCRIPTION
RAID device drivers which support management functionality can register their services with the bio(4) driver. **bioctl** then can be used to manage the RAID controller's properties.

COMMANDS
The following commands are supported:

show [*disks | volumes*]

> Without any argument by default **bioctl** will show information about all volumes and the logical disks used on them. If *disks* is specified, only information about physical disks will be shown. If *volumes* is specified, only information about the volumes will be shown.

alarm [*disable | enable | silence | test*]

> Control the RAID card's alarm functionality, if supported. By default if no argument is specified, its current state will be shown. Optionally the *disable*, *enable*, *silence*, or *test* arguments may be specified to enable, disable, silence, or test the RAID card's alarm.

blink *start channel:target.lun | stop channel:target.lun*

> Instruct the device at *channel:target.lun* to start or cease blinking, if there's ses(4) support in the enclosure.

hotspare *add channel:target.lun | remove channel:target.lun*

> Create or remove a hot-spare drive at location *channel:target.lun*.

passthru *add DISKID channel:target.lun | remove channel:target.lun*

> Create or remove a *pass-through* device. The *DISKID* argument specifies the disk that will be used for the new device, and it will be created at the location *channel:target.lun*. *NOTE*: Removing a pass-through device that has a mounted filesystem will lead to undefined behaviour.

check *start VOLID | stop VOLID*

> Start or stop consistency volume check in the volume with index *VOLID*. *NOTE*: Not many RAID controllers support this feature.

create volume *VOLID DISKIDs [SIZE] STRIPE RAID_LEVEL channel:target.lun*

> Create a volume at index *VOLID*. The *DISKIDs* argument will specify the first and last disk, i.e.: *0-3* will use the disks 0, 1, 2, and 3. The *SIZE* argument is optional and may be specified if not all available disk space is wanted (also dependent of the *RAID_LEVEL*). The volume will have a stripe size defined in the *STRIPE* argument and it will be located at *channel:target.lun*.

remove volume *VOLID channel:target.lun*

> Remove a volume at index *VOLID* and located at *channel:target.lun*. *NOTE*: Removing a RAID volume that has a mounted filesystem will lead to undefined behaviour.

EXAMPLES

The following command, executed from the command line, shows the status of the volumes and its logical disks on the RAID controller:

```
$ bioctl arcmsr0 show
Volume Status       Size        Device/Label    RAID Level Stripe
==================================================================
     0 Building    468G  sd0 ARC-1210-VOL#00        RAID 6  128KB  0% done
   0:0 Online      234G         0:0.0 noencl <WDC WD2500YS-01SHB1 20.06C06>
   0:1 Online      234G         0:1.0 noencl <WDC WD2500YS-01SHB1 20.06C06>
   0:2 Online      234G         0:2.0 noencl <WDC WD2500YS-01SHB1 20.06C06>
   0:3 Online      234G         0:3.0 noencl <WDC WD2500YS-01SHB1 20.06C06>
```

To create a RAID 5 volume on the SCSI 0:15.0 location on the disks 0, 1, 2 and 3, with stripe size of 64Kb on the first volume ID, using all available free space on the disks:

```
$ bioctl arcmsr0 create volume 0 0-3 64 5 0:15.0
```

To remove the volume 0 previously created at the SCSI 0:15.0 location:

```
$ bioctl arcmsr0 remove volume 0 0:15.0
```

SEE ALSO

arcmsr(4), bio(4), cac(4), ciss(4), mfi(4)

HISTORY

The **bioctl** command first appeared in OpenBSD 3.8, it was rewritten for NetBSD 5.0.

AUTHORS

The **bioctl** interface was written by Marco Peereboom ⟨marco@openbsd.org⟩ and was rewritten with multiple features by
Juan Romero Pardines ⟨xtraeme@NetBSD.org⟩.

NAME

   boot — system bootstrapping procedures

DESCRIPTION

This document provides information on using common features in the NetBSD boot loader. Additional information may be found in architecture-specific boot(8) manual pages.

In the native NetBSD boot protocol, options are passed from the boot loader to the kernel via flag bits in the *boothowto* variable (see boothowto(9)).

Interactive mode

In interactive mode, the boot loader will present a prompt, allowing input of these commands:

   boot [*device*:] [*filename*] [**-1234abcdmqsvxz**]

   The default *device* will be set to the disk that the boot loader was loaded from. To boot from an alternate disk, the full name of the device should be given at the prompt. *device* is of the form *xd* [*N*[*x*]] where *xd* is the device from which to boot, *N* is the unit number, and *x* is the partition letter.

   The following list of supported devices may vary from installation to installation:

   hd   Hard disks.
   fd   Floppy drives.

   The default *filename* is netbsd; if the boot loader fails to successfully open that image, it then tries netbsd.gz (expected to be a kernel image compressed by gzip), followed by netbsd.old, netbsd.old.gz, onetbsd, and finally onetbsd.gz. Alternate system images can be loaded by just specifying the name of the image.

   Options are:

   -1   Sets the machine-dependent flag **RB_MD1** in *boothowto*.

   -2   Sets the machine-dependent flag **RB_MD2** in *boothowto*.

   -3   Sets the machine-dependent flag **RB_MD3** in *boothowto*.

   -4   Sets the machine-dependent flag **RB_MD4** in *boothowto*.

   -a   Sets the **RB_ASKNAME** flag in *boothowto*. This causes the kernel to prompt for the root file system device, the system crash dump device, and the path to init(8).

   -b   Sets the **RB_HALT** flag in *boothowto*. This causes subsequent reboot attempts to halt instead of rebooting.

   -c   Sets the **RB_USERCONF** flag in *boothowto*. This causes the kernel to enter the userconf(4) device configuration manager as soon as possible during the boot. userconf(4) allows devices to be enabled or disabled, and allows device locators (such as hardware addresses or bus numbers) to be modified before the kernel attempts to attach the devices.

   -d   Sets the **RB_KDB** flag in *boothowto*. Requests the kernel to enter debug mode, in which it waits for a connection from a kernel debugger; see ddb(4).

   -m   Sets the **RB_MINIROOT** flag in *boothowto*. Informs the kernel that a mini-root file system is present in memory.

   -q   Sets the **AB_QUIET** flag in *boothowto*. Boot the system in quiet mode.

    -s   Sets the **RB_SINGLE** flag in *boothowto*. Boot the system in single-user mode.

    -v   Sets the **AB_VERBOSE** flag in *boothowto*. Boot the system in verbose mode.

    -x   Sets the **AB_DEBUG** flag in *boothowto*. Boot the system with debug messages enabled.

    -z   Sets the **AB_SILENT** flag in *boothowto*. Boot the system in silent mode.

consdev *dev*

> Immediately switch the console to the specified device *dev* and reprint the banner. *dev* must be one of *pc*, *com0*, *com1*, *com2*, *com3*, *com0kbd*, *com1kbd*, *com2kbd*, *com3kbd*, or *auto*. See **Console Selection Policy** in boot_console(8).

dev [*device*]

> Set the default drive and partition for subsequent filesystem operations. Without an argument, print the current setting. *device* is of the form specified in **boot**.

help

> Print an overview about commands and arguments.

ls [path]

> Print a directory listing of path, containing inode number, filename, and file type. path can contain a device specification.

quit

> Reboot the system.

In an emergency, the bootstrap methods described in the NetBSD installation notes for the specific architecture can be used.

FILES

/boot	boot program code loaded by the primary bootstrap
/netbsd	system code
/netbsd.gz	gzip-compressed system code
/usr/mdec/boot	master copy of the boot program (copy to /boot)
/usr/mdec/bootxx_fstype	primary bootstrap for filesystem type fstype, copied to the start of the NetBSD partition by installboot(8).

SEE ALSO

Architecture-specific boot(8) manual pages, ddb(4), userconf(4), halt(8), installboot(8), reboot(8), rescue(8), shutdown(8), boothowto(9)

BUGS

The kernel file name must be specified before, not after, the boot options. Any *filename* specified after the boot options, e.g.:

    boot -d netbsd.test

is ignored, and the default kernel is booted.

BOOT (8)   NetBSD/alpha   BOOT (8)

NAME

boot — Alpha system bootstrapping procedures

DESCRIPTION

DEC Alpha systems can have either of two different firmware systems: ARC (a.k.a. AlphaBIOS), and SRM. Some Alpha systems have both in their flash RAM and can switch between them on command. ARC is used to bootstrap Microsoft Windows NT for Alpha. SRM is used to bootstrap OpenVMS and Ultrix. NetBSD requires SRM.

SRM can bootstrap from supported local storage devices, e.g., IDE disks or CD-ROM drives, SCSI disks or CD-ROM drives, and floppy drives. SRM can also network bootstrap via supported Ethernet interfaces, using BOOTP or MOP. The particular capabilities of SRM will vary from system to system.

When SRM boots the system, it performs a Power On Self Test (POST), probes the system busses to identify devices, and initializes them. SRM includes an x86 instruction emulator in order to run the BIOS initialization routines found in the PROM of any video cards found. In this way, most generic PCI video cards can work in Alpha systems that have PCI bus slots.

SRM then examines the state of one of several variables: `auto_action`. If the value of `auto_action` is "halt" then SRM will stop, print its prompt: ">>>" and wait for commands to be entered on the console. If the value of `auto_action` is "boot" then SRM will automatically bootstrap the operating system specified by various non-volatile environment variables.

SRM device names are not the same as in NetBSD, e.g., **ewa0** is a DEC "tulip" Ethernet interface, **dka0** is a SCSI disk on a recognized controller, **dqa0** is an IDE disk on a recognized controller. The **show device** command will list all the devices that SRM can bootstrap from.

SRM Commands

SRM is somewhat UNIX-like in that it incorporates a simple pipe and I/O redirection, which allows command sequences like:

```
show config | more
show * | more
```

An essential but incomplete list of SRM commands follows:

boot [**-file** *filename*] [**-flags** *value*] [*device*]

Boot an operating system. The default arguments for this command are taken from the SRM environment variables:

```
boot_file       file name to bootstrap.
boot_osflags    flags to pass to the secondary bootstrap program.
bootdef_dev     default bootstrap device.
```

help [*command*]

Invoke the SRM help system.

init

Reset the SRM console, and take actions as specified by SRM variables.

set *variable value* [**-default**]

Set an SRM variable, e.g.,

```
set auto_action boot
set bootdef_dev dka0
set ewa0_mode auto
```

If the **−default** flag is used, the variable will be set to its default value.

show *variable or subsystem*

Show SRM variables and values, or show system state or configuration. If a wildcard is used, then all matching SRM variables are shown, e.g.,

show *	will display all SRM variables.
show b∗	will display all variables whose names begin with *b*.
show config	will display the complete system configuration.
show device	will display all bootable devices.
show memory	will display the system's memory configuration.

SRM Variables

auto_action   What SRM will do at system startup or reset:

boot automatically bootstrap the operating system.

halt after POST, prompt the user on the console for commands to execute.

Some Alpha systems (e.g., AlphaServer 800) have a "halt" switch, which if set, will override the action of this variable, and cause SRM to stop after POST and prompt the user for commands to execute.

bootdef_dev   The default bootstrap device, e.g., **dka0**, **dqa0**, **ewa0**. The **show device** command will list the available and recognized bootable devices.

boot_file   The file to bootstrap from; this is a null string by default.

boot_osflags   The flag passed to the secondary bootstrap program, and the NetBSD kernel:

a   (automatic) multi-user mode bootstrap.

c   crash dump immediately after autoconf(4), if the NetBSD kernel is compiled with DEBUG; See options(4).

d   break into the debugger ASAP, if the NetBSD kernel is compiled with DDB or KGDB; See options(4).

h   on a reboot request from the NetBSD kernel, halt the system instead of rebooting.

i   the NetBSD secondary bootstrap program will stop and prompt for the NetBSD kernel file name to bootstrap.

n   the NetBSD kernel will ask for the root file system's device, the kernel core dump device, and the path to init(8).

q   bootstrap quietly.

s   single-user mode bootstrap.

v   bootstrap verbosely.

These may be used in combinations that are not mutually exclusive. These options are case-insensitive to be compatible with DEC operating systems.

console   What type of console device SRM and NetBSD will use:

graphics use a video card for output, and a PC keyboard for input.

         serial use the first serial port for console.

         Just as with Sun systems, Alpha systems will use the first serial port as a console if there is no keyboard plugged into the keyboard port, even if `console` is set to "graphics".

 `ew*0_mode` The media and speed for DEC "tulip" Ethernet interfaces (e.g., DECchip 21040, 21140, 21143); possible values are: **auto** (IEEE 802.3u "Nway" negotiation), **BNC**, **AUI**, **Twisted-Pair**, **FastFD** (Fast Full Duplex).

 `ew*0_protocols` The protocol to use when netbooting, i.e., MOP (Maintenance Operations Protocol), or BOOTP (Bootstrap Protocol).

         The Alpha SRM firmware is picky about BOOTP responses; the `dhcpd.conf`(5) on the server needs the

           `always-reply-rfc1048 on;`

         directive in the section for netbooting Alpha systems.

 `os_type` This determines which system firmware will be used after the next power-cycle, if both ARC and SRM are present in Flash RAM. This should be set to any of "UNIX", "osf", or "vms" to select the SRM console required for NetBSD. OSF refers to the Open Software Foundation.

After bootstrap

Once the NetBSD/alpha kernel is booted normally it initializes itself and proceeds to start the system. An automatic consistency check of the file systems takes place, and unless this fails, the system comes up to multi-user operation.

The proper way to shut the system down is with the `shutdown`(8) command.

If the system crashes, it will enter the kernel debugger, `ddb`(4), if it is configured in the kernel. If the crash occurred during initialization and the debugger is not present or is exited, the kernel will halt the system.

If the crash occurred during normal operation and the debugger is not present or is exited, the system will attempt a dump to the configured dump device (which will be automatically recovered with `savecore`(8) during the next bootstrap cycle), and after the dump is complete (successful or not) the kernel will attempt a reboot.

FILES

`/boot`	NetBSD secondary bootstrap program (installed)
`/netbsd`	default NetBSD system kernel
`/usr/mdec/bootxx_cd9660`	primary bootstrap for "cd9660" (ISO 9660) file system
`/usr/mdec/bootxx_ffs`	primary bootstrap for "ffs" file system (Berkeley Fast File System)
`/usr/mdec/boot`	secondary bootstrap
`/usr/mdec/netboot`	network bootstrap
`/usr/mdec/ustarboot`	"ustar" disk and tape bootstrap

SEE ALSO

`ddb`(4), `diskless`(8), `init`(8), `installboot`(8), `mkbootimage`(8), `rc`(8), `reboot`(8), `savecore`(8), `setnetbootinfo`(8), `shutdown`(8)

Alpha Architecture Reference Manual Third Edition, *Digital Press*, Alpha Architecture Committee, 1998.

BUGS
   The device names used by NetBSD/alpha and the SRM Console often have no relation to each other.

BOOT (8)   NetBSD/amiga   BOOT (8)

NAME
boot — system bootstrapping procedures

DESCRIPTION
Power fail and crash recovery
When the NetBSD kernel is booted normally (using one of the two methods discussed below), it initializes itself and proceeds to boot the system. An automatic consistency check of the file systems takes place, and unless this fails, the system comes up to multi-user operations. The proper way to shut the system down is with the shutdown(8) command.

If the system crashes, it will enter the kernel debugger, ddb(4), if it is configured in the kernel. If the debugger is not present, or the debugger is exited, the system will attempt a dump to the configured dump device (which will be automatically recovered with savecore(8) during the next boot cycle). After the dump is complete (successful or not), the system will attempt a reboot.

Booting NetBSD using the bootloader
When a bootable NetBSD partition is created by means of HDTOOLBOX or another RDB editing program and a bootblock has been copied there by installboot(8) and the boot priority of the NetBSD partition is either the highest or the NetBSD partition is selected by means of the boot menu, the Amiga ROM will automatically start the NetBSD bootloader. By default it will, after a short timeout, load the kernel image /netbsd and attempt to boot it into multi-user mode. This behaviour can be changed by typing in an alternate command sequence. The command line looks like:

> kernel-path [**-abknpqstvADZ**] [**-c** model] [**-m** memsize] [**-n** memsegments]
> [**-I** mask] [**-S** amount] [**-T** amount]

kernel-path
> This gives you the opportunity to boot another kernel, say: /netbsd.old. The default is /netbsd.

-a   Autoboot into multi-user mode (default).

-b   Prompt for the root file system device, the system crash dump device, and the path to init(8).

-c model
> force machine model. Use 32000+(Qlogic chip revision) for the DraCo.

-k   Reserve the first 4M of fastmem.

-m memsize
> Force fastmem size to be memsize kBytes.

-n   maximum number of segments of memory to use, encoded as follows: 0 (default): 1 segment, 1: 2 segments, 2: 3 or more segments.

-p   Select kernel load segment by priority instead of size.

-q   Boot in quiet mode.

-s   Boot into single-user mode.

-v   Boot in verbose mode.

-D   Enter the kernel debugger (best used with -S)

-I mask
> inhibit sync negotiation as follows: The mask is a bitmap expressed in C notation (e.g., 0xff) with 4*8bits, each bit, if set to 1, disabling sync negotiation for the corresponding target. Note that this only applies to (some of the) real SCSI busses, but not, e.g., to internal IDE. The bytes are used up

from right to left by SCSI bus drivers using this convention.

−s   Load the kernel symbols

Booting NetBSD using the loadbsd program
When you want (or have to) start NetBSD from AmigaOS, you have to use the **loadbsd** program that is supplied in the utils directory of the distribution. The loadbsd command line specification is:

> **loadbsd** [**−abknpstADZ**] [**−c** *model*] [**−m** *memsize*] [**−n** *memsegments*] [**−I** *mask*] [**−S** *amount*] [**−T** *amount*] *kernel−path*

Description of options:

−a   Autoboot into multi-user mode.

−b   Prompt for the root file system device, the system crash dump device, and the path to init(8).

−c   force machine model.

−k   Reserve the first 4M of fastmem.

−m   Force fastmem size to be *memsize* kBytes.

−n   maximum number of *segments* of memory to use, encoded as follows: 0 (default): 1 segment, 1: 2 segments, 2: 3 or more segments.

−p   Select kernel load segment by priority instead of size.

−s   Boot into single-user mode.

−t   Test loading of the kernel but don't start NetBSD.

−A   enable AGA modes.

−D   Enter the kernel debugger after booting. Best with −S.

−I *mask*
        inhibit sync negotiation as follows: The *mask* is a bitmap expressed in hexadecimal (e.g., ff) with 4*8bits, each bit, if set to 1, disabling sync negotiation for the corresponding target. Note that this only applies to (some of the) real SCSI busses, but not, e.g., to internal IDE. The bytes are used up from right to left by SCSI bus drivers using this convention.

−s   include kernel debug symbols (for use by -D).

−Z   Force load via chip memory. Won't work if kernel is larger than the chip memory size or on the DraCo.

Note: Because the loadbsd program can only read kernels from a AmigaOS filesystem, the file */netbsd* is often not the same as the actual kernel booted. This can cause some programs to fail. However, note that you can use third-party Berkeley filesystems such as bffs to access the NetBSD root partition from AmigaOS.

FILES
/netbsd	system kernel
/usr/mdec/bootxx_ffs	RDB device primary boot block
/usr/mdec/bootxx_fd	floppy disk primary boot block
/usr/mdec/boot.amiga	secondary bootstrap
/boot.amiga	secondary bootstrap (installed)

SEE ALSO

    ddb(4), fsck_ffs(8), installboot(8), newfs(8), savecore(8), shutdown(8)

BUGS

    Due to code size restrictions, you can't currently use an old-style file system (created with newfs(8) -O or with NetBSD 0.9) with the boot block. You can use **loadbsd** to boot from AmigaOS, or upgrade the file system with *fsck_ffs -c 2*.

NAME
boot — system bootstrapping procedures

DESCRIPTION
Power fail and crash recovery
When the NetBSD kernel is booted normally (using one of the two methods discussed below), it initializes itself and proceeds to boot the system. An automatic consistency check of the file systems takes place, and unless this fails, the system comes up to multi-user operations. The proper way to shut the system down is with the shutdown(8) command.

If the system crashes, it will enter the kernel debugger, ddb(4), if it is configured in the kernel. If the debugger is not present, or the debugger is exited, the system will attempt a dump to the configured dump device (which will be automatically recovered with savecore(8) during the next boot cycle). After the dump is complete (successful or not), the system will attempt a reboot.

Booting NetBSD using the bootloader
When a bootable NetBSD partition is created by means of installboot(8) and the boot-preference bit in the NVRAM is either invalid or set to NetBSD , the Atari BIOS will automatically start the NetBSD bootloader. By default it will load the kernel image /netbsd and attempts to boot it into multi-user mode. This behaviour can be changed by either keeping the Alternate or the Right-Shift key pressed during the boot. When the Alternate key is pressed, the bootstrap is aborted, causing the BIOS to continue scanning the disks for a bootable partition (this is compatible with AHDI 3.0). Pressing the Right-Shift key during the boot, causes the boot loader to enter the interactive mode. In interactive mode, the command line looks like:

> [*OS-type*] [*boot-path*] [*boot-options*]

Each component of the command can be omitted in which case the defaults indicated will be used.

OS-type:
> .netbsd (the default)
> .linux
> .asv
> .tos

> If something other than .netbsd is specified, control is returned to the BIOS with the boot preference set to the selected type. Due to limitations of the BIOS however, the search for bootblocks is continued rather than restarted.

boot-path   This gives you the opportunity to boot another kernel, say: /netbsd.old. The default is /netbsd

boot-options   These options are a subset of the loadbsd(8) options.
> **-a**   Boot into multi-user mode (the default)
> **-b**   Prompt for the root file system device, the system crash dump device, and the path to init(8).
> **-d**   Enter the kernel debugger
> **-q**   Boot in quiet mode
> **-v**   Boot in verbose mode

Booting using the loadbsd program
When you want (or have to) start NetBSD from GEM, you have to use the loadbsd(8) program that is supplied on the kernel-floppy. The loadbsd command line specification is:

loadbsd [**-abdhqstvwDV**] [**-S** *amount*] [**-T** *amount*] *kernel-path*

Description of options:

-a   Boot automatically into multi-user mode.

-b   Prompt for the root file system device, the system crash dump device, and the path to init(8).

-d   Enter the kernel debugger after booting.

-h   Print a help screen that tries to explain the same options as mentioned here.

-o *outputfile*
        Write all output to the file *outputfile*.

-q   Boot in quiet mode.

-s   Tell NetBSD only to use ST compatible RAM.

-t   Test loading of the kernel but don't start NetBSD.

-v   Boot in verbose mode.

-w   Wait for a keypress before exiting loadbsd. This is useful when starting this program under GEM.

-D   Show debugging output while booting the kernel.

-S *amount*
        Set the amount of available ST compatible RAM in bytes. Normally this value is set automatically
        from the values initialized by the BIOS.

-T *amount*
        Set the amount of available TT compatible RAM in bytes. Normally this value is set automatically
        from the values initialized by the BIOS.

-V   Print the version of loadbsd(8) that you are using.

kernel-path
        This is a GEMDOS path specification of the kernel to boot.

Note: Because the loadbsd program can only read kernels from a GEMDOS filesystem, the file */netbsd* is
usually not the same as the actual kernel booted. This can cause some programs to fail.

FILES
        /netbsd system kernel

SEE ALSO
        ddb(4), savecore(8), shutdown(8)

NAME
boot — system bootstrapping procedures

DESCRIPTION
Cobalt Networks' MIPS-based Microservers (now known as Sun Server Appliances) that can run NetBSD/cobalt can use any of the following boot procedures:

- bootstrap NetBSD from disk using the standard Cobalt Firmware boot sequence

- bootstrap NetBSD from disk using the NetBSD boot loader

- network bootstrap NetBSD using the standard Cobalt Firmware means from a TCP/IP LAN with DHCP and NFS.

- network bootstrap NetBSD using the NetBSD boot loader which can be loaded by the standard Cobalt Firmware with DHCP and NFS.

Power fail and crash recovery
Normally, the system will reboot itself at power-up or after crashes. An automatic consistency check of the file systems will be performed, and unless this fails, the system will resume multi-user operations.

Cobalt Boot Sequence
The first program to take a control after reboot or at power-on is the Cobalt Firmware. The Firmware can load a compressed kernel from disk, subject to a few limitations. The Firmware expects the disk to contain DOS-style partition information with the first partition being a boot one which is special in that it should reside close to the beginning of the disk and must contain an ext2 file system with a `boot` directory which is treated specially by the Firmware. The default sequence is pretty straightforward, the Firmware finds the boot partition, mounts the Ext2 file system from it and tries to load a compressed kernel image from the `boot` directory. The name of the kernel image differs from machine to machine and this is the reason for having multiple copies of NetBSD kernel installed under different names. The following kernel image names are known to be in use by certain Cobalt flavors:

```
/boot/vmlinuz.gz
/boot/vmlinux.gz
/boot/vmlinux-nfsroot.gz
/boot/vmlinux_RAQ.gz
/boot/vmlinux_raq-2800.gz
```

where `/boot` is the directory on the boot partition.

The Firmware console provides the means to alter the default boot sequence and/or to specify boot parameters. Pressing '⟨space⟩' right after the Firmware printed its greeting brings the Firmware console prompt and pressing '?' at the prompt prints a help screen with all commands supported by the Firmware. For example, the 'bfd' command can be used to boot a kernel image:

Cobalt: bfd /boot/<kernel image> [options]

where "options" are the kernel options.

Bootstrap from disk using the standard Firmware sequence
The Firmware enters the standard boot sequence after reboot or at power-on when no front-panel buttons are pressed and the Firmware console is not used to change the boot procedure. At boot time, the Firmware checks the hardware, prints the banner and performs the standard Cobalt boot sequence. There are a few culprits tightly connected to this boot method. First of all, the kernel must be compressed. Second, the Firmware enforces a hard restriction on the kernel size (it cannot exceed approximately 900,000/2,500,000 bytes compressed/uncompressed) resulting in a lock-up should this requirement not be fulfilled. For

NetBSD, another pitfall is that the uncompressed kernel should be copied to the root directory to make certain system binaries (such as e.g. netstat) work, and the kernel images in the `boot` directory should always be in sync with the ones installed in the root directory.

Bootstrap from disk using the NetBSD boot loader

The NetBSD boot loader is an attempt to break through the limitations enforced by the Firmware loader. The main idea is to make the Firmware load the NetBSD boot loader and let the latter take care of loading the kernel. To achieve this goal, multiple copies of the boot loader are installed in the `boot` directory on the boot partition, one copy per each kernel image name the Cobalt Firmware might look for. The NetBSD kernel is located in the root directory (usually `/dev/wd0a`) like it is on other platforms. Once running, the boot loader prints a banner to the serial console similar to the following:

```
>> NetBSD/cobalt 5.0 Bootloader, Revision 0.9 [@0x80f00000]
>> (user@buildhost, builddate)
>> Model:          Cobalt Qube 2
>> Memory:          32768 k
>> PROM boot string:   root=/dev/hda1 ro
Boot [wd0a:netbsd]:
Loading: wd0a:netbsd
3763776+312244 [216944+209676]=0x44b97c
Starting at 0x80001000
```

The boot loader also prints a banner to the LCD panels as the following:

```
NetBSD/cobalt
Bootloader

Loading:
wd0a:netbsd
```

Boot loader Options

It is possible to specify some options and boot devices on the boot loader prompt:

boot [wd0a:netbsd]: [*device:*][*filename*] [**-acdmqsvxz**]

The default *device* will be set to the disk that the boot loader was loaded from. To boot from an alternate disk or partition, the full name of the device should be given at the prompt. *device* is of the form *xdNx* where *xd* is the device from which to boot, *N* is the unit number, and *x* is the partition letter of the NetBSD `disklabel`(5) in the NetBSD partition of the MBR partitions. The NetBSD boot loader recognizes FFS (both UFS1 and UFS2) and Linux Ext2fs.

The following list of supported devices may vary from installation to installation:

wd   IDE hard disks recognized by the Firmware.

The default *filename* is `netbsd`; if the boot loader fails to successfully open that image, it then tries `netbsd.gz` (expected to be a kernel image compressed by `gzip`(1)), followed by `netbsd`, `netbsd.gz`, `onetbsd`, `onetbsd.gz`, `netbsd.bak`, `netbsd.bak.gz`, `netbsd.old`, `netbsd.old.gz`, `netbsd.cobalt`, `netbsd.cobalt.gz`, `netbsd.elf`, and finally `netbsd.elf.gz`. Alternate system images can be loaded by just specifying the name of the image, so it is always a good idea to have a copy of working kernel in the NetBSD root partition before trying a new kernel.

Options are:

-a   Prompt for the root file system device, the system crash dump device, and the path to `init`(8).

-c   Bring the system up into the device configuration manager. From here the device locators can be tuned
to the hardware; see userconf(4).

-d   Bring the system up in debug mode. Here it waits for a kernel debugger connect; see ddb(4).

-q   Boot the system in quiet mode.

-s   Bring the system up in single-user mode.

-v   Boot the system in verbose mode.

As the older version of the boot loader, it is also possible to specify options to the boot loader by breaking
into the Firmware and using the "bfd" command:

Cobalt: bfd /boot/boot.gz [options]

The boot loader allows the following options:

nbsd= [*device*:] [*filename*] [**-acdqsv**]

The device, filename and options on the bfd prompt are same with the boot loader.

It is also a good idea to have a small rescue kernel in the boot directory in the Ext2 partition for the
Firmware boot. In an emergency case, this will allow you to use the Firmware 'bfd' command to boot the rescue image:

Cobalt: bfd /boot/netbsd.gz

Network bootstrap using the standard Firmware sequence

The Cobalt Firmware allows to boot a kernel over the network, with all the limitations of the Firmware loader
described above. The simplest method is to break into the Firmware prompt and use "bfd" command to specify where to boot from:

Cobalt: bfd /netbsd.gz nfsroot=/home/raq/root

The Firmware is picky about syntax and in general, so if things fail mysteriously, try to conform to the conventions described above. For netbooting, you need to NFS-export the directory given to "nfsroot=", and the
named kernel (netbsd.gz) needs to be executable and in that directory. You will also need to setup
dhcpd(8). Once the kernel is loaded with the command line values, the data given via DHCP is used to
mount the root file system. Here is a known working DHCP entry:

```
host raq {
      hardware ethernet 0:10:e0:0:52:62;      # raq MAC
      fixed-address 10.0.0.15;              # raq address
      filename "/netbsd.gz";               # kernel name in root-path
      option root-path "/home/raq/root";      # absolute dir on NFS server
      server-name="10.0.0.3";                 # IP of NFS server
}
```

Another option is to hold down the left and right cursor buttons during power-on which executes the command

bfd /boot/vmlinux.gz root=/dev/nfs nfsroot=/nfsroot,

resulting in a netboot. On RaQ 1's, the default kernel name is vmlinux_RAQ.gz and on RaQ 2's, it is
vmlinux_raq-2800.gz.

Network bootstrap using the NetBSD boot loader

The idea here is the same with the bootstrap from disk using the NetBSD boot loader. Make the firmware
load the NetBSD boot loader via network and let the latter take care of loading the kernel even via network.

A simple method to load the NetBSD boot loader is to use the "bfd" command as well as booting the NetBSD kernel via network as described above:

    Cobalt: bfd /boot/boot.gz nfsroot=/home/raq/root

Note the boot loader binary needs to be `gzip`(1)-compressed. Once the boot loader is successfully loaded it prints a banner as well as booting from disk:

```
>> NetBSD/cobalt 5.0 Bootloader, Revision 0.9 [@0x80f00000]
>> (user@buildhost, builddate)
>> Model:          Cobalt Qube 2
>> Memory:         32768 k
>> PROM boot string:   root=/dev/nfs nfsroot=/nfsroot nfsaddrs=bootp
Boot [nfs:netbsd]:
Loading: nfs:netbsd
3763776+312244 [216944+209676]=0x44b97c
Starting at 0x80001000
```

The boot loader load the NetBSD kernel via NFS which should be specified by the DHCP configuration on the server. Note the nfsroot option specified on the "bfd" prompt will be ignored by the NetBSD boot loader so it's recommended to use the same directory on the "bfd" prompt and in the DHCP configuration.

FILES

`/boot/boot.gz`	boot program code loaded by the Firmware loader
`/boot/netbsd.gz`	`gzip`(1)-compressed rescue system code
`/netbsd`	system code
`/netbsd.gz`	`gzip`(1)-compressed system code
`/usr/mdec/boot`	master copy of the boot program (to be compressed and copied to /boot/boot.gz)

SEE ALSO

    `ddb`(4), `userconf`(4), `dhcpd.conf`(5), `dhcpd`(8), `fdisk`(8), `halt`(8), `reboot`(8), `shutdown`(8), `printf`(9)

        http://www.NetBSD.org/docs/network/netboot/

NAME
boot — system bootstrapping procedures

DESCRIPTION
Dreamcast consoles can only boot from the built-in GD-ROM drive. Insert a bootable CD-R containing the NetBSD kernel and turn on the power.

FILES
/netbsd system code

SEE ALSO
ddb(4), userconf(4), halt(8), reboot(8), shutdown(8)

HISTORY
The **boot** man page appeared in NetBSD 2.0.

BOOT (8)   NetBSD/hp300   BOOT (8)

NAME

> **boot** — system bootstrapping procedures

DESCRIPTION

> **Power fail and crash recovery**
>
>> Normally, the system will reboot itself at power-up or after crashes. An automatic consistency check of the file systems will be performed, and unless this fails, the system will resume multi-user operations.
>
> **Cold starts**
>
>> On an HP300, the boot procedure uses the boot ROM to load a boot program from an LIF format directory at the beginning of an attached disk. The /usr/mdec directory contains a disk boot programs which should be placed in a new pack automatically by newfs(8) when the "a" partition file system on the pack is created.
>>
>> This *boot* program finds the corresponding file on the given device (*netbsd* by default), loads that file into memory, and starts the program at the entry address specified in the program header.
>>
>> The boot program can be interrupted by typing '^C' (ctrl-C). This will force the boot program to interactively prompt for a system to boot. If not interrupted, it will boot from the device from which the boot program itself was loaded.
>>
>> The file specifications used for an interactive boot are of the form:
>>
>>> device(unit, minor)
>>
>> where *device* is the type of the device to be searched, *unit* is 8 * the HP-IB number plus the unit number of the disk or tape, and *minor* is the disk partition or tape file number. Normal line editing characters can be used when typing the file specification. Currently, "rd" and "sd" are the only valid *device* specifiers.
>>
>> For example, to boot from the 'a' file system of unit 0 on HP-IB 2, type rd(16, 0)netbsd to the boot prompt. For tapes, the minor device number gives a file offset.
>>
>> In an emergency, the bootstrap methods described in the paper *Installing 4.3bsd on the HP300* can be used to boot from a distribution tape.

FILES

/netbsd	system code
/usr/mdec/bootrd	LIF format boot block
/usr/mdec/installboot	program to install boot blocks

SEE ALSO

> halt(8), reboot(8), shutdown(8)

NAME

boot — hp700 system bootstrapping procedures

DESCRIPTION

System starts

When powered on, after a panic, or if the system is rebooted via reboot(8) or shutdown(8), the hp700 firmware ("PDC") will proceed to its initialization, and will boot an operating system if autoboot is enabled.

Boot process description

System boot blocks are provided as a "LIF" (Logical Interchange Format) archive, either on a disk device, or via the network, using the *bootp* or *rboot* protocols, depending on the PDC version.

PDC concepts

If autoboot is enabled, the PDC will attempt to boot from the specified "boot path" value. If no "boot path" has been specified, the PDC will then scan for bootable devices and boot from the first found, after a few seconds allowing the user to interrupt the boot process. If autoboot is disabled, the PDC will enter interactive mode, after an optional device scan. In all cases, it is possible to enter interactive mode by holding the escape key during the selftests, or when prompted to do so to abort the current operation, unless the PDC has been configured in "secure mode".

ISL interaction

"ISL" stands for "Initial System Loader" and is the **boot** program in NetBSD. On all versions of the PDC except for the 712 and 725 models the "boot" command (see below) will be followed by the question: "Interact with IPL (Y, N, or Cancel)?>" where a positive answer will invoke an interactive prompt in the **boot** program later and negative will thus suppress it. A cancellation will abort the boot process.

On the 712 and 725 models firmware an additional "isl" argument should be given to the "boot" command to invoke the **boot** interactive prompt. The default behaviour is a non-interactive boot process.

Old PDC operation

This version is used on the following models: 705, 7x0, 715/33/50/75, 725/50/75, 735, 755. There are two levels of interactive commands in this version. The first level is a short menu:

```
b)    Boot from specified device
s)    Search for bootable device
a)    Enter Boot Administration mode
x)    Exit and continue boot sequence

Select from menu:
```

which provides the following commands:

b   boot from a device found during the scan, either with its short "P#" form, or a complete name specification. For example, to boot from the SCSI disk with id 6 off the built-in (first) controller, one would enter **b** *scsi.6.0.*

s   rescan for bootable devices.

a   enter the second part of interactive mode.

x   resume an interrupted boot sequence.

The "Boot Administration" mode, recognizable with its *BOOT_ADMIN>* prompt, controls the various boot options. The complete list of commands depends on the machine and PDC version. The following list only mentions commands impacting the boot process.

AUTOSELECT
Displays or changes the autoboot setting. If autoselect is set to "on", the PDC will always attempt to boot the first bootable device found in this order:
1. Boot device *path* setting.
2. SCSI devices connected to the built-in SCSI controller, the highest ID numbers being preferred.
3. Network *rboot* server (see also `rbootd(8)`).
4. Other SCSI devices connected to secondary controllers, the highest ID numbers being preferred.

If the *primary path* setting defines a bootable device, no device scan will occur.

BOOT
Boots off the specified device. It is similar to the **b** command from the short menu above. The "primary" and "alternate" path settings may be booted with **boot** `pri` and **boot** `alt` respectively.

PATH
Displays or changes the boot and console devices. The boot device is defined as the "primary" path, and another setting may be stored as the "alternate" path for rescue purposes. For example, to define the primary boot path to the SCSI disk with ID 5 connected to the built-in controller, one would enter **path primary** `scsi.5`

When invoked without parameters, **path** will list the various path settings.

Modern PDC operation

Machines equipped with 7100LC, 7200, or 7300LC CPU types are usually blessed with a different kind of PDC. There is only one interactive mode, with a *BOOT_ADMIN>* prompt, which provides both boot settings and commands. The complete list of commands depends on the machine and PDC version. The following list only mentions commands impacting the boot process.

auto boot
Displays or changes the autoboot setting. If **auto boot** is set to "on", the PDC will always attempt to boot. The booted device chosen will depend on the **auto search** setting.

auto search
Displays or changes the device scan setting. If **auto search** is set to "on", the PDC will attempt to boot the first bootable device found in this order:
1. Boot device *path* setting.
2. SCSI devices connected to the built-in SCSI controller, the highest ID numbers being preferred.
3. Network *bootp* server (see also `dhcpd(8)`).
4. Other SCSI devices connected to secondary controllers, the highest ID numbers being preferred.

If **auto search** is set to "off" and the primary boot path points to a bootable device, no device scan will occur.

Note that setting **auto search** to "on" will force autoboot, regardless of the **auto boot** value.

boot
Boots off the specified device. The "primary" and "alternate" path settings may be booted with **boot** `pri` and **boot** `alt` respectively.

path
Displays or changes the boot and console devices. The boot device is defined as the "primary" path, and another setting may be stored as the "alternate" path for rescue purposes. For example, to define the primary boot path to the SCSI disk with ID 5 connected to the built-in controller, one would enter **path pri** `scsi.5`.

When invoked without parameters, **path** will list the various path settings.

Abnormal system termination

If the system crashes, it will enter the kernel debugger, ddb(4), if it is configured in the kernel. If the crash occurred during initialization and the debugger is not present or is exited, the kernel will halt the system. If the crash occurred during normal operation and the debugger is not present or is exited, the system will attempt a dump to the configured dump device (which will be automatically recovered with savecore(8) during the next multi-user boot cycle), and after the dump is complete (successful or not) the kernel will attempt a reboot.

FILES

boot.lif	network bootstrap and kernel combined image
/netbsd	default NetBSD system kernel
/usr/mdec/xxboot	primary bootstrap for "ffs" file system
/usr/mdec/boot	system bootstrap (usually also installed as /boot)

SEE ALSO

ddb(4), dhcpd(8), halt(8), init(8), installboot(8), rbootd(8), reboot(8), savecore(8), shutdown(8)

NAME

boot — system bootstrapping procedures

DESCRIPTION

Windows CE machines with StrongARM CPUs use the hpcboot(8) program to boot NetBSD.

Power fail and crash recovery

Unfortunately, NetBSD can't reboot itself at power-up or after crashes. The machine will go through the cold reset and boot into Windows CE. You will have to restart NetBSD manually using hpcboot(8).

Once NetBSD starts, an automatic consistency check of the file systems will be performed, and unless this fails, the system will resume multi-user operations.

Cold starts

On cold reset Windows CE handheld machines attempt to boot the Windows CE operating system from the boot ROM. The boot ROM is usually not rewritable, so you cannot erase or damage Windows CE image.

You can't boot NetBSD directly, skipping Windows CE. The NetBSD bootloader, hpcboot(8), is provided as a Windows CE application program instead. Though the bootloader is an application program, it blows the entire running Windows CE, its data, and its settings away from RAM (but not ROM!) when the kernel boots successfully. If NetBSD is halted the machine will go through the cold reset and will reboot into Windows CE.

Normal Operation

Please, refer to the hpcboot(8) manual page.

FILES

hpcboot.exe bootloader program for Windows CE

SEE ALSO

hpcboot(8)

BUGS

There is no general way to launch the bootloader automatically, as only a few Windows CE machines provide an "auto run" mechanism.

This port doesn't support kloader(4), which means that when the system is rebooted, it goes back to Windows CE.

NAME

boot — system bootstrapping procedures

DESCRIPTION

Power fail and crash recovery

Unfortunately, on most machines, the system can't reboot itself at power-up or after crashes. You might have to restart the system manually. Once the system starts, an automatic consistency check of the file systems will be performed, and unless this fails, the system will resume multi-user operations.

Cold starts

Typical MIPS based Windows CE Handheld machines attempt to boot Windows CE operating system in its own boot ROM. You can't boot the NetBSD directly skipping Windows CE. The NetBSD bootloaders are provided as application programs on Windows CE instead. You can choose pbsdboot(8) or hpcboot(8). Though the bootloaders are application programs, they blow away the entire Windows CE OS and its settings when the kernel boots successfully.

Normal Operation

Once running, a familiar window will appear. You can choose the machine type, kernel file location and kernel boot options with a GUI and push the button named "[boot]" to boot NetBSD.

Automatic mode

The bootloaders have an "auto boot" option. If you enable this option, the specified kernel will be loaded automatically after a countdown.

FILES

/netbsd	system kernel
/netbsd.gz	gzip-compressed kernel
pbsdboot1.exe	bootloader executable file for Windows CE version 1.01
pbsdboot.exe	bootloader executable file for Windows CE
hpcboot.exe	new bootloader executable file for Windows CE

SEE ALSO

kloader(4), hpcboot(8), pbsdboot(8)

BUGS

There is no general way to launch a bootloader automatically while a few Windows CE machine provide an "auto run" mechanism.

NAME
boot — system bootstrapping procedures

DESCRIPTION
Windows CE machines with SuperH CPUs use the hpcboot(8) program to boot NetBSD. Once running, NetBSD can reboot itself if kloader(4) is configured in the kernel.

Power fail and crash recovery
Unfortunately, NetBSD can't reboot itself at power-up or after crashes. The machine will go through the cold reset and boot into Windows CE. You will have to restart NetBSD manually using hpcboot(8).

Once NetBSD starts, an automatic consistency check of the file systems will be performed, and unless this fails, the system will resume multi-user operations.

Cold starts
On cold reset Windows CE handheld machines attempt to boot the Windows CE operating system from the boot ROM. The boot ROM is usually not rewritable, so you cannot erase or damage Windows CE image.

You can't boot NetBSD directly, skipping Windows CE. The NetBSD bootloader, hpcboot(8), is provided as a Windows CE application program instead. Though the bootloader is an application program, it blows the entire running Windows CE, its data, and its settings away from RAM (but not ROM!) when the kernel boots successfully. If NetBSD is halted the machine will go through the cold reset and will reboot into Windows CE.

Normal Operation
Please, refer to the hpcboot(8) manual page.

FILES
hpcboot.exe bootloader program for Windows CE

SEE ALSO
kloader(4), hpcboot(8)

BUGS
There is no general way to launch the bootloader automatically, as only a few Windows CE machines provide an "auto run" mechanism.

NAME
boot — system bootstrapping procedures

DESCRIPTION
IA-32 computers (the IBM PC and its clones) that can run NetBSD/i386 can use any of the following boot procedures, depending on what the hardware and BIOS support:

boot   bootstrap NetBSD from the system BIOS

dosboot(8)   bootstrap NetBSD from MS-DOS

w95boot(8)   bootstrap NetBSD from Windows 95

pxeboot(8)   network bootstrap NetBSD from a TCP/IP LAN with DHCP, TFTP, and NFS.

Power fail and crash recovery
Normally, the system will reboot itself at power-up or after crashes. An automatic consistency check of the file systems will be performed, and unless this fails, the system will resume multi-user operations.

Cold starts
The 386 PC AT clones attempt to boot the floppy disk drive A (otherwise known as drive 0) first, and failing that, attempt to boot the hard disk C (otherwise known as hard disk controller 1, drive 0). The NetBSD bootblocks are loaded and started either by the BIOS, or by a boot selector program (such as OS-BS, BOOTEASY, the OS/2 Boot Menu or NetBSD's boot-selecting master boot record - see mbr(8)).

Normal Operation
Once running, a banner similar to the following will appear:

> >> NetBSD BIOS Boot, revision 3.0
> >> (user@buildhost, builddate)
> >> Memory: 637/15360 k
> Press return to boot now, any other key for boot menu
> booting hd0a:netbsd - starting in 5

After a countdown, the system image listed will be loaded. In the example above, it will be "hd0a:netbsd" which is the file **netbsd** on partition "a" of the NetBSD MBR partition of the first hard disk known to the BIOS (which is an IDE or similar device - see the **BUGS** section).

Pressing a key within the time limit, or before the boot program starts, will enter interactive mode. When using a short or 0 timeout, it is often useful to interrupt the boot by holding down a shift key, as some BIOSes and BIOS extensions will drain the keystroke buffer at various points during POST.

If present, the file /boot.cfg will be used to configure the behaviour of the boot loader including setting the timeout, choosing a console device, altering the banner text and displaying a menu allowing boot commands to be easily chosen. See boot.cfg(5).

The NetBSD/i386 boot loader can boot a kernel using either the native NetBSD boot protocol, or the "multiboot" protocol (which is compatible with some other operating systems). In the native NetBSD boot protocol, options are passed from the boot loader to the kernel via flag bits in the *boothowto* variable (see boothowto(9)). In the multiboot protocol, options are passed from the boot loader to the kernel as strings.

Diagnostic Output
If the first stage boot fails to load the boot, it will print a terse message indicating the reason for the failure. The possible error messages and their cause are listed in mbr(8).

If the first stage boot succeeds, the banner will be shown and the error messages should be self-explanatory.

Interactive mode

In interactive mode, the boot loader will present a prompt, allowing input of these commands:

boot [*device*:] [*filename*] [**-1234abcdmqsvxz**]

The default *device* will be set to the disk that the boot loader was loaded from. To boot from an alternate disk, the full name of the device should be given at the prompt. *device* is of the form *xd* [*N*[*x*]] where *xd* is the device from which to boot, *N* is the unit number, and *x* is the partition letter.

The following list of supported devices may vary from installation to installation:

hd   Hard disks as numbered by the BIOS. This includes ST506, IDE, ESDI, RLL disks on a WD100[2367] or lookalike controller(s), and SCSI disks on SCSI controllers recognized by the BIOS.

fd   Floppy drives as numbered by the BIOS.

The default *filename* is netbsd; if the boot loader fails to successfully open that image, it then tries netbsd.gz (expected to be a kernel image compressed by gzip), followed by netbsd.old, netbsd.old.gz, onetbsd, and finally onetbsd.gz. Alternate system images can be loaded by just specifying the name of the image.

Options are:

-1   Sets the machine-dependent flag **RB_MD1** in *boothowto*. In NetBSD/i386, this disables multiprocessor boot; the kernel will boot in uniprocessor mode.

-2   Sets the machine-dependent flag **RB_MD2** in *boothowto*. In NetBSD/i386, this disables ACPI.

-3   Sets the machine-dependent flag **RB_MD3** in *boothowto*. In NetBSD/i386, this has no effect.

-4   Sets the machine-dependent flag **RB_MD4** in *boothowto*. In NetBSD/i386, this has no effect.

-a   Sets the **RB_ASKNAME** flag in *boothowto*. This causes the kernel to prompt for the root file system device, the system crash dump device, and the path to init(8).

-b   Sets the **RB_HALT** flag in *boothowto*. This causes subsequent reboot attempts to halt instead of rebooting.

-c   Sets the **RB_USERCONF** flag in *boothowto*. This causes the kernel to enter the userconf(4) device configuration manager as soon as possible during the boot. userconf(4) allows devices to be enabled or disabled, and allows device locators (such as hardware addresses or bus numbers) to be modified before the kernel attempts to attach the devices.

-d   Sets the **RB_KDB** flag in *boothowto*. Requests the kernel to enter debug mode, in which it waits for a connection from a kernel debugger; see ddb(4).

-m   Sets the **RB_MINIROOT** flag in *boothowto*. Informs the kernel that a mini-root file system is present in memory.

-q   Sets the **AB_QUIET** flag in *boothowto*. Boot the system in quiet mode.

-s   Sets the **RB_SINGLE** flag in *boothowto*. Boot the system in single-user mode.

-v   Sets the **AB_VERBOSE** flag in *boothowto*. Boot the system in verbose mode.

-x   Sets the **AB_DEBUG** flag in *boothowto*. Boot the system with debug messages enabled.

-z   Sets the **AB_SILENT** flag in *boothowto*. Boot the system in silent mode.

consdev *dev*

Immediately switch the console to the specified device *dev* and reprint the banner. *dev* must be one of `pc`, `com0`, `com1`, `com2`, `com3`, `com0kbd`, `com1kbd`, `com2kbd`, `com3kbd`, or `auto`. See **Console Selection Policy** in `boot_console`(8).

vesa *modenum | on | off | enabled | disabled | list*

Initialise the video card to the specified resolution and bit depth. The *modenum* should be in the form of `0x100`, `800x600`, `800x600x32`. The values `enabled`, `on` put the display into the default mode, and `disabled`, `off` returns the display into standard vga mode. The value `list` lists all supported modes.

dev [*device*]

Set the default drive and partition for subsequent filesystem operations. Without an argument, print the current setting. *device* is of the form specified in **boot**.

help

Print an overview about commands and arguments.

load *module* [*arguments*]

Load the specified kernel *module*, and pass it the specified *arguments*. If the module name is not an absolute path, `/stand/` ⟨**arch**⟩/⟨**osversion**⟩/modules/⟨**module**⟩/⟨**module**⟩`.kmod` is used. Possible used of the **load** command include loading a memory disk image before booting a kernel, or loading a Xen DOM0 kernel before booting the Xen hypervisor.

ls [*path*]

Print a directory listing of `path`, containing inode number, filename, and file type. `path` can contain a device specification.

multiboot *kernel* [*arguments*]

Boot the specified *kernel*, using the "multiboot" protocol instead of the native NetBSD boot protocol. The *kernel* is specified in the same way as with the **boot** command.

The multiboot protocol may be used in the following cases:

NetBSD/Xen kernels

The Xen DOM0 kernel must be loaded as a module using the **load** command, and the Xen hypervisor must be booted using the **multiboot** command. Options for the DOM0 kernel (such as "-s" for single user mode) must be passed as options to the **load** command. Options for the hypervisor (such as "dom0_mem=256M" to reserve 256 MB of memory for DOM0) must be passed as options to the **multiboot** command. See `boot.cfg`(5) for examples of how to boot NetBSD/Xen.

NetBSD multiboot kernels

A NetBSD kernel that was built with **options MULTIBOOT** (see `multiboot`(8)) may be booted with either the **boot** or **multiboot** command, passing the same arguments in either case.

Non-NetBSD kernels

A kernel for a non-NetBSD operating system that expects to be booted using the multiboot protocol (such as by the GNU "GRUB" boot loader) may be booted using the **multiboot** command. See the foreign operating system's documentation for the available arguments.

>   **quit**
>   Reboot the system.

In an emergency, the bootstrap methods described in the NetBSD installation notes for the i386 architecture can be used to boot from floppy or other media, or over the network.

FILES

/boot	boot program code loaded by the primary bootstrap
/boot.cfg	optional configuration file
/netbsd	system code
/netbsd.gz	gzip-compressed system code
/usr/mdec/boot	master copy of the boot program (copy to /boot)
/usr/mdec/bootxx_fstype	primary bootstrap for filesystem type fstype, copied to the start of the NetBSD partition by installboot(8).

SEE ALSO

ddb(4), userconf(4), boot.cfg(5), boot_console(8), dosboot(8), halt(8), installboot(8), mbr(8), multiboot(8), pxeboot(8), reboot(8), shutdown(8), w95boot(8), boothowto(9)

BUGS

The kernel file name must be specified before, not after, the boot options. Any *filename* specified after the boot options, e.g.:

>   **boot -d netbsd.test**

is ignored, and the default kernel is booted.

Hard disks are always accessed by BIOS functions. Unit numbers are BIOS device numbers which might differ from numbering in the NetBSD kernel or physical parameters (e.g., SCSI slave numbers). There isn't any distinction between "sd" and "wd" devices at the bootloader level. This is less a bug of the bootloader code than a shortcoming of the PC architecture. The default disk device's name printed in the starting message is derived from the "type" field of the NetBSD disklabel (if it is a hard disk).

NAME
boot — system bootstrapping procedures

DESCRIPTION
Power fail and crash recovery
Normally, the NetBSD kernel on the mac68k architecture is booted from the native operating system by means of an application program. When the kernel takes over, it initializes itself and proceeds to boot the system. An automatic consistency check of the file systems takes place, and unless this fails, the system comes up to multi-user operations. The proper way to shut the system down is with the shutdown(8) command.

If the system crashes, it will enter the kernel debugger, ddb(4), if it is configured in the kernel. If the debugger is not present, or the debugger is exited, the system will attempt a dump to the configured dump device (which will be automatically recovered with savecore(8) during the next boot cycle). After the dump is complete (successful or not), the system will attempt a reboot.

On most mac68k machines with "soft-power" after the IIcx, the power switch can be physically rotated and locked in the 'on' position. The native OS can be configured to automatically start the NetBSD boot program. Additionally, the NetBSD boot program can be configured to boot NetBSD without intervention. When a system is so configured, it can crash or lose power and reboot back to a fully multi-user state without any intervention.

The boot application
The boot application runs in the native OS on the system. It has a dialog where booting preferences may be changed and an option whereby these options may be saved. The preferences are stored in the program itself, not in a preferences folder--thus allowing two separate copies of the program to be configured differently (e.g. to boot different netbsd or netbsd.test, or to boot from two different drives).

One option that may be specified is a boot to single-user mode. This stops the boot process very early on and allows system maintenance. If one wishes to provide some security at this phase of the boot, remove the secure option from ttye0 in the ttys(5) file.

Another useful option that may be specified is the "serial console" option. This will allow a serial device (terminal or computer) to act as a console for the system. This device must be configured to use 9600 baud, eight bits, no parity, and one stop bit (9600-N81). Either the printer port or the modem port (tty01 and tty00, respectively) may be used for this.

It is sometimes useful to boot a kernel that resides in a folder in native OS rather than from the usual location in the NetBSD file system. A radio button is supplied for this purpose. Note that some programs will not run properly if the kernel is not found as /netbsd within the NetBSD file system.

FILES
/netbsd system kernel

SEE ALSO
ddb(4), ttys(5), savecore(8), shutdown(8)

NAME
    boot — Macppc system bootstrapping procedures

DESCRIPTION
Power fail and crash recovery
Normally, the system will reboot itself at power-up or after crashes. An automatic consistency check of the file systems will be performed as described in fsck(8), and unless this fails, the system will resume multi-user operations.

Cold starts
The boot ROM performs a Power On Self Test (POST) then loads Open Firmware. Depending on the Open Firmware variable 'auto-boot?' it will either stop at the Open Firmware prompt or attempt to boot an operating system. Depending on the contents of the 'use-nvramrc?', 'boot-command', 'boot-device', and 'boot-file' Open Firmware variables, it will attempt to boot MacOS, MacOS X, or NetBSD.

To boot NetBSD, Open Firmware loads the bootloader ofwboot(8) from the specified 'boot-device'. The bootloader then loads the kernel from the 'boot-file', (if it exists). Otherwise, it tries to load (in the following order): netbsd, netbsd.gz, or netbsd.macppc on the "a" partition of the same device that had the bootloader.

Open Firmware Commands
An essential but incomplete list of Open Firmware commands follows. A more thorough list is contained in the FAQ.
http://www.NetBSD.org/ports/macppc/faq.html#ofw-use

boot [*boot-device* [*boot-file*]] [*options*]

Boot an operating system. The default arguments for this command are taken from the Open Firmware environment variables:
boot-device primary bootloader location
boot-file kernel location
options flags passed to the kernel

reset-all

Reset the system, and proceed as specified by the 'use-nvramrc?' and 'auto-boot?' variables. If 'use-nvramrc?' is set to 'true', then the system will attempt to execute the commands stored in the 'nvramrc' variable. If 'auto-boot?' is set to 'true', the system will attempt to use the values stored in 'boot-command', 'boot-device', and 'boot-file' to boot the system. If 'auto-boot?' is set to 'false', the system will halt at the Open Firmware prompt.

shut-down

Power off the system.

setenv *variable value*

Set an Open Firmware variable, e.g.,

```
setenv auto-boot? false
setenv boot-device hd:,\ofwboot.xcf
setenv boot-file netbsd-GENERIC.gz
```

set-default *variable*

Set an Open Firmware variable to its default value.

printenv [*variable*]

Show Open Firmware variables and values.

eject fd

Eject floppy disk on systems with on-board floppy drives.

mac-boot

Attempt to boot MacOS on an Open Firmware 3 system.

bye

Attempt to boot MacOS on an Open Firmware 1.0.5, 2.0.x, or 2.4 system.

Open Firmware Variables

An essential but incomplete list of Open Firmware variables follows. A more thorough list is contained in the FAQ.

http://www.NetBSD.org/ports/macppc/faq.html#ofw-variables

auto-boot?   What Open Firmware will do at system startup or reset:

             true automatically bootstrap an operating system using values from the 'boot-command', 'boot-device', and 'boot-file' variables.

             false stop at the Open Firmware prompt.

use-nvramrc?   If 'true' runs commands in variable 'nvramrc'.

real-base   Kernel memory location. *Do not modify this value on Open Firmware 3 systems — you may damage your computer.* All other Open Firmware versions should use F00000.

load-base   Bootloader memory location. *Do not modify this value on Open Firmware 3 systems — you may damage your computer.* All other Open Firmware versions should use 600000.

boot-command   The command to use for booting. Typically, the default of 'boot' is used.

boot-device   Device from which to load primary bootloader. Value depends on a variety of factors. See ofwboot(8).

boot-file   Kernel location. Value depends on a variety of factors. See ofwboot(8).

input-device   What type of console input device (ADB keyboard, USB keyboard, or serial port).

             kbd ADB keyboard on models with ADB, USB keyboard on models with USB, and built-in keyboard on laptops. This is the default on some Open Firmware 2.0.x machines and all Open Firmware 2.4 and 3 machines.

             ttya 'Modem' serial port on machines with serial ports. Properties are 38400 bps, 8 bits, no parity, 1 stop bit, no handshaking. This is the default on all Open Firmware 1.0.5 systems and some Open Firmware 2.0.x systems.

             ttyb 'Printer' serial port on machines with serial ports. Properties are the same as the 'Modem' port.

             scca Serial port on Xserve models. Properties are 57600 bps, 8 bits, no parity, 1 stop bit, no handshaking.

BOOT (8)   NetBSD/macppc   BOOT (8)

output-device   What type of console output device (On-board video, AGP video, PCI video, built-in
                     LCD, or serial console). Value depends on a variety of factors. See ofwboot(8) and
                     http://www.NetBSD.org/ports/macppc/faq.html#ofw-input-output-devices

nvramrc   If 'use-nvramrc?' is set to true, these FORTH commands will be run when the
                     computer is reset

Normal Operation

When Open Firmware loads the primary bootloader, it will print something like the following:

```
loading XCOFF
tsize=CC50 dsize=14AC bsize=2668 entry=640000
SECTIONS:
.text   00640000 00640000 0000CC50 000000E0
.data   0064D000 0064D000 000014AC 0000CD30
.bss    0064E4B0 0064E4B0 00002668 00000000
loading .text, done..
loading .data, done..
clearing .bss, done..
```

When ofwboot(8) is started, it prints something like the following:

```
>> NetBSD/macppc OpenFirmware Boot, Revision 1.7
>> (autobuild@tgm.daemon.org, Thu Feb 6 17:50:27 UTC 2003)
```

When ofwboot(8) is loading the kernel, it prints something like the following:

```
4395364+254568 [220144+193803]=0x4d477c
start=0x100000
```

When the NetBSD kernel has started it prints a banner similar to the following:

```
Copyright (c) 1996, 1997, 1998, 1999, 2000, 2001, 2002, 2003
    The NetBSD Foundation, Inc.  All rights reserved.
Copyright (c) 1982, 1986, 1989, 1991, 1993
    The Regents of the University of California.  All rights reserved.

NetBSD 1.6ZC (GENERIC) #0: Tue Sep 30 13:09:10 UTC 2003
        autobuild@tgm.NetBSD.org:/autobuild/HEAD/macppc/OBJ/autobuild/HEAD/sr
```

After bootstrap

Once the NetBSD/macppc kernel is booted normally it initializes itself and proceeds to start the system. An automatic consistency check of the file systems takes place, and unless this fails, the system comes up to multi-user operation.

The proper way to shut the system down is with the shutdown(8) command.

If the system crashes, it will enter the kernel debugger, ddb(4), if it is configured in the kernel. If the crash occurred during initialization and the debugger is not present or is exited, the kernel will halt the system.

If the crash occurred during normal operation and the debugger is not present or is exited, the system will attempt a dump to the configured dump device (which will be automatically recovered with savecore(8) during the next bootstrap cycle), and after the dump is complete (successful or not) the kernel will attempt a reboot.

FILES

/boot	NetBSD secondary bootstrap program (Open Firmware 1.x and 2.x)
/netbsd	default NetBSD system kernel
/usr/mdec/bootxx	NetBSD primary bootstrap program (Open Firmware 1.x and 2.x) a.k.a. "partition zero" bootloader
/usr/mdec/ofwboot	NetBSD secondary bootstrap program (Open Firmware 1.x and 2.x)
/usr/mdec/ofwboot.xcf	primary bootstrap for netboot and "cd9660" (ISO 9660), "MS-DOS", "HFS", and "HFS+" file systems.

SEE ALSO

ddb(4), intro(4), diskless(8), halt(8), init(8), installboot(8), ofwboot(8), rc(8), reboot(8), savecore(8), shutdown(8)

http://www.NetBSD.org/ports/macppc/faq.html
http://www.NetBSD.org/docs/network/netboot/

STANDARDS

IEEE Std 1275-1994 ("Open Firmware")
http://playground.sun.com/1275/home.html

BUGS

The device names used by NetBSD/macppc and Open Firmware often have no relation to each other.

Apple Computer's Open Firmware implementation is easily confused. It is best to reboot your computer after a failed boot attempt, **halt**, or **shutdown -h**. Use the Open Firmware **reset-all** command.

Apple Computer's Open Firmware implementation is notoriously bad. Thorough instructions for installing and booting NetBSD are in the install notes (INSTALL.html) included with every release of NetBSD.

BOOT (8)   NetBSD/mvme68k   BOOT (8)

NAME
boot — system bootstrapping procedures

DESCRIPTION
Power fail and crash recovery
Normally, the system will reboot itself at power-up or after crashes. An automatic consistency check of the file systems will be performed as described in fsck(8). and unless this fails, the system will resume multi-user operations.

Cold starts from disk
The disk-boot program (/usr/mdec/bootsd) will attempt to load netbsd from partition A of the boot device, which must currently be an "sd" disk.

Cold starts from tape
The tape-boot program (/usr/mdec/bootst) will attempt to load netbsd from a SCSI tape drive.

Cold starts over a network
The network boot program (/usr/mdec/netboot) will load netbsd from the NFS root as determined by the procedure described in diskless(8). Note that the MVME147 is unable to boot directly from the network without the help of a small bootloader program (/usr/mdec/sboot).

Boot program options
−a   Prompt for the root file system device, the system crash dump device, and the path to init(8).

−d   Bring the system up in debug mode. Here it waits for a kernel debugger connect; see ddb(4).

−q   Boot the system in quiet mode.

−s   Bring the system up in single-user mode.

−v   Boot the system in verbose mode.

Any extra flags or arguments, or the <boot string> after the -- separator are passed to the boot PROM. Other flags are currently ignored.

At any time you can break to the kernel debugger ddb(4) (assuming **options DDB** was specified in the kernel configuration file) by sending a serial line BREAK character. If you do this accidentally you can continue whatever was in progress by typing 'c' followed by the return key.

FILES
/netbsd	system code
/usr/mdec/bootxx	first-level boot block for disks
/usr/mdec/stboot	first-level boot block for tapes
/usr/mdec/bootsd	second-level boot block for UFS disks
/usr/mdec/bootst	second-level boot block for tapes
/usr/mdec/netboot	boot program for NFS (diskless) boot
/usr/mdec/sboot	network bootstrap program for MVME147
/usr/mdec/installboot	program to install bootxx on a disk

SEE ALSO
disklabel(8), fsck(8), halt(8), init(8), rc(8), shutdown(8), syslogd(8)

NAME

boot — system bootstrapping procedures

DESCRIPTION

Power fail and crash recovery

Normally, the system will reboot itself at power-up or after crashes. An automatic consistency check of the file systems will be performed, and unless this fails, the system will resume multi-user operations.

Cold starts

On an NeXT, the boot procedure uses the boot ROM to load a boot program over the network using BOOTP and TFTP. The /usr/mdec directory contains a network boot program which should be made available via tftp(1). The network boot program will load netbsd from the NFS root as determined by the procedure described in diskless(8).

FILES

```
/netbsd              system code
/usr/mdec/boot       boot program for NFS (diskless) boot
```

SEE ALSO

halt(8), init(8), rc(8), reboot(8), shutdown(8)

NAME

boot — system bootstrapping procedures

DESCRIPTION

The NetBSD kernel is started by placing it near the beginning of physical memory and transferring to the entry point. Since the system is not reenterable, it is necessary to read it in from disk or tape each time it is to be bootstrapped.

Power fail and crash recovery

Normally, the system will boot itself at power-up or after crashes. An automatic consistency check of the file systems will be performed, and unless this fails, the system will resume multi-user operations.

Cold starts

At power up, all DECstation ROMs consult the **haltaction** environment variable in EEPROM to determine whether or not to attempt to boot automatically. If this variable is set to 'h', the ROM prints a prompt on the console and waits for user commands. If set to 'b', the ROM attempts to autoboot.

DECSTATION 2100 and 3100

On the DECstation 2100 and 3100, the path used for automatic booting is stored in the **bootpath** environment variable.

The path is made up of a device type specifier (e.g., rz, tz, mop or tftp) followed by a triplet in the form (x,y,z), followed by a filename to load.

Within the triplet, x is the controller (always 0), y is the SCSI id of the drive to boot from or 0 for net boots, and z is the partition to boot from (usually 0 for SCSI devices, always zero for network booting). For both disk and network boots, () may be specified instead of (0,0,0).

The filename is optional for bootp/tftp and mop booting, since in these cases the network protocol can be used to determine which file to boot. When booting off the tape, no filename should be specified. When booting off of disk, the filename is optional but is usually specified. If no filename is specified when booting off disk, the following filenames are tried in order: **netbsd.pmax**, **netbsd**, **netbsd.gz**, **netbsd.bak**, **netbsd.old**, **onetbsd**, **gennetbsd**. Generally, the kernel is named **netbsd**.

An example bootpath setting would be:

        setenv bootpath rz(0,1,0)netbsd

At the PROM prompt, the user may boot NetBSD with either the **auto** or the **boot** command. If the **auto** command is used, the **−a** argument is passed to the kernel, requesting a multi-user boot; otherwise the **−s** argument is passed, requesting that NetBSD boot to single user mode.

When either the **boot** or the **auto** command is issued with no arguments, the kernel specified in the bootpath environment variable is booted. With the **boot** command, an alternative kernel may be specified with the **−f** flag, followed by the path of the kernel to boot, as described above. For example:

        boot −f rz(0,4,0)netbsd.new

TURBOCHANNEL DECstations

On TurboChannel machines (all DECstation 5000 models), the boot path is specified in the boot environment variable, along with any arguments to be passed to the kernel. Note that to specify boot arguments (e.g., **−a**) when setting the **boot** environment variable, the filename and arguments must be enclosed in quotes. For example:

        setenv boot "3/rz4/netbsd −a"

The device from which to boot is specified as the TurboChannel slot number, a TurboChannel-option-specific device name, and a path to the file to load, all separated by slashes. You can get a list of the devices installed in your TurboChannel slots (as well as any built-in devices which appear as TurboChannel slots) by typing the **cnfg** command at the boot prompt. You can get more detailed information about a specific TurboChannel option by typing **cnfg** followed by the slot number of that option.

For SCSI devices, the option-specific device identifier is either rz# for disks or tz# for tapes, where # is the SCSI id of the device. For network devices, the option-specific protocol identifier is either mop or tftp. Filename requirements are as for the DECstation 2100 and 3100.

To start NetBSD from the boot prompt, the **boot** command must be used. With no arguments, this simply boots the default kernel with the default arguments as set with **setenv boot**. If no boot environment variable is set or if an alternative kernel is to be booted, the path of that kernel may be specified after the boot command as described above, and any arguments may be passed similarly. For example:

```
boot 3/rz4/netbsd.new -a
```

KERNEL ARGUMENTS

The kernel supports the following arguments:

a   Autoboot -- try and boot to multi-user mode without further input.

m   Use a miniroot already present in memory.

n   Prompt for the root file system device, the system crash dump device, and the path to init(8).

N   Do not prompt for the root file system device, the system crash dump device, and the path to init(8). If the configured-in devices are present, use them.

s   Boot only to single-user mode.

Since DECstation PROMs also parse any arguments with a leading "-", and reject unrecognized options, arguments other than "a" or "s" should be specified after the kernel name with no leading "-". For example:

```
boot 3/rz4/netbsd ns
```

SEE ALSO

ddb(4), halt(8), init(8), installboot(8), rc(8), reboot(8), savecore(8), shutdown(8)

HISTORY

The **boot** command is currently under development.

NAME
boot — system bootstrapping procedures

SYNOPSIS
boot

DESCRIPTION

Power fail and crash recovery
Normally, the system will reboot itself at power-up or after crashes. An automatic consistency check of the file systems will be performed as described in fsck(8), and unless this fails, the system will resume multi-user operations.

Cold starts
The prep architecture does not allow the direct booting of a kernel from the hard drive. Instead it requires a complete boot image to be loaded. This boot image contains a NetBSD kernel, which will then provide access to the devices on the machine. The image can be placed on any device that the firmware considers a bootable device. Usually this is either a SCSI disk, tape, CD-ROM, or floppy drive.

Boot program options
The prep architecture and bootloader does not support any option parsing at the boot prompt.

Boot partition
The prep port requires a special boot partition on the primary boot device in order to load the kernel. This partition consists of a PC-style i386 partition label, a small bootloader, and a kernel image. The prep firmware looks for a partition of type 0x41 (65) and expects the bootloader, immediately followed by the kernel, to be there. The mkbootimage(8) command needs to be used to generate this image.

FILES
/netbsd	system code
/usr/mdec/boot	system bootstrap
/usr/mdec/boot_com0	system bootstrap with serial console

SEE ALSO
disklabel(8), fsck(8), halt(8), init(8), installboot(8), mkbootimage(8), rc(8), shutdown(8), syslogd(8)

NAME
boot — sgimips system bootstrapping procedures

DESCRIPTION
Silicon Graphics MIPS-based computers all feature essentially similar firmware systems. However, as of the Indigo R4x00 series (IP20), quasi- ARCS (Advanced RISC Computing Specification) compatible features are also present. All known PROM implementations support loading executables from disk devices, as well as from the network via BOOTP and TFTP.

Disk Booting
SGI provides a small filesystem at the beginning of each bootable disk called a Volume Header, which contains a boot loader and other standalone utilities. Booting NetBSD requires that we write our bootloader into to the volume header using sgivol(8).

Once a bootloader is present in the volume header, it may be executed directly by the PROM either manually, or at boot time using the "OSLoader" PROM environment variable. The NetBSD bootloader will obtain the kernel filename to boot from the PROM or EEPROM. This is specified by setting the PROM environment variable "OSLoadFilename" to an appropriate value. For instance, "/netbsd.ecoff".

For example, the following will configure the PROM to use the bootloader "aoutboot" to load the kernel "netbsd.old"

```
setenv OSLoader aoutboot
setenv OSLoadFilename netbsd.old
```

Network Booting
The system firmware will obtain an IP address, TFTP server address, and an optional filename from the BOOTP server and download it via TFTP. The PROM's configurable network address environment variable "netaddr" must match the address provided by the BOOTP server.

An example BOOTP entry for dhcpd(8) follows:

```
host indigo3k {
        hardware ethernet 08:00:69:42:42:42;
        fixed-address 192.168.0.2;
        option host-name "indigo3k.foo";
        #filename "/netbsd.ecoff";
        next-server 192.168.0.1;
        option root-path "/export/indigo3k/root";
        server-name "192.168.0.1";
}
```

To boot a kernel named "netbsd.ecoff" the user would type:
```
boot -f bootp():/netbsd.ecoff
```

See dhcpd.conf(5) for more information on configuring dhcpd(8) as a BOOTP server.

SEE ALSO
dhcpd.conf(5), dhcpd(8), sgivol(8)

CAVEATS
Some older PROM revisions do not support loading of ELF images. The build system automatically prepares ECOFF versions, which are correctly interpreted.

BUGS

NetBSD does not support booting from disk on systems lacking an ARCS-compatible firmware (presently supported systems include Personal Iris and Indigo R3000). It is possible to work around this by creating a sufficiently large volume header and placing the kernel in it, or by network booting.

Some firmware revisions have a bug, which precludes them from communicating with TFTP servers using ports above 32767. When using NetBSD as the TFTP server, this problem may be worked around as follows:

```
sysctl -w net.inet.ip.anonportmin=20000
sysctl -w net.inet.ip.anonportmax=32767
```

Another bug exists in some firmware revisions, which precludes the PROM from communicating with TFTP servers that employ PMTU (Path MTU) discovery. This bug may be worked around by disabling PMTU on the TFTP server. This does not presently affect NetBSD servers.

This man page is horribly incomplete.

NAME
boot — system bootstrapping procedures

SYNOPSIS
boot [**-adqsv**] [-- ⟨*boot string*⟩]

DESCRIPTION
Power fail and crash recovery
Normally, the system will reboot itself at power-up or after crashes. An automatic consistency check of the file systems will be performed as described in fsck(8), and unless this fails, the system will resume multi-user operations.

Cold starts
The Sun boot firmware, either old-style or new-style (Open Boot Prom), performs a Power On Self Test (POST), and then will boot an operating system according to configuration in Open Firmware environment variables.

Boot program options
-a   Prompt for the root file system device, the system crash dump device, and the path to init(8).

-d   Bring the system up in debug mode. Here it waits for a kernel debugger connect; see gdb(1).

-C   Boot kernel in compat mode. Starting with revision 1.14 (introduced on 2003/03/01), the sparc boot program loads the NetBSD kernel at its linked virtual address. This feature requires a kernel built after 2003/02/21 (corresponding to kernel version 1.6Q). To load older kernels, the **-C** option must be used, which loads the kernel at physical address 0x4000. The size of a kernel loaded in this way is limited to approximately 3MB.

-q   Boot the system in quiet mode.

-s   Bring the system up in single-user mode.

-v   Boot the system in verbose mode.

Any extra flags or arguments, or the ⟨*boot string*⟩ after the -- separator are passed to the boot PROM. Other flags are currently ignored.

The SPARC boot ROM comes in two flavours: an "old-style" ROM is used in sun4 machines, while a "new-style" ROM can be found on sun4c and sun4m models. The "new-style" SPARC boot ROM is a full-featured Forth system with emacs key bindings. It can be put in "old-style" user-interface compatibility mode (in which case it shows a simple '>' prompt), but this is essentially useless. However, by default on sun4c models, the ROM runs in old-mode; to enter new-mode type 'n'. The ROM then shows a Forth-style "ok" prompt. It is recommended to have the ROM always start in its native "new-style" mode. Utter the following incantation in new-mode to force the ROM to always start in new-mode.

    ok setenv sunmon-compat? false

The ROM will normally load the kernel from "sd(0,0,0)vmunix". To change the default so that NetBSD will be loaded from somewhere else, type the following

    ok setenv boot-from sd(0,0,0)netbsd

On newer SPARC machines, there are various aliases to access common devices. A typical list of usable boot devices (extracted from the output of the Open Boot PROM command **devalias**) is:

```
floppy        /obio/SUNW,fdtwo
net-aui       /iommu/sbus/ledma@f,400010:aui/le@f,c00000
net-tpe       /iommu/sbus/ledma@f,400010:tpe/le@f,c00000
```

```
net          /iommu/sbus/ledma@f,400010/le@f,c00000
disk         /iommu/sbus/espdma@f,400000/esp@f,800000/sd@3,0
cdrom        /iommu/sbus/espdma@f,400000/esp@f,800000/sd@6,0:d
tape         /iommu/sbus/espdma@f,400000/esp@f,800000/st@4,0
tape1        /iommu/sbus/espdma@f,400000/esp@f,800000/st@5,0
tape0        /iommu/sbus/espdma@f,400000/esp@f,800000/st@4,0
disk3        /iommu/sbus/espdma@f,400000/esp@f,800000/sd@3,0
disk2        /iommu/sbus/espdma@f,400000/esp@f,800000/sd@2,0
disk1        /iommu/sbus/espdma@f,400000/esp@f,800000/sd@1,0
disk0        /iommu/sbus/espdma@f,400000/esp@f,800000/sd@0,0
```

For new-style machines, if a device specification includes a partition letter (for example *cdrom* in above list), that partition is used by default, otherwise the first (a) partition is used. If booting from the net device, there is no partition involved.

At any time you can break back to the ROM by pressing the 'L1' and 'a' keys at the same time (if the console is a serial port the same is achieved by sending a 'break'). If you do this accidentally you can continue whatever was in progress by typing 'go'.

OPEN BOOT PROM ENVIRONMENT VARIABLES

This section only applies to new-style machines.

All Open Boot PROM environment variables can be printed with the **printenv** command and changed with the **setenv** command. The boot process relevant variables and their suggested value for booting NetBSD are:

```
auto-boot?          true
boot-file
boot-device         disk
diag-switch?        false
```

Of course you may select any other boot device, if you do not want to boot from the device aliased to *disk*, see the discussion on devices above.

OPEN BOOT PROM ABBREVIATED COMMAND SUMMARY

This section only applies to new-style machines.

The following Open Boot PROM commands are related to the boot process:

```
boot                    boot the system from the default device
boot device filename arguments
                        boot the specified device, filename and arguments
probe-ide               list devices on the primary IDE controller
probe-ide-all           list devices on all known IDE controllers
probe-scsi              list devices on the primary SCSI controller
probe-scsi-all          list devices on all known SCSI controllers
reset                   reset the system
```
For disk and tape devices, the boot device is specified as '/path/device@target,lun:partition'.

PROM MONITOR ABBREVIATED COMMAND SUMMARY

This section only applies to old-style machines.

The following PROM monitor commands are related to the boot process:

```
b       boot the system from the default device
b device filename arguments
```

```
                        boot the specified device, filename and arguments
        b?              list boot device types
        k2              reset the system
```

For SCSI disk and tape devices, the boot device is specified as 'device(controller,unit,partition)', where 'unit' is the hexidecimal value of the SCSI id of the target multiplied by eight plus the lun, and 'partition' is the partition number, starting from 0.

FILES

```
    /netbsd     system code
    /boot       system bootstrap
```

SEE ALSO

crash(8), disklabel(8), fsck(8), halt(8), init(8), installboot(8), rc(8), shutdown(8), sparc64/boot(8), syslogd(8)

BUGS

On sun4 machines, the NetBSD sparc boot loader can only boot from RAID partitions that start at the beginning of the disk.

On sun4 and early PROM version sun4c machines, the PROM can only boot from the first 1Gb of the disk.

On later PROM version sun4c and early PROM version sun4m machines, the PROM can only boot from the first 2Gb of the disk.

On later PROM version sun4m machines, the PROM can only boot from the first 4Gb of the disk.

BOOT (8)   NetBSD/sparc64   BOOT (8)

NAME
boot, ofwboot — system bootstrapping procedures

SYNOPSIS
boot [-adqsv] [-- ⟨boot string⟩]

DESCRIPTION
Sun UltraSPARC systems support booting from locally attached storage media (e.g. hard disk, CD-ROM), and booting over Ethernet networks using BOOTP.

Power fail and crash recovery
Normally, the system will reboot itself at power-up or after crashes. An automatic consistency check of the file systems will be performed as described in fsck(8), and unless this fails, the system will resume multi-user operations.

Cold starts
The Sun Open Firmware performs a Power On Self Test (POST), and then will boot an operating system according to configuration in Open Firmware environment variables.

Boot program options
-a   Prompt for the root file system device, the system crash dump device, and the path to init(8).

-d   Bring the system up in debug mode. Here it waits for a kernel debugger connect; see gdb(1).

-q   Boot the system in quiet mode.

-s   Bring the system up in single-user mode.

-v   Boot the system in verbose mode.

Any extra flags or arguments, or the ⟨boot string⟩ after the -- separator are passed to the boot PROM. Other flags are currently ignored.

At any time you can halt the running system and get back to the Open Firmware. If the console is the Sun framebuffer and keyboard, press the 'STOP' and 'A' keys at the same time on the keyboard. On older models of Sun keyboards, the 'STOP' key is labelled 'L1'.

If the console is a serial port the same is achieved by sending a 'BREAK'.

If you do this accidentally, you can continue whatever was in progress with the go command.

BOOT DEVICES
Since machines vary greatly in the way their devices are connected, there are aliases defined by the firmware. You can either use the fully qualified Open Firmware path of a device node, or the alias.

The secondary boot loader, ofwboot, takes boot commands virtually the same as Open Firmware. Thus, the following examples apply equally to ofwboot as well as Open Firmware.

A typical list of usable boot devices (extracted from the output of the Open Firmware command devalias) is:

```
net                    /sbus/SUNW,hme@e,8c00000
disk                   /sbus/SUNW,fas@e,8800000/sd@0,0
cdrom                  /sbus/SUNW,fas@e,8800000/sd@6,0:f
disk6                  /sbus/SUNW,fas@e,8800000/sd@6,0
disk5                  /sbus/SUNW,fas@e,8800000/sd@5,0
disk4                  /sbus/SUNW,fas@e,8800000/sd@4,0
```

```
        disk3                      /sbus/SUNW,fas@e,8800000/sd@3,0
        disk2                      /sbus/SUNW,fas@e,8800000/sd@2,0
        disk1                      /sbus/SUNW,fas@e,8800000/sd@1,0
        disk0                      /sbus/SUNW,fas@e,8800000/sd@0,0
```

If a device specification includes a partition letter (for example *cdrom* in above list), that partition is used by default, otherwise the first (a) partition is used. If booting from the net device, there is no partition involved.

The boot device is an optional first part of the boot string, if no device is specified the default device is used (see below).

FIRMWARE ENVIRONMENT VARIABLES

All Open Firmware environment variables can be printed with the **printenv** command and changed with the **setenv** command. The boot process relevant variables and their suggested value for booting NetBSD are:

```
        boot-command            boot
        auto-boot?              true
        boot-file
        boot-device             disk
        diag-switch?            false
```

Of course you may select any other boot device, if you do not want to boot from the device aliased to *disk*, see the discussion on devices above.

FILES

```
/netbsd                    system code
/ofwboot                   system bootstrap
/usr/mdec/ofwboot.net      alternate bootstrap when booting from the network, see diskless(8)
                           for details.
```

EXAMPLES

Boot from CD-ROM:

```
        boot cdrom
```

Note that some multi-architecture CDs are not able to use the default sparc64 partition for CD-ROMs (f), so they may require an explicit partition letter, for example

```
        boot cdrom:c
```

When using external SCSI CD-ROM drives it is important to know two things: the Sun firmware expects the SCSI ID to be six, and the drive must support 512-byte block reads, in addition to the standard 2048-byte reads.

Use

```
        boot net -sd
```

to boot single user from network and break into the kernel debugger as soon as possible.

Use

```
        boot net tftp:netbsd -a
```

to boot a kernel named netbsd obtained via tftp and have it ask for root filesystem, swap partition and init location once it is up.

During installation from a different operating system

```
boot disk:b
```

is used to boot a "miniroot" filesystem from the swap partition.

SEE ALSO

sparc/boot(8), disklabel(8), diskless(8), fsck(8), halt(8), init(8), installboot(8), rc(8), shutdown(8), syslogd(8)

STANDARDS

Sun developed its firmware and promoted it to become IEEE Std 1275-1994 ("Open Firmware").

```
http://playground.sun.com/1275/
```

BUGS

NetBSD provides no way to boot UltraSPARC systems from floppy disks. This is unlikely to change, due to very low demand for this feature.

The OBP on Ultra 1 and Ultra 2 machines can only boot from the first 4Gb of the disk.

NAME

boot — system bootstrapping procedures

SYNOPSIS

b [*dev* [(*cntrl*, *unit*, *part*)]] [*file*] [**-adqsv**]

DESCRIPTION

Power fail and crash recovery

Normally, the system will reboot itself at power-up or after crashes. An automatic consistency check of the file systems will be performed as described in fsck(8), and unless this fails, the system will resume multi-user operations.

Selecting the device and kernel to boot

Normally, the **b** command alone is sufficient to boot the system, as the PROM chooses a default boot device *dev* if none is specified. The PROM chooses the first device present on the system from the following ordered list:

sd	SCSI disk
ie	Intel Ethernet
ec	3Com Ethernet

Unless specified, the controller number *cntrl*, unit number *unit*, and partition number *part* default to zero, which is almost always correct.

The controller number can be specified if there is more than one of the given device in the system. For example, use "ie(1,,)" to boot off of the second Intel Ethernet in the system.

The unit number specifies one of the many devices attached to a controller. The exact meaning and values vary depending on the device name. For example, "sd(,18,)" boots the disk at target 6 on the first SCSI controller, 18 being the target number 6, multiplied by 4, and given in hexadecimal.

The partition number specifies one of the many partitions on a device. The exact meaning and values vary depending on the device name. For example, "sd(,18,1)" boots the second partition on the disk at target 6 on the first SCSI controller.

The PROM only loads a first-stage boot program, currently either /usr/mdec/bootxx (for a disk boot), or /usr/mdec/bootyy (for a network boot). This first-stage boot program then loads the second-stage boot program from the same device, currently either /usr/mdec/ufsboot (for a disk boot), or /usr/mdec/netboot (for a network boot).

The second-stage boot program will then attempt to load the kernel named *file* (or vmunix if none is specified). The second-stage disk boot program /usr/mdec/ufsboot loads the kernel from the same device that it was loaded from, while the second-stage network boot program /usr/mdec/netboot will load the kernel from the NFS root as determined by the procedure described in diskless(8).

Boot program options

-a Prompt for the root file system device, the system crash dump device, and the path to init(8).

-d Bring the system up in debug mode. Here it waits for a kernel debugger connect; see ddb(4).

-q Boot the system in quiet mode.

-s Bring the system up in single-user mode.

-v Boot the system in verbose mode.

Other flags are currently ignored.

At any time you can break back to the ROM by pressing the 'L1' and 'a' keys at the same time (if the console is a serial port the same is achieved by sending a 'break'). If you do this accidentally you can continue whatever was in progress by typing 'c' followed by the return key.

FILES

`/netbsd`	system code
`/usr/mdec/bootxx`	first-level boot block for disks
`/usr/mdec/bootyy`	first-level boot block for NFS (diskless) boot
`/usr/mdec/netboot`	boot program for NFS (diskless) boot
`/usr/mdec/ufsboot`	second-level boot program for UFS disks
`/usr/sbin/installboot`	program to install bootxx on a disk

SEE ALSO

crash(8), disklabel(8), fsck(8), halt(8), init(8), rc(8), shutdown(8), syslogd(8)

NAME

    boot — system bootstrapping procedures

DESCRIPTION

Power fail and crash recovery

Normally, the system will reboot itself at power-up or after crashes. An automatic consistency check of the file systems will be performed as described in `fsck`(8), and unless this fails, the system will resume multi-user operations.

Cold starts

A disk-boot program (`/usr/mdec/ufsboot`) will attempt to load `netbsd` from partition A of the boot device, which must currently be an "sd" disk. Alternatively, network boot program (`/usr/mdec/netboot`) will load `netbsd` from the NFS root as determined by the procedure described in `diskless`(8).

Boot program options

  -a   Prompt for the root file system device, the system crash dump device, and the path to `init`(8).

  -d   Bring the system up in debug mode. Here it waits for a kernel debugger connect; see `ddb`(4).

  -q   Boot the system in quiet mode.

  -s   Bring the system up in single-user mode.

  -v   Boot the system in verbose mode.

Any extra flags or arguments, or the ⟨*boot string*⟩ after the -- separator are passed to the boot PROM. Other flags are currently ignored.

At any time you can break back to the ROM by pressing the 'L1' and 'a' keys at the same time (if the console is a serial port the same is achieved by sending a 'break'). If you do this accidentally you can continue whatever was in progress by typing 'c' followed by the return key.

FILES

`/netbsd`	system code
`/usr/mdec/bootxx`	first-level boot block for disks
`/usr/mdec/netboot`	boot program for NFS (diskless) boot
`/usr/mdec/ufsboot`	second-level boot program for UFS disks
`/usr/mdec/installboot`	program to install bootxx on a disk

SEE ALSO

`disklabel`(8), `fsck`(8), `halt`(8), `init`(8), `rc`(8), `shutdown`(8), `syslogd`(8)

NAME
boot — system bootstrapping procedures

DESCRIPTION

Power fail and crash recovery

Normally, the system will reboot itself at power-up or after crashes. Provided the auto-restart is enabled on the machine front panel, an automatic consistency check of the file systems will be performed, and unless this fails, the system will resume multi-user operations.

Cold starts

These are processor-type dependent. On an 11/780, there are two floppy files for each disk controller, both of which cause boots from unit 0 of the root file system of a controller located on mba0 or uba0. One gives a single user shell, while the other invokes the multi-user automatic reboot. Thus these files are HPS and HPM for the single and multi-user boot from MASSBUS RP06/RM03/RM05 disks, UPS and UPM for UNIBUS storage module controller and disks such as the EMULEX SC-21 and AMPEX 9300 pair, RAS and RAM to boot from MSCP controllers and disks such as the RA81, or HKS and HKM for RK07 disks. There is also a script for booting from the default device, which is normally a copy of one of the standard multi-user boot scripts, but which may be modified to perform other actions or to boot from a different unit. The situation on the 8600 is similar, with scripts loaded from the console RL02.

Giving the command

```
>>>BOOT HPM
```

would boot the system from (e.g.) an RP06 and run the automatic consistency check as described in fsck(8). (Note that it may be necessary to type control-P and halt the processor to gain the attention of the LSI-11 before getting the >>> prompt.) The command

```
>>>BOOT ANY
```

invokes a version of the boot program in a way which allows you to specify any system as the system to be booted. It reads from the console a device specification (see below) followed immediately by a pathname.

The scripts may be modified for local configuration if necessary. The flags are placed in register 11 (as defined in <sys/reboot.h>). The boot device is specified in register 10. The encoding of this register is also defined in <sys/reboot.h>. The current encoding has a historical basis, and is shown in the following table:

bits	usage
0-7	boot device type (the device major number)
8-15	disk partition
16-19	drive unit
20-23	controller number
24-27	adaptor number (UNIBUS or MASSBUS as appropriate)

The adaptor number corresponds to the normal configuration on the 11/750, and to the order in which adaptors are found on the 11/780 and 8600 (generally the same as the numbers used by UNIX).

On an 11/750, the reset button will boot from the device selected by the front panel boot device switch. In systems with RK07's, position B normally selects the RK07 for boot. This will boot multi-user. To boot from RK07 with boot flags you may specify

```
>>>B/ -n DMA0
```

where, giving a n of 1 causes the boot program to ask for the name of the system to be bootstrapped, giving a n of 2 causes the boot program to come up single user, and a n of 3 causes both of these actions to occur. The "DM" specifies RK07, the "A" represents the adaptor number (UNIBUS or MASSBUS), and the "0" is the drive unit number. Other disk types which may be used are DB (MASSBUS), DD (TU58), and DU

(UDA-50/RA disk). A non-zero disk partition can be used by adding (partition times 1000 hex) to n.

The boot procedure on the Micro VAX II is similar. A switch on the back panel sets the power-up action to autoboot or to halt. When halted, the processor may be booted using the same syntax as on the 11/750.

The 11/750 boot procedure uses the boot ROMs to load block 0 off of the specified device. The /usr/mdec directory contains a number of bootstrap programs for the various disks which should be placed in a new pack by disklabel(8). Similarly, the Micro VAX II boot procedure loads a boot parameter block from block 0 of the disk. The **rdboot** "bootstrap" contains the correct parameters for an MSCP disk such as the RD53.

On any processor, the *boot* program finds the corresponding file on the given device (netbsd by default), loads that file into memory location zero, and starts the program at the entry address specified in the program header (after clearing off the high bit of the specified entry address).

The file specifications used with "BOOT ANY" or "B/3" are of the form:

```
device(adaptor,controller,unit,minor)
```

where *device* is the type of the device to be searched, *adaptor* is the UNIBUS or MASSBUS number of the adaptor to which the device is attached, *controller* is the unit number of the controller or MASSBUS tape formatter on that adaptor, *unit* is the unit number of the disk or transport slave unit of the tape, and *minor* is the disk partition or tape file number. Leading adaptor or controller numbers default to 0. Normal line editing characters can be used when typing the file specification. The following list of supported devices may vary from installation to installation:

hp	MASSBUS disk drive
up	UNIBUS storage module drive
ht	TE16,TU45,TU77 on MASSBUS
kra	storage module on a KDB50
mt	TU78 on MASSBUS
hk	RK07 on UNIBUS
ra	storage module on a MSCP-compatible UNIBUS controller
rb	storage module on a 730 IDC
rl	RL02 on UNIBUS
tm	TM11 emulation tape drives on UNIBUS
tms	TMSCP-compatible tape
ts	TS11 on UNIBUS
ut	UNIBUS TU45 emulator

For example, to boot from a file system which starts at cylinder 0 of unit 0 of a MASSBUS disk, type hp(0,0)netbsd to the boot prompt; hp(2,0,1,0)netbsd would specify drive 1 on MASSBUS adaptor 2; up(0,0)netbsd would specify a UNIBUS drive, hk(0,0)netbsd would specify an RK07 disk drive, ra(1,0,0,0)netbsd would specify a UDA50 disk drive on a second UNIBUS, and rb(0,0)netbsd would specify a disk on a 730 IDC. For tapes, the minor device number gives a file offset; mt(1,2,3,4) would specify the fifth file on slave 3 of the formatter at drive 2 on mba 1.

On an 11/750 with patchable control store, microcode patches will be installed by *boot* if the file psc750.bin exists in the root of the filesystem from which the system is booted.

In an emergency, the bootstrap methods described in the paper *Installing and Operating 4.3bsd* can be used to boot from a distribution tape.

FILES

`/netbsd`	system code
`/boot`	system bootstrap
`/usr/mdec/xxboot`	sector-0 boot block for 750, xx is disk type
`/usr/mdec/bootxx`	second-stage boot for 750, xx is disk type
`/pcs750.bin`	microcode patch file on 750

SEE ALSO

`arff`(8), `halt`(8), `reboot`(8), `shutdown`(8)

HISTORY

The **boot** command appeared in 4.0 BSD.

NAME

boot — system bootstrapping procedures

DESCRIPTION

Power fail and crash recovery

Normally, the system will reboot itself at power-up or after crashes. An automatic consistency check of the file systems will be performed, and unless this fails, the system will resume multi-user operations.

Cold starts

The X68000/X68030 system boots from the device which is determined by the configuration of battery-backuped SRAM. By default, the boot ROM attempts to boot from floppy disk drives (from 0 to 3) first, and then attempts to boot from hard disk (SASI or SCSI). On the NetBSD/x68k, booting from SCSI disks (sd??) and 2HD floppy disks (fd?a, fd?c) is currently supported.

Bootstrapping from a floppy

When the floppy disk is selected as the boot device, the initial program loader of the IOCS (firmware) reads the fdboot_ufs program at the top of the disk, and then the fdboot_ufs program loads the /boot program from the FFS or LFS file system. Normally, the /boot program then loads the NetBSD kernel /netbsd from the same floppy. In addition, the /boot program has abilities to uncompress gzip'ed kernels, to read the kernel from other disks of other file systems etc (see below).

For floppy disks, fdboot_ustar is also provided to read large kernels which do not fit one a single floppy.

Bootstrapping from a SCSI hard disk

When a SCSI hard disk is selected as the boot device, the initial program loader on the SCSI host adapter's ROM reads the operating system-independent IPL menu program at the top of the disk. The IPL menu program recognizes the partition table, and selects the partition to read the operating system kernel. During this phase, when the HELP key on the keyboard is pressed, the IPL menu program displays the partition menu of that disk to prompt the user to select the boot partition (although the NetBSD implementation of the IPL menu, /usr/mdec/mboot, does not have this functionality).

Next, the IPL menu reads the OS-dependent boot program from the top of the selected partition. For NetBSD FFS/LFS file systems sdboot_ufs is used. The sdboot_ufs program then loads the /boot program from that partition.

Normal Operation

Once running, a banner similar to the following will appear:

```
NetBSD Multi-boot, Revision 1.1
(user@buildhost, builddate)
Press return to boot now, any other key for boot menu
booting sd0a:netbsd - starting in 5
```

After a countdown, the system image listed will be loaded. (In the example above, it will be "sd0a:netbsd" which is the file **netbsd** on partition "a" of the NetBSD SCSI hard disk of ID 0. Pressing a key within the time limit will enter interactive mode.

Interactive mode

In interactive mode, the boot loader will present a prompt, allowing input of these commands:

boot [*device*:] [*filename*] [**-adqsv**]

> The default *device* will be set to the disk that the boot loader was loaded from. To boot from an alternate disk, the full name of the device should be given at the prompt. *device* is of the form *xd*[*N*[*x*]] where *xd* is the device from which to boot, *N* is the unit number, and

x is the partition letter.

The following list of supported devices may vary from installation to installation:

sd   SCSI disks on a controller recognized by the IOCS. The unit number is the SCSI ID.

fd   Floppy drives as numbered by the IOCS.

The default `filename` is `netbsd`; if the boot loader fails to successfully open that image, it then tries `netbsd.gz` (expected to be a kernel image compressed by `gzip`(1)). Alternate system images can be loaded by just specifying the name of the image.

Options are:

-a   Prompt for the root file system device, the system crash dump device, and the path to `init`(8).

-d   Bring the system up in debug mode. Here it waits for a kernel debugger connect; see `ddb`(4).

-q   Boot the system in quiet mode.

-s   Bring the system up in single-user mode.

-v   Boot the system in verbose mode.

help   Print an overview about commands and arguments.

ls [path]
Print a directory listing of `path`, containing inode number, filename and file type. `path` can contain a device specification.

halt   Reboot the system.

Model-specific notes

Note for X68030+MC68030 systems: Nothing special to be attended to; you can boot NetBSD just like as other operating systems such as Human68k and OS-9.

Note for X68030/040turbo(68040 accelerator by BEEPs) systems: NetBSD can boot under 040 mode. It can also boot under 030 mode if you have MC68030 on the board.

Note for X68000/Xellent30(68030 accelerator by TSR)+MC68030 systems: In order to boot NetBSD, you must choose 030 mode by using `CH30.SYS`, which must reside in the battery-backuped SRAM.

Note for X68000/Jupiter-X(68040/060 accelerator by FTZ-net) systems: The system must be in 040/060 processor mode.

FILES

`/netbsd`	system code
`/netbsd.gz`	gzip-compressed system code
`/usr/mdec/xxboot_ufs`	boot block (read by installboot), xx is disktype
`/usr/mdec/boot`	source of /boot (can be just copied to the root directory)
`/boot`	main part of the boot program

SEE ALSO

`reboot`(2), `disklabel`(8), `halt`(8), `reboot`(8), `shutdown`(8)

NAME

boot_console — selection of a console device in the i386 bootloader

DESCRIPTION

The NetBSD i386 bootloader selects a console device for its user interaction and passes information about it to the NetBSD kernel. When booting from the system BIOS, the console device and properties are saved in the primary bootstrap by installboot(8). For other boot procedures (such as dosboot(8)) the selection process is controlled by bootloader compile-time options and system setup at the bootloader startup time. The selection may be changed on-the-fly from within the bootloader.

Serial Console Options

The compile-time options (to be set in the booter's "Makefile") are:

SUPPORT_SERIAL=policy

enables support for serial input/output. By default this option is not set and the standard PC keyboard and display are always used as the console device. See **Console Selection Policy** below for valid values of policy.

DIRECT_SERIAL

causes direct hardware access to be used for serial input / output. With this option, software handshake (XON/XOFF) is used for flow control. Without this option, BIOS functions are employed for serial port handling, which require hardware handshake lines to be completely wired.

CONSPEED=integer

sets the baud-rate for the serial console. This option has only an effect when used in combination with the "DIRECT_SERIAL" option above, otherwise, the default setting of 9600 baud is used. The value of integer must be something that makes sense as a serial port baud rate.

COMCONS_KEYPRESS

Require a character input within seven (7) seconds from serial console device to be selected.

Console Selection Policy

The actual policy for the console selection is determined by the value of "SUPPORT_SERIAL" The following options are available:

CONSDEV_PC

Force use of the standard PC keyboard and display as the console.

CONSDEV_COM0 . . . CONSDEV_COM3

Use the serial port with the corresponding BIOS number as the console. No attempt is made to verify connectivity on the selected port. If the port is not known to the BIOS, it falls back to "CONSDEV_PC". (Note: This feature can be deliberately used for console selection if the serial ports have been disabled in the BIOS.)

CONSDEV_COM0KBD . . . CONSDEV_COM3KBD

If the port is known to the BIOS, and output of a character to the port succeeds (and if "DIRECT_SERIAL" is defined the RS-232 "modem ready" status is on after the character is output), the port is used as console. If the port is not known to the BIOS, or the test output fails, it falls back to "CONSDEV_PC".

CONSDEV_AUTO

Auto-select the console. All serial ports known to the BIOS are probed in sequence. If output of a character to the port succeeds (and if "DIRECT_SERIAL" is defined the RS-232 "modem ready" status is on after the character is output), the port is used as console. If no serial port passes the check, "CONSDEV_PC" is used. The progress of the selection process is shown at the PC display as digits corresponding to the serial port number currently probed.

FILES

`/sys/arch/i386/stand/{bios,dos,net}boot/Makefile` compile time options for the boot programs.

SEE ALSO

`console`(4), `boot`(8), `installboot`(8)

BUGS

The value of `SERIAL_POLICY` should be settable through a boot configuration option. However traditionally there was no non-volatile storage available on the PC platform. This requires console auto-selection methods which can be inconvenient and/or unstable in some situations. The selection policy should be adapted to the local hardware configuration, which might require code changes. (Some BIOS versions, particularly those used on large servers and in embedded and single-board industrial computers, have integrated support for serial consoles. The boot loader should query for these settings if possible.)

The serial communication parameters (byte-size, parity, stop-bits) are not settable (either at compile time or run time). The default parameters are "8 N 1".

The baud rate is not settable when using BIOS I/O. It should be settable at compile time with "CONSPEED" just as it is when using "DIRECT_SERIAL". The default speed is 9600 baud (the maximum for BIOS I/O).

NAME

boot26 — Bootloader for NetBSD/acorn26

SYNOPSIS

*boot26 [**-acdqsv**] [*file*]

DESCRIPTION

boot26 is a program that runs under RISC OS and launches the NetBSD/acorn26 kernel. It needs to be installed in a RISC OS filesystem and given file type FFA (Module). The kernel it is to load also needs to be stored in a RISC OS filesystem.

It takes the following options, which set flags in the *boothowto* variable in the booted kernel (see boothowto(9)):

-a   (RB_ASKNAME) Cause the kernel to prompt the user for the name of the device containing the root filesystem. This also causes **boot26** to prompt for the name of the kernel to be loaded.

-s   (RB_SINGLE) Cause the kernel to ask **init** to boot into single-user mode.

-d   (RB_KDB) Cause the kernel to enter the kernel debugger as soon as possible.

-c   (RB_USERCONF) Enter the in-kernel device configuration manager before attaching any devices.

-q   (RB_QUIET) Cause the kernel to emit fewer messages than normal while starting up.

-v   (RB_VERBOSE) Cause the kernel to emit more messages than normal while starting up.

boot26 attempts to load the kernel from the RISC OS file specified as *file*, or from netbsd if *file* is not specified. The file must be an ELF image, and may have been compressed using gzip(1).

Use as a module

boot26 is implemented as a RISC OS relocatable module. It can be loaded into memory by running *RMLoad boot26. After this, NetBSD can be booted by running *boot26 as usual, but the command will be handled by the module.

It should also be possible to arrange for **boot26** to be loaded from ROM (e.g. from the ROM on an expansion card), in which case NetBSD could be made to boot automatically by making **boot26** the configured language using *Configure Language.

Screen display

When it starts up, **boot26** displays the current memory map. Each character in the map represents one page of (physical) RAM. The ticks along the top are to stop you getting lost. The characters in the map indicate what the memory's being used for (actually where it's logically mapped):

```
0 -> zero-page
+ -> boot26 workspace
* -> Free space (boot26 wants to put the kernel here)
d -> RAM disc
s -> System sprite area
m -> RMA
h -> System heap/stack
f -> Font cache
S -> Screen memory
```

On a machine with 32k pages (which is all NetBSD/acorn26 supports), the left half of the first line is potential screen memory, and hence not used by **boot26**. The next page is usually zero page under RISC OS, and is used for zero page under NetBSD as well. The next is usually the system heap under RISC OS, and is used for process 0's kernel stack under NetBSD. The next is used for the message buffer under NetBSD. Pages from there on are used to load the kernel, and must be free if **boot26** is to do so successfully. Future boot-loaders should load the kernel into whatever pages are free, then kick out RISC OS and shuffle them into the right shape. This is left as an exercise for the enthusiastic reader.

FILES
>   /usr/mdec/boot26,ffa   The location of **boot26** in the NetBSD filesystem.

SEE ALSO
>   gzip(1), reboot(2), ddb(4), userconf(4), init(8), boothowto(9)

HISTORY
>   **boot26** was introduced in NetBSD 1.6 as a replacement for the original NetBSD/arm26 bootloader, which was written in BBC BASIC.

BUGS
>   **boot26** cannot load kernels from a NetBSD filesystem.

NAME
   boot32 — Bootloader for NetBSD/acorn32

SYNOPSIS
   *__boot32__ [**-acdqsv**] [*root=rootdir*] [*file*]

DESCRIPTION
   boot32 is a program that runs under RISC OS and launches the NetBSD/acorn32 kernel. It needs to be installed in a RISC OS filesystem and given file type FFA (Module). The kernel it is to load also needs to be stored in a RISC OS filesystem.

   It takes the following standard NetBSD options, which set flags in the *boothowto* variable in the booted kernel (see boothowto(9)). Not all flags may be effective.

   -a   (RB_ASKNAME) Cause the kernel to prompt the user for the name of the device containing the root filesystem. This also causes **boot32** to prompt for the name of the kernel to be loaded.

   -s   (RB_SINGLE) Cause the kernel to ask **init** to boot into single-user mode.

   -d   (RB_KDB) Cause the kernel to enter the kernel debugger as soon as possible.

   -c   (RB_USERCONF) Enter the in-kernel device configuration manager before attaching any devices.

   -q   (RB_QUIET) Cause the kernel to emit fewer messages than normal while starting up.

   -v   (RB_VERBOSE) Cause the kernel to emit more messages than normal while starting up.

   boot32 attempts to load the kernel from the RISC OS file specified as *file*, or from netbsd if *file* is not specified. The file must be an ELF image, and may have been compressed using gzip(1).

Use as a module
   boot32 is implemented as a RISC OS relocatable module. It can be loaded into memory by running *RMLoad boot32. After this, NetBSD can be booted by running *boot32 as usual, but the command will be handled by the module.

   It should also be possible to arrange for **boot32** to be loaded from ROM (e.g., from the ROM on an expansion card), in which case NetBSD could be made to boot automatically by making **boot32** the configured language using *Configure Language.

Screen display
   When it starts up, **boot32** displays the number of 4 kilobyte memory pages it has been delegated by RISC-OS and gives a summary about the memory map as reported by RISC-OS followed by a table of physical memory ranges available to the bootloader. All this information is mainly for bughunting booting problems.

   It then checks its internal structures and kicks out RISC-OS, relocates all memory pages loaded in to their final destinations and kickstarts **boot32**.

FILES
   /usr/mdec/boot32,ffa   The location of **boot32** in the NetBSD filesystem.

SEE ALSO
   gzip(1), reboot(2), ddb(4), userconf(4), init(8), boothowto(9)

HISTORY

      `boot32` was introduced in NetBSD 1.6 as a replacement for the original NetBSD/arm32 bootloader, which was written in BBC BASIC.

BUGS

      `boot32` cannot load kernels from a NetBSD filesystem.

NAME

bootpd, bootpgw – Internet Boot Protocol server/gateway

SYNOPSIS

bootpd [**–i –s –t** timeout **–d** level **–c** chdir–path] [*bootptab* [*dumpfile*]]
bootpgw [**–i –s –t** timeout **–d** level] server

DESCRIPTION

Bootpd implements an Internet Bootstrap Protocol (BOOTP) server as defined in RFC951, RFC1532, and RFC1533. *Bootpgw* implements a simple BOOTP gateway which can be used to forward requests and responses between clients on one subnet and a BOOTP server (i.e. *bootpd*) on another subnet. While either *bootpd* or *bootpgw* will forward BOOTREPLY packets, only *bootpgw* will forward BOOTREQUEST packets.

One host on each network segment is normally configured to run either *bootpd* or *bootpgw* from *inetd* by including one of the following lines in the file */etc/inetd.conf*:

        bootps dgram udp wait root /usr/sbin/bootpd bootpd bootptab
        bootps dgram udp wait root /usr/sbin/bootpgw bootpgw server

This mode of operation is referred to as "inetd mode" and causes *bootpd* (or *bootpgw*) to be started only when a boot request arrives. If it does not receive another packet within fifteen minutes of the last one it received, it will exit to conserve system resources. The **–t** option controls this timeout (see OPTIONS).

It is also possible to run *bootpd* (or *bootpgw*) in "standalone mode" (without *inetd*) by simply invoking it from a shell like any other regular command. Standalone mode is particularly useful when *bootpd* is used with a large configuration database, where the start up delay might otherwise prevent timely response to client requests. (Automatic start up in standalone mode can be done by invoking *bootpd* from within */etc/rc.local*, for example.) Standalone mode is less useful for *bootpgw* which has very little start up delay because it does not read a configuration file.

Either program automatically detects whether it was invoked from inetd or from a shell and automatically selects the appropriate mode. The **–s** or **–i** option may be used to force standalone or inetd mode respectively (see OPTIONS).

OPTIONS

–t *timeout*

> Specifies the *timeout* value (in minutes) that a *bootpd* or *bootpgw* process will wait for a BOOTP packet before exiting. If no packets are received for *timeout* minutes, then the program will exit. A timeout value of zero means "run forever". In standalone mode, this option is forced to zero.

–d *debug–level*

> Sets the *debug–level* variable that controls the amount of debugging messages generated. For example, -d4 or -d 4 will set the debugging level to 4. For compatibility with older versions of *bootpd*, omitting the numeric parameter (i.e. just -d) will simply increment the debug level by one.

–c *chdir–path*

> Sets the current directory used by *bootpd* while checking the existence and size of client boot files. This is useful when client boot files are specified as relative pathnames, and *bootpd* needs to use the same current directory as the TFTP server (typically /tftpboot). This option is not recognized by *bootpgw*.

–i

> Force inetd mode. This option is obsolete, but remains for compatibility with older versions of *bootpd*.

–s

> Force standalone mode. This option is obsolete, but remains for compatibility with older versions of *bootpd*.

bootptab

> Specifies the name of the configuration file from which *bootpd* loads its database of known clients and client options (*bootpd* only).

    dumpfile
Specifies the name of the file that *bootpd* will dump its internal database into when it receives a SIGUSR1 signal (*bootpd* only). This option is only recognized if *bootpd* was compiled with the -DDEBUG flag.

    server   Specifies the name of a BOOTP server to which *bootpgw* will forward all BOOTREQUEST packets it receives (*bootpgw* only).

OPERATION

Both *bootpd* and *bootpgw* operate similarly in that both listen for any packets sent to the *bootps* port, and both simply forward any BOOTREPLY packets. They differ in their handling of BOOTREQUEST packets.

When *bootpgw* is started, it determines the address of a BOOTP server whose name is provided as a command line parameter. When *bootpgw* receives a BOOTREQUEST packet, it sets the "gateway address" and "hop count" fields in the packet and forwards the packet to the BOOTP server at the address determined earlier. Requests are forwarded only if they indicate that the client has been waiting for at least three seconds.

When *bootpd* is started it reads a configuration file, (normally */etc/bootptab*) that initializes the internal database of known clients and client options. This internal database is reloaded from the configuration file when *bootpd* receives a hangup signal (SIGHUP) or when it discovers that the configuration file has changed.

When *bootpd* receives a BOOTREQUEST packet, it looks for a database entry matching the client request. If the client is known, *bootpd* composes a BOOTREPLY packet using the database entry found above, and sends the reply to the client (possibly using a gateway). If the client is unknown, the request is discarded (with a notice if debug > 0).

If *bootpd* is compiled with the -DDEBUG option, receipt of a SIGUSR1 signal causes it to dump its internal database to the file */etc/bootpd.dump* or the dumpfile specified as a command line parameter.

During initialization, both programs determine the UDP port numbers to be used by calling *getservbyname* (which normally uses */etc/services*). Two service names (and port numbers) are used:

        bootps – BOOTP Server listening port
        bootpc – BOOTP Client destination port

If the port numbers cannot be determined using *getservbyname* then the values default to bootps=67 and bootpc=68.

FILES

/etc/bootptab	Database file read by *bootpd*.
/etc/bootpd.dump	Debugging dump file created by *bootpd*.
/etc/services	Internet service numbers.
/tftpboot	Current directory typically used by the TFTP server and *bootpd*.

BUGS

Individual host entries must not exceed 1024 characters.

CREDITS

This distribution is currently maintained by Walter L. Wimer <walt+@cmu.edu>.

The original BOOTP server was created by Bill Croft at Stanford University in January 1986.

The current version of *bootpd* is primarily the work of David Kovar, Drew D. Perkins, and Walter L. Wimer, at Carnegie Mellon University.

Enhancements and bug–fixes have been contributed by:
        (in alphabetical order)
        Danny Backx <db@sunbim.be>

John Brezak <brezak@ch.hp.com>
Frank da Cruz <fdc@cc.columbia.edu>
David R. Linn <drl@vuse.vanderbilt.edu>
Jim McKim <mckim@lerc.nasa.gov>
Gordon W. Ross <gwr@mc.com>
Jason Zions <jazz@hal.com>

SEE ALSO

bootptab(5), inetd(8), tftpd(8)

DARPA Internet Request For Comments:

RFC951   Bootstrap Protocol

RFC1532   Clarifications and Extensions for the Bootstrap Protocol

RFC1533   DHCP Options and BOOTP Vendor Extensions

NAME

bootpef – BOOTP Extension File compiler

SYNOPSIS

bootpef [*-c chdir*] [*-d debug-level*] [*-f config-file*] [*client-name* [*...*]]

DESCRIPTION

bootpef builds the *Extension Path* files described by RFC 1497 (tag 18). If any *client-name* arguments are specified, then *bootpef* compiles the extension files for only those clients.

OPTIONS

−c *chdir−path*

Sets the current directory used by *bootpef* while creating extension files. This is useful when the extension file names are specified as relative pathnames, and *bootpef* needs to use the same current directory as the TFTP server (typically /tftpboot).

−d *debug−level*

Sets the *debug−level* variable that controls the amount of debugging messages generated. For example, -d4 or -d 4 will set the debugging level to 4.

−f *config−file*

Set the name of the config file that specifies the option data to be sent to each client.

SEE ALSO

bootpd(8), tftpd(8)

REFERENCES

RFC951

BOOTSTRAP PROTOCOL (BOOTP)

RFC1497

BOOTP Vendor Information Extensions

NAME
bootpref — set NVRAM boot preference

SYNOPSIS
bootpref [-v] [-b os] [-d delay] [-l lang] [-k kbd] [-s id] [-f fmt] [-1] [-2] [-e sep] [-c colours] [-n]
[-p] [-t] [-v] [-4] [-8] [-o] [-O] [-x] [-X] [-i] [-I]

DESCRIPTION
bootpref views and sets the NVRAM boot preferences.

The program options are:

-v   verbose output (when setting preferences)

-b *netbsd*   set the boot OS to NetBSD

-b *tos*   set the boot OS to TOS

-b *linux*   set the boot OS to Linux

-b *systemv*
                  set the boot OS to System V

-b *none*   set the boot OS to none

-d *delay*   set the boot delay to *delay* seconds, where *delay* is a value between 0 and 255

-l *english*
                  set the language to English

-l *german*   set the language to German

-l *french*   set the language to French

-l *spanish*
                  set the language to Spanish

-l *italian*
                  set the language to Italian

-k *american*
                  set the keyboard layout to American

-k *german*   set the keyboard layout to German

-k *french*   set the keyboard layout to French

-k *british*
                  set the keyboard layout to British

-k *spanish*
                  set the keyboard layout to Spanish

-k *italian*
                  set the keyboard layout to Italian

-k *sw f*

-k *swiss french*
                  set the keyboard layout to Swiss (French)

-k *sw g*

-k *swiss german*
> set the keyboard layout to Swiss (German)

-s *id*　　　　set the SCSI id to *id*, where *id* is a value between 0 and 7

-f *mmddyy*

-f *ddmmyy*

-f *yymmdd*

-f *yyddmm*　set the date format

-1　　　　　　set the date format to 12 hour clock

-2　　　　　　set the date format to 24 hour clock

-e *sep*　　　set the date format separator to *sep*

-c *colours*
> set the number of *colours* - 2, 4, 16, 256 or 65535

-n　　　　　　set the video mode to *NTSC*

-p　　　　　　set the video mode to *PAL*

-t　　　　　　set the video mode to *TV*

-v　　　　　　set the video mode to *VGA*

-4　　　　　　set the video mode to *40 columns*

-8　　　　　　set the video mode to *80 columns*

-o　　　　　　set the video mode to *overscan*

-O　　　　　　set the video mode to *no overscan*

-x　　　　　　set the video mode to *ST compatibility*

-X　　　　　　set the video mode to *no ST compatibility*

-i　　　　　　set the video mode to *interlace* (TV), *double line* (VGA)

-I　　　　　　set the video mode to *no interlace/double line*

All strings can be specified by their shortest abbreviation

If no parameters are specified, **bootpref** shows the current boot preferences.

SEE ALSO
> installboot(8)

HISTORY
> The **bootpref** command first appeared in NetBSD 1.4.

AUTHORS
> Julian Coleman

BUGS

Setting the boot OS to *none* will cause the machine not to boot from the hard disk.

The majority of the parameters are not used under NetBSD.

NAME
bootptest – send BOOTP queries and print responses

SYNOPSIS
bootptest [**–f** *bootfile*] [**–h**] [**–m** *magic_number*] *server–name* [*template-file*]

DESCRIPTION
bootptest sends BOOTP requests to the host specified as *server–name* at one–second intervals until either a response is received, or until ten requests have gone unanswered. After a response is received, **bootptest** will wait one more second listening for additional responses.

OPTIONS
–f *bootfile*

Fill in the boot file field of the request with *bootfile*.

–h   Use the hardware (Ethernet) address to identify the client. By default, the IP address is copied into the request indicating that this client already knows its IP address.

–m *magic_number*

Initialize the first word of the vendor options field with *magic_number*.

A *template-file* may be specified, in which case **bootptest** uses the (binary) contents of this file to initialize the *options* area of the request packet.

CREDITS
The bootptest program is a combination of original and derived works. The main program module (bootptest.c) is original work by Gordon W. Ross <gwr@mc.com>. The packet printing module (print-bootp.c) is a slightly modified version of a file from the BSD tcpdump program.

This program includes software developed by the University of California, Lawrence Berkeley Laboratory and its contributors. (See the copyright notice in print-bootp.c)

SEE ALSO
bootpd(8)

REFERENCES
RFC951

BOOTSTRAP PROTOCOL (BOOTP)

RFC1048

BOOTP Vendor Information Extensions

NAME
bounce – Postfix delivery status reports

SYNOPSIS
bounce [generic Postfix daemon options]

DESCRIPTION
The **bounce**(8) daemon maintains per-message log files with delivery status information. Each log file is named after the queue file that it corresponds to, and is kept in a queue subdirectory named after the service name in the **master.cf** file (either **bounce**, **defer** or **trace**). This program expects to be run from the **master**(8) process manager.

The **bounce**(8) daemon processes two types of service requests:

*   Append a recipient (non-)delivery status record to a per-message log file.

*   Enqueue a delivery status notification message, with a copy of a per-message log file and of the corresponding message. When the delivery status notification message is enqueued successfully, the per-message log file is deleted.

The software does a best notification effort. A non-delivery notification is sent even when the log file or the original message cannot be read.

Optionally, a bounce (defer, trace) client can request that the per-message log file be deleted when the requested operation fails. This is used by clients that cannot retry transactions by themselves, and that depend on retry logic in their own client.

STANDARDS
RFC 822 (ARPA Internet Text Messages)
RFC 2045 (Format of Internet Message Bodies)
RFC 2822 (ARPA Internet Text Messages)
RFC 3462 (Delivery Status Notifications)
RFC 3464 (Delivery Status Notifications)
RFC 3834 (Auto-Submitted: message header)

DIAGNOSTICS
Problems and transactions are logged to **syslogd**(8).

CONFIGURATION PARAMETERS
Changes to **main.cf** are picked up automatically, as **bounce**(8) processes run for only a limited amount of time. Use the command "**postfix reload**" to speed up a change.

The text below provides only a parameter summary. See **postconf**(5) for more details including examples.

2bounce_notice_recipient (postmaster)
The recipient of undeliverable mail that cannot be returned to the sender.

backwards_bounce_logfile_compatibility (yes)
Produce additional **bounce**(8) logfile records that can be read by Postfix versions before 2.0.

bounce_notice_recipient (postmaster)
The recipient of postmaster notifications with the message headers of mail that Postfix did not deliver and of SMTP conversation transcripts of mail that Postfix did not receive.

bounce_size_limit (50000)
The maximal amount of original message text that is sent in a non-delivery notification.

bounce_template_file (empty)
Pathname of a configuration file with bounce message templates.

config_directory (see 'postconf -d' output)
The default location of the Postfix main.cf and master.cf configuration files.

daemon_timeout (18000s)
> How much time a Postfix daemon process may take to handle a request before it is terminated by a built-in watchdog timer.

delay_notice_recipient (postmaster)
> The recipient of postmaster notifications with the message headers of mail that cannot be delivered within $delay_warning_time time units.

deliver_lock_attempts (20)
> The maximal number of attempts to acquire an exclusive lock on a mailbox file or **bounce**(8) logfile.

deliver_lock_delay (1s)
> The time between attempts to acquire an exclusive lock on a mailbox file or **bounce**(8) logfile.

ipc_timeout (3600s)
> The time limit for sending or receiving information over an internal communication channel.

internal_mail_filter_classes (empty)
> What categories of Postfix-generated mail are subject to before-queue content inspection by non_smtpd_milters, header_checks and body_checks.

mail_name (Postfix)
> The mail system name that is displayed in Received: headers, in the SMTP greeting banner, and in bounced mail.

max_idle (100s)
> The maximum amount of time that an idle Postfix daemon process waits for an incoming connection before terminating voluntarily.

max_use (100)
> The maximal number of incoming connections that a Postfix daemon process will service before terminating voluntarily.

notify_classes (resource, software)
> The list of error classes that are reported to the postmaster.

process_id (read-only)
> The process ID of a Postfix command or daemon process.

process_name (read-only)
> The process name of a Postfix command or daemon process.

queue_directory (see 'postconf -d' output)
> The location of the Postfix top-level queue directory.

syslog_facility (mail)
> The syslog facility of Postfix logging.

syslog_name (see 'postconf -d' output)
> The mail system name that is prepended to the process name in syslog records, so that "smtpd" becomes, for example, "postfix/smtpd".

FILES
> /var/spool/postfix/bounce/* non-delivery records
> /var/spool/postfix/defer/* non-delivery records
> /var/spool/postfix/trace/* delivery status records

SEE ALSO
> bounce(5), bounce message template format
> qmgr(8), queue manager
> postconf(5), configuration parameters
> master(5), generic daemon options
> master(8), process manager

syslogd(8), system logging

LICENSE
The Secure Mailer license must be distributed with this software.

AUTHOR(S)
Wietse Venema
IBM T.J. Watson Research
P.O. Box 704
Yorktown Heights, NY 10598, USA

NAME
bpm — menu-based binary package manager

SYNOPSIS
bpm [**-hnVv**] [**-b** *baseURL*] [**-m** *machine*] [**-r** *release*] [**-w** *seconds*]

DESCRIPTION
The **bpm** command is used to locate and install binary packages from any reachable URL.

The following command-line options are supported:

-b *baseURL*
> Specify a base URL from which to download binary packages. The default URL is `ftp://ftp.NetBSD.org/pub/pkgsrc/packages`.

-h   Print a help message and then exit.

-m *machine*
> Use *machine* as the machine architecture to be used, instead of that returned by uname(1).

-n   Don't actually execute the commands to add the package.

-r *release*
> Use *release* as the operating system release to be used, instead of that returned by uname(1).

-V   Print version number and exit.

-v   Turn on verbose output.

-w *seconds*
> The number of *seconds* to wait after displaying an error message and returning to normal menu operations.

bpm provides a menu-based binary package manager for NetBSD. **bpm** first connects to the URL using ftp(1), and displays a list of categories for which binary packages exist. If no categories are displayed, it could be that the machine architecture or operating system release string have been wrongly interpreted, and that it will be necessary to override this values by means of the command line options. Within a category, a list of packages will be displayed, and by selecting one using the number assigned to it, the package will be downloaded automatically, and installed, using the pkg_add(1) utility. It is also possible to change the category currently being examined, and to quit from the utility, simply by selecting the appropriate choices on the menu.

ENVIRONMENT
The environment variables which govern the behavior of ftp(1) and pkg_add(1) are valid for **bpm**.

SEE ALSO
ftp(1), pkg_add(1), uname(1)

AUTHORS
The **bpm** utility was written by Alistair Crooks ⟨agc@NetBSD.org⟩.

NAME

brconfig — configure network bridge parameters

SYNOPSIS

brconfig -a
brconfig *bridge*
brconfig *bridge command* [*args* ...]

DESCRIPTION

The **brconfig** utility is used to configure network bridge parameters and retrieve network bridge parameters and status from the kernel. The bridging function is implemented by the bridge(4) driver.

A network bridge creates a logical link between two or more IEEE 802 networks that use the same (or "similar enough") framing format. For example, it is possible to bridge Ethernet and 802.11 networks together, but it is not possible to bridge Ethernet and Token Ring together.

Bridge interfaces are created using the ifconfig(8) command's "create" sub-command. All other bridge configuration is performed using **brconfig**.

The options are as follows:

-a   Display the status of all bridge devices present on the system. This flag is mutually exclusive with all other sub-commands.

All other operations require that a bridge be specified. If a bridge is specified with no sub-commands, the status of that bridge is displayed. The following sub-commands are available:

up   Start forwarding packets on the bridge.

down   Stop forwarding packets on the bridge.

add *interface*
         Add the interface named by *interface* as a member of the bridge. The interface is put into promiscuous mode so that it can receive every packet sent on the network.

delete *interface*
         Remove the interface named by *interface* from the bridge. Promiscuous mode is disabled on the interface when it is removed from the bridge.

maxaddr *size*
         Set the size of the bridge address cache to *size*. The default is 100 entries.

timeout *seconds*
         Set the timeout of address cache entries to *seconds* seconds. If *seconds* is zero, then address cache entries will not be expired. The default is 1200 seconds.

deladdr *address*
         Delete *address* from the address cache.

flush   Delete all dynamically-learned addresses from the address cache.

flushall
         Delete all addresses, including static addresses, from the address cache.

discover *interface*
         Mark an interface as a "discovering" interface. When the bridge has no address cache entry (either dynamic or static) for the destination address of a packet, the bridge will forward the packet to all member interfaces marked as "discovering". This is the default for all interfaces added to a bridge.

-discover *interface*
> Clear the "discovering" attribute on a member interface. For packets without the "discovering" attribute, the only packets forwarded on the interface are broadcast or multicast packets and packets for which the destination address is known to be on the interface's segment.

ipf
> Enable packet filtering with `pfil`(9) on the bridge. The current implementation passes all ARP and RARP packets through the bridge while filtering IP and IPv6 packets through the configured packet filter, such as `ipf`(4) or `pf`(4). Other packet types are blocked.

learn *interface*
> Mark an interface as a "learning" interface. When a packet arrives on such an interface, the source address of the packet is entered into the address cache as being a destination address on the interface's segment. This is the default for all interfaces added to a bridge.

-learn *interface*
> Clear the "learning" attribute on a member interface.

stp *interface*
> Enable Spanning Tree protocol on *interface*. The `bridge`(4) driver has support for the IEEE 802.1D Spanning Tree protocol (STP). Spanning Tree is used to detect and remove loops in a network topology.

-stp *interface*
> Disable Spanning Tree protocol on *interface*. This is the default for all interfaces added to a bridge.

maxage *seconds*
> Set the time that a Spanning Tree protocol configuration is valid. The default is 20 seconds. The minimum is 1 second and the maximum is 255 seconds.

fwddelay *seconds*
> Set the time that must pass before an interface begins forwarding packets when Spanning Tree is enabled. The default is 15 seconds. The minimum is 1 second and the maximum is 255 seconds.

hellotime *seconds*
> Set the time between broadcasting of Spanning Tree protocol configuration messages. The default is 2 seconds. The minimum is 1 second and the maximum is 255 seconds.

priority *value*
> Set the bridge priority for Spanning Tree. The default is 32768. Allowed numerical values range from 0 (highest priority) to 65535 (lowest priority).

ifpriority *interface value*
> Set the Spanning Tree priority of *interface* to *value*. The default is 128. The minimum is 0 and the maximum is 255.

ifpathcost *interface value*
> Set the Spanning Tree path cost of *interface* to *value*. The default is 55. The minimum is 0 and the maximum is 65535.

EXAMPLES

The following, when placed in the file `/etc/ifconfig.bridge0`, will cause a bridge called 'bridge0' to be created, add the interfaces 'ray0' and 'fxp0' to the bridge, and then enable packet forwarding. Such a configuration could be used to implement a simple 802.11-to-Ethernet bridge (assuming the 802.11 interface is in ad-hoc mode).

```
create
!brconfig $int add ray0 add fxp0 up
```

Consider a system with two 4-port Ethernet boards. The following placed in the file `/etc/ifconfig.bridge0` will cause a bridge consisting of all 8 ports with Spanning Tree enabled to be created:

```
create
!brconfig $int \
    add tlp0 stp tlp0 \
    add tlp1 stp tlp1 \
    add tlp2 stp tlp2 \
    add tlp3 stp tlp3 \
    add tlp4 stp tlp4 \
    add tlp5 stp tlp5 \
    add tlp6 stp tlp6 \
    add tlp7 stp tlp7 \
    up
```

SEE ALSO
`bridge(4)`, `pf(4)`, `ifconfig.if(5)`, `ifconfig(8)`, `ipf(8)`, `pfil(9)`

HISTORY
The **brconfig** utility first appeared in NetBSD 1.6.

AUTHORS
The `bridge(4)` driver and **brconfig** utility were originally written by Jason L. Wright ⟨jason@thought.net⟩ as part of an undergraduate independent study at the University of North Carolina at Greensboro.

This version of the **brconfig** utility was written from scratch by
Jason R. Thorpe ⟨thorpej@wasabisystems.com⟩.

NAME
btattach — attach serial lines as Bluetooth HCI interfaces

SYNOPSIS
btattach [-dFfoPp] [-i *speed*] [*type*] *tty speed*
btattach -t [-dFfoPp] *tty*

DESCRIPTION
btattach is used to assign a *tty* line to a Bluetooth Host Controller Interface using the btuart(4) or bcsp(4) line disciplines, and can optionally initialize the line for a given device *type* before activating the line discipline.

Supported types are:

bcm2035	Broadcom BCM2035
bcsp	Generic BCSP (BlueCore Serial Protocol)
bgb2xx	Philips BGB2xx module
btuart	Generic UART (this is the default)
csr	Cambridge Silicon Radio Casira serial adaptor, or Brainboxes serial dongle (BL642)
ericsson	Ericsson based modules
digi	Digianswer based cards
st	ST Microelectronics minikits based on STLC2410/STLC2415
stlc2500	ST Microelectronics minikits based on STLC2500
swave	Silicon Wave kits
texas	Texas Instruments modules
unistone	Infineon UniStone (PBA31308) modules

When the line discipline is activated, **btattach** detaches and sleeps until it receives a SIGHUP.

The command line options are as follows:

-d   debug mode. print initialization IO and do not detach.

-F   Disable flow control.

-f   Enable flow control.

-i *speed*   Specify an alternate *speed* for the Bluetooth module to use during the initialization phase.

-o   Enable odd parity.

-P   Disable parity.

-p   Enable parity (even parity).

-t   Test mode.

Only the super-user may attach a Bluetooth HCI interface.

Test mode tries to guess the speed using the received link-establish packet from HCI, or btuart(4), if there is no response.

FILES
/var/run/btattach-{tty}.pid

SEE ALSO
bcsp(4), bluetooth(4), btuart(4), btconfig(8)

HISTORY

The **btattach** program was written with reference to `hciattach`(8) as provided with the BlueZ tools for Linux and first appeared in NetBSD 5.0.

AUTHORS

KIYOHARA Takashi ⟨kiyohara@kk.iij4u.or.jp⟩
Iain Hibbert

BUGS

Not all *type* initializations have been tested.

NAME
    btconfig — configure bluetooth devices

SYNOPSIS
    btconfig [**-svz**] [*device* [*parameters*]]
    btconfig [**-l**]

DESCRIPTION
    btconfig is used to configure Bluetooth devices. If the *device* is given, but no parameters, then **btconfig** will print information about the device. If no *device* is given, a basic list of devices will be printed.

    When the **-l** flag is used, just the device names will be printed.

COMMANDS
    The following parameters may be specified with **btconfig**:

up	Enable Bluetooth Device.
down	Disable Bluetooth Device.
pscan	Enable Page Scan. This enables incoming connections to the device.
-pscan	Disable Page Scan.
iscan	Enable Inquiry Scan. This puts the device in Discoverable mode.
-iscan	Disable Inquiry Scan.
encrypt	Enable encryption. This will cause the device to request encryption on all baseband connections, and will only work if authentication is also enabled.
-encrypt	Disable encryption.
auth	Enable authentication. This will cause the device to request authentication for all baseband connections.
-auth	Disable authentication.
switch	Enable Role Switching. In a Bluetooth piconet there is one Master and up to seven Slaves, and normally the device that initiates a connection will take the Master role. Enabling this option allows remote devices to switch connection roles.
-switch	Disable Role Switching.
master	Request the Master role when accepting connections.
-master	Do not request Master role.
hold	Enable Hold Mode.
-hold	Disable Hold Mode.
sniff	Enable Sniff Mode.
-sniff	Disable Sniff Mode.
park	Enable Park Mode.
-park	Disable Park Mode.

name *name*   Set human readable name of device.

ptype *type*   Set packet types. *type* is a 16 bit hex value specifying packet types that will be requested by outgoing ACL connections. By default, all packet types that the device supports are enabled, see bluetooth specifications for more information if you want to change this.

class *class*   Set class of device. *class* is a 6 digit hex value the value of which declares the device capabilities. See the "Assigned Numbers - Baseband" document at http://www.bluetooth.com/ for details of constructing a Class of Device value. As a starter, 0x020104 means Desktop Computer, with Networking available.

fixed   Set fixed pin type.

variable   Set variable pin type.

inquiry   Perform device Discovery from the specified device and print details.

imode *type*   Set inquiry mode type to control which event formats are generated during a device inquiry. The *type* can be:

        std   Standard Inquiry Result Event format.

        rssi   Enable Remote Signal Strength Indicator (RSSI) in inquiry results. This will only work if the device features indicate ⟨RSSI with inquiry result⟩.

        ext   Inquiry Result with RSSI format or Extended Inquiry Result fomat. This will only work where the device features indicate ⟨extended inquiry⟩, and the Extended Inquiry Result will only occur when the remote device provides the extended information.

reset   Perform a hard reset on the device and re-initialise system state.

voice   Set Voice Setting. [This should be 0x0060 for now]

pto   Set Page Timeout value. This is a decimal value in milliseconds.

scomtu   Change SCO mtu value. This is a decimal value, see ubt(4) for reasons why you may need to do this.

All parameters are parsed before any device operations take place. Each time the **-v** flag is given, verbosity levels will be increased.

Super-user privileges are required to change device configurations.

DIAGNOSTICS

Messages indicating the specified device does not exist, the requested address is unknown, or the user is not privileged and tried to alter an device's configuration.

SEE ALSO

bcsp(4), bluetooth(4), bt3c(4), btbc(4), btuart(4), sbt(4), ubt(4)

HISTORY

The **btconfig** command was written for NetBSD 4.0 by Iain Hibbert under the sponsorship of Itronix, Inc.

BUGS

The output is very messy.

NAME
btdevctl — Bluetooth remote device control utility

SYNOPSIS
btdevctl [**-A** | **-D**] [**-qv**] [**-m** *mode*] **-a** *address* **-d** *device* **-s** *service*

DESCRIPTION
The **btdevctl** utility is used to configure bluetooth devices in the system. Normally, **btdevctl** will perform an SDP query to the remote device as needed, and cache the results in the /var/db/btdevctl.plist file for later use. If neither Attach nor Detach is specified, **btdevctl** will display the configuration.

The options are:

-A   Attach device

-a *address*
            Remote device address. The *address* may be given as BDADDR or a name. If a name was specified, **btdevctl** attempts to resolve the name via bt_gethostbyname(3).

-D   Detach device

-d *device*
            Local device address. May be given as BDADDR or device name.

-m *mode*   Connection link mode. The following modes are supported:

            none   clear previously set mode.
            auth   require devices be paired, see btpin(1).
            encrypt   auth, plus enable encryption.
            secure   encryption, plus change of link key.

            When configuring the HID service, **btdevctl** will set 'auth' by default, or 'encrypt' for keyboard devices.

-q   Ignore any cached data and perform a SDP query for the given *service*.

-s *service*
            Service to configure. Known services are:

            HID   Human Interface Device.
            HF   Handsfree.
            HSET   Headset.

-v   Be verbose.

For device configurations to persist across boots, add entries to the /etc/bluetooth/btdevctl.conf file and set the rc.conf(5) variable **btdevctl** to YES.

EXIT STATUS
The **btdevctl** utility exits 0 on success, and >0 if an error occurs.

FILES
/etc/bluetooth/btdevctl.conf
/dev/bthub
/var/db/btdevctl.plist

SEE ALSO

btpin(1), bthidev(4), bthub(4), btsco(4), rc.conf(5)

HISTORY

Parts of the **btdevctl** program originated in the FreeBSD **bthidcontrol** program.

AUTHORS

Iain Hibbert for Itronix, Inc.

Maksim Yevmenkin ⟨m_evmenkin@yahoo.com⟩

NAME

bthcid — Bluetooth Link Key/PIN Code Manager

SYNOPSIS

bthcid [**-fn**] [**-d** *device*] [**-m** *mode*] [**-s** *socket_name*]
bthcid [**-h**]

DESCRIPTION

The **bthcid** daemon handles Link Key and PIN code requests for Bluetooth devices. It opens a raw HCI socket and listens for the following HCI events.

Link_Key_Request

> **bthcid** scans the /var/db/bthcid.keys file for a cached link key matching the remote device BD_ADDR and, if found, the Link_Key_Request_Reply will be sent back to the device, otherwise the Link_Key_Request_Negative_Reply will be sent.

Link_Key_Notification

> When a new link key is created by the device, it will be cached for future use in the /var/db/bthcid.keys link keys file, which will be created if it does not already exist.

PIN_Code_Request

> The **bthcid** daemon checks its PIN cache for a matching remote device entry. If no PIN is found, the **bthcid** daemon will send a message to any PIN clients that have registered, with the device details and a timeout value. When no clients are available or the timeout has expired, **bthcid** will send a PIN_Code_Request_Negative_Reply back to the device. When a PIN is found, or if a client responds within the timeout period, a PIN_Code_Request_Reply will be sent back to the device.

> PINs received from clients will be cached for 5 minutes until used, and may be added to the cache prior to pairing with the btpin(1) utility.

Some of the functionality of **bthcid** can be handled by the Bluetooth controller directly, and cached Link Keys may be examined, deleted or moved to device storage using the btkey(1) program.

The command line options are as follows:

-d *device*
> Specify the local Bluetooth device address. The default is BDADDR_ANY.

-f   Run in foreground (do not detach).

-h   Display usage message and exit.

-m   Specify the file mode access bits for the PIN client socket. The default is to allow readwrite access to user and group (0660).

-n   Do not listen for PIN clients.

-s *socket_name*
> Specify the socket name to listen on for PIN clients. The default path is /var/run/bthcid.

FILES

/var/db/bthcid.keys
/var/run/bthcid
/var/run/bthcid.pid

SEE ALSO
> btkey(1), btpin(1), bluetooth(4), btconfig(8)

HISTORY
> The **bthcid** daemon first appeared in FreeBSD 5.3 as **hcsecd**. It was ported to NetBSD 4.0 with its present name and extended to support PIN clients by Iain Hibbert under the sponsorship of Itronix, Inc.

AUTHORS
> Maksim Yevmenkin ⟨m_evmenkin@yahoo.com⟩
> Iain Hibbert

NAME
   btpand — Bluetooth PAN daemon

SYNOPSIS
   btpand [**-i** *ifname*] [**-m** *mode*] **-a** *addr* **-d** *device*
           { **-s** *service* | **-S** *service* [**-p** *psm*]}
   btpand [**-c** *path*] [**-i** *ifname*] [**-l** *limit*] [**-m** *mode*] [**-p** *psm*] **-d** *device*
           { **-s** *service* | **-S** *service*}

DESCRIPTION
   The **btpand** daemon handles Bluetooth Personal Area Networking services in the system. It can operate in client mode as a Personal Area Networking User (PANU) or in server mode as Network Access Point (NAP), Group ad-hoc Network (GN) or PANU host. **btpand** connects to the system via a tap(4) virtual Ethernet device and forwards Ethernet packets to remote Bluetooth devices using the Bluetooth Network Encapsulation Protocol (BNEP).

   The PANU client is the device that uses either the NAP or GN service, or can talk directly to a PANU host in a crossover cable fashion.

   A GN host forwards Ethernet packets to each of the connected PAN users as needed but does not provide access to any additional networks.

   The NAP service provides some of the features of an Ethernet bridge, with the NAP host forwarding Ethernet packets between each of the connected PAN users, and a different network media.

   Note, the only differences between NAP and GN services as implemented by **btpand** are in the SDP service record. The bridging of packets by the NAP must be configured separately with brconfig(4).

   The options are as follows:

   -a *address*   In client mode, address of remote server. May be given as BDADDR or name, in which case **btpand** will attempt to resolve the address via the bt_gethostbyname(3) call.

   -c *path*   In server mode, specify *path* to the sdpd(8) control socket. The default path is /var/run/sdp.

   -d *device*   Restrict connections to the local *device*. May be given as BDADDR or name, in which case **btpand** will attempt to resolve the address via the bt_devaddr(3) call. **btpand** will set the tap(4) interface physical address to the BDADDR of the Bluetooth radio.

   -i *ifname*   **btpand** uses the tap(4) driver to create a new network interface for use. Use this option to select a specific tap(4) device interface which must already be created.

   -l *limit*   In server mode, limit the number of simultaneous connections. The default limit is 7 for NAP and GN servers, and 1 for a PANU server.

   -m *mode*   Set L2CAP connection link mode. Supported modes are:

                       auth   require devices to be paired.
                       encrypt   auth, plus enable encryption.
                       secure   encryption, plus change of link key.

   -p *psm*   Use an alternative L2CAP Protocol/Service Multiplexer (PSM) for server mode or client mode (when not using Service Discovery). The default PSM for BNEP is 15 (0x000f).

   -s *service*   Name of *service* to provide or connect to, the following services are recognised:

GN	Group ad-hoc Network.
NAP	Network Access Point.
PANU	Personal Area Networking User.

-S *service*   As per **-s** except that **btpand** will not use SDP services for connection setup.

When providing networking services, the Bluetooth PAN profile says that the 'Class of Device' property of the bluetooth controller SHALL include Networking capability (set bit 0x020000). See btconfig(8) for details.

After **btpand** has set up the client or server connection and opened the tap(4) interface, it will create a pid file and detach.

EXIT STATUS

The **btpand** utility exits 0 on success, and >0 if an error occurs.

FILES

```
/dev/tap
/etc/bluetooth/hosts
/var/run/sdp
/var/run/tapN.pid
```

EXAMPLES

```
ifconfig tap1 create
btpand -a host -d ubt0 -s NAP -m encrypt -i tap1
dhclient -q -o -w -nw tap1
```

Will create an encrypted connection to the NAP on *host*, and link that to the *tap1* interface.

```
btpand -d ubt0 -s GN -m auth
```

Will create a Group Network requiring authentication to join and register the GN service with the local SDP server.

SEE ALSO

bluetooth(3), bluetooth(4), tap(4), bridge(4), btconfig(8), brconfig(8), dhclient(8), dhcpd(8), ifconfig(8), sdpd(8)

The "Personal Area Networking Profile" and "Bluetooth Network Encapsulation Protocol" specifications are available at

```
http://www.bluetooth.com/
```

AUTHORS

Iain Hibbert

BUGS

There is no way to supply alternative values for the SDP record.

There is no way to set net type or multicast address filters.

btpand does not do any address routing except to directly connected unicast addresses. All other packets are multicast.

As **btpand** uses the BDADDR of the Bluetooth radio as the physical address of the tap, only one instance can be run per radio.

btpand can only provide a single service.

NAME

    catman — format cat pages from man pages

SYNOPSIS

    catman [**-knpsw**] [**-m** *directory*] [*sections*]

    catman [**-knpsw**] [**-M** *directory*] [*sections*]

DESCRIPTION

    catman creates formatted versions of the on-line manual pages from their nroff(1) source. Manual pages whose formatted versions are missing or out of date are regenerated. If manual pages are regenerated, **catman** also regenerates the whatis database.

    The optional *sections* argument is one word, and contains the section numbers of all the sections to be checked. For example, if *sections* is "13f8", the manual pages in sections 1, 3f, and 8 will be checked and regenerated. If no *sections* argument is provided, **catman** will try to operate on all of the known manual sections.

    The options are as follows:

    -k   Ignore errors from nroff when building manpages.

    -n   Do not create the whatis database.

    -p   Display the commands that would have been executed, but do not actually execute them.

    -s   Perform work silently; do not echo commands as they are executed. This flag is ignored if **-p** is specified.

    -w   Only create the whatis database.

    -m *directory*

        Add *directory* to the set of directories to be updated.

    -M *directory*

        Update manual pages in *directory*.

SEE ALSO

    apropos(1), man(1), whatis(1)

BUGS

    Currently does not handle hard links.

NAME
ccdconfig — configuration utility for the concatenated disk driver

SYNOPSIS
ccdconfig [-cv] ccd ileave [flags] dev [. . .]
ccdconfig -C [-v] [-f config_file]
ccdconfig -u [-v] ccd [. . .]
ccdconfig -U [-v] [-f config_file]
ccdconfig -g [-M core] [-N system] [ccd [...]]

DESCRIPTION
ccdconfig is used to dynamically configure and unconfigure concatenated disk devices, or ccds. For more information about the ccd, see ccd(4).

The options are as follows:

-c   Configure a ccd. This is the default behavior of ccdconfig.

-C   Configure all ccd devices listed in the ccd configuration file.

-f config_file
      When configuring or unconfiguring all devices, read the file config_file instead of the default /etc/ccd.conf.

-g   Dump the current ccd configuration in a format suitable for use as the ccd configuration file. If no arguments are specified, every configured ccd is dumped. Otherwise, the configuration of each listed ccd is dumped.

-M core
      Extract values associated with the name list from core instead of the default /dev/mem.

-N system
      Extract the name list from system instead of the default /netbsd.

-u   Unconfigure a ccd.

-U   Unconfigure all ccd devices listed the ccd configuration file.

-v   Causes ccdconfig to be verbose.

A ccd is described on the command line and in the ccd configuration file by the name of the ccd, the interleave factor, the ccd configuration flags, and a list of one or more devices. The flags may be represented as a decimal number, a hexadecimal number, a comma-separated list of strings, or the word "none". The flags are as follows:

Symbolic	Numeric	Comment
CCDF_UNIFORM	0x02	Use uniform interleave. The size of all components is clamped to that of the smallest component.
CCDF_NOLABEL	0x04	Ignore raw disklabel. Useful when creating a new ccd.

/etc/ccd.conf
The file /etc/ccd.conf is used to configure ccdconfig if -C or -U is used. Each line of the configuration file contains arguments as per the -c argument: ccd ileave [flags] dev [. . .]

A '#' is a comment, and everything to end of line is ignored. A '\' at the end of a line indicates that the next line should be concatenated with the current. A '\' preceding any character (other than the end of line) prevents that character's special meaning from taking effect.

See **EXAMPLES** for an example of `/etc/ccd.conf`.

FILES

/etc/ccd.conf - default ccd configuration file.

EXAMPLES

The following command, executed from the command line, would configure ccd0 with 4 components (/dev/sd2e, /dev/sd3e, /dev/sd4e, /dev/sd5e), and an interleave factor of 32 blocks.

```
# ccdconfig ccd0 32 0 /dev/sd2e /dev/sd3e /dev/sd4e /dev/sd5e
```

An example `/etc/ccd.conf`:

```
#
# /etc/ccd.conf
# Configuration file for concatenated disk devices
#

# ccd      ileave flags  component devices
ccd0       16     none   /dev/sd2e /dev/sd3e
```

SEE ALSO

ccd(4), ccd.conf(5), rc(8)

HISTORY

The **ccdconfig** command first appeared in NetBSD 1.1.

NAME

    cgdconfig — configuration utility for the cryptographic disk driver

SYNOPSIS

    cgdconfig [**-npv**] [**-V** *vmeth*] *cgd dev* [*paramsfile*]
    cgdconfig -C [**-nv**] [**-f** *configfile*]
    cgdconfig -U [**-nv**] [**-f** *configfile*]
    cgdconfig -G [**-nv**] [**-i** *ivmeth*] [**-k** *kgmeth*] [**-o** *outfile*] *paramsfile*
    cgdconfig -g [**-nv**] [**-i** *ivmeth*] [**-k** *kgmeth*] [**-o** *outfile*] *alg* [*keylen*]
    cgdconfig -s [**-nv**] [**-i** *ivmeth*] *cgd dev alg* [*keylen*]
    cgdconfig -u [**-nv**] *cgd*

DESCRIPTION

    cgdconfig is used to configure and unconfigure cryptographic disk devices (cgds) and to maintain the configuration files that are associated with them. For more information about cryptographic disk devices see cgd(4).

    The options are as follows:

    -C   Configure all the devices listed in the cgd configuration file.

    -f *configfile*   Specify the configuration file explicitly, rather than using the default configuration file /etc/cgd/cgd.conf.

    -G   Generate a new paramsfile (to stdout) using the values from *paramsfile* which will generate the same key. This may need to prompt for multiple passphrases.

    -g   Generate a paramsfile (to stdout).

    -i *ivmeth*   Specify the IV method (default: encblkno1).

    -k *kgmeth*   Specify the key generation method (default: pkcs5_pbkdf2/sha1).

    -n   Do not actually configure or unconfigure a cryptographic disk device, but instead report the steps that would be taken.

    -o *outfile*   When generating a *paramsfile*, store it in *outfile*.

    -p   Read all passphrases from stdin rather than /dev/tty. Passphrases are separated by newlines. Users of this flag must be able to predict the order in which passphrases are prompted. If this flag is specified then verification errors will cause the device in question to be unconfigured rather than prompting for the passphrase again.

    -s   Read the key from stdin.

    -U   Unconfigure all the devices listed in the cgd configuration file.

    -u   Unconfigure a cgd.

    -V *vmeth*   Specify the verification method (default: none).

    -v   Be verbose. May be specified multiple times.

    For more information about the cryptographic algorithms and IV methods supported, please refer to cgd(4).

Key Generation Methods

    To generate the key which it will use, **cgdconfig** evaluates all of the key generation methods in the parameters file and uses the exclusive-or of the outputs of all the methods. The methods and descriptions are as follows:

pkcs5_pbkdf2/sha1	This method requires a passphrase which is entered at configuration time. It is a salted hmac-based scheme detailed in "PKCS#5 v2.0: Password-Based Cryptography Standard", RSA Laboratories, March 25, 1999, pages 8-10. PKCS #5 was also republished as RFC 2898.
pkcs5_pbkdf2	This is an earlier, slightly incorrect and deprecated implementation of the above algorithm. It is retained for backwards compatibility with existing parameters files, and will be removed. Existing parameters files should be converted to use the correct method using the −G option, and a new passphrase.
storedkey	This method stores its key in the parameters file.
randomkey	The method simply reads /dev/random and uses the resulting bits as the key. It does not require a passphrase to be entered. This method is typically used to present disk devices that do not need to survive a reboot, such as the swap partition. It is also handy to facilitate overwriting the contents of a disk volume with meaningless data prior to use.
urandomkey	The method simply reads /dev/urandom and uses the resulting bits as the key. This is similar to the randomkey method, but it guarantees that cgdconfig will not stall waiting for hard-random bits (useful when configuring a cgd for swap at boot time). Note, however, that some or all of the bits used to generate the key may be obtained from a pseudo-random number generator, which may not be as secure as the entropy based hard-random number generator.
shell_cmd	This method executes a shell command via popen(3) and reads the key from stdout.

Verification Method

The verification method is how **cgdconfig** determines if the generated key is correct. If the newly configured disk fails to verify, then **cgdconfig** will regenerate the key and re-configure the device. It only makes sense to specify a verification method if at least of the key generation methods is error prone, e.g., uses a user-entered passphrase. The following verification methods are supported:

none	perform no verification.
disklabel	scan for a valid disklabel.
ffs	scan for a valid FFS file system.
re-enter	prompt for passphrase twice, and ensure entered passphrases are identical. This method only works with the pkcs5_pbkdf2/sha1 and pkcs5_pbkdf2 key generators.

/etc/cgd/cgd.conf

The file /etc/cgd/cgd.conf is used to configure **cgdconfig** if either of −C or −U are specified. Each line of the file is composed of either two or three tokens: cgd, target, and optional paramsfile.

A '#' character is interpreted as a comment and indicates that the rest of the line should be ignored. A '\' at the end of a line indicates that the next line is a continuation of the current line.

See **EXAMPLES** for an example of /etc/cgd/cgd.conf.

Parameters File

The Parameters File contains the required information to generate the key and configure a device. These files are typically generated by the −g flag and not edited by hand. When a device is configured the default parameters file is constructed by taking the basename of the target disk and prepending /etc/cgd/ to it. E.g., if the target is /dev/sd0h, then the default parameters file will be /etc/cgd/sd0h.

It is possible to have more than one parameters file for a given disk which use different key generation methods but will generate the same key. To create a parameters file that is equivalent to an existing parameters file, use **cgdconfig** with the **-G** flag. See **EXAMPLES** for an example of this usage.

The parameters file contains a list of statements each terminated with a semi-colon. Some statements can contain statement-blocks which are either a single unadorned statement, or a brace-enclosed list of semicolon terminated statements. Three types of data are understood:

integer   a 32 bit signed integer.
string   a string.
base64   a length-encoded base64 string.

The following statements are defined:

algorithm *string*
        Defines the cryptographic algorithm.

iv-method *string*
        Defines the IV generation method.

keylength *integer*
        Defines the length of the key.

verify_method *string*
        Defines the verification method.

keygen *string statement_block*
        Defines a key generation method. The *statement_block* contains statements that are specific to the key generation method.

The keygen statement's statement block may contain the following statements:

key *string*
        The key. Only used for the storedkey key generation method.

cmd *string*
        The command to execute. Only used for the shell_cmd key generation method.

iterations *integer*
        The number of iterations. Only used for pkcs5_pbkdf2/sha1 and pkcs5_pbkdf2.

salt *base64*
        The salt. Only used for pkcs5_pbkdf2/sha1 and pkcs5_pbkdf2.

FILES
    /etc/cgd/   configuration directory, used to store paramsfiles.
    /etc/cgd/cgd.conf   cgd configuration file.

EXAMPLES
    To set up and configure a cgd that uses AES with a 192 bit key in CBC mode with the IV Method 'encblkno1' (encrypted block number):

            # cgdconfig -g -o /etc/cgd/wd0e aes-cbc 192
            # cgdconfig cgd0 /dev/wd0e
            /dev/wd0e's passphrase:

    When using verification methods, the first time that we configure the disk the verification method will fail. We overcome this by supplying **-V** *re-enter* when we configure the first time to set up the disk. Here is the sequence of commands that is recommended:

```
# cgdconfig -g -o /etc/cgd/wd0e -V disklabel aes-cbc
# cgdconfig -V re-enter cgd0 /dev/wd0e
/dev/wd0e's passphrase:
re-enter device's passphrase:
# disklabel -e -I cgd0
# cgdconfig -u cgd0
# cgdconfig cgd0 /dev/wd0e
/dev/wd0e's passphrase:
```

To create a new parameters file that will generate the same key as an old parameters file:

```
# cgdconfig -G -o newparamsfile oldparamsfile
old file's passphrase:
new file's passphrase:
```

To configure a cgd that uses Blowfish with a 200 bit key that it reads from stdin:

```
# cgdconfig -s cgd0 /dev/sd0h blowfish-cbc 200
```

An example parameters file which uses PKCS#5 PBKDF2:

```
algorithm aes-cbc;
iv-method encblkno1;
keylength 128;
verify_method none;
keygen pkcs5_pbkdf2/sha1 {
        iterations 39361;
        salt AAAAgMoHiYonye6Kog \
            dYJAobCHE=;
};
```

An example parameters file which stores its key locally:

```
algorithm       aes-cbc;
iv-method       encblkno1;
keylength       256;
verify_method   none;
keygen storedkey key AAABAK3QO6d7xzLfrXTdsgg4 \
                ly2TdxkFqOkYYcbyUKu/f60L;
```

An example /etc/cgd/cgd.conf:

```
#
# /etc/cgd/cgd.conf
# Configuration file for cryptographic disk devices
#

# cgd         target          [paramsfile]
cgd0          /dev/wd0e
cgd1          /dev/sd0h       /usr/local/etc/cgd/sd0h
```

Note that this will store the parameters file as /etc/cgd/wd0e. And use the entered passphrase to generate the key.

DIAGNOSTICS

cgdconfig: could not calibrate pkcs5_pbkdf2 An error greater than 5% in calibration occured. This could be the result of dynamic processor frequency scaling technology. Ensure that the processor clock frequency remains static throughout the program's execution.

SEE ALSO

cgd(4)

"PKCS #5 v2.0: Password-Based Cryptography Standard", RSA Laboratories, March 25, 1999.

HISTORY

The **cgdconfig** utility appeared in NetBSD 2.0.

BUGS

Since **cgdconfig** uses getpass(3) to read in the passphrase, it is limited to 128 characters.

NAME

chat – Automated conversational script with a modem

SYNOPSIS

chat [*options*] *script*

DESCRIPTION

The *chat* program defines a conversational exchange between the computer and the modem. Its primary purpose is to establish the connection between the Point-to-Point Protocol Daemon (*pppd*) and the remote's *pppd* process.

OPTIONS

–f *<chat file>*

Read the chat script from the chat *file*. The use of this option is mutually exclusive with the chat script parameters. The user must have read access to the file. Multiple lines are permitted in the file. Space or horizontal tab characters should be used to separate the strings.

–t *<timeout>*

Set the timeout for the expected string to be received. If the string is not received within the time limit then the reply string is not sent. An alternate reply may be sent or the script will fail if there is no alternate reply string. A failed script will cause the *chat* program to terminate with a non-zero error code.

–r *<report file>*

Set the file for output of the report strings. If you use the keyword *REPORT*, the resulting strings are written to this file. If this option is not used and you still use *REPORT* keywords, the *stderr* file is used for the report strings.

–e

Start with the echo option turned on. Echoing may also be turned on or off at specific points in the chat script by using the *ECHO* keyword. When echoing is enabled, all output from the modem is echoed to *stderr*.

–E

Enables environment variable substitution within chat scripts using the standard $*xxx* syntax.

–v

Request that the *chat* script be executed in a verbose mode. The *chat* program will then log the execution state of the chat script as well as all text received from the modem and the output strings sent to the modem. The default is to log through the SYSLOG; the logging method may be altered with the –S and –s flags. SYSLOGs are logged to facility LOG_LOCAL2.

–V

Request that the *chat* script be executed in a stderr verbose mode. The *chat* program will then log all text received from the modem and the output strings sent to the modem to the stderr device. This device is usually the local console at the station running the chat or pppd program.

–s

Use stderr. All log messages from '–v' and all error messages will be sent to stderr.

–S

Do not use the SYSLOG. By default, error messages are sent to the SYSLOG. The use of –S will prevent both log messages from '–v' and error messages from being sent to the SYSLOG (to facility LOG_LOCAL2).

–T *<phone number>*

Pass in an arbitrary string, usually a phone number, that will be substituted for the \T substitution metacharacter in a send string.

–U *<phone number 2>*

Pass in a second string, usually a phone number, that will be substituted for the \U substitution metacharacter in a send string. This is useful when dialing an ISDN terminal adapter that requires two numbers.

script

If the script is not specified in a file with the *–f* option then the script is included as parameters to the *chat* program.

CHAT SCRIPT

The *chat* script defines the communications.

A script consists of one or more "expect–send" pairs of strings, separated by spaces, with an optional "subexpect–subsend" string pair, separated by a dash as in the following example:

    ogin:–BREAK–ogin: ppp ssword: hello2u2

This line indicates that the *chat* program should expect the string "ogin:". If it fails to receive a login prompt within the time interval allotted, it is to send a break sequence to the remote and then expect the string "ogin:". If the first "ogin:" is received then the break sequence is not generated.

Once it received the login prompt the *chat* program will send the string ppp and then expect the prompt "ssword:". When it receives the prompt for the password, it will send the password hello2u2.

A carriage return is normally sent following the reply string. It is not expected in the "expect" string unless it is specifically requested by using the \r character sequence.

The expect sequence should contain only what is needed to identify the string. Since it is normally stored on a disk file, it should not contain variable information. It is generally not acceptable to look for time strings, network identification strings, or other variable pieces of data as an expect string.

To help correct for characters which may be corrupted during the initial sequence, look for the string "ogin:" rather than "login:". It is possible that the leading "l" character may be received in error and you may never find the string even though it was sent by the system. For this reason, scripts look for "ogin:" rather than "login:" and "ssword:" rather than "password:".

A very simple script might look like this:

    ogin: ppp ssword: hello2u2

In other words, expect ....ogin:, send ppp, expect ...ssword:, send hello2u2.

In actual practice, simple scripts are rare. At the vary least, you should include sub-expect sequences should the original string not be received. For example, consider the following script:

    ogin:––ogin: ppp ssword: hello2u2

This would be a better script than the simple one used earlier. This would look for the same login: prompt, however, if one was not received, a single return sequence is sent and then it will look for login: again. Should line noise obscure the first login prompt then sending the empty line will usually generate a login prompt again.

COMMENTS

Comments can be embedded in the chat script. A comment is a line which starts with the # (hash) character in column 1. Such comment lines are just ignored by the chat program. If a '#' character is to be expected as the first character of the expect sequence, you should quote the expect string. If you want to wait for a prompt that starts with a # (hash) character, you would have to write something like this:

        # Now wait for the prompt and send logout string
        '# ' logout

SENDING DATA FROM A FILE

If the string to send starts with an at sign (@), the rest of the string is taken to be the name of a file to read to get the string to send. If the last character of the data read is a newline, it is removed. The file can be a named pipe (or fifo) instead of a regular file. This provides a way for **chat** to communicate with another program, for example, a program to prompt the user and receive a password typed in.

ABORT STRINGS

Many modems will report the status of the call as a string. These strings may be **CONNECTED** or **NO CARRIER** or **BUSY**. It is often desirable to terminate the script should the modem fail to connect to the remote. The difficulty is that a script would not know exactly which modem string it may receive. On one attempt, it may receive **BUSY** while the next time it may receive **NO CARRIER**.

These "abort" strings may be specified in the script using the *ABORT* sequence. It is written in the script as in the following example:

ABORT BUSY ABORT 'NO CARRIER' '' ATZ OK ATDT5551212 CONNECT

This sequence will expect nothing; and then send the string ATZ. The expected response to this is the string *OK*. When it receives *OK*, the string ATDT5551212 to dial the telephone. The expected string is *CONNECT*. If the string *CONNECT* is received the remainder of the script is executed. However, should the modem find a busy telephone, it will send the string *BUSY*. This will cause the string to match the abort character sequence. The script will then fail because it found a match to the abort string. If it received the string *NO CARRIER*, it will abort for the same reason. Either string may be received. Either string will terminate the *chat* script.

CLR_ABORT STRINGS

This sequence allows for clearing previously set **ABORT** strings. **ABORT** strings are kept in an array of a pre-determined size (at compilation time); **CLR_ABORT** will reclaim the space for cleared entries so that new strings can use that space.

SAY STRINGS

The **SAY** directive allows the script to send strings to the user at the terminal via standard error. If **chat** is being run by pppd, and pppd is running as a daemon (detached from its controlling terminal), standard error will normally be redirected to the file /etc/ppp/connect-errors.

SAY strings must be enclosed in single or double quotes. If carriage return and line feed are needed in the string to be output, you must explicitly add them to your string.

The SAY strings could be used to give progress messages in sections of the script where you want to have 'ECHO OFF' but still let the user know what is happening. An example is:

```
ABORT BUSY
ECHO OFF
SAY "Dialing your ISP...\n"
'' ATDT5551212
TIMEOUT 120
SAY "Waiting up to 2 minutes for connection ... "
CONNECT ''
SAY "Connected, now logging in ...\n"
ogin: account
ssword: pass
$ SAY "Logged in OK ...\n" etc ...
```

This sequence will only present the SAY strings to the user and all the details of the script will remain hidden. For example, if the above script works, the user will see:

Dialing your ISP...
Waiting up to 2 minutes for connection ... Connected, now logging in ...
Logged in OK ...

REPORT STRINGS

A **report** string is similar to the ABORT string. The difference is that the strings, and all characters to the next control character such as a carriage return, are written to the report file.

The report strings may be used to isolate the transmission rate of the modem's connect string and return the value to the chat user. The analysis of the report string logic occurs in conjunction with the other string processing such as looking for the expect string. The use of the same string for a report and abort sequence is probably not very useful, however, it is possible.

The report strings to no change the completion code of the program.

These "report" strings may be specified in the script using the *REPORT* sequence. It is written in the script as in the following example:

REPORT CONNECT ABORT BUSY '' ATDT5551212 CONNECT '' ogin: account

This sequence will expect nothing; and then send the string ATDT5551212 to dial the telephone. The expected string is *CONNECT*. If the string *CONNECT* is received the remainder of the script is executed. In addition the program will write to the expect–file the string "CONNECT" plus any characters which follow it such as the connection rate.

CLR_REPORT STRINGS

This sequence allows for clearing previously set **REPORT** strings. **REPORT** strings are kept in an array of a pre-determined size (at compilation time); **CLR_REPORT** will reclaim the space for cleared entries so that new strings can use that space.

ECHO

The echo options controls whether the output from the modem is echoed to *stderr*. This option may be set with the *–e* option, but it can also be controlled by the *ECHO* keyword. The "expect–send" pair *ECHO ON* enables echoing, and *ECHO OFF* disables it. With this keyword you can select which parts of the conversation should be visible. For instance, with the following script:

ABORT 'BUSY'
ABORT 'NO CARRIER'
OK\r\n ATD1234567
\r\n \c
ECHO ON
CONNECT \c
ogin: account

all output resulting from modem configuration and dialing is not visible, but starting with the *CONNECT* (or *BUSY*) message, everything will be echoed.

HANGUP

The HANGUP options control whether a modem hangup should be considered as an error or not. This option is useful in scripts for dialing systems which will hang up and call your system back. The HANGUP options can be **ON** or **OFF**.

When HANGUP is set OFF and the modem hangs up (e.g., after the first stage of logging in to a callback system), **chat** will continue running the script (e.g., waiting for the incoming call and second stage login prompt). As soon as the incoming call is connected, you should use the **HANGUP ON** directive to reinstall normal hang up signal behavior. Here is an (simple) example script:

ABORT 'BUSY'
OK\r\n ATD1234567
\r\n \c
CONNECT \c
'Callback login:' call_back_ID
HANGUP OFF
ABORT "Bad Login"
'Callback Password:' Call_back_password
TIMEOUT 120
CONNECT \c
HANGUP ON
ABORT "NO CARRIER"
ogin:––BREAK––ogin: real_account
etc ...

TIMEOUT

The initial timeout value is 45 seconds. This may be changed using the **–t** parameter.

To change the timeout value for the next expect string, the following example may be used:

> ATZ OK ATDT5551212 CONNECT TIMEOUT 10 ogin:---ogin: TIMEOUT 5 assword: hello2u2

This will change the timeout to 10 seconds when it expects the login: prompt. The timeout is then changed to 5 seconds when it looks for the password prompt.

The timeout, once changed, remains in effect until it is changed again.

SENDING EOT

The special reply string of *EOT* indicates that the chat program should send an EOT character to the remote. This is normally the End-of-file character sequence. A return character is not sent following the EOT.

The EOT sequence may be embedded into the send string using the sequence ^D.

GENERATING BREAK

The special reply string of *BREAK* will cause a break condition to be sent. The break is a special signal on the transmitter. The normal processing on the receiver is to change the transmission rate. It may be used to cycle through the available transmission rates on the remote until you are able to receive a valid login prompt.

The break sequence may be embedded into the send string using the \K sequence.

ESCAPE SEQUENCES

The expect and reply strings may contain escape sequences. All of the sequences are legal in the reply string. Many are legal in the expect. Those which are not valid in the expect sequence are so indicated.

"	Expects or sends a null string. If you send a null string then it will still send the return character. This sequence may either be a pair of apostrophe or quote characters.
\b	represents a backspace character.
\c	Suppresses the newline at the end of the reply string. This is the only method to send a string without a trailing return character. It must be at the end of the send string. For example, the sequence hello\c will simply send the characters h, e, l, l, o. *(not valid in expect.)*
\d	Delay for one second. The program uses sleep(1) which will delay to a maximum of one second. *(not valid in expect.)*
\K	Insert a BREAK *(not valid in expect.)*
\n	Send a newline or linefeed character.
\N	Send a null character. The same sequence may be represented by \0. *(not valid in expect.)*
\p	Pause for a fraction of a second. The delay is 1/10th of a second. *(not valid in expect.)*
\q	Suppress writing the string to the SYSLOG. The string ?????? is written to the log in its place. *(not valid in expect.)*
\r	Send or expect a carriage return.
\s	Represents a space character in the string. This may be used when it is not desirable to quote the strings which contains spaces. The sequence 'HI TIM' and HI\sTIM are the same.
\t	Send or expect a tab character.
\T	Send the phone number string as specified with the −T option *(not valid in expect.)*
\U	Send the phone number 2 string as specified with the −U option *(not valid in expect.)*
\\	Send or expect a backslash character.
\ddd	Collapse the octal digits (ddd) into a single ASCII character and send that character. *(some characters are not valid in expect.)*
^C	Substitute the sequence with the control character represented by C. For example, the character DC1 (17) is shown as ^Q. *(some characters are not valid in expect.)*

ENVIRONMENT VARIABLES

Environment variables are available within chat scripts, if the $-E$ option was specified in the command line. The metacharacter $ is used to introduce the name of the environment variable to substitute. If the substitution fails, because the requested environment variable is not set, *nothing* is replaced for the variable.

TERMINATION CODES

The *chat* program will terminate with the following completion codes.

0   The normal termination of the program. This indicates that the script was executed without error to the normal conclusion.

1   One or more of the parameters are invalid or an expect string was too large for the internal buffers. This indicates that the program as not properly executed.

2   An error occurred during the execution of the program. This may be due to a read or write operation failing for some reason or chat receiving a signal such as SIGINT.

3   A timeout event occurred when there was an *expect* string without having a "−subsend" string. This may mean that you did not program the script correctly for the condition or that some unexpected event has occurred and the expected string could not be found.

4   The first string marked as an *ABORT* condition occurred.

5   The second string marked as an *ABORT* condition occurred.

6   The third string marked as an *ABORT* condition occurred.

7   The fourth string marked as an *ABORT* condition occurred.

...   The other termination codes are also strings marked as an *ABORT* condition.

Using the termination code, it is possible to determine which event terminated the script. It is possible to decide if the string "BUSY" was received from the modem as opposed to "NO DIAL TONE". While the first event may be retried, the second will probably have little chance of succeeding during a retry.

COPYRIGHT

The *chat* program is in public domain. This is not the GNU public license. If it breaks then you get to keep both pieces.

NAME

    chown — change file owner and group

SYNOPSIS

    chown [**-R** [**-H** | **-L** | **-P**]] [**-fhv**] *owner*[*:group*] *file* . . .
    chown [**-R** [**-H** | **-L** | **-P**]] [**-fhv**] *:group file* . . .

DESCRIPTION

    chown sets the user ID and/or the group ID of the specified files.

    The options are as follows:

    -H   If the **-R** option is specified, symbolic links on the command line are followed. (Symbolic links encountered in the tree traversal are not followed.)

    -L   If the **-R** option is specified, all symbolic links are followed.

    -P   If the **-R** option is specified, no symbolic links are followed.

    -R   Change the user ID and/or the group ID for the file hierarchies rooted in the files instead of just the files themselves.

    -f   Don't report any failure to change file owner or group, nor modify the exit status to reflect such failures.

    -h   If *file* is a symbolic link, the owner and/or group of the link is changed.

    -v   Cause **chown** to be verbose, showing files as they are processed.

    The **-H**, **-L** and **-P** options are ignored unless the **-R** option is specified. In addition, these options override each other and the command's actions are determined by the last one specified.

    The **-L** option cannot be used together with the **-h** option.

    The *owner* and *group* operands are both optional, however, one must be specified. If the *group* operand is specified, it must be preceded by a colon (":") character.

    The *owner* may be either a user name or a numeric user ID. The *group* may be either a group name or a numeric group ID. Since it is valid to have a user or group name that is numeric (and doesn't have the numeric ID that matches its name) the name lookup is always done first. Preceding an ID with a "#" character will force it to be taken as a number.

    The ownership of a file may only be altered by a super-user for obvious security reasons.

    Unless invoked by the super-user, **chown** clears the set-user-id and set-group-id bits on a file to prevent accidental or mischievous creation of set-user-id and set-group-id programs.

    The **chown** utility exits 0 on success, and >0 if an error occurs.

COMPATIBILITY

    Previous versions of the **chown** utility used the dot (".") character to distinguish the group name. This has been changed to be a colon (":") character so that user and group names may contain the dot character.

SEE ALSO

    chflags(1), chgrp(1), find(1), chown(2), lchown(2), fts(3), symlink(7)

STANDARDS

    The **chown** command is expected to be POSIX 1003.2 compliant.

The **−v** option and the use of "#" to force a numeric lookup are extensions to IEEE Std 1003.2 ("POSIX.2").

NAME
   chroot — change root directory

SYNOPSIS
   chroot [**-u** *user*] [**-g** *group*] [**-G** *group, group, . . .*] *newroot* [*command*]

DESCRIPTION
   The **chroot** command changes its root directory to the supplied directory *newroot* and exec's *command*, if supplied, or an interactive copy of your shell.

   If the **-u**, **-g** or **-G** options are given, the user, group and group list of the process are set to these values after the chroot has taken place. See setgid(2), setgroups(2), setuid(2), getgrnam(3) and getpwnam(3).

   Note, *command* or the shell are run as your real-user-id.

ENVIRONMENT
   The following environment variable is referenced by **chroot**:

   SHELL   If set, the string specified by SHELL is interpreted as the name of the shell to exec. If the variable SHELL is not set, /bin/sh is used.

SEE ALSO
   chdir(2), chroot(2), environ(7)

HISTORY
   The **chroot** utility first appeared in 4.4BSD.

SECURITY CONSIDERATIONS
   chroot should never be installed setuid root, as it would then be possible to exploit the program to gain root privileges.

NAME

chrtbl — create character classification and upper <-> lower conversion tables

SYNOPSIS

chrtbl [-o *ofile*] *ifile*

DESCRIPTION

chrtbl creates character classification and upper <-> lower conversion tables for single byte files. The chrtbl command is modelled after the Solaris/SVR4 command. The input file is similar and contains a keyword per line followed by characters or ranges. Valid keywords are:

LC_CTYPE *filename*
> Set the filename for the character classification output.

LC_NUMERIC *filename*
> Set the filename for the numeric formatting output.

isupper *begin-char* [- *end-char*]
> Set the attribute of the specified characters range(s) to be upper case.

islower *begin-char* [- *end-char*]
> Set the attribute of the specified characters range(s) to be lower case.

isdigit *begin-char* [- *end-char*]
> Set the attribute of the specified characters range(s) to be numeric.

isspace *begin-char* [- *end-char*]
> Set the attribute of the specified characters range(s) to be space.

ispunct *begin-char* [- *end-char*]
> Set the attribute of the specified characters range(s) to be punctuation.

iscntrl *begin-char* [- *end-char*]
> Set the attribute of the specified characters range(s) to be control.

isxdigit *begin-char* [- *end-char*]
> Set the attribute of the specified characters range(s) to be hexadecimal digits.

isblank *begin-char* [- *end-char*]
> Set the attribute of the specified characters range(s) to be blank.

ul <*upper-char lower-char*> ...
> Specify a case correspondence between upper and lower char.

cswidth *n1,s1:n2,s2:n3,s3*
> Specify the character set byte width (n1,n2,n3) and the screen width(s1,s2,s3) for the 3 character sets.

decimal_point *char*
> Specify the decimal point numeric formatting character.

thousands_sep *char*
> Specify the thousands separator numeric formatting character.

Available options

-o *ofile*
> Print the conversion tables in a human readable (C source) form.

SEE ALSO
    setlocale(3)

BUGS
    Preliminary support of LC_NUMERIC is present, but not currently fully implemented. No support for wide character locales. Support for alternate localized character sets and numeric formatting is currently not implemented.

NAME

cleanup – canonicalize and enqueue Postfix message

SYNOPSIS

cleanup [generic Postfix daemon options]

DESCRIPTION

The **cleanup**(8) daemon processes inbound mail, inserts it into the **incoming** mail queue, and informs the queue manager of its arrival.

The **cleanup**(8) daemon always performs the following transformations:

- Insert missing message headers: (**Resent-**) **From:**, **To:**, **Message-Id:**, and **Date:**.

- Transform envelope and header addresses to the standard *user@fully-qualified-domain* form that is expected by other Postfix programs. This task is delegated to the **trivial-rewrite**(8) daemon.

- Eliminate duplicate envelope recipient addresses.

The following address transformations are optional:

- Optionally, rewrite all envelope and header addresses according to the mappings specified in the **canonical**(5) lookup tables.

- Optionally, masquerade envelope sender addresses and message header addresses (i.e. strip host or domain information below all domains listed in the **masquerade_domains** parameter, except for user names listed in **masquerade_exceptions**). By default, address masquerading does not affect envelope recipients.

- Optionally, expand envelope recipients according to information found in the **virtual**(5) lookup tables.

The **cleanup**(8) daemon performs sanity checks on the content of each message. When it finds a problem, by default it returns a diagnostic status to the client, and leaves it up to the client to deal with the problem. Alternatively, the client can request the **cleanup**(8) daemon to bounce the message back to the sender in case of trouble.

STANDARDS

RFC 822 (ARPA Internet Text Messages)
RFC 2045 (MIME: Format of Internet Message Bodies)
RFC 2046 (MIME: Media Types)
RFC 3463 (Enhanced Status Codes)
RFC 3464 (Delivery status notifications)

DIAGNOSTICS

Problems and transactions are logged to **syslogd**(8).

BUGS

Table-driven rewriting rules make it hard to express **if then else** and other logical relationships.

CONFIGURATION PARAMETERS

Changes to **main.cf** are picked up automatically, as **cleanup**(8) processes run for only a limited amount of time. Use the command "**postfix reload**" to speed up a change.

The text below provides only a parameter summary. See **postconf**(5) for more details including examples.

COMPATIBILITY CONTROLS

undisclosed_recipients_header (To: undisclosed-recipients:;)

Message header that the Postfix **cleanup**(8) server inserts when a message contains no To: or Cc: message header.

Available in Postfix version 2.1 only:

enable_errors_to (no)
> Report mail delivery errors to the address specified with the non-standard Errors-To: message header, instead of the envelope sender address (this feature is removed with Postfix version 2.2, is turned off by default with Postfix version 2.1, and is always turned on with older Postfix versions).

Available in Postfix version 2.6 and later:

always_add_missing_headers (no)
> Always add (Resent-) From:, To:, Date: or Message-ID: headers when not present.

BUILT-IN CONTENT FILTERING CONTROLS

Postfix built-in content filtering is meant to stop a flood of worms or viruses. It is not a general content filter.

body_checks (empty)
> Optional lookup tables for content inspection as specified in the **body_checks**(5) manual page.

header_checks (empty)
> Optional lookup tables for content inspection of primary non-MIME message headers, as specified in the **header_checks**(5) manual page.

Available in Postfix version 2.0 and later:

body_checks_size_limit (51200)
> How much text in a message body segment (or attachment, if you prefer to use that term) is subjected to body_checks inspection.

mime_header_checks ($header_checks)
> Optional lookup tables for content inspection of MIME related message headers, as described in the **header_checks**(5) manual page.

nested_header_checks ($header_checks)
> Optional lookup tables for content inspection of non-MIME message headers in attached messages, as described in the **header_checks**(5) manual page.

Available in Postfix version 2.3 and later:

message_reject_characters (empty)
> The set of characters that Postfix will reject in message content.

message_strip_characters (empty)
> The set of characters that Postfix will remove from message content.

BEFORE QUEUE MILTER CONTROLS

As of version 2.3, Postfix supports the Sendmail version 8 Milter (mail filter) protocol. When mail is not received via the smtpd(8) server, the cleanup(8) server will simulate SMTP events to the extent that this is possible. For details see the MILTER_README document.

non_smtpd_milters (empty)
> A list of Milter (mail filter) applications for new mail that does not arrive via the Postfix **smtpd**(8) server.

milter_protocol (6)
> The mail filter protocol version and optional protocol extensions for communication with a Milter application; prior to Postfix 2.6 the default protocol is 2.

milter_default_action (tempfail)
> The default action when a Milter (mail filter) application is unavailable or mis-configured.

milter_macro_daemon_name ($myhostname)
> The {daemon_name} macro value for Milter (mail filter) applications.

milter_macro_v ($mail_name $mail_version)
> The {v} macro value for Milter (mail filter) applications.

milter_connect_timeout (30s)
> The time limit for connecting to a Milter (mail filter) application, and for negotiating protocol options.

milter_command_timeout (30s)
> The time limit for sending an SMTP command to a Milter (mail filter) application, and for receiving the response.

milter_content_timeout (300s)
> The time limit for sending message content to a Milter (mail filter) application, and for receiving the response.

milter_connect_macros (see 'postconf -d' output)
> The macros that are sent to Milter (mail filter) applications after completion of an SMTP connection.

milter_helo_macros (see 'postconf -d' output)
> The macros that are sent to Milter (mail filter) applications after the SMTP HELO or EHLO command.

milter_mail_macros (see 'postconf -d' output)
> The macros that are sent to Milter (mail filter) applications after the SMTP MAIL FROM command.

milter_rcpt_macros (see 'postconf -d' output)
> The macros that are sent to Milter (mail filter) applications after the SMTP RCPT TO command.

milter_data_macros (see 'postconf -d' output)
> The macros that are sent to version 4 or higher Milter (mail filter) applications after the SMTP DATA command.

milter_unknown_command_macros (see 'postconf -d' output)
> The macros that are sent to version 3 or higher Milter (mail filter) applications after an unknown SMTP command.

milter_end_of_data_macros (see 'postconf -d' output)
> The macros that are sent to Milter (mail filter) applications after the message end-of-data.

Available in Postfix version 2.5 and later:

milter_end_of_header_macros (see 'postconf -d' output)
> The macros that are sent to Milter (mail filter) applications after the end of the message header.

MIME PROCESSING CONTROLS
Available in Postfix version 2.0 and later:

disable_mime_input_processing (no)
> Turn off MIME processing while receiving mail.

mime_boundary_length_limit (2048)
> The maximal length of MIME multipart boundary strings.

mime_nesting_limit (100)
> The maximal recursion level that the MIME processor will handle.

strict_8bitmime (no)
> Enable both strict_7bit_headers and strict_8bitmime_body.

strict_7bit_headers (no)
> Reject mail with 8-bit text in message headers.

strict_8bitmime_body (no)
> Reject 8-bit message body text without 8-bit MIME content encoding information.

strict_mime_encoding_domain (no)
> Reject mail with invalid Content-Transfer-Encoding: information for the message/* or multipart/* MIME content types.

Available in Postfix version 2.5 and later:

detect_8bit_encoding_header (yes)
> Automatically detect 8BITMIME body content by looking at Content-Transfer-Encoding: message headers; historically, this behavior was hard-coded to be "always on".

AUTOMATIC BCC RECIPIENT CONTROLS
Postfix can automatically add BCC (blind carbon copy) when mail enters the mail system:

always_bcc (empty)
> Optional address that receives a "blind carbon copy" of each message that is received by the Postfix mail system.

Available in Postfix version 2.1 and later:

sender_bcc_maps (empty)
> Optional BCC (blind carbon-copy) address lookup tables, indexed by sender address.

recipient_bcc_maps (empty)
> Optional BCC (blind carbon-copy) address lookup tables, indexed by recipient address.

ADDRESS TRANSFORMATION CONTROLS
Address rewriting is delegated to the **trivial-rewrite**(8) daemon. The **cleanup**(8) server implements table driven address mapping.

empty_address_recipient (MAILER-DAEMON)
> The recipient of mail addressed to the null address.

canonical_maps (empty)
> Optional address mapping lookup tables for message headers and envelopes.

recipient_canonical_maps (empty)
> Optional address mapping lookup tables for envelope and header recipient addresses.

sender_canonical_maps (empty)
> Optional address mapping lookup tables for envelope and header sender addresses.

masquerade_classes (envelope_sender, header_sender, header_recipient)
> What addresses are subject to address masquerading.

masquerade_domains (empty)
> Optional list of domains whose subdomain structure will be stripped off in email addresses.

masquerade_exceptions (empty)
> Optional list of user names that are not subjected to address masquerading, even when their address matches $masquerade_domains.

propagate_unmatched_extensions (canonical, virtual)
> What address lookup tables copy an address extension from the lookup key to the lookup result.

Available before Postfix version 2.0:

virtual_maps (empty)
> Optional lookup tables with a) names of domains for which all addresses are aliased to addresses in other local or remote domains, and b) addresses that are aliased to addresses in other local or remote domains.

Available in Postfix version 2.0 and later:

virtual_alias_maps ($virtual_maps)
> Optional lookup tables that alias specific mail addresses or domains to other local or remote address.

Available in Postfix version 2.2 and later:

canonical_classes (envelope_sender, envelope_recipient, header_sender, header_recipient)
    What addresses are subject to canonical_maps address mapping.

recipient_canonical_classes (envelope_recipient, header_recipient)
    What addresses are subject to recipient_canonical_maps address mapping.

sender_canonical_classes (envelope_sender, header_sender)
    What addresses are subject to sender_canonical_maps address mapping.

remote_header_rewrite_domain (empty)
    Don't rewrite message headers from remote clients at all when this parameter is empty; otherwise, rewrite message headers and append the specified domain name to incomplete addresses.

RESOURCE AND RATE CONTROLS
duplicate_filter_limit (1000)
    The maximal number of addresses remembered by the address duplicate filter for **aliases**(5) or **virtual**(5) alias expansion, or for **showq**(8) queue displays.

header_size_limit (102400)
    The maximal amount of memory in bytes for storing a message header.

hopcount_limit (50)
    The maximal number of Received: message headers that is allowed in the primary message headers.

in_flow_delay (1s)
    Time to pause before accepting a new message, when the message arrival rate exceeds the message delivery rate.

message_size_limit (10240000)
    The maximal size in bytes of a message, including envelope information.

Available in Postfix version 2.0 and later:

header_address_token_limit (10240)
    The maximal number of address tokens are allowed in an address message header.

mime_boundary_length_limit (2048)
    The maximal length of MIME multipart boundary strings.

mime_nesting_limit (100)
    The maximal recursion level that the MIME processor will handle.

queue_file_attribute_count_limit (100)
    The maximal number of (name=value) attributes that may be stored in a Postfix queue file.

Available in Postfix version 2.1 and later:

virtual_alias_expansion_limit (1000)
    The maximal number of addresses that virtual alias expansion produces from each original recipient.

virtual_alias_recursion_limit (1000)
    The maximal nesting depth of virtual alias expansion.

MISCELLANEOUS CONTROLS
config_directory (see 'postconf -d' output)
    The default location of the Postfix main.cf and master.cf configuration files.

daemon_timeout (18000s)
    How much time a Postfix daemon process may take to handle a request before it is terminated by a built-in watchdog timer.

delay_logging_resolution_limit (2)
> The maximal number of digits after the decimal point when logging sub-second delay values.

delay_warning_time (0h)
> The time after which the sender receives the message headers of mail that is still queued.

ipc_timeout (3600s)
> The time limit for sending or receiving information over an internal communication channel.

max_idle (100s)
> The maximum amount of time that an idle Postfix daemon process waits for an incoming connection before terminating voluntarily.

max_use (100)
> The maximal number of incoming connections that a Postfix daemon process will service before terminating voluntarily.

myhostname (see 'postconf -d' output)
> The internet hostname of this mail system.

myorigin ($myhostname)
> The domain name that locally-posted mail appears to come from, and that locally posted mail is delivered to.

process_id (read-only)
> The process ID of a Postfix command or daemon process.

process_name (read-only)
> The process name of a Postfix command or daemon process.

queue_directory (see 'postconf -d' output)
> The location of the Postfix top-level queue directory.

soft_bounce (no)
> Safety net to keep mail queued that would otherwise be returned to the sender.

syslog_facility (mail)
> The syslog facility of Postfix logging.

syslog_name (see 'postconf -d' output)
> The mail system name that is prepended to the process name in syslog records, so that "smtpd" becomes, for example, "postfix/smtpd".

Available in Postfix version 2.1 and later:

enable_original_recipient (yes)
> Enable support for the X-Original-To message header.

FILES
> /etc/postfix/canonical*, canonical mapping table
> /etc/postfix/virtual*, virtual mapping table

SEE ALSO
> trivial-rewrite(8), address rewriting
> qmgr(8), queue manager
> header_checks(5), message header content inspection
> body_checks(5), body parts content inspection
> canonical(5), canonical address lookup table format
> virtual(5), virtual alias lookup table format
> postconf(5), configuration parameters
> master(5), generic daemon options
> master(8), process manager
> syslogd(8), system logging

README FILES

Use "**postconf readme_directory**" or "**postconf html_directory**" to locate this information.

ADDRESS_REWRITING_README Postfix address manipulation

CONTENT_INSPECTION_README content inspection

LICENSE

The Secure Mailer license must be distributed with this software.

AUTHOR(S)

Wietse Venema

IBM T.J. Watson Research

P.O. Box 704

Yorktown Heights, NY 10598, USA

NAME
clri — clear an inode

SYNOPSIS
clri *special_device inode_number* ...

DESCRIPTION
clri is obsoleted for normal file system repair work by fsck(**8**).

clri zeros out the inodes with the specified inode number(s) on the filesystem residing on the given *special_device*. The fsck(8) utility is usually run after **clri** to reclaim the zero'ed inode(s) and the blocks previously claimed by those inode(s). Both read and write permission are required on the specified *special_device*.

The primary purpose of this routine is to remove a file which for some reason is not being properly handled by fsck(8). Once removed, it is anticipated that fsck(8) will be able to clean up the resulting mess.

SEE ALSO
fsck(8), fsdb(8)

BUGS
If the file is open, the work of **clri** will be lost when the inode is written back to disk from the inode cache.

NAME
      cnwctl — display statistics and control Netwave AirSurfer PC Cards

SYNOPSIS
      cnwctl [**-d** *domain*] [**-i** *interface*] [**-k** *scramble-key*] [**-sS** [*rate*]]

DESCRIPTION
      The **cnwctl** utility is used to control Netwave AirSurfer PC Cards as well as display statistics. The following options are available:

      -d   Set the domain of the card to *domain*. The domain must be between 0x000 and 0x1ff. The domains 0x000 through 0x0ff are for access to an add-hoc network. The domains 0x100 through 0x1ff are for access to a Netwave Access Point. The default domain is 0x000. A card may only talk to the access point in its domain, or other cards in its add-hoc domain.

      -i   Use *interface* as the interface rather than cnw0.

      -k   Set the scramble key to *scramble-key*. The scramble key must be between 0x0000 and 0xffff. Both the source and the destination must use the same scramble key in order to communicate.

      -s   Display statistics. When the optional argument *rate* (which must be the last argument to the end of the command line) is specified as a non-zero value, statistics will be displayed every *rate* seconds. At the top of each "page" of statistics, column labels will be displayed. The first row of statistics will be totals since boot, subsequent lines are deltas from the previous row. If *rate* is not specified, or is 0 (zero), a single page of statistics will be displayed. These statistics are more detailed and include:

      domain   The domain this card is part of.

      rx   Number of packets received.

      rxoverflow
              Number of overflows detected.

      rxoverrun
              Number of overruns detected.

      rxcrcerror
              Number of CRC errors detected. Random noise can cause these errors.

      rxframe   Number of framing errors detected.

      rxerrors Number of generic errors detected.

      rxavail   Number of times a packet was available.

      tx   Number of packets requested to be sent.

      txokay   Number of packets sent.

      txabort   Number of packets aborted (not sent within 9 tries).

      txlostcd Number of times carrier detect was lost.

      txerrors Number of generic transmit errors detected.

      txretries Total number of retries.

      *N*x retries
              Number of packets which were retried N times.

−s   Display status read from the hardware. This option is only available to the super user. The *rate*
argument is used as with the **−s** option. The following fields are displayed

link integrity field (lif)
          A 0 value implies no links.

connection quality (cq)
          Probably indicates the quality of the connection to the access point.

spu   Unknown meaning.

link quality (lq)
          Probably indicated the quality of the link to the access point.

hhc   Unknown meaning.

mhs   Unknown meaning.

revision   The revision numbers of the card.

id   The ID of the card.

SEE ALSO
      cnw(4)

NAME
compat_30 — setup procedure for backward compatibility on post-3.0 release

SYNOPSIS
options COMPAT_30

DESCRIPTION
The **compat_30** module allows NetBSD to run NetBSD 3.0 executables.

The support is present if the kernel was built with option COMPAT_30. It is not available as a loadable module.

Static executables typically need no additional setup. Dynamic binaries may require shared libraries whose major version number changed since NetBSD 3.0, which are listed below. A shadow directory under /emul is not used; the libraries can be obtained from a NetBSD 3.0 distribution and installed in the original directories shown, as the major version number in the file name will prevent conflicts. If an upgrade installation from NetBSD 3.0 has been done and these libraries are still present, nothing more need be done.

Libraries needed from 3.0
```
/lib/libcrypto.so.2.1 /lib/libcrypto.so.2

/usr/lib/libcrypto.so.2.1 /usr/lib/libcrypto.so.2

/lib/libevent.so.0.2 /lib/libevent.so.0

/usr/lib/libevent.so.0.2 /usr/lib/libevent.so.0

/usr/lib/libg2c.so.2.0 /usr/lib/libg2c.so.2

/usr/lib/libkadm.so.5.0 /usr/lib/libkadm.so.5

/usr/lib/libkafs.so.6.0 /usr/lib/libkafs.so.6

/usr/lib/libkdb.so.5.0 /usr/lib/libkdb.so.5

/usr/lib/libkrb5.so.19.1 /usr/lib/libkrb5.so.19

/usr/lib/libkrb.so.6.0 /usr/lib/libkrb.so.6

/usr/lib/libkstream.so.2.0 /usr/lib/libkstream.so.2

/usr/lib/libmagic.so.0.1 /usr/lib/libmagic.so.0

/usr/lib/libpcap.so.1.4 /usr/lib/libpcap.so.1

/lib/libradius.so.0.0 /lib/libradius.so.0

/usr/lib/libradius.so.0.0 /usr/lib/libradius.so.0

/usr/lib/libssh.so.1.0 /usr/lib/libssh.so.1

/usr/lib/libssl.so.3.0 /usr/lib/libssl.so.3

/usr/lib/libstdc++.so.5.0 /usr/lib/libstdc++.so.5

/lib/libz.so.0.4 /lib/libz.so.0

/usr/lib/libz.so.0.4 /usr/lib/libz.so.0

/usr/lib/libamu.so.2.1 /usr/lib/libamu.so.2
```

IMPLEMENTATION NOTES

COMPAT_30 enables the NetBSD 3.0 versions of the following system calls, whose syscall numbers and argument structures were changed after the 3.0 release to accommodate 64-bit filesystems: fhstat(2), fstat(2), getdents(2), lstat(2), stat(2).

The filehandle structure (formerly *fhandle_t*) was made opaque to userland and variable-sized. A *fh_size* argument was added to related syscalls: fhstat(2), fhstatvfs(2), fhstatvfs1(2), fhopen(2), getfh(2). This changes the API and ABI of those syscalls, COMPAT_30 enables binary compatibility with the old ABI. Source compatibility is not provided, as use of those syscalls is supposed to be rare.

The error code from the socket(2) syscall changed from EPROTONOSUPPORT to EAFNOSUPPORT in the case of an unsupported address family. COMPAT_30 enables binary compatibility with the old ABI. Source compatiblility is not provided.

The *struct ntptimeval* used by ntp_gettime(2) changed with the implementation of timecounters.

SEE ALSO

config(1), fhstat(2), fstat(2), getdents(2), lstat(2), stat(2), options(4)

HISTORY

NetBSD offers back-compatibility options back to NetBSD 0.9, but the first to be documented with a manual page is **compat_30**.

BUGS

The compatible getdents(2) is unable to see directory entries beneath the top layer of a union, even though the real 3.0 **getdents**() did not have that problem.

SECURITY CONSIDERATIONS

Programs with security impact that receive incorrect directory contents from **getdents**() may behave improperly, as when they are unable to find, or find the wrong versions of, important files.

NAME
compat_darwin — setup procedure for running Darwin binaries from MacOS X

DESCRIPTION
NetBSD supports running Darwin binaries. This works on PowerPC ports, and i386 should be supported in the future. For now, most text based and X11 based program should work. Applications using the Quartz displaying system may work, but local display is not yet supported: running MacOS X's Quartz display server on NetBSD is a work in progress.

The Darwin compatibility feature is active for kernels compiled with the COMPAT_DARWIN, COMPAT_MACH, and EXEC_MACHO options enabled.

All Darwin binaries are dynamically linked. As COMPAT_DARWIN only emulates the Darwin system calls, you will need various Darwin userland files, such as the shared libraries and the dynamic linker. Theses files are kept in a "shadow root" directory, named /emul/darwin. Each time a Darwin binary has to use a file, it will look it up in /emul/darwin first. This feature is used to prevent conflict between native and foreign libraries and configuration files.

There are two ways of setting up the /emul/darwin tree.

1. The easiest way is to install the Darwin library package in pkgsrc/emulators/darwin_lib. This package uses files provided by the OpenDarwin project. Therefore, it does not contain Apple's MacOS X proprietary libraries, which are required in order to run any Quartz-based application. If you need some files not installed by the package, read on.

2. You can also install Darwin or MacOS X files in /emul/darwin by hand. To do this, you need a Darwin system. In order to know what libraries a program needs, just use the
        otool -L program
    command on Darwin. Alternatively, you can use ktrace(1) and kdump(1) to discover what files the program attempts to open.

Please note that you need a valid MacOS X license if you copy Apple proprietary libraries and programs from a MacOS X system.

SEE ALSO
kdump(1), ktrace(1), options(4)

AUTHORS
COMPAT_DARWIN and COMPAT_MACH layers were written by Emmanuel Dreyfus ⟨manu@NetBSD.org⟩ with some help from
Christos Zoulas ⟨christos@NetBSD.org⟩

EXEC_MACHO was integrated into NetBSD by
Christos Zoulas ⟨christos@NetBSD.org⟩.

The pkgsrc/emulators/darwin_lib package was created by
James Whitwell ⟨abacau@yahoo.com.au⟩.

BUGS
Many. COMPAT_DARWIN is still very experimental.

NAME

> `compat_freebsd` — setup procedure for running FreeBSD binaries

DESCRIPTION

> NetBSD supports running FreeBSD binaries. Most binaries should work, except programs that use FreeBSD-specific features. These include i386-specific calls, such as syscons utilities. The FreeBSD compatibility feature is active for kernels compiled with the `COMPAT_FREEBSD` option enabled.

> A lot of programs are dynamically linked. This means, that you will also need the FreeBSD shared libraries that the program depends on, and the runtime linker. Also, you will need to create a "shadow root" directory for FreeBSD binaries on your NetBSD system. This directory is named `/emul/freebsd`. Any file operations done by FreeBSD programs run under NetBSD will look in this directory first. So, if a FreeBSD program opens, for example, `/etc/passwd`, NetBSD will first try to open `/emul/freebsd/etc/passwd`, and if that does not exist open the 'real' `/etc/passwd` file. It is recommended that you install FreeBSD packages that include configuration files, etc under `/emul/freebsd`, to avoid naming conflicts with possible NetBSD counterparts. Shared libraries should also be installed in the shadow tree.

> Generally, you will need to look for the shared libraries that FreeBSD binaries depend on only the first few times that you install a FreeBSD program on your NetBSD system. After a while, you will have a sufficient set of FreeBSD shared libraries on your system to be able to run newly imported FreeBSD binaries without any extra work.

Setting up shared libraries

> How to get to know which shared libraries FreeBSD binaries need, and where to get them? Basically, there are 2 possibilities (when following these instructions: you will need to be root on your NetBSD system to do the necessary installation steps).

> 1. You have access to a FreeBSD system. In this case you can temporarily install the binary there, see what shared libraries it needs, and copy them to your NetBSD system. Example: you have just ftp-ed the FreeBSD binary of SimCity. Put it on the FreeBSD system you have access to, and check which shared libraries it needs by running 'ldd sim':

> >   me@freebsd% ldd /usr/local/lib/SimCity/res/sim
> >   /usr/local/lib/SimCity/res/sim:
> >   -lXext.6 => /usr/X11R6/lib/libXext.so.6.0 (0x100c1000)
> >   -lX11.6 => /usr/X11R6/lib/libX11.so.6.0 (0x100c9000)
> >   -lc.2 => /usr/lib/libc.so.2.1 (0x10144000)
> >   -lm.2 => /usr/lib/libm.so.2.0 (0x101a7000)
> >   -lgcc.261 => /usr/lib/libgcc.so.261.0 (0x101bf000)

> You would need go get all the files from the last column, and put them under `/emul/freebsd`. This means you eventually have these files on your NetBSD system:
>
> ```
> /emul/freebsd/usr/X11R6/lib/libXext.so.6.0
> /emul/freebsd/usr/X11R6/lib/libX11.so.6.0
> /emul/freebsd/usr/lib/libc.so.2.1
> /emul/freebsd/usr/lib/libm.so.2.0
> /emul/freebsd/usr/lib/libgcc.so.261.0
> ```

> Note that if you already have a FreeBSD shared library with a matching major revision number to the first column of the `ldd` output, you won't need to copy the file named in the last column to your system, the one you already have should work. It is advisable to copy the shared library anyway if it is a newer version, though. You can remove the old one. So, if you have these libraries on your system:

`/emul/freebsd/usr/lib/libc.so.2.0`

and you find that the ldd output for a new binary you want to install is:

−lc.2 => /usr/lib/libc.so.2.1 (0x10144000)

You won't need to worry about copying `/usr/lib/libc.so.2.1` too, because the program should work fine with the slightly older version. You can decide to replace the libc.so anyway, and that should leave you with:
`/emul/freebsd/usr/lib/libc.so.2.1`

Finally, you must make sure that you have the FreeBSD runtime linker and its config files on your system. You should copy these files from the FreeBSD system to their appropriate place on your NetBSD system (in the `/emul/freebsd` tree):
`usr/libexec/ld.so`
`var/run/ld.so.hints`

2.   You don't have access to a FreeBSD system. In that case, you should get the extra files you need from various ftp sites. Information on where to look for the various files is appended below. For now, let's assume you know where to get the files.

Retrieve the following files (from _one_ ftp site to avoid any version mismatches), and install them under `/emul/freebsd` (i.e. `foo/bar` is installed as `/emul/freebsd/foo/bar`):
`sbin/ldconfig`
`usr/bin/ldd`
`usr/lib/libc.so.x.y.z`
`usr/libexec/ld.so`

ldconfig and **ldd** don't necessarily need to be under `/emul/freebsd`, you can install them elsewhere in the system too. Just make sure they don't conflict with their NetBSD counterparts. A good idea would be to install them in `/usr/local/bin` as **ldconfig-freebsd** and **ldd-freebsd**.

Run the FreeBSD ldconfig program with directory arguments in which the FreeBSD runtime linker should look for shared libs. `/usr/lib` are standard, you could run like the following:

        me@netbsd% mkdir -p /emul/freebsd/var/run
        me@netbsd% touch /emul/freebsd/var/run/ld.so.hints
        me@netbsd% ldconfig-freebsd /usr/X11R6/lib /usr/local/lib

Note that argument directories of ldconfig are mapped to `/emul/freebsd/XXXX` by NetBSD's compat code, and should exist as such on your system. Make sure `/emul/freebsd/var/run/ld.so.hints` is existing when you run FreeBSD's ldconfig, if not, you may lose NetBSD's `/var/run/ld.so.hints`. FreeBSD **ldconfig** should be statically linked, so it doesn't need any shared libraries by itself. It will create the file `/emul/freebsd/var/run/ld.so.hints`. You should rerun the FreeBSD version of the ldconfig program each time you add a new shared library.

You should now be set up for FreeBSD binaries which only need a shared libc. You can test this by running the FreeBSD **ldd** on itself. Suppose that you have it installed as **ldd-freebsd**, it should produce something like:

        me@netbsd% ldd-freebsd 'which ldd-freebsd'
               /usr/local/bin/ldd-freebsd:
                      -lc.2 => /usr/lib/libc.so.2.1 (0x1001a000)

This being done, you are ready to install new FreeBSD binaries. Whenever you install a new FreeBSD program, you should check if it needs shared libraries, and if so, whether you have them installed in the `/emul/freebsd` tree. To do this, you run the FreeBSD version **ldd** on the new program, and watch its output. **ldd** (see also the manual page for ldd(1)) will print a list of shared libraries that the program depends on, in the form -l<majorname> => <fullname>.

If it prints "not found" instead of <fullname> it means that you need an extra library. Which library this is, is shown in <majorname>, which will be of the form XXXX.<N> You will need to find a libXXXX.so.<N>.<mm> on a FreeBSD ftp site, and install it on your system. The XXXX (name) and <N> (major revision number) should match; the minor number(s) <mm> are less important, though it is advised to take the most recent version.

3. In some cases, FreeBSD binary needs access to certain device file. For example, FreeBSD X server software needs FreeBSD /dev/ttyv0 for ioctls. In this case, create a symbolic link from /emul/freebsd/dev/ttyv0 to a wscons(4) device file like /dev/ttyE0. You will need to have at least **options WSDISPLAY_COMPAT_SYSCONS** and probably also **options WSDISPLAY_COMPAT_USL** in your kernel (see options(4) and wscons(4)).

Finding the necessary files

Note: the information below is valid as of the time this document was written (June, 1995), but certain details such as names of ftp sites, directories and distribution names may have changed by the time you read this.

The FreeBSD distribution is available on a lot of ftp sites. Sometimes the files are unpacked, and you can get the individual files you need, but mostly they are stored in distribution sets, usually consisting of subdirectories with gzipped tar files in them. The primary ftp sites for the distributions are:

        ftp.freebsd.org:/pub/FreeBSD

Mirror sites are described on:

        ftp.freebsd.org:/pub/FreeBSD/MIRROR.SITES

This distribution consists of a number of tar-ed and gzipped files, Normally, they're controlled by an install program, but you can retrieve files "by hand" too. The way to look something up is to retrieve all the files in the distribution, and "tar ztvf" through them for the file you need. Here is an example of a list of files that you might need.

```
Needed               Files

ld.so                2.0-RELEASE/bindist/bindist.??
ldconfig             2.0-RELEASE/bindist/bindist.??
ldd                  2.0-RELEASE/bindist/bindist.??
libc.so.2            2.0-RELEASE/bindist/bindist.??
libX11.so.6.0        2.0-RELEASE/XFree86-3.1/XFree86-3.1-bin.tar.gz
libX11.so.6.0        XFree86-3.1.1/X311bin.tgz
libXt.so.6.0         2.0-RELEASE/XFree86-3.1/XFree86-3.1-bin.tar.gz
libXt.so.6.0         XFree86-3.1.1/X311bin.tgz
```

The files called "bindist.??" are tar-ed, gzipped and split, so you can extract contents by "cat bindist.?? | tar zpxf -".

Extract the files from these gzipped tarfiles in your /emul/freebsd directory (possibly omitting or afterwards removing files you don't need), and you are done.

BUGS

The information about FreeBSD distributions may become outdated.

NAME

compat_ibcs2 — setup procedure for running iBCS2 binaries

DESCRIPTION

NetBSD supports running Intel Binary Compatibility Standard 2 (iBCS2) binaries. This only applies to i386 systems for now. Binaries are supported from SCO UNIX and other systems derived from AT&T System V.3 UNIX. iBCS2 support is only well tested using SCO binaries. XENIX binaries are also supported although not as well tested. SVR4 binaries are supported by the COMPAT_SVR4 option.

iBCS2 supports COFF, ELF, and x.out (XENIX) binary formats. Binaries from SCO OpenServer (version 5.x) are the only ELF binaries that have been tested. Most programs should work, but not ones that use or depend on:

> kernel internal data structures
> STREAMS drivers (other than TCP/IP sockets)
> local X displays (uses a STREAMS pipe)
> virtual 8086 mode

The iBCS2 compatibility feature is active for kernels compiled with the COMPAT_IBCS2 option enabled. If support for iBCS2 ELF executables is desired, the EXEC_ELF32 option should be enabled in addition to COMPAT_IBCS2.

Many COFF-format programs and most ELF-format programs are dynamically linked. This means that you will also need the shared libraries that the program depends on. Also, you will need to create a "shadow root" directory for iBCS2 binaries on your NetBSD system. This directory is named /emul/ibcs2. Any file operations done by iBCS2 programs run under NetBSD will look in this directory first. So, if an iBCS2 program opens, for example, /etc/passwd, NetBSD will first try to open /emul/ibcs2/etc/passwd, and if that does not exist open the 'real' /etc/passwd file. It is recommended that you install iBCS2 packages that include configuration files, etc. under /emul/ibcs2, to avoid naming conflicts with possible NetBSD counterparts. Shared libraries should also be installed in the shadow tree.

Generally, you will need to look for the shared libraries that iBCS2 binaries depend on only the first few times that you install an iBCS2 program on your NetBSD system. After a while, you will have a sufficient set of iBCS2 shared libraries on your system to be able to run newly imported iBCS2 binaries without any extra work.

Setting up shared libraries

How to get to know which shared libraries iBCS2 binaries need, and where to get them? Depending on the file type of the executable, there are different possibilities (when following these instructions: you will need to be root on your NetBSD system to do the necessary installation steps).

COFF binaries   You can simply copy all of the available shared libraries since they are fairly small in size. The COFF shared libraries are typically found in /shlib and can be obtained from the following sources:

> SCO UNIX version 3.x (aka ODT)
> SCO UNIX version 5.x (aka OpenServer)
> SCO UnixWare
> Many versions of SVR4.2/x86

After copying the shared libraries, you should have at least the following files on your system:

```
/emul/ibcs2/shlib/libc_s
/emul/ibcs2/shlib/libnsl_s
/emul/ibcs2/shlib/protlib_s
```

ELF binaries   You can simply copy all of the available shared libraries from the source system or distribution or use `ldd`(1) to determine the libraries required by a specific binary.

After copying the shared libraries, you should have at least the following files on your system:

```
/emul/ibcs2/usr/lib/libc.so.1
/emul/ibcs2/usr/lib/libcrypt.so
/emul/ibcs2/usr/lib/libndbm.so
/emul/ibcs2/usr/lib/libsocket.so.1
```

If you don't have access to a SCO system, you will need to get the extra files you need from a SCO distribution. As of January 1998, SCO sells a copy of SCO OpenServer (iBCS2) and/or SCO UnixWare (SVR4) for personal/non-commercial use for only the cost of shipping (about $20US). The distribution comes on an ISO9660-format CDROM which can be mounted and used to copy the necessary files.

Run the following script to copy the basic set of files from a SCO distribution directory mounted somewhere locally:

/usr/share/examples/emul/ibcs2/ibcs2-setup [directory]

You should now be set up for SCO binaries which only need standard shared libs.

BUGS

The information about SCO distributions may become outdated.

Attempting to a use a nameserver on the local host does not currently work due to an absurd shortcut taken by the iBCS2 network code (remember that there are no kernel sockets).

16/32/64 bit offsets may not be handled correctly in all cases.

NAME
compat_linux — setup procedure for running Linux binaries

DESCRIPTION
NetBSD supports running Linux binaries. This applies to amd64, arm, alpha, i386, m68k, and powerpc systems for now. Both the a.out and ELF binary formats are supported. Most programs should work, including the ones that use the Linux SVGAlib (only on i386). NetBSD amd64 can execute both 32bit and 64bit linux programs. Programs that will not work include some that use i386-specific calls, such as enabling virtual 8086 mode. Currently, sound is only partially supported for Linux binaries (they will probably run, depending on what Linux sound support features are used).

The Linux compatibility feature is active for kernels compiled with the COMPAT_LINUX option enabled. If support for Linux a.out executables is desired, the EXEC_AOUT option should be enabled in addition to option COMPAT_LINUX. Similarly, if support for Linux 32-bit and/or 64-bit ELF executables is desired, the EXEC_ELF32 and/or EXEC_ELF64 options (respectively) should be enabled in addition to COMPAT_LINUX.

A lot of programs are dynamically linked. This means that you will also need the Linux shared libraries that the program depends on, and the runtime linker. Also, you will need to create a "shadow root" directory for Linux binaries on your NetBSD system. This directory is named /emul/linux or /emul/linux32 for 32bit emulation on 64bit systems. Any file operations done by Linux programs run under NetBSD will look in this directory first. So, if a Linux program opens, for example, /etc/passwd, NetBSD will first try to open /emul/linux/etc/passwd, and if that does not exist open the 'real' /etc/passwd file. It is recommended that you install Linux packages that include configuration files, etc under /emul/linux, to avoid naming conflicts with possible NetBSD counterparts. Shared libraries should also be installed in the shadow tree. Filenames that start "/../" are only looked up in the real root.

Generally, you will need to look for the shared libraries that Linux binaries depend on only the first few times that you install a Linux program on your NetBSD system. After a while, you will have a sufficient set of Linux shared libraries on your system to be able to run newly imported Linux binaries without any extra work.

Setting up shared libraries
How to get to know which shared libraries Linux binaries need, and where to get them? Basically, there are 2 possibilities (when following these instructions: you will need to be root on your NetBSD system to do the necessary installation steps).

1. For i386, you can simply install the SuSE shared libs using the pkgsrc/emulators/suse100_linux package(s). On PowerPC ports, the pkgsrc/emulators/linuxppc_lib will install the needed libraries. If you are on other platforms, or this doesn't supply you with all the needed libraries, read on.

2. You have access to a Linux system. In this case you can temporarily install the binary there, see what shared libraries it needs, and copy them to your NetBSD system. Example: you have just ftp-ed the Linux binary of Doom. Put it on the Linux system you have access to, and check which shared libraries it needs by running 'ldd linuxxdoom':

   > (me@linux) ldd linuxxdoom
   >   libXt.so.3 (DLL Jump 3.1) => /usr/X11/lib/libXt.so.3.1.0
   >   libX11.so.3 (DLL Jump 3.1) => /usr/X11/lib/libX11.so.3.1.0
   >   libc.so.4 (DLL Jump 4.5pl26) => /lib/libc.so.4.6.29

   You would need go get all the files from the last column, and put them under /emul/linux, with the names in the first column as symbolic links pointing to them. This means you eventually have these files on your NetBSD system:

```
/emul/linux/usr/X11/lib/libXt.so.3.1.0
/emul/linux/usr/X11/lib/libXt.so.3 (symbolic link to the above)
/emul/linux/usr/X11/lib/libX11.so.3.1.0
/emul/linux/usr/X11/lib/libX11.so.3 (symbolic link to the above)
/emul/linux/lib/libc.so.4.6.29
/emul/linux/lib/libc.so.4 (symbolic link to the above)
```

Note that if you already have a Linux shared library with a matching major revision number to the first column of the `ldd`(1) output, you won't need to copy the file named in the last column to your system, the one you already have should work. It is advisable to copy the shared library anyway if it is a newer version, though. You can remove the old one, as long as you make the symbolic link point to the new one. So, if you have these libraries on your system:

```
/emul/linux/lib/libc.so.4.6.27
/emul/linux/lib/libc.so.4 -> /emul/linux/lib/libc.so.4.6.27
```

and you find that the **ldd** output for a new binary you want to install is:

libc.so.4 (DLL Jump 4.5pl26) => /lib/libc.so.4.6.29

you won't need to worry about copying `/lib/libc.so.4.6.29` too, because the program should work fine with the slightly older version. You can decide to replace the libc.so anyway, and that should leave you with:

```
/emul/linux/lib/libc.so.4.6.29
/emul/linux/lib/libc.so.4 -> /emul/linux/lib/libc.so.4.6.29
```

Please note that the symbolic link mechanism is *only* needed for Linux binaries, the NetBSD runtime linker takes care of looking for matching major revision numbers itself, you don't need to worry about that.

Finally, you must make sure that you have the Linux runtime linker and its config files on your system. You should copy these files from the Linux system to their appropriate place on your NetBSD system (in the `/emul/linux` tree):

```
/lib/ld.so
/etc/ld.so.cache
/etc/ld.so.config
```

3.   You don't have access to a Linux system. In that case, you should get the extra files you need from various ftp sites. Information on where to look for the various files is appended below. For now, let's assume you know where to get the files.

Retrieve the following files (from _one_ ftp site to avoid any version mismatches), and install them under `/emul/linux` (i.e. `/foo/bar` is installed as `/emul/linux/foo/bar`):

```
/sbin/ldconfig
/usr/bin/ldd
/lib/libc.so.x.y.z
/lib/ld.so
```

ldconfig and **ldd** don't necessarily need to be under `/emul/linux`, you can install them elsewhere in the system too. Just make sure they don't conflict with their NetBSD counterparts. A good idea would be to install them in `/usr/local/bin` as **ldconfig-linux** and **ldd-linux**.

Create the file `/emul/linux/etc/ld.so.conf`, containing the directories in which the Linux runtime linker should look for shared libs. It is a plain text file, containing a directory name on each line. `/lib` and `/usr/lib` are standard, you could add the following:

```
/usr/X11/lib
/usr/local/lib
```

Note that these are mapped to `/emul/linux/XXXX` by NetBSD's compat code, and should exist as such on your system.

Run the Linux **ldconfig** program. It should be statically linked, so it doesn't need any shared libraries by itself. It will create the file `/emul/linux/etc/ld.so.cache` You should rerun the Linux version of **ldconfig** each time you add a new shared library.

You should now be set up for Linux binaries which only need a shared libc. You can test this by running the Linux **ldd** on itself. Suppose that you have it installed as **ldd-linux**, it should produce something like:

> (me@netbsd) ldd-linux 'which ldd-linux'
>   libc.so.4 (DLL Jump 4.5pl26) => /lib/libc.so.4.6.29

This being done, you are ready to install new Linux binaries. Whenever you install a new Linux program, you should check if it needs shared libraries, and if so, whether you have them installed in the `/emul/linux` tree. To do this, you run the Linux **ldd** on the new program, and watch its output. **ldd** (see also the manual page for `ldd(1)`) will print a list of shared libraries that the program depends on, in the form ⟨majorname⟩ (⟨jumpversion⟩) => ⟨fullname⟩.

If it prints "not found" instead of ⟨fullname⟩ it means that you need an extra library. Which library this is, is shown in ⟨majorname⟩, which will be of the form libXXXX.so.<N> You will need to find a libXXXX.so.<N>.<mm> on a Linux ftp site, and install it on your system. The XXXX (name) and ⟨N⟩ (major revision number) should match; the minor number(s) ⟨mm⟩ are less important, though it is advised to take the most recent version.

4.   Set up linux specific devices:

> (me@netbsd) cd /usr/share/examples/emul/linux/etc
> (me@netbsd) cp LINUX_MAKEDEV /emul/linux/dev
> (me@netbsd) cd /emul/linux/dev && sh LINUX_MAKEDEV all

Setting up procfs

Some Linux binaries expect procfs to be mounted and that it would contain some Linux specific stuff. If it's not the case, they behave unexpectedly or even crash.

Mount procfs on NetBSD using following command:

> (me@netbsd) mount_procfs -o linux procfs /emul/linux/proc

You can also set up your system so that procfs is mounted automatically on system boot, by putting an entry like the one below to `/etc/fstab`.

> procfs /emul/linux/proc procfs ro,linux

See `mount_procfs`(8) for further information.

Setting up other files

Newer version of Linux use `/etc/nsswitch.conf` for network information, such as NIS and DNS. You must create or get a valid copy of this file and put it in `/emul/linux/etc`.

Finding the necessary files

Note: the information below is valid as of the time this document was first written (March, 1995), but certain details such as names of ftp sites, directories and distribution names may have changed by the time you read this.

Linux is distributed by several groups that make their own set of binaries that they distribute. Each distribution has its own name, like "Slackware" or "Yggdrasil". The distributions are available on a lot of ftp sites. Sometimes the files are unpacked, and you can get the individual files you need, but mostly they are stored in distribution sets, usually consisting of subdirectories with gzipped tar files in them. The primary ftp sites for the distributions are:

```
sunsite.unc.edu:/pub/Linux/distributions
tsx-11.mit.edu:/pub/linux/distributions
```

Some European mirrors:

```
ftp.luth.se:/pub/linux/distributions
ftp.demon.co.uk:/pub/linux/distributions
src.doc.ic.ac.uk:/packages/linux/distributions
```

For simplicity, let's concentrate on Slackware here. This distribution consists of a number of subdirectories, containing separate packages. Normally, they're controlled by an install program, but you can retrieve files "by hand" too. First of all, you will need to look in the contents subdir of the distribution. You will find a lot of small textfiles here describing the contents of the separate packages. The fastest way to look something up is to retrieve all the files in the contents subdirectory, and grep through them for the file you need. Here is an example of a list of files that you might need, and in which contents-file you will find it by grepping through them:

```
Needed                    Package

ld.so                     ldso
ldconfig                  ldso
ldd                       ldso
libc.so.4                 shlibs
libX11.so.6.0             xf_lib
libXt.so.6.0              xf_lib
libX11.so.3               oldlibs
libXt.so.3                oldlibs
```

So, in this case, you will need the packages ldso, shlibs, xf_lib and oldlibs. In each of the contents-files for these packages, look for a line saying "PACKAGE LOCATION", it will tell you on which 'disk' the package is, in our case it will tell us in which subdirectory we need to look. For our example, we would find the following locations:

```
Package                   Location

ldso                      diska2
shlibs                    diska2
oldlibs                   diskx6
xf_lib                    diskx9
```

The locations called diskXX refer to the slakware/XX subdirectories of the distribution, others may be found in the contrib subdirectory. In this case, we could now retrieve the packages we need by retrieving the following files (relative to the root of the Slackware distribution tree):

```
slakware/a2/ldso.tgz
slakware/a2/shlibs.tgz
slakware/x6/oldlibs/tgz
slakware/x9/xf_lib.tgz
```

Extract the files from these gzipped tarfiles in your /emul/linux directory (possibly omitting or afterwards removing files you don't need), and you are done.

Programs using SVGAlib

SVGAlib binaries require some extra care. You need to have **options WSDISPLAY_COMPAT_USL** in your kernel (see `wscons(4)`), and you will also have to create some symbolic links in the `/emul/linux/dev` directory, namely:

`/emul/linux/dev/console` -> `/dev/tty`

`/emul/linux/dev/mouse` -> whatever device your mouse is connected to

`/emul/linux/dev/ttyS0` -> `/dev/tty00`

`/emul/linux/dev/ttyS1` -> `/dev/tty01`

Be warned: the first link mentioned here makes SVGAlib binaries work, but may confuse others, so you may have to remove it again at some point.

BUGS

The information about Linux distributions may become outdated.

Absolute pathnames pointed to by symbolic links are only looked up in the shadow root when the symbolic link itself was found by an absolute pathname inside the shadow root. This is not consistent.

Linux executables cannot handle directory offset cookies > 32 bits. Should such an offset occur, you will see the message "linux_getdents: dir offset too large for emulated program". Currently, this can only happen on NFS mounted file systems, mounted from servers that return offsets with information in the upper 32 bits. These errors should rarely happen, but can be avoided by mounting this file system with offset translation enabled. See the **−X** option to `mount_nfs(8)`. The **−2** option to `mount_nfs(8)` will also have the desired effect, but is less preferable.

NAME
compat_netbsd32 — setup procedure for 32-bit compatibility on 64-bit platform

DESCRIPTION
The **compat_netbsd32** module allows NetBSD/sparc64 to run NetBSD/sparc executables, and NetBSD/amd64 to run NetBSD/i386 executables.

To use **compat_netbsd32**, one must either have COMPAT_NETBSD32 and EXEC_ELF32 in the kernel, or load the compat_netbsd32 and exec_netbsd32 kernel modules.

Static executables typically need no additional setup. Dynamic binaries require the dynamic linker plus shared libraries. Most of these files will need to be placed under /emul/netbsd32.

The easiest method of installing support for these is via the emulators/netbsd32_compat14, emulators/netbsd32_compat15, and emulators/netbsd32_compat16 packages, provided in the NetBSD packages collection. These install 32-bit a.out and ELF compatibility libraries, respectively. The details of what is actually necessary for correct operation are given below. This obviously is handled by the emulator packages.

For a.out compatibility, /usr/libexec/ld.so from a 32-bit distribution is required to exist as /emul/netbsd32/usr/libexec/ld.so.   For   32-bit   ELF   compatibility, /usr/libexec/ld.elf_so needs to be in /emul/netbsd32/usr/libexec/ld.elf_so.

The shared libraries for a.out binaries do not live under the /emul/netbsd32 directory, but under the /emul/aout directory, where the a.out dynamic linker will find them.

BUGS
A list of things which fail to work in compatibility mode should be here.

IPC is not well supported.

sysctl(3) is not well supported.

NAME

compat_osf1 — setup procedure for running OSF/1 binaries

DESCRIPTION

NetBSD supports running OSF/1 (a.k.a Digital Unix, a.k.a. Tru64) binaries on NetBSD/alpha systems. Most programs should work, including the ones that use the shared object libraries. Programs that make direct MACH system calls will not work. The OSF/1 compatibility feature is active for kernels compiled with the COMPAT_OSF1 option enabled (see options(4)).

To run dynamically linked programs, you will need the OSF/1 shared libraries, runtime linker, and certain configuration files found in /etc. These are installed in a "shadow root" directory called /emul/osf1. Any file operations done by OSF/1 programs run under NetBSD will look in this directory first, and fall back to the file system proper. So, if an OSF/1 program opens /etc/svc.conf, NetBSD will first try to open /emul/osf1/etc/svc.conf, and if that file does not exist it will then try /etc/svc.conf. Shared libraries and configuration specific to OSF/1 should be installed in the shadow tree.

Setting up /emul/osf1

The simple technique is to install pkgsrc/emulators/osf1_lib. (You may also want to install pkgsrc/www/navigator and/or pkgsrc/www/communicator.)

Alternatively, if you have access to an OSF/1 machine and if the licensing details permit, you can copy the contents of:

```
/shlib
/usr/shlib
/etc/sia
/usr/lib/X11/locale
```

(The latter is required to run Netscape Navigator or Communicator.)

Also copy

```
/etc/svc.conf
/usr/ccs/lib/cmplrs/otabase/libots.so
/sbin/loader
```

Or, simply NFS mount the appropriate directories under /emul/osf1.

SEE ALSO

config(1), options(4)

BUGS

Your hostname(1) *must* contain a dot *or* your resolv.conf(5) must contain a search line. Without one of those, the OSF/1 resolver will die and no hostname resolution will be possible.

Certain values in /emul/osf1/etc/svc.conf can cause programs to fail with "Bad system call".

Pathnames pointed to by symbolic links are not looked up in the shadow root when running an OSF/1 executable. This is not consistent.

NAME

> `compat_pecoff` — setup procedure for running Win32 applications (a.k.a. PEACE)

DESCRIPTION

> NetBSD has partial support for running Win32 applications. This manual page describes how to run Win32 (and hopefully WinCE in the future) applications on NetBSD. Note that PE (Portable Executable) is a Microsoft extension to the COFF executable file format.

BRIEF INTRODUCTION TO THE WIN32 API

> The Win32 API is an application program interface (API) for 32-bit applications for Microsoft Windows 9x/Me/NT/2000. The Win32 API is provided via a set of core DLLs (Dynamically Linked Libraries), including `KERNEL32.DLL`, `USER32.DLL` and `GDI32.DLL`.

> The structure of these core DLLs and the interface between the operating system kernel and userland is implementation-dependent. Each implementation must provide its own core DLLs. Therefore, these DLLs are different for Windows 98 and Windows 2000.

> `KERNEL32.DLL` is used by all Win32 applications; it provides basic kernel interface such as file access, process control, memory management etc.

> `USER32.DLL` is used by most Win32 applications; it provides basic userland functions such as GUI and messaging.

> `GDI32.DLL` provides functions to draw images and characters.

> `SHELL32.DLL` is the Windows shell support, including file association.

> `COMCTL32.DLL` and `COMDLG32.DLL` are GUI components which are commonly used in many applications. `WSOCK32.DLL` provides the networking API. `DDRAW.DLL`, `DSOUND.DLL`, and `DINPUT.DLL` are for DirectX.

> Most other DLLs are compatible among all the implementations and therefore can be shared.

NETBSD SUPPORT FOR THE WIN32 API

> NetBSD support for Win32 applications is developed by the PEACE Project, and is under active development. Currently it can run some console applications including the Windows 2000 `CMD.EXE` as well as a small number of GUI applications.

> The PEACE system consists of three parts: the kernel part, the dynamic loader and the core DLLs.

> The kernel part provides loading and executing PE/COFF format executable binaries; i.e. it extends the `execve`(2) system call, just like other binary compatibility options. It is activated by enabling the `COMPAT_PECOFF` kernel option (see `options`(4)). The dynamic loader is the PE/COFF version of `ld.so`(1). It reads the file header of the executable binary, and loads required DLLs.

> The core DLLs implement the actual Win32 API functions as described in the previous section. Since the kernel part does not provide any additional system calls and other kernel interface, all Win32 API functions are implemented on top of the existing NetBSD APIs (system calls and standard libraries such as `libc` and `libX11`).

PREPARING THE PEACE DYNAMIC LOADER AND CORE DLLS

> Development snapshots of the dynamic loader can be retrieved from `http://sourceforge.net/project/showfiles.php?group_id=21711`. The file name of snapshot is `peace-i386-ld.so.dll-*.gz`, where '*' is replaced with the snapshot date. Simply `gunzip`(1) the file and copy the resulting file to `/usr/libexec/ld.so.dll`.

COMPAT_PECOFF (8)   NetBSD   COMPAT_PECOFF (8)

The   core   DLLs   archives   can   also   be   retrieved   from `http://sourceforge.net/project/showfiles.php?group_id=21711` as `peace-i386-sysdll-*.tgz` and `peace-i386-dll-*.tgz`. The dynamic loader searches for required DLLs from the following directories:

1.   directories listed in the environment variable `DLLPATH` (separated by colons)
2.   `/usr/lib`
3.   the directory where the executable is located

The core DLLs are required to be installed into `/usr/lib`, in order to use `CMD.EXE` (or another Win32 application) as the login shell.

According to the development phase, some other PEACE-specific DLLs might be distributed separately. Please check the announcements on the Web or the mailing list.

Other DLLs can be stored in arbitrary directories specified by the environment variable `DLLPATH`. To use Windows NT/2000 DLLs installed on a separate partition of the local disk directly for NetBSD, type:

```
mount -t ntfs -o ro /dev/wd0h /nthd
setenv DLLPATH /nthd/WINNT/SYSTEM32:/nthd/WINNT
```

(assuming `csh`(1)).

SEE ALSO
config(1), gunzip(1), ld.so(1), execve(2), options(4), modload(8), mount_ntfs(8), `http://chiharu.hauN.org/peace/`

HISTORY
Kernel support for PE/COFF appeared in NetBSD 1.5.

AUTHORS
Implementation of Win32 binary compatibility support for NetBSD was started by Masaru OKI. The PEACE Project is founded by him to implement the enormous number of functions in the Win32/WinCE API.

BUGS
–   Currently only the i386 platform is supported.
–   Most functions in Win32 are missing.
–   The dynamic loader and core DLLs are not provided in the standard distribution of NetBSD. This is because a cross-compiler is required to build them.

NAME

    `compat_sunos` — setup procedure for m68k, sparc and sparc64 architectures

DESCRIPTION

    NetBSD/sparc64, NetBSD/sparc and some of the NetBSD/m68k architectures can run SunOS executables. Most executables will work.

    The exceptions include programs that use the SunOS kvm library, and various system calls, `ioctl`()'s, or kernel semantics that are difficult to emulate. The number of reasons why a program might fail to work is (thankfully) longer than the number of programs that fail to run.

    Static executables will normally run without any extra setup. This procedure details the directories and files that must be set up to allow dynamically linked executables to work.

    The files you need are on your SunOS machine. You need to worry about the legal issues of ensuring that you have a right to use the required files on your machine. On your NetBSD machine, do the following:

    1.   `mkdir -p /emul/sunos/usr/lib /emul/sunos/usr/5lib`

    2.   `cp SunOS:/usr/lib/lib*.so.*.* NetBSD:/emul/sunos/usr/lib`

    3.   `cp SunOS:/usr/5lib/lib*.so.*.* NetBSD:/emul/sunos/usr/5lib`

    4.   `cp SunOS:/usr/lib/ld.so NetBSD:/emul/sunos/usr/lib/ld.so`

    5.   If you ever expect to use YP, you will want to create a link:
        `ln -s /var/run/ypbind.lock /etc/ypbind.lock`

    Alternatively, you can use an NFS mount to accomplish the same effect. On your NetBSD machine, do the following:

    1.   `mkdir -p /emul/sunos/usr`

    2.   `mount SunOS:/usr /emul/sunos/usr`

    This will place the SunOS libraries on your NetBSD machine in a location where the SunOS compatibility code will look for first, where they do not conflict with the standard libraries.

NOTES

    When using `compat_sunos` on NetBSD/sparc64, the `COMPAT_NETBSD32` option must also be used.

BUGS

    A list of things which fail to work in compatibility mode should be here.

    SunOS executables can not handle directory offset cookies > 32 bits. Should such an offset occur, you will see the message "sunos_getdents: dir offset too large for emulated program". Currently, this can only happen on NFS mounted filesystems, mounted from servers that return offsets with information in the upper 32 bits. These errors should rarely happen, but can be avoided by mounting this filesystem with offset translation enabled. See the **-X** option to `mount_nfs`(8). The **-2** option to `mount_nfs`(8) will also have the desired effect, but is less preferable.

    The NetBSD/sparc64 support is less complete than the other ports.

COMPAT_SVR4 (8)   NetBSD   COMPAT_SVR4 (8)

NAME

    compat_svr4 — setup procedure for running SVR4/iBCS2 binaries **compat_svr4_32** — setup proce-
dure for running 32-bit SVR4/iBCS2 binaries

DESCRIPTION

    NetBSD supports running SVR4/iBCS2 binaries. This code has been tested on i386 (with binaries from SCO
OpenServer and XENIX), m68k (with binaries from AMIX) and sparc (with binaries from Solaris) systems.
Most programs should work, but not ones that use or depend on:

> kernel internal data structures
> the `/proc` filesystem
> the ticotsord loopback RPC mechanism (NIS uses this)
> sound and video interfaces
> threads (ttsession uses threads)
> the streams administrative driver

    The SVR4 compatibility feature is active for kernels compiled with the `COMPAT_SVR4` option enabled.
Since support for ELF executables is included only if the kernel is compiled with the `EXEC_ELF32` or
`EXEC_ELF64` options enabled, kernels which include `COMPAT_SVR4` should also typically include
`EXEC_ELF32` (for 32-bit ELF support) and/or `EXEC_ELF64` (for 64-bit ELF support).

    Another compatibility feature is `COMPAT_SVR4_32`, which allows the execution of 32-bit SVR4 binaries
on a machine with a 64-bit kernel. This requires `EXEC_ELF32` and `COMPAT_NETBSD32` options as well as
`COMPAT_SVR4`. It is configured the same way as `COMPAT_SVR4` but uses the `/emul/svr4_32` directory instead of `/emul/svr4`. But typically, `/emul/svr4_32` can be made to point to `/emul/svr4` if
the operating system donating the libraries has support for both 32-bit and 64-bit binaries.

    Execution of 32-bit SVR4 binaries on a machine with a 32-bit kernel uses `COMPAT_SVR4`, not
`COMPAT_SVR4_32`.

    Most SVR4 programs are dynamically linked. This means that you will also need the shared libraries that the
program depends on and the runtime linker. Also, you will need to create a "shadow root" directory for
SVR4 binaries on your NetBSD system. This directory is named `/emul/svr4`. Any file operations done by
SVR4 programs run under NetBSD will look in this directory first. So, if a SVR4 program opens, for example, `/etc/passwd`, NetBSD will first try to open `/emul/svr4/etc/passwd`, and if that does not exist
open the 'real' `/etc/passwd` file. It is recommended that you install SVR4 packages that include configuration files, etc under `/emul/svr4`, to avoid naming conflicts with possible NetBSD counterparts. Shared
libraries should also be installed in the shadow tree.

    The simplest way to set up your system for SVR4 binaries is:
1.   Make the necessary directories:

> (me@netbsd) mkdir -p /emul/svr4/{dev,etc}
> (me@netbsd) mkdir -p /emul/svr4/usr/{bin,lib,ucblib}
> (me@netbsd) mkdir -p /emul/svr4/usr/openwin/{bin,lib}
> (me@netbsd) mkdir -p /emul/svr4/usr/dt/{bin,lib}

2.   Copy files from an svr4 system:

> (me@svr4) cd /usr/lib
> (me@svr4) tar -cf - . | \
>   rsh netbsd 'cd /emul/svr4/usr/lib && tar -xpf -'

        (me@svr4) cd /usr/ucblib
        (me@svr4) tar -cf - . | \
                rsh netbsd 'cd /emul/svr4/usr/ucblib && tar -xpf -'

If you are running openwindows:

        (me@svr4) cd /usr/openwin/lib
        (me@svr4) tar -cf - . | \
                rsh netbsd 'cd /emul/svr4/usr/openwin/lib && tar -xpf -'
        (me@svr4) cd /usr/dt/lib
        (me@svr4) tar -cf - . | \
                rsh netbsd 'cd /emul/svr4/usr/dt/lib && tar -xpf -'

3.   You will also probably need the timezone files from your Solaris system, otherwise emulated binaries will run on UTC time.

        (me@netbsd) mkdir -p /emul/svr4/usr/share/lib/zoneinfo
        (me@netbsd) mkdir -p /emul/svr4/etc/default
        (me@svr4) cd /usr/share/lib/zoneinfo
        (me@solaris) tar -cf -. | \
                rsh netbsd 'cd /emul/svr4/usr/share/lib/zoneinfo &&
                tar -xpf -'
        (me@netbsd) echo TZ=US/Pacific > /emul/svr4/etc/default/init

4.   Set up the configuration files and devices:

        (me@netbsd) cd /usr/share/examples/emul/svr4/etc
        (me@netbsd) cp netconfig nsswitch.conf /emul/svr4/etc
        (me@netbsd) cp SVR4_MAKEDEV /emul/svr4/dev
        (me@netbsd) cd /emul/svr4/dev && sh SVR4_MAKEDEV all

As the major number allocated for emulation of SVR4 devices may vary between NetBSD platforms, the SVR4_MAKEDEV script uses the uname(1) command to determine the architecture the devices nodes are being created for; this can be overridden by setting the MACHINE environment variable accordingly.

An alternative method is to mount a whole SVR4 partition in /emul/svr4 and then override with other mounts /emul/svr4/etc and /emul/svr4/dev.

BUGS

Many system calls are still not emulated. The streams emulation is incomplete (socketpair does not work yet).

Most SVR4 executables can not handle directory offset cookies > 32 bits. More recent ones, compiled for large file support (Solaris 2.6 and up) can. With older programs, you will see the message "svr4_getdents: dir offset too large for emulated program"" when this happens. Currently, this can only happen on NFS mounted filesystems, mounted from servers that return offsets with information in the upper 32 bits. These errors should rarely happen, but can be avoided by mounting this filesystem with offset translation enabled. See the **−X** option to mount_nfs(8). The **−2** option to mount_nfs(8) will also have the desired effect, but is less preferable.

NAME
compat_ultrix — setup procedure for ULTRIX compatibility on MIPS and VAX architectures

DESCRIPTION
NetBSD/mips and NetBSD/vax architectures can run Risc ULTRIX and VAX ULTRIX executables, respectively. However, you have to worry about the legal issues of ensuring that you have a right to use any ULTRIX binaries on your machine.

Most executables will work. The exceptions include programs that use proprietary, ULTRIX-specific features (LAT, CI support, DECnet support) and various system calls, **ioctl**()'s, or ULTRIX kernel semantics that are difficult to emulate (e.g. ULTRIX packetfilter) or buggy (e.g. ULTRIX NIS).

All ULTRIX executables are static, so no shared libraries are required for ULTRIX compatibility. However, ULTRIX is based on a 4.3 BSD alpha release. ULTRIX commands and libraries are often much older than their NetBSD or even SunOS 4.x equivalents, and may require incompatible configuration files.

SYSTEM CONFIGURATION FILES
Set up `resolv.conf` and `svc.conf` as below:

```
# mkdir -p /emul/ultrix/etc
# cd /emul/ultrix/etc
# egrep 'domain|nameserver' /etc/resolv.conf > ./resolv.conf
# cp -p /usr/share/examples/emul/ultrix/etc/* ./
```

/etc/resolv.conf
The ULTRIX resolver library only understands **domain** and **nameserver** lines in `resolv.conf`(5). You should create a copy of `/etc/resolv.conf` containing only those commands and put it in `/emul/ultrix/etc/resolv.conf`. Note that the domain search order used by ULTRIX executables may not be the same as native binaries; there is no good way around this.

/etc/svc.conf
ULTRIX uses `/etc/svc.conf` to select an ordered search of NIS, Hesiod, or local flat-file mappings. You should create an `/emul/ultrix/etc/svc.conf` specifying either local files or bind (DNS) lookups for all ULTRIX name services.

SEE ALSO
`resolv.conf`(5)

BUGS
RISC ULTRIX NIS (YP) is known to not work. The ULTRIX NIS libraries have a consistent endian-ness bug. ULTRIX NIS client will not inter-operate with the NetBSD `ypbind`(8) process. The only workaround is to use `/etc/svc.conf` to disable NIS (YP).

The ndbm hashed-password file used by ULTRIX are incompatible with the db hashed-password file used by NetBSD. There is no good solution for this. NIS would be a good one, if ULTRIX NIS worked.

The API used by Xservers to talk to the kernel is currently compatible with ULTRIX 4.1. An implementation of the ULTRIX 4.2 Xws interface (used by X11R6) is in progress.

A complete list of things which fail to work in ULTRIX compatibility mode should be added here.

NAME
    comsat — biff server

SYNOPSIS
    comsat [**-l**]

DESCRIPTION
    comsat is the server process which receives reports of incoming mail and notifies users if they have requested this service. **comsat** receives messages on a datagram port associated with the "biff" service specification (see services(5) and inetd(8)). The one line messages are of the form:

        user@mailbox-offset

    If the *user* specified is logged in to the system and the associated terminal has the owner execute bit turned on (by a "biff y"), the *offset* is used as a seek offset into the appropriate mailbox file and the first 7 lines or 560 characters of the message are printed on the user's terminal. Lines which appear to be part of the message header other than the "From" or "Subject" lines are not included in the displayed message.

OPTIONS
    The **comsat** program supports this option:

    -l   The **-l** option turns on syslogd(8) log messages.

FILES
    To find out who's logged on and on what terminals **comsat** consults:

    /var/run/utmp
    /var/run/utmpx

SEE ALSO
    biff(1), inetd(8), syslogd(8)

HISTORY
    The **comsat** command appeared in 4.2 BSD.

BUGS
    The message header filtering is prone to error. The density of the information presented is near the theoretical minimum.

    Users should be notified of mail which arrives on other machines than the one to which they are currently logged in.

    The notification should appear in a separate window so it does not mess up the screen.

    comsat runs as root so that it can open the users maildrop.

NAME
      cpuctl — program to control CPUs

SYNOPSIS
      cpuctl *command* [*arguments*]

DESCRIPTION
      The **cpuctl** command can be used to control and inspect the state of CPUs in the system.

      The first argument, *command*, specifies the action to take. Valid commands are:

      identify *cpu*   Output information on the specified CPU's features and capabilities. Not available on all architectures.

      list   For each CPU in the system, display the current state and time of the last state change.

      offline *cpuno*   Set the specified CPU off line.

            Unbound LWPs (lightweight processes) will not be executed on the CPU while it is off line. Bound LWPs will continue to be executed on the CPU, and device interrupts routed to the CPU will continue to be handled. A future release of the system may allow device interrupts to be re-routed away from individual CPUs.

            At least one CPU in the system must remain on line.

      online *cpuno*   Set the specified CPU on line, making it available to run unbound LWPs.

FILES
      /dev/cpuctl control device

SEE ALSO
      psrset(8), schedctl(8)

HISTORY
      The **cpuctl** command first appeared in NetBSD 5.0.

NAME

    crash — examine and debug system images

SYNOPSIS

    crash [**-M** *core*] [**-N** *system*]

DESCRIPTION

The **crash** command is used to examine and debug system images.

If run without any arguments, **crash** operates on the running system.

The options are as follows:

-M *core*   Operate on the specified crash dump instead of the default /dev/mem. Crash dumps should be from the same version of the system and same machine architecture as the running version of **crash**, and must be uncompressed.

-N *kernel*   Extract the name list from the specified kernel instead of the default /dev/ksyms.

The command syntax used by **crash** is the same as the in-kernel debugger. See the ddb(4) manual page for more information.

Operations and facilities that require a running system, such as breakpoints, are not supported by **crash**.

crash does not provide pagination. However, by using the pipe symbol, output may be sent to commands available from the shell. For example:

```
crash> ps | more
crash> ps | grep ioflush
```

SEE ALSO

ps(1), vmstat(1), ddb(4), pstat(8)

HISTORY

The **crash** command appeared in NetBSD 6.0.

NAME
crash — UNIX system failures

DESCRIPTION
This section explains a bit about system crashes and (very briefly) how to analyze crash dumps.

When the system crashes voluntarily it prints a message of the form

        panic: why i gave up the ghost

on the console, takes a dump on a mass storage peripheral, and then invokes an automatic reboot procedure as described in `reboot`(8). Unless some unexpected inconsistency is encountered in the state of the file systems due to hardware or software failure, the system will then resume multi-user operations.

The system has a large number of internal consistency checks; if one of these fails, then it will panic with a very short message indicating which one failed. In many instances, this will be the name of the routine which detected the error, or a two-word description of the inconsistency. A full understanding of most panic messages requires perusal of the source code for the system.

The most common cause of system failures is hardware failure, which can reflect itself in different ways. Here are the messages which are most likely, with some hints as to causes. Left unstated in all cases is the possibility that hardware or software error produced the message in some unexpected way.

iinit This cryptic panic message results from a failure to mount the root filesystem during the bootstrap process. Either the root filesystem has been corrupted, or the system is attempting to use the wrong device as root filesystem. Usually, an alternative copy of the system binary or an alternative root filesystem can be used to bring up the system to investigate.

Can't exec /sbin/init
This is not a panic message, as reboots are likely to be futile. Late in the bootstrap procedure, the system was unable to locate and execute the initialization process, `init`(8). The root filesystem is incorrect or has been corrupted, or the mode or type of `/sbin/init` forbids execution.

IO err in push
hard IO err in swap
The system encountered an error trying to write to the paging device or an error in reading critical information from a disk drive. The offending disk should be fixed if it is broken or unreliable.

realloccg: bad optim
ialloc: dup alloc
alloccgblk:cyl groups corrupted
ialloccg: map corrupted
free: freeing free block
free: freeing free frag
ifree: freeing free inode
alloccg: map corrupted
These panic messages are among those that may be produced when filesystem inconsistencies are detected. The problem generally results from a failure to repair damaged filesystems after a crash, hardware failures, or other condition that should not normally occur. A filesystem check will normally correct the problem.

timeout table overflow
This really shouldn't be a panic, but until the data structure involved is made to be extensible, running out of entries causes a crash. If this happens, make the timeout table bigger.

trap type %d, code = %x, v = %x
> An unexpected trap has occurred within the system; the trap types are:

> | | |
> |---|---|
> | 0 | bus error |
> | 1 | address error |
> | 2 | illegal instruction |
> | 3 | divide by zero |
> | 4 | *chk* instruction |
> | 5 | *trapv* instruction |
> | 6 | privileged instruction |
> | 7 | trace trap |
> | 8 | MMU fault |
> | 9 | simulated software interrupt |
> | 10 | format error |
> | 11 | FP coprocessor fault |
> | 12 | coprocessor fault |
> | 13 | simulated AST |

The favorite trap type in system crashes is trap type 8, indicating a wild reference. "code" (hex) is the concatenation of the MMU status register (see <hp300/cpu.h>) in the high 16 bits and the 68020 special status word (see the 68020 manual, page 6-17) in the low 16. "v" (hex) is the virtual address which caused the fault. Additionally, the kernel will dump about a screenful of semi-useful information. "pid" (decimal) is the process id of the process running at the time of the exception. Note that if we panic in an interrupt routine, this process may not be related to the panic. "ps" (hex) is the 68020 processor status register "ps". "pc" (hex) is the value of the program counter saved on the hardware exception frame. It may *not* be the PC of the instruction causing the fault. "sfc" and "dfc" (hex) are the 68020 source/destination function codes. They should always be one. "p0" and "p1" are the VAX-like region registers. They are of the form:

> <length> '@' <kernel VA>

where both are in hex. Following these values are a dump of the processor registers (hex). Finally, is a dump of the stack (user/kernel) at the time of the offense.

init died
> The system initialization process has exited. This is bad news, as no new users will then be able to log in. Rebooting is the only fix, so the system just does it right away.

out of mbufs: map full
> The network has exhausted its private page map for network buffers. This usually indicates that buffers are being lost, and rather than allow the system to slowly degrade, it reboots immediately. The map may be made larger if necessary.

That completes the list of panic types you are likely to see.

When the system crashes it writes (or at least attempts to write) an image of memory into the back end of the dump device, usually the same as the primary swap area. After the system is rebooted, the program savecore(8) runs and preserves a copy of this core image and the current system in a specified directory for later perusal. See savecore(8) for details.

To analyze a dump you should begin by running adb(1) with the **−k** flag on the system load image and core dump. If the core image is the result of a panic, the panic message is printed. Normally the command "$c" will provide a stack trace from the point of the crash and this will provide a clue as to what went wrong. For more details consult *Using ADB to Debug the UNIX Kernel.*

SEE ALSO

adb(1), reboot(8)

MC68020 32-bit Microprocessor User's Manual.

Using ADB to Debug the UNIX Kernel.

4.3BSD for the HP300.

HISTORY

A **crash** man page appeared in Version 6 AT&T UNIX.

NAME

    crash — UNIX system failures

DESCRIPTION

    This section explains what happens when the system crashes and (very briefly) how to analyze crash dumps.

    When the system crashes voluntarily it prints a message of the form

```
panic: why i gave up the ghost
```

on the console, takes a dump on a mass storage peripheral, and then invokes an automatic reboot procedure as described in reboot(8). (If auto-reboot is disabled on the front panel of the machine the system will simply halt at this point.) Unless some unexpected inconsistency is encountered in the state of the file systems due to hardware or software failure, the system will then resume multi-user operations.

    The system has a large number of internal consistency checks; if one of these fails, then it will panic with a very short message indicating which one failed. In many instances, this will be the name of the routine which detected the error, or a two-word description of the inconsistency. A full understanding of most panic messages requires perusal of the source code for the system.

    The most common cause of system failures is hardware failure, which can reflect itself in different ways. Here are the messages which are most likely, with some hints as to causes. Left unstated in all cases is the possibility that hardware or software error produced the message in some unexpected way.

iinit   This cryptic panic message results from a failure to mount the root filesystem during the bootstrap process. Either the root filesystem has been corrupted, or the system is attempting to use the wrong device as root filesystem. Usually, an alternative copy of the system binary or an alternative root filesystem can be used to bring up the system to investigate.

Can't exec /sbin/init

        This is not a panic message, as reboots are likely to be futile. Late in the bootstrap procedure, the system was unable to locate and execute the initialization process, init(8). The root filesystem is incorrect or has been corrupted, or the mode or type of /sbin/init forbids execution.

IO err in push

hard IO err in swap

        The system encountered an error trying to write to the paging device or an error in reading critical information from a disk drive. The offending disk should be fixed if it is broken or unreliable.

realloccg: bad optim

ialloc: dup alloc

alloccgblk: cyl groups corrupted

ialloccg: map corrupted

free: freeing free block

free: freeing free frag

ifree: freeing free inode

alloccg: map corrupted

        These panic messages are among those that may be produced when filesystem inconsistencies are detected. The problem generally results from a failure to repair damaged filesystems after a crash, hardware failures, or other condition that should not normally occur. A filesystem check will normally correct the problem.

timeout table overflow

        This really shouldn't be a panic, but until the data structure involved is made to be extensible, running out of entries causes a crash. If this happens, make the timeout table bigger.

KSP not valid

SBI fault

CHM? in kernel
> These indicate either a serious bug in the system or, more often, a glitch or failing hardware. If SBI faults recur, check out the hardware or call field service. If the other faults recur, there is likely a bug somewhere in the system, although these can be caused by a flakey processor. Run processor microdiagnostics.

machine check %x: *description*
> machine dependent machine-check information
>> Machine checks are different on each type of CPU. Most of the internal processor registers are saved at the time of the fault and are printed on the console. For most processors, there is one line that summarizes the type of machine check. Often, the nature of the problem is apparent from this message and/or the contents of key registers. The VAX Hardware Handbook should be consulted, and, if necessary, your friendly field service people should be informed of the problem.

trap type %d, code=%x, pc=%x
> A unexpected trap has occurred within the system; the trap types are:

0	reserved addressing fault
1	privileged instruction fault
2	reserved operand fault
3	bpt instruction fault
4	xfc instruction fault
5	system call trap
6	arithmetic trap
7	ast delivery trap
8	segmentation fault
9	protection fault
10	trace trap
11	compatibility mode fault
12	page fault
13	page table fault

> The favorite trap types in system crashes are trap types 8 and 9, indicating a wild reference. The code is the referenced address, and the pc at the time of the fault is printed. These problems tend to be easy to track down if they are kernel bugs since the processor stops cold, but random flakiness seems to cause this sometimes. The debugger can be used to locate the instruction and subroutine corresponding to the PC value. If that is insufficient to suggest the nature of the problem, more detailed examination of the system status at the time of the trap usually can produce an explanation.

init died   The system initialization process has exited. This is bad news, as no new users will then be able to log in. Rebooting is the only fix, so the system just does it right away.

out of mbufs: map full
> The network has exhausted its private page map for network buffers. This usually indicates that buffers are being lost, and rather than allow the system to slowly degrade, it reboots immediately. The map may be made larger if necessary.

That completes the list of panic types you are likely to see.

When the system crashes it writes (or at least attempts to write) an image of memory into the back end of the dump device, usually the same as the primary swap area. After the system is rebooted, the program savecore(8) runs and preserves a copy of this core image and the current system in a specified directory for later perusal. See savecore(8) for details.

To analyze a dump you should begin by running **adb** with the **−k** flag on the system load image and core dump. If the core image is the result of a panic, the panic message is printed. Normally the command "$c" will provide a stack trace from the point of the crash and this will provide a clue as to what went wrong. For more detail see "Using ADB to Debug the UNIX Kernel".

SEE ALSO

gdb(1), reboot(8)

"VAX 11/780 System Maintenance Guide" and "VAX Hardware Handbook" for more information about machine checks.

"Using ADB to Debug the UNIX Kernel"

NAME
cron — daemon to execute scheduled commands (ISC Cron V4.1)

SYNOPSIS
cron [-n] [-x *debugflags*]

DESCRIPTION
cron is normally started during system boot by rc.d(8) framework, if cron is switched on in rc.conf(5).

It will return immediately so you don't have to start it with '&'.

cron searches /var/cron/tabs for crontab files which are named after accounts in /etc/passwd. Crontabs found are loaded into memory. cron also searches for /etc/crontab which is in a different format (see crontab(5)). cron then wakes up every minute, examining all stored crontabs, checking each command to see if it should be run in the current minute. When executing commands, any output is mailed to the owner of the crontab (or to the user named in the MAILTO environment variable in the crontab, if such exists).

Events such as START and FINISH are recorded in the /var/log/cron log file with date and time details. This information is useful for a number of reasons, such as determining the amount of time required to run a particular job. By default, root has an hourly job that rotates these log files with compression to preserve disk space.

Additionally, cron checks each minute to see if its spool directory's modtime (or the modtime on /etc/crontab) has changed, and if it has, cron will then examine the modtime on all crontabs and reload those which have changed. Thus cron need not be restarted whenever a crontab file is modified. Note that the crontab(1) command updates the modtime of the spool directory whenever it changes a crontab.

The following options are available:

-x   This flag turns on some debugging flags. *debugflags* is comma-separated list of debugging flags to turn on. If a flag is turned on, cron writes some additional debugging information to system log during its work. Available debugging flags are:
          sch   scheduling
          proc process control
          pars parsing
          load database loading
          misc miscellaneous
          test test mode - do not actually execute any commands
          bit   show how various bits are set (long)
          ext   print extended debugging information

-n   Stay in the foreground and don't daemonize cron.

Daylight Saving Time and other time changes
Local time changes of less than three hours, such as those caused by the start or end of Daylight Saving Time, are handled specially. This only applies to jobs that run at a specific time and jobs that are run with a granularity greater than one hour. Jobs that run more frequently are scheduled normally.

If time has moved forward, those jobs that would have run in the interval that has been skipped will be run immediately. Conversely, if time has moved backward, care is taken to avoid running jobs twice.

Time changes of more than 3 hours are considered to be corrections to the clock or timezone, and the new time is used immediately.

SIGNALS
> On receipt of a `SIGHUP`, the cron daemon will close and reopen its log file. This is useful in scripts which rotate and age log files. Naturally this is not relevant if cron was built to use `syslog`(3).

FILES
> `/var/cron/tabs` **cron** spool directory
> `/etc/crontab`   system crontab
> `/var/log/cron`   log file for cron events

SEE ALSO
> `crontab`(1), `crontab`(5)

AUTHORS
> Paul Vixie ⟨vixie@isc.org⟩

NAME

cvsbug – send problem report (PR) about CVS to a central support site

SYNOPSIS

cvsbug [*site*] [**–f** *problem-report*] [**–t** *mail-address*]
[**–P**] [**–L**] [**––request-id**] [**–v**]

DESCRIPTION

cvsbug is a tool used to submit *problem reports* (PRs) to a central support site. In most cases the correct *site* will be the default. This argument indicates the support site which is responsible for the category of problem involved. Some sites may use a local address as a default. *site* values are defined by using the **aliases**(5).

cvsbug invokes an editor on a problem report template (after trying to fill in some fields with reasonable default values). When you exit the editor, **cvsbug** sends the completed form to the *Problem Report Management System* (**GNATS**) at a central support site. At the support site, the PR is assigned a unique number and is stored in the **GNATS** database according to its category and submitter-id. **GNATS** automatically replies with an acknowledgement, citing the category and the PR number.

To ensure that a PR is handled promptly, it should contain your (unique) *submitter-id* and one of the available *categories* to identify the problem area. (Use '**cvsbug -L**' to see a list of categories.)

The **cvsbug** template at your site should already be customized with your submitter-id (running ' **install-sid** *submitter-id*' to accomplish this is part of the installation procedures for **cvsbug**). If this hasn't been done, see your system administrator for your submitter-id, or request one from your support site by invoking '**cvsbug ––request–id**'. If your site does not distinguish between different user sites, or if you are not affiliated with the support site, use '**net**' for this field.

The more precise your problem description and the more complete your information, the faster your support team can solve your problems.

OPTIONS

–f *problem-report*

specify a file (*problem-report*) which already contains a complete problem report. **cvsbug** sends the contents of the file without invoking the editor. If the value for *problem-report* is ' **–** ', then **cvsbug** reads from standard input.

–t *mail-address*

Change mail address at the support site for problem reports. The default *mail-address* is the address used for the default *site*. Use the *site* argument rather than this option in nearly all cases.

–P   print the form specified by the environment variable **PR_FORM** on standard output. If **PR_FORM** is not set, print the standard blank PR template. No mail is sent.

-L   print the list of available categories. No mail is sent.

––request–id

sends mail to the default support site, or *site* if specified, with a request for your *submitter-id*. If you are not affiliated with *site*, use a *submitter-id* of **net** '.

–v   Display the **cvsbug** version number.

Note: use **cvsbug** to submit problem reports rather than mailing them directly. Using both the template and **cvsbug** itself will help ensure all necessary information will reach the support site.

ENVIRONMENT

The environment variable **EDITOR** specifies the editor to invoke on the template.
default: **vi**

If the environment variable **PR_FORM** is set, then its value is used as the file name of the template for your problem-report editing session. You can use this to start with a partially completed form (for example, a form with the identification fields already completed).

HOW TO FILL OUT A PROBLEM REPORT

Problem reports have to be in a particular form so that a program can easily manage them. Please remember the following guidelines:

- describe only **one problem** with each problem report.

- For follow-up mail, use the same subject line as the one in the automatic acknowledgement. It consists of category, PR number and the original synopsis line. This allows the support site to relate several mail messages to a particular PR and to record them automatically.

- Please try to be as accurate as possible in the subject and/or synopsis line.

- The subject and the synopsis line are not confidential. This is because open-bugs lists are compiled from them. Avoid confidential information there.

See the GNU **Info** file **cvsbug.info** or the document *Reporting Problems With cvsbug* for detailed information on reporting problems

HOW TO SUBMIT TEST CASES, CODE, ETC.

Submit small code samples with the PR. Contact the support site for instructions on submitting larger test cases and problematic source code.

FILES

/tmp/p$$ copy of PR used in editing session
/tmp/pf$$ copy of empty PR form, for testing purposes
/tmp/pbad$$ file for rejected PRs

INSTALLATION AND CONFIGURATION

See **INSTALL** for installation instructions.

SEE ALSO

gnats(l), **query-pr**(1), **edit-pr**(1), **gnats**(8), **queue-pr**(8), **at-pr**(8), **mkcat**(8), **mkdist**(8).

AUTHORS

Jeffrey Osier, Brendan Kehoe, Jason Merrill, Heinz G. Seidl (Cygnus Support)

COPYING

Copyright (c) 1992, 1993 Free Software Foundation, Inc.

Permission is granted to make and distribute verbatim copies of this manual provided the copyright notice and this permission notice are preserved on all copies.

Permission is granted to copy and distribute modified versions of this manual under the conditions for verbatim copying, provided that the entire resulting derived work is distributed under the terms of a permission notice identical to this one.

Permission is granted to copy and distribute translations of this manual into another language, under the above conditions for modified versions, except that this permission notice may be included in translations approved by the Free Software Foundation instead of in the original English.

NAME
     daicctl — ISDN control, test and statistics utility

SYNOPSIS
     under construction

DESCRIPTION
     under construction.

     Call it with -? to get minimal help.

SEE ALSO
     daic(4)

HISTORY
     The **daicctl** utility is not yet published.

AUTHORS
     The **daicctl** utility was written by Martin Husemann.

NAME

  dbsym — copy kernel symbol table into db_symtab space

SYNOPSIS

  dbsym [**−v**] [**−b** *bfdname*] *kernel*

DESCRIPTION

  dbsym is used to copy the symbol table in a newly linked kernel into the *db_symtab* array (in the data section) so that the ddb(4) kernel debugger can find the symbols. This program is only used on systems for which the boot program does not load the symbol table into memory with the kernel. The space for these symbols is reserved in the data segment using a config option like:

```
options              SYMTAB_SPACE=72000
```

  The size of the db_symtab array (the value of **SYMTAB_SPACE**) must be at least as large as the kernel symbol table. If insufficient space is reserved, dbsym will refuse to copy the symbol table.

  To recognize kernel executable format, the **−b** flag specifies BFD name of kernel.

  If the **−v** flag is given, **dbsym** will print out status information as it is copying the symbol table.

  Note that debugging symbols are not useful to the ddb(4) kernel debugger, so to minimize the size of the kernel, one should either compile the kernel without debugging symbols (no **−g** flag) or use the strip(1) command to strip debugging symbols from the kernel before **dbsym** is used to copy the symbol table. The command

```
strip -d netbsd
```

  will strip out debugging symbols.

SEE ALSO

  strip(1), ddb(4)

NAME
dev_mkdb — create /dev database

SYNOPSIS
dev_mkdb [-o *database*] [directory]

DESCRIPTION
The **dev_mkdb** command creates a db(3) hash access method database in "/var/run/dev.db" which contains the names of all of the character and block special files in the specified directory, using the file type and the *st_rdev* field as the key. If no directory is specified, the "/dev" directory is used.

Keys are a structure containing a mode_t followed by a dev_t, with any padding zero'd out. The former is the type of the file (st_mode & S_IFMT), the latter is the st_rdev field.

The options are as follows:

-o *database*
> Put the output databases in the named file.

FILES
/dev   Device directory.
/var/run/dev.db Database file.

SEE ALSO
ps(1), stat(2), db(3), devname(3), kvm_nlist(3), ttyname(3), kvm_mkdb(8)

HISTORY
The **dev_mkdb** command appeared in 4.4BSD.

NAME

dhclient - Dynamic Host Configuration Protocol (DHCP) Client

SYNOPSIS

dhclient [**-p** *port*] [**-d**] [**-q**] [**-1**] [**-o**] [**-r**] [**-lf** *lease-file*] [**-pf** *pid-file*] [**-cf** *config-file*] [**-sf** *script-file*] [**-s** server] [**-g** relay] [**-n**] [**-nw**] [**-w**] [*if0* [*...ifN*]]

DESCRIPTION

The Internet Systems Consortium DHCP Client, dhclient, provides a means for configuring one or more network interfaces using the Dynamic Host Configuration Protocol, BOOTP protocol, or if these protocols fail, by statically assigning an address.

SYSTEM REQUIREMENTS

You must have the Berkeley Packet Filter (bpf) configured in your NetBSD kernel.

OPERATION

The DHCP protocol allows a host to contact a central server which maintains a list of IP addresses which may be assigned on one or more subnets. A DHCP client may request an address from this pool, and then use it on a temporary basis for communication on network. The DHCP protocol also provides a mechanism whereby a client can learn important details about the network to which it is attached, such as the location of a default router, the location of a name server, and so on.

On startup, dhclient reads the *dhclient.conf* for configuration instructions. It then gets a list of all the network interfaces that are configured in the current system. For each interface, it attempts to configure the interface using the DHCP protocol.

In order to keep track of leases across system reboots and server restarts, dhclient keeps a list of leases it has been assigned in the dhclient.leases(5) file. On startup, after reading the dhclient.conf file, dhclient reads the dhclient.leases file to refresh its memory about what leases it has been assigned.

When a new lease is acquired, it is appended to the end of the dhclient.leases file. In order to prevent the file from becoming arbitrarily large, from time to time dhclient creates a new dhclient.leases file from its in-core lease database. The old version of the dhclient.leases file is retained under the name *dhclient.leases~* until the next time dhclient rewrites the database.

Old leases are kept around in case the DHCP server is unavailable when dhclient is first invoked (generally during the initial system boot process). In that event, old leases from the dhclient.leases file which have not yet expired are tested, and if they are determined to be valid, they are used until either they expire or the DHCP server becomes available.

A mobile host which may sometimes need to access a network on which no DHCP server exists may be preloaded with a lease for a fixed address on that network. When all attempts to contact a DHCP server have failed, dhclient will try to validate the static lease, and if it succeeds, will use that lease until it is restarted.

A mobile host may also travel to some networks on which DHCP is not available but BOOTP is. In that case, it may be advantageous to arrange with the network administrator for an entry on the BOOTP database, so that the host can boot quickly on that network rather than cycling through the list of old leases.

COMMAND LINE

The names of the network interfaces that dhclient should attempt to configure may be specified on the command line. If no interface names are specified on the command line dhclient will normally identify all network interfaces, eliminating non-broadcast interfaces if possible, and attempt to configure each interface.

It is also possible to specify interfaces by name in the **dhclient.conf(5)** file. If interfaces are specified in this way, then the client will only configure interfaces that are either specified in the configuration file or on the command line, and will ignore all other interfaces.

If the DHCP client should listen and transmit on a port other than the standard (port 68), the **-p** flag may used. It should be followed by the udp port number that dhclient should use. This is mostly useful for debugging purposes. If a different port is specified for the client to listen on and transmit on, the client will also use a different destination port - one greater than the specified destination port.

The DHCP client normally transmits any protocol messages it sends before acquiring an IP address to, 255.255.255.255, the IP limited broadcast address. For debugging purposes, it may be useful to have the server transmit these messages to some other address. This can be specified with the **-s** flag, followed by the IP address or domain name of the destination.

For testing purposes, the giaddr field of all packets that the client sends can be set using the **-g** flag, followed by the IP address to send. This is only useful for testing, and should not be expected to work in any consistent or useful way.

The DHCP client will normally run in the foreground until it has configured an interface, and then will revert to running in the background. To run force dhclient to always run as a foreground process, the **-d** flag should be specified. This is useful when running the client under a debugger, or when running it out of inittab on System V systems.

The client normally prints a startup message and displays the protocol sequence to the standard error descriptor until it has acquired an address, and then only logs messages using the **syslog (3)** facility. The **-q** flag prevents any messages other than errors from being printed to the standard error descriptor.

The client normally doesn't release the current lease as it is not required by the DHCP protocol. Some cable ISPs require their clients to notify the server if they wish to release an assigned IP address. The **-r** flag explicitly releases the current lease, and once the lease has been released, the client exits.

The **-1** flag cause dhclient to try once to get a lease. If it fails, dhclient exits with exit code two.

The **-o** flag cause dhclient to assume that it's been given a fixed lease, so once it installs the lease, it exits. This is really only useful on very small systems, and only works on a single interface at a time - if you want it to support multiple interfaces, run dhclient on each interface in succession.

The DHCP client normally gets its configuration information from **/etc/dhclient.conf,** its lease database from **/var/db/dhclient.leases,** stores its process ID in a file called **/var/run/dhclient.pid,** and configures the network interface using **/sbin/dhclient-script** To specify different names and/or locations for these files, use the **-cf, -lf, -pf** and **-sf** flags, respectively, followed by the name of the file. This can be particularly useful if, for example, **/var/db** or **/var/run** has not yet been mounted when the DHCP client is started.

The DHCP client normally exits if it isn't able to identify any network interfaces to configure. On laptop computers and other computers with hot-swappable I/O buses, it is possible that a broadcast interface may be added after system startup. The **-w** flag can be used to cause the client not to exit when it doesn't find any such interfaces. The **omshell (1)** program can then be used to notify the client when a network interface has been added or removed, so that the client can attempt to configure an IP address on that interface.

The DHCP client can be directed not to attempt to configure any interfaces using the **-n** flag. This is most likely to be useful in combination with the **-w** flag.

The client can also be instructed to become a daemon immediately, rather than waiting until it has acquired an IP address. This can be done by supplying the **-nw** flag.

CONFIGURATION
The syntax of the dhclient.conf(5) file is discussed separately.

OMAPI
The DHCP client provides some ability to control it while it is running, without stopping it. This capability is provided using OMAPI, an API for manipulating remote objects. OMAPI clients connect to the client using TCP/IP, authenticate, and can then examine the client's current status and make changes to it.

Rather than implementing the underlying OMAPI protocol directly, user programs should use the dhcpctl API or OMAPI itself. Dhcpctl is a wrapper that handles some of the housekeeping chores that OMAPI does not do automatically. Dhcpctl and OMAPI are documented in **dhcpctl(3)** and **omapi(3)**. Most things you'd want to do with the client can be done directly using the **omshell(1)** command, rather than having to write a special program.

THE CONTROL OBJECT
The control object allows you to shut the client down, releasing all leases that it holds and deleting any DNS records it may have added. It also allows you to pause the client - this unconfigures any interfaces the

client is using. You can then restart it, which causes it to reconfigure those interfaces. You would normally pause the client prior to going into hibernation or sleep on a laptop computer. You would then
resume it after the power comes back. This allows PC cards to be shut down while the computer is hiber-
nating or sleeping, and then reinitialized to their previous state once the computer comes out of hibernation
or sleep.

The control object has one attribute - the state attribute. To shut the client down, set its state attribute to 2.
It will automatically do a DHCPRELEASE. To pause it, set its state attribute to 3. To resume it, set its
state attribute to 4.

FILES

/sbin/dhclient-script,   /etc/dhclient.conf,   /var/db/dhclient.leases,   /var/run/dhclient.pid,
/var/db/dhclient.leases˜.

SEE ALSO

dhcpd(8), dhcrelay(8), dhclient-script(8), dhclient.conf(5), dhclient.leases(5).

AUTHOR

dhclient(8) has been written for Internet Systems Consortium by Ted Lemon in cooperation with Vixie
Enterprises. To learn more about Internet Systems Consortium, see **http://www.isc.org** To learn more
about Vixie Enterprises, see **http://www.vix.com.**

This client was substantially modified and enhanced by Elliot Poger for use on Linux while he was working
on the MosquitoNet project at Stanford.

The current version owes much to Elliot's Linux enhancements, but was substantially reorganized and partially rewritten by Ted Lemon so as to use the same networking framework that the Internet Systems Consortium DHCP server uses. Much system-specific configuration code was moved into a shell script so that
as support for more operating systems is added, it will not be necessary to port and maintain system-specific configuration code to these operating systems - instead, the shell script can invoke the native tools to
accomplish the same purpose.

NAME

dhclient-script - DHCP client network configuration script

DESCRIPTION

The DHCP client network configuration script is invoked from time to time by **dhclient(8)**. This script is used by the dhcp client to set each interface's initial configuration prior to requesting an address, to test the address once it has been offered, and to set the interface's final configuration once a lease has been acquired. If no lease is acquired, the script is used to test predefined leases, if any, and also called once if no valid lease can be identified.

This script is not meant to be customized by the end user. If local customizations are needed, they should be possible using the enter and exit hooks provided (see HOOKS for details). These hooks will allow the user to override the default behaviour of the client in creating a **/etc/resolv.conf** file.

No standard client script exists for some operating systems, even though the actual client may work, so a pioneering user may well need to create a new script or modify an existing one. In general, customizations specific to a particular computer should be done in the **/etc/dhclient.conf** file. If you find that you can't make such a customization without customizing **/etc/dhclient.conf** or using the enter and exit hooks, please submit a bug report.

HOOKS

When it starts, the client script first defines a shell function, **make_resolv_conf** , which is later used to create the **/etc/resolv.conf** file. To override the default behaviour, redefine this function in the enter hook script.

On after defining the make_resolv_conf function, the client script checks for the presence of an executable **/etc/dhclient-enter-hooks** script, and if present, it invokes the script inline, using the Bourne shell '.' command. The entire environment documented under OPERATION is available to this script, which may modify the environment if needed to change the behaviour of the script. If an error occurs during the execution of the script, it can set the exit_status variable to a nonzero value, and **/sbin/dhclient-script** will exit with that error code immediately after the client script exits.

After all processing has completed, **/sbin/dhclient-script** checks for the presence of an executable **/etc/dhclient-exit-hooks** script, which if present is invoked using the '.' command. The exit status of dhclient-script will be passed to dhclient-exit-hooks in the exit_status shell variable, and will always be zero if the script succeeded at the task for which it was invoked. The rest of the environment as described previously for dhclient-enter-hooks is also present. The **/etc/dhclient-exit-hooks** script can modify the valid of exit_status to change the exit status of dhclient-script.

OPERATION

When dhclient needs to invoke the client configuration script, it defines a set of variables in the environment, and then invokes **CLIENTBINDIR/dhclient-script.** In all cases, $reason is set to the name of the reason why the script has been invoked. The following reasons are currently defined: MEDIUM, PREINIT, BOUND, RENEW, REBIND, REBOOT, EXPIRE, FAIL and TIMEOUT.

MEDIUM

The DHCP client is requesting that an interface's media type be set. The interface name is passed in $interface, and the media type is passed in $medium.

PREINIT

The DHCP client is requesting that an interface be configured as required in order to send packets prior to receiving an actual address. For clients which use the BSD socket library, this means configuring the interface with an IP address of 0.0.0.0 and a broadcast address of 255.255.255.255. For other clients, it may be possible to simply configure the interface up without actually giving it an IP address at all. The interface name is passed in $interface, and the media type in $medium.

If an IP alias has been declared in dhclient.conf, its address will be passed in $alias_ip_address, and that ip alias should be deleted from the interface, along with any routes to it.

1

BOUND

The DHCP client has done an initial binding to a new address. The new ip address is passed in $new_ip_address, and the interface name is passed in $interface. The media type is passed in $medium. Any options acquired from the server are passed using the option name described in **dhcp-options**, except that dashes ('-') are replaced by underscores ('_') in order to make valid shell variables, and the variable names start with new_. So for example, the new subnet mask would be passed in $new_subnet_mask.

Before actually configuring the address, dhclient-script should somehow ARP for it and exit with a nonzero status if it receives a reply. In this case, the client will send a DHCPDECLINE message to the server and acquire a different address. This may also be done in the RENEW, REBIND, or REBOOT states, but is not required, and indeed may not be desirable.

When a binding has been completed, a lot of network parameters are likely to need to be set up. A new /etc/resolv.conf needs to be created, using the values of $new_domain_name and $new_domain_name_servers (which may list more than one server, separated by spaces). A default route should be set using $new_routers, and static routes may need to be set up using $new_static_routes.

If an IP alias has been declared, it must be set up here. The alias IP address will be written as $alias_ip_address, and other DHCP options that are set for the alias (e.g., subnet mask) will be passed in variables named as described previously except starting with $alias_ instead of $new_. Care should be taken that the alias IP address not be used if it is identical to the bound IP address ($new_ip_address), since the other alias parameters may be incorrect in this case.

RENEW

When a binding has been renewed, the script is called as in BOUND, except that in addition to all the variables starting with $new_, there is another set of variables starting with $old_. Persistent settings that may have changed need to be deleted - for example, if a local route to the bound address is being configured, the old local route should be deleted. If the default route has changed, the old default route should be deleted. If the static routes have changed, the old ones should be deleted. Otherwise, processing can be done as with BOUND.

REBIND

The DHCP client has rebound to a new DHCP server. This can be handled as with RENEW, except that if the IP address has changed, the ARP table should be cleared.

REBOOT

The DHCP client has successfully reacquired its old address after a reboot. This can be processed as with BOUND.

EXPIRE

The DHCP client has failed to renew its lease or acquire a new one, and the lease has expired. The IP address must be relinquished, and all related parameters should be deleted, as in RENEW and REBIND.

FAIL

The DHCP client has been unable to contact any DHCP servers, and any leases that have been tested have not proved to be valid. The parameters from the last lease tested should be deconfigured. This can be handled in the same way as EXPIRE.

TIMEOUT

The DHCP client has been unable to contact any DHCP servers. However, an old lease has been identified, and its parameters have been passed in as with BOUND. The client configuration script should test these parameters and, if it has reason to believe they are valid, should exit with a value of zero. If not, it should exit with a nonzero value.

The usual way to test a lease is to set up the network as with REBIND (since this may be called to test more than one lease) and then ping the first router defined in $routers. If a response is received, the lease must be valid for the network to which the interface is currently connected. It would be more complete to try to ping all of the routers listed in $new_routers, as well as those listed in $new_static_routes, but current scripts do not do this.

FILES

Each operating system should generally have its own script file, although the script files for similar operating systems may be similar or even identical. The script files included in Internet Systems Consortium DHCP distribution appear in the distribution tree under client/scripts, and bear the names of the operating systems on which they are intended to work.

BUGS

If more than one interface is being used, there's no obvious way to avoid clashes between server-supplied configuration parameters - for example, the stock dhclient-script rewrites /etc/resolv.conf. If more than one interface is being configured, /etc/resolv.conf will be repeatedly initialized to the values provided by one server, and then the other. Assuming the information provided by both servers is valid, this shouldn't cause any real problems, but it could be confusing.

SEE ALSO

dhclient(8), dhcpd(8), dhcrelay(8), dhclient.conf(5) and dhclient.leases(5).

AUTHOR

dhclient-script(8) has been written for Internet Systems Consortium by Ted Lemon in cooperation with Vixie Enterprises. To learn more about Internet Systems Consortium, see **http://www.isc.org.** To learn more about Vixie Enterprises, see **http://www.vix.com.**

NAME

dhcpcd — an RFC 2131 compliant DHCP client

SYNOPSIS

dhcpcd [**-bdgknpqwABDEGHJKLTV**] [**-c**, **--script** *script*] [**-e**, **--env** *value*]
      [**-f**, **--config** *file*] [**-h**, **--hostname** *hostname*]
      [**-i**, **--vendorclassid** *vendorclassid*] [**-l**, **--leasetime** *seconds*]
      [**-m**, **--metric** *metric*] [**-o**, **--option** *option*] [**-r**, **--request** *address*]
      [**-s**, **--inform** *address[/cidr]*] [**-t**, **--timeout** *seconds*]
      [**-u**, **--userclass** *class*] [**-v**, **--vendor** *code, value*]
      [**-y**, **--reboot** *seconds*] [**-z**, **--allowinterfaces** *pattern*]
      [**-C**, **--nohook** *hook*] [**-F**, **--fqdn** *FQDN*] [**-I**, **--clientid** *clientid*]
      [**-O**, **--nooption** *option*] [**-Q**, **--require** *option*] [**-S**, **--static** *value*]
      [**-W**, **--whitelist** *address[/cidr]*] [**-X**, **--blacklist** *address[/cidr]*]
      [**-Z**, **--denyinterfaces** *pattern*] [interface] [...]
dhcpcd -k, **--release** [interface]
dhcpcd -x, **--exit** [interface]

DESCRIPTION

dhcpcd is an implementation of the DHCP client specified in RFC 2131. **dhcpcd** gets the host information (IP address, routes, etc) from a DHCP server and configures the network *interface* of the machine on which it is running. **dhcpcd** then runs the configuration script which writes DNS information to resolvconf(8), if available, otherwise directly to /etc/resolv.conf. If the hostname is currently blank, (null) or localhost, or *force_hostname* is YES or TRUE or 1 then **dhcpcd** sets the hostname to the one supplied by the DHCP server. **dhcpcd** then daemonises and waits for the lease renewal time to lapse. It will then attempt to renew its lease and reconfigure if the new lease changes.

dhcpcd is also an implementation of the BOOTP client specified in RFC 951.

Local Link configuration

If **dhcpcd** failed to obtain a lease, it probes for a valid IPv4LL address (aka ZeroConf, aka APIPA). Once obtained it restarts the process of looking for a DHCP server to get a proper address.

When using IPv4LL, **dhcpcd** nearly always succeeds and returns an exit code of 0. In the rare case it fails, it normally means that there is a reverse ARP proxy installed which always defeats IPv4LL probing. To disable this behaviour, you can use the **-L**, **--noipv4ll** option.

Multiple interfaces

If a list of interfaces are given on the command line, then **dhcpcd** only works with those interfaces, otherwise **dhcpcd** discovers available Ethernet interfaces. If any interface reports a working carrier then **dhcpcd** will try and obtain a lease before forking to the background, otherwise it will fork right away. This behaviour can be modified with the **-b**, **--background** and **-w**, **--waitip** options.

If a single interface is given then **dhcpcd** only works for that interface and runs as a separate instance. The **-w**, **--waitip** option is enabled in this instance to maintain compatibility with older versions.

Interfaces are preferred by carrier, DHCP lease/IPv4LL and then lowest metric. For systems that support route metrics, each route will be tagged with the metric, otherwise **dhcpcd** changes the routes to use the interface with the same route and the lowest metric. See options below for controlling which interfaces we allow and deny through the use of patterns.

Hooking into DHCP events

    dhcpcd runs /libexec/dhcpcd-run-hooks, or the script specified by the **-c**, **--script** option. This script runs each script found in /libexec/dhcpcd-hooks in a lexical order. The default installation supplies the scripts 01-test, 10-mtu, 20-resolv.conf and 30-hostname. You can disable each script by using the **-C**, **--nohook** option. See dhcpcd-run-hooks(8) for details on how these scripts work. **dhcpcd** currently ignores the exit code of the script.

Fine tuning

    You can fine-tune the behaviour of **dhcpcd** with the following options:

-b, **--background**
> Background immediately. This is useful for startup scripts which don't disable link messages for carrier status.

-c, **--script** *script*
> Use this *script* instead of the default /libexec/dhcpcd-run-hooks.

-d, **--debug**
> Echo debug messages to the stderr and syslog.

-e, **--env** *value*
> Push *value* to the environment for use in dhcpcd-run-hooks(8). For example, you can force the hostname hook to always set the hostname with *-e force_hostname=YES*.

-g, **--reconfigure**
> **dhcpcd** will re-apply IP address, routing and run dhcpcd-run-hooks(8) for each interface. This is useful so that a 3rd party such as PPP or VPN can change the routing table and / or DNS, etc and then instruct **dhcpcd** to put things back afterwards. **dhcpcd** does not read a new configuration when this happens - you should rebind if you need that functionality.

-f, **--config** *file*
> Specify a config to load instead of /etc/dhcpcd.conf. **dhcpcd** always processes the config file before any command line options.

-h, **--hostname** *hostname*
> Sends *hostname* to the DHCP server so it can be registered in DNS. If *hostname* is an empty string then the current system hostname is sent. If *hostname* is a FQDN (ie, contains a .) then it will be encoded as such.

-i, **--vendorclassid** *vendorclassid*
> Override the *vendorclassid* field sent. The default is dhcpcd <version>. If not set then none is sent.

-k, **--release**
> This causes an existing **dhcpcd** process running on the *interface* to release its lease, de-configure the *interface* and then exit. **dhcpcd** then waits until this process has exited.

-l, **--leasetime** *seconds*
> Request a specific lease time in *seconds*. By default **dhcpcd** does not request any lease time and leaves it in the hands of the DHCP server.

-m, **--metric** *metric*
> Metrics are used to prefer an interface over another one, lowest wins. **dhcpcd** will supply a default metic of 200 + if_nametoindex(3). An extra 100 will be added for wireless interfaces.

-o, **--option** *option*
> Request the DHCP *option* variable for use in /libexec/dhcpcd-run-hooks.

-n, --rebind
> Notifies an existing **dhcpcd** process running on the *interface* to rebind its lease. **dhcpcd** will not re-configure itself or use any other command line arguments. **dhcpcd** will timeout the rebind after 30 seconds at which point the lease will be expired and **dhcpcd** will enter the discovery state to obtain a new lease. Use the **-t, --timeout** option to change this. If **dhcpcd** is not running, then it starts up as normal. This option used to be renew, but rebind is more accurate as we need to broadcast the request instead of unicasting.

-p, --persistent
> **dhcpcd** normally de-configures the *interface* and configuration when it exits. Sometimes, this isn't desirable if, for example, you have root mounted over NFS. You can use this option to stop this from happening.

-r, --request [*address*]
> **dhcpcd** normally sends a DHCP DISCOVER to find servers to offer an address. **dhcpcd** then requests the address used. You can use this option to skip the DISCOVER phase and just request the *address*. The downside is if you request an *address* the DHCP server does not know about or the DHCP server is not authoritative, it will remain silent. In this situation, we go back to the init state and DISCOVER again. If no *address* is given then the first address currently assigned to the *interface* is used.

-s, --inform [*address*[*/cidr*]]
> Behaves like **-r, --request** as above, but sends a DHCP INFORM instead of a REQUEST. This does not get a lease as such, just notifies the DHCP server of the *address* in use. You should also include the optional *cidr* network number in case the address is not already configured on the interface. **dhcpcd** remains running and pretends it has an infinite lease. **dhcpcd** will not de-configure the interface when it exits. If **dhcpcd** fails to contact a DHCP server then it returns a failure instead of falling back on IPv4LL.

-t, --timeout *seconds*
> Timeout after *seconds*, instead of the default 30. A setting of 0 *seconds* causes **dhcpcd** to wait forever to get a lease.

-u, --userclass *class*
> Tags the DHCP message with the userclass *class*. DHCP servers use this to give members of the class DHCP options other than the default, without having to know things like hardware address or hostname.

-v, --vendor *code,value*
> Add an encapsulated vendor option. *code* should be between 1 and 254 inclusive. To add a raw vendor string, omit *code* but keep the comma. Examples.
>
> Set the vendor option 01 with an IP address.
>   dhcpcd −v 01,192.168.0.2 eth0
> Set the vendor option 02 with a hex code.
>   dhcpcd −v 02,01:02:03:04:05 eth0
> Set the vendor option 03 with an IP address as a string.
>   dhcpcd −v 03,\"192.168.0.2\" eth0
> Set un-encapsulated vendor option to hello world.
>   dhcpcd −v ,"hello world" eth0

-w, --waitip
> Wait for an address to be assigned before forking to the background.

-x, --exit
> This will signal an existing **dhcpcd** process running on the *interface* to de-configure the *interface* and exit. **dhcpcd** then waits until this process has exited.

-y, --reboot *seconds*
> Allow *reboot* seconds before moving to the discover phase if we have an old lease to use. The default is 10 seconds. A setting of 0 seconds causes **dhcpcd** to skip the reboot phase and go straight into discover.

-D, --duid
> Generate an RFC 4361 compliant clientid. This requires persistent storage and not all DHCP servers work with it so it is not enabled by default. **dhcpcd** generates the DUID and stores it in /etc/dhcpcd.duid. This file should not be copied to other hosts.

-E, --lastlease
> If **dhcpcd** cannot obtain a lease, then try to use the last lease acquired for the interface. If the **-p, --persistent** option is not given then the lease is used if it hasn't expired.

-F, --fqdn *fqdn*
> Requests that the DHCP server updates DNS using FQDN instead of just a hostname. Valid values for *fqdn* are disable, none, ptr and both. **dhcpcd** itself never does any DNS updates. **dhcpcd** encodes the FQDN hostname as specified in RFC1035.

-I, --clientid *clientid*
> Send the *clientid*. If the string is of the format 01:02:03 then it is encoded as hex. For interfaces whose hardware address is longer than 8 bytes, or if the *clientid* is an empty string then **dhcpcd** sends a default *clientid* of the hardware family and the hardware address.

Restricting behaviour

dhcpcd will try to do as much as it can by default. However, there are sometimes situations where you don't want the things to be configured exactly how the the DHCP server wants. Here are some options that deal with turning these bits off.

-q, --quiet
> Quiet **dhcpcd** on the command line, only warnings and errors will be displayed. The messages are still logged though.

-z, --allowinterfaces *pattern*
> When discovering interfaces, the interface name must match *pattern* which is a space or comma separated list of patterns passed to fnmatch(3). If the same interface is matched in **-Z, --denyinterfaces** then it is still denied.

-A, --noarp
> Don't request or claim the address by ARP. This also disables IPv4LL.

-B, --nobackground
> Don't run in the background when we acquire a lease. This is mainly useful for running under the control of another process, such as a debugger or a network manager.

-C, --nohook *script*
> Don't run this hook script. Matches full name, or prefixed with 2 numbers optionally ending with .sh.

> So to stop **dhcpcd** from touching your DNS or MTU settings you would do:-
>> dhcpcd -C resolv.conf -C mtu eth0

-G, --nogateway
>   Don't set any default routes.

-H, --xidhwaddr
>   Use the last four bytes of the hardware address as the DHCP xid instead of a randomly generated number.

-J, --broadcast
>   Instructs the DHCP server to broadcast replies back to the client. Normally this is only set for non Ethernet interfaces, such as FireWire and InfiniBand. In most instances, **dhcpcd** will set this automatically.

-K, --nolink
>   Don't receive link messages for carrier status. You should only have to use this with buggy device drivers or running **dhcpcd** through a network manager.

-L, --noipv4ll
>   Don't use IPv4LL (aka APIPA, aka Bonjour, aka ZeroConf).

-O, --nooption *option*
>   Don't request the specified option. If no option given, then don't request any options other than those to configure the interface and routing.

-Q, --require *option*
>   Requires the *option* to be present in all DHCP messages, otherwise the message is ignored. To enforce that **dhcpcd** only responds to DHCP servers and not BOOTP servers, you can **-Q** *dhcp_message_type*.

-S, --static *value*
>   Configures a static *value*. If you set **ip_address** then **dhcpcd** will not attempt to obtain a lease and just use the value for the address with an infinite lease time.
>
>   Here is an example which configures a static address, routes and dns.
>   dhcpcd -S ip_address=192.168.0.10/24 \
>   -S routers=192.168.0.1 \
>   -S domain_name_servers=192.168.0.1 \
>   eth0

-T, --test
>   On receipt of DHCP messages just call /libexec/dhcpcd-run-hooks with the reason of TEST which echos the DHCP variables found in the message to the console. The interface configuration isn't touched and neither are any configuration files. To test INFORM the interface needs to be configured with the desired address before starting **dhcpcd**.

-V, --variables
>   Display a list of option codes and the associated variable for use in dhcpcd-run-hooks(8). Variables are prefixed with new_ and old_ unless the option number is -. Variables without an option are part of the DHCP message and cannot be directly requested.

-W, --whitelist *address*[/cidr]
>   Only accept packets from *address*[/cidr]. **-X, --blacklist** is ignored if **-W, --whitelist** is set.

-X, --blacklist *address*[*/cidr*]
>   Ignore all packets from *address*[*/cidr*].

-Z, --denyinterfaces *pattern*
> When discovering interfaces, the interface name must not match *pattern* which is a space or comma separated list of patterns passed to fnmatch(3).

3RDPARTY LINK MANAGEMENT
Some interfaces require configuration by 3rd parties, such as PPP or VPN. When an interface configuration in **dhcpcd** is marked as STATIC or INFORM without an address then **dhcpcd** will monitor the interface until an address is added or removed from it and act accordingly. For point to point interfaces (like PPP), a default route to its destination is automatically added to the configuration. If the point to point interface if configured for INFORM, then **dhcpcd** unicasts INFORM to the destination, otherwise it defaults to STATIC.

NOTES
dhcpcd requires a Berkley Packet Filter, or BPF device on BSD based systems and a Linux Socket Filter, or LPF device on Linux based systems.

FILES
/etc/dhcpcd.conf
Configuration file for dhcpcd. If you always use the same options, put them here.

/etc/dhcpcd.duid
Text file that holds the DUID used to identify the host.

/libexec/dhcpcd-run-hooks
Bourne shell script that is run to configure or de-configure an interface.

/libexec/dhcpcd-hooks
A directory containing bourne shell scripts that are run by the above script. Each script can be disabled by using the **-C, --nohook** option described above.

/var/db/dhcpcd-*interface*.lease
The actual DHCP message send by the server. We use this when reading the last lease and use the files mtime as when it was issued.

/var/run/dhcpcd.pid
Stores the PID of **dhcpcd** running on all interfaces.

/var/run/dhcpcd-*interface*.pid
Stores the PID of **dhcpcd** running on the *interface*.

SEE ALSO
dhcpcd.conf(5), dhcpcd-run-hooks(8), resolv.conf(5), resolvconf(8), if_nametoindex(3), fnmatch(3)

STANDARDS
RFC 951, RFC 1534, RFC 2131, RFC 2132, RFC 2855, RFC 3004, RFC 3361, RFC 3396, RFC 3397, RFC 3442, RFC 3927, RFC 4361, RFC 4390, RFC 4702.

AUTHORS
Roy Marples ⟨roy@marples.name⟩

BUGS
Please report them to http://roy.marples.name/projects/dhcpcd

NAME

dhcpcd-run-hooks — DHCP client configuration script

DESCRIPTION

dhcpcd-run-hooks is used by dhcpcd(8) to run any system and user defined hook scripts. System hook scripts are found in /libexec/dhcpcd-hooks and the user defined hooks are /etc/dhcpcd.enter-hook. and /etc/dhcpcd.exit-hook. The default install supplies hook scripts for configuring /etc/resolv.conf and the hostname. Your distribution may have included other hook scripts to say configure ntp or ypbind. A test hook is also supplied that simply echos the dhcp variables to the console from DISCOVER message.

Each time **dhcpcd-run-hooks** is invoked, $interface is set to the interface that **dhcpcd** is run on and $reason is to the reason why **dhcpcd-run-hooks** was invoked. DHCP information to be configured is held in variables starting with the word new_ and old DHCP information to be removed is held in variables starting with the word old_. **dhcpcd** can display the full list of variables it knows how about by using the **-V**, **--variables** argument.

Here's a list of reasons why **dhcpcd-run-hooks** could be invoked:

PREINIT   dhcpcd is starting up and any pre-initialisation should be done.

CARRIER   dhcpcd has detected the carrier is up. This is generally just a notification and no action need be taken.

INFORM   dhcpcd informed a DHCP server about it's address and obtained other configuration details.

BOUND   dhcpcd obtained a new lease from a DHCP server.

RENEW   dhcpcd renewed it's lease.

REBIND   dhcpcd has rebound to a new DHCP server.

REBOOT   dhcpcd successfully requested a lease from a DHCP server.

IPV4LL   dhcpcd failed to contact any DHCP servers but did obtain an IPV4LL address.

STATIC   dhcpcd has been configured with a static configuration which has not been obtained from a DHCP server.

3RDPARTY

        dhcpcd is monitoring the interface for a 3rd party to give it an IP address.

TIMEOUT   dhcpcd failed to contact any DHCP servers but was able to use an old lease.

EXPIRE   dhcpcd's lease or state expired and it failed to obtain a new one.

NAK   dhcpcd received a NAK from the DHCP server. This should be treated as EXPIRE.

NOCARRIER

        dhcpcd lost the carrier. The cable may have been unplugged or association to the wireless point lost.

FAIL   dhcpcd failed to operate on the interface. This normally happens when dhcpcd does not support the raw interface, which means it cannot work as a DHCP or ZeroConf client. Static configuration and DHCP INFORM is still allowed.

STOP   dhcpcd stopped running on the interface.

TEST   dhcpcd received an OFFER from a DHCP server but will not configure the interface. This is primarily used to test the variables are filled correctly for the script to process them.

FILES

When **dhcpcd-run-hooks** runs, it loads `/etc/dhcpcd.enter-hook` and any scripts found in `/libexec/dhcpcd-hooks` in a lexical order and then finally `/etc/dhcpcd.exit-hook`

SEE ALSO

dhcpcd(8)

AUTHORS

Roy Marples ⟨roy@marples.name⟩

BUGS

Please report them to http://roy.marples.name/projects/dhcpcd

NAME

dhcpd - Dynamic Host Configuration Protocol Server

SYNOPSIS

dhcpd [**-p** *port*] [**-f**] [**-d**] [**-q**] [**-t** | **-T**] [**-cf** *config-file*] [**-lf** *lease-file*] [**-tf** *trace-output-file*] [**-play** *trace-playback-file*] [*if0* [*...ifN*]]

DESCRIPTION

The Internet Systems Consortium DHCP Server, dhcpd, implements the Dynamic Host Configuration Protocol (DHCP) and the Internet Bootstrap Protocol (BOOTP). DHCP allows hosts on a TCP/IP network to request and be assigned IP addresses, and also to discover information about the network to which they are attached. BOOTP provides similar functionality, with certain restrictions.

CONTRIBUTIONS

This software is free software. At various times its development has been underwritten by various organizations, including the ISC and Vixie Enterprises. The development of 3.0 has been funded almost entirely by Nominum, Inc.

At this point development is being shepherded by Ted Lemon, and hosted by the ISC, but the future of this project depends on you. If you have features you want, please consider implementing them.

OPERATION

The DHCP protocol allows a host which is unknown to the network administrator to be automatically assigned a new IP address out of a pool of IP addresses for its network. In order for this to work, the network administrator allocates address pools in each subnet and enters them into the dhcpd.conf(5) file.

On startup, dhcpd reads the *dhcpd.conf* file and stores a list of available addresses on each subnet in memory. When a client requests an address using the DHCP protocol, dhcpd allocates an address for it. Each client is assigned a lease, which expires after an amount of time chosen by the administrator (by default, one day). Before leases expire, the clients to which leases are assigned are expected to renew them in order to continue to use the addresses. Once a lease has expired, the client to which that lease was assigned is no longer permitted to use the leased IP address.

In order to keep track of leases across system reboots and server restarts, dhcpd keeps a list of leases it has assigned in the dhcpd.leases(5) file. Before dhcpd grants a lease to a host, it records the lease in this file and makes sure that the contents of the file are flushed to disk. This ensures that even in the event of a system crash, dhcpd will not forget about a lease that it has assigned. On startup, after reading the dhcpd.conf file, dhcpd reads the dhcpd.leases file to refresh its memory about what leases have been assigned.

New leases are appended to the end of the dhcpd.leases file. In order to prevent the file from becoming arbitrarily large, from time to time dhcpd creates a new dhcpd.leases file from its in-core lease database. Once this file has been written to disk, the old file is renamed *dhcpd.leases~*, and the new file is renamed dhcpd.leases. If the system crashes in the middle of this process, whichever dhcpd.leases file remains will contain all the lease information, so there is no need for a special crash recovery process.

BOOTP support is also provided by this server. Unlike DHCP, the BOOTP protocol does not provide a protocol for recovering dynamically-assigned addresses once they are no longer needed. It is still possible to dynamically assign addresses to BOOTP clients, but some administrative process for reclaiming addresses is required. By default, leases are granted to BOOTP clients in perpetuity, although the network administrator may set an earlier cutoff date or a shorter lease length for BOOTP leases if that makes sense.

BOOTP clients may also be served in the old standard way, which is to simply provide a declaration in the dhcpd.conf file for each BOOTP client, permanently assigning an address to each client.

Whenever changes are made to the dhcpd.conf file, dhcpd must be restarted. To restart dhcpd, send a SIGTERM (signal 15) to the process ID contained in */var/run/dhcpd.pid*, and then re-invoke dhcpd. Because the DHCP server database is not as lightweight as a BOOTP database, dhcpd does not automatically restart itself when it sees a change to the dhcpd.conf file.

Note: We get a lot of complaints about this. We realize that it would be nice if one could send a SIGHUP to the server and have it reload the database. This is not technically impossible, but it would require a great deal of work, our resources are extremely limited, and they can be better spent elsewhere. So please don't complain about this on the mailing list unless you're prepared to fund a project to implement this feature, or prepared to do it yourself.

COMMAND LINE

The names of the network interfaces on which dhcpd should listen for broadcasts may be specified on the command line. This should be done on systems where dhcpd is unable to identify non-broadcast interfaces, but should not be required on other systems. If no interface names are specified on the command line dhcpd will identify all network interfaces which are up, eliminating non-broadcast interfaces if possible, and listen for DHCP broadcasts on each interface.

If dhcpd should listen on a port other than the standard (port 67), the **-p** flag may used. It should be followed by the udp port number on which dhcpd should listen. This is mostly useful for debugging purposes.

To run dhcpd as a foreground process, rather than allowing it to run as a daemon in the background, the **-f** flag should be specified. This is useful when running dhcpd under a debugger, or when running it out of inittab on System V systems.

To have dhcpd log to the standard error descriptor, specify the **-d** flag. This can be useful for debugging, and also at sites where a complete log of all dhcp activity must be kept but syslogd is not reliable or otherwise cannot be used. Normally, dhcpd will log all output using the syslog(3) function with the log facility set to LOG_DAEMON.

Dhcpd can be made to use an alternate configuration file with the **-cf** flag, or an alternate lease file with the **-lf** flag. Because of the importance of using the same lease database at all times when running dhcpd in production, these options should be used **only** for testing lease files or database files in a non-production environment.

When starting dhcpd up from a system startup script (e.g., /etc/rc), it may not be desirable to print out the entire copyright message on startup. To avoid printing this message, the **-q** flag may be specified.

The DHCP server reads two files on startup: a configuration file, and a lease database. If the **-t** flag is specified, the server will simply test the configuration file for correct syntax, but will not attempt to perform any network operations. This can be used to test the a new configuration file automatically before installing it.

The **-T** flag can be used to test the lease database file in a similar way.

The **-tf** and **-play** options allow you to specify a file into which the entire startup state of the server and all the transactions it processes are either logged or played back from. This can be useful in submitting bug reports - if you are getting a core dump every so often, you can start the server with the **-tf** option and then, when the server dumps core, the trace file will contain all the transactions that led up to it dumping core, so that the problem can be easily debugged with **-play**.

The **-play** option must be specified with an alternate lease file, using the **-lf** switch, so that the DHCP server doesn't wipe out your existing lease file with its test data. The DHCP server will refuse to operate in playback mode unless you specify an alternate lease file.

CONFIGURATION

The syntax of the dhcpd.conf(5) file is discussed separately. This section should be used as an overview of the configuration process, and the dhcpd.conf(5) documentation should be consulted for detailed reference information.

Subnets

dhcpd needs to know the subnet numbers and netmasks of all subnets for which it will be providing service. In addition, in order to dynamically allocate addresses, it must be assigned one or more ranges of addresses on each subnet which it can in turn assign to client hosts as they boot. Thus, a very simple configuration providing DHCP support might look like this:

```
subnet 239.252.197.0 netmask 255.255.255.0 {
  range 239.252.197.10 239.252.197.250;
}
```

Multiple address ranges may be specified like this:

```
subnet 239.252.197.0 netmask 255.255.255.0 {
  range 239.252.197.10 239.252.197.107;
  range 239.252.197.113 239.252.197.250;
}
```

If a subnet will only be provided with BOOTP service and no dynamic address assignment, the range clause can be left out entirely, but the subnet statement must appear.

Lease Lengths

DHCP leases can be assigned almost any length from zero seconds to infinity. What lease length makes sense for any given subnet, or for any given installation, will vary depending on the kinds of hosts being served.

For example, in an office environment where systems are added from time to time and removed from time to time, but move relatively infrequently, it might make sense to allow lease times of a month of more. In a final test environment on a manufacturing floor, it may make more sense to assign a maximum lease length of 30 minutes - enough time to go through a simple test procedure on a network appliance before packaging it up for delivery.

It is possible to specify two lease lengths: the default length that will be assigned if a client doesn't ask for any particular lease length, and a maximum lease length. These are specified as clauses to the subnet command:

```
subnet 239.252.197.0 netmask 255.255.255.0 {
  range 239.252.197.10 239.252.197.107;
  default-lease-time 600;
  max-lease-time 7200;
}
```

This particular subnet declaration specifies a default lease time of 600 seconds (ten minutes), and a maximum lease time of 7200 seconds (two hours). Other common values would be 86400 (one day), 604800 (one week) and 2592000 (30 days).

Each subnet need not have the same lease—in the case of an office environment and a manufacturing environment served by the same DHCP server, it might make sense to have widely disparate values for default and maximum lease times on each subnet.

BOOTP Support

Each BOOTP client must be explicitly declared in the dhcpd.conf file. A very basic client declaration will specify the client network interface's hardware address and the IP address to assign to that client. If the client needs to be able to load a boot file from the server, that file's name must be specified. A simple bootp client declaration might look like this:

```
host haagen {
  hardware ethernet 08:00:2b:4c:59:23;
  fixed-address 239.252.197.9;
  filename "/tftpboot/haagen.boot";
}
```

Options

DHCP (and also BOOTP with Vendor Extensions) provide a mechanism whereby the server can provide the client with information about how to configure its network interface (e.g., subnet mask), and also how the client can access various network services (e.g., DNS, IP routers, and so on).

These options can be specified on a per-subnet basis, and, for BOOTP clients, also on a per-client basis. In the event that a BOOTP client declaration specifies options that are also specified in its subnet declaration, the options specified in the client declaration take precedence. A reasonably complete DHCP configuration might look something like this:

```
        subnet 239.252.197.0 netmask 255.255.255.0 {
          range 239.252.197.10 239.252.197.250;
          default-lease-time 600 max-lease-time 7200;
          option subnet-mask 255.255.255.0;
          option broadcast-address 239.252.197.255;
          option routers 239.252.197.1;
          option domain-name-servers 239.252.197.2, 239.252.197.3;
          option domain-name "isc.org";
        }
```

A bootp host on that subnet that needs to be in a different domain and use a different name server might be declared as follows:

```
        host haagen {
          hardware ethernet 08:00:2b:4c:59:23;
          fixed-address 239.252.197.9;
          filename "/tftpboot/haagen.boot";
          option domain-name-servers 192.5.5.1;
          option domain-name "vix.com";
        }
```

A more complete description of the dhcpd.conf file syntax is provided in dhcpd.conf(5).

OMAPI

The DHCP server provides the capability to modify some of its configuration while it is running, without stopping it, modifying its database files, and restarting it. This capability is currently provided using OMAPI - an API for manipulating remote objects. OMAPI clients connect to the server using TCP/IP, authenticate, and can then examine the server's current status and make changes to it.

Rather than implementing the underlying OMAPI protocol directly, user programs should use the dhcpctl API or OMAPI itself. Dhcpctl is a wrapper that handles some of the housekeeping chores that OMAPI does not do automatically. Dhcpctl and OMAPI are documented in **dhcpctl(3)** and **omapi(3)**.

OMAPI exports objects, which can then be examined and modified. The DHCP server exports the following objects: lease, host, failover-state and group. Each object has a number of methods that are provided: lookup, create, and destroy. In addition, it is possible to look at attributes that are stored on objects, and in some cases to modify those attributes.

THE LEASE OBJECT

Leases can't currently be created or destroyed, but they can be looked up to examine and modify their state.

Leases have the following attributes:

state *integer* lookup, examine
> 1 = free
> 2 = active
> 3 = expired
> 4 = released
> 5 = abandoned
> 6 = reset
> 7 = backup
> 8 = reserved
> 9 = bootp

ip-address *data* lookup, examine
> The IP address of the lease.

dhcp-client-identifier *data* lookup, examine, update
> The client identifier that the client used when it acquired the lease. Not all clients send client identifiers, so this may be empty.

4

client-hostname *data* examine, update
> The value the client sent in the host-name option.

host *handle* examine
> the host declaration associated with this lease, if any.

subnet *handle* examine
> the subnet object associated with this lease (the subnet object is not currently supported).

pool *handle* examine
> the pool object associated with this lease (the pool object is not currently supported).

billing-class *handle* examine
> the handle to the class to which this lease is currently billed, if any (the class object is not currently supported).

hardware-address *data* examine, update
> the hardware address (chaddr) field sent by the client when it acquired its lease.

hardware-type *integer* examine, update
> the type of the network interface that the client reported when it acquired its lease.

ends *time* examine
> the time when the lease's current state ends, as understood by the client.

tstp *time* examine
> the time when the lease's current state ends, as understood by the server.

tsfp *time* examine
> the time when the lease's current state ends, as understood by the failover peer (if there is no failover peer, this value is undefined).

cltt *time* examine
> The time of the last transaction with the client on this lease.

THE HOST OBJECT

Hosts can be created, destroyed, looked up, examined and modified. If a host declaration is created or deleted using OMAPI, that information will be recorded in the dhcpd.leases file. It is permissible to delete host declarations that are declared in the dhcpd.conf file.

Hosts have the following attributes:

name *data* lookup, examine, modify
> the name of the host declaration. This name must be unique among all host declarations.

group *handle* examine, modify
> the named group associated with the host declaration, if there is one.

hardware-address *data* lookup, examine, modify
> the link-layer address that will be used to match the client, if any. Only valid if hardware-type is also present.

hardware-type *integer* lookup, examine, modify
> the type of the network interface that will be used to match the client, if any. Only valid if hardware-address is also present.

dhcp-client-identifier *data* lookup, examine, modify
> the dhcp-client-identifier option that will be used to match the client, if any.

ip-address *data* examine, modify
> a fixed IP address which is reserved for a DHCP client that matches this host declaration. The IP address will only be assigned to the client if it is valid for the network segment to which the client is connected.

statements *data* modify
> a list of statements in the format of the dhcpd.conf file that will be executed whenever a message

from the client is being processed.

known *integer* examine, modify

if nonzero, indicates that a client matching this host declaration will be treated as *known* in pool permit lists. If zero, the client will not be treated as known.

THE GROUP OBJECT

Named groups can be created, destroyed, looked up, examined and modified. If a group declaration is created or deleted using OMAPI, that information will be recorded in the dhcpd.leases file. It is permissible to delete group declarations that are declared in the dhcpd.conf file.

Named groups currently can only be associated with hosts - this allows one set of statements to be efficiently attached to more than one host declaration.

Groups have the following attributes:

name *data*

the name of the group. All groups that are created using OMAPI must have names, and the names must be unique among all groups.

statements *data*

a list of statements in the format of the dhcpd.conf file that will be executed whenever a message from a client whose host declaration references this group is processed.

THE CONTROL OBJECT

The control object allows you to shut the server down. If the server is doing failover with another peer, it will make a clean transition into the shutdown state and notify its peer, so that the peer can go into partner down, and then record the "recover" state in the lease file so that when the server is restarted, it will automatically resynchronize with its peer.

On shutdown the server will also attempt to cleanly shut down all OMAPI connections. If these connections do not go down cleanly after five seconds, they are shut down pre-emptively. It can take as much as 25 seconds from the beginning of the shutdown process to the time that the server actually exits.

To shut the server down, open its control object and set the state attribute to 2.

THE FAILOVER-STATE OBJECT

The failover-state object is the object that tracks the state of the failover protocol as it is being managed for a given failover peer. The failover object has the following attributes (please see **dhcpd.conf (5)** for explanations about what these attributes mean):

name *data* examine

Indicates the name of the failover peer relationship, as described in the server's **dhcpd.conf** file.

partner-address *data* examine

Indicates the failover partner's IP address.

local-address *data* examine

Indicates the IP address that is being used by the DHCP server for this failover pair.

partner-port *data* examine

Indicates the TCP port on which the failover partner is listening for failover protocol connections.

local-port *data* examine

Indicates the TCP port on which the DHCP server is listening for failover protocol connections for this failover pair.

max-outstanding-updates *integer* examine

Indicates the number of updates that can be outstanding and unacknowledged at any given time, in this failover relationship.

mclt *integer* examine

Indicates the maximum client lead time in this failover relationship.

load-balance-max-secs *integer* examine

Indicates the maximum value for the secs field in a client request before load balancing is bypassed.

load-balance-hba *data* examine
Indicates the load balancing hash bucket array for this failover relationship.

local-state *integer* examine, modify
Indicates the present state of the DHCP server in this failover relationship. Possible values for state are:

> 1 - partner down
> 2 - normal
> 3 - communications interrupted
> 4 - resolution interrupted
> 5 - potential conflict
> 6 - recover
> 7 - recover done
> 8 - shutdown
> 9 - paused
> 10 - startup
> 11 - recover wait

In general it is not a good idea to make changes to this state. However, in the case that the failover partner is known to be down, it can be useful to set the DHCP server's failover state to partner down. At this point the DHCP server will take over service of the failover partner's leases as soon as possible, and will give out normal leases, not leases that are restricted by MCLT. If you do put the DHCP server into the partner-down when the other DHCP server is not in the partner-down state, but is not reachable, IP address assignment conflicts are possible, even likely. Once a server has been put into partner-down mode, its failover partner must not be brought back online until communication is possible between the two servers.

partner-state *integer* examine
Indicates the present state of the failover partner.

local-stos *integer* examine
Indicates the time at which the DHCP server entered its present state in this failover relationship.

partner-stos *integer* examine
Indicates the time at which the failover partner entered its present state.

hierarchy *integer* examine
Indicates whether the DHCP server is primary (0) or secondary (1) in this failover relationship.

last-packet-sent *integer* examine
Indicates the time at which the most recent failover packet was sent by this DHCP server to its failover partner.

last-timestamp-received *integer* examine
Indicates the timestamp that was on the failover message most recently received from the failover partner.

skew *integer* examine
Indicates the skew between the failover partner's clock and this DHCP server's clock

max-response-delay *integer* examine
Indicates the time in seconds after which, if no message is received from the failover partner, the partner is assumed to be out of communication.

cur-unacked-updates *integer* examine
Indicates the number of update messages that have been received from the failover partner but not yet processed.

FILES

/etc/dhcpd.conf, /var/db/dhcpd.leases, /var/run/dhcpd.pid, /var/db/dhcpd.leases˜.

SEE ALSO

dhclient(8), dhcrelay(8), dhcpd.conf(5), dhcpd.leases(5)

AUTHOR

dhcpd(8) was originally written by Ted Lemon under a contract with Vixie Labs. Funding for this project was provided by Internet Systems Consortium. Version 3 of the DHCP server was funded by Nominum, Inc. Information about Internet Systems Consortium is available at **http://www.isc.org/**. Information about Nominum can be found at **http://www.nominum.com/**.

NAME

dhcrelay - Dynamic Host Configuration Protocol Relay Agent

SYNOPSIS

dhcrelay [**-p** *port*] [**-d**] [**-q**] [**-i** *if0* [**...** **-i** *ifN*]] [**-a**] [**-c** *count*] [**-A** *length*] [**-D**] [**-m** *append* |
replace | *forward* | *discard*] *server0* [*...serverN*]

DESCRIPTION

The Internet Systems Consortium DHCP Relay Agent, dhcrelay, provides a means for relaying DHCP and
BOOTP requests from a subnet to which no DHCP server is directly connected to one or more DHCP
servers on other subnets.

SYSTEM REQUIREMENTS

You must have the Berkeley Packet Filter (bpf) configured in your NetBSD kernel.

OPERATION

The DHCP Relay Agent listens for DHCP and BOOTP queries and responses. When a query is received
from a client, dhcrelay forwards it to the list of DHCP servers specified on the command line. When a
reply is received from a server, it is broadcast or unicast (according to the relay agent's ability or the client's
request) on the network from which the original request came.

COMMAND LINE

The names of the network interfaces that dhcrelay should attempt to configure may be specified on the
command line using the **-i** option. If no interface names are specified on the command line dhcrelay will
identify all network interfaces, elimininating non-broadcast interfaces if possible, and attempt to configure
each interface.

The **-i** flag can be used to specify the network interfaces on which the relay agent should listen. In general,
it must listen not only on those network interfaces to which clients are attached, but also on those network
interfaces to which the server (or the router that reaches the server) is attached. However, in some cases it
may be necessary to exclude some networks; in this case, you must list all those network interfaces that
should *not* be excluded using the **-i** flag.

In some cases it *is* helpful for the relay agent to forward requests from networks on which a DHCP server is
running to other DHCP servers. This would be the case if two DHCP servers on different networks were
being used to provide backup service for each other's networks.

If dhcrelay should listen and transmit on a port other than the standard (port 67), the **-p** flag may used. It
should be followed by the udp port number that dhcrelay should use. This is mostly useful for debugging
purposes.

Dhcrelay will normally run in the foreground until it has configured an interface, and then will revert to
running in the background. To force dhcrelay to always run as a foreground process, the **-d** flag should be
specified. This is useful when running dhcrelay under a debugger, or when running it out of inittab on System V systems.

Dhcrelay will normally print its network configuration on startup. This can be unhelpful in a system startup
script - to disable this behaviour, specify the **-q** flag.

RELAY AGENT INFORMATION OPTIONS

If the **-a** flag is set the relay agent will append an agent option field to each request before forwarding it to
the server. Agent option fields in responses sent from servers to clients will be stripped before forwarding
such responses back to the client.

The agent option field will contain two agent options: the Circuit ID suboption and the Remote ID suboption. Currently, the Circuit ID will be the printable name of the interface on which the client request was
received. The client supports inclusion of a Remote ID suboption as well, but this is not used by default.

When forwarding packets, dhcrelay discards packets which have reached a hop count of 10. If a lower or
higher threshold (up to 255) is desired, depending on your environment, you can specify the max hop count
threshold as a number following the **-c** option.

Relay Agent options are added to a DHCP packet without the knowledge of the DHCP client. The client may have filled the DHCP packet option buffer completely, in which case there theoretically isn't any space to add Agent options. However, the DHCP server may be able to handle a much larger packet than most DHCP clients would send. The current Agent Options draft requires that the relay agent use a maximum packet size of 576 bytes.

It is recommended that with the Internet Systems Consortium DHCP server, the maximum packet size be set to about 1400, allowing plenty of extra space in which the relay agent can put the agent option field, while still fitting into the Ethernet MTU size. This can be done by specifying the **-A** flag, followed by the desired maximum packet size (e.g., 1400).

Note that this is reasonably safe to do even if the MTU between the server and the client is less than 1500, as long as the hosts on which the server and client are running support IP fragmentation (and they should). With some knowledge as to how large the agent options might get in a particular configuration, this parameter can be tuned as finely as necessary.

It is possible for a relay agent to receive a packet which already contains an agent option field. If this packet does not have a giaddr set, the standard requires that the packet be discarded.

If giaddr is set, the server may handle the situation in one of four ways: it may *append* its own set of relay options to the packet, leaving the supplied option field intact. It may *replace* the existing agent option field. It may *forward* the packet unchanged. Or, it may *discard* it.

Which of these behaviours is followed by the Internet Systems Consortium DHCP Relay Agent may be configured with the **-m** flag, followed by one of the four keywords specified in *italics* above.

When the relay agent receives a reply from a server that it's supposed to forward to a client, and Relay Agent Information option processing is enabled, the relay agent scans the packet for Relay Agent Information options and removes them. As it's scanning, if it finds a Relay Agent Information option field containing an Agent ID suboption that matches one of its IP addresses, that option is recognized as its own. If no such option is found, the relay agent can either drop the packet, or relay it anyway. If the **-D** option is specified, all packets that don't contain a match will be dropped.

SPECIFYING DHCP SERVERS
The name or IP address of at least one DHCP server to which DHCP and BOOTP requests should be relayed must be specified on the command line.

SEE ALSO
dhclient(8), dhcpd(8), RFC2132, RFC2131, draft-ietf-dhc-agent-options-03.txt.

BUGS
It should be possible for the user to define the Circuit ID and Remote ID values on a per-interface basis.

The relay agent should not relay packets received on a physical network to DHCP servers on the same physical network - if they do, the server will receive duplicate packets. In order to fix this, however, the relay agent needs to be able to learn about the network topology, which requires that it have a configuration file.

AUTHOR
dhcrelay(8) has been written for Internet Systems Consortium by Ted Lemon in cooperation with Vixie Enterprises. To learn more about Internet Systems Consortium, see **http://www.isc.org/isc.** To learn more about Vixie Enterprises, see **http://www.vix.com.**

NAME

    discard – Postfix discard mail delivery agent

SYNOPSIS

    discard [generic Postfix daemon options]

DESCRIPTION

    The Postfix **discard**(8) delivery agent processes delivery requests from the queue manager. Each request specifies a queue file, a sender address, a domain or host name that is treated as the reason for discarding the mail, and recipient information. The reason may be prefixed with an RFC 3463-compatible detail code. This program expects to be run from the **master**(8) process manager.

    The **discard**(8) delivery agent pretends to deliver all recipients in the delivery request, logs the "next-hop" domain or host information as the reason for discarding the mail, updates the queue file and marks recipients as finished or informs the queue manager that delivery should be tried again at a later time.

    Delivery status reports are sent to the **trace**(8) daemon as appropriate.

SECURITY

    The **discard**(8) mailer is not security-sensitive. It does not talk to the network, and can be run chrooted at fixed low privilege.

STANDARDS

    None.

DIAGNOSTICS

    Problems and transactions are logged to **syslogd**(8).

    Depending on the setting of the **notify_classes** parameter, the postmaster is notified of bounces and of other trouble.

CONFIGURATION PARAMETERS

    Changes to **main.cf** are picked up automatically as **discard**(8) processes run for only a limited amount of time. Use the command "**postfix reload**" to speed up a change.

    The text below provides only a parameter summary. See **postconf**(5) for more details including examples.

    config_directory (see 'postconf -d' output)

        The default location of the Postfix main.cf and master.cf configuration files.

    daemon_timeout (18000s)

        How much time a Postfix daemon process may take to handle a request before it is terminated by a built-in watchdog timer.

    delay_logging_resolution_limit (2)

        The maximal number of digits after the decimal point when logging sub-second delay values.

    double_bounce_sender (double-bounce)

        The sender address of postmaster notifications that are generated by the mail system.

    ipc_timeout (3600s)

        The time limit for sending or receiving information over an internal communication channel.

    max_idle (100s)

        The maximum amount of time that an idle Postfix daemon process waits for an incoming connection before terminating voluntarily.

    max_use (100)

        The maximal number of incoming connections that a Postfix daemon process will service before terminating voluntarily.

      process_id (read-only)

          The process ID of a Postfix command or daemon process.

      process_name (read-only)

          The process name of a Postfix command or daemon process.

      queue_directory (see 'postconf -d' output)

          The location of the Postfix top-level queue directory.

      syslog_facility (mail)

          The syslog facility of Postfix logging.

      syslog_name (see 'postconf -d' output)

          The mail system name that is prepended to the process name in syslog records, so that "smtpd" becomes, for example, "postfix/smtpd".

SEE ALSO

      qmgr(8), queue manager

      bounce(8), delivery status reports

      error(8), Postfix error delivery agent

      postconf(5), configuration parameters

      master(5), generic daemon options

      master(8), process manager

      syslogd(8), system logging

LICENSE

      The Secure Mailer license must be distributed with this software.

HISTORY

      This service was introduced with Postfix version 2.2.

AUTHOR(S)

      Victor Duchovni

      Morgan Stanley

      Based on code by:

      Wietse Venema

      IBM T.J. Watson Research

      P.O. Box 704

      Yorktown Heights, NY 10598, USA

NAME
disklabel — read and write disk pack label

SYNOPSIS
disklabel [**-ACDFrtv**] *disk*
disklabel **-e** [**-CDFIrv**] *disk*
disklabel **-i** [**-DFIrv**] *disk*
disklabel **-R** [**-DFrv**] *disk protofile*
disklabel **-w** [**-DFrv**] [**-f** *disktab*] *disk disktype* [*packid*]
disklabel [**-NW**] *disk*
disklabel **-l**

DESCRIPTION
disklabel can be used to install, examine, or modify the label on a disk drive or pack. When writing the label, it can be used to change the drive identification, the disk partitions on the drive, or to replace a damaged label.

The **-e**, **-i**, **-l**, **-R**, **-w**, **-N**, and **-W** options determine the basic operation. If none are specified the label is displayed.

-e   Edit the existing label (using EDITOR) and write it back to the disk. If EDITOR is undefined, then vi(1) is used.

-i   Interactively update the existing label and write it back to the disk.

-l   Show all known file system types (those that can be specified along a partition within the label) and exit.

-R   Write (restore) a label by reading it from *protofile*. The file should be in the same format as the default output.

-w   Write a standard label for the specified *disktype*. See disktab(5).

-N   Disallow writes to the disk sector that contains the label. This is the default state.

-W   Allow writes to the disk sector that contains the label. This state may not persist if no programs have the disk open.

The majority of the rest of the options affect more than one form of the command:

-A   Read all labels from the disk, including ones deleted with **disklabel -D**. Implies **-r**.

-C   Output the partition offset and size values in ⟨cylinder/head/sector⟩ format. Note this format is always accepted on input with either the **-e** or **-R** flags.

-D   Delete all existing labels (by 1's complementing the magic number) before writing any labels to their default location. Implies **-r**. If **-D** is specified without a request to write the label, then existing labels are just deleted.

-F   Treat *disk* as a regular file. This suppresses all ioctl(2) calls, and is the default if *disk* is a regular file. *disk* is always opened using opendisk(3) even if **-F** is specified. Implies **-r**.

-I   If a label cannot be read from *disk* request the default one from the kernel. Implies **-r**.

-f *disktab*
        Specify the name of a file to use instead of /etc/disktab.

-r   Read/write the disk directly rather than using ioctl(2) requests on the kernel. When writing a label, the kernel will be told about the label before the label is written and asked to write afterwards. This is the historic behaviour and can be supressed by specifying **-F**.

-t   Format the output as a disktab(5) entry.

-v   Be verbose about the operations being done, in particular the disk sectors being read and written. Specifying **-v** more than once will increase the verbosity.

On systems that expect to have disks with MBR partitions (see fdisk(8)) **disklabel** will find, and update if requested, labels in the first 8k of type 169 (NetBSD) MBR labels and within the first 8k of the physical disk. On other systems **disklabel** will only look at the start of the disk. The offset at which the labels are written is also system dependent.

disklabel will detect byteswapped labels, but currently cannot display them.

Previous versions of **disklabel** could update the bootstrap code on some architectures. This functionality has been subsumed by installboot(8).

EXIT STATUS
The exit status of **disklabel** is set to indicate any errors or warnings. The values used are:

0   The **disklabel** utility has completed successfully.

1   A fatal error has occurred, such as unknown options passed on the command line, or writing the disklabel failed.

4   An I/O error of some sort occurred.

101..n   One or more warnings occured while reading the disklabel. Subtract 100 to get the number of warnings detected.

FILES
/etc/disktab

EXAMPLES
disklabel sd0

Display the in-core label for sd0 as obtained via /dev/rsd0c.

disklabel -i -r sd0

Read the on-disk label for sd0, edit it using the built-in interactive editor and reinstall in-core as well as on-disk.

disklabel -i -I sd0

As previous, but don't fail if there was no label on the disk yet; provide some default values instead.

disklabel -e -I sd0

As previous, only edit using $EDITOR

disklabel -w -r /dev/rsd0c sd2212 foo

Create a label for sd0 based on information for "sd2212" found in /etc/disktab, using foo as the disk pack label. If you do not have an entry for your disk in /etc/disktab, you can use this style to put an initial label onto a new disk. Then dump the label to a file (using **disklabel sd0 > protofile**), editing the file, and replacing the label with **disklabel -R sd0 protofile**.

disklabel -R sd0 mylabel

Restore the on-disk and in-core label for sd0 from information in mylabel.

DIAGNOSTICS

The kernel device drivers will not allow the size of a disk partition to be decreased or the offset of a partition to be changed while it is open. Some device drivers create a label containing only a single large partition if a disk is unlabeled; thus, the label must be written to the "a" partition of the disk while it is open. This sometimes requires the desired label to be set in two steps, the first one creating at least one other partition, and the second setting the label on the new partition while shrinking the "a" partition.

SEE ALSO

opendisk(3), disklabel(5), disktab(5), dkctl(8), fdisk(8), installboot(8), mbrlabel(8), mscdlabel(8)

BUGS

If the disk partition is not specified in the disk name (i.e., *xy0* instead of */dev/rxy0c*), **disklabel** will construct the full pathname of the disk and use the "d" partition on i386, hpcmips, or arc, and the "c" partition on all others.

On the sparc, sparc64, sun2, and sun3 NetBSD systems, the size of each partition must be a multiple of the number of sectors per cylinder (i.e., each partition must be an integer number of cylinders), or the boot ROMs will declare the label invalid and fail to boot the system.

In addition, the **−r** option should never be used on a sparc, sparc64, sun2, or sun3 system boot disk - the NetBSD kernel translates the NetBSD disk label into a SunOS compatible format (which is required by the boot PROMs) when it writes the label. Using the **−r** flag causes **disklabel** to write directly to disk, and bypass the format translation. This will result in a disk label that the PROMs will not recognize, and that therefore cannot be booted from.

NAME

diskless — booting a system over the network

DESCRIPTION

The ability to boot a system over the network is useful for two kinds of systems:

diskless   a system with no attached mass storage media to boot or run from (e.g. a network computer).

dataless   a system with a hard drive that only contains system and application software, and user data is mounted over the network from a central server.

It can also be done as a temporary measure while repairing or re-installing file systems on a local disk. This capability is necessarily platform dependent because of its dependence on system firmware support; not all platforms supported by NetBSD are capable of being network booted.

The protocols used to obtain a network address (e.g. an IP host address), include, but are not limited to:

RARP   Reverse Address Resolution Protocol (ARP)
DHCP   Dynamic Host Configuration Protocol
BOOTP Bootstrap Protocol

This information can also be derived from non-volatile RAM or by a transform of a network interface (e.g. Ethernet) MAC address.

The protocols used to load a NetBSD kernel over a network include, but are not limited to:

TFTP   Trivial File Transfer Protocol
NFS   Sun Network File System
RMP   HP Remote Maintenance Protocol
MOP   DEC Maintenance Operations Protocol

Derivation of the filename of the secondary bootstrap program can be done by a transform of a network interface MAC address (or other protocol address), or provided by a server as with BOOTP, and DHCP. How this is done is platform dependent; see boot(8).

The NetBSD kernel doesn't care how it gets loaded and started. The protocols used to boot NetBSD can be completely different than the ones that NetBSD uses operationally, i.e. you can netboot the system using HP RMP and the NetBSD kernel can use IP to communicate after bootstrap.

There is no standard way to pass all the required information from a boot loader to an operating system kernel, so the NetBSD kernel usually has to recapitulate the same (or similar) protocol exchanges over the network to obtain a network address, determine which servers to use, and so on. NetBSD supports obtaining this information from RARP, BOOTP, DHCP, and Sun RPC "bootparams". See options(4) for a list of methods that can be compiled into a NetBSD kernel.

NetBSD only supports the Sun Network File System (NFS) for mounting its root file system over a network. NetBSD can use any local mass storage device for which it has a driver, after bootstrap, even if that device is not supported by the system's firmware for booting.

N.B. DHCP is essentially a series of extensions to BOOTP; the NetBSD dhcpd(8) is capable of responding to both kinds of protocol requests.

In the majority of configurations, network boot servers and clients are attached to the same LAN so that broadcast queries from the clients can be heard by the servers. Unless specially configured, routers block broadcasts from propagating from LAN to LAN; some routers can be configured to "forward" broadcast BOOTP packets to another LAN attached to that router, which permits a server on that remote LAN to respond to the client's broadcast query.

OPERATION

When booting a system over the network, there are three phases of interaction between client and server:

1. The system firmware (or stage-1 bootstrap) loads a boot program.
2. The boot program loads a NetBSD kernel.
3. The NetBSD kernel performs an NFS mount of the root file system.

Each of these phases are described in further detail below.

1. loading a boot program

In phase 1, the system firmware loads a boot program. Firmware designs vary widely, so this phase is inherently machine-specific. Some examples:

DEC Alpha systems use BOOTP to determine the client's IP address and then use TFTP load a secondary bootstrap program from the server and filename specified in the BOOTP reply. DEC Alpha systems can also use MOP to load a program to run the system.

Sun systems use RARP to determine the client's IP address, transform that address to a hexadecimal string to form the filename of the secondary boot program, and then use TFTP to download the boot program from the server that sent the RARP reply.

HP 300-series systems use the HP RMP to download a boot program.

Typical personal computers may load a network boot program either from diskette or from a PROM on a Network Interface Card (NIC). Some BIOSes support booting from a network interface.

2. loading a kernel

In phase 2, the secondary boot program loads a kernel. Operation in this phase depends on the design of the boot program (the design described here is the one used by Sun and NetBSD/hp300). The boot program:

1. gets the client IP address using RARP.
2. gets the client name and server IP address by broadcasting an RPC / BOOTPARAMS / WHOAMI request with the client IP address.
3. gets the server path for this client's root using an RPC / BOOTPARAMS / GETFILE request with the client name.
4. gets the root file handle by calling mountd(8) with the server path for the client root file system.
5. gets the kernel file handle by calling NFS **lookup**() on the root file handle.
6. loads the kernel using NFS read calls on the kernel file handle.
7. transfers control to the kernel entry point.

A BOOTP and/or DHCP secondary bootstrap program will do the following:

1. query for the client's bootstrap parameters. The response must include the client's IP address, and a TFTP server to load the NetBSD kernel from.
2. loads the NetBSD kernel from the TFTP server.
3. transfers control to the kernel entry point.

3. NFS mounting the root file system

In phase 3, the kernel performs an NFS mount of the root file system. The kernel repeats much of the work done by the boot program because there is no standard way for the boot program to pass the information it gathered on to the kernel.

In general, the GENERIC kernel config(1) file for any particular architecture will specify compile-time options to use the same protocol used by the secondary boot program for that architecture. A NetBSD kernel can be compiled to use any of BOOTP, DHCP, or Sun RPC BOOTPARAMS; see options(4).

The procedure typically used by the kernel is as follows:

1. The kernel finds a boot server using the same procedures as described above to determine the client's IP address, an NFS server, etc.
2. The kernel gets the NFS file handle for root using the same procedure as described above.
3. The kernel calls the NFS **getattr**() function to get the last-modified time of the root directory, and uses it to check the system clock.

SERVER CONFIGURATION

Before a client can bootstrap over the network, its server must be configured. Each daemon that implements these protocols must be set up so that it can answer queries from the clients. Some of these daemons are invoked as packets come in, by inetd(8), and some must run independently, started from /etc/rc; see rc.conf(5).

Protocol	Program	Startup
RARP	rarpd	rc.conf(5)
DHCP	dhcpd	rc.conf(5)
BOOTP	bootpd	inetd.conf(5)
TFTP	tftpd	inetd.conf(5)
Sun RPC	rpcbind	rc.conf(5)
Sun RPC	rpc.bootparamd	rc.conf(5)
Sun NFS	mountd	rc.conf(5)
Sun NFS	nfsiod	rc.conf(5)
HP RMP	rbootd	rc.conf(5)

N.B. DHCP is essentially a series of extensions to BOOTP; the NetBSD dhcpd(8) is capable of responding to both kinds of protocol requests. Since they both bind to the same UDP port, only one may be run on a given server.

In the following examples, the client's hostname is **myclient**; the server is **myserver**, and the addresses are all fictional. In these examples the hostnames may be Fully Qualified Domain Names (FQDN, e.g. "myclient.mydomain.com") provided that they are used consistently.

RARP

For clients that use RARP to obtain their IP address, an entry must be added for each client to /etc/ethers with the client's Ethernet MAC address and Internet hostname:

        8:0:20:7:c5:c7   myclient

This will be used by rarpd(8) to reply to queries from the clients. There must be one entry per client system.

A client system's Ethernet MAC address is often printed on the system case, or on a chip on its motherboard, or on the NIC. If not, "sniffing" the network with tcpdump(8) when the client is powered-on should reveal its Ethernet MAC address.

Each client system that uses RARP must have its own, unique IP address assigned to it. Assign an IP address for myclient in your /etc/hosts file, or in the master file for your DNS zone. For /etc/hosts the entry should look like:

        192.197.96.12   myclient

DHCP/BOOTP

The NetBSD DHCP server dhcpd(8) was developed by the Internet Software Consortium (ISC); http://www.isc.org/

DHCP can provide a wide range of information to a requesting client; the key data for bootstrapping a diskless client are:

1. an IP address
2. a subnet mask
3. a TFTP server address for loading the secondary bootstrap and the NetBSD kernel
4. a filename of the secondary bootstrap
5. an NFS server address for the client's file system
6. the client's root file system path, to be NFS mounted.

An example for /etc/dhcpd.conf

```
host myclient {
        hardware ethernet 8:0:20:7:c5:c7;
        fixed-address myclient;                # client's assigned IP address
        filename "myclient.netboot";  # secondary bootstrap
        next-server myserver;         # TFTP server for secondary bootstrap
        option swap-server myserver;  # NFS server for root filesystem
        option root-path "/export/myclient/root";
}
```

That **host** declaration goes inside a **subnet** declaration, which gives parameters for all hosts on the subnet that will be using DHCP, such as the "routers" (the default route), "subnet-mask", "broadcast-address", "domain-name-servers", etc. See dhcpd.conf(5) for details. In that example, **myclient** has an assigned IP address.

The DHCP parameters required for network bootstrapping a system will vary from platform to platform, as dictated by each system's firmware. In particular, because the DHCP is extensible, some hardware vendors have specified DHCP options to return information to requesting clients that are specific to that platform. Please see your platform's boot(8) for details.

TFTP

If booting a Sun system, or other system that expects to use TFTP, ensure that inetd(8) is configured to run tftpd(8). The tftpd(8) server should be set up to serve the directory /tftpboot.

If booting a SPARC system, install a copy of the appropriate diskless secondary boot loader (such as /usr/mdec/boot or ofwboot.net) in the /tftpboot directory. Make a link such that the boot program is accessible by a filename composed of the client's IP address in hexadecimal, a dot, and the architecture name (all upper case). For example:

```
# cd /tftpboot
# ln -s boot C0C5600C.SUN4
```

For a Sun-3 or UltraSPARC system, the filename would be just C0C5600C (these systems' firmware does not append the architecture name). The name used is architecture dependent, it simply has to match what the booting client's system firmware wishes to it to be.

If the client's system firmware fails to fetch the expected file, tcpdump(8) can be used to discover which filename the client is being requested. Also, examination of tftpd(8) log entries (typically in /var/log/messages) should show whether the server is hearing the client system, and what filename the client is asking for.

HP RMP

If booting an HP 300-series system, ensure that /etc/rbootd.conf is configured properly to transfer the boot program to the client. An entry might look like this:

```
08:00:09:01:23:E6      SYS_UBOOT       # myclient
```

The secondary bootstrap program for an HP 300-series system SYS_UBOOT (which may be called uboot.lif before installation) must be installed in the directory /usr/mdec/rbootd.

See the rbootd(8) manual page for more information.

Sun RPC BOOTPARAMS

Add **myclient** to the bootparams database in /etc/bootparams:

```
myclient   root=myserver:/export/myclient/root \
           swap=myserver:/export/myclient/root/swap \
           dump=myserver:/export/myclient/root/swap
```

and ensure that rpc.bootparamd(8) and rpcbind(8) are running. Both **myclient** and **myserver** must have IP addresses in the DNS or /etc/hosts.

Diskless Client File Systems

Build the swap file for **myclient** on the NFS server:

```
# cd /export/myclient/root
# dd if=/dev/zero of=swap bs=16k count=1024
```

This creates a 16 megabyte swap file.

Populate **myclient**'s root file system on the NFS server. How this is done depends on the client architecture and the version of the NetBSD distribution. It can be as simple as copying and modifying the server's root file system, or unpack a complete NetBSD binary distribution for the appropriate platform.

If the NFS server is going to support multiple different architectures (e.g. Alpha, PowerPC, SPARC, MIPS), then it is important to think carefully about how to lay out the NFS server's exported file systems, to share what can be shared (e.g. text files, configuration files, user home directories), and separate that which is distinct to each architecture (e.g. binary executables, libraries).

NFS

Export the client-populated file systems on the NFS server in /etc/exports:

```
/usr -ro myclient
# for SunOS:
# /export/myclient -rw=myclient,root=myclient
# for NetBSD:
/export/myclient -maproot=root -alldirs myclient
```

If the server and client are of the same architecture, then the client can share the server's /usr file system (as is done above). If not, you must build a properly fleshed out /usr partition for the client in some other part of the server's file system, to serve to the client.

If your server is a SPARC, and your client a Sun-3, you might create and fill /export/usr.sun3 and then use the following /etc/exports lines:

```
/export/usr.sun3 -ro myclient
/export/myclient -rw=myclient,root=myclient
```

Of course, in either case you will have to have an NFS server running on the server side.

CLIENT CONFIGURATION

Copy and customize at least the following files in /export/myclient/root:

```
# cd /export/myclient/root/etc
# vi fstab
# cp /etc/hosts hosts
# echo 'hostname="myclient"' >> rc.conf
# echo "inet 192.197.96.12" > ifconfig.le0
```

Note that "le0" above should be replaced with the name of the network interface that the client will use for booting; the network interface name is device dependent in NetBSD.

Correct the critical mount points and the swap file in the client's /etc/fstab (which will be /export/myclient/root/etc/fstab) i.e.

```
myserver:/export/myclient/root    /     nfs   rw 0 0
myserver:/usr                     /usr nfs   rw 0 0
/swap                             none swap sw 0 0
```

Note, you *must* specify the swap file in /etc/fstab or it will not be used! See swapctl(8).

FILES
/etc/hosts	table of associated IP addresses and IP host names; see hosts(5)
/etc/ethers	table of associated Ethernet MAC addresses and IP host names used by rarpd(8); see ethers(5)
/etc/bootparams	client root pathname and swap pathname; see bootparams(5)
/etc/exports	exported NFS mount points; see exports(5)
/etc/rbootd.conf	configuration file for HP RMP; see rbootd(8)
/usr/mdec/rbootd	location of boot programs offered by rbootd(8)
/tftpboot	location of boot programs offered by tftpd(8)

SEE ALSO
bootparams(5), dhcpd.conf(5), ethers(5), exports(5), fstab(5), hosts(5), networks(5), boot(8), dhcpd(8), mopd(8), mountd(8), nfsd(8), rarpd(8), rbootd(8), reboot(8), rpc.bootparamd(8), tftpd(8)

Reverse Address Resolution Protocol, RFC, 903, June 1984.

Bootstrap Loading using TFTP, RFC, 906, June 1984.

Bootstrap Protocol, RFC, 951, September 1985.

The TFTP Protocol (Revision 2), RFC, 1350, July 1992.

Dynamic Host Configuration Protocol, RFC, 2131, March 1997.

DHCP Options and BOOTP Vendor Extensions, RFC, 2132, March 1997.

http://www.rfc-editor.org/

NAME

diskpart — calculate default disk partition sizes

SYNOPSIS

diskpart [**-d**] [**-p**] [**-s** *size*] *disk-type*

DESCRIPTION

diskpart is used to calculate the disk partition sizes based on the default rules used at Berkeley.

Available options and operands:

-d   An entry suitable for inclusion in the disk description file /etc/disktab is generated; for example, disktab(5).

-p   Tables suitable for inclusion in a device driver are produced.

-s *size* The size of the disk may be limited to *size* with the **-s** option.

On disks that use bad144(8) type of bad-sector forwarding, space is normally left in the last partition on the disk for a bad sector forwarding table, although this space is not reflected in the tables produced. The space reserved is one track for the replicated copies of the table and sufficient tracks to hold a pool of 126 sectors to which bad sectors are mapped. For more information, see bad144(8). The **-s** option is intended for other controllers which reserve some space at the end of the disk for bad-sector replacements or other control areas, even if not a multiple of cylinders.

The disk partition sizes are based on the total amount of space on the disk as given in the table below (all values are supplied in units of sectors). The 'c' partition is, by convention, used to access the entire physical disk. The device driver tables include the space reserved for the bad sector forwarding table in the 'c' partition; those used in the disktab and default formats exclude reserved tracks. In normal operation, either the 'g' partition is used, or the 'd', 'e', and 'f' partitions are used. The 'g' and 'f' partitions are variable-sized, occupying whatever space remains after allocation of the fixed sized partitions. If the disk is smaller than 20 Megabytes, then **diskpart** aborts with the message "disk too small, calculate by hand".

Partition	20-60 MB	61-205 MB	206-355 MB	356+ MB
a	15884	15884	15884	15884
b	10032	33440	33440	66880
d	15884	15884	15884	15884
e	unused	55936	55936	307200
h	unused	unused	291346	291346

If an unknown disk type is specified, **diskpart** will prompt for the required disk geometry information.

SEE ALSO

disktab(5), bad144(8)

HISTORY

The **diskpart** command appeared in 4.2 BSD.

BUGS

Most default partition sizes are based on historical artifacts (like the RP06), and may result in unsatisfactory layouts.

When using the **-d** flag, alternative disk names are not included in the output.

NAME
dkctl — program to manipulate disks

SYNOPSIS
dkctl *device*
dkctl *device command* [*arg* [...]]

DESCRIPTION
dkctl allows a user or system administrator to manipulate and configure disks in various ways. It is used by specifying a disk to manipulate, the command to perform, and any arguments the command may require. If **dkctl** is called without any command, it displays strategy, cache, and all of the wedges of the specified device.

COMMANDS
The following commands are supported:

getcache   Get and display the cache enables for the specified device.

setcache *none* | *r* | *w* | *rw* [*save*]
                            Set the cache enables for the specified device. The enables are as follows:

      none   Disable all caches on the disk.

      r   Enable the read cache, and disable all other caches on the disk.

      w   Enable the write cache, and disable all other caches on the disk.

      rw   Enable both the read and write caches on the disk.

      save   If specified, and the cache enables are savable, saves the cache enables in the disk's non-volatile parameter storage.

synccache [*force*]   Causes the cache on the disk to be synchronized, flushing all dirty write cache blocks to the media. If *force* is specified, the cache synchronization command will be issued even if the kernel does not believe that there are any dirty cache blocks in the disk's cache.

keeplabel [*yes* | *no*]
                            Specify to keep or drop the in-core disklabel on the last close of the disk device. (Keep if *yes* is specified, drop if *no* is specified.)

badsector *flush* | *list* | *retry*
                            Used for managing the kernel's bad sector list for wd(4) devices. The software bad sector list is only maintained if the option "WD_SOFTBADSECT" was specified on kernel configuration.

      flush   Clears the in kernel list of bad sectors.

      list   Prints out the list of bad sector ranges recorded by the kernel.

      retry   Flushes the in kernel list and then retries all of the previously recorded bad sectors, causing the list to self update. This option *can only* be used with character devices.

addwedge *name startblk blkcnt ptype*
                            Define a "wedge" on the specified disk starting at block number *startblk* and spanning *blkcnt* blocks. The wedge will have the volume name *name* and the

partition type *ptype*. Valid choices for ptype would be *unused*, *swap*, *ffs*, *lfs*, *ext2fs*, *cd9660*, *ados*, *hfs*, *msdos*, *filecore*, *raidframe*, *ccd*, *appleufs*, *ntfs*, and *cgd*.

The device name of the virtual block device assigned to the wedge will be displayed after the wedge has been successfully created. See dk(4) for more information about disk wedges.

delwedge *dk*   Delete the wedge specified by its device name *dk* from the specified disk.

getwedgeinfo   Display information about the specified disk wedge.

listwedges   List all of the wedges configured on the specified disk.

strategy [*name*]   Get and set the disk I/O scheduler (buffer queue strategy) on the drive. If you do not provide a *name* argument, the currently selected strategy will be shown. To set the bufq strategy, the *name* argument must be specified. *name* must be the name of one of the built-in kernel disk I/O schedulers. To get the list of supported schedulers, use the following command:

```
$ sysctl kern.bufq.strategies
```

Note: The **addwedge** and **delwedge** commands only modify the in-kernel representation of disks; for modifying information on the disks themselves, refer to fdisk(8) or gpt(8).

SEE ALSO

ioctl(2), dk(4), sd(4), wd(4), disklabel(5), atactl(8), fdisk(8), gpt(8), scsictl(8)

HISTORY

The **dkctl** command first appeared in NetBSD 1.6.

AUTHORS

The **dkctl** command was written by Jason R. Thorpe of Wasabi Systems, Inc.

NAME

    dkscan_bsdlabel — program to create wedges from a BSD disklabel

SYNOPSIS

    dkscan_bsdlabel [**-nv**] *device*

DESCRIPTION

    dkscan_bsdlabel scans a disk for a BSD disklabel, which does not need to be the label variant used on the architecture currently running, or even the same endianess.

    The following options are supported:

    -n   No execution - list the wedges, but do not create them.

    -v   Be more verbose - print additional information.

    The argument *device* specifices the disk on which the disklabel is scanned and to which the wedges are added.

EXAMPLES

        dkscan_bsdlabel -v *wd1*

    Create wedges from all recognized partitions on wd1

SEE ALSO

    dk(4), disklabel(5), dkctl(8)

HISTORY

    The **dkscan_bsdlabel** command first appeared in NetBSD 5.0.

AUTHORS

    Martin Huseman wrote the **dkscan_bsdlabel** utility. It is reusing a lot of kernel code written by Jason R. Thorpe.

NAME

dm — dungeon master

SYNOPSIS

ln -s dm *game*

DESCRIPTION

dm is a program used to regulate game playing. **dm** expects to be invoked with the name of a game that a user wishes to play. This is done by creating symbolic links to **dm**, in the directory /usr/games for all of the regulated games. The actual binaries for these games should be placed in a "hidden" directory, /usr/games/hide, that may only be accessed by the **dm** program. **dm** determines if the requested game is available and, if so, runs it. The file /etc/dm.conf controls the conditions under which games may be run.

The file /etc/nogames may be used to "turn off" game playing. If the file exists, no game playing is allowed; the contents of the file will be displayed to any user requesting a game.

FILES

/etc/dm.conf	configuration file
/etc/nogames	turns off game playing
/usr/games/hide	directory of "real" binaries
/var/log/games.log	game logging file

SEE ALSO

dm.conf(5)

HISTORY

The **dm** command appeared in 4.3 BSD–Tahoe.

SECURITY CONSIDERATIONS

Two issues result from **dm** running the games setgid "games". First, all games that allow users to run UNIX commands should carefully set both the real and effective group ids immediately before executing those commands. Probably more important is that **dm** never be setgid anything but "games" so that compromising a game will result only in the user's ability to play games at will. Secondly, games which previously had no reason to run setgid and which accessed user files may have to be modified.

NAME

dmesg — display the system message buffer

SYNOPSIS

dmesg [**-M** core] [**-N** system]

DESCRIPTION

dmesg displays the contents of the system message buffer.

The options are as follows:

-M   Extract values associated with the name list from the specified core instead of the default "/dev/mem".

-N   Extract the name list from the specified system instead of the default "/netbsd".

The system message buffer is a circular buffer of a fixed size. If the buffer has been filled, the first line of the **dmesg** output may not be complete. The size of the message buffer is configurable at compile-time on most systems with the MSGBUFSIZE kernel option. Look for MSGBUFSIZE in options(4) for details.

FILES

/var/run/dmesg.boot copy of dmesg at the time of last boot.

SEE ALSO

options(4), syslogd(8)

HISTORY

The **dmesg** command appeared in 4.0BSD.

NAME
dmsetup – low level logical volume management

SYNOPSIS
dmsetup help *[-c|-C|--columns]*
dmsetup create *device_name [-u uuid] [--notable | --table <table> | table_file]*
dmsetup remove *[-f|--force] device_name*
dmsetup remove_all *[-f|--force]*
dmsetup suspend *[--nolockfs] [--noflush] device_name*
dmsetup resume *device_name*
dmsetup load *device_name [--table <table> | table_file]*
dmsetup clear *device_name*
dmsetup reload *device_name [--table <table> | table_file]*
dmsetup rename *device_name new_name*
dmsetup message *device_name sector message*
dmsetup ls *[--target target_type] [--exec command] [--tree [-o options]]*
dmsetup info *[device_name]*
dmsetup info -c|-C|--columns *[--noheadings] [--separator separator] [-o fields] [-O|--sort sort_fields]*
[device_name]
dmsetup deps *[device_name]*
dmsetup status *[--target target_type] [device_name]*
dmsetup table *[--target target_type] [device_name]*
dmsetup wait *device_name [event_nr]*
dmsetup mknodes *[device_name]*
dmsetup targets
dmsetup version
dmsetup setgeometry *device_name cyl head sect start*

devmap_name *major minor*
devmap_name *major:minor*

DESCRIPTION
dmsetup manages logical devices that use the device-mapper driver. Devices are created by loading a table that specifies a target for each sector (512 bytes) in the logical device.

The first argument to dmsetup is a command. The second argument is the logical device name or uuid.

Invoking the command as **devmap_name** is equivalent to
dmsetup info -c --noheadings -j *major* **-m** *minor*.

OPTIONS
-c|-C|--columns
Display output in columns rather than as Field: Value lines.

-j|--major *major*
Specify the major number.

-m|--minor *minor*
Specify the minor number.

-n|--noheadings
Suppress the headings line when using columnar output.

--noopencount
Tell the kernel not to supply the open reference count for the device.

--notable
When creating a device, don't load any table.

-o|--options
> Specify which fields to display.

-r|--readonly
> Set the table being loaded read-only.

--readahead [+]<sectors>|auto|none
> Specify read ahead size in units of sectors. The default value is "auto" which allows the kernel to choose a suitable value automatically. The + prefix lets you specify a minimum value which will not be used if it is smaller than the value chosen by the kernel. "None" is equivalent to specifying zero.

--table <table>
> Specify a one-line table directly on the command line.

-u|--uuid
> Specify the uuid.

-v|--verbose [-v|--verbose]
> Produce additional output.

--version
> Display the library and kernel driver version.

COMMANDS

create   *device_name [-u uuid] [--notable | --table <table> | table_file]*
> Creates a device with the given name. If table_file or <table> is supplied, the table is loaded and made live. Otherwise a table is read from standard input unless --notable is used. The optional uuid can be used in place of device_name in subsequent dmsetup commands. If successful a device will appear as /dev/device-mapper/<device-name>. See below for information on the table format.

deps   *[device_name]*
> Outputs a list of (major, minor) pairs for devices referenced by the live table for the specified device.

help   *[-c|-C|--columns]*
> Outputs a summary of the commands available, optionally including the list of report fields.

info   *[device_name]*
> Outputs some brief information about the device in the form:
> > State: SUSPENDED|ACTIVE, READ-ONLY
> > Tables present: LIVE and/or INACTIVE
> > Open reference count
> > Last event sequence number (used by **wait**)
> > Major and minor device number
> > Number of targets in the live table
> > UUID

info   *[--noheadings] [--separator separator] [-o fields] [-O|--sort sort_fields] [device_name]*
> Output you can customise. Fields are comma-separated and chosen from the following list: name, major, minor, attr, open, segments, events, uuid. Attributes are: (L)ive, (I)nactive, (s)uspended, (r)ead-only, read-(w)rite. Precede the list with '+' to append to the default selection of columns instead of replacing it. Precede any sort_field with - for a reverse sort on that column.

ls   *[--target target_type] [--exec command] [--tree [-o options]]*
> List device names. Optionally only list devices that have at least one target of the specified type. Optionally execute a command for each device. The device name is appended to the supplied command. --tree displays dependencies between devices as a tree. It accepts a comma-separate list of options. Some specify the information displayed against each node: device/nodevice; active, open, rw, uuid. Others specify how the tree is displayed: ascii, utf, vt100; compact, inverted, notrunc.

load|reload

> *device_name [--table <table> | table_file]*
> Loads <table> or table_file into the inactive table slot for device_name. If neither is supplied, reads a table from standard input.

message

> *device_name sector message*
> Send message to target. If sector not needed use 0.

mknodes

> *[device_name]*
> Ensure that the node in /dev/mapper for device_name is correct. If no device_name is supplied, ensure that all nodes in /dev/mapper correspond to mapped devices currently loaded by the device-mapper kernel driver, adding, changing or removing nodes as necessary.

remove

> *[-f|--force] device_name*
> Removes a device. It will no longer be visible to dmsetup. Open devices cannot be removed except with older kernels that contain a version of device-mapper prior to 4.8.0. In this case the device will be deleted when its open_count drops to zero. From version 4.8.0 onwards, if a device can't be removed because an uninterruptible process is waiting for I/O to return from it, adding --force will replace the table with one that fails all I/O, which might allow the process to be killed.

remove_all

> *[-f|--force]*
> Attempts to remove all device definitions i.e. reset the driver. Use with care! From version 4.8.0 onwards, if devices can't be removed because uninterruptible processess are waiting for I/O to return from them, adding --force will replace the table with one that fails all I/O, which might allow the process to be killed. This also runs **mknodes** afterwards.

rename

> *device_name new_name*
> Renames a device.

resume *device_name*

> Un-suspends a device. If an inactive table has been loaded, it becomes live. Postponed I/O then gets re-queued for processing.

setgeometry

> *device_name cyl head sect start*
> Sets the device geometry to C/H/S.

status   *[--target target_type] [device_name]*

> Outputs status information for each of the device's targets. With --target, only information relating to the specified target type is displayed.

suspend

> *[--nolockfs] [--noflush] device_name*
> Suspends a device. Any I/O that has already been mapped by the device but has not yet completed will be flushed. Any further I/O to that device will be postponed for as long as the device is suspended. If there's a filesystem on the device which supports the operation, an attempt will be made to sync it first unless --nolockfs is specified. Some targets such as recent (October 2006) versions of multipath may support the --noflush option. This lets outstanding I/O that has not yet reached the device to remain unflushed.

table   *[--target target_type] [device_name]*

> Outputs the current table for the device in a format that can be fed back in using the create or load commands. With --target, only information relating to the specified target type is displayed.

targets

> Displays the names and versions of the currently-loaded targets.

version
> Outputs version information.

wait *device_name [event_nr]*
> Sleeps until the event counter for device_name exceeds event_nr. Use -v to see the event number returned. To wait until the next event is triggered, use **info** to find the last event number.

TABLE FORMAT
Each line of the table specifies a single target and is of the form:
>   logical_start_sector num_sectors target_type target_args

There are currently three simple target types available together with more complex optional ones that implement snapshots and mirrors.

linear *destination_device start_sector*
> The traditional linear mapping.

striped *num_stripes chunk_size [destination start_sector]+*
> Creates a striped area.
> e.g. striped 2 32 /dev/hda1 0 /dev/hdb1 0 will map the first chunk (16k) as follows:
>   LV chunk 1 -> hda1, chunk 1
>   LV chunk 2 -> hdb1, chunk 1
>   LV chunk 3 -> hda1, chunk 2
>   LV chunk 4 -> hdb1, chunk 2
>   etc.

error
> Errors any I/O that goes to this area. Useful for testing or for creating devices with holes in them.

EXAMPLES
> # A table to join two disks together
> 0 1028160 linear /dev/hda 0
> 1028160 3903762 linear /dev/hdb 0
>
>
> # A table to stripe across the two disks,
> # and add the spare space from
> # hdb to the back of the volume
>
> 0 2056320 striped 2 32 /dev/hda 0 /dev/hdb 0
> 2056320 2875602 linear /dev/hdb 1028160

ENVIRONMENT VARIABLES
DM_DEV_DIR
> The device directory name. Defaults to "/dev" and must be an absolute path.

AUTHORS
> Original version: Joe Thornber (thornber@sistina.com)

SEE ALSO
> Device-mapper resource page: http://sources.redhat.com/dm/

NAME
dnssec–dsfromkey – DNSSEC DS RR generation tool

SYNOPSIS
dnssec–dsfromkey [–**v** *level*] [–**1**] [–**2**] [–**a** *alg*] [–**l** *domain*] {keyfile}

dnssec–dsfromkey {–s} [–**1**] [–**2**] [–**a** *alg*] [–**K** *directory*] [–**l** *domain*] [–**s**] [–**c** *class*] [–**f** *file*] [–**A**]
[–**v** *level*] {dnsname}

DESCRIPTION
dnssec–dsfromkey outputs the Delegation Signer (DS) resource record (RR), as defined in RFC 3658 and RFC 4509, for the given key(s).

OPTIONS
–1
> Use SHA–1 as the digest algorithm (the default is to use both SHA–1 and SHA–256).

–2
> Use SHA–256 as the digest algorithm.

–a *algorithm*
> Select the digest algorithm. The value of **algorithm** must be one of SHA–1 (SHA1) or SHA–256 (SHA256). These values are case insensitive.

–K *directory*
> Look for key files (or, in keyset mode, *keyset–* files) in **directory**.

–f *file*
> Zone file mode: in place of the keyfile name, the argument is the DNS domain name of a zone master file, which can be read from **file**. If the zone name is the same as **file**, then it may be omitted.

–A
> Include ZSK's when generating DS records. Without this option, only keys which have the KSK flag set will be converted to DS records and printed. Useful only in zone file mode.

–l *domain*
> Generate a DLV set instead of a DS set. The specified **domain** is appended to the name for each record in the set. The DNSSEC Lookaside Validation (DLV) RR is described in RFC 4431.

–s
> Keyset mode: in place of the keyfile name, the argument is the DNS domain name of a keyset file.

–c *class*
> Specifies the DNS class (default is IN). Useful only in keyset or zone file mode.

–v *level*
> Sets the debugging level.

EXAMPLE
To build the SHA–256 DS RR from the **Kexample.com.+003+26160** keyfile name, the following command would be issued:

dnssec–dsfromkey –2 Kexample.com.+003+26160

The command would print something like:

example.com. IN DS 26160 5 2
3A1EADA7A74B8D0BA86726B0C227AA85AB8BBD2B2004F41A868A54F0 C5EA0B94

FILES
The keyfile can be designed by the key identification *Knnnn.+aaa+iiii* or the full file name *Knnnn.+aaa+iiii.key* as generated by dnssec–keygen(8).

The keyset file name is built from the **directory**, the string *keyset–* and the **dnsname**.

CAVEAT

A keyfile error can give a "file not found" even if the file exists.

SEE ALSO

dnssec−keygen(8), **dnssec−signzone**(8), BIND 9 Administrator Reference Manual, RFC 3658, RFC 4431. RFC 4509.

AUTHOR

Internet Systems Consortium

COPYRIGHT

Copyright © 2008, 2009 Internet Systems Consortium, Inc. ("ISC")

DNSSEC–KEYFROMLABEL(8)   BIND9   DNSSEC–KEYFROMLABEL(8)

NAME
dnssec–keyfromlabel – DNSSEC key generation tool

SYNOPSIS
dnssec–keyfromlabel {–l *label*} [**–3**] [**–a** *algorithm*] [**–A** *date/offset*] [**–c** *class*] [**–D** *date/offset*] [**–E** *engine*] [**–f** *flag*] [**–G**] [**–I** *date/offset*] [**–k**] [**–K** *directory*] [**–n** *nametype*] [**–P** *date/offset*] [**–p** *protocol*] [**–R** *date/offset*] [**–t** *type*] [**–v** *level*] {name}

DESCRIPTION
dnssec–keyfromlabel gets keys with the given label from a crypto hardware and builds key files for DNSSEC (Secure DNS), as defined in RFC 2535 and RFC 4034.

The **name** of the key is specified on the command line. This must match the name of the zone for which the key is being generated.

OPTIONS
–a *algorithm*

Selects the cryptographic algorithm. The value of **algorithm** must be one of RSAMD5, RSASHA1, DSA, NSEC3RSASHA1, NSEC3DSA, RSASHA256 or RSASHA512. These values are case insensitive.

If no algorithm is specified, then RSASHA1 will be used by default, unless the **–3** option is specified, in which case NSEC3RSASHA1 will be used instead. (If **–3** is used and an algorithm is specified, that algorithm will be checked for compatibility with NSEC3.)

Note 1: that for DNSSEC, RSASHA1 is a mandatory to implement algorithm, and DSA is recommended.

Note 2: DH automatically sets the –k flag.

–3

Use an NSEC3–capable algorithm to generate a DNSSEC key. If this option is used and no algorithm is explicitly set on the command line, NSEC3RSASHA1 will be used by default.

–E *engine*

Specifies the name of the crypto hardware (OpenSSL engine). When compiled with PKCS#11 support it defaults to "pkcs11".

–l *label*

Specifies the label of the key pair in the crypto hardware. The label may be preceded by an optional OpenSSL engine name, separated by a colon, as in "pkcs11:keylabel".

–n *nametype*

Specifies the owner type of the key. The value of **nametype** must either be ZONE (for a DNSSEC zone key (KEY/DNSKEY)), HOST or ENTITY (for a key associated with a host (KEY)), USER (for a key associated with a user(KEY)) or OTHER (DNSKEY). These values are case insensitive.

–C

Compatibility mode: generates an old–style key, without any metadata. By default, **dnssec–keyfromlabel** will include the key's creation date in the metadata stored with the private key, and other dates may be set there as well (publication date, activation date, etc). Keys that include this data may be incompatible with older versions of BIND; the **–C** option suppresses them.

–c *class*

Indicates that the DNS record containing the key should have the specified class. If not specified, class IN is used.

–f *flag*

Set the specified flag in the flag field of the KEY/DNSKEY record. The only recognized flags are KSK (Key Signing Key) and REVOKE.

–G

Generate a key, but do not publish it or sign with it. This option is incompatible with −P and −A.

−h

Prints a short summary of the options and arguments to **dnssec–keyfromlabel**.

−K *directory*

Sets the directory in which the key files are to be written.

−k

Generate KEY records rather than DNSKEY records.

−p *protocol*

Sets the protocol value for the key. The protocol is a number between 0 and 255. The default is 3 (DNSSEC). Other possible values for this argument are listed in RFC 2535 and its successors.

−t *type*

Indicates the use of the key. **type** must be one of AUTHCONF, NOAUTHCONF, NOAUTH, or NOCONF. The default is AUTHCONF. AUTH refers to the ability to authenticate data, and CONF the ability to encrypt data.

−v *level*

Sets the debugging level.

TIMING OPTIONS

Dates can be expressed in the format YYYYMMDD or YYYYMMDDHHMMSS. If the argument begins with a '+' or '−', it is interpreted as an offset from the present time. For convenience, if such an offset is followed by one of the suffixes 'y', 'mo', 'w', 'd', 'h', or 'mi', then the offset is computed in years (defined as 365 24−hour days, ignoring leap years), months (defined as 30 24−hour days), weeks, days, hours, or minutes, respectively. Without a suffix, the offset is computed in seconds.

−P *date/offset*

Sets the date on which a key is to be published to the zone. After that date, the key will be included in the zone but will not be used to sign it. If not set, and if the −G option has not been used, the default is "now".

−A *date/offset*

Sets the date on which the key is to be activated. After that date, the key will be included in the zone and used to sign it. If not set, and if the −G option has not been used, the default is "now".

−R *date/offset*

Sets the date on which the key is to be revoked. After that date, the key will be flagged as revoked. It will be included in the zone and will be used to sign it.

−U *date/offset*

Sets the date on which the key is to be retired. After that date, the key will still be included in the zone, but it will not be used to sign it.

−D *date/offset*

Sets the date on which the key is to be deleted. After that date, the key will no longer be included in the zone. (It may remain in the key repository, however.)

GENERATED KEY FILES

When **dnssec–keyfromlabel** completes successfully, it prints a string of the form *Knnnn.+aaa+iiiii* to the standard output. This is an identification string for the key files it has generated.

- *nnnn* is the key name.

- *aaa* is the numeric representation of the algorithm.

- *iiiii* is the key identifier (or footprint).

dnssec–keyfromlabel creates two files, with names based on the printed string. *Knnnn.+aaa+iiiii.key* contains the public key, and *Knnnn.+aaa+iiiii.private* contains the private key.

The *.key* file contains a DNS KEY record that can be inserted into a zone file (directly or with a

DNSSEC–KEYFROMLABEL(8)   BIND9   DNSSEC–KEYFROMLABEL(8)

$INCLUDE statement).

The *.private* file contains algorithm–specific fields. For obvious security reasons, this file does not have general read permission.

SEE ALSO

dnssec–keygen(8), **dnssec–signzone**(8), BIND 9 Administrator Reference Manual, RFC 4034.

AUTHOR

Internet Systems Consortium

COPYRIGHT

Copyright © 2008, 2009 Internet Systems Consortium, Inc. ("ISC")

NAME

dnssec–keygen – DNSSEC key generation tool

SYNOPSIS

dnssec–keygen [–**a** *algorithm*] [–**b** *keysize*] [–**n** *nametype*] [–**3**] [–**A** *date/offset*] [–**C**] [–**c** *class*]
[–**D** *date/offset*] [–**E** *engine*] [–**e**] [–**f** *flag*] [–**G**] [–**g** *generator*] [–**h**] [–**I** *date/offset*]
[–**K** *directory*] [–**k**] [–**P** *date/offset*] [–**p** *protocol*] [–**q**] [–**R** *date/offset*] [–**r** *randomdev*]
[–**s** *strength*] [–**t** *type*] [–**v** *level*] [–**z**] {name}

DESCRIPTION

dnssec–keygen generates keys for DNSSEC (Secure DNS), as defined in RFC 2535 and RFC 4034. It can
also generate keys for use with TSIG (Transaction Signatures) as defined in RFC 2845, or TKEY
(Transaction Key) as defined in RFC 2930.

The **name** of the key is specified on the command line. For DNSSEC keys, this must match the name of the
zone for which the key is being generated.

OPTIONS

–a *algorithm*

Selects the cryptographic algorithm. For DNSSEC keys, the value of **algorithm** must be one of
RSAMD5, RSASHA1, DSA, NSEC3RSASHA1, NSEC3DSA, RSASHA256 or RSASHA512. For
TSIG/TKEY, the value must be DH (Diffie Hellman), HMAC–MD5, HMAC–SHA1,
HMAC–SHA224, HMAC–SHA256, HMAC–SHA384, or HMAC–SHA512. These values are case
insensitive.

If no algorithm is specified, then RSASHA1 will be used by default, unless the –3 option is specified,
in which case NSEC3RSASHA1 will be used instead. (If –3 is used and an algorithm is specified, that
algorithm will be checked for compatibility with NSEC3.)

Note 1: that for DNSSEC, RSASHA1 is a mandatory to implement algorithm, and DSA is
recommended. For TSIG, HMAC–MD5 is mandatory.

Note 2: DH, HMAC–MD5, and HMAC–SHA1 through HMAC–SHA512 automatically set the –T
KEY option.

–b *keysize*

Specifies the number of bits in the key. The choice of key size depends on the algorithm used. RSA
keys must be between 512 and 2048 bits. Diffie Hellman keys must be between 128 and 4096 bits.
DSA keys must be between 512 and 1024 bits and an exact multiple of 64. HMAC keys must be
between 1 and 512 bits.

The key size does not need to be specified if using a default algorithm. The default key size is 1024
bits for zone signing keys (ZSK's) and 2048 bits for key signing keys (KSK's, generated with –**f**
KSK). However, if an algorithm is explicitly specified with the –**a**, then there is no default key size,
and the –**b** must be used.

–n *nametype*

Specifies the owner type of the key. The value of **nametype** must either be ZONE (for a DNSSEC
zone key (KEY/DNSKEY)), HOST or ENTITY (for a key associated with a host (KEY)), USER (for a
key associated with a user(KEY)) or OTHER (DNSKEY). These values are case insensitive. Defaults
to ZONE for DNSKEY generation.

–3

Use an NSEC3–capable algorithm to generate a DNSSEC key. If this option is used and no algorithm
is explicitly set on the command line, NSEC3RSASHA1 will be used by default. Note that
RSASHA256 and RSASHA512 algorithms are NSEC3–capable.

–C

Compatibility mode: generates an old–style key, without any metadata. By default, **dnssec–keygen** will include the key's creation date in the metadata stored with the private key, and other dates may be set there as well (publication date, activation date, etc). Keys that include this data may be incompatible with older versions of BIND; the **–C** option suppresses them.

–c *class*

Indicates that the DNS record containing the key should have the specified class. If not specified, class IN is used.

–E *engine*

Uses a crypto hardware (OpenSSL engine) for random number and, when supported, key generation. When compiled with PKCS#11 support it defaults to pkcs11; the empty name resets it to no engine.

–e

If generating an RSAMD5/RSASHA1 key, use a large exponent.

–f *flag*

Set the specified flag in the flag field of the KEY/DNSKEY record. The only recognized flags are KSK (Key Signing Key) and REVOKE.

–G

Generate a key, but do not publish it or sign with it. This option is incompatible with –P and –A.

–g *generator*

If generating a Diffie Hellman key, use this generator. Allowed values are 2 and 5. If no generator is specified, a known prime from RFC 2539 will be used if possible; otherwise the default is 2.

–h

Prints a short summary of the options and arguments to **dnssec–keygen**.

–K *directory*

Sets the directory in which the key files are to be written.

–k

Deprecated in favor of –T KEY.

–p *protocol*

Sets the protocol value for the generated key. The protocol is a number between 0 and 255. The default is 3 (DNSSEC). Other possible values for this argument are listed in RFC 2535 and its successors.

–q

Quiet mode: Suppresses unnecessary output, including progress indication. Without this option, when **dnssec–keygen** is run interactively to generate an RSA or DSA key pair, it will print a string of symbols to *stderr* indicating the progress of the key generation. A '.' indicates that a random number has been found which passed an initial sieve test; '+' means a number has passed a single round of the Miller–Rabin primality test; a space means that the number has passed all the tests and is a satisfactory key.

–r *randomdev*

Specifies the source of randomness. If the operating system does not provide a */dev/random* or equivalent device, the default source of randomness is keyboard input. *randomdev* specifies the name of a character device or file containing random data to be used instead of the default. The special value *keyboard* indicates that keyboard input should be used.

–s *strength*

Specifies the strength value of the key. The strength is a number between 0 and 15, and currently has no defined purpose in DNSSEC.

–T *rrtype*

Specifies the resource record type to use for the key. **rrtype** must be either DNSKEY or KEY. The default is DNSKEY when using a DNSSEC algorithm, but it can be overridden to KEY for use with SIG(0). Using any TSIG algorithm (HMAC–* or DH) forces this option to KEY.

–t *type*

Indicates the use of the key. **type** must be one of AUTHCONF, NOAUTHCONF, NOAUTH, or NOCONF. The default is AUTHCONF. AUTH refers to the ability to authenticate data, and CONF the ability to encrypt data.

−v *level*
> Sets the debugging level.

TIMING OPTIONS

Dates can be expressed in the format YYYYMMDD or YYYYMMDDHHMMSS. If the argument begins with a '+' or '−', it is interpreted as an offset from the present time. For convenience, if such an offset is followed by one of the suffixes 'y', 'mo', 'w', 'd', 'h', or 'mi', then the offset is computed in years (defined as 365 24−hour days, ignoring leap years), months (defined as 30 24−hour days), weeks, days, hours, or minutes, respectively. Without a suffix, the offset is computed in seconds.

−P *date/offset*
> Sets the date on which a key is to be published to the zone. After that date, the key will be included in the zone but will not be used to sign it. If not set, and if the −G option has not been used, the default is "now".

−A *date/offset*
> Sets the date on which the key is to be activated. After that date, the key will be included in the zone and used to sign it. If not set, and if the −G option has not been used, the default is "now".

−R *date/offset*
> Sets the date on which the key is to be revoked. After that date, the key will be flagged as revoked. It will be included in the zone and will be used to sign it.

−I *date/offset*
> Sets the date on which the key is to be retired. After that date, the key will still be included in the zone, but it will not be used to sign it.

−D *date/offset*
> Sets the date on which the key is to be deleted. After that date, the key will no longer be included in the zone. (It may remain in the key repository, however.)

GENERATED KEYS

When **dnssec–keygen** completes successfully, it prints a string of the form *Knnnn.+aaa+iiiii* to the standard output. This is an identification string for the key it has generated.

- *nnnn* is the key name.

- *aaa* is the numeric representation of the algorithm.

- *iiiii* is the key identifier (or footprint).

dnssec–keygen creates two files, with names based on the printed string. *Knnnn.+aaa+iiiii.key* contains the public key, and *Knnnn.+aaa+iiiii.private* contains the private key.

The *.key* file contains a DNS KEY record that can be inserted into a zone file (directly or with a $INCLUDE statement).

The *.private* file contains algorithm−specific fields. For obvious security reasons, this file does not have general read permission.

Both *.key* and *.private* files are generated for symmetric encryption algorithms such as HMAC−MD5, even though the public and private key are equivalent.

EXAMPLE

To generate a 768−bit DSA key for the domain **example.com**, the following command would be issued:

dnssec–keygen −a DSA −b 768 −n ZONE example.com

The command would print a string of the form:

Kexample.com.+003+26160

DNSSEC–KEYGEN(8)   BIND9   DNSSEC–KEYGEN(8)

       In this example, **dnssec–keygen** creates the files *Kexample.com.+003+26160.key* and
       Kexample.com.+003+26160.private.

SEE ALSO

       dnssec–signzone(8), BIND 9 Administrator Reference Manual, RFC 2539, RFC 2845, RFC 4034.

AUTHOR

       Internet Systems Consortium

COPYRIGHT

       Copyright © 2004, 2005, 2007–2009 Internet Systems Consortium, Inc. ("ISC")
       Copyright © 2000–2003 Internet Software Consortium.

NAME

dnssec–revoke – Set the REVOKED bit on a DNSSEC key

SYNOPSIS

dnssec–revoke [**–hr**] [**–v** *level*] [**–K** *directory*] [**–E** *engine*] [**–f**] {keyfile}

DESCRIPTION

dnssec–revoke reads a DNSSEC key file, sets the REVOKED bit on the key as defined in RFC 5011, and creates a new pair of key files containing the now–revoked key.

OPTIONS

–h

Emit usage message and exit.

–K *directory*

Sets the directory in which the key files are to reside.

–r

After writing the new keyset files remove the original keyset files.

–v *level*

Sets the debugging level.

–E *engine*

Use the given OpenSSL engine. When compiled with PKCS#11 support it defaults to pkcs11; the empty name resets it to no engine.

–f

Force overwrite: Causes **dnssec–revoke** to write the new key pair even if a file already exists matching the algorithm and key ID of the revoked key.

SEE ALSO

dnssec–keygen(8), BIND 9 Administrator Reference Manual, RFC 5011.

AUTHOR

Internet Systems Consortium

COPYRIGHT

Copyright © 2009 Internet Systems Consortium, Inc. ("ISC")

NAME
dnssec−settime − Set the key timing metadata for a DNSSEC key

SYNOPSIS
dnssec−settime [−**f**] [−**K** *directory*] [−**P** *date/offset*] [−**A** *date/offset*] [−**R** *date/offset*] [−**I** *date/offset*]
[−**D** *date/offset*] [−**h**] [−**v** *level*] [−**E** *engine*] {keyfile}

DESCRIPTION
dnssec−settime reads a DNSSEC private key file and sets the key timing metadata as specified by the −**P**, −**A**, −**R**, −**I**, and −**D** options. The metadata can then be used by **dnssec−signzone** or other signing software to determine when a key is to be published, whether it should be used for signing a zone, etc.

If none of these options is set on the command line, then **dnssec−settime** simply prints the key timing metadata already stored in the key.

When key metadata fields are changed, both files of a key pair (*Knnnn.+aaa+iiiii.key* and *Knnnn.+aaa+iiiii.private*) are regenerated. Metadata fields are stored in the private file. A human−readable description of the metadata is also placed in comments in the key file.

OPTIONS
−**f**

Force an update of an old−format key with no metadata fields. Without this option, **dnssec−settime** will fail when attempting to update a legacy key. With this option, the key will be recreated in the new format, but with the original key data retained. The key's creation date will be set to the present time.

−**K** *directory*

Sets the directory in which the key files are to reside.

−**h**

Emit usage message and exit.

−**v** *level*

Sets the debugging level.

−**E** *engine*

Use the given OpenSSL engine. When compiled with PKCS#11 support it defaults to pkcs11; the empty name resets it to no engine.

TIMING OPTIONS
Dates can be expressed in the format YYYYMMDD or YYYYMMDDHHMMSS. If the argument begins with a '+' or '−', it is interpreted as an offset from the present time. For convenience, if such an offset is followed by one of the suffixes 'y', 'mo', 'w', 'd', 'h', or 'mi', then the offset is computed in years (defined as 365 24−hour days, ignoring leap years), months (defined as 30 24−hour days), weeks, days, hours, or minutes, respectively. Without a suffix, the offset is computed in seconds. To unset a date, use 'none'.

−**P** *date/offset*

Sets the date on which a key is to be published to the zone. After that date, the key will be included in the zone but will not be used to sign it.

−**A** *date/offset*

Sets the date on which the key is to be activated. After that date, the key will be included in the zone and used to sign it.

−**R** *date/offset*

Sets the date on which the key is to be revoked. After that date, the key will be flagged as revoked. It will be included in the zone and will be used to sign it.

−**I** *date/offset*

Sets the date on which the key is to be retired. After that date, the key will still be included in the zone, but it will not be used to sign it.

−**D** *date/offset*

Sets the date on which the key is to be deleted. After that date, the key will no longer be included in the zone. (It may remain in the key repository, however.)

PRINTING OPTIONS

dnssec–settime can also be used to print the timing metadata associated with a key.

−u

Print times in UNIX epoch format.

−p *C/P/A/R/U/D/all*

Print a specific metadata value or set of metadata values. The **−p** option may be followed by one or more of the following letters to indicate which value or values to print: **C** for the creation date, **P** for the publication date, **A** for the activation date, **R** for the revokation date, **U** for the unpublication date, or **D** for the deletion date. To print all of the metadata, use **−p all**.

SEE ALSO

dnssec–keygen(8), **dnssec–signzone**(8), BIND 9 Administrator Reference Manual, RFC 5011.

AUTHOR

Internet Systems Consortium

COPYRIGHT

Copyright © 2009 Internet Systems Consortium, Inc. ("ISC")

DNSSEC–SIGNZONE(8)   BIND9   DNSSEC–SIGNZONE(8)

NAME
dnssec–signzone – DNSSEC zone signing tool

SYNOPSIS
dnssec–signzone [–**a**] [–**c** *class*] [–**d** *directory*] [–**E** *engine*] [–**e** *end–time*] [–**f** *output–file*] [–**g**] [–**h**]
[–**K** *directory*] [–**k** *key*] [–**l** *domain*] [–**i** *interval*] [–**I** *input–format*] [–**j** *jitter*]
[–**N** *soa–serial–format*] [–**o** *origin*] [–**O** *output–format*] [–**p**] [–**P**] [–**r** *randomdev*]
[–**S**] [–**s** *start–time*] [–**T** *ttl*] [–**t**] [–**u**] [–**v** *level*] [–**x**] [–**z**] [–**3** *salt*] [–**H** *iterations*]
[–**A**] {zonefile} [key...]

DESCRIPTION
dnssec–signzone signs a zone. It generates NSEC and RRSIG records and produces a signed version of the
zone. The security status of delegations from the signed zone (that is, whether the child zones are secure or
not) is determined by the presence or absence of a *keyset* file for each child zone.

OPTIONS
–a
> Verify all generated signatures.

–c *class*
> Specifies the DNS class of the zone.

–C
> Compatibility mode: Generate a *keyset–zonename* file in addition to *dsset–zonename* when signing a
> zone, for use by older versions of **dnssec–signzone**.

–d *directory*
> Look for *dsset–* or *keyset–* files in **directory**.

–E *engine*
> Uses a crypto hardware (OpenSSL engine) for the crypto operations it supports, for instance signing
> with private keys from a secure key store. When compiled with PKCS#11 support it defaults to
> pkcs11; the empty name resets it to no engine.

–g
> Generate DS records for child zones from *dsset–* or *keyset–* file. Existing DS records will be removed.

–K *directory*
> Key repository: Specify a directory to search for DNSSEC keys. If not specified, defaults to the current
> directory.

–k *key*
> Treat specified key as a key signing key ignoring any key flags. This option may be specified multiple
> times.

–l *domain*
> Generate a DLV set in addition to the key (DNSKEY) and DS sets. The domain is appended to the
> name of the records.

–s *start–time*
> Specify the date and time when the generated RRSIG records become valid. This can be either an
> absolute or relative time. An absolute start time is indicated by a number in YYYYMMDDHHMMSS
> notation; 20000530144500 denotes 14:45:00 UTC on May 30th, 2000. A relative start time is
> indicated by +N, which is N seconds from the current time. If no **start–time** is specified, the current
> time minus 1 hour (to allow for clock skew) is used.

–e *end–time*
> Specify the date and time when the generated RRSIG records expire. As with **start–time**, an absolute
> time is indicated in YYYYMMDDHHMMSS notation. A time relative to the start time is indicated
> with +N, which is N seconds from the start time. A time relative to the current time is indicated with
> now+N. If no **end–time** is specified, 30 days from the start time is used as a default. **end–time** must
> be later than **start–time**.

−f *output−file*

    The name of the output file containing the signed zone. The default is to append *.signed* to the input filename.

−h

    Prints a short summary of the options and arguments to **dnssec–signzone**.

−i *interval*

    When a previously–signed zone is passed as input, records may be resigned. The **interval** option specifies the cycle interval as an offset from the current time (in seconds). If a RRSIG record expires after the cycle interval, it is retained. Otherwise, it is considered to be expiring soon, and it will be replaced.

    The default cycle interval is one quarter of the difference between the signature end and start times. So if neither **end–time** or **start–time** are specified, **dnssec–signzone** generates signatures that are valid for 30 days, with a cycle interval of 7.5 days. Therefore, if any existing RRSIG records are due to expire in less than 7.5 days, they would be replaced.

−I *input–format*

    The format of the input zone file. Possible formats are **"text"** (default) and **"raw"**. This option is primarily intended to be used for dynamic signed zones so that the dumped zone file in a non–text format containing updates can be signed directly. The use of this option does not make much sense for non–dynamic zones.

−j *jitter*

    When signing a zone with a fixed signature lifetime, all RRSIG records issued at the time of signing expires simultaneously. If the zone is incrementally signed, i.e. a previously–signed zone is passed as input to the signer, all expired signatures have to be regenerated at about the same time. The **jitter** option specifies a jitter window that will be used to randomize the signature expire time, thus spreading incremental signature regeneration over time.

    Signature lifetime jitter also to some extent benefits validators and servers by spreading out cache expiration, i.e. if large numbers of RRSIGs don't expire at the same time from all caches there will be less congestion than if all validators need to refetch at mostly the same time.

−n *ncpus*

    Specifies the number of threads to use. By default, one thread is started for each detected CPU.

−N *soa−serial−format*

    The SOA serial number format of the signed zone. Possible formats are **"keep"** (default), **"increment"** and **"unixtime"**.

        "keep"

        Do not modify the SOA serial number.

        "increment"

        Increment the SOA serial number using RFC 1982 arithmetics.

        "unixtime"

        Set the SOA serial number to the number of seconds since epoch.

−o *origin*

    The zone origin. If not specified, the name of the zone file is assumed to be the origin.

−O *output−format*

    The format of the output file containing the signed zone. Possible formats are **"text"** (default) and **"raw"**.

−p

    Use pseudo–random data when signing the zone. This is faster, but less secure, than using real random data. This option may be useful when signing large zones or when the entropy source is limited.

–P

Disable post sign verification tests.

The post sign verification test ensures that for each algorithm in use there is at least one non revoked self signed KSK key, that all revoked KSK keys are self signed, and that all records in the zone are signed by the algorithm. This option skips these tests.

–r *randomdev*

Specifies the source of randomness. If the operating system does not provide a */dev/random* or equivalent device, the default source of randomness is keyboard input. *randomdev* specifies the name of a character device or file containing random data to be used instead of the default. The special value *keyboard* indicates that keyboard input should be used.

–S

Smart signing: Instructs **dnssec–signzone** to search the key repository for keys that match the zone being signed, and to include them in the zone if appropriate.

When a key is found, its timing metadata is examined to determine how it should be used, according to the following rules. Each successive rule takes priority over the prior ones:

If no timing metadata has been set for the key, the key is published in the zone and used to sign the zone.

If the key's publication date is set and is in the past, the key is published in the zone.

If the key's activation date is set and in the past, the key is published (regardless of publication date) and used to sign the zone.

If the key's revocation date is set and in the past, and the key is published, then the key is revoked, and the revoked key is used to sign the zone.

If either of the key's unpublication or deletion dates are set and in the past, the key is NOT published or used to sign the zone, regardless of any other metadata.

–T *ttl*

Specifies the TTL to be used for new DNSKEY records imported into the zone from the key repository. If not specified, the default is the minimum TTL value from the zone's SOA record. This option is ignored when signing without –S, since DNSKEY records are not imported from the key repository in that case. It is also ignored if there are any pre–existing DNSKEY records at the zone apex, in which case new records' TTL values will be set to match them.

–t

Print statistics at completion.

–u

Update NSEC/NSEC3 chain when re–signing a previously signed zone. With this option, a zone signed with NSEC can be switched to NSEC3, or a zone signed with NSEC3 can be switch to NSEC or to NSEC3 with different parameters. Without this option, **dnssec–signzone** will retain the existing chain when re–signing.

–v *level*

Sets the debugging level.

–x

Only sign the DNSKEY RRset with key–signing keys, and omit signatures from zone–signing keys. (This is similar to the **dnssec–dnskey–kskonly yes;** zone option in **named**.)

–z

Ignore KSK flag on key when determining what to sign. This causes KSK–flagged keys to sign all records, not just the DNSKEY RRset. (This is similar to the **update–check–ksk no;** zone option in **named**.)

–3 *salt*

DNSSEC–SIGNZONE(8)   BIND9   DNSSEC–SIGNZONE(8)

Generate an NSEC3 chain with the given hex encoded salt. A dash (*salt*) can be used to indicate that no salt is to be used when generating the NSEC3 chain.

−H *iterations*

When generating an NSEC3 chain, use this many interations. The default is 10.

−A

When generating an NSEC3 chain set the OPTOUT flag on all NSEC3 records and do not generate NSEC3 records for insecure delegations.

Using this option twice (i.e., **−AA**) turns the OPTOUT flag off for all records. This is useful when using the **−u** option to modify an NSEC3 chain which previously had OPTOUT set.

zonefile

The file containing the zone to be signed.

key

Specify which keys should be used to sign the zone. If no keys are specified, then the zone will be examined for DNSKEY records at the zone apex. If these are found and there are matching private keys, in the current directory, then these will be used for signing.

EXAMPLE

The following command signs the **example.com** zone with the DSA key generated by **dnssec–keygen** (Kexample.com.+003+17247). Because the **−S** option is not being used, the zone's keys must be in the master file (*db.example.com*). This invocation looks for *dsset* files, in the current directory, so that DS records can be imported from them (**−g**).

```
% dnssec–signzone −g −o example.com db.example.com \
Kexample.com.+003+17247
db.example.com.signed
%
```

In the above example, **dnssec–signzone** creates the file *db.example.com.signed*. This file should be referenced in a zone statement in a *named.conf* file.

This example re–signs a previously signed zone with default parameters. The private keys are assumed to be in the current directory.

```
% cp db.example.com.signed db.example.com
% dnssec–signzone −o example.com db.example.com
db.example.com.signed
%
```

SEE ALSO

dnssec–keygen(8), BIND 9 Administrator Reference Manual, RFC 4033.

AUTHOR

Internet Systems Consortium

COPYRIGHT

Copyright © 2004–2009 Internet Systems Consortium, Inc. ("ISC")
Copyright © 2000–2003 Internet Software Consortium.

NAME
dosboot — boot NetBSD/i386 from DOS

SYNOPSIS
dosboot [-u] [-c *command*] [-i] [*path* [-adqsv]]

DESCRIPTION
dosboot is an MS-DOS program. It is a boot loader for NetBSD/i386 designed to permit NetBSD to be booted directly from MS-DOS. By default, it boots a file with name NETBSD in the current MS-DOS directory. dosboot shares common code with the standard boot loader, boot(8).

The recognized options are:

-c   Execute *command* (see below).

-i   Enter interactive mode. dosboot will present a prompt, allowing input of commands (see below).

-u   Boot from a UFS filesystem instead of an MS-DOS filesystem.

path Specifies the kernel file. In MS-DOS mode (default) a normal MS-DOS filename (with or without drive specification) is accepted. In UFS mode (after -u or after a **mode ufs** command), a path in a NetBSD filesystem is expected. By default, the file is looked up in partition 'a' of the first harddisk. Another device or partition can be specified by prepending a block device name in terms of NetBSD, followed by a colon (see boot(8) and examples).

-adqsv
        Flags passed to the kernel, see boot(8).

The commands accepted after the -c flag or in interactive mode are:

boot [*device*:] [*filename*] [-1234abcdmqsvxz]
        Boot NetBSD. See **boot** in boot(8) for full details.

dev [device]
        Set the default device and partition for subsequent filesystem operations. Without an operand, print the current setting. This setting doesn't apply to MS-DOS mode.

help
        Print an overview about commands and arguments.

ls [path]
        Print a directory listing of path, containing inode number, filename and file type. This command works in UFS mode only. path can contain a device specification.

mode *fstype*
        Switch filesystem type; *fstype* should be one of *dos* or *ufs*.

quit
        Leave the dosboot program and exit to MS-DOS.

dosboot is also installed in the release(7) hierarchy, under installation/misc/dosboot.com.

FILES
/usr/mdec/dosboot.com

EXAMPLES

To boot a NetBSD kernel located on MS-DOS drive D, one would issue:

```
dosboot D:\NODOS\NETBSD
```

To boot from a NetBSD floppy into single user mode, type e.g.:

```
dosboot -u fd0a:netbsd -s
```

SEE ALSO

release(7), boot(8), w95boot(8)

HISTORY

The NetBSD/i386 **dosboot** command first appeared in NetBSD 1.3.

BUGS

dosboot assumes that the processor is in real mode at startup. It does not work well in the presence of MS-DOS extenders and memory managers.

dosboot does not run directly under Windows 95. See w95boot(8) for a method of starting NetBSD from Windows 95 using dosboot.

In UFS mode, files can only be loaded from devices known to the BIOS. The device names do not necessarily comply with the names later used by the booted NetBSD kernel.

In MS-DOS mode, no useful boot device specification is passed to NetBSD. It is necessary to have the root device hardwired into the kernel configuration or to enter it manually.

NAME

   drtest — stand-alone disk test program

DESCRIPTION

   drtest is a stand-alone program used to read a disk track by track. It was primarily intended as a test program for new stand-alone drivers, but has shown useful in other contexts as well, such as verifying disks and
   running speed tests. For example, when a disk has been formatted (by format(8)), you can check that hard
   errors has been taken care of by running **drtest**. No hard errors should be found, but in many cases quite a
   few soft ECC errors will be reported.

   While **drtest** is running, the cylinder number is printed on the console for every 10th cylinder read.

EXAMPLES

   A sample run of **drtest** is shown below. In this example (using a 750), **drtest** is loaded from the root
   file system; usually it will be loaded from the machine's console storage device. Boldface means user input.
   As usual, "#" and "@" may be used to edit input.

   ```
   >>>B/3
   %%
   loading hk(0,0)boot
   Boot
   :  hk(0,0)drtest
   Test program for stand-alone up and hp driver

   Debugging level (1=bse, 2=ecc, 3=bse+ecc)?
   Enter disk name [type(adapter,unit), e.g. hp(1,3)]? hp(0,0)
   Device data: #cylinders=1024, #tracks=16, #sectors=32
   Testing hp(0,0), chunk size is 16384 bytes.
   ```
   (chunk size is the number of bytes read per disk access)
   ```
   Start ...Make sure hp(0,0) is online
    . . .
   ```
   (errors are reported as they occur)
   ```
    . . .
   ```
   (...program restarts to allow checking other disks)
   (...to abort halt machine with ^P)

DIAGNOSTICS

   The diagnostics are intended to be self explanatory. Note, however, that the device number in the diagnostic
   messages is identified as *typeX* instead of *type(a,u)* where $X = a*8+u$, e.g., hp(1,3) becomes hp11.

SEE ALSO

   bad144(8), format(8)

HISTORY

   The **drtest** command appeared in 4.2 BSD.

AUTHORS

   Helge Skrivervik

NAME

   drvctl — tool to rescan busses and detach devices on user request

SYNOPSIS

   drvctl **-r** [**-a** *attribute*] *busdevice* [locator ...]
   drvctl **-d** *device*
   drvctl [**-n**] **-l** [*device*]
   drvctl **-p** *device*
   drvctl **-Q** *device*
   drvctl **-R** *device*
   drvctl **-S** *device*

DESCRIPTION

   The **drvctl** program works with the drvctl(4) pseudo-driver, and allows to rescan busses and to detach
   drivers from devices.

   The following options are available:

   -a   Give the interface attribute where children are to be attached to (and which defines the interpreta-
            tion of the locator information). This will only be needed in rare cases where the bus has multiple
            attributes.

   -d   Detach the device driver from the device given by the *device* argument.

   -l   List the children of the device specified by the *device* argument. If *device* is not specified, list
            roots of the device tree instead. Output comes in two columns. The first column is *device*, or
            "root" if *device* is not specified. The second column is the child.

   -n   Suppress first column in **-l** output.

   -p   Get the properties for the device specified by the *device* argument. The properties are displayed
            as an XML property list.

   -Q   Resume the ancestors of *device*, *device* itself, and all of its descendants.

   -R   Resume both the ancestors of *device* and *device* itself.

   -r   Rescan the bus given by the *busdevice* argument. The scan range can be restricted by an
            optional *locator* list.

   -S   Suspend both the descendants of *device* and *device* itself.

FILES

   /dev/drvctl

SEE ALSO

   proplib(3), autoconf(9)

BUGS

   Currently, there is no good way to get information about locator lengths and default values (which is present
   at kernel configuration time) out of a running kernel. Thus the locator handling is less intelligent as it could
   be.

DTMFDECODE (1)   NetBSD General Commands Manual   DTMFDECODE (1)

NAME
dtmfdecode — decodes DTMF tones from A-law audio data

SYNOPSIS
dtmfdecode

DESCRIPTION
dtmfdecode is part of the isdn4bsd package and is used to detect DTMF tones in the audio stream.

It reads audio G.711 A-law coded data from stdin and outputs the detected numbers values as ASCII characters to stdout.

The detector is implemented as 8 narrow band-pass filters realized with an integer double-cross recursive algorithm. Various ad-hoc methods are employed to provide hysteresis and anti-bounce for the detected signals.

EXAMPLES
The command:

```
dtmfdecode < beep.al
```

will print a "1" to stdout.

STANDARDS
ITU Recommendations G.711

AUTHORS
The **dtmfdecode** utility was written by Poul-Henning Kamp ⟨phk@freebsd.org⟩. This man page was written by
Hellmuth Michaelis ⟨hm@freebsd.org⟩.

NAME

dump, **rdump** — file system backup

SYNOPSIS

dump [**-0123456789aceFinStuX**] [**-B** *records*] [**-b** *blocksize*] [**-d** *density*]
    [**-f** *file*] [**-h** *level*] [**-k** *read-blocksize*] [**-L** *label*] [**-l** *timeout*]
    [**-r** *cachesize*] [**-s** *feet*] [**-T** *date*] [**-x** *snap-backup*] *files-to-dump*
dump [**-W** | **-w**]

(The 4.3 BSD option syntax is implemented for backward compatibility, but is not documented here).

DESCRIPTION

dump examines files on a file system and determines which files need to be backed up. These files are copied to the given disk, tape or other storage medium for safe keeping (see the **-f** option below for doing remote backups). A dump that is larger than the output medium is broken into multiple volumes. On most media the size is determined by writing until an end-of-media indication is returned. This can be enforced by using the **-a** option.

On media that cannot reliably return an end-of-media indication (such as some cartridge tape drives) each volume is of a fixed size; the actual size is determined by the tape size and density and/or block count options below. By default, the same output file name is used for each volume after prompting the operator to change media.

files-to-dump is either a single file system, or a list of files and directories on a single file system to be backed up as a subset of the file system. In the former case, *files-to-dump* may be the device of a file system, the path to a currently mounted file system, the path to an unmounted file system listed in /etc/fstab, or, if **-F** is given, a file system image. In the latter case, certain restrictions are placed on the backup: **-u** is ignored, the only dump level that is supported is **-0**, and all of the files must reside on the same file system.

Any files with the superuser "log" flag (SF_LOG) set will be skipped. These files are assumed to be wapbl(4) journal files and will not be backed up.

The following options are supported by **dump**:

-0-9   Dump levels. A level 0, full backup, guarantees the entire file system is copied (but see also the **-h** option below). A level number above 0, incremental backup, tells dump to copy all files new or modified since the last dump of a lower level (but see also the **-i** option below). The default level is 9.

-a   "auto-size". Bypass all tape length considerations, and enforce writing until an end-of-media indication is returned. This fits best for most modern tape drives. Use of this option is particularly recommended when appending to an existing tape, or using a tape drive with hardware compression (where you can never be sure about the compression ratio).

-B *records*
    The number of kilobytes per volume, rounded down to a multiple of the blocksize. This option overrides the calculation of tape size based on length and density.

-b *blocksize*
    The number of kilobytes per dump record.

-c   Modify the calculation of the default density and tape size to be more appropriate for cartridge tapes.

-d *density*
Set tape density to *density*. The default is 1600 Bits Per Inch (BPI).

-e Eject tape automatically if a tape change is required.

-F Indicates that *files-to-dump* is a file system image.

-f *file*
Write the backup to *file*; *file* may be a special device file like /dev/rst0 (a tape drive), /dev/rsd1c (a disk drive), an ordinary file, or '-' (the standard output). Multiple file names may be given as a single argument separated by commas. Each file will be used for one dump volume in the order listed; if the dump requires more volumes than the number of names given, the last file name will used for all remaining volumes after prompting for media changes. If the name of the file is of the form "host:file", or "user@host:file", **dump** writes to the named file on the remote host using rmt(8). Note that methods more secure than rsh(1) (such as ssh(1)) can be used to invoke rmt(8) on the remote host, via the environment variable RCMD_CMD. See rcmd(3) for more details.

-h *level*
Honor the user "nodump" flag (UF_NODUMP) only for dumps at or above the given *level*. The default honor level is 1, so that incremental backups omit such files but full backups retain them.

-i The dump is treated as level 9 but takes into account a previous level 9, if one exists. This makes it possible to perform a "true incremental" dump.

-k *read-blocksize*
The size in kilobyte of the read buffers, rounded up to a multiple of the file system block size. Default is 32k.

-l *timeout*
If a tape change is required, eject the tape and wait for the drive to be ready again. This is to be used with tape changers which automatically load the next tape when the tape is ejected. If after the timeout (in seconds) the drive is not ready **dump** falls back to the default behavior, and prompts the operator for the next tape.

-L *label*
The user-supplied text string *label* is placed into the dump header, where tools like restore(8) and file(1) can access it. Note that this label is limited to be at most **LBLSIZE** (currently 16) characters, which must include the terminating '\0'.

-n Whenever **dump** requires operator attention, notify all operators in the group "operator" using wall(1).

-r *cachesize*
Use that many buffers for read cache operations. A value of zero disables the read cache altogether, higher values improve read performance by reading larger data blocks from the disk and maintaining them in an LRU cache. See the **-k** option for the size of the buffers. Maximum is 512, the size of the cache is limited to 15% of the avail RAM by default.

-s *feet*
Attempt to calculate the amount of tape needed at a particular density. If this amount is exceeded, **dump** prompts for a new tape. It is recommended to be a bit conservative on this option. The default tape length is 2300 feet.

-S Display an estimate of the backup size and the number of tapes required, and exit without actually performing the dump.

-t   All informational log messages printed by **dump** will have the time prepended to them. Also, the completion time interval estimations will have the estimated time at which the dump will complete printed at the end of the line.

-T *date*

Use the specified date as the starting time for the dump instead of the time determined from looking in /etc/dumpdates. The format of date is the same as that of ctime(3). This option is useful for automated dump scripts that wish to dump over a specific period of time. The **-T** option is mutually exclusive from the **-u** option.

-u   Update the file /etc/dumpdates after a successful dump. The format of /etc/dumpdates is readable by people, consisting of one free format record per line: file system name, increment level and ctime(3) format dump date. There may be only one entry per file system at each level. The file /etc/dumpdates may be edited to change any of the fields, if necessary. If a list of files or subdirectories is being dumped (as opposed to an entire file system), then **-u** is ignored.

-x *snap-backup*

Use a snapshot with *snap-backup* as backup for this dump. See fss(4) for more details. Snapshot support is *experimental*. Be sure you have a backup before you use it.

-X   Similar to **-x** but uses a file system internal snapshot on the file system to be dumped.

-W   **dump** tells the operator what file systems need to be dumped. This information is gleaned from the files /etc/dumpdates and /etc/fstab. The **-W** option causes **dump** to print out, for each file system in /etc/dumpdates the most recent dump date and level, and highlights those file systems that should be dumped. If the **-W** option is set, all other options are ignored, and **dump** exits immediately.

-w   Is like W, but prints only those file systems which need to be dumped.

If **dump** honors the "nodump" flag (UF_NODUMP), files with the "nodump" flag will not be backed up. If a directory has the "nodump" flag, this directory and any file or directory under it will not be backed up.

dump requires operator intervention on these conditions: end of tape, end of dump, tape write error, tape open error or disk read error (if there are more than a threshold of 32). In addition to alerting all operators implied by the **-n** option, **dump** interacts with the operator on **dump**'s control terminal at times when **dump** can no longer proceed, or if something is grossly wrong. All questions **dump** poses *must* be answered by typing "yes" or "no", appropriately.

Since making a dump involves a lot of time and effort for full dumps, **dump** checkpoints itself at the start of each tape volume. If writing that volume fails for some reason, **dump** will, with operator permission, restart itself from the checkpoint after the old tape has been rewound and removed, and a new tape has been mounted.

dump tells the operator what is going on at periodic intervals, including usually low estimates of the number of blocks to write, the number of tapes it will take, the time to completion, and the time to the tape change. The output is verbose, so that others know that the terminal controlling **dump** is busy, and will be for some time.

In the event of a catastrophic disk event, the time required to restore all the necessary backup tapes or files to disk can be kept to a minimum by staggering the incremental dumps. An efficient method of staggering incremental dumps to minimize the number of tapes follows:

• Always start with a level 0 backup, for example:

```
/sbin/dump -0u -f /dev/nrst1 /usr/src
```

This should be done at set intervals, say once a month or once every two months, and on a set of fresh tapes that is saved forever.

- After a level 0, dumps of active file systems are taken on a daily basis, using a modified Tower of Hanoi algorithm, with this sequence of dump levels:

  3 2 5 4 7 6 9 8 9 9 ...

  For the daily dumps, it should be possible to use a fixed number of tapes for each day, used on a weekly basis. Each week, a level 1 dump is taken, and the daily Hanoi sequence repeats beginning with 3. For weekly dumps, another fixed set of tapes per dumped file system is used, also on a cyclical basis.

After several months or so, the daily and weekly tapes should get rotated out of the dump cycle and fresh tapes brought in.

If **dump** receives a SIGINFO signal (see the "status" argument of stty(1)) whilst a backup is in progress, statistics on the amount completed, current transfer rate, and estimated finished time, will be written to the standard error output.

ENVIRONMENT

If the following environment variables exist, they are used by **dump**.

TAPE   If no -f option was specified, **dump** will use the device specified via TAPE as the dump device. TAPE may be of the form "tapename", "host:tapename", or "user@host:tapename".

RCMD_CMD **dump** will use RCMD_CMD rather than rsh(1) to invoke rmt(8) on the remote machine.

TIMEFORMAT

can be used to control the format of the timestamps produced by the −t option. TIMEFORMAT is a string containing embedded formatting commands for strftime(3). The total formatted string is limited to about 80 characters, if this limit is exceeded then "ERROR: TIMEFORMAT too long, reverting to default" will be printed and the time format will revert to the default one. If TIMEFORMAT is not set then the format string defaults to "%T %Z"

FILES

/dev/nrst0	default tape unit to use. Taken from _PATH_DEFTAPE in /usr/include/paths.h.
/dev/rst*	raw SCSI tape interface
/etc/dumpdates	dump date records
/etc/fstab	dump table: file systems and frequency
/etc/group	to find group *operator*

DIAGNOSTICS

Many, and verbose.

dump exits with zero status on success. Startup errors are indicated with an exit code of 1; abnormal termination is indicated with an exit code of 3.

SEE ALSO

chflags(1), rcmd(1), stty(1), wall(1), fts(3), rcmd(3), fss(4), st(4), fstab(5), environ(7), restore(8), rmt(8)

HISTORY

A **dump** command appeared in Version 6 AT&T UNIX.

The **−i** flag was inspired by the **−x** flag from Sun's Solstice Backup utility.

BUGS

At least the following caveats can be mentioned.

- Fewer than 32 read errors on the file system are ignored.

- Each reel requires a new process, so parent processes for reels already written just hang around until the entire tape is written.

- **dump** with the **−W** or **−w** options does not report file systems that have never been recorded in /etc/dumpdates, even if listed in /etc/fstab.

- When dumping a list of files or subdirectories, access privileges are required to scan the directory (as this is done via the fts(3) routines rather than directly accessing the file system).

- It would be nice if **dump** knew about the dump sequence, kept track of the tapes scribbled on, told the operator which tape to mount when, and provided more assistance for the operator running restore(8).

- Snapshot support is *experimental*. Be sure you have a backup before you use it.

NAME

    dump_lfs, **rdump_lfs** — filesystem backup

SYNOPSIS

    dump_lfs [**-0123456789aceFnStuX**] [**-B** *records*] [**-b** *blocksize*] [**-d** *density*]
          [**-f** *file*] [**-h** *level*] [**-k** *read-blocksize*] [**-L** *label*] [**-l** *timeout*]
          [**-r** *cachesize*] [**-s** *feet*] [**-T** *date*] [**-x** *snap-backup*] *files-to-dump*
    dump_lfs [**-W** | **-w**]

    (The 4.3 BSD option syntax is implemented for backward compatibility, but is not documented here).

DESCRIPTION

    dump_lfs examines files on a file system and determines which files need to be backed up. These files are
copied to the given disk, tape or other storage medium for safe keeping (see the **-f** option below for doing
remote backups). A dump that is larger than the output medium is broken into multiple volumes. On most
media the size is determined by writing until an end-of-media indication is returned. This can be enforced by
using the **-a** option.

    On media that cannot reliably return an end-of-media indication (such as some cartridge tape drives) each
volume is of a fixed size; the actual size is determined by the tape size and density and/or block count options
below. By default, the same output file name is used for each volume after prompting the operator to change
media.

    files-to-dump is either a single file system, or a list of files and directories on a single file system to be
backed up as a subset of the file system. In the former case, *files-to-dump* may be the device of a file
system, the path to a currently mounted file system, the path to an unmounted file system listed in
/etc/fstab, or, if **-F** is given, a file system image. In the latter case, certain restrictions are placed on
the backup: **-u** is ignored, the only dump level that is supported is **-0**, and all of the files must reside on the
same file system.

    The following options are supported by **dump_lfs**:

    -0-9   Dump levels. A level 0, full backup, guarantees the entire file system is copied (but see also the **-h**
           option below). A level number above 0, incremental backup, tells dump to copy all files new or
           modified since the last dump of a lower level. The default level is 9.

    -a   "auto-size". Bypass all tape length considerations, and enforce writing until an end-of-media indi-
           cation is returned. This fits best for most modern tape drives. Use of this option is particularly rec-
           ommended when appending to an existing tape, or using a tape drive with hardware compression
           (where you can never be sure about the compression ratio).

    -B *records*
           The number of kilobytes per volume, rounded down to a multiple of the blocksize. This option
           overrides the calculation of tape size based on length and density.

    -b *blocksize*
           The number of kilobytes per dump record.

    -c   Modify the calculation of the default density and tape size to be more appropriate for cartridge
           tapes.

    -d *density*
           Set tape density to *density*. The default is 1600 Bits Per Inch (BPI).

    -e   Eject tape automatically if a tape change is required.

-F   Indicates that *files-to-dump* is a file system image.

-f *file*

    Write the backup to *file*; *file* may be a special device file like /dev/rst0 (a tape drive), /dev/rsd1c (a disk drive), an ordinary file, or '-' (the standard output). Multiple file names may be given as a single argument separated by commas. Each file will be used for one dump volume in the order listed; if the dump requires more volumes than the number of names given, the last file name will used for all remaining volumes after prompting for media changes. If the name of the file is of the form "host:file", or "user@host:file", **dump_lfs** writes to the named file on the remote host using rmt(8). Note that methods more secure than rsh(1) (such as ssh(1)) can be used to invoke rmt(8) on the remote host, via the environment variable RCMD_CMD. See rcmd(3) for more details.

-h *level*

    Honor the user "nodump" flag (UF_NODUMP) only for dumps at or above the given *level*. The default honor level is 1, so that incremental backups omit such files but full backups retain them.

-k *read-blocksize*

    The size in kilobyte of the read buffers, rounded up to a multiple of the file system block size. Default is 32k.

-l *timeout*

    If a tape change is required, eject the tape and wait for the drive to be ready again. This is to be used with tape changers which automatically load the next tape when the tape is ejected. If after the timeout (in seconds) the drive is not ready **dump_lfs** falls back to the default behavior, and prompts the operator for the next tape.

-L *label*

    The user-supplied text string *label* is placed into the dump header, where tools like restore(8) and file(1) can access it. Note that this label is limited to be at most LBLSIZE (currently 16) characters, which must include the terminating '\0'.

-n   Whenever **dump_lfs** requires operator attention, notify all operators in the group "operator" using wall(1).

-r *cachesize*

    Use that many buffers for read cache operations. A value of zero disables the read cache altogether, higher values improve read performance by reading larger data blocks from the disk and maintaining them in an LRU cache. See the **-k** option for the size of the buffers. Maximum is 512, the size of the cache is limited to 15% of the avail RAM by default.

-s *feet*

    Attempt to calculate the amount of tape needed at a particular density. If this amount is exceeded, **dump_lfs** prompts for a new tape. It is recommended to be a bit conservative on this option. The default tape length is 2300 feet.

-S   Display an estimate of the backup size and the number of tapes required, and exit without actually performing the dump.

-t   All informational log messages printed by **dump_lfs** will have the time prepended to them. Also, the completion time interval estimations will have the estimated time at which the dump will complete printed at the end of the line.

-T *date*

    Use the specified date as the starting time for the dump instead of the time determined from looking in /etc/dumpdates. The format of date is the same as that of ctime(3). This option is useful for automated dump scripts that wish to dump over a specific period of time. The **-T** option is mutually exclusive from the **−u** option.

−u   Update the file /etc/dumpdates after a successful dump. The format of /etc/dumpdates is readable by people, consisting of one free format record per line: file system name, increment level and ctime(3) format dump date. There may be only one entry per file system at each level. The file /etc/dumpdates may be edited to change any of the fields, if necessary. If a list of files or subdirectories is being dumped (as opposed to an entire file system), then **−u** is ignored.

−X   Prevent the log from wrapping until the dump completes, guaranteeing a consistent backup. Processes that write to the filesystem will continue as usual until the entire log is full, after which they will block until the dump is complete. This functionality is analogous to what fss(4) provides for other file systems. The **−x** flag is provided for compatibility with dump(8); it functions exactly as the **−X** flag does (its argument is ignored).

−W   **dump_lfs** tells the operator what file systems need to be dumped. This information is gleaned from the files /etc/dumpdates and /etc/fstab. The **−W** option causes **dump_lfs** to print out, for each file system in /etc/dumpdates the most recent dump date and level, and highlights those file systems that should be dumped. If the **−W** option is set, all other options are ignored, and **dump_lfs** exits immediately.

−w   Is like W, but prints only those file systems which need to be dumped.

If **dump_lfs** honors the "nodump" flag (UF_NODUMP), files with the "nodump" flag will not be backed up. If a directory has the "nodump" flag, this directory and any file or directory under it will not be backed up.

dump_lfs requires operator intervention on these conditions: end of tape, end of dump, tape write error, tape open error or disk read error (if there are more than a threshold of 32). In addition to alerting all operators implied by the **−n** option, **dump_lfs** interacts with the operator on **dump_lfs**'s control terminal at times when **dump_lfs** can no longer proceed, or if something is grossly wrong. All questions **dump_lfs** poses *must* be answered by typing "yes" or "no", appropriately.

Since making a dump involves a lot of time and effort for full dumps, **dump_lfs** checkpoints itself at the start of each tape volume. If writing that volume fails for some reason, **dump_lfs** will, with operator permission, restart itself from the checkpoint after the old tape has been rewound and removed, and a new tape has been mounted.

dump_lfs tells the operator what is going on at periodic intervals, including usually low estimates of the number of blocks to write, the number of tapes it will take, the time to completion, and the time to the tape change. The output is verbose, so that others know that the terminal controlling **dump_lfs** is busy, and will be for some time.

In the event of a catastrophic disk event, the time required to restore all the necessary backup tapes or files to disk can be kept to a minimum by staggering the incremental dumps. An efficient method of staggering incremental dumps to minimize the number of tapes follows:

• Always start with a level 0 backup, for example:

      /sbin/dump −0u −f /dev/nrst1 /usr/src

  This should be done at set intervals, say once a month or once every two months, and on a set of fresh tapes that is saved forever.

• After a level 0, dumps of active file systems are taken on a daily basis, using a modified Tower of Hanoi algorithm, with this sequence of dump levels:

      3 2 5 4 7 6 9 8 9 9 ...

For the daily dumps, it should be possible to use a fixed number of tapes for each day, used on a weekly basis. Each week, a level 1 dump is taken, and the daily Hanoi sequence repeats beginning with 3. For weekly dumps, another fixed set of tapes per dumped file system is used, also on a cyclical basis.

After several months or so, the daily and weekly tapes should get rotated out of the dump cycle and fresh tapes brought in.

If **dump_lfs** receives a SIGINFO signal (see the "status" argument of stty(1)) whilst a backup is in progress, statistics on the amount completed, current transfer rate, and estimated finished time, will be written to the standard error output.

ENVIRONMENT

If the following environment variables exist, they are used by **dump_lfs**.

TAPE   If no -f option was specified, **dump_lfs** will use the device specified via TAPE as the dump device. TAPE may be of the form "tapename", "host:tapename", or "user@host:tapename".

RCMD_CMD **dump_lfs** will use RCMD_CMD rather than rsh(1) to invoke rmt(8) on the remote machine.

TIMEFORMAT
                can be used to control the format of the timestamps produced by the **-t** option. TIMEFORMAT is a string containing embedded formatting commands for strftime(3). The total formatted string is limited to about 80 characters, if this limit is exceeded then "ERROR: TIMEFORMAT too long, reverting to default" will be printed and the time format will revert to the default one. If TIMEFORMAT is not set then the format string defaults to "%T %Z"

FILES

/dev/nrst0	default tape unit to use. Taken from _PATH_DEFTAPE in /usr/include/paths.h.
/dev/rst*	raw SCSI tape interface
/etc/dumpdates	dump date records
/etc/fstab	dump table: file systems and frequency
/etc/group	to find group *operator*

DIAGNOSTICS

Many, and verbose.

dump_lfs exits with zero status on success. Startup errors are indicated with an exit code of 1; abnormal termination is indicated with an exit code of 3.

SEE ALSO

chflags(1), rcmd(1), stty(1), wall(1), fts(3), rcmd(3), st(4), fstab(5), environ(7), restore(8), rmt(8)

HISTORY

A **dump_lfs** command appeared in NetBSD 1.5.

BUGS

Fewer than 32 read errors on the file system are ignored.

Each reel requires a new process, so parent processes for reels already written just hang around until the entire tape is written.

dump_lfs with the −W or −w options does not report file systems that have never been recorded in /etc/dumpdates, even if listed in /etc/fstab.

When dumping a list of files or subdirectories, access privileges are required to scan the directory (as this is done via the fts(3) routines rather than directly accessing the file system).

It would be nice if dump_lfs knew about the dump sequence, kept track of the tapes scribbled on, told the operator which tape to mount when, and provided more assistance for the operator running restore(8).

NAME

dumpfs — dump file system information

SYNOPSIS

dumpfs [**-acFijmsv**] *filesys* | *device* [. . .]

DESCRIPTION

dumpfs prints out detailed information about the specified filesystems.

Options:

-a   Print details from each alternate superblock.

-c   Print details of each cylinder group.

-F   Dump a file system image from a file, not a special device.

-i   Print details of each allocated inode.

-j   Print details of the WAPBL journal.

-m   Print details of the cylinder group summary.

-s   Print details of the superblock.

-v   Be even more verbose.

If none of **-a**, **-c**, **-i**, **-j**, **-m**, or **-s** are given, then **dumpfs** defaults to **-cmsv**.

dumpfs is useful mostly for finding out certain file system information such as the file system block size, minimum free space percentage, and the file system level that can be upgraded with the **-c** option of fsck_ffs(8). All of this information is output by **dumpfs -s**.

SEE ALSO

disktab(5), fs(5), disklabel(8), fsck(8), fsck_ffs(8), newfs(8), tunefs(8)

HISTORY

The **dumpfs** command appeared in 4.2BSD. The **-a**, **-c**, **-i**, **-m**, and **-s** options, and the inode dump were added for NetBSD 2.0. The **-j**, option was added for NetBSD 6.0.

NAME
   dumplfs — dump file system information

SYNOPSIS
   dumplfs [**-adiS**] [**-b** *blkno*] [**-I** *blkno*] [**-s** *segno*] *filesys* | *device*

DESCRIPTION
   dumplfs prints out the file system layout information for the LFS file system or special device specified.
   The listing is very long and detailed. This command is useful mostly for finding out certain file system information such as the file system block size.

   The following flags are interpreted by **dumplfs**.

   -a   Dump the contents of all superblocks, not just the first. Superblocks appear in the dumplfs output
             with the segment containing them.

   -b   Use the block specified immediately after the flag as the super block for the filesystem.

   -d   Check partial segment data checksums and report mismatches. This makes **dumplfs** operate
             much more slowly.

   -I   Use the block specified immediately after the flag as the inode block containing the index file
             inode.

   -i   Dump information about the inode free list.

   -S   Dump information about the segment table.

   -s   Add the segment number immediately following the flag to a list of segments to dump. This flag
             may be specified more than once to dump more than one segment. The default is to dump all seg-
             ments.

SEE ALSO
   disktab(5), fs(5), disklabel(8), newfs_lfs(8)

HISTORY
   The **dumplfs** command appeared in 4.4 BSD.

NAME
    edquota — edit user quotas

SYNOPSIS
    edquota [**-u**] [**-f** *filesystem*] [**-p** *proto-username*] *username* ...

    edquota -g [**-f** *filesystem*] [**-p** *proto-groupname*] *groupname* ...

    edquota [**-u**] [**-f** *filesystem*] [**-h** *block#/inode#*] [**-s** *block#/inode#*] *username*
        ...

    edquota -g [**-f** *filesystem*] [**-h** *block#/inode#*] [**-s** *block#/inode#*] *groupname*
        ...

    edquota [**-u**] [**-f** *filesystem*] **-t**

    edquota -g [**-f** *filesystem*] **-t**

DESCRIPTION
    edquota is a quota editor. By default, or if the **-u** flag is specified, one or more users may be specified on the command line. Unless **-h** or **-s** are used, a temporary file is created for each user with an ASCII representation of the current disk quotas for that user. The list of filesystems with user quotas is determined from /etc/fstab. By default, quota for all quota-enabled filesystems are edited; the **-f** option can be used to restrict it to a single filesystem. An editor is invoked on the ASCII file. The editor invoked is vi(1) unless the environment variable EDITOR specifies otherwise.

    The quotas may then be modified, new quotas added, etc. Setting a quota to zero indicates that no quota should be imposed. Setting a hard limit to one indicates that no allocations should be permitted. Setting a soft limit to one with a hard limit of zero indicates that allocations should be permitted on only a temporary basis (see **-t** below). The current usage information in the file is for informational purposes; only the hard and soft limits can be changed.

    On leaving the editor, **edquota** reads the temporary file and modifies the binary quota files to reflect the changes made.

    If the **-p** flag is specified, **edquota** will duplicate the quotas of the prototypical user specified for each user specified. This is the normal mechanism used to initialize quotas for groups of users.

    The **-h** and **-s** flags can be used to change quota limits (hard and soft, respectively) without user interaction, for usage in e.g. batch scripts. The arguments are the new block and inode number limit, separated by a slash.

    If the **-g** flag is specified, **edquota** is invoked to edit the quotas of one or more groups specified on the command line. The **-p** flag can be specified in conjunction with the **-g** flag to specify a prototypical group to be duplicated among the listed set of groups.

    Users are permitted to exceed their soft limits for a grace period that may be specified per filesystem. Once the grace period has expired, the soft limit is enforced as a hard limit. The default grace period for a filesystem is specified in /usr/include/ufs/ufs/quota.h. The **-t** flag can be used to change the grace period. By default, or when invoked with the **-u** flag, the grace period is set for all the filesystems with user quotas specified in /etc/fstab. When invoked with the **-g** flag the grace period is set for all the filesystems with group quotas specified in /etc/fstab. The grace period may be specified in days, hours, minutes, or seconds. Setting a grace period to zero indicates that the default grace period should be imposed. Setting a grace period to one second indicates that no grace period should be granted.

    Only the super-user may edit quotas.

FILES

`quota.user`	at the filesystem root with user quotas
`quota.group`	at the filesystem root with group quotas
`/etc/fstab`	to find filesystem names and locations

DIAGNOSTICS

Various messages about inaccessible files; self-explanatory.

SEE ALSO

`quota`(1), `quotactl`(2), `fstab`(5), `quotacheck`(8), `quotaon`(8), `repquota`(8)

NAME

eeprom — display or modify contents of the EEPROM or openprom

SUN 3 SYNOPSIS

eeprom [-] [-c] [-f *device*] [-i] [*field*[=*value*] ...]

SPARC, SPARC64, MACPPC and PREP SYNOPSIS

eeprom [-] [-c] [-f *device*] [-i] [-v] [*field*[=*value*] ...]

DESCRIPTION

eeprom provides an interface for displaying and changing the contents of the EEPROM or openprom. The eeprom tool is only installed on supported platforms.

Without any arguments, eeprom will list all of the known fields and their corresponding values. When given the name of a specific field, eeprom will display that value or set it if the field name is followed by '=' and a value. Only the super-user may modify the contents of the EEPROM or openprom.

The options are as follows:

-      Commands are taken from stdin and displayed on stdout.

-c   eeprom will fix incorrect checksum values and exit. This flag is quietly ignored on systems with an openprom.

-f *device*   On systems with an EEPROM, use *device* instead of the default /dev/eeprom. On systems with an openprom, use *device* instead of the default /dev/openprom.

-i   If checksum values are incorrect, eeprom will ignore them and continue after displaying a warning. This flag is quietly ignored on systems with an openprom.

The following options are valid only on the SPARC and will produce an error when used on a Sun 3:

-v   On systems with an openprom, be verbose when setting a value. Systems with an EEPROM are always verbose.

The -v option is also present on sparc64, macppc, and prep systems.

FIELDS AND VALUES

The following fields and values are for systems with an EEPROM:

hwupdate   A valid date, such as "7/12/95". The strings "today" and "now" are also acceptable.

memsize   How much memory, in megabytes, is installed in the system.

memtest   How much memory, in megabytes, is to be tested upon power-up.

scrsize   The size of the screen. Acceptable values are "1024x1024", "1152x900", "1600x1280", and "1440x1440".

watchdog_reboot   If true, the system will reboot upon reset. Otherwise, the system will fall into the monitor.

default_boot   If true, the system will use the boot device stored in bootdev.

bootdev   Specifies the default boot device in the form cc(x,x,x), where 'cc' is a combination of two letters such as 'sd' or 'le' and each 'x' is a hexadecimal number between 0 and ff, less the prepending '0x'.

kbdtype	This value is "0" for all Sun keyboards.
console	Specifies the console type. Valid values are "b&w", "ttya", "ttyb", "color", and "p4opt".
keyclick	If true, the keys click annoyingly.
diagdev	This is a string very similar to that used by `bootdev`. It specifies the default boot device when the diagnostic switch is turned on.
diagpath	A 40-character, NULL-terminated string specifying the kernel or standalone program to load when the diagnostic switch is turned on.
columns	An 8-bit integer specifying the number of columns on the console.
rows	An 8-bit integer specifying the number of rows on the console.
ttya_use_baud	Use the baud rate stored in `ttya_baud` instead of the default 9600.
ttya_baud	A 16-bit integer specifying the baud rate to use on ttya.
ttya_no_rtsdtr	If true, disables RTS/DTR.
ttyb_use_baud	Similar to `ttya_use_baud`, but for ttyb.
ttyb_baud	Similar to `ttya_baud`, but for ttyb.
ttyb_no_rtsdtr	Similar to `ttya_no_rtsdtr`, but for ttyb.
banner	An 80-character, NULL-terminated string to use at power-up instead of the default Sun banner.

Note that the `secure`, `bad_login`, and `password` fields are not currently supported.

Since the openprom is designed such that the field names are arbitrary, explaining them here is dubious. Below are field names and values that one is likely to see on a system with an openprom. NOTE: this list may be incomplete or incorrect due to differences between revisions of the openprom.

sunmon-compat?	If true, the old EEPROM-style interface will be used while in the monitor, rather than the openprom-style interface.
selftest-#megs	A 32-bit integer specifying the number of megabytes of memory to test upon power-up.
oem-logo	A 64bitx64bit bitmap in Sun Iconedit format. To set the bitmap, give the pathname of the file containing the image. NOTE: this property is not yet supported.
oem-logo?	If true, enables the use of the bitmap stored in `oem-logo` rather than the default Sun logo.
oem-banner	A string to use at power up, rather than the default Sun banner.
oem-banner?	If true, enables the use of the banner stored in `oem-banner` rather than the default Sun banner.
ttya-mode	A string of five comma separated fields in the format "9600,8,n,1,-". The first field is the baud rate. The second field is the number of data bits. The third field is the parity; acceptable values for parity are 'n' (none), 'e' (even), 'o' (odd), 'm' (mark), and 's' (space). The fourth field is the number of stop bits. The fifth field is the 'handshake' field; acceptable values are '-' (none), 'h' (RTS/CTS), and 's' (Xon/Xoff).

ttya-rts-dtr-off	If true, the system will ignore RTS/DTR.
ttya-ignore-cd	If true, the system will ignore carrier detect.
ttyb-mode	Similar to `ttya-mode`, but for ttyb.
ttyb-rts-dtr-off	Similar to `ttya-rts-dtr-off`, but for ttyb.
ttyb-ignore-cd	Similar to `ttya-ignore-cd`, but for ttyb.
sbus-probe-list	Four digits in the format "0123" specifying which order to probe the sbus at power-up. It is unlikely that this value should ever be changed.
screen-#columns	An 8-bit integer specifying the number of columns on the console.
screen-#rows	An 8-bit integer specifying the number of rows on the console.
auto-boot?	If true, the system will boot automatically at power-up.
watchdog-reboot?	If true, the system will reboot upon reset. Otherwise, system will fall into the monitor.
input-device	One of the strings "keyboard", "ttya", or "ttyb" specifying the default console input device.
output-device	One of the strings "screen", "ttya", or "ttyb" specifying the default console output device.
keyboard-click?	If true, the keys click annoyingly.
sd-targets	A string in the format "31204567" describing the translation of physical to logical target.
st-targets	Similar to `sd-targets`, but for tapes. The default translation is "45670123".
scsi-initiator-id	The SCSI ID of the on-board SCSI controller.
hardware-revision	A 7-character string describing a date, such as "25May95".
last-hardware-update	Similar to `hardware-revision`, describing when the CPU was last updated.
diag-switch?	If true, the system will boot and run in diagnostic mode.

FILES

/dev/eeprom	The EEPROM device on systems with an EEPROM.
/dev/openprom	The openprom device on systems with an openprom.
/dev/nvram	The nvram device on PReP systems.

SEE ALSO

`ofctl`(8)

BUGS

The fields and their values are not necessarily well defined on systems with an openprom. Your mileage may vary.

There are a few fields known to exist in some revisions of the EEPROM and/or openprom that are not yet supported. Most notable are those relating to password protection of the EEPROM or openprom.

Avoid gratuitously changing the contents of the EEPROM. It has a limited number of write cycles.

The date parser isn't very intelligent.

NAME

envstat — utility to handle environmental sensors

SYNOPSIS

envstat [**-DfIlSTWx**] [**-c** *file*] [**-d** *device*] [**-i** *interval*]
[**-s** *device:sensor,...*] [**-w** *width*]

DESCRIPTION

envstat is a utility that handles various aspects of the sensors registered with the envsys(4) framework. It is capable of displaying sensor values as well as changing parameters and setting critical limits for the sensors.

In display mode, column widths as well as displayed sensors are fully customizable. Critical limits or other properties can be set via the configuration file. If critical limits were set previously, the display mode will show the critical limits in addition to the current values.

The following options are available:

-c   Accepts a file as argument to set properties for sensors in devices registered with the framework. See the envsys.conf(5) manual page for more information.

-D   Display the names of the drivers that were registered with the envsys(4) framework, one per line and some properties for the driver: refresh timeout value, for example.

-d *device*
    Display only the sensors for the given *device*. This is useful when there are multiple devices registered and you want to only see results from a specific device.

-f   Display temperature values in degrees Fahrenheit. The default is to display temperature values in degrees Celsius.

-I   This flag skips the sensors with invalid state, these are normally shown using the "N/A" string by default.

-i *interval*
    Repeat the display every *interval* seconds. Note that some devices do not provide fresh values on demand. See the individual device's manual page for meaningful values for *interval*. If not specified, or specified as 0, **envstat** produces one round of values and exits.

-k   Display temperature values in Kelvin. The default is to display temperature values in degrees Celsius.

-l   List the names of all supported sensors, one per line. Use of this flag causes **envstat** to ignore all other option flags.

-r   This flag is provided for compatibility reasons and there's no need to use it. In the previous implementation, it was used to enable the row mode; this mode is now the default.

-S   This flag is used to restore defaults to all devices registered with the framework. This will remove all properties that were set in the configuration file to the setting that the drivers use by default.

-s *device:sensor,...*
    Restrict the display to the named sensors. The pair device and sensor description must be supplied as a comma separated list. Device as well as sensor descriptions are case sensitive.

-T   Create and display max, min and average statistics for a sensor. Must be used with an *interval*, otherwise statistics cannot be collected up. Please note that to get realistic values a lower interval value should be used, but that will also increase overhead.

-w *width*
      Use *width* as the column width for the output. Each column is additionally separated by a single space. The default is the length of the longest sensor name.

-W   This option has no effect. It is retained for historical reasons.

-x   Shows the property list used by the `sysmon_envsys`(9) framework that contains details about all registered drivers and sensors.

EXAMPLES

To display the "charge" sensor of the driver `acpibat0` in one line every ten seconds:

```
$ envstat -s "acpibat0:charge" -i 10
```

To list the drivers that are currently registered with `envsys`(4):

```
$ envstat -D
```

To display the sensors of the driver `aibs0`:

```
$ envstat -d aibs0
```

To set all properties specified in the configuration file:

```
$ envstat -c /etc/envsys.conf
```

To remove all properties that were set previously in the configuration file:

```
$ envstat -S
```

To display statistics for all sensors and ignoring sensors with invalid states every second:

```
$ envstat -ITi1
```

SEE ALSO

`proplib`(3), `acpiacad`(4), `acpibat`(4), `acpitz`(4), `admtemp`(4), `aibs`(4), `amdtemp`(4), `aps`(4), `arcmsr`(4), `battery_pmu`(4), `cac`(4), `coretemp`(4), `dbcool`(4), `envctrl`(4), `envsys`(4), `finsio`(4), `ipmi`(4), `itesio`(4), `lm`(4), `lmtemp`(4), `mfi`(4), `nsclpcsio`(4), `owtemp`(4), `pic16lc`(4), `smsc`(4), `tctrl`(4), `thinkpad`(4), `tm121temp`(4), `ug`(4), `viaenv`(4), `envsys.conf`(5)

HISTORY

envstat appeared in NetBSD 1.5. It was completely rewritten from scratch for NetBSD 5.0.

AUTHORS

The **envstat** utility that appeared in NetBSD 5.0 was written by Juan Romero Pardines. The previous version was written by Bill Squier.

NAME

    error − Postfix error/retry mail delivery agent

SYNOPSIS

    error [generic Postfix daemon options]

DESCRIPTION

    The Postfix **error**(8) delivery agent processes delivery requests from the queue manager. Each request specifies a queue file, a sender address, the reason for non-delivery (specified as the next-hop destination), and recipient information. The reason may be prefixed with an RFC 3463-compatible detail code; if none is specified a default 4.0.0 or 5.0.0 code is used instead. This program expects to be run from the **master**(8) process manager.

    Depending on the service name in master.cf, **error** or **retry**, the server bounces or defers all recipients in the delivery request using the "next-hop" information as the reason for non-delivery. The **retry** service name is supported as of Postfix 2.4.

    Delivery status reports are sent to the **bounce**(8), **defer**(8) or **trace**(8) daemon as appropriate.

SECURITY

    The **error**(8) mailer is not security-sensitive. It does not talk to the network, and can be run chrooted at fixed low privilege.

STANDARDS

    RFC 3463 (Enhanced Status Codes)

DIAGNOSTICS

    Problems and transactions are logged to **syslogd**(8).

    Depending on the setting of the **notify_classes** parameter, the postmaster is notified of bounces and of other trouble.

CONFIGURATION PARAMETERS

    Changes to **main.cf** are picked up automatically as **error**(8) processes run for only a limited amount of time. Use the command "**postfix reload**" to speed up a change.

    The text below provides only a parameter summary. See **postconf**(5) for more details including examples.

    2bounce_notice_recipient (postmaster)

        The recipient of undeliverable mail that cannot be returned to the sender.

    bounce_notice_recipient (postmaster)

        The recipient of postmaster notifications with the message headers of mail that Postfix did not deliver and of SMTP conversation transcripts of mail that Postfix did not receive.

    config_directory (see 'postconf -d' output)

        The default location of the Postfix main.cf and master.cf configuration files.

    daemon_timeout (18000s)

        How much time a Postfix daemon process may take to handle a request before it is terminated by a built-in watchdog timer.

    delay_logging_resolution_limit (2)

        The maximal number of digits after the decimal point when logging sub-second delay values.

    double_bounce_sender (double-bounce)

        The sender address of postmaster notifications that are generated by the mail system.

    ipc_timeout (3600s)

        The time limit for sending or receiving information over an internal communication channel.

max_idle (100s)

> The maximum amount of time that an idle Postfix daemon process waits for an incoming connection before terminating voluntarily.

max_use (100)

> The maximal number of incoming connections that a Postfix daemon process will service before terminating voluntarily.

notify_classes (resource, software)

> The list of error classes that are reported to the postmaster.

process_id (read-only)

> The process ID of a Postfix command or daemon process.

process_name (read-only)

> The process name of a Postfix command or daemon process.

queue_directory (see 'postconf -d' output)

> The location of the Postfix top-level queue directory.

syslog_facility (mail)

> The syslog facility of Postfix logging.

syslog_name (see 'postconf -d' output)

> The mail system name that is prepended to the process name in syslog records, so that "smtpd" becomes, for example, "postfix/smtpd".

SEE ALSO

qmgr(8), queue manager
bounce(8), delivery status reports
discard(8), Postfix discard delivery agent
postconf(5), configuration parameters
master(5), generic daemon options
master(8), process manager
syslogd(8), system logging

LICENSE

The Secure Mailer license must be distributed with this software.

AUTHOR(S)

Wietse Venema
IBM T.J. Watson Research
P.O. Box 704
Yorktown Heights, NY 10598, USA

NAME
> eshconfig — configure Essential Communications' HIPPI network interface

SYNOPSIS
> eshconfig [-estx] [-b *bytes*] [-c *bytes*] [-d *filename*] [-i *usecs*] [-m *bytes*]
> [-r *bytes*] [-u *filename*] [-w *bytes*] [*interface*]

DESCRIPTION
> eshconfig is used to configure device-specific parameters and download new firmware to the Essential
> Communications RoadRunner-based HIPPI network interface. The interface is very sensitive to the DMA
> performance characteristics of the host, and so requires careful tuning to achieve reasonable performance. In
> addition, firmware is likely to change frequently, which necessitates a reasonably easy way to update that
> firmware.

> Available operands for eshconfig:

> -b *bytes*
>> Adjust the burst size for read (by NIC of host memory) DMA.

> -c *bytes*
>> Adjust the burst size for write (by NIC of host memory) DMA.

> -d *filename*
>> Filename for file to download into NIC firmware. This must be a file in the standard Essential for-
>> mat, with :04 preceding every line, and a tag line at the end indicating the characteristics of the
>> firmware file.

> -e
>> Write data to EEPROM. Normally, setting tuning parameters will only persist until the system is
>> rebooted. Setting this parameter ensures that the changes will be written to EEPROM.

> -i *usecs*
>> Interrupt delay in microseconds.

> -m *bytes*
>> Minimum number of bytes to DMA in one direction (read or write) before allowing a DMA in the
>> other direction. Tuning this prevents one direction from dominating the flow of bytes, and artifi-
>> cially throttling the NIC.

> -r *bytes*
>> Bytes before DMA starts for read (from host to NIC). This controls how soon the DMA is trig-
>> gered; until this many bytes are requested, the DMA will not begin.

> -s
>> Show statistics for the HIPPI NIC. Repeat the option to suppress non-zero statistics.

> -t
>> Show current tuning parameters on the host.

> -u *filename*
>> Name of file to which the NIC firmware should be uploaded. Not currently supported.

> -w *bytes*
>> Number of bytes required before write (from NIC to host) DMA is started. Until this many bytes
>> are ready to be written, the DMA will not start.

> -x
>> Reset the NIC. This is necessary for the HIPPI-FP support, as ifconfig(8) will no longer physi-
>> cally reset the NIC when the interfaces goes up and down.

> Only the super-user may modify the configuration of a network interface.

DIAGNOSTICS

Messages indicating the specified interface does not exist or the user is not privileged and tried to alter an interface's configuration.

SEE ALSO

esh(4), ifconfig(8)

HISTORY

The **eshconfig** command first appeared in NetBSD 1.4.

NAME

etcupdate — update the configuration and startup files in /etc

SYNOPSIS

etcupdate [**-ahlv**] [**-p** *pager*] [**-s** {*srcdir* | *tgzdir* | *tgzfile*}] [**-t** *temproot*]
[**-w** *width*]

DESCRIPTION

etcupdate is a tool that lets the administrator update the configuration and startup files in /etc (and some other directories like /dev, /root and /var) without having to manually check and modify every file. The administrator should run this script after performing an operating system update (e.g. after running make build in /usr/src or after extracting new binary distribution files) to update to the latest configuration and startup files.

etcupdate compares the new configuration files against the currently installed files. The user is given the option of installing, merging or deleting each modified or missing file. The user can also view the differences between the files. By default, it shows the differences in the unified diff format. The default format can be toggled to show the differences in unified, context, or side by side formats or an user-defined command may be used to view differences. (And if **wdiff** is installed, it can also show differences on a word by word basis.)

etcupdate also detects if the user installs certain special files and performs corresponding tasks like remaking device nodes or rebuilding a database from the aliases(5) file. Finally, **etcupdate** runs postinstall(8) to check the results.

etcupdate needs a clean set of new configuration files to compare the existing files against. These files, called the "reference files" in this manual, may be derived from either a source or binary distribution of NetBSD.

If the user is updating from sources (which is the default mode), **etcupdate** will first create a copy of the reference files by running make distribution in /usr/src/etc, installing the files to a so-called temproot. (See usage of the **-s** *srcdir* and **-t** *temproot* options later in this manual page.) Although this is the default mode, it is not recommended (see the "BUGS" section).

Instead of using sources, it is recommended that the user should extract one or more binary distribution sets in a special location and use those as the reference files (see usage of the **-s** *tgzdir* option later in this manual page), or specify one or more binary distribution sets directly (see usage of the **-s** *tgzfile* option later in this manual page).

The following options are available:

-a   **etcupdate** can automatically update files which have not been modified locally. The **-a** flag instructs **etcupdate** to store MD5 checksums in /var/etcupdate and use these checksums to determine if there have been any local modifications.

-h   Prints a help text.

-l   Automatically skip files with unchanged RCS IDs. This has the effect of leaving alone files that have been altered locally but which have not been changed in the reference files. Since this works using RCS IDs, files without RCS IDs will not be skipped even if only modified locally. This flag may be used together with the **-a** flag described above.

-p *pager*   The pager to use when displaying files. By default this is more(1) but it can be changed either with this option or by defining the PAGER variable.

-s {*srcdir* | *tgzdir* | *tgzfile*}

        The location of the reference files, or the NetBSD source files used to create the reference files. This may be specified in one of three ways:

        -s *srcdir*   The top level directory of the NetBSD source tree. By default this is `/usr/src` but it can be changed either with this option or the `SRCDIR` variable. The reference files will be created by running "make distribution" in the *srcdir*/etc directory. Note that *srcdir* should refer to the top of the source directory tree; earlier versions of **etcupdate** expected *srcdir* to refer to the `etc` subdirectory within the source tree.

        -s *tgzdir*   A directory in which reference files have been extracted from a binary distribution of NetBSD. The files that are distributed in the "etc.tgz" set file must be present. The files that are distributed in the "xetc.tgz" set file are optional. The reference files from the specified directory will be copied to the `temproot` directory.

        -s *tgzfile*   The location of a set file (or "tgz file") such as "etc.tgz" or "xetc.tgz" from a binary distribution of NetBSD. Each set file is a compressed archive containing reference files, which will be extracted to the `temproot` directory. Multiple **-s** options may be used to specify multiple set files. The "etc.tgz" set file must be specified. The "xetc.tgz" set file is optional.

-t *temproot*   Specifies the location of the `temproot` directory. This directory will be used for a temporary copy of the reference files created by running "make distribution" in the source directory specified by **-s** *srcdir*, or a temporary copy of the reference files extracted from the binary sets specified by **-s** *tgzfile*, or a temporary copy of the reference files from the directory specified by **-s** *tempdir*. By default this is `/tmp/temproot` but can be changed either with this option or the `TEMPROOT` environment variable.

-v   Makes **etcupdate** verbose about its actions.

-w *width*   Sets screen width used during interactive merge. By default this is the number of columns `stty`(1) reports but it can be changed either with this option or by defining the `WIDTH` variable. This is useful for `xterm`(1) users with wider shell windows.

ENVIRONMENT

    `TEMPROOT`   Sets a default value for `temproot`. See **-t** above.

    `SRCDIR`   The location of the NetBSD sources files. See **-s** above.

    `PAGER`   The pager to use when displaying files. See **-p** above.

    `WIDTH`   The screen width used during interactive merge. See **-w** above.

    `IGNOREFILES`   A list of files that **etcupdate** should ignore. Files listed in this variable will never be considered for updating by **etcupdate**.

FILES

    The environment variables can also be defined in the following configuration files. The user's personal configuration file settings override the global settings.

    /etc/etcupdate.conf

~/.etcupdaterc

EXAMPLES

You have just upgraded your NetBSD host from 3.0 to 4.0 and now it's time to update the configuration files as well. To update the configuration files from the sources (if you have the /usr/src/etc directory):

```
etcupdate
```

The default location of the source files is /usr/src but this may be overridden with the **-s** *srcdir* command line argument:

```
etcupdate -s /some/where/src
```

To update the configuration files from binary distribution sets do something like this:

```
etcupdate -s /some/where/etc.tgz -s /some/where/xetc.tgz
```

or like this:

```
mkdir /tmp/temproot
cd /tmp/temproot
tar -xpzf /some/where/etc.tgz
tar -xpzf /some/where/xetc.tgz
etcupdate -s /tmp/temproot
```

You have modified only few files in the /etc directory so you would like install most of the updates without being asked. To automatically update the unmodified configuration files:

```
etcupdate -a
```

To get a better idea what's going on, use the **-v** flag:

```
etcupdate -v
```

SEE ALSO

cmp(1), more(1), rcs(1), sdiff(1), stty(1), aliases(5), postinstall(8)

HISTORY

The **etcupdate** command appeared in NetBSD 1.6.

In NetBSD 4.0, the **-s** *tgzfile* option was added, the **-b** *tempdir* option was converted to **-s** *tgzdir*, and the **-s** *srcdir* option was changed to refer to the top of the source directory tree rather than to the etc subdirectory.

In NetBSD 5.0, the ability to specify multiple colon-separated files with a single **-s** option was deprecated, and options deprecated in NetBSD 4.0 were removed.

AUTHORS

The script was written by Martti Kuparinen ⟨martti@NetBSD.org⟩ and improved by several other NetBSD users.

The idea for this script (including code fragments, variable names etc.) came from the FreeBSD mergemaster (by Douglas Barton). Unlike the FreeBSD mergemaster, this does not use CVS version tags by default to compare if the files need to be updated. Files are compared with cmp(1) as this is more reliable and the only way if the version numbers are the same even though the files are different.

BUGS

If a source directory is specified via the "**−s** *srcdir*" option (or if the /usr/src directory is used by default), then **etcupdate** will run "make distribution" in the etc subdirectory of the source directory, but it will not use the same options or environment variables that would be used during a full build of the operating system. For this reason, use of the "**−s** *srcdir*" option is not recommended, and use of the "**−s** *tgzdir*" or "**−s** *tgzfile*" options is recommended.

NAME

   extattrctl — manage UFS1 extended attributes

SYNOPSIS

   extattrctl start *path*
   extattrctl stop *path*
   extattrctl initattr [**-f**] [**-p** *path*] *attrsize attrfile*
   extattrctl showattr *attrfile*
   extattrctl enable *path attrnamespace attrname attrfile*
   extattrctl disable *path attrnamespace attrname*

DESCRIPTION

   The **extattrctl** utility is the management utility for extended attributes over the UFS1 file system. It allows the starting and stopping of extended attributes on a file system, as well as initialization of attribute backing files, and enabling and disabling of specific extended attributes on a file system.

   The first argument on the command line indicates the operation to be performed. Operation must be one of the following:

   start *path*
   > Start extended attribute support on the file system named using *path*. The file system must be a UFS1 file system, and the UFS_EXTATTR kernel option must have been enabled.

   stop *path*
   > Stop extended attribute support on the file system named using *path*. Extended attribute support must previously have been started.

   initattr [**-f**][**-p** *path*] *attrsize attrfile*
   > Create and initialize a file to use as an attribute backing file. You must specify a maximum per-inode size for the attribute in bytes in *attrsize*, as well as the file where the attribute will be stored, using *attrfile*.

   > The **-f** argument may be used to indicate that it is alright to overwrite an existing attribute backing file; otherwise, if the target file exists, an error will be returned.

   > The **-p** *path* argument may be used to preallocate space for all attributes rather than relying on sparse files to conserve space. This has the advantage of guaranteeing that space will be available for attributes when they are written, preventing low disk space conditions from denying attribute service.

   > This file should not exist before running **initattr**.

   showattr *attrfile*
   > Show the attribute header values in the attribute file named by *attrfile*.

   enable *path attrnamespace attrname attrfile*
   > Enable an attribute named *attrname* in the namespace *attrnamespace* on the file system identified using *path*, and backed by initialized attribute file *attrfile*. Available namespaces are "user" and "system". The backing file must have been initialized using **initattr** before its first use. Attributes must have been started on the file system prior to the enabling of any attributes.

   disable *path attrnamespace attrname*
   > Disable the attributed named *attrname* in namespace *attrnamespace* on the file system identified by *path*. Available namespaces are "user" and "system". The file system must have attributes started on it, and the attribute most have been enabled using **enable**.

The kernel also includes support for automatic starting of extended attributes on a file system at mount time once configured with **extattrctl**. If the kernel is built with the `UFS_EXTATTR_AUTOSTART` option, UFS will search for a `.attribute` sub-directory of the file system root during the mount operation. If found, extended attribute support will be started for the file system. UFS will then search for `system` and `user` sub-directories of the `.attribute` directory for any potential backing files and enable an extended attribute for each valid backing file with the backing file name as the attribute name.

EXAMPLES

```
extattrctl start /
```

Start extended attributes on the root file system.

```
extattrctl initattr 17 /.attribute/system/md5
```

Create an attribute backing file in `/.attribute/system/md5`, and set the maximum size of each attribute to 17 bytes, with a sparse file used for storing the attributes.

```
extattrctl enable / system md5 /.attribute/system/md5
```

Enable an attribute named md5 on the root file system, backed from the file `/.attribute/system/md5`.

```
extattrctl disable / md5
```

Disable the attribute named md5 on the root file system.

```
extattrctl stop /
```

Stop extended attributes on the root file system.

SEE ALSO

`extattr_get_file`(2), `getextattr`(8), `extattr`(9)

HISTORY

Extended attribute support was developed as part of the TrustedBSD Project, and introduced in FreeBSD 5.0 and NetBSD 4.0. It was developed to support security extensions requiring additional labels to be associated with each file or directory.

AUTHORS

Robert N M Watson

BUGS

extattrctl works only on UFS1 file systems. The kernel support for extended attribute backing files and this control program should be generalized for any file system that lacks native extended attribute support.

NAME
faithd — FAITH IPv6/v4 translator daemon

SYNOPSIS
faithd [-dp] [-f *configfile*] *service* [*serverpath* [*serverargs*]]
faithd

DESCRIPTION
The **faithd** utility provides IPv6-to-IPv4 TCP relaying. It can only be used on an IPv4/v6 dual stack router.

When **faithd** receives TCPv6 traffic, it will relay the TCPv6 traffic to TCPv4. The destination for the relayed TCPv4 connection will be determined by the last 4 octets of the original IPv6 destination. For example, if 2001:0db8:4819:ffff:: is reserved for **faithd**, and the TCPv6 destination address is 2001:0db8:4819:ffff::0a01:0101, the traffic will be relayed to IPv4 destination 10.1.1.1.

To use the **faithd** translation service, an IPv6 address prefix must be reserved for mapping IPv4 addresses into. The kernel must be properly configured to route all the TCP connections toward the reserved IPv6 address prefix into the faith(4) pseudo interface, using the route(8) command. Also, sysctl(8) should be used to configure net.inet6.ip6.keepfaith to 1.

The router must be configured to capture all the TCP traffic for the reserved IPv6 address prefix, by using route(8) and sysctl(8) commands.

The **faithd** utility needs special name-to-address translation logic, so that hostnames gets resolved into the special IPv6 address prefix. For small-scale installations, use hosts(5); For large-scale installations, it is useful to have a DNS server with special address translation support. An implementation called **totd** is available at http://www.vermicelli.pasta.cs.uit.no/software/totd.html. Make sure you do not propagate translated DNS records over to normal DNS, as it can cause severe problems.

Daemon mode
When **faithd** is invoked as a standalone program, **faithd** will daemonize itself. **faithd** will listen to TCPv6 port *service*. If TCPv6 traffic to port *service* is found, it relays the connection.

Since **faithd** listens to TCP port *service*, it is not possible to run local TCP daemons for port *service* on the router, using inetd(8) or other standard mechanisms. By specifying *serverpath* to **faithd**, you can run local daemons on the router. The **faithd** utility will invoke ia local daemon at *serverpath* if the destination address is a local interface address, and will perform translation to IPv4 TCP in other cases. You can also specify *serverargs* for the arguments for the local daemon.

The following options are available:

-d   Debugging information will be generated using syslog(3).

-f *configfile*
      Specify a configuration file for access control. See below.

-p   Use privileged TCP port number as source port, for IPv4 TCP connection toward final destination. For relaying ftp(1) this flag is not necessary as special program code is supplied.

faithd will relay both normal and out-of-band TCP data. It is capable of emulating TCP half close as well. **faithd** includes special support for protocols used by ftp(1). When translating the FTP protocol, **faithd** translates network level addresses in PORT/LPRT/EPRT and PASV/LPSV/EPSV commands.

Inactive sessions will be disconnected in 30 minutes, to prevent stale sessions from chewing up resources. This may be inappropriate for some services (should this be configurable?).

inetd mode

When **faithd** is invoked via inetd(8), **faithd** will handle connections passed from standard input. If the connection endpoint is in the reserved IPv6 address prefix, **faithd** will relay the connection. Otherwise, **faithd** will invoke a service-specific daemon like telnetd(8), by using the command argument passed from inetd(8).

faithd determines operation mode by the local TCP port number, and enables special protocol handling whenever necessary/possible. For example, if **faithd** is invoked via inetd(8) on the FTP port, it will operate as an FTP relay.

Access control

To prevent malicious access, **faithd** implements a simple address-based access control. With /etc/faithd.conf (or configfile specified by **−f**), **faithd** will avoid relaying unwanted traffic. The faithd.conf configuration file contains directives of the following format:

- *src/slen* deny *dst/dlen*

  If the source address of a query matches *src/slen*, and the translated destination address matches *dst/dlen*, deny the connection.

- *src/slen* permit *dst/dlen*

  If the source address of a query matches *src/slen*, and the translated destination address matches *dst/dlen*, permit the connection.

The directives are evaluated in sequence, and the first matching entry will be effective. If there is no match (if we reach the end of the ruleset) the traffic will be denied.

With inetd mode, traffic may be filtered by using access control functionality in inetd(8).

EXIT STATUS

faithd exits with EXIT_SUCCESS (0) on success, and EXIT_FAILURE (1) on error.

EXAMPLES

Before invoking **faithd**, the faith(4) interface has to be configured properly.

```
# sysctl −w net.inet6.ip6.accept_rtadv=0
# sysctl −w net.inet6.ip6.forwarding=1
# sysctl −w net.inet6.ip6.keepfaith=1
# ifconfig faith0 create up
# route add −inet6 2001:0db8:4819:ffff:: −prefixlen 96 ::1
# route change −inet6 2001:0db8:4819:ffff:: −prefixlen 96 −ifp faith0
```

Daemon mode samples

To translate telnet service, and provide no local telnet service, invoke **faithd** as follows:

```
# faithd telnet
```

If you would like to provide local telnet service via telnetd(8) on /usr/libexec/telnetd, use the following command line:

```
# faithd telnet /usr/libexec/telnetd telnetd
```

If you would like to pass extra arguments to the local daemon:

```
# faithd ftp /usr/libexec/ftpd ftpd −l
```

Here are some other examples. You may need **-p** if the service checks the source port range.

```
# faithd ssh
# faithd telnet /usr/libexec/telnetd telnetd
```

inetd mode samples

Add the following lines into inetd.conf(5).

```
telnet   stream   faith/tcp6   nowait   root   faithd   telnetd
ftp      stream   faith/tcp6   nowait   root   faithd   ftpd -l
ssh      stream   faith/tcp6   nowait   root   faithd   /usr/sbin/sshd -i
```

inetd(8) will open listening sockets with kernel TCP relay support enabled. Whenever a connection comes in, **faithd** will be invoked by inetd(8). If the connection endpoint is in the reserved IPv6 address prefix. **faithd** will relay the connection. Otherwise, **faithd** will invoke service-specific daemon like telnetd(8).

Access control samples

The following illustrates a simple faithd.conf setting.

```
# permit anyone from 2001:0db8:ffff::/48 to use the translator,
# to connect to the following IPv4 destinations:
# - any location except 10.0.0.0/8 and 127.0.0.0/8.
# Permit no other connections.
#
2001:0db8:ffff::/48 deny 10.0.0.0/8
2001:0db8:ffff::/48 deny 127.0.0.0/8
2001:0db8:ffff::/48 permit 0.0.0.0/0
```

SEE ALSO

faith(4), route(8), sysctl(8), pkgsrc/net/totd

Jun-ichiro itojun Hagino and Kazu Yamamoto, "An IPv6-to-IPv4 transport relay translator", *RFC 3142*, June 2001.

HISTORY

The **faithd** utility first appeared in the WIDE Hydrangea IPv6 protocol stack kit.

SECURITY CONSIDERATIONS

It is very insecure to use IP-address based authentication, for connections relayed by **faithd**, and any other TCP relaying services.

Administrators are advised to limit accesses to **faithd** using faithd.conf, or by using IPv6 packet filters, to protect the **faithd** service from malicious parties, and to avoid theft of service/bandwidth. IPv6 destination addresses can be limited by carefully configuring routing entries that point to faith(4), using route(8). The IPv6 source address needs to be filtered using packet filters. The documents listed in **SEE ALSO** have more information on this topic.

NAME

    fastboot, **fasthalt** — reboot/halt the system without checking the disks

SYNOPSIS

    fastboot [*boot-options*]
    fasthalt [*halt-options*]

DESCRIPTION

    fastboot and **fasthalt** are shell scripts which reboot or halt the system, and when next started, the system will skip the normal the file systems checks. This is done by creating a file /fastboot, then invoking the reboot(8) program. The system startup script, /etc/rc, looks for this file and, if present, skips the normal invocation of fsck(8).

SEE ALSO

    halt(8), rc(8), reboot(8)

HISTORY

    The **fastboot** command appeared in 4.2BSD.

NAME

fdisk — MS-DOS partition maintenance program

SYNOPSIS

fdisk [-aBFfiSuv][-0 | -1 | -2 | -3 | -E *number*
     [-s *id/start/size[/bootmenu]*]][-r *file* | -w *file*]
     [-A *ptn_alignment[/ptn_0_offset]*][-b *cylinders/heads/sectors*]
     [-c *bootcode*][-T *disktype*][-t *disktab*][*device*]
fdisk -l

DESCRIPTION

The **fdisk** program is used to display or update the *master boot record* or *MBR* in the first sector (sector 0) of a disk that uses the MBR style of partitioning. The following NetBSD ports use this style of disk partitioning: amd64, arc, bebox, cobalt, hpcarm, hpcmips, hpcsh, i386, macppc, mvmeppc, netwinder, ofppc, and prep.

The MBR contains bootable code, a partition table, an indication of which partition is 'active', and (optionally, depending on the boot code) a menu for selecting a partition to be booted. There can be at most 4 partitions defined in sector 0, one of which can be an extended partition which can be split into any number of sub-partitions.

The boot code in the MBR is usually invoked by the BIOS or firmware, and the MBR passes control to the next stage boot code stored in the first sector of the partition to be booted (the *partition boot record* or *PBR*).

After booting, NetBSD does not use the partitioning done by **fdisk**, instead it uses a NetBSD disklabel saved in sector 1 of the NetBSD partition. See mbrlabel(8) for a way of using information from the MBR to construct a NetBSD disklabel.

The standard MBR boot code will only boot the 'active' partition. However, NetBSD contains additional boot programs which allow the user to interactively select which of the partitions to boot. The 'mbr_ext' code will also boot NetBSD from an extended partition but will not work on old systems that do not support LBA reads, the 'mbr_com0' and 'mbr_com0_9600' will read and write from a serial port. At the start the **fdisk** program will determine whether the disk sector 0 is valid as a boot sector. (This is determined by checking the magic number.) If not, **fdisk** will initialise the boot code as well as the partition table. During this, all four partitions will be marked empty.

The flags -a, -i or -u are used to indicate that the partition data is to be updated. The **fdisk** program will enter an interactive conversational mode. This mode is designed not to change any data unless you explicitly tell it to; **fdisk** selects defaults for its questions to guarantee that behaviour.

If partition data is going to be updated and the disk carries GUID Partition Tables, **fdisk** will remove both primary and backup GPT headers from the disk. See gpt(8) for information on how to manipulate GUID Partition Tables.

fdisk will calculate the correct *cylinder*, *head*, and *sector* values for any partition you edit. If you specify -v you will be asked whether you want to specify them yourself.

Finally, when all the data for the first sector has been accumulated, **fdisk** will ask if you really want to write the new partition table. Only if you reply affirmatively to this question will **fdisk** write anything to the disk.

Available options:

-0   Specify partition slot 0 to be printed or updated.

-1   Specify partition slot 1 to be printed or updated.

-2   Specify partition slot 2 to be printed or updated.

-3   Specify partition slot 3 to be printed or updated.

-A *ptn_alignment*[/*ptn_0_offset*]

Specify the alignment for all partitions and optionally the offset for the first partition of the disk and of extended partitions. If *ptn_alignment* is specified and *ptn_0_offset* is not specified, then the offset is set to the alignment. If -A isn't specified, then the alignment of the first partition is inspected. If it ends on a 2048 sector boundary, then the alignment is set to 2048, if the start is a power of 2 less than, or equal to 2048 then the offset is set to the start sector. If the first partition isn't defined then the alignment and offset for disks larger than 128GB is set to 2048 (1MB). In all other cases the alignment default to a cylinder and the offset to a track (both using the BIOS geometry). The 1MB alignment is the same as that used by recent windows versions.

-a   Change the active partition. In interactive mode this question will be asked after the partitions have been processed.

-B   On an i386 or amd64 system, interactively update the boot selector settings. (The boot selector permits the user to interactively select the boot partition, and thus which operating system is run, at system boot time; see mbr(8) for more information.)

-b *cylinders/heads/sectors*

Specify the BIOS geometry parameters for *cylinders*, *heads*, and *sectors*. It is used only in conjunction with the -u flag. If not specified the BIOS geometry will be obtained using sysctl (i386 and amd64) or by solving the simultaenous equations from the existing partition information. If that fails then either the geometry from the disklabel or 63 sectors and 16 heads is used.

-c *bootcode*

Specify the filename that **fdisk** should read the bootcode from. If the name of a directory is specified, then **fdisk** will look for files with the default names in that directory. The default is to read from /usr/mdec/mbr, /usr/mdec/mbr_bootsel or /usr/mdec/mbr_ext depending on whether *bootmenu* was specified for any partitions on an i386 machine, and leave the bootcode empty for other machines.

-E *number*

Specify extended partition *number* to be printed or updated. If the specified extended partition doesn't exist on updating partition data an additional extended partition will be created.

-F   Indicate that *device* is a regular file. Unless the geometry of *device* is told to **fdisk** by -T *disktype*, **fdisk** will count the 512-byte sectors in *device* and produce a fake geometry. If *device* is a regular file, -F will be used implicitly.

-f   Run **fdisk** in a non-interactive mode. In this mode, you can only change the disk parameters by using the -b flag. This is provided only so scripts or other programs may use **fdisk** as part of an automatic installation process.

Using the -f flag with -u makes it impossible to specify the starting and ending *cylinder*, *head*, and *sector* fields (only *start* and *size* can be specified by -s option). They will be automatically computed using the BIOS geometry.

-i   Explicitly request initialisation of the master boot code (similar to what **fdisk /mbr** does under MS-DOS), even if the magic number in the first sector is ok. The partition table is left alone by this (but see above).

-l   Lists known *sysid* values and exit.

-r *file*
Read the boot record from file *file* instead of the specified disk. The geometry information used is still that of the disk volume. Any changes are written back to the file.

-S   When used with no other flags print a series of /bin/sh commands for setting variables to the partition information. This could be used by installation scripts.

-s *id/start/size[/bootmenu]*
Specify the partition *id*, *start*, *size*, and optionally *bootmenu*. This flag requires the use of a partition selection flag (**-0**, **-1**, **-2**, **-3**, or **-E** *number*).

-T *disktype*
Use the disklabel *disktype* instead of the disklabel on *device*.

-t *disktab*
Read *disktype* from the named disktab(5) file instead of from /etc/disktab.

-u   Update partition data, including *id*, *start*, and *size*. Unless **-f** option (non-interactive mode) is specified, **fdisk** will display the partitions and interactively ask which one you want to edit. **fdisk** will step through each field showing the old value and asking for a new one. The *start* and *size* can be specified in blocks (NN), cylinders (NNc or NNcyl), megabytes (NNm or NNMB), or gigabytes (NNg or NNGB), values in megabytes and gigabytes will be rounded to the nearest cylinder boundary. The *size* may be specified as $ in which case the partition will extend to the end of the available free space.

In a non-interactive mode (specified by **-f** option), partition data should be specified by **-s** option. A partition selection option (**-0**, **-1**, **-2**, **-3**, or **-E** *number*) should also be specified to select a partition slot to be updated.

fdisk will not allow you to create partitions which overlap. If **-u** and **-s** are specified in a non-interactive mode then the details of the specified partition will be changed. Any other partitions which overlap the requested part of the disk will be silently deleted.

If *bootmenu* is specified for any partition **fdisk** will determine whether the installed boot code supports the bootselect code, if it doesn't you will be asked whether you want to install the required boot code. To remove a *bootmenu* label, simply press ⟨space⟩ followed by ⟨return⟩.

-v   Be more verbose, specifying **-v** more than once may increase the amount of output.

Using **-v** with **-u** allows the user to change more parameters than normally permitted.

-w *file*
Write the modified partition table to file *file* instead of the disk.

When called with no arguments, it prints the partition table. An example follows:

```
Disk: /dev/rwd0d
NetBSD disklabel disk geometry:
cylinders: 16383, heads: 16, sectors/track: 63 (1008 sectors/cylinder)
total sectors: 40032696

BIOS disk geometry:
cylinders: 1023, heads: 255, sectors/track: 63 (16065 sectors/cylinder)
total sectors: 40032696

Partition table:
0: NetBSD (sysid 169)
```

```
        bootmenu: net 1.5.
        start 4209030, size 8289540 (4048 MB, Cyls 262-778), Active
1: Primary DOS with 32 bit FAT (sysid 11)
        bootmenu: win98
        start 63, size 4208967 (2055 MB, Cyls 0-262)
2: NetBSD (sysid 169)
        bootmenu: current
        start 32515560, size 7517136 (3670 MB, Cyls 2024-2491/234/40)
3: Ext. partition - LBA (sysid 15)
        start 12498570, size 20016990 (9774 MB, Cyls 778-2024)
Extended partition table:
E0: NetBSD (sysid 169)
        bootmenu: test
        start 12498633, size 12305727 (6009 MB, Cyls 778-1544)
E1: Primary DOS with 32 bit FAT (sysid 11)
        start 24804423, size 4096512 (2000 MB, Cyls 1544-1799)
E2: Primary DOS with 32 bit FAT (sysid 11)
        start 28900998, size 3614562 (1765 MB, Cyls 1799-2024)
Bootselector enabled, infinite timeout.
First active partition: 0
```

This example disk is divided into four partitions, the last of which is an extended partition. The sub-partitions of the extended partition are also shown. In this case there is no free space in either the disk or in the extended partition.

The various fields in each partition entry are:

> *ptn_number*: *id_name* (sysid *id_number*)
> > bootmenu: *bootmenu*
> > start *start*, size *size* (*MB* MB, Cyls *first-next*) [, Active]

ptn_number
> is the number of the partition.

id_name   is the name of the filesystem type or operating system that uses this partition.

id_number   is the number that identifies the partition type. 169 decimal is used for NetBSD partitions, 15 decimal to create an extended partition and 0 to mark a partition as unused. Use **fdisk −l** to list the known partition types.

bootmenu   is the menu prompt output by the interactive boot code for this partition. This line is omitted if the prompt is not defined.

start, *size*   are the start address and size of the partition in sectors.

MB   is the size of the partition in megabytes.

first, *next* are the bounds of this partition displayed as cylinder/head/sector. If the partition starts (or ends) on a cylinder boundary the head and sector values are omitted. If −**v** is not specified the start of extended partitions and the first partition on the disk are rounded down to include the mandatory red tape in the preceding track.

Active   is output if this is the active partition.

If the −**v** flag is specified, the beginning and end of each partition are also displayed as follows:
> beg: cylinder *cylinder*, head *head*, sector *sector*
> end: cylinder *cylinder*, head *head*, sector *sector*

cylinder, *head*, *sector*

> are the beginning or ending address of a partition.

> *Note:* these numbers are read from the bootblock, so are the values calculated by a previous run of **fdisk**.

fdisk attempts to check whether each partition is bootable, by checking the magic number and some other characteristics of the first sector of each partition (the PBR). If the partition does not appear to be bootable, **fdisk** will print a line containing "PBR is not bootable" followed by an error message. If the partition is bootable, and if the **-v** flag is specified, **fdisk** will print "PBR appears to be bootable". If the **-v** flag is specified more than once, **fdisk** will print the heading "Information from PBR:" followed by one or more lines of information gleaned from the PBR; this additional information may be incorrect or misleading, because different operating systems use different PBR formats. Note that, even if no errors are reported, an attempt to boot from the partition might fail. NetBSD partitions may be made bootable using installboot(8).

NOTES

This program is only available (and useful) on systems with PC-platform-style MBR partitioning.

Traditionally the partition boundaries should be on cylinder boundaries using the BIOS geometry, with the exception of the first partition, which traditionally begins in the second track of the first cylinder (cylinder 0, head 1, sector 1). Although the BIOS geometry is typically different from the geometry reported by the drive, neither will match the actual physical geometry for modern disks (the actual geometry will vary across the disk). Keeping the partition boundaries on cylinder boundaries makes partitioning a driver easier as only relatively small numbers need be entered.

The automatic calculation of the starting cylinder and other parameters uses a set of figures that represent what the BIOS thinks is the geometry of the drive. The default values should be correct for the system on which **fdisk** is run; however, if you move the disk to a different system, the BIOS of that system might use a different geometry translation.

If you run the equivalent of **fdisk** on a different operating system then the *bootmenu* strings associated with extended partitions may be lost.

Editing an existing partition is risky, and may cause you to lose all the data in that partition.

You should run this program interactively once or twice to see how it works. This is completely safe as long as you answer the last question in the negative. You can also specify **-w** *file* to write the output to a file and later specify **-r** *file* to read back the updated information. This can be done without having write access to the disk volume.

FILES

/usr/mdec/mbr	Default location of i386 bootcode
/usr/mdec/mbr_bootsel	Default location of i386 bootselect code
/usr/mdec/mbr_ext	Default location of i386 bootselect for extended partitions

EXAMPLES

Update MBR partition data of /dev/rwd0d in interactive mode:

> **fdisk -u /dev/rwd0d**

Change active MBR partition of /dev/rwd0d in interactive mode:

> **fdisk -a /dev/rwd0d**

Install MBR bootcode /usr/mdec/mbr_bootsel into /dev/rwd0d:

```
fdisk -c /usr/mdec/mbr_bootsel /dev/rwd0d
```

Set MBR partition data for slot 0 of /dev/rwd0d specifying values without prompt:

```
fdisk -f -u -0 -s 169/63/2097089 /dev/rwd0d
```

Make partition slot 0 of /dev/rwd0d active without prompt:

```
fdisk -f -a -0 /dev/rwd0d
```

Initialize and create MBR partition data using bootcode destdir/usr/mdec/mbr without prompt against 1GB disk image file diskimg:

```
fdisk -f -i -b 130/255/63 -c destdir/usr/mdec/mbr -F diskimg
```

Create MBR partition data for slot 0 which has an active NetBSD partition using whole disk without prompt against 1GB disk image file diskimg:

```
fdisk -f -a -u -0 -s 169/63/2097089 -F diskimg
```

SEE ALSO

disktab(5), boot(8), disklabel(8), gpt(8), installboot(8), mbr(8), mbrlabel(8)

BUGS

The word 'partition' is used to mean both an MBR partition and a NetBSD partition, sometimes in the same sentence.

There are subtleties that the program detects that are not explained in this manual page.

NAME
fingerd — remote user information server

SYNOPSIS
fingerd [-8ghlmpSsu] [-P *filename*]

DESCRIPTION
fingerd is a simple protocol based on RFC 1288 that provides an interface to the Name and Finger programs at several network sites. The program is supposed to return a friendly, human-oriented status report on either the system at the moment or a particular person in depth. There is no required format and the protocol consists mostly of specifying a single "command line".

fingerd is started by inetd(8), which listens for TCP requests at port 79. Once handed a connection, fingerd reads a single command line terminated by a ⟨CRLF⟩ which it then passes to finger(1). fingerd closes its connections as soon as the output is finished.

If the line is null (i.e., just a ⟨CRLF⟩ is sent) then finger(1) returns a "default" report that lists all people logged into the system at that moment.

If a user name is specified (e.g., eric⟨CRLF⟩) then the response lists more extended information for only that particular user, whether logged in or not. Allowable "names" in the command line include both "login names" and "user names". If a name is ambiguous, all possible derivations are returned.

The following options may be passed to fingerd as server program arguments in /etc/inetd.conf:

-8   Enable 8-bit output.

-g   Do not show any gecos information besides the users' real names.

-h   Display the name of the remote host in short mode, instead of the office location and office phone.

-l   Enable logging. The name of the host originating the query, and the actual request is reported via syslog(3) at LOG_NOTICE priority. A request of the form '/W' or '/w' will return long output. Empty requests will return all currently logged in users. All other requests look for specific users. See RFC 1288 for details.

-m   Prevent matching of *user* names. *User* is usually a login name; however, matching will also be done on the users' real names, unless the **-m** option is supplied.

-P *filename* Use an alternate program as the local information provider. The default local program executed by fingerd is finger(1). By specifying a customized local server, this option allows a system manager to have more control over what information is provided to remote sites.

-p   Prevents finger(1) from displaying the contents of the ".plan" and ".project" files.

-S   Prints user information in short mode, one line per user. This overrides the "Whois switch" that may be passed in from the remote client.

-s   Disable forwarding of queries to other remote hosts.

-u   Queries without a user name are rejected.

SEE ALSO
finger(1), inetd(8)

HISTORY

The **fingerd** command appeared in 4.3 BSD.

BUGS

Connecting directly to the server from a TIP or an equally narrow-minded TELNET-protocol user program can result in meaningless attempts at option negotiation being sent to the server, which will foul up the command line interpretation. **fingerd** should be taught to filter out IAC's and perhaps even respond negatively (IAC WON'T) to all option commands received.

NAME
fixmount – fix remote mount entries

SYNOPSIS
fixmount [**−adervq**] [**−h** *name*] *host* ...

DESCRIPTION
fixmount is a variant of **showmount**(8) that can delete bogus mount entries in remote **mountd**(8) daemons. The actions specified by the options are performed for each *host* in turn.

OPTIONS
−a −d −e

These options work as in **showmount**(8) except that only entries pertaining to the local host are printed.

−r

Removes those remote mount entries on *host* that do not correspond to current mounts, i.e., which are left-over from a crash or are the result of improper mount protocol. The actuality of mounts is verified using the entries in **/etc/mtab**.

−v

Verify remote mounts. Similar to **−r** except that only a notification message is printed for each bogus entry found. The remote mount table is not changed.

−A

Issues a command to the remote mountd declaring that ALL of its filesystems have been unmounted. This should be used with caution, as it removes all remote mount entries pertaining to the local system, whether or not any filesystems are still mounted locally.

−q

Be quiet. Suppresses error messages due to timeouts and "Program not registered", i.e., due to remote hosts not supporting RPC or not running mountd.

−h *name*

Pretend the local hostname is *name*. This is useful after the local hostname has been changed and rmtab entries using the old name remain on a remote machine. Unfortunately, most mountd's won't be able to successfully handle removal of such entries, so this option is useful in combination with **−v** only.

This option also saves time as comparisons of remotely recorded and local hostnames by address are avoided.

FILES
/etc/mtab	List of current mounts.
/etc/rmtab	Backup file for remote mount entries on NFS server.

SEE ALSO
showmount(8), **mtab**(5), **rmtab**(5), **mountd**(8C).

"am-utils" **info**(1) entry.

Linux NFS and Automounter Administration by Erez Zadok, ISBN 0-7821-2739-8, (Sybex, 2001).

http://www.am-utils.org

Amd − The 4.4 BSD Automounter

BUGS
No attempt is made to verify the information in **/etc/mtab** itself.

Since swap file mounts are not recorded in **/etc/mtab**, a heuristic specific to SunOS is used to determine whether such a mount is actual (replacing the string "swap" with "root" and verifying the resulting path).

Symbolic links on the server will cause the path in the remote entry to differ from the one in **/etc/mtab**. To catch those cases, a filesystem is also deemed mounted if its *local* mount point is identical to the remote entry. I.e., on a SunOS diskless client, **server:/export/share/sunos.4.1.1** is actually **/usr/share**. Since the local mount point is **/usr/share** as well this will be handled correctly.

There is no way to clear a stale entry in a remote mountd after the local hostname (or whatever reverse name resolution returns for it) has been changed. To take care of these cases, the remote /etc/rmtab file has to be edited and mountd restarted.

The RPC timeouts for mountd calls can only be changed by recompiling. The defaults are 2 seconds for client handle creation and 5 seconds for RPC calls.

AUTHORS

Andreas Stolcke <stolcke@icsi.berkeley.edu>.

Erez Zadok <ezk@cs.sunysb.edu>, Computer Science Department, Stony Brook University, Stony Brook, New York, USA.

Other authors and contributors to am-utils are listed in the **AUTHORS** file distributed with am-utils.

NAME

flush – Postfix fast flush server

SYNOPSIS

flush [generic Postfix daemon options]

DESCRIPTION

The **flush**(8) server maintains a record of deferred mail by destination. This information is used to improve the performance of the SMTP **ETRN** request, and of its command-line equivalent, "**sendmail -qR**" or "**postqueue -f**". This program expects to be run from the **master**(8) process manager.

The record is implemented as a per-destination logfile with as contents the queue IDs of deferred mail. A logfile is append-only, and is truncated when delivery is requested for the corresponding destination. A destination is the part on the right-hand side of the right-most @ in an email address.

Per-destination logfiles of deferred mail are maintained only for eligible destinations. The list of eligible destinations is specified with the **fast_flush_domains** configuration parameter, which defaults to **$relay_domains**.

This server implements the following requests:

add *sitename queueid*

Inform the **flush**(8) server that the message with the specified queue ID is queued for the specified destination.

send_site *sitename*

Request delivery of mail that is queued for the specified destination.

send_file *queueid*

Request delivery of the specified deferred message.

refresh Refresh non-empty per-destination logfiles that were not read in **$fast_flush_refresh_time** hours, by simulating send requests (see above) for the corresponding destinations.

Delete empty per-destination logfiles that were not updated in **$fast_flush_purge_time** days.

This request completes in the background.

purge Do a **refresh** for all per-destination logfiles.

SECURITY

The **flush**(8) server is not security-sensitive. It does not talk to the network, and it does not talk to local users. The fast flush server can run chrooted at fixed low privilege.

DIAGNOSTICS

Problems and transactions are logged to **syslogd**(8).

BUGS

Fast flush logfiles are truncated only after a "send" request, not when mail is actually delivered, and therefore can accumulate outdated or redundant data. In order to maintain sanity, "refresh" must be executed periodically. This can be automated with a suitable wakeup timer setting in the **master.cf** configuration file.

Upon receipt of a request to deliver mail for an eligible destination, the **flush**(8) server requests delivery of all messages that are listed in that destination's logfile, regardless of the recipients of those messages. This is not an issue for mail that is sent to a **relay_domains** destination because such mail typically only has recipients in one domain.

CONFIGURATION PARAMETERS

Changes to **main.cf** are picked up automatically as **flush**(8) processes run for only a limited amount of time. Use the command "**postfix reload**" to speed up a change.

The text below provides only a parameter summary. See **postconf**(5) for more details including examples.

config_directory (see 'postconf -d' output)
> The default location of the Postfix main.cf and master.cf configuration files.

daemon_timeout (18000s)
> How much time a Postfix daemon process may take to handle a request before it is terminated by a built-in watchdog timer.

fast_flush_domains ($relay_domains)
> Optional list of destinations that are eligible for per-destination logfiles with mail that is queued to those destinations.

fast_flush_refresh_time (12h)
> The time after which a non-empty but unread per-destination "fast flush" logfile needs to be refreshed.

fast_flush_purge_time (7d)
> The time after which an empty per-destination "fast flush" logfile is deleted.

ipc_timeout (3600s)
> The time limit for sending or receiving information over an internal communication channel.

max_idle (100s)
> The maximum amount of time that an idle Postfix daemon process waits for an incoming connection before terminating voluntarily.

max_use (100)
> The maximal number of incoming connections that a Postfix daemon process will service before terminating voluntarily.

parent_domain_matches_subdomains (see 'postconf -d' output)
> What Postfix features match subdomains of "domain.tld" automatically, instead of requiring an explicit ".domain.tld" pattern.

process_id (read-only)
> The process ID of a Postfix command or daemon process.

process_name (read-only)
> The process name of a Postfix command or daemon process.

queue_directory (see 'postconf -d' output)
> The location of the Postfix top-level queue directory.

syslog_facility (mail)
> The syslog facility of Postfix logging.

syslog_name (see 'postconf -d' output)
> The mail system name that is prepended to the process name in syslog records, so that "smtpd" becomes, for example, "postfix/smtpd".

FILES
/var/spool/postfix/flush, "fast flush" logfiles.

SEE ALSO
smtpd(8), SMTP server
qmgr(8), queue manager
postconf(5), configuration parameters
master(5), generic daemon options
master(8), process manager
syslogd(8), system logging

README FILES
Use "**postconf readme_directory**" or "**postconf html_directory**" to locate this information.
ETRN_README, Postfix ETRN howto

LICENSE

      The Secure Mailer license must be distributed with this software.

HISTORY

      This service was introduced with Postfix version 1.0.

AUTHOR(S)

      Wietse Venema
      IBM T.J. Watson Research
      P.O. Box 704
      Yorktown Heights, NY 10598, USA

NAME
    format — how to format disks and tapes

DESCRIPTION
    Currently, there are no "native" NetBSD media formatting utilities. Formatting of both disks and cartridge tapes must be done either stand-alone or under HP-UX using the *mediainit* utility distributed by HP. Note that HP-brand cartridge tapes come pre-formatted, and HP disks are supposed to.

HISTORY
    The **format** utility first appeared in 4.4 BSD.

NAME

 format — how to format disk packs

DESCRIPTION

There are two ways to format disk packs. The simplest is to use the **format** program. The alternative is to use the DEC standard formatting software which operates under the DEC diagnostic supervisor. This manual page describes the operation of **format**, then concludes with some remarks about using the DEC formatter.

format is a standalone program used to format and check disks prior to constructing file systems. In addition to the formatting operation, **format** records any bad sectors encountered according to DEC standard 144. Formatting is performed one track at a time by writing the appropriate headers and a test pattern and then checking the sector by reading and verifying the pattern, using the controller's ECC for error detection. A sector is marked bad if an unrecoverable media error is detected, or if a correctable ECC error too many bits in length is detected (such errors are indicated as "ECC" in the summary printed upon completing the format operation). After the entire disk has been formatted and checked, the total number of errors are reported, any bad sectors and skip sectors are marked, and a bad sector forwarding table is written to the disk in the first five even numbered sectors of the last track. It is also possible to reformat sections of the disk in units of tracks. **format** may be used on any UNIBUS or MASSBUS drive supported by the *up* and *hp* device drivers which uses 4-byte headers (everything except RP's).

The test pattern used during the media check may be selected from one of: 0xf00f (RH750 worst case), 0xec6d (media worst case), and 0xa5a5 (alternating 1's and 0's). Normally the media worst case pattern is used.

format also has an option to perform an extended "severe burn-in", which makes a number of passes using different patterns. The number of passes can be selected at run time, up to a maximum of 48, with provision for additional passes or termination after the preselected number of passes. This test runs for many hours, depending on the disk and processor.

Each time **format** is run to format an entire disk, a completely new bad sector table is generated based on errors encountered while formatting. The device driver, however, will always attempt to read any existing bad sector table when the device is first opened. Thus, if a disk pack has never previously been formatted, or has been formatted with different sectoring, five error messages will be printed when the driver attempts to read the bad sector table; these diagnostics should be ignored.

Formatting a 400 megabyte disk on a MASSBUS disk controller usually takes about 20 minutes. Formatting on a UNIBUS disk controller takes significantly longer. For every hundredth cylinder formatted **format** prints a message indicating the current cylinder being formatted. (This message is just to reassure people that nothing is amiss.)

format uses the standard notation of the standalone I/O library in identifying a drive to be formatted. A drive is specified as *zz(x,y)*, where *zz* refers to the controller type (either *hp* or *up*), *x* is the unit number of the drive; 8 times the UNIBUS or MASSBUS adaptor number plus the MASSBUS drive number or UNIBUS drive unit number; and *y* is the file system partition on drive *x* (this should always be 0). For example, "hp(1,0)" indicates that drive 1 on MASSBUS adaptor 0 should be formatted; while "up(10,0)" indicates that UNIBUS drive 2 on UNIBUS adaptor 1 should be formatted.

Before each formatting attempt, **format** prompts the user in case debugging should be enabled in the appropriate device driver. A carriage return disables debugging information.

format should be used prior to building file systems (with newfs(8) to ensure that all sectors with uncorrectable media errors are remapped. If a drive develops uncorrectable defects after formatting, either bad144(8) or badsect(8) should be able to avoid the bad sectors.

EXAMPLES

A sample run of **format** is shown below. In this example (using a VAX-11/780), **format** is loaded from the console floppy; on an 11/750 **format** will be loaded from the root file system with boot(8) following a "B/3" command. Boldface means user input. As usual, "#" and "@" may be used to edit input.

>>>**L FORMAT**
                          LOAD DONE, 00004400 BYTES LOADED
>>>**S 2**
Disk format/check utility

Enable debugging (0=none, 1=bse, 2=ecc, 3=bse+ecc)? **0**
Device to format? **hp(8,0)**
(*error messages may occur as old bad sector table is read*)
Formatting drive hp0 on adaptor 1: verify (yes/no)? **yes**
Device data: #cylinders=842, #tracks=20, #sectors=48
Starting cylinder (0):
Starting track (0):
Ending cylinder (841):
Ending track (19):
Available test patterns are:
                          1 - (f00f) RH750 worst case
                          2 - (ec6d) media worst case
                          3 - (a5a5) alternating 1's and 0's
                          4 - (ffff) Severe burnin (up to 48 passes)
Pattern (one of the above, other to restart)? **2**
Maximum number of bit errors to allow for soft ECC (3):
Start formatting...make sure the drive is online

  ...
(*soft ecc's and other errors are reported as they occur*)
  ...
(*if 4 write check errors were found, the program terminates like this...*)
  ...
Errors:
Bad sector: 0
Write check: 4
Hard ECC: 0
Other hard: 0
Marked bad: 0
Skipped: 0
Total of 4 hard errors revectored.
Writing bad sector table at block 808272
(*808272 is the block # of the first block in the bad sector table*)
Done
(*...program restarts to allow formatting other disks*)
(*...to abort halt machine with ^P*)

DIAGNOSTICS

The diagnostics are intended to be self explanatory.

USING DEC SOFTWARE TO FORMAT

Warning: These instructions are for people with 11/780 CPUs. The steps needed for 11/750 or 11/730 CPU's are similar, but not covered in detail here.

The formatting procedures are different for each type of disk. Listed here are the formatting procedures for RK07's, RP0X, and RM0X disks.

You should shut down UNIX and halt the machine to do any disk formatting. Make certain you put in the pack you want formatted. It is also a good idea to spin down or write protect the disks you don't want to format, just in case.

Formatting an RK07

Load the console floppy labeled, "RX11 VAX DSK LD DEV #1" in the console disk drive, and type the following commands:

```
>>>BOOT
DIAGNOSTIC SUPERVISOR.  ZZ-ESSAA-X5.0-119  23-JAN-1980 12:44:40.03
DS>ATTACH DW780 SBI DW0 3 5
DS>ATTACH RK611 DMA
DS>ATTACH RK07 DW0 DMA0
DS>SELECT DMA0
DS>LOAD EVRAC
DS>START/SEC:PACKINIT
```

Formatting an RP0X

Follow the above procedures except that the ATTACH and SELECT lines should read:

```
DS>ATTACH RH780 SBI RH0 8 5
DS>ATTACH RP0X RH0 DBA0                     (RP0X is, e.g., RP06)
DS>SELECT DBA0
```

This is for drive 0 on mba0; use 9 instead of 8 for mba1, etc.

Formatting an RM0X

Follow the above procedures except that the ATTACH and SELECT lines should read:

```
DS>ATTACH RH780 SBI RH0 8 5
DS>ATTACH RM0X RH0 DRA0
DS>SELECT DRA0
```

Don't forget to put your UNIX console floppy back in the floppy disk drive.

SEE ALSO

bad144(8), badsect(8), newfs(8)

BUGS

An equivalent facility should be available which operates under a running UNIX system.

It should be possible to reformat or verify part or all of a disk, then update the existing bad sector table.

NAME

    fsck — file system consistency check and interactive repair

SYNOPSIS

    fsck [**-dfnPpqvy**] [**-l** *maxparallel*] [**-T** *fstype:fsoptions*] [**-t** *fstype*]
        [**-x** *mountpoint*] [special | node ...]

DESCRIPTION

The **fsck** command invokes file system-specific programs to check the special devices listed in the fstab(5) file or in the command line for consistency.

It is normally used in the script /etc/rc during automatic reboot. If no file systems are specified, and "preen" mode is enabled (**-p** option) **fsck** reads the table /etc/fstab to determine which file systems to check, in what order. Only partitions in fstab that are mounted "rw," "rq" or "ro" and that have non-zero pass number are checked. File systems with pass number 1 (normally just the root file system) are checked one at a time. When pass 1 completes, all remaining file systems are checked, running one process per disk drive. By default, file systems which are already mounted read-write are not checked. The disk drive containing each file system is inferred from the longest prefix of the device name that ends in a digit; the remaining characters are assumed to be the partition designator.

The options are as follows:

-d   Debugging mode. Just print the commands without executing them.

-f   Force checking of file systems, even when they are marked clean (for file systems that support this), or when they are mounted read-write.

-l *maxparallel*
      Limit the number of parallel checks to the number specified in the following argument. By default, the limit is the number of disks, running one process per disk. If a smaller limit is given, the disks are checked round-robin, one file system at a time.

-n   Causes **fsck** to assume no as the answer to all operator questions, except "CONTINUE?".

-P   Display a progress meter for each file system check. This option also disables parallel checking. Note that progress meters are not supported by all file system types.

-p   Enter preen mode. In preen mode, **fsck** will check all file systems listed in /etc/fstab according to their pass number, and will make minor repairs without human intervention.

-q   Quiet mode, do not output any messages for clean filesystems.

-T *fstype:fsoptions*
      List of comma separated file system specific options for the specified file system type, in the same format as mount(8).

-t *fstype*
      Invoke **fsck** only for the comma separated list of file system types. If the list starts with "no" then invoke **fsck** for the file system types that are not specified in the list.

-v   Print the commands before executing them.

-x *mountpoint*
      Exclude the filesystem which has a *mountpoint* the same as in /etc/fstab. Used only in "preen" mode.

-y   Causes **fsck** to assume yes as the answer to all operator questions.

EXIT STATUS

fsck exits with 0 on success. Any major problems will cause **fsck** to exit with the following non-zero exit(3) codes, so as to alert any invoking program or script that human intervention is required.

1   Usage problem.

2   Unresolved errors while checking the filesystem. Re-running **fsck** on the filesystem(s) is required.

4   The root filesystem was changed in the process of checking, and updating the mount was unsuccessful. A reboot (without sync) is required.

8   The filesystem check has failed, and a subsequent check is required that will require human intervention.

12   **fsck** exited because of the result of a signal (usually SIGINT or SIGQUIT from the terminal).

FILES

/etc/fstab file system table

SEE ALSO

fstab(5), fsck_ext2fs(8), fsck_ffs(8), fsck_lfs(8), fsck_msdos(8), mount(8)

NAME
  fsck_ext2fs — ext2 File System consistency check and interactive repair

SYNOPSIS
  fsck_ext2fs [**-dfnpUy**] [**-b** *block#*] [**-c** *level*] [**-m** *mode*] *filesystem* . . .

DESCRIPTION
  fsck_ext2fs performs interactive filesystem consistency checks and repair for each of the filesystems specified on the command line. It is normally invoked from fsck(8).

  The kernel takes care that only a restricted class of innocuous filesystem inconsistencies can happen unless hardware or software failures intervene. These are limited to the following:

Unreferenced inodes
Link counts in inodes too large
Missing blocks in the free map
Blocks in the free map also in files
Counts in the super-block wrong

  These are the only inconsistencies that **fsck_ext2fs** in "preen" mode (with the **-p** option) will correct; if it encounters other inconsistencies, it exits with an abnormal return status. For each corrected inconsistency one or more lines will be printed identifying the filesystem on which the correction will take place, and the nature of the correction. After successfully correcting a filesystem, **fsck_ext2fs** will print the number of files on that filesystem and the number of used and free blocks.

  If sent a QUIT signal, **fsck_ext2fs** will finish the filesystem checks, then exit with an abnormal return status.

  Without the **-p** option, **fsck_ext2fs** audits and interactively repairs inconsistent conditions for filesystems. If the filesystem is inconsistent the operator is prompted for concurrence before each correction is attempted. It should be noted that some of the corrective actions which are not correctable under the **-p** option will result in some loss of data. The amount and severity of data lost may be determined from the diagnostic output. The default action for each consistency correction is to wait for the operator to respond yes or no. If the operator does not have write permission on the filesystem **fsck_ext2fs** will default to a **-n** action.

  The following flags are interpreted by **fsck_ext2fs**.

  -b Use the block specified immediately after the flag as the super block for the filesystem. Block 8193 is usually an alternate super block.

  -d Print debugging output.

  -f Force checking of file systems. Normally, if a file system is cleanly unmounted, the kernel will set a "clean flag" in the file system superblock, and **fsck_ext2fs** will not check the file system. This option forces **fsck_ext2fs** to check the file system, regardless of the state of the clean flag.

  -m Use the mode specified in octal immediately after the flag as the permission bits to use when creating the lost+found directory rather than the default 1777. In particular, systems that do not wish to have lost files accessible by all users on the system should use a more restrictive set of permissions such as 700.

  -n Assume a no response to all questions asked by **fsck_ext2fs** except for CONTINUE?, which is assumed to be affirmative; do not open the filesystem for writing.

-p   Specify "preen" mode, described above.

-U   Resolve numeric userids to usernames.

-y   Assume a yes response to all questions asked by **fsck_ext2fs**; this should be used with great
          caution as this is a free license to continue after essentially unlimited trouble has been encoun-
          tered.

Inconsistencies checked are as follows:
1. Blocks claimed by more than one inode or the free map.
2. Blocks claimed by an inode outside the range of the filesystem.
3. Incorrect link counts.
4. Size checks:
   Directory size not a multiple of filesystem block size.
   Partially truncated file.
5. Bad inode format.
6. Blocks not accounted for anywhere.
7. Directory checks:
   File pointing to unallocated inode.
   Inode number out of range.
   Dot or dot-dot not the first two entries of a directory or having the wrong inode number.
8. Super Block checks:
   More blocks for inodes than there are in the filesystem.
   Bad free block map format.
   Total free block and/or free inode count incorrect.

Orphaned files and directories (allocated but unreferenced) are, with the operator's concurrence, reconnected
by placing them in the lost+found directory. The name assigned is the inode number. If the
lost+found directory does not exist, it is created. If there is insufficient space its size is increased.

Because of inconsistencies between the block device and the buffer cache, the raw device should always be
used.

DIAGNOSTICS

The diagnostics produced by **fsck_ext2fs** are fully enumerated and explained in Appendix A of *Fsck –
The UNIX File System Check Program.*

SEE ALSO

fs(5), fstab(5), fsck(8), fsdb(8), newfs(8), reboot(8)

NAME

fsck_ffs — Fast File System consistency check and interactive repair

SYNOPSIS

fsck_ffs [**-adFfPpqUX**] [**-B** *byteorder*] [**-b** *block*] [**-c** *level*] [**-m** *mode*]
      [**-x** *snap-backup*] [**-y** | **-n**] *filesystem* . . .

DESCRIPTION

fsck_ffs performs interactive file system consistency checks and repair for each of the file systems specified on the command line. It is normally invoked from fsck(8).

The kernel takes care that only a restricted class of innocuous file system inconsistencies can happen unless hardware or software failures intervene. These are limited to the following:

> Unreferenced inodes
> Link counts in inodes too large
> Missing blocks in the free map
> Blocks in the free map also in files
> Counts in the super-block wrong

These are the only inconsistencies that **fsck_ffs** in "preen" mode (with the **-p** option) will correct; if it encounters other inconsistencies, it exits with an abnormal return status. For each corrected inconsistency one or more lines will be printed identifying the file system on which the correction will take place, and the nature of the correction. After successfully correcting a file system, **fsck_ffs** will print the number of files on that file system, the number of used and free blocks, and the percentage of fragmentation.

If sent a QUIT signal, **fsck_ffs** will finish the file system checks, then exit with an abnormal return status.

If **fsck_ffs** receives a SIGINFO signal (see the **status** argument for stty(1)), a line will be written to the standard error output indicating the name of the device currently being checked, the current phase number and phase-specific progress information.

Without the **-p** option, **fsck_ffs** audits and interactively repairs inconsistent conditions for file systems. If the file system is inconsistent the operator is prompted for concurrence before each correction is attempted. It should be noted that some of the corrective actions which are not correctable under the **-p** option will result in some loss of data. The amount and severity of data lost may be determined from the diagnostic output. The default action for each consistency correction is to wait for the operator to respond yes or no. If the operator does not have write permission on the file system **fsck_ffs** will default to a **-n** action.

fsck_ffs has more consistency checks than its predecessors *check*, *dcheck*, *fcheck*, and *icheck* combined.

The following flags are interpreted by **fsck_ffs**.

-a	Interpret the filesystem as an Apple UFS filesystem, even if there is no Apple UFS volume label present.
-B *byteorder*	Convert the file system metadata to *byteorder* byte order if needed. Valid byte orders are "be" and "le". If **fsck_ffs** is interrupted while swapping the metadata byte order, the file system cannot be recovered. **fsck_ffs** will print a message in interactive mode if the file system is not in host byte order.
-b *block*	Use the block number *block* as the super block for the file system. Block 32 is usually an alternative super block.
-c *level*	Convert the FFSv1 file system to the level *level*. Note that the level of a file system can only be raised. There are currently five levels defined:

0   The file system is in the old (static table) format.

1   The file system is in the new (dynamic table) format.

2   The file system supports 32-bit UIDs and GIDs, short symbolic links are stored in the inode, and directories have an added field showing the file type.

3   If maxcontig is greater than one, build the free segment maps to aid in finding contiguous sets of blocks. If maxcontig is equal to one, delete any existing segment maps.

4   Rearrange the super block to the same layout as FFSv2; disable the rotational layout tables and per cylinder group block totals.

In interactive mode, **fsck_ffs** will list the conversion to be made and ask whether the conversion should be done. If a negative answer is given, no further operations are done on the file system. In preen mode, the conversion is listed and done if possible without user interaction. Conversion in preen mode is best used when all the file systems are being converted at once.

The output of dumpfs(8) can be examined to determine the format of the file system ("format" in the second line) and the file system level ("fslevel" in the sixth line).

-d   Print debugging output.

-F   Indicates that *filesystem* is a file system image, rather than a raw character device. *filesystem* will be accessed 'as-is', and no attempts will be made to read a disklabel.

-f   Force checking of file systems. Normally, if a file system is cleanly unmounted, the kernel will set a "clean flag" in the file system super block, and **fsck_ffs** will not check the file system. This option forces **fsck_ffs** to check the file system, regardless of the state of the clean flag.

-m *mode*   Use the octal value *mode* as the permission bits to use when creating the lost+found directory rather than the default 1700. In particular, systems that do not wish to have lost files accessible by all users on the system should use a more restrictive set of permissions such as 700.

-n   Assume a no response to all questions asked by **fsck_ffs** except for CONTINUE?, which is assumed to be affirmative; do not open the file system for writing.

-P   Display a progress meter for the file system check. A new meter is displayed for each of the 5 file system check passes, unless **-p** is specified, in which case only one meter for overall progress is displayed. Progress meters are disabled if the **-d** option is specified.

-p   Specify "preen" mode, described above.

-x *snap-backup*
                Use a snapshot with *snap-backup* as backup to check a read-write mounted filesystem. Must be used with **-n**. See fss(4) for more details. The point is to check an internally-consistent version of the filesystem to find out if it is damaged; on failure one should unmount the filesystem and repair it.

-U   Resolve user ids to usernames.

-X   Similar to -x but uses a file system internal snapshot on the file system to be
                            checked.

-y   Assume a yes response to all questions asked by **fsck_ffs**; this should be
                            used with great caution as this is a free license to continue after essentially
                            unlimited trouble has been encountered.

Inconsistencies checked are as follows:
1. Blocks claimed by more than one inode or the free map.
2. Blocks claimed by an inode outside the range of the file system.
3. Incorrect link counts.
4. Size checks:
        Directory size not a multiple of DIRBLKSIZ.
        Partially truncated file.
5. Bad inode format.
6. Blocks not accounted for anywhere.
7. Directory checks:
        File pointing to unallocated inode.
        Inode number out of range.
        Dot or dot-dot not the first two entries of a directory or having the wrong inode number.
8. Super Block checks:
        More blocks for inodes than there are in the file system.
        Bad free block map format.
        Total free block and/or free inode count incorrect.

Orphaned files and directories (allocated but unreferenced) are, with the operator's concurrence, reconnected
by placing them in the `lost+found` directory. The name assigned is the inode number. If the
`lost+found` directory does not exist, it is created. If there is insufficient space its size is increased.

Because of inconsistencies between the block device and the buffer cache, the raw device should always be
used.

DIAGNOSTICS
     The diagnostics produced by **fsck_ffs** are fully enumerated and explained in Appendix A of *Fsck – The
     UNIX File System Check Program*.

SEE ALSO
     `fss`(4), `fs`(5), `fstab`(5), `dumpfs`(8), `fsck`(8), `fsdb`(8), `newfs`(8), `reboot`(8)

NAME

    fsck_lfs — Log-structured File System consistency check and interactive repair

SYNOPSIS

    fsck_lfs [**-dfpqU**] [**-b** *block*] [**-m** *mode*] [**-y** | **-n**] *filesystem* . . .

DESCRIPTION

    fsck_lfs performs interactive filesystem consistency checks and repair for each of the filesystems speci-
fied on the command line. It is normally invoked from fsck(8).

    The design of LFS takes care that no filesystem inconsistencies can happen unless hardware or software fail-
ures intervene. **fsck_lfs** will report and optionally correct any such inconsistencies.

    For each corrected inconsistency one or more lines will be printed identifying the filesystem on which the
correction will take place, and the nature of the correction. After successfully correcting a filesystem,
fsck_lfs will print the number of files on that filesystem, the number of used and free blocks, and the percentage of fragmentation.

    If sent a QUIT signal, **fsck_lfs** will finish the filesystem checks, then exit with an abnormal return status.

    Without the **-p** option, **fsck_lfs** audits and interactively repairs inconsistent conditions for filesystems.
If the filesystem is inconsistent, the operator is prompted for concurrence before each correction is attempted.
It should be noted that some of the corrective actions will result in some loss of data. The amount and severity of data lost may be determined from the diagnostic output. The default action for each consistency correction is to wait for the operator to respond yes or no. If the operator does not have write permission on
the filesystem **fsck_lfs** will default to a **-n** action.

    The following flags are interpreted by **fsck_lfs**:

    -b *block*   Use *block* as the super block for the filesystem.

    -d   Print debugging output.

    -f   Force checking of file systems. Normally, if a file system is cleanly unmounted, the kernel
                   will set a "clean flag" in the file system superblock, and **fsck_lfs** will not check the file
                   system. This option forces **fsck_lfs** to check the file system, regardless of the state of the
                   clean flag.

    -m *mode*   Use *mode* specified in octal as the permission bits to use when creating the lost+found
                   directory rather than the default 1700. In particular, systems that do not wish to have lost
                   files accessible by all users on the system should use a more restrictive set of permissions
                   such as 700.

    -n   Assume a no response to all questions asked by **fsck_lfs** except for CONTINUE?, which
                   is assumed to be affirmative; do not open the filesystem for writing.

    -p   Specify "preen" mode. Currently, in this mode **fsck_lfs** rolls forward from the older
                   checkpoint, and performs no other action.

    -q   Quiet mode, do not output any messages for clean filesystems.

    -U   Resolve user ids to user names.

    -y   Assume a yes response to all questions asked by **fsck_lfs**; this should be used with great
                   caution as this is a free license to continue after essentially unlimited trouble has been
                   encountered.

    Inconsistencies checked are as follows:

1. Blocks claimed by more than one inode.
2. Blocks claimed by an inode outside the range of the filesystem.
3. Incorrect link counts.
4. Size checks:
   Directory size not a multiple of DIRBLKSIZ.
   Partially truncated file.
5. Bad inode format.
6. Directory checks:
   File pointing to unallocated inode.
   Inode number out of range.
   Dot or dot-dot not the first two entries of a directory or having the wrong inode number.
7. Super Block checks:
   More blocks for inodes than there are in the filesystem.
8. Index File checks:
   "In use" inodes on free list, or free inodes not on free list.
   Segment block counts incorrect, or "clean" segments containing live data.

Orphaned files and directories (allocated but unreferenced) are, with the operator's concurrence, reconnected by placing them in the `lost+found` directory. The name assigned is the inode number. If the `lost+found` directory does not exist, it is created. If there is insufficient space its size is increased.

Because of inconsistencies between the block device and the buffer cache, the raw device should always be used.

DIAGNOSTICS

The diagnostics produced by **fsck_lfs** are fully enumerated and explained in Appendix A of *Fsck − The UNIX File System Check Program.*

SEE ALSO

`fstab`(5), `fsck`(8), `newfs_lfs`(8), `reboot`(8)

HISTORY

The **fsck_lfs** program was first made available in NetBSD 1.4.

AUTHORS

Most of the **fsck_lfs** program was taken from `fsck_ffs`(8); what was not was written by Konrad Schroder ⟨perseant@NetBSD.org⟩.

FSCK_MSDOS (8)   NetBSD   FSCK_MSDOS (8)

NAME
　　　　fsck_msdos — DOS/Windows (FAT) filesystem consistency checker

SYNOPSIS
　　　　fsck_msdos **-p** [**-f**] *filesystem* . . .
　　　　fsck_msdos [**-fny**] [**-x** *snap-backup*] *filesystem* . . .

DESCRIPTION
　　　　The **fsck_msdos** utility verifies and repairs FAT filesystems (more commonly known as DOS filesystems).

　　　　The first form of **fsck_msdos** preens the specified filesystems. It is normally started by fsck(8) run from /etc/rc during automatic reboot, when a FAT filesystem is detected. When preening file systems, **fsck_msdos** will fix common inconsistencies non-interactively. If more serious problems are found, **fsck_msdos** does not try to fix them, indicates that it was not successful, and exits.

　　　　The second form of **fsck_msdos** checks the specified file systems and tries to repair all detected inconsistencies, requesting confirmation before making any changes.

　　　　The options are as follows:

　　　　-f　　　　　　　　This option is ignored by **fsck_msdos**, and is present only for compatibility with programs that check other file system types for consistency, such as fsck_ffs(8).

　　　　-n　　　　　　　　Causes **fsck_msdos** to assume no as the answer to all operator questions, except "CONTINUE?".

　　　　-p　　　　　　　　Preen the specified filesystems.

　　　　-x *snap-backup*　Use a snapshot with *snap-backup* as backup to check a read-write mounted filesystem. Must be used with **-n**. See fss(4) for more details. The point is to check an internally-consistent version of the filesystem to find out if it is damaged; on failure one should unmount the filesystem and repair it.

　　　　-y　　　　　　　　Causes **fsck_msdos** to assume yes as the answer to all operator questions.

SEE ALSO
　　　　fss(4), fsck(8), fsck_ffs(8), mount_msdos(8)

BUGS
　　　　fsck_msdos is still under construction.

NAME

fsdb — FFS debugging/editing tool

SYNOPSIS

fsdb [**-dFn**] **-f** *fsname*

DESCRIPTION

fsdb opens *fsname* (usually a raw disk partition) and runs a command loop allowing manipulation of the file system's inode data. You are prompted to enter a command with "fsdb (inum X)>" where *X* is the currently selected i-number. The initial selected inode is the root of the filesystem (i-number 2). The command processor uses the editline(3) library, so you can use command line editing to reduce typing if desired. When you exit the command loop, the file system superblock is marked dirty and any buffered blocks are written to the file system.

The **-d** option enables additional debugging output (which comes primarily from fsck(8)-derived code).

The **-F** option indicates that *filesystem* is a file system image, rather than a raw character device. It will be accessed 'as-is', and no attempts will be made to read a disklabel.

The **-n** option disables writing to the device, preventing any changes from being made to the filesystem.

COMMANDS

Besides the built-in editline(3) commands, **fsdb** supports these commands:

help   Print out the list of accepted commands.

inode *i-number*
> Select inode *i-number* as the new current inode.

back   Revert to the previously current inode.

clri   Clear the current inode.

lookup *name*
cd *name*
> Find *name* in the current directory and make its inode the current inode. *Name* may be a multi-component name or may begin with slash to indicate that the root inode should be used to start the lookup. If some component along the pathname is not found, the last valid directory encountered is left as the active inode.
> This command is valid only if the starting inode is a directory.

active
print   Print out the active inode.

uplink Increment the active inode's link count.

downlink
> Decrement the active inode's link count.

linkcount *number*
> Set the active inode's link count to *number*.

ls   List the current inode's directory entries. This command is valid only if the current inode is a directory.

blks   List the current inode's blocks numbers.

findblk *disk block number ...*
> Find the inode(s) owning the specified disk block(s) number(s). Note that these are not absolute disk blocks numbers, but offsets from the start of the partition.

rm *name*
del *name*
> Remove the entry *name* from the current directory inode. This command is valid only if the current inode is a directory.

ln *ino name*
> Create a link to inode *ino* under the name *name* in the current directory inode. This command is valid only if the current inode is a directory.

chinum *dirslot inum*
> Change the i-number in directory entry *dirslot* to *inum*.

chname *dirslot name*
> Change the name in directory entry *dirslot* to *name*. This command cannot expand a directory entry. You can only rename an entry if the name will fit into the existing directory slot.

chtype *type*
> Change the type of the current inode to *type*. *type* may be one of: *file*, *dir*, *socket*, or *fifo*.

chmod *mode*
> Change the mode bits of the current inode to *mode*. You cannot change the file type with this subcommand; use **chtype** to do that.

chflags *flags*
> Change the file flags of the current inode to *flags*.

chown *uid*
> Change the owner of the current inode to *uid*.

chgrp *gid*
> Change the group of the current inode to *gid*.

chgen *gen*
> Change the generation number of the current inode to *gen*.

mtime *time*
ctime *time*
atime *time*
> Change the modification, change, or access time (respectively) on the current inode to *time*. *Time* should be in the format *YYYYMMDDHHMMSS[.nsec]* where *nsec* is an optional nanosecond specification. If no nanoseconds are specified, the *mtimensec*, *ctimensec*, or *atimensec* field will be set to zero.

quit, q, exit, ⟨*EOF*⟩
> Exit the program.

SEE ALSO
editline(3), fs(5), clri(8), fsck(8)

HISTORY
fsdb uses the source code for fsck(8) to implement most of the file system manipulation code. The remainder of **fsdb** first appeared in NetBSD 1.1.

WARNING

Use this tool with extreme caution -- you can damage an FFS file system beyond what fsck(8) can repair.

BUGS

Manipulation of "short" symlinks doesn't work (in particular, don't try changing a symlink's type).

You must specify modes as numbers rather than symbolic names.

There are a bunch of other things that you might want to do which **fsdb** doesn't implement.

NAME

fsinfo – coordinate site-wide filesystem information

SYNOPSIS

fsinfo [**–v**] [**–a** *autodir*] [**–b** *bootparams*] [**–d** *dumpsets*] [**–e** *exports*] [**–f** *fstabs*] [**–h** *hostname*] [**–m** *automounts*] [**–I** *dir*] [**–D** *string[=string]*] [**–U** *string[=string]*] *config* ...

DESCRIPTION

The **fsinfo** utility takes a set of system configuration information, and generates a coordinated set of *amd* , *mount* and *mountd* configuration files.

The **fsinfo** command is fully described in the document *Amd - The 4.4BSD Automounter*

SEE ALSO

amd(8), **mount**(8), **mountd**(8).

"am-utils" **info**(1) entry.

Linux NFS and Automounter Administration by Erez Zadok, ISBN 0-7821-2739-8, (Sybex, 2001).

http://www.am-utils.org

Amd – The 4.4 BSD Automounter

HISTORY

The **fsinfo** command first appeared in 4.4BSD.

AUTHORS

Jan-Simon Pendry <jsp@doc.ic.ac.uk>, Department of Computing, Imperial College, London, UK.

Erez Zadok <ezk@cs.sunysb.edu>, Computer Science Department, Stony Brook University, Stony Brook, New York, USA.

Other authors and contributors to am-utils are listed in the **AUTHORS** file distributed with am-utils.

NAME
  fsirand — install random inode generation numbers in a filesystem

SYNOPSIS
  fsirand [**-F**] [**-p**] [**-x** *constant*] *special*

DESCRIPTION
  fsirand writes random inode generation numbers for all the inodes on device *special*. These random numbers make the NFS filehandles less predictable, increasing security of exported filesystems.

  fsirand should be run on a clean and unmounted filesystem.

  The options are as follows:

  -F   Indicates that *special* is a file system image, rather than a device name. *special* will be accessed 'as-is', without requiring that it is a raw character device and without attempting to read a disklabel.

  -p   Print the current inode generation numbers; the filesystem is not modified.

  -x *constant*
          Exclusive-or the given constant with the random number used in the generation process.

  fsirand exits zero on success, non-zero on failure.

  If **fsirand** receives a SIGINFO signal, statistics on the amount of work completed and estimated completion time (in minutes:seconds) will be written to the standard error output.

SEE ALSO
  fsck_ffs(8), newfs(8)

NAME

    fssconfig — configure file system snapshot devices

SYNOPSIS

    fssconfig [**-cxv**] *device path backup* [*cluster* [*size*]]
    fssconfig -u [**-v**] *device*
    fssconfig -l [**-v**] [*device*]

DESCRIPTION

The **fssconfig** command configures file system snapshot pseudo disk devices. It will associate the file system snapshot disk *device* with a snapshot of *path* allowing the latter to be accessed as though it were a disk.

If *backup* resides on the snapshotted file system a persistent snapshot will be created. This snapshot is active until *backup* is unlinked. This snapshot mode is only supported for ffs files systems.

Otherwise data written through the *path* will be saved in *backup*. If *backup* is a regular file, it will be created with length *size*. Default size is the size of *path*. Data is saved to *backup* in units of *cluster* bytes.

Options indicate an action to be performed:

-c Configures the device. If successful, references to *device* will access the contents of *path* at the time the snapshot was taken. If *backup* is a directory, a temporary file will be created in this directory. This file will be unlinked on exit.

-l List the snapshot devices and indicate which ones are in use. If a specific *device* is given, then only that will be described.

-u Unconfigures the *device*.

-v Be more verbose listing the snapshot devices.

-x Unlink *backup* after the *device* is configured.

If no action option is given, **-c** is assumed.

FILES

    /dev/rfss?
    /dev/fss?

EXAMPLES

        fssconfig fss0 /usr /tmp/back

Configures the snapshot device fss0 for a snapshot of the /usr file system. Data written through /usr will be backed up in /tmp/back.

        fssconfig fss1 / /dev/rsd0e 8192

Configures the snapshot device fss1 for a snapshot of the / file system. Data written through / will be backed up in /dev/rsd0e. The backup will take place in units of 8192 bytes.

        fssconfig -u fss0

Unconfigures the fss0 device.

SEE ALSO
> opendisk(3), fss(4), mount(8), umount(8)

HISTORY
> The **fssconfig** command appeared in NetBSD 2.0.

BUGS
> The fss(4) driver is *experimental*. Be sure you have a backup before you use it.

NAME
ftp-proxy — Internet File Transfer Protocol proxy daemon

SYNOPSIS
ftp-proxy [**-6Adrv**] [**-a** *address*] [**-b** *address*] [**-D** *level*] [**-i** *netif*]
        [**-m** *maxsessions*] [**-P** *port*] [**-p** *port*] [**-q** *queue*] [**-R** *address*]
        [**-T** *tag*] [**-t** *timeout*]

DESCRIPTION
ftp-proxy is a proxy for the Internet File Transfer Protocol. FTP control connections should be redirected into the proxy using the ipnat(4) or pf(4) *rdr* command, after which the proxy connects to the server on behalf of the client.

The proxy allows data connections to pass, rewriting and redirecting them so that the right addresses are used. All connections from the client to the server have their source address rewritten so they appear to come from the proxy. Consequently, all connections from the server to the proxy have their destination address rewritten, so they are redirected to the client. The proxy uses the pf(4) *anchor* facility for this, unless the option **-i** is specified, it will then use the ipnat(4) interface.

Assuming the FTP control connection is from $client to $server, the proxy connected to the server using the $proxy source address, and $port is negotiated, then **ftp-proxy** adds the following rules to the various anchors. (These example rules use inet, but the proxy also supports inet6.)

In case of active mode (PORT or EPRT):

```
rdr from $server to $proxy port $port -> $client
pass quick inet proto tcp \
    from $server to $client port $port
```

In case of passive mode (PASV or EPSV):

```
nat from $client to $server port $port -> $proxy
pass in quick inet proto tcp \
    from $client to $server port $port
pass out quick inet proto tcp \
    from $proxy to $server port $port
```

The options are as follows:

-6   IPv6 mode. The proxy will expect and use IPv6 addresses for all communication. Only the extended FTP modes EPSV and EPRT are allowed with IPv6. The proxy is in IPv4 mode by default.

-A   Only permit anonymous FTP connections. Either user "ftp" or user "anonymous" is allowed.

-a *address*
        The proxy will use this as the source address for the control connection to a server.

-b *address*
        Address where the proxy will listen for redirected control connections. The default is 127.0.0.1, or ::1 in IPv6 mode.

-D *level*
        Debug level, ranging from 0 to 7. Higher is more verbose. The default is 5. (These levels correspond to the syslog(3) levels.)

-d   Do not daemonize. The process will stay in the foreground, logging to standard error.

-i *netif*

    Set **ftp-proxy** for use with IP-Filter. The argument *netif* should be set to the name of the network interface where rdr is applied on.

-m *maxsessions*

    Maximum number of concurrent FTP sessions. When the proxy reaches this limit, new connections are denied. The default is 100 sessions. The limit can be lowered to a minimum of 1, or raised to a maximum of 500.

-P *port*

    Fixed server port. Only used in combination with **-R**. The default is port 21.

-p *port*

    Port where the proxy will listen for redirected connections. The default is port 8021.

-q *queue*

    Create rules with queue *queue* appended, so that data connections can be queued.

-R *address*

    Fixed server address, also known as reverse mode. The proxy will always connect to the same server, regardless of where the client wanted to connect to (before it was redirected). Use this option to proxy for a server behind NAT, or to forward all connections to another proxy.

-r   Rewrite sourceport to 20 in active mode to suit ancient clients that insist on this RFC property.

-T *tag*

    Automatically tag packets passing through the pf(4) rule with the name supplied.

-t *timeout*

    Number of seconds that the control connection can be idle, before the proxy will disconnect. The maximum is 86400 seconds, which is also the default. Do not set this too low, because the control connection is usually idle when large data transfers are taking place.

-v   Set the 'log' flag on pf rules committed by **ftp-proxy**. Use twice to set the 'log-all' flag. The pf rules do not log by default.

CONFIGURATION

To make use of the proxy using pf(4), pf.conf(5) needs the following rules. All anchors are mandatory. Adjust the rules as needed.

In the NAT section:

```
nat-anchor "ftp-proxy/*"
rdr-anchor "ftp-proxy/*"
rdr pass on $int_if proto tcp from $lan to any port 21 -> \
    127.0.0.1 port 8021
```

In the rule section:

```
anchor "ftp-proxy/*"
pass out proto tcp from $proxy to any port 21
```

To make use of the proxy using ipnat(4), ipnat.conf(5) need the following rule:

```
rdr $int_if any port 21 -> 127.0.0.1 port 8021 tcp
```

SEE ALSO

ftp(1), ipnat(4), pf(4), ipnat.conf(5), pf.conf(5)

CAVEATS

ipnat(4) and pf(4) does not allow the ruleset to be modified if the system is running at a securelevel higher than 1. At that level **ftp-proxy** cannot add rules to the anchors and FTP data connections may get blocked.

Negotiated data connection ports below 1024 are not allowed.

The negotiated IP address for active modes is ignored for security reasons. This makes third party file transfers impossible.

ftp-proxy chroots to "/var/chroot/ftp-proxy" and changes to user "_proxy" to drop privileges.

NAME

ftpd — Internet File Transfer Protocol server

SYNOPSIS

ftpd [**-46DdHlnQqrsUuWwX**] [**-a** *anondir*] [**-C** *user*[*@host*]] [**-c** *confdir*]
[**-e** *emailaddr*] [**-h** *hostname*] [**-L** *xferlogfile*] [**-P** *dataport*]
[**-V** *version*]

DESCRIPTION

ftpd is the Internet File Transfer Protocol server process. The server uses the TCP protocol and listens at the port specified in the "ftp" service specification; see services(5).

Available options:

-4   When **-D** is specified, bind to IPv4 addresses only.

-6   When **-D** is specified, bind to IPv6 addresses only.

-a *anondir*
Define *anondir* as the directory to chroot(2) into for anonymous logins. Default is the home directory for the ftp user. This can also be specified with the ftpd.conf(5) **chroot** directive.

-C *user*[*@host*]
Check whether *user* (as if connecting from *host*, if provided) would be granted access under the restrictions given in ftpusers(5), and exit without attempting a connection. **ftpd** exits with an exit code of 0 if access would be granted, or 1 otherwise. This can be useful for testing configurations.

-c *confdir*
Change the root directory of the configuration files from "/etc" to *confdir*. This changes the directory for the following files: /etc/ftpchroot, /etc/ftpusers, /etc/ftpwelcome, /etc/motd, and the file specified by the ftpd.conf(5) **limit** directive.

-D   Run as daemon. **ftpd** will listen on the default FTP port for incoming connections and fork a child for each connection. This is lower overhead than starting **ftpd** from inetd(8) and thus might be useful on busy servers to reduce load.

-d   Debugging information is written to the syslog using a facility of LOG_FTP.

-e *emailaddr*
Use *emailaddr* for the "%E" escape sequence (see **Display file escape sequences**)

-H   Equivalent to "-h 'hostname'".

-h *hostname*
Explicitly set the hostname to advertise as to *hostname*. The default is the hostname associated with the IP address that **ftpd** is listening on. This ability (with or without **-h**), in conjunction with **-c** *confdir*, is useful when configuring 'virtual' FTP servers, each listening on separate addresses as separate names. Refer to inetd.conf(5) for more information on starting services to listen on specific IP addresses.

-L *xferlogfile*
Log wu-ftpd style 'xferlog' entries to *xferlogfile*.

-l   Each successful and failed FTP session is logged using syslog with a facility of LOG_FTP. If this option is specified more than once, the retrieve (get), store (put), append, delete, make directory, remove directory and rename operations and their file name arguments are also logged.

-n   Don't attempt translation of IP addresses to hostnames.

-P *dataport*

        Use *dataport* as the data port, overriding the default of using the port one less that the port **ftpd** is listening on.

-Q   Disable the use of pid files for keeping track of the number of logged-in users per class. This may reduce the load on heavily loaded FTP servers.

-q   Enable the use of pid files for keeping track of the number of logged-in users per class. This is the default.

-r   Permanently drop root privileges once the user is logged in. The use of this option may result in the server using a port other than the (listening-port - 1) for **PORT** style commands, which is contrary to the **RFC 959** specification, but in practice very few clients rely upon this behaviour. See **SECURITY CONSIDERATIONS** below for more details.

-s   Require a secure authentication mechanism like Kerberos or S/Key to be used.

-U   Don't log each concurrent FTP session to /var/run/utmp. This is the default.

-u   Log each concurrent FTP session to /var/run/utmp, making them visible to commands such as who(1).

-V *version*

        Use *version* as the version to advertise in the login banner and in the output of **STAT** and **SYST** instead of the default version information. If *version* is empty or '-' then don't display any version information.

-W   Don't log each FTP session to /var/log/wtmp.

-w   Log each FTP session to /var/log/wtmp, making them visible to commands such as last(1). This is the default.

-X   Log wu-ftpd style 'xferlog' entries to the syslog, prefixed with "xferlog: ", using a facility of LOG_FTP. These syslog entries can be converted to a wu-ftpd style xferlog file suitable for input into a third-party log analysis tool with a command similar to:

```
            sed -ne 's/^.*xferlog: //p' /var/log/xferlog > wuxferlog
```

The file /etc/nologin can be used to disable FTP access. If the file exists, **ftpd** displays it and exits. If the file /etc/ftpwelcome exists, **ftpd** prints it before issuing the "ready" message. If the file /etc/motd exists (under the chroot directory if applicable), **ftpd** prints it after a successful login. This may be changed with the ftpd.conf(5) directive **motd**.

The **ftpd** server currently supports the following FTP requests. The case of the requests is ignored.

Request	Description
ABOR	abort previous command
ACCT	specify account (ignored)
ALLO	allocate storage (vacuously)
APPE	append to a file
CDUP	change to parent of current working directory
CWD	change working directory
DELE	delete a file
EPSV	prepare for server-to-server transfer
EPRT	specify data connection port

FEAT	list extra features that are not defined in **RFC 959**
HELP	give help information
LIST	give list files in a directory ("`ls -lA`")
LPSV	prepare for server-to-server transfer
LPRT	specify data connection port
MLSD	list contents of directory in a machine-processable form
MLST	show a pathname in a machine-processable form
MKD	make a directory
MDTM	show last modification time of file
MODE	specify data transfer *mode*
NLST	give name list of files in directory
NOOP	do nothing
OPTS	define persistent options for a given command
PASS	specify password
PASV	prepare for server-to-server transfer
PORT	specify data connection port
PWD	print the current working directory
QUIT	terminate session
REST	restart incomplete transfer
RETR	retrieve a file
RMD	remove a directory
RNFR	specify rename-from file name
RNTO	specify rename-to file name
SITE	non-standard commands (see next section)
SIZE	return size of file
STAT	return status of server
STOR	store a file
STOU	store a file with a unique name
STRU	specify data transfer *structure*
SYST	show operating system type of server system
TYPE	specify data transfer *type*
USER	specify user name
XCUP	change to parent of current working directory (deprecated)
XCWD	change working directory (deprecated)
XMKD	make a directory (deprecated)
XPWD	print the current working directory (deprecated)
XRMD	remove a directory (deprecated)

The following non-standard or UNIX specific commands are supported by the SITE request.

Request	Description
CHMOD	change mode of a file, e.g. "SITE CHMOD 755 filename"
HELP	give help information.
IDLE	set idle-timer, e.g. "SITE IDLE 60"
RATEGET	set maximum get rate throttle in bytes/second, e.g. "SITE RATEGET 5k"
RATEPUT	set maximum put rate throttle in bytes/second, e.g. "SITE RATEPUT 5k"
UMASK	change umask, e.g. "SITE UMASK 002"

The following FTP requests (as specified in **RFC 959** and **RFC 2228**) are recognized, but are not implemented: **ACCT**, **ADAT**, **AUTH**, **CCC**, **CONF**, **ENC**, **MIC**, **PBSZ**, **PROT**, **REIN**, and **SMNT**.

The **ftpd** server will abort an active file transfer only when the **ABOR** command is preceded by a Telnet "Interrupt Process" (IP) signal and a Telnet "Synch" signal in the command Telnet stream, as described in Internet **RFC 959**. If a **STAT** command is received during a data transfer, preceded by a Telnet IP and

Synch, transfer status will be returned.

ftpd interprets file names according to the "globbing" conventions used by csh(1). This allows users to use the metacharacters "* ? [ ] { } ~".

User authentication
ftpd authenticates users according to five rules.

1. The login name must be in the password data base, passwd(5), and not have a null password. In this case a password must be provided by the client before any file operations may be performed. If the user has an S/Key key, the response from a successful **USER** command will include an S/Key challenge. The client may choose to respond with a **PASS** command giving either a standard password or an S/Key one-time password. The server will automatically determine which type of password it has been given and attempt to authenticate accordingly. See skey(1) for more information on S/Key authentication. S/Key is a Trademark of Bellcore.

2. The login name must be allowed based on the information in ftpusers(5).

3. The user must have a standard shell returned by getusershell(3). If the user's shell field in the password database is empty, the shell is assumed to be /bin/sh. As per shells(5), the user's shell must be listed with full path in /etc/shells.

4. If directed by the file ftpchroot(5) the session's root directory will be changed by chroot(2) to the directory specified in the ftpd.conf(5) **chroot** directive (if set), or to the home directory of the user. This facility may also be triggered by enabling the boolean **ftp-chroot** in login.conf(5). However, the user must still supply a password. This feature is intended as a compromise between a fully anonymous account and a fully privileged account. The account should also be set up as for an anonymous account.

5. If the user name is "anonymous" or "ftp", an anonymous FTP account must be present in the password file (user "ftp"). In this case the user is allowed to log in by specifying any password (by convention an email address for the user should be used as the password).

    The server performs a chroot(2) to the directory specified in the ftpd.conf(5) **chroot** directive (if set), the **-a** *anondir* directory (if set), or to the home directory of the "ftp" user.

    The server then performs a chdir(2) to the directory specified in the ftpd.conf(5) **homedir** directive (if set), otherwise to /.

    If other restrictions are required (such as disabling of certain commands and the setting of a specific umask), then appropriate entries in ftpd.conf(5) are required.

    If the first character of the password supplied by an anonymous user is "-", then the verbose messages displayed at login and upon a **CWD** command are suppressed.

Display file escape sequences
When **ftpd** displays various files back to the client (such as /etc/ftpwelcome and /etc/motd), various escape strings are replaced with information pertinent to the current connection.

The supported escape strings are:

Escape	Description
%c	Class name.
%C	Current working directory.
%E	Email address given with **-e**.
%L	Local hostname.

%M	Maximum number of users for this class. Displays "unlimited" if there's no limit.
%N	Current number of users for this class.
%R	Remote hostname.
%s	If the result of the most recent "%M" or "%N" was not "1", print an "s".
%S	If the result of the most recent "%M" or "%N" was not "1", print an "S".
%T	Current time.
%U	User name.
%%	A "%" character.

Setting up a restricted ftp subtree

In order that system security is not breached, it is recommended that the subtrees for the "ftp" and "chroot" accounts be constructed with care, following these rules (replace "ftp" in the following directory names with the appropriate account name for 'chroot' users):

˜ftp	Make the home directory owned by "root" and unwritable by anyone.
˜ftp/bin	Make this directory owned by "root" and unwritable by anyone (mode 555). Generally any conversion commands should be installed here (mode 111).
˜ftp/etc	Make this directory owned by "root" and unwritable by anyone (mode 555). The files pwd.db (see passwd(5)) and group (see group(5)) must be present for the **LIST** command to be able to display owner and group names instead of numbers. The password field in passwd(5) is not used, and should not contain real passwords. The file motd, if present, will be printed after a successful login. These files should be mode 444.
˜ftp/pub	This directory and the subdirectories beneath it should be owned by the users and groups responsible for placing files in them, and be writable only by them (mode 755 or 775). They should *not* be owned or writable by ftp or its group.
˜ftp/incoming	This directory is where anonymous users place files they upload. The owners should be the user "ftp" and an appropriate group. Members of this group will be the only users with access to these files after they have been uploaded; these should be people who know how to deal with them appropriately. If you wish anonymous FTP users to be able to see the names of the files in this directory the permissions should be 770, otherwise they should be 370.

The following ftpd.conf(5) directives should be used:

```
modify guest off
umask  guest 0707
upload guest on
```

This will result in anonymous users being able to upload files to this directory, but they will not be able to download them, delete them, or overwrite them, due to the umask and disabling of the commands mentioned above.

˜ftp/tmp	This directory is used to create temporary files which contain the error messages generated by a conversion or **LIST** command. The owner should be the user "ftp". The permissions should be 300.

If you don't enable conversion commands, or don't want anonymous users uploading files here (see ˜ftp/incoming above), then don't create this directory. However, error messages from conversion or **LIST** commands won't be returned to the user. (This is the traditional behaviour.) Note that the ftpd.conf(5) directive **upload** can be used to prevent users uploading here.

To set up "ftp-only" accounts that provide only FTP, but no valid shell login, you can copy/link `/sbin/nologin` to `/sbin/ftplogin`, and enter `/sbin/ftplogin` to `/etc/shells` to allow logging-in via FTP into the accounts, which must have `/sbin/ftplogin` as login shell.

FILES

`/etc/ftpchroot`	List of normal users whose root directory should be changed via `chroot`(2).
`/etc/ftpd.conf`	Configure file conversions and other settings.
`/etc/ftpusers`	List of unwelcome/restricted users.
`/etc/ftpwelcome`	Welcome notice before login.
`/etc/motd`	Welcome notice after login.
`/etc/nologin`	If it exists, displayed and access is refused.
`/var/run/ftpd.pids-CLASS`	
	State file of logged-in processes for the **ftpd** class 'CLASS'.
`/var/run/utmp`	List of logged-in users on the system.
`/var/log/wtmp`	Login history database.

SEE ALSO

`ftp`(1), `skey`(1), `who`(1), `getusershell`(3), `ftpchroot`(5), `ftpd.conf`(5), `ftpusers`(5), `login.conf`(5), `syslogd`(8)

STANDARDS

ftpd recognizes all commands in **RFC 959**, follows the guidelines in **RFC 1123**, recognizes all commands in **RFC 2228** (although they are not supported yet), and supports the extensions from **RFC 2389**, **RFC 2428**, and **RFC 3659**.

HISTORY

The **ftpd** command appeared in 4.2 BSD.

Various features such as the `ftpd.conf`(5) functionality, **RFC 2389**, and **RFC 3659** support was implemented in NetBSD 1.3 and later releases by Luke Mewburn.

BUGS

The server must run as the super-user to create sockets with privileged port numbers (i.e, those less than `IPPORT_RESERVED`, which is 1024). If **ftpd** is listening on a privileged port it maintains an effective user id of the logged in user, reverting to the super-user only when binding addresses to privileged sockets. The **-r** option can be used to override this behaviour and force privileges to be permanently revoked; see **SECURITY CONSIDERATIONS** below for more details.

ftpd may have trouble handling connections from scoped IPv6 addresses, or IPv4 mapped addresses (IPv4 connection on `AF_INET6` socket). For the latter case, running two daemons, one for IPv4 and one for IPv6, will avoid the problem.

SECURITY CONSIDERATIONS

RFC 959 provides no restrictions on the **PORT** command, and this can lead to security problems, as **ftpd** can be fooled into connecting to any service on any host. With the "checkportcmd" feature of the `ftpd.conf`(5), **PORT** commands with different host addresses, or TCP ports lower than `IPPORT_RESERVED` will be rejected. This also prevents 'third-party proxy ftp' from working. Use of this option is *strongly* recommended, and enabled by default.

By default **ftpd** uses a port that is one less than the port it is listening on to communicate back to the client for the **EPRT**, **LPRT**, and **PORT** commands, unless overridden with **-P** *dataport*. As the default port for **ftpd** (21) is a privileged port below `IPPORT_RESERVED`, **ftpd** retains the ability to switch back to root privileges to bind these ports. In order to increase security by reducing the potential for a bug in **ftpd** providing a remote root compromise, **ftpd** will permanently drop root privileges if one of the following is true:

1. **ftpd** is running on a port greater than IPPORT_RESERVED and the user has logged in as a 'guest' or 'chroot' user.

2. **ftpd** was invoked with **-r**.

Don't create ˜ftp/tmp if you don't want anonymous users to upload files there. That directory is only necessary if you want to display the error messages of conversion commands to the user. Note that if uploads are disabled with the ftpd.conf(5) directive **upload**, then this directory cannot be abused by the user in this way, so it should be safe to create.

To avoid possible denial-of-service attacks, **SIZE** requests against files larger than 10240 bytes will be denied if the current transfer **TYPE** is 'A' (ASCII).

NAME

      `fusermount` — manage librefuse mount items

SYNOPSIS

      `fusermount` [`-chpVx`] [`-d` *name*] *refuseoptions*
      `fusermount -u` *mountpoint(s)*

DESCRIPTION

      The **fusermount** utility acts as a frontend to the `refuse`(3) library, allowing mounting and unmounting of refuse-based file systems.

      There are essentially two forms of the **fusermount** command. The first, and default option, is to mount a refuse-based file system. By using the **-u** argument, the file system can be unmounted.

      The arguments to **fusermount** are as follows:

      -c   Set a flag to enable kernel caching of files. At present this option has no effect.

      -d *name*
           Make the name argument appear as the file system name in `mount`(8) and `df`(1) output.

      -h   Print a usage message and exit.

      -p   Check the file permissions. At present this option has no effect.

      -V   Display the **fusermount** version on stdout, and then exit successfully.

      -x   Allow mortal (non-root) users to access the file system. At present, this option has no effect.

      The **fusermount** utility is included mainly for compatibility reasons, since some file systems demand its existence.

EXIT STATUS

      fusermount returns 0 for successful operation, or non-zero if one of the operations did not complete successfully.

EXAMPLES

      The command

           `fusermount -d ntfs-3g unused mount.ntfs-3g ntfs.img /mnt`

      will mount the file `ntfs.img` on the directory `/mnt`. Please note the `unused` argument in the command, which is necessary for compatibility with other implementations of the **fusermount** command.

SEE ALSO

      `df`(1), `puffs`(3), `refuse`(3), `mount`(8)

HISTORY

      The **fusermount** utility first appeared in NetBSD 5.0.

AUTHORS

      The **fusermount** utility was written by Alistair Crooks ⟨agc@NetBSD.org⟩.

FWCTL (8)   NetBSD   FWCTL (8)

NAME

fwctl — IEEE1394 control utility

SYNOPSIS

fwctl [**-prt**] [**-b** *pri_req*] [**-c** *node*] [**-d** *node*] [**-g** *gap_count*] [**-l** *file*]
    [**-M** *mode*] [**-m** *EUI64* | *hostname*] [**-o** *node*] [**-R** *filename*] [**-S** *filename*]
    [**-s** *node*] [**-u** *bus_num*]

DESCRIPTION

The **fwctl** utility is designed to provide a way for users to access and control the NetBSD IEEE1394 subsystem. Without options, **fwctl** will output a list of devices that are/were connected to the bus.

The following options are available:

-b *pri_req*	Set the PRIORITY_BUDGET register on all supported nodes.
-c *node*	Show the configuration ROM on the node.
-d *node*	Hex dump of the configuration ROM.
-g *gap_count*	Broadcast *gap_count* by phy_config packet.
-l *file*	Load hex dump file of the configuration ROM and parse it.
-M *mode*	Explicitly specify either *dv* or *mpeg* mode for the incoming stream. Only meaningful in case of and must precede the **-R** option. If not specified, the program will try to guess. If you get an error complaining about "format 0x20", try to force the *mpeg* mode.
-m *EUI64*	*hostname*	Set default fwmem target. Hostname will be converted to EUI64.
-o *node*	Send a link-on PHY packet to the node.
-p	Dump PHY registers.
-R *filename*	Receive DV or MPEG TS stream and dump it to a file. Use Ctrl-C to stop receiving. Some DV cameras seem not to send the stream if a bus manager exits. If you cannot get the stream, try the following commands:

```
sysctl hw.ieee1394if.try_bmr=0
fwctl -r
```

The resulting file contains raw DV data excluding isochronous header and CIP header. It can be handled by the `pkgsrc/multimedia/libdv` package. The resulting MPEG TS stream can be played and sent over a network using the VideoLAN tool (`pkgsrc/multimedia/vlc`). The stream can be piped directly to **vlc**, see **EXAMPLES**.

-r	Initiate bus reset.
-S *filename*	Send a DV file as isochronous stream.
-s *node*	Write to the RESET_START register on the node.
-t	Show the topology map.

       -u *bus_num*   Specify the IEEE1394 bus number to be operated on.

FILES
```
/dev/fw0.0
```

EXAMPLES
Each DV frame has a fixed size and it is easy to edit the frame order.
```
fwctl -R original.dv
```
Receive a DV stream with DV camera attached.
```
dd if=original.dv of=first.dv bs=120000 count=30
```
Get first 30 frames (NTSC).
```
dd if=original.dv of=second.dv bs=120000 skip=30 count=30
```
Get second 30 frames (NTSC).
```
cat second.dv first.dv | fwctl -S /dev/stdin
```
Swap first and second 30 frames and send them to DV recorder.

For PAL, replace "bs=120000" with "bs=144000".
```
fwcontrol -R file.m2t
```
Receive an MPEG TS stream from a camera producing MPEG transport stream. This has been tested with SONY HDR-FX1E camera that produces HD MPEG-2 stream at 25 Mbps bandwidth.

To send the stream from the camera over the network using TCP (which supprisingly works better with vlc), you can use
```
fwcontrol -R - | nc 192.168.10.11 9000
```
with `pkgsrc/net/netcat` and to receive the stream, use
```
nc -l -p 9000 | vlc -
```

To netcast via UDP, you need to use `pkgsrc/misc/buffer`, since vlc is not fast enough to read UDP packets from buffers and thus it experiences dropouts when run directly. The sending side can use
```
fwcontrol -R - | nc 192.168.10.11 9000
```
and to receive the stream, use
```
nc -l -u -p 9000 | buffer -s 10k -b 1000 -m 20m -p 5 | vlc -
```

For more information on how to work with **vlc** see its documentation.

SEE ALSO
mplayer(1), vlc(1), fwip(4), fwohci(4), ieee1394if(4), sbp(4)

HISTORY
The **fwctl** command first appeared in FreeBSD 5.0, as **fwcontrol**. It was added to NetBSD 4.0 under its present name.

AUTHORS
Hidetoshi Shimokawa ⟨simokawa@FreeBSD.org⟩
Petr Holub ⟨hopet@ics.muni.cz⟩ - MPEG TS mode.
KIYOHARA Takashi ⟨kiyohara@NetBSD.org⟩

BUGS

This utility is still under development and provided for debugging purposes. Especially MPEG TS reception support is very rudimental and supports only high-bandwidth MPEG-2 streams (fn field in CIP header equals 3).

NAME
    getencstat — get SCSI Environmental Services Device enclosure status

SYNOPSIS
    getencstat [**−v**] *device* [*device* . . .]

DESCRIPTION
    getencstat gets summary and detailed SCSI Environmental Services (or SAF-TE) device enclosure status. The overall status is printed out. If the overall status is considered okay, nothing else is printed out (unless the **−v** option is used).

    A SCSI Environmental Services device enclosure may be either in the state of being **OK,** or in one or more of the states of **INFORMATIONAL, NON-CRITICAL, CRITICAL,** or **UNRECOVERABLE** states. These overall states reflect a summary of the states of each object within such a device (such as power supplies or disk drives).

    With the **−v** option, the status of all objects within the device is printed, whether **OK** or not. Along with the status of each object is the object identifier.

    The user may then use setencstat(8) to try and clear overall device status, or may use setobjstat(8) to set specific object status.

FILES
    /dev/ses*N* SCSI Environmental Services Devices

SEE ALSO
    ses(4), sesd(8), setencstat(8), setobjstat(8)

NAME

getNAME — get NAME sections from manual source for whatis/apropos data base

SYNOPSIS

getNAME [-itvw] path [path ...]

DESCRIPTION

The getNAME utility looks inside manual page sources to find the name of the page. It can be used to create a table of contents, report the style of manual, or to create an introductory manual page. By default, getNAME returns data for use in an apropos(1) database. getNAME is designed to be called from manual grovelling tools, not to be used directly.

Historically, makewhatis(8) used to use getNAME to get manpage names, but that's no longer the case.

OPTIONS

The following options are available:

-i   Print information useful in creating an introduction manual. See intro(1), intro(2), etc. for examples.

-t   Print information useful for creating a table of contents.

-v   Complain about incorrectly formatted man pages.

-w   Print information whether the manpage uses traditional man ("OLD"), new mandoc ("NEW"), or some unknown ("UNKNOWN") macros.

SEE ALSO

man(1), catman(8), makewhatis(8)

HISTORY

The getNAME command first appeared in 2.0BSD.

BUGS

It would be nice if getNAME could deal with compressed and/or preformatted manual pages. Looks for .S[Hh] NAME for consistency checking, but that breaks man pages in other languages.

NAME

getty, uugetty — set terminal modes for system access

SYNOPSIS

getty [*type* [*tty*]]
uugetty [*type* [*tty*]]

DESCRIPTION

The **getty** program is called by init(8) to open and initialize the tty line, read a login name, and invoke login(1). The devices on which to run **getty** are normally determined by ttys(5).

The **getty** program can also recognize a Point to Point Protocol (PPP) negotiation, and, if the **pp** attribute in gettytab(5) is set, invoke the program given by that string, e.g., pppd(8), instead of login(1). This makes it possible to use a single serial port for either a "shell" account with command line interface, or a PPP network link.

The argument *tty* is the special device file in /dev to open for the terminal (for example, "ttyh0"). If there is no argument or the argument is ' – ', the tty line is assumed to be open as file descriptor 0.

The *type* argument can be used to make **getty** treat the terminal line specially. This argument is used as an index into the gettytab(5) database, to determine the characteristics of the line. If there is no argument, or there is no such table, the *default* table is used. If there is no /etc/gettytab a set of system defaults is used. If indicated by the table located, **getty** will clear the terminal screen, print a banner heading, and prompt for a login name. Usually either the banner or the login prompt will include the system hostname.

getty uses the ttyaction(3) facility with an action of "getty" and user "root" to execute site-specific commands when it starts.

Most of the default actions of **getty** can be circumvented, or modified, by a suitable gettytab(5) table.

The **getty** program can be set to timeout after some interval, which will cause dial up lines to hang up if the login name is not entered reasonably quickly.

The **uugetty** program is the same, except that it uses pidlock(3) to respect the locks in /var/spool/lock of processes that dial out on that tty.

FILES

/etc/gettytab
/etc/ttys
/var/spool/lock/LCK..ttyXX

DIAGNOSTICS

ttyxx: No such device or address.
ttyxx: No such file or address. A terminal which is turned on in the ttys(5) file cannot be opened, likely because the requisite lines are either not configured into the system, the associated device was not attached during boot-time system configuration, or the special file in /dev does not exist.

SEE ALSO

login(1), ioctl(2), pidlock(3), ttyaction(3), tty(4), gettytab(5), ttys(5), init(8), pppd(8)

HISTORY

A **getty** program appeared in Version 6 AT&T UNIX.

NAME
gpioctl — control GPIO devices

SYNOPSIS
gpioctl [**-q**] *device* attach *device offset mask*
gpioctl [**-q**] *device* detach *device*
gpioctl [**-q**] *device pin* [*0* | *1* | *2*]
gpioctl [**-q**] *device pin* [*on* | *off* | *toggle*]
gpioctl [**-q**] *device pin* set [*flags*] [*name*]
gpioctl [**-q**] *device pin* unset

DESCRIPTION
The **gpioctl** program allows manipulation of GPIO (General Purpose Input/Output) device pins. Such devices can be either part of the chipset or embedded CPU, or a separate chip. The usual way of using GPIO is to connect some simple devices such as LEDs and 1-wire thermal sensors to its pins.

Each GPIO device has an associated device file in the /dev directory. *device* can be specified with or without the /dev prefix. For example, /dev/gpio0 or gpio0.

GPIO pins can be either "read" or "written" with the values of logical 0 or 1. If only a *pin* number is specified on the command line, the pin state will be read from the GPIO controller and displayed. To write to a pin, a value must be specified after the *pin* number. Values can be either 0 or 1. A value of 2 has a special meaning: it "toggles" the pin, i.e. changes its state to the opposite. Instead of the numerical values, the word *on*, *off*, or *toggle* can be used.

Only pins that have been configured at securelevel 0, typically during system startup, are accessible once the securelevel has been raised. Pins can be given symbolic names for easier use. Besides using individual pins, device drivers that use GPIO pins can be attached to a gpio(4) device using the **gpioctl** command.

The following configuration *flags* are supported by the GPIO framework:

in	input direction
out	output direction
inout	bi-directional
od	open-drain output
pp	push-pull output
tri	tri-state (output disabled)
pu	internal pull-up enabled
pd	internal pull-down enabled
iin	invert input
iout	invert output
pulsate	pulsate output at a hardware-defined frequency and duty cycle

Note that not all the flags may be supported by the particular GPIO controller.

When executed with only the gpio(4) device name as argument, **gpioctl** reads information about the GPIO device and displays it. At securelevel 0 the number of physically available pins is displayed, at higher securelevels the number of configured (set) pins is displayed.

The options are as follows:

-q   Operate quietly i.e. nothing is printed to stdout.

FILES

/dev/gpio*u*   GPIO device unit *u* file.

EXAMPLES

Configure pin 20 to have push-pull output:

```
# gpioctl gpio0 20 set out pp
```

Write logical 1 to pin 20:

```
# gpioctl gpio0 20 1
```

Attach a onewire(4) bus on a gpioow(4) device on pin 4:

```
# gpioctl gpio0 attach gpioow 4 0x01
```

Detach the gpioow0 device:

```
# gpioctl gpio0 detach gpioow0
```

Configure pin 5 as output and name it error_led:

```
# gpioctl gpio0 5 set out error_led
```

Toggle the error_led:

```
# gpioctl gpio0 error_led 2
```

SEE ALSO

gpio(4)

HISTORY

The **gpioctl** command first appeared in OpenBSD 3.6 and NetBSD 4.0.

AUTHORS

The **gpioctl** program was written by Alexander Yurchenko ⟨grange@openbsd.org⟩. Device attachment was added by
Marc Balmer ⟨marc@msys.ch⟩.

NAME

    `gpt` — GUID partition table maintenance utility

SYNOPSIS

    `gpt [general_options] command [command_options] device ...`

DESCRIPTION

    The **gpt** utility provides the necessary functionality to manipulate GUID partition tables (GPTs), but see **BUGS** below for how and where functionality is missing. The basic usage model of the **gpt** tool follows that of the cvs(1) tool. The general options are described in the following paragraph. The remaining paragraphs describe the individual commands with their options. Here we conclude by mentioning that a *device* is either a special file corresponding to a disk-like device or a regular file. The command is applied to each *device* listed on the command line.

General Options

    The general options allow the user to change default settings or otherwise change the behaviour that is applicable to all commands. Not all commands use all default settings, so some general options may not have an effect on all commands.

    The **-p** *count* option allows the user to change the number of partitions the GPT can accommodate. This is used whenever a new GPT is created. By default, the **gpt** utility will create space for 128 partitions (or 32 sectors of 512 bytes).

    The **-r** option causes the **gpt** utility to open the device for reading only. Currently this option is primarily useful for the **show** command, but the intent is to use it to implement dry-run behaviour.

    The **-v** option controls the verbosity level. The level increases with every occurrence of this option. There is no formalized definition of the different levels yet.

Commands

    `gpt add [-b number][-i index][-s count][-t type] device ...`

        The **add** command allows the user to add a new partition to an existing table. By default, it will create a UFS partition covering the first available block of an unused disk space. The command-specific options can be used to control this behaviour.

        The **-b** *number* option allows the user to specify the starting (beginning) sector number of the partition. The minimum sector number is 1, but has to fall inside an unused region of disk space that is covered by the GPT.

        The **-i** *index* option allows the user to specify which (free) entry in the GPT table is to be used for the new partition. By default, the first free entry is selected.

        The **-s** *count* option allows the user to specify the size of the partition in sectors. The minimum size is 1.

        The **-t** *type* option allows the user to specify the partition type. The type is given as an UUID, but **gpt** accepts **efi**, **swap**, **ufs**, **hfs**, **linux**, and **windows** as aliases for the most commonly used partition types.

    `gpt create [-fp] device ...`

        The **create** command allows the user to create a new (empty) GPT. By default, one cannot create a GPT when the device contains a MBR, however this can be overridden with the **-f** option. If the **-f** option is specified, an existing MBR is destroyed and any partitions described by the MBR are lost.

The **-p** option tells **gpt** to create only the primary table and not the backup table. This option is only useful for debugging and should not be used otherwise.

gpt destroy [**-r**] *device* . . .

The **destroy** command allows the user to destroy an existing, possibly not empty GPT.

The **-r** option instructs **gpt** to destroy the table in a way that it can be recovered.

gpt label [**-a**]⟨**-f** *file* | **-l** *label*⟩ *device* . . .

gpt label [**-b** *number*] [**-i** *index*] [**-s** *count*] [**-t** *type*] ⟨**-f** *file* | **-l** *label*⟩ *device* . . .

The **label** command allows the user to label any partitions that match the selection. At least one of the following selection options must be specified.

The **-a** option specifies that all partitions should be labeled. It is mutually exclusive with all other selection options.

The **-b** *number* option selects the partition that starts at the given block number.

The **-i** *index* option selects the partition with the given partition number.

The **-s** *count* option selects all partitions that have the given size. This can cause multiple partitions to be removed.

The **-t** *type* option selects all partitions that have the given type. The type is given as an UUID or by the aliases that the **add** command accepts. This can cause multiple partitions to be removed.

The **-f** *file* or **-l** *label* options specify the new label to be assigned to the selected partitions. The **-f** *file* option is used to read the label from the specified file. Only the first line is read from the file and the trailing newline character is stripped. If the file name is the dash or minus sign (**-**), the label is read from the standard input. The **-l** *label* option is used to specify the label in the command line. The label is assumed to be encoded in UTF-8.

gpt migrate [**-fs**] *device* . . .

The **migrate** command allows the user to migrate an MBR-based disk partitioning into a GPT-based partitioning. By default, the MBR is not migrated when it contains partitions of an unknown type. This can be overridden with the **-f** option. Specifying the **-f** option will cause unknown partitions to be ignored and any data in it to be lost.

The **-s** option prevents migrating BSD disk labels into GPT partitions by creating the GPT equivalent of a slice.

gpt remove [**-a**] *device* . . .

gpt remove [**-b** *number*] [**-i** *index*] [**-s** *count*] [**-t** *type*] *device* . . .

The **remove** command allows the user to remove any and all partitions that match the selection. It uses the same selection options as the **label** command. See above for a description of these options. Partitions are removed by clearing the partition type. No other information is changed.

gpt show [**-lu**] *device* . . .

The **show** command displays the current partitioning on the listed devices and gives an overall view of the disk contents. With the **-l** option the GPT partition label will be displayed instead of the GPT partition type. The option has no effect on non-GPT partitions. With the **-u** option the GPT partition type is displayed as an UUID instead of in a user friendly form. The **-l** option takes precedence over the **-u** option.

SEE ALSO

fdisk(8), mount(8), newfs(8), swapon(8)

HISTORY

The **gpt** utility appeared in FreeBSD 5.0 for ia64.

BUGS

The development of the **gpt** utility is still work in progress. Many necessary features are missing or partially implemented. In practice this means that the manual page, supposed to describe these features, is farther removed from being complete or useful. As such, missing functionality is not even documented as missing. However, it is believed that the currently present functionality is reliable and stable enough that this tool can be used without bullet-proof footware if one thinks one does not make mistakes.

It is expected that the basic usage model does not change, but it is possible that future versions will not be compatible in the strictest sense of the word. For example, the **−p** *count* option may be changed to a command option rather than a generic option. There are only two commands that use it so there is a chance that the natural tendency for people is to use it as a command option. Also, options primarily intended for diagnostic or debug purposes may be removed in future versions.

Another possibility is that the current usage model is accompanied by other interfaces to make the tool usable as a back-end. This all depends on demand and thus feedback.

NAME

grfconfig — alter grf device screen mode definitions at run time

SYNOPSIS

grfconfig [**-r**] *device* [*file*]

DESCRIPTION

grfconfig is used to change or view the screen mode definition list contained in a grf device. You may alter the console screen definition as well as the definitions for the graphic screen. The console will automatically reinitialize itself to the new screen mode.

The following flags and arguments are interpreted by **grfconfig**:

-r Print out a raw listing of the mode definitions instead of the pretty list normally shown.

device The grf device to manipulate. This argument is required.

file The file which contains the mode definitions. If this argument is not specified, **grfconfig** will print out of a list of the modes currently loaded into the grf device.

MODE DEFINITION FILE

The mode definitions are taken from a file which has lines of the format:

num clk wid hi dep hbs hss hse ht vbs vss vse vt flags

num The mode number or 'c' for the console mode.

clk The pixel clock in Hz.

wid The screen mode's width.

hi The screen mode's height.

dep The bitdepth of the mode. Use 4 for a text console mode.

hbs hss hse ht
The horizontal timing parameters for the mode in pixel values. All the values are relative to the end of the horizontal blank (beginning of the displayed area).

vbs vss vse vt
The vertical timing parameters for the mode in line values. All the values are relative to the end of vertical blank (beginning of the displayed area).

flags By default every mode uses negative horizontal and vertical sync pulses, it is non-interlaced and does not use scandoubling.

default	Use the default flags: -hsync -vsync
doublescan	Doublescan mode
interlace	Interlace mode
+hsync	Positive horizontal sync pulses
-hsync	Negative horizontal sync pulses
+vsync	Positive vertical sync pulses
-vsync	Negative vertical sync pulses

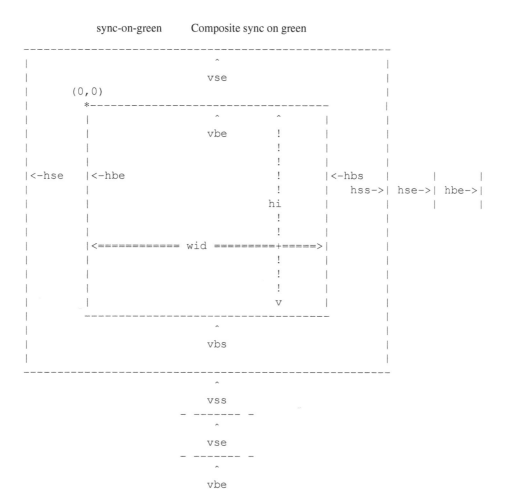

SEE ALSO

    console(4), grfcl(4), grfcv(4), grfcv3d(4), grfet(4), grfrh(4), grfrt(4), grful(4), iteconfig(8)

HISTORY

    The **grfconfig** command first appeared in NetBSD 1.0.

    The mode definition file changed two times.

    In NetBSD 1.0 all horizontal values were videoclock cycle values instead of pixel values:

```
num clk     wid hi  dep hbs hss hse hbe ht  vbs vss vse vbe  vt
 1   31000000 640 480  8   80  86  96 102 104 480 489 492 517  520
 2   31000000 640 480  8   80  86  96 102 104 240 244 246 258  260
 3   31000000 640 480  8   80  86  96 102 104 960 978 984 1034 1040
```

    In NetBSD 1.1 and NetBSD 1.2:

num clk   wid hi dep hbs hss hse hbe ht vbs vss vse vbe vt
1   31000000 640 480 8   640 688 768 816 832 480 489 492 517 520
2   31000000 640 480 8   640 688 768 816 832 240 244 246 258 260
3   31000000 640 480 8   640 688 768 816 832 960 978 984 1034 1040

the vertical values were used to select the interlace or doublescan mode. All vertical values were half the
width for the interlace mode and twice the width for the doublescan mode.

Beginning with NetBSD 1.3:

num clk   wid hi dep hbs hss hse ht vbs vss vse vt flags
1   31000000 640 480 8   640 688 768 832 480 489 492 520 default
2   31000000 640 480 8   640 688 768 832 480 489 492 520 interlace
3   31000000 640 480 8   640 688 768 832 480 489 492 520 doublescan
4   31000000 640 480 8   640 688 768 832 480 489 492 520 +hsync +vsync

hbe and vbe are computed in the grf drivers.

BUGS

 grfconfig can not set the modes for /dev/grf1, /dev/grf2 and /dev/grf4 and it will not work
 for /dev/grf0.

NAME
    group — manage group information on the system

SYNOPSIS
    group add [options] *group*
    group del [options] *group*
    group info [options] *group*
    group mod [options] *group*

DESCRIPTION
    The **group** utility acts as a frontend to the groupadd(8), groupmod(8), groupinfo(8), and groupdel(8) commands. The utilities by default are built with EXTENSIONS. This allows for further functionality.

    For a full explanation of the options available, please see the relevant manual page.

EXIT STATUS
    The **group** utility exits 0 on success, and >0 if an error occurs.

SEE ALSO
    group(5), groupadd(8), groupdel(8), groupinfo(8), groupmod(8)

HISTORY
    The **group** utility first appeared in NetBSD 1.5. It is based on the *addnerd* package by the same author.

AUTHORS
    The **group** utility was written by Alistair G. Crooks ⟨agc@NetBSD.org⟩.

NAME
groupadd — add a group to the system

SYNOPSIS
groupadd [**-ov**] [**-g** *gid*] [**-r** *lowgid..highgid*] *group*

DESCRIPTION
The **groupadd** utility adds a group to the system. See group(8) for more information about EXTENSIONS. The options are as follows:

-g *gid*
> Give the numeric group identifier to be used for the new group.

-o   Allow the new group to have a gid which is already in use for another group.

-r *lowgid..highgid*
> Set the low and high bounds of a gid range for new groups. A new group can only be created if there are gids which can be assigned inside the range. This option is included if built with EXTENSIONS.

-v   Enable verbose mode - explain the commands as they are executed. This option is included if built with EXTENSIONS.

EXIT STATUS
The **groupadd** utility exits 0 on success, and >0 if an error occurs.

SEE ALSO
group(5), group(8), user(8)

HISTORY
The **groupadd** utility first appeared in NetBSD 1.5. It is based on the *addnerd* package by the same author.

AUTHORS
The **groupadd** utility was written by Alistair G. Crooks ⟨agc@NetBSD.org⟩.

NAME
     groupdel — remove a group from the system

SYNOPSIS
     groupdel [**−v**] *group*

DESCRIPTION
     The **groupdel** utility removes a group from the system. See group(8) for more information about EXTENSIONS. The options are as follows:

     −v   Enable verbose mode - explain the commands as they are executed. This option is included if built with EXTENSIONS.

EXIT STATUS
     The **groupdel** utility exits 0 on success, and >0 if an error occurs.

SEE ALSO
     group(5), group(8), user(8)

HISTORY
     The **groupdel** utility first appeared in NetBSD 1.5. It is based on the *addnerd* package by the same author.

AUTHORS
     The **groupdel** utility was written by Alistair G. Crooks ⟨agc@NetBSD.org⟩.

NAME

groupinfo — displays group information

SYNOPSIS

groupinfo [**-ev**] *group*

DESCRIPTION

The **groupinfo** utility retrieves the group information from the system. The **groupinfo** utility is only available if built with EXTENSIONS. See group(8) for more information.

The following command line options are recognised:

-e   Return 0 if the group exists, and non-zero if the group does not exist, on the system. No information is displayed. This form of the command is useful for scripts which need to check whether a particular group name or gid is already in use on the system.

-v   Perform any actions in a verbose manner.

The *group* argument may either be a group's name, or a gid.

EXIT STATUS

The **groupinfo** utility exits 0 on success, and >0 if an error occurs.

FILES

/etc/usermgmt.conf

SEE ALSO

passwd(5), group(8)

HISTORY

The **groupinfo** utility first appeared in NetBSD 1.5. It is based on the *addnerd* package by the same author.

AUTHORS

The **groupinfo** utility was written by Alistair G. Crooks ⟨agc@NetBSD.org⟩.

NAME
groupmod — modify an existing group on the system

SYNOPSIS
groupmod [**-ov**] [**-g** *gid*] [**-n** *newname*] *group*

DESCRIPTION
The **groupmod** utility modifies an existing group on the system. See group(8) for more information about EXTENSIONS. The options are as follows:

-g *gid*
> Give the numeric group identifier to be used for the new group.

-n *new-group-name*
> Give the new name which the group shall have.

-o   Allow the new group to have a gid which is already in use for another group.

-v   Enable verbose mode - explain the commands as they are executed. This option is included if built with EXTENSIONS.

EXIT STATUS
The **groupmod** utility exits 0 on success, and >0 if an error occurs.

SEE ALSO
group(5), group(8), user(8)

HISTORY
The **groupmod** utility first appeared in NetBSD 1.5. It is based on the *addnerd* package by the same author.

AUTHORS
The **groupmod** utility was written by Alistair G. Crooks ⟨agc@NetBSD.org⟩.

NAME
gspa — assembler for the GSP chip

SYNOPSIS
gspa [**-c** *c_array_name*] [**-l** *list_file*] [**-o** *hex_file*] [infile]

DESCRIPTION
gspa is an assembler for the TMS34010 and TMS34020 graphics processor chips.

The supported options are:

-c *c_array_name*

    Create a pre-initialized C-structure *c_array_name* with the hex code of the assembler output.

-l *list_file*

    Create commented (with the input file) hex code of the assembler output in *list_file*.

-o *hex_file*

    Create the output in *hex_file*. If **-c** is used, C code will be written to *hex_file*, otherwise uncommented hex code of the assembler output will be written.

If no **-o** option is given, output will be written to stdout.

If no *infile* is given, input will be read from stdin.

HISTORY
gspa appeared in NetBSD 1.1.

AUTHORS
gspa was written by Paul Mackerras. The **-c** mode was added by Ignatios Souvatzis ⟨is@NetBSD.org⟩. This man page was written by Thomas Klausner ⟨wiz@NetBSD.org⟩.

NAME
   hdaudioctl — program to manipulate hdaudio(4) devices.

SYNOPSIS
   hdaudioctl [*-f device*] *command* [*arguments*]

DESCRIPTION
   The **hdaudioctl** command can be used to inspect and reconfigure High Definition Audio devices and
   their child codecs.

   The mandatory *command* argument specifies the action to take. Valid commands are:

   list   For each child codec of the chosen hdaudio(4) device, display the nid, vendor,
                              product, subsystem and device IDs.

   get *codecid nid*   Retrieve and display the current codec configuration as a proplib(3) XML plist.

   set *codecid nid* [*plist*]
                              Detach the specified hdafg(4) codec and then re-attach with its widgets explic-
                              itly configured according to the specified plist. If no plist is given, the in-built
                              widget parsing rules based on the High Definition Audio specification will be
                              used.

   graph *codecid nid*   Output a DOT file suitable processing by graphviz. The resulting image will
                              graphically show the structure and interconnections of the widgets that form the
                              chosen hdafg(4) codec.

FILES
   /dev/hdaudioX control devices

SEE ALSO
   audio(4), hdaudio(4), pkgsrc/graphics/graphviz

HISTORY
   The **hdaudioctl** command first appeared in NetBSD 5.1.

AUTHORS
   hdaudioctl is based on two separate programs written by Jared McNeill ⟨jmcneill@NetBSD.org⟩ under
   contract by
   Precedence Technologies Ltd ⟨http://www.precedence.co.uk/⟩. Integration into one program and writing this
   manual page was done by
   Stephen Borrill ⟨sborrill@NetBSD.org⟩.

CAVEATS
   When a plist is loaded and the hdafg(4) codec reattaches, all mixer controls will be returned to their default
   values.

NAME

hlfsd – home-link file system daemon

SYNOPSIS

hlfsd [**–fhnpvC**] [**–a** *alt_dir*] [**–c** *cache-interval*] [**–g** *group*] [**–i** *reload-interval*] [**–l** *logfile*] [**–o**
mount-options] [**–x** *log-options*] [**–D** *debug-options*] [**–P** *password-file*] [*linkname* [*subdir*]]

DESCRIPTION

Hlfsd is a daemon which implements a filesystem containing a symbolic link to subdirectory within a
user's home directory, depending on the user which accessed that link. It was primarily designed to redirect
incoming mail to users' home directories, so that it can read from anywhere.

Hlfsd operates by mounting itself as an NFS server for the directory containing *linkname*, which defaults to
/hlfs/home. Lookups within that directory are handled by **hlfsd**, which uses the password map to determine how to resolve the lookup. The directory will be created if it doesn't already exist. The symbolic link
will be to the accessing user's home directory, with *subdir* appended to it. If not specified, *subdir* defaults
to **.hlfsdir**. This directory will also be created if it does not already exist.

A SIGTERM sent to **hlfsd** will cause it to shutdown. A SIGHUP will flush the internal caches, and reload
the password map. It will also close and reopen the log file, to enable the original log file to be removed or
rotated. A SIGUSR1 will cause it to dump its internal table of user IDs and home directories to the file
/usr/tmp/hlfsd.dump.XXXXXX.

OPTIONS

–a *alt_dir*

Alternate directory. The name of the directory to which the symbolic link returned by **hlfsd** will
point, if it cannot access the home directory of the user. This defaults to **/var/hlfs**. This directory
will be created if it doesn't exist. It is expected that either users will read these files, or the system
administrators will run a script to resend this "lost mail" to its owner.

–c *cache-interval*

Caching interval. **Hlfsd** will cache the validity of home directories for this interval, in seconds.
Entries which have been verified within the last *cache-interval* seconds will not be verified again,
since the operation could be expensive, and the entries are most likely still valid. After the interval
has expired, **hlfsd** will re-verify the validity of the user's home directory, and reset the cache time-
counter. The default value for *cache-interval* is 300 seconds (5 minutes).

–f

Force fast startup. This option tells **hlfsd** to skip startup-time consistency checks such as existence
of mount directory, alternate spool directory, symlink to be hidden under the mount directory, their
permissions and validity.

–g *group*

Set the special group HLFS_GID to *group*. Programs such as **from** or **comsat**, which access the
mailboxes of other users) must be setgid HLFS_GID to work properly. The default group is
"hlfs". If no group is provided, and there is no group "hlfs", this feature is disabled.

–h

Help. Print a brief help message, and exit.

–i *reload-interval*

Map-reloading interval. Each *reload-interval* seconds, **hlfsd** will reload the password map. **Hlfsd**
needs the password map for the UIDs and home directory pathnames. **Hlfsd** schedules a
SIGALRM to reload the password maps. A SIGHUP sent to **hlfsd** will force it to reload the maps
immediately. The default value for *reload-interval* is 900 seconds (15 minutes.)

–l *logfile*

Specify a log file to which **hlfsd** will record events. If *logfile* is the string **syslog** then the log messages will be sent to the system log daemon by *syslog*(3), using the LOG_DAEMON facility. This
is also the default.

–n

No verify. **Hlfsd** will not verify the validity of the symbolic link it will be returning, or that the
user's home directory contains sufficient disk-space for spooling. This can speed up **hlfsd** at the
cost of possibly returning symbolic links to home directories which are not currently accessible or

are full. By default, **hlfsd** validates the symbolic-link in the background. The **−n** option overrides the meaning of the **−c** option, since no caching is necessary.

−o *mount-options*

> Mount options. Mount options which **hlfsd** will use to mount itself on top of *dirname*. By default, *mount-options* is set to "ro". If the system supports symbolic-link caching, default options are set to "ro,nocache".

−p   Print PID. Outputs the process-id of **hlfsd** to standard output where it can be saved into a file.

−v   Version. Displays version information to standard error.

−x *log-options*

> Specify run-time logging options. The options are a comma separated list chosen from: fatal, error, user, warn, info, map, stats, all.

−C   Force **hlfsd** to run on systems that cannot turn off the NFS attribute-cache. Use of this option on those systems is discouraged, as it may result in loss or mis-delivery of mail. The option is ignored on systems that can turn off the attribute-cache.

−D *log-options*

> Select from a variety of debugging options. Prefixing an option with the string **no** reverses the effect of that option. Options are cumulative. The most useful option is **all**. Since this option is only used for debugging other options are not documented here. A fuller description is available in the program source. A SIGUSR1 sent to **hlfsd** will cause it to dump its internal password map to the file **/usr/tmp/hlfsd.dump.XXXXXX**.

−P *password-file*

> Read the user-name, user-id, and home directory information from the file *password-file*. Normally, **hlfsd** will use *getpwent*(3) to read the password database. This option allows you to override the default database, and is useful if you want to map users' mail files to a directory other than their home directory. Only the username, uid, and home-directory fields of the file *password-file* are read and checked. All other fields are ignored. The file *password-file* must otherwise be compliant with Unix System 7 colon-delimited format *passwd*(5).

FILES

/hlfs   directory under which **hlfsd** mounts itself and manages the symbolic link **home**.

.hlfsdir

> default sub-directory in the user's home directory, to which the **home** symbolic link returned by **hlfsd** points.

/var/hlfs

> directory to which **home** symbolic link returned by **hlfsd** points if it is unable to verify the that user's home directory is accessible.

SEE ALSO

mail(1), **getgrent**(3), **getpwent**(3), **passwd**(5), **amd**(8), **cron(8)**, **mount**(8), **sendmail**(8), **umount**(8).

HLFSD: Delivering Email to Your $HOME, in *Proc. LISA-VII, The 7th Usenix System Administration Conference*, November 1993.

"am-utils" **info**(1) entry.

Linux NFS and Automounter Administration by Erez Zadok, ISBN 0-7821-2739-8, (Sybex, 2001).

http://www.am-utils.org

AUTHORS

Erez Zadok <ezk@cs.sunysb.edu>, Computer Science Department, Stony Brook University, Stony Brook, New York, USA. and Alexander Dupuy <dupuy@smarts.com>, System Management ARTS, White Plains, New York, USA.

Other authors and contributors to am-utils are listed in the **AUTHORS** file distributed with am-utils.

NAME

hostapd — authenticator for IEEE 802.11 networks

SYNOPSIS

hostapd [**-BdhKtv**] *config-file* ...

DESCRIPTION

The **hostapd** utility is an authenticator for IEEE 802.11 networks. It provides full support for WPA/IEEE 802.11i and can also act as an IEEE 802.1X Authenticator with a suitable backend Authentication Server (typically FreeRADIUS). The **hostapd** utility implements the authentication protocols that piggyback on top of the normal IEEE 802.11 protocol mechanisms. To use **hostapd** as an authenticator, the underlying device must support some basic functionality such as the ability to set security information in the 802.11 management frames. Beware that not all devices have this support.

The **hostapd** utility is designed to be a "daemon" program that runs in the background and acts as the backend component controlling the wireless connection. It supports separate frontend programs such as the text-based frontend, hostapd_cli(8).

The following arguments must be specified on the command line:

config-file

Use the settings in the specified configuration file; the name of the specified wireless interface is contained in this file. See hostapd.conf(5) for a description of the configuration file syntax.

Changes to the configuration file can be reloaded by sending a SIGHUP to the **hostapd** processor or with the hostapd_cli(8) utility, using "hostapd_cli reconfigure".

OPTIONS

The options are as follows:

-d   Enable debugging messages. If this option is supplied twice, more verbose messages are displayed.

-h   Show help text.

-t   Include timestamps in debugging output.

-v   Display version information on the terminal and exit.

-B   Detach from the controlling terminal and run as a daemon process in the background.

-K   Include key information in debugging output.

SEE ALSO

ath(4), ipw(4), iwi(4), ral(4), wi(4), hostapd.conf(5), hostapd_cli(8), ifconfig(8)

HISTORY

The **hostapd** utility first appeared in NetBSD 4.0.

AUTHORS

The **hostapd** utility was written by Jouni Malinen ⟨jkmaline@cc.hut.fi⟩. This manual page is derived from the README file included in the **hostapd** distribution.

NAME

hostapd_cli — text-based frontend program for interacting with hostapd(8)

SYNOPSIS

hostapd_cli [*commands*]

DESCRIPTION

The **hostapd_cli** utility is a text-based frontend program for interacting with hostapd(8). It is used to query the current status.

The **hostapd_cli** utility can show the current authentication status, dot11 and dot1x MIBs, etc.

The **hostapd_cli** utility supports two modes: interactive and command line. Both modes share the same command set.

Interactive mode is started when **hostapd_cli** is executed without any parameters on the command line. Commands are then entered from the controlling terminal in response to the **hostapd_cli** prompt. In command line mode, the same commands are entered as command line arguments.

COMMANDS

The following commands may be supplied on the command line or at a prompt when operating interactively.

mib   Report MIB variables (dot1x, dot11) for the current interface.

sta *addr*
          Report the MIB variables for the associated station with MAC address *addr*.

all_sta
          Report the MIB variables for all associated stations.

help   Show usage help.

interface [*ifname*]
          Show available interfaces and/or set the current interface when multiple are available.

level *debug_level*
          Change the debugging level in hostapd(8). Larger numbers generate more messages.

license
          Display the full license for **hostapd_cli**.

quit   Exit **hostapd_cli**.

SEE ALSO

hostapd.conf(5), hostapd(8)

HISTORY

The **hostapd_cli** utility first appeared in NetBSD 4.0.

AUTHORS

The **hostapd_cli** utility was written by Jouni Malinen ⟨jkmaline@cc.hut.fi⟩. This manual page is derived from the README file included in the **hostapd** distribution.

NAME
hpcboot — load and boot kernel from Windows CE

SYNOPSIS
hpcboot.exe

DESCRIPTION
hpcboot is a program that runs on Windows CE. It loads and executes the specified NetBSD kernel. **hpcboot** supports hpcarm, hpcmips, and hpcsh ports.

Click on the "Boot" button to start the boot process with selected options. Click on the "Cancel" button to exit **hpcboot**.

"Kernel" Tab
On this tab you can select the kernel to boot and options to pass to the kernel.

Directory
> In this combobox you specify the "current" directory. The kernel and miniroot image pathnames are taken to be relative to this directory.
>
> **hpcboot** can load kernel and miniroot from FAT and UFS filesystems, and via HTTP.

Kernel
> In this text field you specify the name of the kernel to load. Kernels compressed with gzip(1) are supported.

Model
> Select your H/PC model in this combobox.

Root File System
> This group of controls lets you specify the desired root file system type. You can select wd(4), sd(4), md(4), and NFS root.
>
> If you select md(4) memory disk root file system, you should specify the path name of the file system image in the text field below. Miniroot images compressed with gzip(1) are supported.

Kernel Boot Flags
> This group of controls is used to pass boot flags to the kernel.

"Option" Tab
On this tab you can specify miscellaneous options that mostly control the **hpcboot** program itself.

Auto Boot
> If this option is selected **hpcboot** will automatically boot NetBSD after the specified timeout.

Reverse Video
> Tells kernel if it should use the framebuffer in reverse video mode.

Pause Before Boot
> If selected, a warning dialog will be presented *before* anything is done, right after the "Boot" button is pressed.

Load Debug Info
> This option currently does nothing.

Safety Message
> If selected, a warning dialog will be presented *after* the kernel has been loaded and prepared to be started. This will be your last chance to cancel the boot.

    Extra Kernel Options

        In this text field you can specify additional options to pass to the kernel.

"Console" Tab

    This tab gets its name from the big text area that **hpcboot** uses as the "console" to report its progress.

    Save To File

        If checked, the progress log will be sent to the specified file instead.

    "Checkboxes Anonymous"

        The row of 8 checkboxes controls debugging options for **hpcboot** itself. They control the bits of an internal variable, the leftmost checkbox being the 7th bit.

    "Buttons Anonymous"

        The buttons "a" to "d" control 4 "hooks" a developer might want to use during **hpcboot** development.

SEE ALSO

    `kloader`(4), `boot`(8)

HISTORY

    The **hpcboot** utility first appeared in NetBSD 1.6.

BUGS

    hpcboot reads the entire kernel image at once, and requires enough free area on the main memory.

NAME
hprop — propagate the KDC database

SYNOPSIS
hprop [**-m** *file* | **--master-key**=file] [**-d** *file* | **--database**=file]
    [**--source**=*heimdal* | *mit-dump* | *krb4-dump* | *kaserver*] [**-r** *string* |
    --v4-realm=*string*] [**-c** *cell* | **--cell**=*cell*] [**-S** | **--kaspecials**] [**-k**
    keytab | **--keytab**=*keytab*] [**-R** *string* | **--v5-realm**=*string*]
    [**-D** | **--decrypt**] [**-E** | **--encrypt**] [**-n** | **--stdout**] [**-v** | **--verbose**]
    [**--version**] [**-h** | **--help**] [*host*[*:port*]] . . .

DESCRIPTION
hprop takes a principal database in a specified format and converts it into a stream of Heimdal database records. This stream can either be written to standard out, or (more commonly) be propagated to a hpropd(8) server running on a different machine.

If propagating, it connects to all *hosts* specified on the command by opening a TCP connection to port 754 (service hprop) and sends the database in encrypted form.

Supported options:

-m *file*, **--master-key**=file
    Where to find the master key to encrypt or decrypt keys with.

-d *file*, **--database**=file
    The database to be propagated.

--source=*heimdal* | *mit-dump* | *krb4-dump* | *kaserver*
    Specifies the type of the source database. Alternatives include:

        heimdal   a Heimdal database
        mit-dump   a MIT Kerberos 5 dump file
        krb4-dump   a Kerberos 4 dump file
        kaserver   an AFS kaserver database

-k *keytab*, **--keytab**=*keytab*
    The keytab to use for fetching the key to be used for authenticating to the propagation daemon(s). The key kadmin/hprop is used from this keytab. The default is to fetch the key from the KDC database.

-R *string*, **--v5-realm**=*string*
    Local realm override.

-D, **--decrypt**
    The encryption keys in the database can either be in clear, or encrypted with a master key. This option transmits the database with unencrypted keys.

-E, **--encrypt**
    This option transmits the database with encrypted keys.

-n, **--stdout**
    Dump the database on stdout, in a format that can be fed to hpropd.

The following options are only valid if **hprop** is compiled with support for Kerberos 4 (kaserver).

-r *string*, **--v4-realm**=*string*
    v4 realm to use.

-c *cell*, --**cell**=*cell*
>   The AFS cell name, used if reading a kaserver database.

-**S**, --**kaspecials**
>   Also dump the principals marked as special in the kaserver database.

-**K**, --**ka-db**
>   Deprecated, identical to '--source=kaserver'.

EXAMPLES
>   The following will propagate a database to another machine (which should run hpropd(8)):

```
$ hprop slave-1 slave-2
```

Convert a Kerberos 4 dump-file for use with a Heimdal KDC:

```
$ hprop -n --source=krb4-dump -d /var/kerberos/principal.dump \
    --master-key=/.k | hpropd -n
```

SEE ALSO
>   hpropd(8)

NAME
    hpropd — receive a propagated database

SYNOPSIS
    hpropd [**-d** *file* | **--database=***file*] [**-n** | **--stdin**] [**--print**] [**-i** | **--no-inetd**]
        [**-k** *keytab* | **--keytab=***keytab*] [**-4** | **--v4dump**]

DESCRIPTION
    hpropd receives a database sent by **hprop**. and writes it as a local database.

    By default, **hpropd** expects to be started from **inetd** if stdin is a socket and expects to receive the dumped database over stdin otherwise. If the database is sent over the network, it is authenticated and encrypted. Only connections authenticated with the principal **kadmin/hprop** are accepted.

    Options supported:

    -d *file*, **--database=***file*
        database

    -n, **--stdin**
        read from stdin

    --print
        print dump to stdout

    -i, **--no-inetd**
        not started from inetd

    -k *keytab*, **--keytab=***keytab*
        keytab to use for authentication

    -4, **--v4dump**
        create v4 type DB

SEE ALSO
    hprop(8)

NAME

httpd — hyper text transfer protocol version 1.1 daemon

SYNOPSIS

httpd [**-befHnrsuVX**] [**-C** *suffix cgihandler*] [**-c** *cgibin*] [**-I** *port*]
      [**-i** *address*] [**-M** *suffix type encoding encoding11*] [**-p** *pubdir*]
      [**-S** *server_software*] [**-t** *chrootdir*] [**-v** *virtualroot*] [**-x** *index*]
      [**-Z** *cert privkey*] *slashdir* [*myname*]

DESCRIPTION

The **httpd** program reads a *HTTP* request from the standard input, and sends a reply to the standard output. Besides ˜user translation and virtual hosting support (see below), all file requests are from *slashdir* directory. The server uses *myname* as its name, which defaults to the local hostname, obtained from gethostname(3) (but see the **-v** option for virtual hosting.) **httpd** is designed to be small, simple and relatively featureless, hopefully increasing its security.

OPTIONS

The following options are available:

-b
    This option enables daemon mode, where **httpd** detaches from the current terminal, running in the background and servicing HTTP requests.

-C *suffix cgihandler*
    This option adds a new CGI handler program for a particular file type. The *suffix* should be any normal file suffix, and the *cgihandler* should be a full path to an interpreter. This option is the only way to enable CGI programs that exist outside of the cgibin directory to be executed. Multiple **-C** options may be passed.

-c *cgibin*
    This option enables the CGI/1.1 interface. The *cgibin* directory is expected to contain the CGI programs to be used. **httpd** looks for URL's in the form of */cgi-bin/<scriptname>* where ⟨scriptname⟩ is a valid CGI program in the *cgibin* directory. In other words, all CGI URL's must begin with */cgi-bin/*. Note that the CGI/1.1 interface is not available with ˜user translation.

-e
    This option causes **httpd** to not clear the environment when used with either the **-t** or **-U** options.

-f
    This option stops the **-b** flag from **httpd** detaching from the tty and going into the background.

-H
    This option causes directory index mode to hide files and directories that start with a period, except for ... Also see **-X**.

-I *port*
    This option is only valid with the **-b** option. It causes *port* to use used as the port to bind daemon mode. The default is the "http" port.

-i *address*
    This option is only valid with the **-b** option. It causes *address* to use used as the address to bind daemon mode. If otherwise unspecified, the address used to bind is derived from the *myname*, which defaults to the name returned by gethostname(3). Only the last **-i** option is used.

-M *suffix type encoding encoding11*
    This option adds a new entry to the table that converts file suffixes to content type and encoding. This option takes four additional arguments containing the file prefix, its "Content-Type",

"Content-Encoding", and "Content-Encoding" for HTTP/1.1 connections, respectively. If any of these are a single dash ("-"), the empty string is used instead. Multiple **−M** options may be passed.

−n This option stops **httpd** from doing IP address to name resolution of hosts for setting the REMOTE_HOST variable before running a CGI program. This option has no effect without the **−c** option.

−p *pubdir*
This option changes the default user directory for /˜*user*/ translations from "public_html" to *pubdir*.

−r This option forces pages besides the "index.html" (see the **−X** option) page to require that the Referrer: header be present and refer to this web server, otherwise a redirect to the "index.html" page will be returned instead.

−S *server_software*
This option sets the internal server version to *server_software*.

−s This option forces logging to be set to stderr always.

−t *chrootdir*
When this option is used, **httpd** will chroot to the specified directory before answering requests. Every other path should be specified relative to the new root, if this option is used. Note that the current environment is normally replaced with an empty environment with this option, unless the **−e** option is also used.

−U *username*
This option causes **httpd** to switch to the user and the groups of *username* after initialization. This option, like **−t** above, causes **httpd** to clear the environment unless the **−e** option is given.

−u This option enables the transformation of Uniform Resource Locators of the form /˜*user*/ into the directory ˜user/public_html (but see the **−p** option above).

−V This option sets the default virtual host directory to *slashdir*. If no directory exists in *virtualroot* for the request, then *slashdir* will be used. The default behaviour is to return 404 (Not Found.)

−v *virtualroot*
This option enables virtual hosting support. Directories in *virtualroot* will be searched for a matching virtual host name, when parsing the HTML request. If a matching name is found, it will be used as both the server's real name, [*myname*], and as the *slashdir*. See the **EXAMPLES** section for an example of using this option.

−X This option enables directory indexing. A directory index will be generated only when the default file (i.e. index.html normally) is not present.

−x *index* This option changes the default file read for directories from "index.html" to *index*.

−Z *certificate_path privatekey_path*
This option sets the path to the server certificate file and the private key file in pem format. It also causes **httpd** to start SSL mode.

Note that in **httpd** versions 20031005 and prior that supported the **−C** and **−M** options, they took a single space-separated argument that was parsed. since version 20040828, they take multiple options (2 in the case of **−C** and 4 in the case of **−M**.)

INETD CONFIGURATION

As **httpd** uses inetd(8) by default to process incoming TCP connections for HTTP requests (but see the **−b** option), **httpd** has little internal networking knowledge. (Indeed, you can run it on the command line with little change of functionality.) A typical inetd.conf(5) entry would be:

```
http stream tcp  nowait:600 _httpd /usr/libexec/httpd httpd /var/www
http stream tcp6 nowait:600 _httpd /usr/libexec/httpd httpd /var/www
```

This would serve web pages from /var/www on both IPv4 and IPv6 ports. The *:600* changes the requests per minute to 600, up from the inetd(8) default of 40.

Using the NetBSD inetd(8), you can provide multiple IP-address based HTTP servers by having multiple listening ports with different configurations.

NOTES

This server supports the *HTTP/0.9*, *HTTP/1.0*, and *HTTP/1.1* standards. Support for these protocols is very minimal and many optional features are not supported.

httpd can be compiled without CGI support (NO_CGIBIN_SUPPORT), user transformations (NO_USER_SUPPORT), directory index support (NO_DIRINDEX_SUPPORT), daemon mode support (NO_DAEMON_MODE), and dynamic MIME content (NO_DYNAMIC_CONTENT), and SSL support (NO_SSL_SUPPORT) by defining the listed macros when building **httpd**.

HTTP BASIC AUTHORISATION

httpd has support for HTTP Basic Authorisation. If a file named .htpasswd exists in the directory of the current request, **httpd** will restrict access to documents in that directory using the RFC 2617 HTTP "Basic" authentication scheme.

Note: This does not recursively protect any sub-directories.

The .htpasswd file contains lines delimited with a colon containing usernames and passwords hashed with crypt(3), for example:

```
heather:$1$pZWI4tH/$DzDP163i6VvVRv2lJNV7k1
jeremy:A.xewbx2DpQ8I
```

On NetBSD, the pwhash(1) utility may be used to generate hashed passwords.

While **httpd** distributed with NetBSD has support for HTTP Basic Authorisation enabled by default, in the portable distribution it is excluded. Compile **httpd** with "-DDO_HTPASSWD" on the compiler command line to enable this support. It may require linking with the crypt library, using "-lcrypt".

SSL SUPPORT

httpd has support for SSLv2, SSLv3, and TLSv1 protocols that is included by default. It requires linking with the crypto and ssl library, using "-lcrypto -lssl". To disable SSL SUPPORT compile **httpd** with "-DNO_SSL_SUPPORT" on the compiler command line.

FILES

httpd looks for a couple of special files in directories that allow certain features to be provided on a per-directory basis. In addition to the .htpasswd used by HTTP basic authorisation, if a .bzdirect file is found (contents are irrelevant) **httpd** will allow direct access even with the **−r** option. If a .bzredirect symbolic link is found, **httpd** will perform a smart redirect to the target of this symlink. The target is assumed to live on the same server. If a .bzabsredirect symbolic link is found, **httpd** will redirect to the absolute url pointed to by this symlink. This is useful to redirect to different servers.

EXAMPLES

To configure set of virtual hosts, one would use an `inetd.conf`(5) entry like:

```
http stream tcp  nowait:600 _httpd /usr/libexec/httpd httpd -v /var/vroot /var/www
```

and inside `/var/vroot` create a directory (or a symlink to a directory) with the same name as the virtual host, for each virtual host. Lookups for these names are done in a case-insensitive manner.

To use **httpd** with PHP, one must use the **-C** option to specify a CGI handler for a particular file type. Typically this, this will be like:

```
httpd -C .php /usr/pkg/bin/php /var/www
```

SEE ALSO

`inetd.conf`(5), `inetd`(8)

HISTORY

The **httpd** program is actually called "bozohttpd". It was first written in perl, based on another perl http server called "tinyhttpd". It was then rewritten from scratch in perl, and then once again in C. From "bozohttpd" version 20060517, it has been integrated into NetBSD. The focus has always been simplicity and security, with minimal features and regular code audits. This manual documents **httpd** version 20100512.

AUTHORS

httpd was written by Matthew R. Green ⟨mrg@eterna.com.au⟩.

The large list of contributors includes:

– Arnaud Lacombe ⟨alc@netbsd.org⟩ provided some clean up for memory leaks

– Christoph Badura ⟨bad@bsd.de⟩ provided Range: header support

– Julian Coleman ⟨jdc@coris.org.uk⟩ provided an IPv6 bugfix

– Chuck Cranor ⟨chuck@research.att.com⟩ provided cgi-bin support fixes, and more

– DEGROOTE Arnaud ⟨degroote@netbsd.org⟩ provided a fix for daemon mode

– Andrew Doran ⟨ad@netbsd.org⟩ provided directory indexing support

– Per Ekman ⟨pek@pdc.kth.se⟩ provided a fix for a minor (non-security) buffer overflow condition

– Alistair G. Crooks ⟨agc@netbsd.org⟩ cleaned up many internal interfaces, made bozohttpd linkable as a library and provided the lua binding.

– Jun-ichiro itojun Hagino, KAME ⟨itojun@iijlab.net⟩ provided initial IPv6 support

– Martin Husemann ⟨martin@netbsd.org⟩ provided .bzabsredirect support

– Arto Huusko ⟨arto.huusko@pp2.inet.fi⟩ provided fixes cgi-bin

– Roland Illig ⟨roland.illig@gmx.de⟩ provided some off-by-one fixes

– Zak Johnson ⟨zakj@nox.cx⟩ provided cgi-bin enhancements

– Nicolas Jombart ⟨ecu@ipv42.net⟩ provided fixes for HTTP basic authorisation support

– Thomas Klausner ⟨wiz@danbala.ifoer.tuwien.ac.at⟩ provided many fixes and enhancements for the man page

- Johnny Lam ⟨jlam@netbsd.org⟩ provided man page fixes

- Luke Mewburn ⟨lukem@netbsd.org⟩ provided many various fixes, including cgi-bin fixes and enhancements, HTTP basic authorisation support and much code clean up

- Jeremy C. Reed ⟨reed@netbsd.org⟩ provided several clean up fixes, and man page updates

- Scott Reynolds ⟨scottr@netbsd.org⟩ provided various fixes

- Tyler Retzlaff ⟨rtr@eterna.com.au⟩ provided SSL support, cgi-bin fixes and much other random other stuff

- Steve Rumble ⟨rumble@ephemeral.org⟩ provided the **-v** option.

- Joerg Sonnenberger ⟨joerg@netbsd.org⟩ implemented If-Modified-Since support

- ISIHARA Takanori ⟨ishit@oak.dti.ne.jp⟩ provided a man page fix

- Holger Weiss ⟨holger@CIS.FU-Berlin.DE⟩ provided http authorisation fixes

- ⟨xs@kittenz.org⟩ provided chroot and change-to-user support, and other various fixes

- Coyote Point provided various CGI fixes

There are probably others I have forgotten (let me know if you care)

Please send all updates to **httpd** to ⟨mrg@eterna.com.au⟩ for inclusion in future releaases.

BUGS

httpd does not handled HTTP/1.1 chunked input from the client yet.

NAME

iasl — Intel ASL compiler and disassembler (iASL)

SYNOPSIS

iasl [*options*]⟨*input file*⟩

DESCRIPTION

The **iasl** is a fully-featured compiler for the ACPI Source Language (ASL). It translates ASL to ACPI
Machine Language (AML), but **iasl** can also act as a disassembler, translating AML to ASL.

OPTIONS

Global

−@ *file*	Specify command file.
−I *dir*	Specify additional include directory.

General Output

−p *prefix*	Specify a path or filename *prefix* for all output files.
−va	Disable all errors and warnings in the summary.
−vi	Use less verbose errors and warnings.
−vo	Enable optimization comments.
−vr	Disable remarks.
−vs	Disable signon.
−w *1	2	3*	Set warning reporting level.

AML Output Files

−s *a	c*	Create AML in assembler (*.asm) or C (*.c) source file.
−i *a	c*	Create assembler (*.inc) or C (*.h) include file.
−t *a	c*	Create AML in assembler or C hex table (*.hex).

AML Code Generation

−oa	Disable all optimizations (compatibility mode).
−of	Disable constant folding.
−oi	Disable integer optimization to operation codes.
−on	Disable named reference string optimization.
−r *revision*	Override table header *revision* (1-255).

Listings

−l	Create mixed, ASL and AML, listing file (*.lst).
−ln	Create namespace file (*.nsp).
−ls	Create combined source file (*.src).

AML Disassembler

−d *file*	Disassemble binary ACPI table to a *file* (*.dsl).
−dc *file*	Disassemble AML and immediately compile it.
−e *f1, f2*	Include ACPI table(s) for external symbol resolution.
−2	Emit ACPI 2.0 compatible ASL code.
−g	Get ACPI tables and write to files (*.dat).

Help

-h	Display additional help and compiler debug options.
-hc	Display operators allowed in constant expressions.
-hr	Display ACPI reserved method names.

SEE ALSO

acpi(4), acpidump(8), amldb(8)

Intel Corporation, *iASL Compiler/Disassembler User Reference*, Revision 2.00, September 18, 2009.

HISTORY

The **iasl** compiler/disassembler is part of the Intel ACPI Component Architecture (ACPICA). It first appeared in NetBSD 6.0.

AUTHORS

Among Intel engineers, Robert Moore ⟨robert.moore@intel.com⟩ was the chief architect behind **iasl**. This manual page was written for NetBSD by
Jukka Ruohonen ⟨jruohonen@iki.fi⟩.

NAME

identd — TCP/IP Ident protocol server

SYNOPSIS

identd [**-46beIilNnr**] [**-a** address] [**-c** charset] [**-F** format] [**-f** username]
        [**-g** uid] [**-L** username] [**-m** filter] [**-o** osname] [**-P** address]
        [**-p** portno] [**-t** seconds] [**-u** uid]

DESCRIPTION

identd is a TCP/IP server which implements the user identification protocol as specified in RFC 1413.

identd operates by looking up specific TCP/IP connections and returning information which may or may not be associated with the process owning the connection.

The following options are available:

-4   Bind to IPv4 addresses only (valid with flag **-b**).

-6   Bind to IPv6 addresses only (valid with flag **-b**).

-a address   Bind to the specified address. This may be an IPv4 or IPv6 address or even a hostname. If a hostname is specified then **identd** will resolve it to an address (or addresses) and will bind this address (valid with flag **-b**).

-b   Run in the background (as daemon).

-c charset   Specify an optional character set designator to be included in replies. charset should be a valid charset set as described in the MIME RFC in upper case characters.

-e   Return "UNKNOWN-ERROR" instead of the usual "NO-USER" or "INVALID-PORT" error replies.

-F format   Specify the format to display info. The allowed format specifiers are:

```
%u      print user name
%U      print user number
%g      print (primary) group name
%G      print (primary) group number
%l      print list of all groups by name
%L      print list of all groups by number
```

The lists of groups (%l, %L) are comma-separated, and start with the primary group which is not repeated. Any other characters (preceded by %, and those not preceded by it) are printed literally.

-f username   Specify a fall back username. If the lookup fails then this username will be returned. This can be useful for when running this service on a NAT host and not using the forward/proxy functionality.

-g gid   Specify the group id number or name which the server should switch to after binding itself to the TCP/IP port.

-I   Same as **-i** but without the restriction that the username in .ident must not match an existing user.

-i   If the .ident file exists in the home directory of the identified user, return the username found in that file instead of the real username. If the username found in .ident is that of an existing user, then the real username will be returned.

-L *username*   Specify a "lie" *username*. **identd** will return this name for all valid ident requests.

-l   Use syslogd(8) for logging purposes.

-m *filter*   Enables forwarding of ident queries. The *filter* argument specifies which packet filter should be used to lookup the connections, currently 'pf' and 'ipfilter' are supported packet filters. Note that **identd** changes the ident queries to use the local port on the NAT host instead of the local port on the forwarding host. This is needed because otherwise we can't do a lookup on the proxy host. On the proxy host, "proxy mode" should be enabled with the **-P** flag or "lying mode" with the **-L** flag.

-N   Enable .noident files. If this file exists in the home directory of the identified user then return "HIDDEN-USER" instead of the normal USERID response.

-n   Return numeric user IDs instead of usernames.

-o *osname*   Return *osname* instead of the default "UNIX".

-P *address*   Specify a proxy server which will be used to receive proxied ident queries from. See also the **-m** flag how this operates.

-p *portno*   Specify an alternative port number under which the server should run. The default is port 113 (valid with flag **-b**).

-r   Return a random name of alphanumeric characters. If the **-n** flag is also enabled then a random number will be returned.

-t *seconds*   Specify a timeout for the service. The default timeout is 30 seconds.

-u *uid*   Specify the user id number or name to which the server should switch after binding itself to the TCP/IP port.

FILES
    /etc/inetd.conf

EXAMPLES
    identd operates from inetd(8) or as standalone daemon. Put the following lines into inetd.conf(5) to enable **identd** as an IPv4 and IPv6 service via inetd:

    ident stream tcp nowait nobody /usr/libexec/identd identd -l

    ident stream tcp6 nowait nobody /usr/libexec/identd identd -l

    To run **identd** as standalone daemon, use the **-b** flag.

SEE ALSO
    inetd.conf(5), inetd(8)

AUTHORS
    This implementation of **identd** is written by Peter Postma ⟨peter@NetBSD.org⟩.

CAVEATS
    Since **identd** should typically not be run as a privileged user or group, .ident files for use when running with the **-I** or **-i** flags will need to be world accessible. The same applies for .noident files when running with the **-N** flag.

    When forwarding is enabled with the **-m** flag then **identd** will need access to either /etc/pf (pf) or /etc/ipnat (ipfilter). Since it's not a good idea to run **identd** under root, you'll need to adjust group owner/permissions to the device(s) and run **identd** under that group.

NAME

   ifconfig — configure network interface parameters

SYNOPSIS

   ifconfig [**-N**] *interface address_family* [*address* [*dest_address*]] [*parameters*]
   ifconfig [**-hLmNvz**] *interface* [*protocol_family*]
   ifconfig -a [**-bdhLNmsuvz**] [*protocol_family*]
   ifconfig -l [**-bdsu**]
   ifconfig -s *interface*
   ifconfig -C

DESCRIPTION

   ifconfig is used to assign an address to a network interface and/or configure network interface parameters. **ifconfig** must be used at boot time to define the network address of each interface present on a
   machine; it may also be used at a later time to redefine an interface's address or other operating parameters.

   Available operands for **ifconfig**:

address

   For the DARPA-Internet family, the address is either a host name present in the host name data base,
   hosts(5), or a DARPA Internet address expressed in the Internet standard "dot notation". For the
   Xerox Network Systems(tm) family, addresses are *net:a.b.c.d.e.f*, where *net* is the
   assigned network number (in decimal), and each of the six bytes of the host number, *a* through *f*,
   are specified in hexadecimal. The host number may be omitted on Ethernet interfaces, which use
   the hardware physical address, and on interfaces other than the first. For the ISO family, addresses
   are specified as a long hexadecimal string, as in the Xerox family. However, two consecutive dots
   imply a zero byte, and the dots are optional, if the user wishes to (carefully) count out long strings
   of digits in network byte order.

address_family

   Specifies the *address_family* which affects interpretation of the remaining parameters. Since
   an interface can receive transmissions in differing protocols with different naming schemes, specifying the address family is recommended. The address or protocol families currently supported are
   "inet", "inet6", "atalk", "iso", and "link".

interface

   The *interface* parameter is a string of the form "name unit", for example, "en0"

   The following parameters may be set with **ifconfig**:

active   This keyword applies when **ifconfig** adds or modifies any link-layer address. It
                            indicates that **ifconfig** should "activate" the address. Activation makes an address
                            the default source for transmissions on the interface. You may not delete the active
                            address from an interface. You must activate some other address, first.

advbase *n*   If the driver is a carp(4) pseudo-device, set the base advertisement interval to *n* sec-
                            onds. This ia an 8-bit number; the default value is 1 second.

advskew *n*   If the driver is a carp(4) pseudo-device, skew the advertisement interval by *n*. This is
                            an 8-bit number; the default value is 0.

                            Taken together the **advbase** indicate how frequently, in seconds, the host will adver-
                            tise the fact that it considers itself the master of the virtual host. The formula is
                            advbase + (**advskew** / 256). If the master does not advertise within three times this
                            interval, this host will begin advertising as master.

alias	Establish an additional network address for this interface. This is sometimes useful when changing network numbers, and one wishes to accept packets addressed to the old interface.
–alias	Remove the specified network address alias.
arp	Enable the use of the Address Resolution Protocol in mapping between network level addresses and link level addresses (default). This is currently implemented for mapping between DARPA Internet addresses and Ethernet addresses.
–arp	Disable the use of the Address Resolution Protocol.
anycast	(inet6 only) Set the IPv6 anycast address bit.
–anycast	(inet6 only) Clear the IPv6 anycast address bit.
broadcast *mask*	(Inet only) Specify the address to use to represent broadcasts to the network. The default broadcast address is the address with a host part of all 1's.
carpdev *iface*	If the driver is a carp(4) pseudo-device, attach it to *iface*. If not specified, the kernel will attempt to select an interface with a subnet matching that of the carp interface.
debug	Enable driver dependent debugging code; usually, this turns on extra console error logging.
–debug	Disable driver dependent debugging code.
delete	Remove the network address specified. This would be used if you incorrectly specified an alias, or it was no longer needed. If you have incorrectly set an NS address having the side effect of specifying the host portion, removing all NS addresses will allow you to respecify the host portion. **delete** does not work for IPv6 addresses. Use **–alias** with explicit IPv6 address instead.
dest_address	Specify the address of the correspondent on the other end of a point to point link.
down	Mark an interface "down". When an interface is marked "down", the system will not attempt to transmit messages through that interface. If possible, the interface will be reset to disable reception as well. This action does not automatically disable routes using the interface.
ipdst	This is used to specify an Internet host who is willing to receive ip packets encapsulating NS packets bound for a remote network. An apparent point to point link is constructed, and the address specified will be taken as the NS address and network of the destination. IP encapsulation of CLNP packets is done differently.
media *type*	Set the media type of the interface to *type*. Some interfaces support the mutually exclusive use of one of several different physical media connectors. For example, a 10Mb/s Ethernet interface might support the use of either AUI or twisted pair connectors. Setting the media type to "10base5" or "AUI" would change the currently active connector to the AUI port. Setting it to "10baseT" or "UTP" would activate twisted pair. Refer to the interfaces' driver specific man page for a complete list of the available types and the ifmedia(4) manual page for a list of media types. See the **–m** flag below.
mediaopt *opts*	Set the specified media options on the interface. *opts* is a comma delimited list of options to apply to the interface. Refer to the interfaces' driver specific man page for a complete list of available options. Also see the ifmedia(4) manual page for a list of media options.

−mediaopt *opts*
　　　　　　　　　Disable the specified media options on the interface.

mode *mode*　　If the driver supports the media selection system, set the specified operating mode on
　　　　　　　　　the interface to *mode*. For IEEE 802.11 wireless interfaces that support multiple oper-
　　　　　　　　　ating modes this directive is used to select between 802.11a ("11a"), 802.11b
　　　　　　　　　("11b"), and 802.11g ("11g") operating modes.

instance *minst* Set the media instance to *minst*. This is useful for devices which have multiple phys-
　　　　　　　　　ical layer interfaces (PHYs). Setting the instance on such devices may not be strictly
　　　　　　　　　required by the network interface driver as the driver may take care of this automati-
　　　　　　　　　cally; see the driver's manual page for more information.

metric *n*　　　Set the routing metric of the interface to *n*, default 0. The routing metric is used by the
　　　　　　　　　routing protocol (routed(8)). Higher metrics have the effect of making a route less
　　　　　　　　　favorable; metrics are counted as addition hops to the destination network or host.

mtu *n*　　　　Set the maximum transmission unit of the interface to *n*. Most interfaces don't support
　　　　　　　　　this option.

netmask *mask*　(inet, inet6, and ISO) Specify how much of the address to reserve for subdividing
　　　　　　　　　networks into sub-networks. The mask includes the network part of the local address
　　　　　　　　　and the subnet part, which is taken from the host field of the address. The mask can be
　　　　　　　　　specified as a single hexadecimal number with a leading 0x, with a dot-notation Inter-
　　　　　　　　　net address, or with a pseudo-network name listed in the network table networks(5).
　　　　　　　　　The mask contains 1's for the bit positions in the 32-bit address which are to be used
　　　　　　　　　for the network and subnet parts, and 0's for the host part. The mask should contain at
　　　　　　　　　least the standard network portion, and the subnet field should be contiguous with the
　　　　　　　　　network portion.

　　　　　　　　　For INET and INET6 addresses, the netmask can also be given with slash-notation
　　　　　　　　　after the address (e.g 192.168.17.3/24).

nsellength *n*　(ISO only) This specifies a trailing number of bytes for a received NSAP used for local
　　　　　　　　　identification, the remaining leading part of which is taken to be the NET (Network
　　　　　　　　　Entity Title). The default value is 1, which is conformant to US GOSIP. When an
　　　　　　　　　ISO address is set in an ifconfig command, it is really the NSAP which is being speci-
　　　　　　　　　fied. For example, in US GOSIP, 20 hex digits should be specified in the ISO NSAP to
　　　　　　　　　be assigned to the interface. There is some evidence that a number different from 1
　　　　　　　　　may be useful for AFI 37 type addresses.

state *state*　　Explicitly force the carp(4) pseudo-device to enter this state. Valid states are *init*,
　　　　　　　　　backup, and *master*.

frag *threshold*　(IEEE 802.11 devices only) Configure the fragmentation threshold for IEEE
　　　　　　　　　802.11-based wireless network interfaces.

rts *threshold*　(IEEE 802.11 devices only) Configure the RTS/CTS threshold for IEEE
　　　　　　　　　802.11-based wireless network interfaces. This controls the number of bytes used for
　　　　　　　　　the RTS/CTS handshake boundary. The *threshold* can be any value between 0 and
　　　　　　　　　2347. The default is 2347, which indicates the RTS/CTS mechanism should not be
　　　　　　　　　used.

ssid *id*　　　　(IEEE 802.11 devices only) Configure the Service Set Identifier (a.k.a. the network
　　　　　　　　　name) for IEEE 802.11-based wireless network interfaces. The *id* can either be any
　　　　　　　　　text string up to 32 characters in length, or a series of up to 64 hexadecimal digits pre-
　　　　　　　　　ceded by "0x". Setting *id* to the empty string allows the interface to connect to any

available access point.

nwid *id*   Synonym for "ssid".

hidessid   (IEEE 802.11 devices only) When operating as an access point, do not broadcast the
                          SSID in beacon frames or respond to probe request frames unless they are directed to
                          the ap (i.e., they include the ap's SSID). By default, the SSID is included in beacon
                          frames and undirected probe request frames are answered.

−hidessid   (IEEE 802.11 devices only) When operating as an access point, broadcast the SSID
                          in beacon frames and answer and respond to undirected probe request frames (default).

nwkey *key*   (IEEE 802.11 devices only) Enable WEP encryption for IEEE 802.11-based wireless
                          network interfaces with the *key*. The *key* can either be a string, a series of hexadeci-
                          mal digits preceded by "0x", or a set of keys in the form *n:k1,k2,k3,k4*, where *n*
                          specifies which of keys will be used for all transmitted packets, and four keys, *k1*
                          through *k4*, are configured as WEP keys. Note that the order must be match within
                          same network if multiple keys are used. For IEEE 802.11 wireless network, the length
                          of each key is restricted to 40 bits, i.e. 5-character string or 10 hexadecimal digits,
                          while the WaveLAN/IEEE Gold cards accept the 104 bits (13 characters) key.

nwkey persist   (IEEE 802.11 devices only) Enable WEP encryption for IEEE 802.11-based wireless
                          network interfaces with the persistent key written in the network card.

nwkey persist:*key*
                          (IEEE 802.11 devices only) Write the *key* to the persistent memory of the network
                          card, and enable WEP encryption for IEEE 802.11-based wireless network interfaces
                          with the *key*.

−nwkey   (IEEE 802.11 devices only) Disable WEP encryption for IEEE 802.11-based wire-
                          less network interfaces.

apbridge   (IEEE 802.11 devices only) When operating as an access point, pass packets between
                          wireless clients directly (default).

−apbridge   (IEEE 802.11 devices only) When operating as an access point, pass packets through
                          the system so that they can be forwared using some other mechanism. Disabling the
                          internal bridging is useful when traffic is to be processed with packet filtering.

pass *passphrase*
                          If the driver is a carp(4) pseudo-device, set the authentication key to *passphrase*.
                          There is no passphrase by default

powersave   (IEEE 802.11 devices only) Enable 802.11 power saving mode.

−powersave   (IEEE 802.11 devices only) Disable 802.11 power saving mode.

powersavesleep *duration*
                          (IEEE 802.11 devices only) Set the receiver sleep duration in milliseconds for 802.11
                          power saving mode.

bssid *bssid*   (IEEE 802.11 devices only) Set the desired BSSID for IEEE 802.11-based wireless
                          network interfaces.

−bssid   (IEEE 802.11 devices only) Unset the desired BSSID for IEEE 802.11-based wire-
                          less network interfaces. The interface will automatically select a BSSID in this mode,
                          which is the default.

chan *chan*   (IEEE 802.11 devices only) Select the channel (radio frequency) to be used for
                      IEEE 802.11-based wireless network interfaces.

–chan   (IEEE 802.11 devices only) Unset the desired channel to be used for IEEE
                      802.11-based wireless network interfaces. It doesn't affect the channel to be created
                      for IBSS or hostap mode.

list scan   (IEEE 802.11 devices only) Display the access points and/or ad-hoc neighbors
                      located in the vicinity. The **–v** flag may be used to display long SSIDs. **–v** also
                      causes received information elements to be displayed symbolicaly. Only the super-
                      user can use this command.

tunnel *src_addr[,src_port]*
                      dest_addr[,dest_port] (IP tunnel devices only) Configure the physical
                      source and destination address for IP tunnel interfaces, including gif(4). The argu-
                      ments *src_addr* and *dest_addr* are interpreted as the outer source/destination for
                      the encapsulating IPv4/IPv6 header.

                      On a gre(4) interface in UDP mode, the arguments *src_port* and *dest_port* are
                      interpreted as the outer source/destination port for the encapsulating UDP header.

deletetunnel   Unconfigure the physical source and destination address for IP tunnel interfaces previ-
                      ously configured with **tunnel**.

create   Create the specified network pseudo-device.

destroy   Destroy the specified network pseudo-device.

pltime *n*   (inet6 only) Set preferred lifetime for the address.

prefixlen *n*   (inet and inet6 only) Effect is similar to **netmask**. but you can specify by prefix
                      length by digits.

deprecated   (inet6 only) Set the IPv6 deprecated address bit.

–deprecated   (inet6 only) Clear the IPv6 deprecated address bit.

tentative   (inet6 only) Set the IPv6 tentative address bit.

–tentative   (inet6 only) Clear the IPv6 tentative address bit.

eui64   (inet6 only) Fill interface index (lowermost 64bit of an IPv6 address) automatically.

link[0-2]   Enable special processing of the link level of the interface. These three options are
                      interface specific in actual effect, however, they are in general used to select special
                      modes of operation. An example of this is to enable SLIP compression, or to select the
                      connector type for some Ethernet cards. Refer to the man page for the specific driver
                      for more information.

–link[0-2]   Disable special processing at the link level with the specified interface.

up   Mark an interface "up". This may be used to enable an interface after an "ifconfig
                      down." It happens automatically when setting the first address on an interface. If the
                      interface was reset when previously marked down, the hardware will be re-initialized.

vhid *n*   If the driver is a carp(4) pseudo-device, set the virtual host ID to *n*. Acceptable val-
                      ues are 1 to 255.

vlan *vid*   If the interface is a vlan(4) pseudo-interface, set the VLAN identifier to *vid*. These
                      are the first 12 bits (0-4095) from a 16-bit integer used to create an 802.1Q VLAN
                      header for packets sent from the vlan(4) interface. Note that **vlan** and **vlanif**

	must be set at the same time.
vlanif *iface*	If the interface is a vlan(4) pseudo-interface, associate the physical interface *iface* with it. Packets transmitted through the vlan(4) interface will be diverted to the specified physical interface *iface* with 802.1Q VLAN encapsulation. Packets with 802.1Q encapsulation received by the physical interface with the correct VLAN tag will be diverted to the associated vlan(4) pseudo-interface. The VLAN interface is assigned a copy of the physical interface's flags and Ethernet address. If the vlan(4) interface already has a physical interface associated with it, this command will fail. To change the association to another physical interface, the existing association must be cleared first. Note that **vlanif** and **vlan** must be set at the same time.
agrport *iface*	Add *iface* to the agr(4) interface.
-agrport *iface*	Remove *iface* from the agr(4) interface.
vltime *n*	(inet6 only) Set valid lifetime for the address.
ip4csum	Shorthand of "ip4csum-tx ip4csum-rx"
-ip4csum	Shorthand of "-ip4csum-tx -ip4csum-rx"
tcp4csum	Shorthand of "tcp4csum-tx tcp4csum-rx"
-tcp4csum	Shorthand of "-tcp4csum-tx -tcp4csum-rx"
udp4csum	Shorthand of "udp4csum-tx udp4csum-rx"
-udp4csum	Shorthand of "-udp4csum-tx -udp4csum-rx"
tcp6csum	Shorthand of "tcp6csum-tx tcp6csum-rx"
-tcp6csum	Shorthand of "-tcp6csum-tx -tcp6csum-rx"
udp6csum	Shorthand of "udp6csum-tx udp6csum-rx"
-udp6csum	Shorthand of "-udp6csum-tx -udp6csum-rx"
ip4csum-tx	Enable hardware-assisted IPv4 header checksums for the out-bound direction.
-ip4csum-tx	Disable hardware-assisted IPv4 header checksums for the out-bound direction.
ip4csum-rx	Enable hardware-assisted IPv4 header checksums for the in-bound direction.
-ip4csum-rx	Disable hardware-assisted IPv4 header checksums for the in-bound direction.
tcp4csum-tx	Enable hardware-assisted TCP/IPv4 checksums for the out-bound direction.
-tcp4csum-tx	Disable hardware-assisted TCP/IPv4 checksums for the out-bound direction.
tcp4csum-rx	Enable hardware-assisted TCP/IPv4 checksums for the in-bound direction.
-tcp4csum-rx	Disable hardware-assisted TCP/IPv4 checksums for the in-bound direction.
udp4csum-tx	Enable hardware-assisted UDP/IPv4 checksums for the out-bound direction.
-udp4csum-tx	Disable hardware-assisted UDP/IPv4 checksums for the out-bound direction.
udp4csum-rx	Enable hardware-assisted UDP/IPv4 checksums for the in-bound direction.
-udp4csum-rx	Disable hardware-assisted UDP/IPv4 checksums for the in-bound direction.
tcp6csum-tx	Enable hardware-assisted TCP/IPv6 checksums for the out-bound direction.

-tcp6csum-tx	Disable hardware-assisted TCP/IPv6 checksums for the out-bound direction.
tcp6csum-rx	Enable hardware-assisted TCP/IPv6 checksums for the in-bound direction.
-tcp6csum-rx	Disable hardware-assisted TCP/IPv6 checksums for the in-bound direction.
udp6csum-tx	Enable hardware-assisted UDP/IPv6 checksums for the out-bound direction.
-udp6csum-tx	Disable hardware-assisted UDP/IPv6 checksums for the out-bound direction.
udp6csum-rx	Enable hardware-assisted UDP/IPv6 checksums for the in-bound direction.
-udp6csum-rx	Disable hardware-assisted UDP/IPv6 checksums for the in-bound direction.
tso4	Enable hardware-assisted TCP/IPv4 segmentation on interfaces that support it.
-tso4	Disable hardware-assisted TCP/IPv4 segmentation on interfaces that support it.
tso6	Enable hardware-assisted TCP/IPv6 segmentation on interfaces that support it.
-tso6	Disable hardware-assisted TCP/IPv6 segmentation on interfaces that support it.

maxupd *n*   If the driver is a pfsync(4) pseudo-device, indicate the maximum number of updates for a single state which can be collapsed into one. This is an 8-bit number; the default value is 128.

syncdev *iface*   If the driver is a pfsync(4) pseudo-device, use the specified interface to send and receive pfsync state synchronisation messages.

-syncdev   If the driver is a pfsync(4) pseudo-device, stop sending pfsync state synchronisation messages over the network.

syncpeer *peer_address*

If the driver is a pfsync(4) pseudo-device, make the pfsync link point-to-point rather than using multicast to broadcast the state synchronisation messages. The peer_address is the IP address of the other host taking part in the pfsync cluster. With this option, pfsync(4) traffic can be protected using ipsec(4).

-syncpeer   If the driver is a pfsync(4) pseudo-device, broadcast the packets using multicast.

ifconfig displays the current configuration for a network interface when no optional parameters are supplied. If a protocol family is specified, **ifconfig** will report only the details specific to that protocol family.

If the **-s** flag is passed before an interface name, **ifconfig** will attempt to query the interface for its media status. If the interface supports reporting media status, and it reports that it does not appear to be connected to a network, **ifconfig** will exit with status of 1 (false); otherwise, it will exit with a zero (true) exit status. Not all interface drivers support media status reporting.

If the **-m** flag is passed before an interface name, **ifconfig** will display all of the supported media for the specified interface. If the **-L** flag is supplied, address lifetime is displayed for IPv6 addresses, as time offset string.

Optionally, the **-a** flag may be used instead of an interface name. This flag instructs **ifconfig** to display information about all interfaces in the system. **-d** limits this to interfaces that are down, **-u** limits this to interfaces that are up, **-b** limits this to broadcast interfaces, and **-s** omits interfaces which appear not to be connected to a network.

The **-l** flag may be used to list all available interfaces on the system, with no other additional information. Use of this flag is mutually exclusive with all other flags and commands, except for **-d** (only list interfaces that are down), **-u** (only list interfaces that are up), **-s** (only list interfaces that may be connected), **-b** (only list broadcast interfaces).

The **−C** flag may be used to list all of the interface cloners available on the system, with no additional information. Use of this flag is mutually exclusive with all other flags and commands.

The **−v** flag prints statistics on packets sent and received on the given interface. If **−h** is used in conjunction with **−v**, the byte statistics will be printed in "human-readable" format. The **−z** flag is identical to the **−v** flag except that it zeros the interface input and output statistics after printing them.

The **−N** flag is just the opposite of the **−n** flag in netstat(1) or in route(8): it tells **ifconfig** to try to resolve numbers to hostnames or to service names. The default **ifconfig** behavior is to print numbers instead of names.

Only the super-user may modify the configuration of a network interface.

EXAMPLES

Add a link-layer (MAC) address to an Ethernet:

ifconfig sip0 link 00:11:22:33:44:55

Add and activate a link-layer (MAC) address:

ifconfig sip0 link 00:11:22:33:44:55 active

DIAGNOSTICS

Messages indicating the specified interface does not exist, the requested address is unknown, or the user is not privileged and tried to alter an interface's configuration.

SEE ALSO

netstat(1), agr(4), carp(4), ifmedia(4), netintro(4), pfsync(4), vlan(4), ifconfig.if(5), rc(8), routed(8)

HISTORY

The **ifconfig** command appeared in 4.2 BSD.

NAME

ifmcstat — dump multicast group management statistics per interface

SYNOPSIS

ifmcstat

DESCRIPTION

The **ifmcstat** command dumps multicast group information in the kernel.

There are no command-line options.

NAME
ifwatchd — watch for addresses added to or deleted from interfaces and call up/down-scripts for them

SYNOPSIS
ifwatchd [**-hiqv**] [**-A** *arrival-script*] [**-c** *carrier-script*]
       [**-D** *departure-script*] [**-d** *down-script*] [**-u** *up-script*]
       [**-n** *no-carrier-script*] *ifname(s)*

DESCRIPTION
ifwatchd is used to monitor dynamic interfaces (for example PPP interfaces) for address changes, and to monitor static interfaces for carrier changes. Sometimes these interfaces are accompanied by a daemon program, which can take care of running any necessary scripts (like pppd(8) or isdnd(8)), but sometimes the interfaces run completely autonomously (like pppoe(4)).

ifwatchd provides a generic way to watch these types of changes. It works by monitoring the routing socket and interpreting RTM_NEWADDR (address added), RTM_DELADDR (address deleted) and RTM_IFINFO (carrier detect or loss of carrier) messages. It does not need special privileges to do this. The scripts called for up or down events are run with the same user id as **ifwatchd** is run.

The following options are available:

-A *arrival-script*
    Specify the command to invoke on arrival of new interfaces (like PCMCIA cards).

-c *carrier-script*
    Specify the command to invoke when the carrier status transitions from no carrier to carrier.

-D *departure-script*
    Specify the command to invoke when an interface departs (for example a PCMCIA card is removed.)

-d *down-script*
    Specify the command to invoke on "interface down" events (or: deletion of an address from an interface).

-h   Show the synopsis.

-i   Inhibit a call to the up-script on startup for all watched interfaces already marked up. If this option is not given, **ifwatchd** will check all watched interfaces on startup whether they are already marked up and, if they are, call the up-script with appropriate parameters. Additionally, if the interface is up and has a link, **ifwatchd** will run the carrier script.

    Since ifwatchd typically is started late in the system boot sequence, some of the monitored interfaces may already have come up when it finally starts, but their up-scripts have not been called. By default **ifwatchd** calls them on startup to account for this (and make the scripts easier.)

-n *no-carrier-script*
    Specify the command to invoke when the carrier status transitions from carrier to no carrier.

-q   Be quiet and don't log non-error messages to syslog.

-u *up-script*
    Specify the command to invoke on "interface up" events (or: addition of an address to an interface).

-v   Run in verbose debug mode and do not detach from the controlling terminal. Output verbose progress messages and flag errors ignored during normal operation. *You do not want to use this option in* /etc/rc.conf!

ifname(s)
>   The name of the interface to watch. Multiple interfaces may be specified. Events for other interfaces are ignored.

EXAMPLES
```
# ifwatchd -u /etc/ppp/ip-up -d /etc/ppp/ip-down pppoe0
```

If your pppoe0 interface is your main connection to the internet, the typical use of the up/down scripts is to add and remove a default route. This is an example for an up script doing this:
```
#! /bin/sh
/sbin/route add default $5
/sbin/route add -inet6 default fe80::2 -iface ifp $1
```

As described below the fifth command line parameter will contain the peer address of the pppoe link. The corresponding ip-down script is:
```
#! /bin/sh
/sbin/route delete default $5
/sbin/route delete -inet6 default fe80::2
```

Note that this is not a good idea if you have pppoe0 configured to connect only on demand (via the link1 flag), but works well for all permanent connected cases. Use
```
! /sbin/route add default -iface 0.0.0.1
```
in your /etc/ifconfig.pppoe0 file in the on-demand case.

The next example is for dhclient users.
```
# ifwatchd -i -c /etc/dhcp/carrier-detect tlp0
```

With the above command, the carrier-detect script will be invoked when a carrier is detected on the interface *tlp0*. Note that the **-i** flag prevents any action based on the initial state. A script like the following should work for most users, although it will not work for machines with multiple interfaces running **dhclient**.
```
#! /bin/sh
# Arguments:  ifname tty speed address destination
# If there is a dhclient already running, kill it.
# (This step could be put in a distinct no-carrier script,
# if desired.)
if [ -f /var/run/dhclient.pid ]; then
        /bin/kill '/bin/cat /var/run/dhclient.pid'
fi
# Start dhclient again on this interface
/sbin/dhclient $1
```

PARAMETERS PASSED TO SCRIPTS
The invoked scripts get passed these parameters:

ifname   The name of the interface this change is for (this allows to share the same script for multiple interfaces watched and dispatching on the interface name in the script).

tty   Dummy parameter for compatibility with pppd(8) which will always be */dev/null*.

speed   Dummy parameter for compatibility with pppd(8) which will always be *9600*.

address   The new address if this is an up event, or the no longer valid old address if this is a down event.

The format of the address depends on the address family, for IPv4 it is the usual dotted quad notation, for IPv6 the colon separated standard notation.

destination   For point to point interfaces, this is the remote address of the interface. For other interfaces it is the broadcast address.

ERRORS
The program logs to the syslog daemon as facility "daemon". For detailed debugging use the **−v** (verbose) option.

SEE ALSO
pppoe(4), route(4), ifconfig.if(5), rc.d(8), route(8)

HISTORY
The **ifwatchd** utility appeared in NetBSD 1.6.

AUTHORS
The program was written by Martin Husemann ⟨martin@NetBSD.org⟩.

CAVEATS
Due to the nature of the program a lot of stupid errors can not easily be caught in advance without removing the provided facility for advanced uses. For example typing errors in the interface name can not be detected by checking against the list of installed interfaces, because it is possible for a pcmcia card with the name given to be inserted later.

NAME
    `inetd`, `inetd.conf` — internet "super-server"

SYNOPSIS
    `inetd` [`-d`] [`-l`] [`configuration file`]

DESCRIPTION
    `inetd` should be run at boot time by `/etc/rc` (see `rc`(8)). It then opens sockets according to its configuration and listens for connections. When a connection is found on one of its sockets, it decides what service the socket corresponds to, and invokes a program to service the request. After the program is finished, it continues to listen on the socket (except in some cases which will be described below). Essentially, `inetd` allows running one daemon to invoke several others, reducing load on the system.

    The options available for `inetd`:

`-d`   Turns on debugging.

`-l`   Turns on libwrap connection logging.

    Upon execution, `inetd` reads its configuration information from a configuration file which, by default, is `/etc/inetd.conf`. The path given for this configuration file must be absolute, unless the `-d` option is also given on the command line. There must be an entry for each field of the configuration file, with entries for each field separated by a tab or a space. Comments are denoted by a "#" at the beginning of a line. There must be an entry for each field (except for one special case, described below). The fields of the configuration file are as follows:

        [addr:]service-name
        socket-type[:accept_filter]
        protocol[,sndbuf=size][,rcvbuf=size]
        wait/nowait[:max]
        user[:group]
        server-program
        server program arguments

    To specify an *Sun-RPC* based service, the entry would contain these fields:

        service-name/version
        socket-type
        rpc/protocol[,sndbuf=size][,rcvbuf=size]
        wait/nowait[:max]
        user[:group]
        server-program
        server program arguments

    To specify a UNIX-domain (local) socket, the entry would contain these fields:

        path
        socket-type
        unix[,sndbuf=size][,rcvbuf=size]
        wait/nowait[:max]
        user[:group]
        server-program
        server program arguments

    For Internet services, the first field of the line may also have a host address specifier prefixed to it, separated from the service name by a colon. If this is done, the string before the colon in the first field indicates what local address `inetd` should use when listening for that service, or the single character "*" to indicate

INADDR_ANY, meaning 'all local addresses'. To avoid repeating an address that occurs frequently, a line with a host address specifier and colon, but no further fields, causes the host address specifier to be remembered and used for all further lines with no explicit host specifier (until another such line or the end of the file). A line

        *:

is implicitly provided at the top of the file; thus, traditional configuration files (which have no host address specifiers) will be interpreted in the traditional manner, with all services listened for on all local addresses.

The *service-name* entry is the name of a valid service in the file /etc/services. For "internal" services (discussed below), the service name *must* be the official name of the service (that is, the first entry in /etc/services). When used to specify a *Sun-RPC* based service, this field is a valid RPC service name in the file /etc/rpc. The part on the right of the "/" is the RPC version number. This can simply be a single numeric argument or a range of versions. A range is bounded by the low version to the high version – "rusers/1-3".

The *socket-type* should be one of "stream", "dgram", "raw", "rdm", or "seqpacket", depending on whether the socket is a stream, datagram, raw, reliably delivered message, or sequenced packet socket.

Optionally, an accept_filter(9) can be specified by appending a colon to the socket-type, followed by the name of the desired accept filter. In this case **inetd** will not see new connections for the specified service until the accept filter decides they are ready to be handled.

The *protocol* must be a valid protocol as given in /etc/protocols or the string "unix". Examples might be "tcp" and "udp". Rpc based services are specified with the "rpc/tcp" or "rpc/udp" service type. "tcp" and "udp" will be recognized as "TCP or UDP over default IP version". It is currently IPv4, but in the future it will be IPv6. If you need to specify IPv4 or IPv6 explicitly, use something like "tcp4" or "udp6". If you would like to enable special support for faithd(8), prepend a keyword "faith" into *protocol*, like "faith/tcp6".

In addition to the protocol, the configuration file may specify the send and receive socket buffer sizes for the listening socket. This is especially useful for TCP as the window scale factor, which is based on the receive socket buffer size, is advertised when the connection handshake occurs, thus the socket buffer size for the server must be set on the listen socket. By increasing the socket buffer sizes, better TCP performance may be realized in some situations. The socket buffer sizes are specified by appending their values to the protocol specification as follows:

```
tcp,rcvbuf=16384
tcp,sndbuf=64k
tcp,rcvbuf=64k,sndbuf=1m
```

A literal value may be specified, or modified using 'k' to indicate kilobytes or 'm' to indicate megabytes. Socket buffer sizes may be specified for all services and protocols except for tcpmux services.

The *wait/nowait* entry is used to tell **inetd** if it should wait for the server program to return, or continue processing connections on the socket. If a datagram server connects to its peer, freeing the socket so **inetd** can receive further messages on the socket, it is said to be a "multi-threaded" server, and should use the "nowait" entry. For datagram servers which process all incoming datagrams on a socket and eventually time out, the server is said to be "single-threaded" and should use a "wait" entry. comsat(8) (biff(1)) and ntalkd(8) are both examples of the latter type of datagram server. tftpd(8) is an exception; it is a datagram server that establishes pseudo-connections. It must be listed as "wait" in order to avoid a race; the server reads the first packet, creates a new socket, and then forks and exits to allow **inetd** to check for new service requests to spawn new servers. The optional "max" suffix (separated from "wait" or "nowait" by a dot or a colon) specifies the maximum number of server instances that may be spawned from **inetd** within an interval of 60 seconds. When omitted, "max" defaults to 40. If it reaches this maximum spawn rate, **inetd** will log the problem (via the syslogger using the LOG_DAEMON facility and LOG_ERR level) and stop handling the specific service for ten minutes.

Stream servers are usually marked as "nowait" but if a single server process is to handle multiple connections, it may be marked as "wait". The master socket will then be passed as fd 0 to the server, which will then need to accept the incoming connection. The server should eventually time out and exit when no more connections are active. **inetd** will continue to listen on the master socket for connections, so the server should not close it when it exits. identd(8) is usually the only stream server marked as wait.

The *user* entry should contain the user name of the user as whom the server should run. This allows for servers to be given less permission than root. Optionally, a group can be specified by appending a colon to the user name, followed by the group name (it is possible to use a dot (".") in lieu of a colon, however this feature is provided only for backward compatibility). This allows for servers to run with a different (primary) group id than specified in the password file. If a group is specified and *user* is not root, the supplementary groups associated with that user will still be set.

The *server-program* entry should contain the pathname of the program which is to be executed by **inetd** when a request is found on its socket. If **inetd** provides this service internally, this entry should be "internal".

The *server program arguments* should be just as arguments normally are, starting with argv[0], which is the name of the program. If the service is provided internally, the word "internal" should take the place of this entry. It is possible to quote an argument using either single or double quotes. This allows you to have, e.g., spaces in paths and parameters.

Internal Services

inetd provides several "trivial" services internally by use of routines within itself. These services are "echo", "discard", "chargen" (character generator), "daytime" (human readable time), and "time" (machine readable time, in the form of the number of seconds since midnight, January 1, 1900 GMT). For details of these services, consult the appropriate RFC.

TCP services without official port numbers can be handled with the RFC1078-based tcpmux internal service. TCPmux listens on port 1 for requests. When a connection is made from a foreign host, the service name requested is passed to TCPmux, which performs a lookup in the service name table provided by /etc/inetd.conf and returns the proper entry for the service. TCPmux returns a negative reply if the service doesn't exist, otherwise the invoked server is expected to return the positive reply if the service type in /etc/inetd.conf file has the prefix "tcpmux/". If the service type has the prefix "tcpmux/+", TCPmux will return the positive reply for the process; this is for compatibility with older server code, and also allows you to invoke programs that use stdin/stdout without putting any special server code in them. Services that use TCPmux are "nowait" because they do not have a well-known port number and hence cannot listen for new requests.

inetd rereads its configuration file when it receives a hangup signal, SIGHUP. Services may be added, deleted or modified when the configuration file is reread. **inetd** creates a file */var/run/inetd.pid* that contains its process identifier.

libwrap

Support for TCP wrappers is included with **inetd** to provide internal tcpd-like access control functionality. An external tcpd program is not needed. You do not need to change the /etc/inetd.conf server-program entry to enable this capability. **inetd** uses /etc/hosts.allow and /etc/hosts.deny for access control facility configurations, as described in hosts_access(5).

Nota Bene: TCP wrappers do not affect/restrict UDP or internal services.

IPsec

The implementation includes a tiny hack to support IPsec policy settings for each socket. A special form of the comment line, starting with "# @", is used as a policy specifier. The content of the above comment line will be treated as a IPsec policy string, as described in ipsec_set_policy(3). Multiple IPsec policy strings may be specified by using a semicolon as a separator. If conflicting policy strings are found in a single line, the last string will take effect. A #@ line affects all of the following lines in /etc/inetd.conf, so you may want to reset the IPsec policy by using a comment line containing only #@ (with no policy string).

If an invalid IPsec policy string appears in /etc/inetd.conf, **inetd** logs an error message using syslog(3) and terminates itself.

IPv6 TCP/UDP behavior

If you wish to run a server for both IPv4 and IPv6 traffic, you will need to run two separate processes for the same server program, specified as two separate lines in /etc/inetd.conf using "tcp4" and "tcp6" respectively. Plain "tcp" means TCP on top of the current default IP version, which is, at this moment, IPv4.

Under various combination of IPv4/v6 daemon settings, **inetd** will behave as follows:

- If you have only one server on "tcp4", IPv4 traffic will be routed to the server. IPv6 traffic will not be accepted.
- If you have two servers on "tcp4" and "tcp6", IPv4 traffic will be routed to the server on "tcp4", and IPv6 traffic will go to server on "tcp6".
- If you have only one server on "tcp6", only IPv6 traffic will be routed to the server. The kernel may route to the server IPv4 traffic as well, under certain configuration. See ip6(4) for details.

FILES

/etc/inetd.conf	configuration file for all **inetd** provided services
/etc/services	service name to protocol and port number mappings.
/etc/protocols	protocol name to protocol number mappings
/etc/rpc	Sun-RPC service name to service number mappings.
/etc/hosts.allow	explicit remote host access list.
/etc/hosts.deny	explicit remote host denial of service list.

SEE ALSO

hosts_access(5), hosts_options(5), protocols(5), rpc(5), services(5), comsat(8), fingerd(8), ftpd(8), rexecd(8), rlogind(8), rshd(8), telnetd(8), tftpd(8)

J. Postel, *Echo Protocol*, RFC, 862, May 1983.

J. Postel, *Discard Protocol*, RFC, 863, May 1983.

J. Postel, *Character Generator Protocol*, RFC, 864, May 1983.

J. Postel, *Daytime Protocol*, RFC, 867, May 1983.

J. Postel and K. Harrenstien, *Time Protocol*, RFC, 868, May 1983.

M. Lottor, *TCP port service Multiplexer (TCPMUX)*, RFC, 1078, November 1988.

HISTORY

The **inetd** command appeared in 4.3BSD. Support for *Sun-RPC* based services is modeled after that provided by SunOS 4.1. Support for specifying the socket buffer sizes was added in NetBSD 1.4. In November 1996, libwrap support was added to provide internal tcpd-like access control functionality; libwrap is based on Wietse Venema's tcp_wrappers. IPv6 support and IPsec hack was made by KAME project, in 1999.

BUGS

Host address specifiers, while they make conceptual sense for RPC services, do not work entirely correctly. This is largely because the portmapper interface does not provide a way to register different ports for the same service on different local addresses. Provided you never have more than one entry for a given RPC service, everything should work correctly (Note that default host address specifiers do apply to RPC lines with no explicit specifier.)

"tcpmux" on IPv6 is not tested enough.

SECURITY CONSIDERATIONS
Enabling the "echo", "discard", and "chargen" built-in trivial services is not recommended because remote users may abuse these to cause a denial of network service to or from the local host.

NAME
init — process control initialization

SYNOPSIS
init

DESCRIPTION
The **init** program is the last stage of the boot process (after the kernel loads and initializes all the devices). It normally begins multi-user operation.

The following table describes the state machine used by **init**:

1. Single user shell. **init** may be passed **-s** from the boot program to prevent the system from going multi-user and to instead execute a single user shell without starting the normal daemons. If the kernel is in a secure mode, **init** will downgrade it to securelevel 0 (insecure mode). The system is then quiescent for maintenance work and may later be made to go to state 2 (multi-user) by exiting the single-user shell (with ^D).

2. Multi-user boot (default operation). Executes /etc/rc (see rc(8)). If this was the first state entered (as opposed to entering here after state 1), then /etc/rc will be invoked with its first argument being 'autoboot'. If /etc/rc exits with a non-zero (error) exit code, commence single user operation by giving the super-user a shell on the console by going to state 1 (single user). Otherwise, proceed to state 3.

    If value of the "init.root" sysctl node is not equal to / at this point, the /etc/rc process will be run inside a chroot(2) indicated by sysctl with the same error handling as above.

    If the administrator has not set the security level to −1 to indicate that the kernel should not run multi-user in secure mode, and the /etc/rc script has not set a higher level of security than level 1, then **init** will put the kernel into securelevel mode 1. See rc.conf(5) and secmodel_securelevel(9) for more information.

3. Set up ttys as specified in ttys(5). See below for more information. On completion, continue to state 4. If we did chroot in state 2, each getty(8) process will be run in the same chroot(2) path as in 2 (that is, the value of "init.root" sysctl is not re-read).

4. Multi-user operation. Depending upon the signal received, change state appropriately; on SIGTERM, go to state 7; on SIGHUP, go to state 5; on SIGTSTP, go to state 6.

5. Clean-up mode; re-read ttys(5), killing off the controlling processes on lines that are now 'off', and starting processes that are newly 'on'. On completion, go to state 4.

6. 'Boring' mode; no new sessions. Signals as per state 4.

7. Shutdown mode. Send SIGHUP to all controlling processes, reap the processes for 30 seconds, and then go to state 1 (single user); warning if not all the processes died.

If the 'console' entry in the ttys(5) file is marked "insecure", then **init** will require that the superuser password be entered before the system will start a single-user shell. The password check is skipped if the 'console' is marked as "secure".

It should be noted that while **init** has the ability to start multi-user operation inside a chroot(2) environment, the **init** process itself will always run in the "original root directory". This also implies that single-user mode is always started in the original root, giving the possibility to create multi-user sessions in different root directories over time. The "init.root" sysctl node is fabricated by **init** at startup and re-created any time it's found to be missing. Type of the node is string capable of holding full pathname, and is only accessible by the superuser (unless explicitly destroyed and re-created with different specification).

In multi-user operation, **init** maintains processes for the terminal ports found in the file ttys(5). **init** reads this file, and executes the command found in the second field. This command is usually getty(8); it opens and initializes the tty line and executes the login(1) program. The login(1) program, when a valid user logs in, executes a shell for that user. When this shell dies, either because the user logged out or an abnormal termination occurred (a signal), the **init** program wakes up, deletes the user from the utmp(5) and utmpx(5) files of current users and records the logout in the wtmp(5) and wtmpx(5) files. The cycle is then restarted by **init** executing a new getty(8) for the line.

Line status (on, off, secure, getty, or window information) may be changed in the ttys(5) file without a reboot by sending the signal SIGHUP to **init** with the command "kill -s HUP 1". This is referenced in the table above as state 5. On receipt of this signal, **init** re-reads the ttys(5) file. When a line is turned off in ttys(5), **init** will send a SIGHUP signal to the controlling process for the session associated with the line. For any lines that were previously turned off in the ttys(5) file and are now on, **init** executes a new getty(8) to enable a new login. If the getty or window field for a line is changed, the change takes effect at the end of the current login session (e.g., the next time **init** starts a process on the line). If a line is commented out or deleted from ttys(5), **init** will not do anything at all to that line. However, it will complain that the relationship between lines in the ttys(5) file and records in the utmp(5) file is out of sync, so this practice is not recommended.

init will terminate multi-user operations and resume single-user mode if sent a terminate (TERM) signal, for example, "kill -s TERM 1". If there are processes outstanding that are deadlocked (because of hardware or software failure), **init** will not wait for them all to die (which might take forever), but will time out after 30 seconds and print a warning message.

init will cease creating new getty(8)'s and allow the system to slowly die away, if it is sent a terminal stop (TSTP) signal, i.e. "kill -s TSTP 1". A later hangup will resume full multi-user operations, or a terminate will start a single user shell. This hook is used by reboot(8) and halt(8).

The role of **init** is so critical that if it dies, the system will reboot itself automatically. If, at bootstrap time, the **init** process cannot be located, or exits during its initialisation, the system will panic with the message "panic: init died (signal %d, exit %d)".

If /dev/console does not exist, **init** will cd to /dev and run "MAKEDEV -MM init". MAKEDEV(8) will use mount_tmpfs(8) or mount_mfs(8) to create a memory file system mounted over /dev that contains the standard devices considered necessary to boot the system.

FILES
/dev/console	System console device.
/dev/tty*	Terminal ports found in ttys(5).
/var/run/utmp{,x}	Record of current users on the system.
/var/log/wtmp{,x}	Record of all logins and logouts.
/etc/ttys	The terminal initialization information file.
/etc/rc	System startup commands.

DIAGNOSTICS
getty repeating too quickly on port %s, sleeping A process being started to service a line is exiting quickly each time it is started. This is often caused by a ringing or noisy terminal line. *Init will sleep for 10 seconds, then continue trying to start the process.*

some processes would not die; ps axl advised. A process is hung and could not be killed when the system was shutting down. This condition is usually caused by a process that is stuck in a device driver because of a persistent device error condition.

SEE ALSO
config(1), kill(1), login(1), sh(1), options(4), ttys(5), getty(8), halt(8), MAKEDEV(8), MAKEDEV.local(8), mount_mfs(8), mount_tmpfs(8), rc(8), reboot(8), rescue(8), shutdown(8), sysctl(8), secmodel_bsd44(9), secmodel_securelevel(9)

HISTORY
A **init** command appeared in Version 6 AT&T UNIX.

NAME
   installboot — install disk bootstrap software

SYNOPSIS
   installboot [**-fnv**] [**-B** *s2bno*] [**-b** *s1bno*] [**-m** *machine*] [**-o** *options*]
                 [**-t** *fstype*] *filesystem primary* [*secondary*]
   installboot **-c** [**-fnv**] [**-m** *machine*] [**-o** *options*] [**-t** *fstype*] *filesystem*
   installboot **-e** [**-fnv**] [**-m** *machine*] [**-o** *options*] *bootstrap*

DESCRIPTION
   The **installboot** utility installs and removes NetBSD disk bootstrap software into a file system.
   installboot can install *primary* into *filesystem*, or disable an existing bootstrap in
   filesystem.

   One some architectures the options of an existing installed bootstrap, or those of a bootstrap file can be
   changed.

   Generally, NetBSD disk bootstrap software consists of two parts: a "primary" bootstrap program usually written into the disklabel area of the file system by **installboot**, and a "secondary" bootstrap program that
   usually resides as an ordinary file in the file system.

   When booting, the primary bootstrap program is loaded and invoked by the machine's PROM or BIOS.
   After receiving control of the system it loads and runs the secondary bootstrap program, which in turn loads
   and runs the kernel. The secondary bootstrap may allow control over various boot parameters passed to the
   kernel.

   Perform the following steps to make a file system bootable:

   1.   Copy the secondary bootstrap (usually /usr/mdec/boot.**MACHINE** or /usr/mdec/boot) to
        the root directory of the target file system.

   2.   Use   **installboot**   to   install   the   primary   bootstrap   program   (usually
        /usr/mdec/boot**xx**_**FSTYPE**) into *filesystem*.

        The following platforms do not require this step if the primary bootstrap already exists and the sec-
        ondary bootstrap file is just being updated: **alpha**, **amd64**, **amiga**, **i386**, **pmax**, **sparc64**, and **vax**.

        The following platform does not require the first step since a single bootstrap file is used. The single
        bootstrap is installed like the primary bootstrap on other platforms: **next68k**.

   The options and arguments recognized by **installboot** are as follows:

   -B *s2bno*   When hard-coding the blocks of *secondary* into *primary*, start from block *s2bno*
                 instead of trying to determine the block numbers occupied by *secondary* by examining
                 filesystem. If this option is supplied, *secondary* should refer to an actual secondary
                 bootstrap (rather than the file name of the one present in *filesystem*) so that its size can
                 be determined.

   -b *s1bno*   Install *primary* at block number *s1bno* instead of the default location for the machine and
                 file system type. [**alpha**, **pmax**, **vax**]

   -c   Clear (remove) any existing bootstrap instead of installing one.

   -e   Edit the options of an existing bootstrap. This can be use to change the options in
                 bootxx_xxxfs files, raw disk partitions, and the pxeboot_ia32.bin file. [**amd64**, **i386**]

   -f   Forces **installboot** to ignore some errors.

-m *machine*

Use *machine* as the target machine type. The default machine is determined from uname(3) and then MACHINE. The following machines are currently supported by **installboot**:

alpha, amd64, amiga, ews4800mips, hp300, hp700, i386, landisk, macppc, news68k, newsmips, next68k, pmax, sparc, sparc64, sun2, sun3, vax, x68k

-n   Do not write to *filesystem*.

-o *options*

Machine specific **installboot** options, comma separated.

Supported options are (with the machines for they are valid in brackets):

alphasum   [**alpha**] Recalculate and restore the Alpha checksum. This is the default for NetBSD/alpha.

append   [**alpha**, **pmax**, **vax**] Append *primary* to the end of *filesystem*, which must be a regular file in this case.

command=<boot command>
          [**amiga**] Modify the default boot command line.

console=<console name>
          [**amd64**, **i386**] Set the console device, <console name> must be one of: pc, com0, com1, com2, com3, com0kbd, com1kbd, com2kbd or com3kbd.

ioaddr=<ioaddr>
          [**amd64**, **i386**] Set the IO address to be used for the console serial port. Defaults to the IO address used by the system BIOS for the specified port.

keymap=<keymap>
          [**amd64**, **i386**] Set a boot time keyboard translation map. Each character in <keymap> will be replaced by the one following it. For example, an argument of "zyz" would swap the lowercase letters 'y' and 'z'.

password=<password>
          [**amd64**, **i386**] Set the password which must be entered before the boot menu can be accessed.

resetvideo [**amd64**, **i386**] Reset the video before booting.

speed=<baud rate>
          [**amd64**, **i386**] Set the baud rate for the serial console. If a value of zero is specified, then the current baud rate (set by the BIOS) will be used.

sunsum   [**alpha**, **pmax**, **vax**] Recalculate and restore the Sun and NetBSD/sparc compatible checksum. *Note*: The existing NetBSD/sparc disklabel should use no more than 4 partitions.

timeout=<seconds>
          [**amd64**, **i386**] Set the timeout before the automatic boot begins to the given number of seconds.

modules   [**amd64**, **i386**] (Don't) load kernel modules.

                    bootconf   [**amd64**, **i386**] (Don't) read a "boot.cfg" file.

-t *fstype* Use *fstype* as the type of *filesystem*. The default operation is to attempt to auto-detect this setting. The following file system types are currently supported by **installboot**:

            ffs   BSD Fast File System.

            raid   Mirrored RAIDframe File System.

            raw   'Raw' image. Note: if a platform needs to hard-code the block offset of the secondary bootstrap, it cannot be searched for on this file system type, and must be provided with **-B** *s2bno*.

-v   Verbose operation.

filesystem The path name of the device or file system image that **installboot** is to operate on. It is not necessary for *filesystem* to be a currently mounted file system.

primary   The path name of the "primary" boot block to install. The path name must refer to a file in a file system that is currently mounted.

secondary The path name of the "secondary" boot block, relative to the root of the file system in the device or image specified by the *filesystem* argument. Note that this may refer to a file in a file system that is not mounted. Most systems require *secondary* to be in the "root" directory of the file system, so the leading "/" is not necessary on *secondary*.

            Only certain combinations of platform (**-m** *machine*) and file system type (**-t** *fstype*) require that the name of the secondary bootstrap is supplied as *secondary*, so that information such as the disk block numbers occupied by the secondary bootstrap can be stored in the primary bootstrap. These are:

Platform	File systems
macppc	ffs, raw
news68k	ffs, raw
newsmips	ffs, raw
sparc	ffs, raid, raw
sun2	ffs, raw
sun3	ffs, raw

installboot exits 0 on success, and >0 if an error occurs.

ENVIRONMENT

    installboot uses the following environment variables:

    MACHINE Default value for *machine*, overriding the result from uname(3).

FILES

    Most NetBSD ports will contain variations of the following files:

    /usr/mdec/bootxx_**FSTYPE** Primary bootstrap for file system type **FSTYPE**. Installed into the bootstrap area of the file system by **installboot**.

    /usr/mdec/bootxx_fat16   Primary bootstrap for MS-DOS **FAT16** file systems. This differs from **bootxx_msdos** in that it doesn't require the filesystem to have been initialised with any reserved sectors. It also uses the information in the Boot Parameter Block to get the media and filesytem properties.

`/usr/mdec/bootxx_ffsv1`	Primary bootstrap for **FFSv1** file systems (the "traditional" NetBSD file system). Use dumpfs(8) to confirm the file system format is **FFSv1**.
`/usr/mdec/bootxx_ffsv2`	Primary bootstrap for **FFSv2** file systems. Use dumpfs(8) to confirm the file system format is **FFSv2**.
`/usr/mdec/bootxx_lfsv1`	Primary bootstrap for **LFSv1** file systems.
`/usr/mdec/bootxx_lfsv2`	Primary bootstrap for **LFSv2** file systems (the default LFS version).
`/usr/mdec/bootxx_msdos`	Primary bootstrap for MS-DOS **FAT** file systems.
`/usr/mdec/bootxx_ustarfs`	Primary bootstrap for **TARFS** boot images. This is used by various install media.
`/usr/mdec/boot.`**MACHINE**	Secondary bootstrap for machine type **MACHINE**. This should be installed into the file system before **installboot** is run.
`/usr/mdec/boot`	Synonym for `/usr/mdec/boot.`**MACHINE**
`/boot.`**MACHINE**	Installed copy of secondary bootstrap for machine type **MACHINE**.
`/boot`	Installed copy of secondary bootstrap. Searched for by the primary bootstrap if `/boot.`**MACHINE** is not found.

NetBSD/macppc files

`/usr/mdec/bootxx`	NetBSD/macppc primary bootstrap.
`/usr/mdec/ofwboot`	NetBSD/macppc secondary bootstrap.
`/ofwboot`	Installed copy of NetBSD/macppc secondary bootstrap.

NetBSD/next68k files

`/usr/mdec/boot`	NetBSD/next68k bootstrap.

NetBSD/sparc64 files

`/usr/mdec/bootblk`	NetBSD/sparc64 primary bootstrap.
`/usr/mdec/ofwboot`	NetBSD/sparc64 secondary bootstrap.
`/ofwboot`	Installed copy of NetBSD/sparc64 secondary bootstrap.

EXAMPLES
common
Verbosely install the Berkeley Fast File System primary bootstrap on to disk 'sd0':

```
installboot -v /dev/rsd0c /usr/mdec/bootxx_ffs
```
Note: the "whole disk" partition (c on some ports, d on others) is used here, since the a partition probably is already opened (mounted as /), so **installboot** would not be able to access it.

Remove the primary bootstrap from disk 'sd1':

```
installboot -c /dev/rsd1c
```

NetBSD/amiga
Modify the command line to change the default from "netbsd -ASn2" to "netbsd -S":

```
installboot    -m    amiga    -o    command="netbsd    -S"    /dev/rsd0a
/usr/mdec/bootxx_ffs
```

NetBSD/ews4800mips

Install the System V Boot File System primary bootstrap on to disk 'sd0', with the secondary bootstrap '/boot' already present in the SysVBFS partition on the disk:

```
installboot /dev/rsd0c /usr/mdec/bootxx_bfs
```

NetBSD/i386 and NetBSD/amd64

Install new boot blocks on an existing mounted root file system on 'wd0', setting the timeout to five seconds, after copying a new secondary bootstrap:

```
cp /usr/mdec/boot /boot
installboot -v -o timeout=5 /dev/rwd0a /usr/mdec/bootxx_ffsv1
```

Create a bootable CD-ROM with an ISO9660 file system for an i386 system with a serial console:

```
mkdir cdrom
cp sys/arch/i386/compile/mykernel/netbsd cdrom/netbsd
cp /usr/mdec/boot cdrom/boot
cp /usr/mdec/bootxx_cd9660 bootxx
installboot -o console=com0,speed=19200 -m i386 -e bootxx
makefs -t cd9660 -o 'bootimage=i386;bootxx,no-emul-boot' boot.iso
      cdrom
```

Create a bootable floppy disk with an FFSv1 file system for a small custom kernel (note: bigger kernels needing multiple disks are handled with the ustarfs file system):

```
newfs -s 1440k /dev/rfd0a
```

Note: Ignore the warnings that newfs(8) displays; it can not write a disklabel, which is not a problem for a floppy disk.

```
mount /dev/fd0a /mnt
cp /usr/mdec/boot /mnt/boot
gzip -9 < sys/arch/i386/compile/mykernel/netbsd > /mnt/netbsd.gz
umount /mnt
installboot -v /dev/rfd0a /usr/mdec/bootxx_ffsv1
```

Create a bootable FAT file system on 'wd1a', which should have the same offset and size as a FAT primary partition in the Master Boot Record (MBR):

```
newfs_msdos -r 16 /dev/rwd1a
```

Notes: The -r 16 is to reserve space for the primary bootstrap. newfs_msdos(8) will display an "MBR type" such as '1', '4', or '6'; the MBR partition type of the appropriate primary partition should be changed to this value.

```
mount -t msdos /dev/wd1a /mnt
cp /usr/mdec/boot /mnt/boot
cp path/to/kernel /mnt/netbsd
umount /mnt
installboot -t raw /dev/rwd1a /usr/mdec/bootxx_msdos
```

Make the existing FAT16 filesystem on 'sd0e' bootable. This can be used to make USB memory bootable provided it has 512 byte sectors and that the manufacturer correctly initialised the file system.

```
mount -t msdos /dev/sd0e /mnt
cp /usr/mdec/boot /mnt/boot
cp path/to/kernel /mnt/netbsd
umount /mnt
installboot /dev/rsd0e /usr/mdec/bootxx_fat16
```

It may also be necessary to use **fdisk** to make the device itself bootable.

Switch the existing installed bootstrap to use a serial console without reinstalling or altering other options such as timeout.

```
installboot -e -o console=com0 /dev/rwd0a
```

NetBSD/macppc

Note the **installboot** utility is only required for macppc machines with OpenFirmware version 2 to boot. OpenFirmware 3 cannot load bootblocks specified in the Apple partition map.

Install the Berkeley Fast File System primary bootstrap on to disk 'wd0':
```
installboot /dev/rwd0c /usr/mdec/bootxx /ofwboot
```

The secondary NetBSD/macppc bootstrap is located in /usr/mdec/ofwboot.

The primary bootstrap requires the raw ofwboot for the secondary bootstrap, not ofwboot.xcf, which is used for the OpenFirmware to load kernels.

NetBSD/next68k

Install the bootstrap on to disk 'sd0':
```
installboot /dev/rsd0c /usr/mdec/boot
```

NetBSD/pmax

Install the Berkeley Fast File System primary bootstrap on to disk 'sd0':
```
installboot /dev/rsd0c /usr/mdec/bootxx_ffs
```

NetBSD/pmax requires that this file system starts at block 0 of the disk.

Install the ISO 9660 primary bootstrap in the file /tmp/cd-image:
```
installboot -m pmax /tmp/cd-image /usr/mdec/bootxx_cd9660
```

Make an ISO 9660 filesystem in the file /tmp/cd-image and install the ISO 9660 primary bootstrap in the filesystem, where the source directory for the ISO 9660 filesystem contains a kernel, the primary bootstrap bootxx_cd9660 and the secondary bootstrap boot.pmax:
```
mkisofs -o /tmp/cd-image -a -l -v iso-source-dir
. . .
48 51 iso-source-dir/bootxx_cd9660
. . .
installboot -b `expr 48 \* 4` /tmp/cd-image /usr/mdec/bootxx_cd9660
```

NetBSD/sparc

Install the Berkeley Fast File System primary bootstrap on to disk 'sd0', with the secondary bootstrap '/boot' already present:
```
installboot /dev/rsd0c /usr/mdec/bootxx /boot
```

NetBSD/sparc64

Install the Berkeley Fast File System primary bootstrap on to disk 'wd0':
```
installboot /dev/rwd0c /usr/mdec/bootblk
```

The secondary NetBSD/sparc64 bootstrap is located in /usr/mdec/ofwboot.

NetBSD/sun2 and NetBSD/sun3

Install the Berkeley Fast File System primary bootstrap on to disk 'sd0', with the secondary bootstrap '/boot' already present:
```
installboot /dev/rsd0c /usr/mdec/bootxx /boot
```

SEE ALSO

uname(3), boot(8), disklabel(8), dumpfs(8), fdisk(8), pxeboot(8)

HISTORY

This implementation of **installboot** appeared in NetBSD 1.6.

AUTHORS

The machine independent portion of this implementation of **installboot** was written by Luke Mewburn. The following people contributed to the various machine dependent back-ends: Simon Burge (pmax), Chris Demetriou (alpha), Matthew Fredette (sun2, sun3), Matthew Green (sparc64), Ross Harvey (alpha), Michael Hitch (amiga), Paul Kranenburg (sparc), David Laight (i386), Christian Limpach (next68k), Luke Mewburn (macppc), Matt Thomas (vax), Izumi Tsutsui (news68k, newsmips), and UCHIYAMA Yasushi (ews4800mips).

BUGS

There are not currently primary bootstraps to support all file systems types which are capable of being the root file system.

If a disk has been converted from **FFS** to **RAID** without the contents of the disk erased, then the original **FFS** installation may be auto-detected instead of the **RAID** installation. In this case, the **-t** *raid* option must be provided.

NetBSD/alpha

The NetBSD/alpha primary bootstrap program can only load the secondary bootstrap program from file systems starting at the beginning (block 0) of disks. Similarly, the secondary bootstrap program can only load kernels from file systems starting at the beginning of disks.

The size of primary bootstrap programs is restricted to 7.5KB, even though some file systems (e.g., ISO 9660) are able to accommodate larger ones.

NetBSD/hp300

The disk must have a boot partition large enough to hold the bootstrap code. Currently the primary bootstrap must be a **LIF** format file.

NetBSD/i386 and NetBSD/amd64

The bootstrap must be installed in the NetBSD partition that starts at the beginning of the mbr partition. If that is a valid filesystem and contains the /boot program then it will be used as the root filesystem, otherwise the 'a' partition will be booted.

The size of primary bootstrap programs is restricted to 8KB, even though some file systems (e.g., ISO 9660) are able to accommodate larger ones.

NetBSD/macppc

Due to restrictions in **installboot** and the secondary bootstrap implementation, file systems where kernels exist must start at the beginning of disks.

Currently, **installboot** doesn't recognize an existing Apple partition map on the disk and always writes a faked map to make disks bootable.

The NetBSD/macppc bootstrap program can't load kernels from **FFSv2** partitions.

NetBSD/next68k

The size of bootstrap programs is restricted to the free space before the file system at the beginning of the disk minus 8KB.

NetBSD/pmax

    The NetBSD/pmax secondary bootstrap program can only load kernels from file systems starting at the beginning of disks.

    The size of primary bootstrap programs is restricted to 7.5KB, even though some file systems (e.g., ISO 9660) are able to accommodate larger ones.

NetBSD/sun2 and NetBSD/sun3

    The NetBSD/sun2 and NetBSD/sun3 secondary bootstrap program can only load kernels from file systems starting at the beginning of disks.

NetBSD/vax

    The NetBSD/vax secondary bootstrap program can only load kernels from file systems starting at the beginning of disks.

    The size of primary bootstrap programs is restricted to 7.5KB, even though some file systems (e.g., ISO 9660) are able to accommodate larger ones.

NAME

installboot — install a bootstrap on an FFS filesystem partition

SYNOPSIS

/usr/mdec/installboot [-l *newcommandline*] *bootblock device*

DESCRIPTION

installboot copies the bootblock to a bootable partition. The bootstrap is written into the bootblock area on the partition, right in front of the superblock, and hence limited in size to 8192 bytes.

The bootstrap resides in the first few blocks on the partition (as specified by Commodore-Amiga Inc.) The bootstrap is loaded into memory by the ROM from bootable devices: RDB devices, where the partition is marked as bootable, or (not on the DraCo) floppy disks in Amiga format (880K/1760k).

In the presence of more than one bootable partition/floppy disk, the partition is chosen by the bootpriority (from the RDB), which can be overridden by the operator from the boot menu (on Amiga machines, hold down the outer mouse buttons during boot; on DraCo machines, press the left mouse button when prompted).

On RDB devices, the whole bootblock is loaded by the ROM. The number of boot blocks in the RDB partition entry must be correct.

On floppy disks, the ROM always loads the first two blocks (1024 bytes), and the bootblock allocates memory and loads the whole bootblock on startup.

After receiving control, the bootblock uses the stand-alone filesystem code in "libsa.a" to load the kernel from the filesystem on the partition it was started from. The code for the boot program can be found in /usr/mdec/bootxx_fd (floppy disk code) or /usr/mdec/bootxx_ffs (generic RDB disk code).

The arguments are:

-l *newcommandline*
          Specify a different command line to replace the default.

bootblock The file containing the bootblock (normally /usr/mdec/bootxx_ffs for RDB devices).

device   The name of the character special device specifying the partition on which the bootstrap is to be installed.

EXAMPLES

The following command will install the boot program in the bootblock area on "sd0a":

          installboot /usr/mdec/bootxx_ffs /dev/rsd0a

SEE ALSO

dd(1), boot(8)

HISTORY

The installboot command first appeared in NetBSD 1.3.

BUGS

If installboot is accidentally used on the whole disk partition, the RDB will be overwritten, making your system unusable after the next reboot.

Some third-party accelerator boards are not autoconfiguring. You won't be able to use their memory when booting from the bootblock after a cold start.

Some third-party disk controllers don't support bootblock booting.

DraCo ROMs don't support bootblock booting from floppy disks.

Most 68060 boards, unlike the DraCo, don't set the SysBase->AttnFlags bit for the 68060 CPU (a patch program which is called during AmigaOS startup does this). You need to add options BB060STUPIDROM to your kernel to boot on such a machine.

There is currently no easy way to edit the RDB from within NetBSD. Therefore, you have to use HDTOOL-BOX or a similar tool to set the partition to bootable, "use custom bootblocks" and the number of bootblocks to 16 (for bootxx_ffs) or 2 (for bootxx_fd), at least the first time you install the bootblock.

As normal dd is used to install the bootblock, you can only install onto your currently used root (or any other mounted) partition from single-user mode, or while otherwise running in insecure mode.

NAME
    installboot — install a bootstrap on an FFS filesystem partition

SYNOPSIS
    /usr/mdec/installboot [**–Nmtuv**] *device*

DESCRIPTION
    installboot prepares the (physically) first partition on a device for boot-strapping from the TOS-ROM. The bootstrap is written into the bootblock area on the partition, right in front of the disk pack label, and hence limited in size to LABELOFFSET bytes. A disk pack label should be created (see disklabel(8)) before installing the bootstrap.

    The bootstrap is split into three parts: a small first-stage program that resides in the (physically) first 512 bytes on the device (as specified by Atari Corp.), a second-stage program that immediately follows the first-stage program, and a third-stage program that resides on the root filesystem. The first-stage program is loaded into memory by the ROM. After receiving control, it loads the second-stage program and the disk label. The second-stage boot program uses the stand-alone filesystem code in "libsa.a" to load the third-stage boot program from the root-filesystem on the device. The third-stage boot program then loads the kernel. The prototype code for the first-stage boot program can be found in /usr/mdec/std/fdboot (floppy disk code), /usr/mdec/std/sdboot (SCSI disk code) and /usr/mdec/std/wdboot (IDE disk code). The second-stage boot program is stored in /usr/mdec/std/bootxx. and the third-stage boot program is stored in /usr/mdec/std/boot.atari. The boot code for Milan machines is different from the other machines and the files for the Milan can be found in the directory /usr/mdec/milan. Note that the Milan uses the SCSI disk code for both SCSI and IDE disks.

    For backwards compatibility with the vendor specific AHDI disk label, a special first-stage boot program is provided in /usr/mdec/std/xxboot.ahdi. Together with the general second-stage boot program, it is installed in the AHDI partition where the NetBSD disk label lives. Furthermore, the AHDI specifications require an additional bootstrap, which is written into the AHDI root sector (disk block zero). The prototype code for this AHDI compliant bootstrap can be found in /usr/mdec/std/sdb00t.ahdi and /usr/mdec/std/wdb00t.ahdi, or the equivalents in /usr/mdec/milan.

    Perform the following steps to make a file system bootable:

1. Copy the secondary bootstrap (either /usr/mdec/std/boot.atari or /usr/mdec/milan/boot.atari) to the root directory of the target file system.

2. Use **installboot** to install the primary and secondary bootstrap programs (from /usr/mdec/std or /usr/mdec/milan) into the *filesystem*.

    The options are as follows:

    –N   Do not actually write anything on the disk.

    –m   Use Milan boot code.

    –t   Number of tracks per cylinder (IDE disk).

    –u   Number of sectors per track (IDE disk).

    –v   Verbose mode.

    The arguments are:

    device The name of the device on which the bootstrap is to be installed.

EXAMPLES
>   The following command will install the first-stage and second-stage boot programs in the bootblock area on
>   "sd0c":

>   installboot sd0

SEE ALSO
>   bootpref(8), disklabel(8)

HISTORY
>   The **installboot** command first appeared in NetBSD 1.1

BUGS
>   **installboot** knows too much about kernel internal details, forcing it to check the running kernel's
>   release and revision.
>
>   Because neither the floppy disk driver nor disklabel(8) are capable of creating a disk pack label on a
>   floppy disk, **installboot** has to create a fictitious label, that is not used by the kernel.
>
>   Except for installation of the bootcode on floppy, **installboot** automatically sets the boot preference in
>   NVRAM to NetBSD.

NAME
   installboot — install a bootstrap on a UFS disk

SYNOPSIS
   /usr/mdec/installboot -n | **-v** *ufsboot bootxx rawdev*

DESCRIPTION
   installboot is used to install a "first-stage" boot program into the boot area of a UFS disk partition, and initialize the table of block numbers the *bootxx* program uses to load the second-stage boot program.

   The options are as follows:

   -n   Do not actually write anything on the disk.

   -v   Be verbose, printing out the block numbers that *bootxx* will use to load *ufsboot*.

   The arguments are:

   ufsboot   the name of the second-stage boot program in the file system where the first-stage boot program is to be installed.

   bootxx   the name of the prototype file for the first stage boot program.

   rawdev   the name of the raw device in which the first-stage boot program is to be installed. This should correspond to the block device on which the file system containing *ufsboot* is mounted.

SEE ALSO
   disklabel(8), init(8)

BUGS
   installboot requires simultaneous access to the mounted file system and the raw device, but that is not allowed with the kernel securelevel variable set to a value greater than zero (the default), so **installboot** only works in single-user mode (or insecure mode - see init(8)).

NAME

iopctl — a program to control IOP devices

SYNOPSIS

iopctl [**-f** *ctldev*] *command* [*tid*]

DESCRIPTION

The **iopctl** command can be used to interrogate and control I2O devices.

The following options are available:

-f *ctldev*   Specify the control device to use. The default is /dev/iop0.

The following commands are available:

reconfig   Reconfigure the IOP: ask all bus ports to rescan their busses, and attach or detach devices to and from the system as necessary.

showddmid *tid*
Retrieve and display the DDM (device driver module) identity parameter group from the specified target.

showdevid *tid*
Retrieve and display the device identity parameter group from the specified target.

showlct   Display the driver's private copy of the logical configuration table. This copy of the LCT matches the current device configuration, but is not necessarily the latest available version of the LCT.

showstatus
Display the current status of the IOP.

showtidmap
Display the device to TID map.

FILES

/dev/iop*u* control device for IOP unit *u*

SEE ALSO

ioctl(2), iop(4), iopsp(4), ld(4)

The sysutils/i2ocfg package.

HISTORY

The **iopctl** command first appeared in NetBSD 1.5.3.

NAME

    iostat — report I/O statistics

SYNOPSIS

    iostat [**-CdDITx**] [**-c** *count*] [**-M** *core*] [**-N** *system*] [**-w** *wait*] [*drives*]

DESCRIPTION

    iostat displays kernel I/O statistics on terminal, disk and CPU operations. By default, **iostat** displays one line of statistics averaged over the machine's run time. The use of **-c** presents successive lines averaged over the *wait* period. The **-I** option causes **iostat** to print raw, unaveraged values.

    Only the last disk option specified (**-d**, **-D**, or **-x**) is used.

    The options are as follows:

-c *count*	Repeat the display *count* times. Unless the **-I** flag is in effect, the first display is for the time since a reboot and each subsequent report is for the time period since the last display. If no *wait* interval is specified, the default is 1 second.
-C	Show CPU statistics. This is enabled by default unless the **-d**, **-D**, **-T**, or **-x** flags are used.
-d	Show disk statistics. This is the default. Displays kilobytes per transfer, number of transfers, and megabytes transferred. Use of this flag disables display of CPU and tty statistics.
-D	Show alternative disk statistics. Displays kilobytes transferred, number of transfers, and time spent in transfers. Use of this flag disables the default display.
-I	Show the running total values, rather than an average.
-M *core*	Extract values associated with the name list from the specified core instead of the default "/dev/mem".
-N *system*	Extract the name list from the specified system instead of the default "/netbsd".
-T	Show tty statistics. This is enabled by default unless the **-C**, **-d**, or **-D** flags are used.
-w *wait*	Pause *wait* seconds between each display. If no repeat *count* is specified, the default is infinity.
-x	Show extended disk statistics. Each disk is displayed on a line of its own with all available statistics. This option overrides all other display options, and all disks are displayed unless specific disks are provided as arguments. Additionally, separate read and write statistics are displayed.

    iostat displays its information in the following format:

tty

tin	characters read from terminals
tout	characters written to terminals

disks Disk operations. The header of the field is the disk name and unit number. If more than four disk drives are configured in the system, **iostat** displays only the first four drives. To force **iostat** to display specific drives, their names may be supplied on the command line.

KB/t	Kilobytes transferred per disk transfer
t/s	transfers per second

        MB/s   Megabytes transferred per second

        The alternative display format, (selected with **−D**), presents the following values.
        KB   Kilobytes transferred
        xfr   Disk transfers
        time   Seconds spent in disk activity

  cpu
        us   % of CPU time in user mode
        ni   % of CPU time in user mode running niced processes
        sy   % of CPU time in system mode
        id   % of CPU time in idle mode

FILES
    `/netbsd` Default kernel namelist.
    `/dev/mem` Default memory file.

SEE ALSO
    `fstat`(1), `netstat`(1), `nfsstat`(1), `ps`(1), `systat`(1), `vmstat`(1), `pstat`(8)

    The sections starting with "Interpreting system activity" in *Installing and Operating 4.3BSD*.

HISTORY
    iostat appeared in Version 6 AT&T UNIX. The **−x** option was added in NetBSD 1.4.

NAME
ipf – alters packet filtering lists for IP packet input and output

SYNOPSIS
ipf [**–6AcdDEInoPrsvVyzZ**] [**–l** <block|pass|nomatch>] [**–T** <optionlist>] [**–F** <i|o|a|s|S>] **–f** <*file-name*> [**–f** <*filename*> [...]]

DESCRIPTION
ipf opens the filenames listed (treating "–" as stdin) and parses the file for a set of rules which are to be added or removed from the packet filter rule set.

Each rule processed by **ipf** is added to the kernel's internal lists if there are no parsing problems. Rules are added to the end of the internal lists, matching the order in which they appear when given to **ipf**.

OPTIONS

–6   This option is required to parse IPv6 rules and to have them loaded.

–A   Set the list to make changes to the active list (default).

–c <language>
             This option causes **ipf** to generate output files for a compiler that supports **language**. *At present, the only target language supported is* **C (-cc) for which two files - ip_rules.c and ip_rules.h are generated in the CURRENT DIRECTORY when ipf is being run. These files can be used with the IPFILTER_COMPILED kernel option to build filter rules staticly into the kernel.**

–d   Turn debug mode on. Causes a hexdump of filter rules to be generated as it processes each one.

–D   Disable the filter (if enabled). Not effective for loadable kernel versions.

–E   Enable the filter (if disabled). Not effective for loadable kernel versions.

–F <i|o|a>
             This option specifies which filter list to flush. The parameter should either be "i" (input), "o" (output) or "a" (remove all filter rules). Either a single letter or an entire word starting with the appropriate letter maybe used. This option maybe before, or after, any other with the order on the command line being that used to execute options.

–F <s|S>
             To flush entries from the state table, the **-F** option is used in conjunction with either "s" (removes state information about any non-fully established connections) or "S" (deletes the entire state table). Only one of the two options may be given. A fully established connection will show up in **ipfstat -s** output as 5/5, with deviations either way indicating it is not fully established any more.

–F<5|6|7|8|9|10|11>
             For the TCP states that represent the closing of a connection has begun, be it only one side or the complete connection, it is possible to flush those states directly using the number corresponding to that state. The numbers relate to the states as follows: 5 = close-wait, 6 = fin-wait-1, 7 = closing, 8 = last-ack, 9 = fin-wait-2, 10 = time-wait, 11 = closed.

–F<number>
             If the argument supplied to **-F** is greater than 30, then state table entries that have been idle for more than this many seconds will be flushed.

–f <filename>
             This option specifies which files **ipf** should use to get input from for modifying the packet filter rule lists.

–I   Set the list to make changes to the inactive list.

–l <pass|block|nomatch>
             Use of the **-l** flag toggles default logging of packets. Valid arguments to this option are **pass**, **block** and **nomatch**. When an option is set, any packet which exits filtering and matches the set category is logged. This is most useful for causing all packets which don't match any of the loaded rules to be logged.

    −n   This flag (no-change) prevents **ipf** from actually making any ioctl calls or doing anything which would alter the currently running kernel.

    −o   Force rules by default to be added/deleted to/from the output list, rather than the (default) input list.

    −P   Add rules as temporary entries in the authentication rule table.

    −r   Remove matching filter rules rather than add them to the internal lists

    −s   Swap the active filter list in use to be the "other" one.

    −T <optionlist>

            This option allows run-time changing of IPFilter kernel variables. Some variables require IPFilter to be in a disabled state (**-D**) for changing, others do not. The optionlist parameter is a comma separated list of tuning commands. A tuning command is either "list" (retrieve a list of all variables in the kernel, their maximum, minimum and current value), a single variable name (retrieve its current value) and a variable name with a following assignment to set a new value. Some examples follow.

            # Print out all IPFilter kernel tunable parameters
            ipf -T list
            # Display the current TCP idle timeout and then set it to 3600
            ipf -D -T fr_tcpidletimeout,fr_tcpidletimeout=3600 -E
            # Display current values for fr_pass and fr_chksrc, then set fr_chksrc to 1.
            ipf -T fr_pass,fr_chksrc,fr_chksrc=1

    −v   Turn verbose mode on. Displays information relating to rule processing.

    −V   Show version information. This will display the version information compiled into the ipf binary and retrieve it from the kernel code (if running/present). If it is present in the kernel, information about its current state will be displayed (whether logging is active, default filtering, etc).

    −y   Manually resync the in-kernel interface list maintained by IP Filter with the current interface status list.

    −z   For each rule in the input file, reset the statistics for it to zero and display the statistics prior to them being zeroed.

    −Z   Zero global statistics held in the kernel for filtering only (this doesn't affect fragment or state statistics).

FILES
    /dev/ipauth
    /dev/ipl
    /dev/ipstate

# SEE ALSO
    ipftest(1), mkfilters(1), ipf(4), ipl(4), ipf(5), ipf.conf(5), ipf6.conf(5), ipfstat(8), ipmon(8), ipnat(8)

DIAGNOSTICS
    Needs to be run as root for the packet filtering lists to actually be affected inside the kernel.

BUGS
    If you find any, please send email to me at darrenr@pobox.com

NAME
ipfs – saves and restores information for NAT and state tables.

SYNOPSIS
ipfs [-nv] -l

ipfs [-nv] -u

ipfs [-nv] [**–d** *<dirname>*] -R

ipfs [-nv] [**–d** *<dirname>*] -W

ipfs [-nNSv] [**–f** *<filename>*] -r

ipfs [-nNSv] [**–f** *<filename>*] -w

ipfs [-nNSv] **–f** *<filename>* **–i** <if1>,<if2>

DESCRIPTION
ipfs allows state information created for NAT entries and rules using *keep state* to be locked (modification prevented) and then saved to disk, allowing for the system to experience a reboot, followed by the restoration of that information, resulting in connections not being interrupted.

OPTIONS
–d   Change the default directory used with **–R** and **–W** options for saving state information.

–n   Don't actually take any action that would affect information stored in the kernel or on disk.

–v   Provides a verbose description of what's being done.

–i <ifname1>,<ifname2>
Change all instances of interface name ifname1 in the state save file to ifname2. Useful if you're restoring state information after a hardware reconfiguration or change.

–N   Operate on NAT information.

–S   Operate on filtering state information.

–u   Unlock state tables in the kernel.

–l   Lock state tables in the kernel.

–r   Read information in from the specified file and load it into the kernel. This requires the state tables to have already been locked and does not change the lock once complete.

–w   Write information out to the specified file and from the kernel. This requires the state tables to have already been locked and does not change the lock once complete.

–R   Restores all saved state information, if any, from two files, *ipstate.ipf* and *ipnat.ipf*, stored in the */var/db/ipf* directory unless otherwise specified by the **–d** option. The state tables are locked at the beginning of this operation and unlocked once complete.

–W   Saves in-kernel state information, if any, out to two files, *ipstate.ipf* and *ipnat.ipf*, stored in the */var/db/ipf* directory unless otherwise specified by the **–d** option. The state tables are locked at the beginning of this operation and unlocked once complete.

FILES
/var/db/ipf/ipstate.ipf
/var/db/ipf/ipnat.ipf
/dev/ipl
/dev/ipstate
/dev/ipnat

SEE ALSO
ipf(8), ipl(4), ipmon(8), ipnat(8)

DIAGNOSTICS

Perhaps the -W and -R operations should set the locking but rather than undo it, restore it to what it was previously. Fragment table information is currently not saved.

BUGS

If you find any, please send email to me at darrenr@pobox.com

NAME
ipfstat – reports on packet filter statistics and filter list

SYNOPSIS
ipfstat [**–6aAdfghIilnoRsv**]

ipfstat -t [**–6C**] [**–D** <addrport>] [**–P** <protocol>] [**–S** <addrport>] [**–T** <refresh time>]

DESCRIPTION
ipfstat examines /dev/kmem using the symbols **_fr_flags**, **_frstats**, **_filterin**, and **_filterout**. To run and work, it needs to be able to read both /dev/kmem and the kernel itself. The kernel name defaults to **/netbsd**.

The default behaviour of **ipfstat** is to retrieve and display the accumulated statistics which have been accumulated over time as the kernel has put packets through the filter.

OPTIONS

–6   Display filter lists and states for IPv6, if available.

–a   Display the accounting filter list and show bytes counted against each rule.

–A   Display packet authentication statistics.

–C   This option is only valid in combination with **–t**. Display "closed" states as well in the top. Normally, a TCP connection is not displayed when it reaches the CLOSE_WAIT protocol state. With this option enabled, all state entries are displayed.

–d   Produce debugging output when displaying data.

–D <addrport>
          This option is only valid in combination with **–t**. Limit the state top display to show only state entries whose destination IP address and port match the addrport argument. The addrport specification is of the form ipaddress[,port]. The ipaddress and port should be either numerical or the string "any" (specifying any IP address resp. any port). If the **–D** option is not specified, it defaults to "**–D** any,any".

–f   Show fragment state information (statistics) and held state information (in the kernel) if any is present.

–g   Show groups currently configured (both active and inactive).

–h   Show per-rule the number of times each one scores a "hit". For use in combination with **–i**.

–i   Display the filter list used for the input side of the kernel IP processing.

–I   Swap between retrieving "inactive"/"active" filter list details. For use in combination with **–i**.

–n   Show the "rule number" for each rule as it is printed.

–o   Display the filter list used for the output side of the kernel IP processing.

–P <protocol>
          This option is only valid in combination with **–t**. Limit the state top display to show only state entries that match a specific protocol. The argument can be a protocol name (as defined in **/etc/protocols**) or a protocol number. If this option is not specified, state entries for any protocol are specified.

–R   Don't try to resolve addresses to hostnames and ports to services while printing statistics.

–s   Show packet/flow state information (statistics only).

–sl   Show held state information (in the kernel) if any is present (no statistics).

–S <addrport>
          This option is only valid in combination with **–t**. Limit the state top display to show only state entries whose source IP address and port match the addrport argument. The addrport specification is of the form ipaddress[,port]. The ipaddress and port should be either numerical or the string "any" (specifying any IP address resp. any port). If the **–S** option is not specified, it defaults to "**–S** any,any".

> **−t**   Show the state table in a way similar to the way **top(1)** shows the process table. States can be sorted using a number of different ways. This option requires **curses(3)** and needs to be compiled in. It may not be available on all operating systems. See below, for more information on the keys that can be used while ipfstat is in top mode.

> **−T** <refreshtime>
> This option is only valid in combination with **−t**. Specifies how often the state top display should be updated. The refresh time is the number of seconds between an update. Any positive integer can be used. The default (and minimal update time) is 1.

> **−v**   Turn verbose mode on. Displays more debugging information. When used with either **-i** or **-o**, counters associated with the rule, such as the number of times it has been matched and the number of bytes from such packets is displayed. For "keep state" rules, a count of the number of state sessions active against the rule is also displayed.

SYNOPSIS

The role of **ipfstat** is to display current kernel statistics gathered as a result of applying the filters in place (if any) to packets going in and out of the kernel. This is the default operation when no command line parameters are present.

When supplied with either **−i** or **−o**, it will retrieve and display the appropriate list of filter rules currently installed and in use by the kernel.

One of the statistics that **ipfstat** shows is **ticks**. This number indicates how long the filter has been enabled. The number is incremented every half−second.

STATE TOP

Using the **−t** option **ipfstat** will enter the state top mode. In this mode the state table is displayed similar to the way **top** displays the process table. The **−C**, **−D**, **−P**, **−S** and **−T** command line options can be used to restrict the state entries that will be shown and to specify the frequency of display updates.

In state top mode, the following keys can be used to influence the displayed information:

b show packets/bytes from backward direction.

f show packets/bytes from forward direction. (default)

l redraw the screen.

q quit the program.

s switch between different sorting criterion.

r reverse the sorting criterion.

States can be sorted by protocol number, by number of IP packets, by number of bytes and by time-to-live of the state entry. The default is to sort by the number of bytes. States are sorted in descending order, but you can use the **r** key to sort them in ascending order.

STATE TOP LIMITATIONS

It is currently not possible to interactively change the source, destination and protocol filters or the refresh frequency. This must be done from the command line.

The screen must have at least 80 columns. This is however not checked. When running state top in IPv6 mode, the screen must be much wider to display the very long IPv6 addresses.

Only the first X-5 entries that match the sort and filter criteria are displayed (where X is the number of rows on the display. The only way to see more entries is to resize the screen.

FILES

/dev/kmem
/dev/ipl
/dev/ipstate
/netbsd

ipfstat(8)   ipfstat(8)

SEE ALSO
        ipf(8)

BUGS
        none known.

NAME
ipftest – test packet filter rules with arbitrary input.

SYNOPSIS
ipftest [**–6bCdDoRvx**] [**–F** input-format] [**–i** <filename>] [**–I** interface] [**–l** <filename>] [**–N** <file-name>] [**–P** <filename>] [**–r** <filename>] [**–S** <ip_address>] [**–T** <optionlist>]

DESCRIPTION
ipftest is provided for the purpose of being able to test a set of filter rules without having to put them in place, in operation and proceed to test their effectiveness. The hope is that this minimises disruptions in providing a secure IP environment.

ipftest will parse any standard ruleset for use with **ipf**, **ipnat** and/or **ippool** and apply input, returning output as to the result. However, **ipftest** will return one of three values for packets passed through the filter: pass, block or nomatch. This is intended to give the operator a better idea of what is happening with packets passing through their filter ruleset.

At least one of **–N**, **-P** or **–r** must be specified.

OPTIONS
–6 Use IPv6.

–b Cause the output to be a brief summary (one-word) of the result of passing the packet through the filter; either "pass", "block" or "nomatch". This is used in the regression testing.

–C Force the checksums to be (re)calculated for all packets being input into **ipftest**. This may be necessary if pcap files from tcpdump are being fed in where there are partial checksums present due to hardware offloading.

–d Turn on filter rule debugging. Currently, this only shows you what caused the rule to not match in the IP header checking (addresses/netmasks, etc).

–D Dump internal tables before exiting. This excludes log messages.

–F This option is used to select which input format the input file is in. The following formats are available: etherfind, hex, pcap, snoop, tcpdump,text.

    etherfind
      The input file is to be text output from etherfind. The text formats which are currently supported are those which result from the following etherfind option combinations:

        etherfind -n
        etherfind -n -t

    hex The input file is to be hex digits, representing the binary makeup of the packet. No length correction is made, if an incorrect length is put in the IP header. A packet may be broken up over several lines of hex digits, a blank line indicating the end of the packet. It is possible to specify both the interface name and direction of the packet (for filtering purposes) at the start of the line using this format: [direction,interface] To define a packet going in on le0, we would use **[in,le0]** - the []'s are required and part of the input syntax.

    pcap The input file specified by **–i** is a binary file produced using libpcap (i.e., tcpdump version 3). Packets are read from this file as being input (for rule purposes). An interface maybe specified using **–I**.

    snoop The input file is to be in "snoop" format (see RFC 1761). Packets are read from this file and used as input from any interface. This is perhaps the most useful input type, currently.

    tcpdump
      The input file is to be text output from tcpdump. The text formats which are currently supported are those which result from the following tcpdump option combinations:

        tcpdump -n
        tcpdump -nq

```
                              tcpdump -nqt
                              tcpdump -nqtt
                              tcpdump -nqte
```

    text   The input file is in **ipftest** text input format. This is the default if no **−F** argument is specified. The format used is as follows:

          "in"|"out" "on" if ["tcp"|"udp"|"icmp"]
              srchost[,srcport] dsthost[,destport] [FSRPAU]

This allows for a packet going "in" or "out" of an interface (if) to be generated, being one of the three main protocols (optionally), and if either TCP or UDP, a port parameter is also expected. If TCP is selected, it is possible to (optionally) supply TCP flags at the end. Some examples are:

      # a UDP packet coming in on le0
      in on le0 udp 10.1.1.1,2210 10.2.1.5,23
      # an IP packet coming in on le0 from localhost - hmm :)
      in on le0 localhost 10.4.12.1
      # a TCP packet going out of le0 with the SYN flag set.
      out on le0 tcp 10.4.12.1,2245 10.1.1.1,23 S

−i <filename>
    Specify the filename from which to take input. Default is stdin.

−I <interface>
    Set the interface name (used in rule matching) to be the name supplied. This is useful where it is not otherwise possible to associate a packet with an interface. Normal "text packets" can override this setting.

−l <filename>
    Dump log messages generated during testing to the specified file.

−N <filename>
    Specify the filename from which to read NAT rules in **ipnat**(5) format.

−o   Save output packets that would have been written to each interface in a file /tmp/*interface_name* in raw format.

−P <filename>
    Read IP pool configuration information in **ippool**(5) format from the specified file.

−r <filename>
    Specify the filename from which to read filter rules in **ipf**(5) format.

−R   Don't attempt to convert IP addresses to hostnames.

−S <ip_address>
    The IP address specifived with this option is used by ipftest to determine whether a packet should be treated as "input" or "output". If the source address in an IP packet matches then it is considered to be inbound. If it does not match then it is considered to be outbound. This is primarily for use with tcpdump (pcap) files where there is no in/out information saved with each packet.

−T <optionlist>
    This option simulates the run-time changing of IPFilter kernel variables available with the **−T** option of **ipf**. The optionlist parameter is a comma separated list of tuning commands. A tuning command is either "list" (retrieve a list of all variables in the kernel, their maximum, minimum and current value), a single variable name (retrieve its current value) and a variable name with a following assignment to set a new value. See **ipf**(8) for examples.

−v   Verbose mode. This provides more information about which parts of rule matching the input packet passes and fails.

−x   Print a hex dump of each packet before printing the decoded contents.

SEE ALSO

ipf(5), ipf(8), tcpdump(8),

BUGS

Not all of the input formats are sufficiently capable of introducing a wide enough variety of packets for them to be all useful in testing.

NAME

ipmon – monitors /dev/ipl for logged packets

SYNOPSIS

ipmon [–abBDFhnpstvxX] [–N <device>] [–L <facility>] [–o [NSI]] [–O [NSI]] [–P <pidfile>]
[–S <device>] [–f <device>] [<filename>]

DESCRIPTION

ipmon opens **/dev/ipl** for reading and awaits data to be saved from the packet filter. The binary data read from the device is reprinted in human readable for, however, IP#'s are not mapped back to hostnames, nor are ports mapped back to service names. The output goes to standard output by default or a filename, if given on the command line. Should the –s option be used, output is instead sent to **syslogd(8)**. Messages sent via syslog have the day, month and year removed from the message, but the time (including microseconds), as recorded in the log, is still included.

Messages generated by ipmon consist of whitespace separated fields. Fields common to all messages are:

1. The date of packet receipt. This is suppressed when the message is sent to syslog.

2. The time of packet receipt. This is in the form HH:MM:SS.F, for hours, minutes seconds, and fractions of a second (which can be several digits long).

3. The name of the interface the packet was processed on, e.g., **we1**.

4. The group and rule number of the rule, e.g., **@0:17**. These can be viewed with **ipfstat -n**.

5. The action: **p** for passed, **b** for blocked, for a short packet, **n** did not match any rules or **L** for a log rule.

6. The addresses. This is actually three fields: the source address and port (separated by a comma), the **->** symbol, and the destination address and port. E.g.: **209.53.17.22,80 -> 198.73.220.17,1722**.

7. **PR** followed by the protocol name or number, e.g., **PR tcp**.

8. **len** followed by the header length and total length of the packet, e.g., **len 20 40**.

If the packet is a TCP packet, there will be an additional field starting with a hyphen followed by letters corresponding to any flags that were set. See the ipf.conf manual page for a list of letters and their flags.

If the packet is an ICMP packet, there will be two fields at the end, the first always being 'icmp', and the next being the ICMP message and submessage type, separated by a slash, e.g., **icmp 3/3** for a port unreachable message.

In order for **ipmon** to properly work, the kernel option **IPFILTER_LOG** must be turned on in your kernel. Please see **options(4)** for more details.

ipmon reopens its log file(s) and rereads its configuration file when it receives a SIGHUP signal.

OPTIONS

–a   Open all of the device logfiles for reading log entries from. All entries are displayed to the same output 'device' (stderr or syslog).

–b   For rules which log the body of a packet, generate hex output representing the packet contents after the headers.

–B <binarylogfilename>

Enable logging of the raw, unformatted binary data to the specified <*binarylogfilename*> file. This can be read, later, using **ipmon** with the **-f** option.

–D   Cause ipmon to turn itself into a daemon. Using subshells or backgrounding of ipmon is not required to turn it into an orphan so it can run indefinitely.

–f <device>

specify an alternative device/file from which to read the log information for normal IP Filter log records.

–F   Flush the current packet log buffer. The number of bytes flushed is displayed, even should the result be zero.

−L <facility>
 Using this option allows you to change the default syslog facility that ipmon uses for syslog messages. The default is local0.

−n IP addresses and port numbers will be mapped, where possible, back into hostnames and service names.

−N <device>
 Set the logfile to be opened for reading NAT log records from to <device>.

−o Specify which log files to actually read data from. N - NAT logfile, S - State logfile, I - normal IP Filter logfile. The **-a** option is equivalent to using **-o NSI**.

−O Specify which log files you do not wish to read from. This is most sensibly used with the **-a**. Letters available as parameters to this are the same as for **-o**.

−p Cause the port number in log messages to always be printed as a number and never attempt to look it up as from */etc/services*, etc.

−P <pidfile>
 Write the pid of the ipmon process to a file. By default this is *//etc/opt/ipf/ipmon.pid* (Solaris), */var/run/ipmon.pid* (44BSD or later) or */etc/ipmon.pid* for all others.

−s Packet information read in will be sent through syslogd rather than saved to a file. The default facility when compiled and installed is **local0**. The following levels are used:

 LOG_INFO – packets logged using the "log" keyword as the action rather than pass or block.

 LOG_NOTICE – packets logged which are also passed

 LOG_WARNING – packets logged which are also blocked

 LOG_ERR – packets which have been logged and which can be considered "short".

−S <device>
 Set the logfile to be opened for reading state log records from to <device>.

−t read the input file/device in a manner akin to tail(1).

−v show tcp window, ack and sequence fields.

−x show the packet data in hex.

−X show the log header record data in hex.

DIAGNOSTICS
 ipmon expects data that it reads to be consistent with how it should be saved and will abort if it fails an assertion which detects an anomaly in the recorded data.

FILES
 /dev/ipl
 /dev/ipnat
 /dev/ipstate
 /etc/services

SEE ALSO
 ipl(4), ipf(8), ipfstat(8), ipnat(8)

BUGS
 If you find any, please send email to me at darrenr@pobox.com

2

NAME

ipnat – user interface to the NAT subsystem

SYNOPSIS

ipnat [**–dhlnrsvCF**] [**–M core**] [**–N system**] **–f** <*filename*>

DESCRIPTION

ipnat opens the filename given (treating "–" as stdin) and parses the file for a set of rules which are to be added or removed from the IP NAT.

Each rule processed by **ipnat** is added to the kernels internal lists if there are no parsing problems. Rules are added to the end of the internal lists, matching the order in which they appear when given to **ipnat**.

Note that **ipf(8)** must be enabled (with **ipf -E**) before NAT is configured, as the same kernel facilities are used for NAT functionality. In addition, packet forwarding must be enabled. These details may be handled automatically when **ipnat** is run by **rc** at normal system startup. See **options(4)**, **sysctl(8)**, and **rc.conf(5)** for more information.

OPTIONS

–C	delete all entries in the current NAT rule listing (NAT rules)
–d	Enable printing of some extra debugging information.
–F	delete all active entries in the current NAT translation table (currently active NAT mappings)
–h	Print number of hits for each MAP/Redirect filter.
–l	Show the list of current NAT table entry mappings.
–n	This flag (no-change) prevents **ipf** from actually making any ioctl calls or doing anything which would alter the currently running kernel.
–r	Remove matching NAT rules rather than add them to the internal lists.
–s	Retrieve and display NAT statistics.
–v	Turn verbose mode on. Displays information relating to rule processing and active rules/table entries.

FILES

/dev/ipnat
/usr/share/examples/ipf Directory with examples.

DIAGNOSTICS

ioctl(SIOCGNATS): Input/output error Ensure that the necessary kernel functionality is present and **ipf** enabled with **ipf -E**.

SEE ALSO

ipnat(5), rc.conf(5), ipf(8), ipfstat(8)

NAME
ippool – user interface to the IPFilter pools

SYNOPSIS
ippool -a [-dnv] [-m <name>] [-o <role>] -i <ipaddr>[/<netmask>]
ippool -A [-dnv] [-m <name>] [-o <role>] [-S <seed>] [-t <type>]
ippool -f <file> [-dnuv]
ippool -F [-dv] [-o <role>] [-t <type>]
ippool -l [-dv] [-m <name>] [-t <type>]
ippool -r [-dnv] [-m <name>] [-o <role>] -i <ipaddr>[/<netmask>]
ippool -R [-dnv] [-m <name>] [-o <role>] [-t <type>]
ippool -s [-dtv] [-M <core>] [-N <namelist>]

DESCRIPTION
Ippool is used to manage information stored in the IP pools subsystem of IPFilter. Configuration file information may be parsed and loaded into the kernel, currently configured pools removed or changed as well as inspected.

The command line options used are broken into two sections: the global options and the instance specific options.

GLOBAL OPTIONS
–d   Toggle debugging of processing the configuration file.

–n   This flag (no-change) prevents **ippool** from actually making any ioctl calls or doing anything which would alter the currently running kernel.

–v   Turn verbose mode on.

COMMAND OPTIONS
-a   Add a new data node to an existing pool in the kernel.

-A   Add a new (empty) pool to the kernel.

-f <file>
          Read in IP pool configuration information from the file and load it into the kernel.

-F   Flush loaded pools from the kernel.

-l   Display a list of pools currently loaded into the kernel.

-r   Remove an existing data node from a pool in the kernel.

-R   Remove an existing pool from within the kernel.

-s   Display IP pool statistical information.

OPTIONS
-i <ipaddr>[/<netmask>]
          Sets the IP address for the operation being undertaken with an all-one's mask or, optionally, a specific netmask given in either the dotted-quad notation or a single integer.

-m <name>
          Sets the pool name for the current operation.

-M <core>
          Specify an alternative path to /dev/kmem to retrieve statistical information from.

-N <namelist>
          Specify an alternative path to lookup symbol name information from when retrieving statistical information.

-o <role>
          Sets the role with which this pool is to be used. Currently only **ipf, auth** and **count** are accepted as arguments to this option.

> **-S <seed>**
>> Sets the hashing seed to the number specified. Only for use with **hash** type pools.
>
> **-t <type>**
>> Sets the type of pool being defined. Myst be one of **tree, hash, group-map.**
>
> **-u**   When parsing a configuration file, rather than load new pool data into the kernel, unload it.

FILES
> /dev/iplookup
> /etc/ippool.conf

SEE ALSO
> ippool(5), ipf(8), ipfstat(8)

NAME
ipresend – resend IP packets out to network

SYNOPSIS
ipresend [**–EHPRSTX**] [**–d** <device>] [**–g** <*gateway*>] [**–m** <*MTU*>] [**–r** <*filename*>]

DESCRIPTION
ipresend was designed to allow packets to be resent, once captured, back out onto the network for use in testing. *ipresend* supports a number of different file formats as input, including saved snoop/tcpdump binary data.

OPTIONS
–d <interface>

Set the interface name to be the name supplied. This is useful with the **–P, –S, –T** and **–E** options, where it is not otherwise possible to associate a packet with an interface. Normal "text packets" can override this setting.

–g <gateway>

Specify the hostname of the gateway through which to route packets. This is required whenever the destination host isn't directly attached to the same network as the host from which you're sending.

–m <MTU>

Specify the MTU to be used when sending out packets. This option allows you to set a fake MTU, allowing the simulation of network interfaces with small MTU's without setting them so.

–r <filename>

Specify the filename from which to take input. Default is stdin.

–E   The input file is to be text output from etherfind. The text formats which are currently supported are those which result from the following etherfind option combinations:

etherfind -n
etherfind -n -t

–H   The input file is to be hex digits, representing the binary makeup of the packet. No length correction is made, if an incorrect length is put in the IP header.

–P   The input file specified by **–i** is a binary file produced using libpcap (i.e., tcpdump version 3). Packets are read from this file as being input (for rule purposes).

–R   When sending packets out, send them out "raw" (the way they came in). The only real significance here is that it will expect the link layer (i.e. ethernet) headers to be prepended to the IP packet being output.

–S   The input file is to be in "snoop" format (see RFC 1761). Packets are read from this file and used as input from any interface. This is perhaps the most useful input type, currently.

–T   The input file is to be text output from tcpdump. The text formats which are currently supported are those which result from the following tcpdump option combinations:

tcpdump -n
tcpdump -nq
tcpdump -nqt
tcpdump -nqtt
tcpdump -nqte

–X   The input file is composed of text descriptions of IP packets.

SEE ALSO
ipftest(1), ipsend(1), iptest(1), bpf(4), ipsend(5), tcpdump(8)

DIAGNOSTICS

Needs to be run as root.

BUGS

Not all of the input formats are sufficiently capable of introducing a wide enough variety of packets for them to be all useful in testing. If you find any, please send email to me at darrenr@pobox.com

NAME

iprop, **ipropd-master**, **ipropd-slave** — propagate changes to a Heimdal Kerberos master KDC to slave KDCs

SYNOPSIS

ipropd-master [**-c** *string* | **--config-file**=*string*] [**-r** *string* |
                  --realm=*string*] [**-k** *kspec* | **--keytab**=*kspec*] [**-d** *file* |
                  --database=*file*] [**--slave-stats-file**=*file*]
                  [**--time-missing**=*time*] [**--time-gone**=*time*] [**--detach**]
                  [**--version**] [**--help**]
ipropd-slave [**-c** *string* | **--config-file**=*string*] [**-r** *string* |
                 --realm=*string*] [**-k** *kspec* | **--keytab**=*kspec*]
                 [**--time-lost**=*time*] [**--detach**] [**--version**] [**--help**] *master*

DESCRIPTION

ipropd-master is used to propagate changes to a Heimdal Kerberos database from the master Kerberos server on which it runs to slave Kerberos servers running **ipropd-slave**.

The slaves are specified by the contents of the slaves file in the KDC's database directory, e.g. /var/heimdal/slaves. This has principals one per-line of the form

        iprop/*slave*@*REALM*

where *slave* is the hostname of the slave server in the given *REALM*, e.g.

        iprop/kerberos-1.example.com@EXAMPLE.COM

On a slave, the argument *master* specifies the hostname of the master server from which to receive updates.

In contrast to hprop(8), which sends the whole database to the slaves regularly, **iprop** normally sends only the changes as they happen on the master. The master keeps track of all the changes by assigning a version number to every change to the database. The slaves know which was the latest version they saw, and in this way it can be determined if they are in sync or not. A log of all the changes is kept on the master. When a slave is at an older version than the oldest one in the log, the whole database has to be sent.

The changes are propagated over a secure channel (on port 2121 by default). This should normally be defined as "iprop/tcp" in /etc/services or another source of the services database. The master and slaves must each have access to a keytab with keys for the **iprop** service principal on the local host.

There is a keep-alive feature logged in the master's slave-stats file (e.g. /var/heimdal/slave-stats).

Supported options for **ipropd-master**:

-c *string*, **--config-file**=*string*

-r *string*, **--realm**=*string*

-k *kspec*, **--keytab**=*kspec*
        keytab to get authentication from

-d *file*, **--database**=*file*
        Database (default per KDC)

--slave-stats-file=*file*
        file for slave status information

--time-missing=*time*
        time before slave is polled for presence (default 2 min)

--time-gone=_time_
>   time of inactivity after which a slave is considered gone (default 5 min)

--detach
>   detach from console

--version

--help

Supported options for **ipropd-slave**:

-c _string_, **--config-file=**_string_

-r _string_, **--realm=**_string_

-k _kspec_, **--keytab=**_kspec_
>   keytab to get authentication from

--time-lost=_time_
>   time before server is considered lost (default 5 min)

--detach
>   detach from console

--version

--help
Time arguments for the relevant options above may be specified in forms like 5 min, 300 s, or simply a number of seconds.

FILES
>   slaves, slave-stats in the database directory.

SEE ALSO
>   krb5.conf(5), hprop(8), hpropd(8), iprop-log(8), kdc(8)

NAME

iprop-log — maintain the iprop log file

SYNOPSIS

iprop-log [**--version**] [**-h** | **--help**] *command*

iprop-log truncate [**-c** *file* | **--config-file**=*file*] [**-r** *string* |
      --realm=*string*] [**-h** | **--help**]

iprop-log dump [**-c** *file* | **--config-file**=*file*] [**-r** *string* | **--realm**=*string*]
      [**-h** | **--help**]

iprop-log replay [**--start-version**=*version-number*]
      [**--end-version**=*version-number*] [**-c** *file* | **--config-file**=*file*] [**-r**
      string | **--realm**=*string*] [**-h** | **--help**]

DESCRIPTION

Supported options:

--version

-h, **--help**

command can be one of the following:

truncate

    -c *file*, **--config-file**=*file*
      configuration file

    -r *string*, **--realm**=*string*
      realm

Truncates the log. Sets the new logs version number for the to the last entry of the old log. If
the log is truncted by emptying the file, the log will start over at the first version (0).

dump

    -c *file*, **--config-file**=*file*
      configuration file

    -r *string*, **--realm**=*string*
      realm

Print out all entires in the log to standard output.

replay

    --start-version=*version-number*
      start replay with this version

    --end-version=*version-number*
      end replay with this version

    -c *file*, **--config-file**=*file*
      configuration file

    -r *string*, **--realm**=*string*
      realm

Replay the changes from specified entries (or all if none is specified) in the transaction log to the database.

last-version

-**c** *file*, --**config-file**=*file*
  configuration file

-**r** *string*, --**realm**=*string*
  realm

prints the version of the last log entry.

SEE ALSO
iprop(8)

NAME

ipsend – sends IP packets

SYNOPSIS

ipsend [**–dITUv**] [**–i** <interface>] [**–f** <*offset*>] [**–g** <*gateway*>] [**–m** <*MTU*>] [**–o** <*option*>] [**–P** <protocol>] [**–s** <*source*>] [**–t** <*dest. port*>] [**–w** <*window*>] <destination> [TCP-flags]

DESCRIPTION

ipsend can be compiled in two ways. The first is used to send one-off packets to a destination host, using command line options to specify various attributes present in the headers. The *destination* must be given as the last command line option, except for when TCP flags are specified as a combination of A, S, F, U, P and R, last.

The other way it may be compiled, with DOSOCKET defined, is to allow an attempt at making a TCP connection using a with ipsend resending the SYN packet as per the command line options.

OPTIONS

–d   enable debugging mode.

–f <offset>

The *-f* allows the IP offset field in the IP header to be set to an arbitrary value, which can be specified in decimal or hexadecimal.

–g <gateway>

Specify the hostname of the gateway through which to route packets. This is required whenever the destination host isn't directly attached to the same network as the host from which you're sending.

–i <interface>

Set the interface name to be the name supplied.

–m <MTU>

Specify the MTU to be used when sending out packets. This option allows you to set a fake MTU, allowing the simulation of network interfaces with small MTU's without setting them so.

–o <option>

Specify options to be included at the end of the IP header. An EOL option is automatically appended and need not be given. If an option would also have data associated with it (source as an IP# for a lsrr option), then this will not be initialised.

–s <source>

Set the source address in the packet to that provided - maybe either a hostname or IP#.

–t <dest.**port**>

Set the destination port for TCP/UDP packets.

–w <window>

Set the window size for TCP packets.

–I   Set the protocol to ICMP.

–P <protocol>

Set the protocol to the value given. If the parameter is a name, the name is looked up in the */etc/protocols* file.

–T   Set the protocol to TCP.

–U   Set the protocol to UDP.

–v   enable verbose mode.

SEE ALSO

ipresend(1), iptest(1), bpf(4), protocols(5), ipsend(5)

DIAGNOSTICS

      Needs to be run as root.

BUGS

      If you find any, please send email to me at darrenr@pobox.com

NAME
iptest – automatically generate a packets to test IP functionality

SYNOPSIS
iptest [**–1234567**] [**–d** <device>] [**–g** <gateway>] [**–m** *<MTU>*] [**–p** *<pointtest>*] [**–s** *<source>*] <destination>

DESCRIPTION
iptest ...

OPTIONS
–1   Run IP test group #1. This group of tests generates packets with the IP header fields set to invalid values given other packet characteristics. The point tests are: 1 (ip_hl < ip_len), 2 (ip_hl > ip_len), 3 (ip_v < 4), 4 (ip_v > 4), 5 (ip_len < packetsize, long packets), 6 (ip_len > packet size, short packets), 7 (Zero length fragments), 8 (packet > 64k after reassembly), 9 (IP offset with MSB set), 10 (ttl variations).

–2   Run IP test group #2. This group of tests generates packets with the IP options constructed with invalid values given other packet characteristics. The point tests are: 1 (option length > packet length), 2 (option length = 0).

–3   Run IP test group #3. This group of tests generates packets with the ICMP header fields set to non-standard values. The point tests are: 1 (ICMP types 0-31 & 255), 2 (type 3 & code 0 - 31), 3 (type 4 & code 0, 127, 128, 255), 4 (type 5 & code 0, 127, 128, 255), 5 (types 8-10,13-18 with codes 0, 127, 128 and 255), 6 (type 12 & code 0, 127, 128, 129, 255) and 7 (type 3 & codes 9-10, 13-14 and 17-18 - shortened packets).

–4   Run IP test group #4. This group of tests generates packets with the UDP header fields set to non-standard values. The point tests are: 1 (UDP length > packet size), 2 (UDP length < packetsize), 3 (sport = 0, 1, 32767, 32768, 65535), 4 (dport = 0, 1, 32767, 32768, 65535) and 5 (sizeof(struct ip) <= MTU <= sizeof(struct udphdr) + sizeof(struct ip)).

–5   Run IP test group #5. This group of tests generates packets with the TCP header fields set to non-standard values. The point tests are: 1 (TCP flags variations, all combinations), 2 (seq = 0, 0x7fffffff, 0x8000000, 0xa0000000, 0xffffffff), 3 (ack = 0, 0x7fffffff, 0x8000000, 0xa0000000, 0xffffffff), 4 (SYN packet with window of 0, 32768, 65535), 5 (set urgent pointer to 1, 0x7fff, 0x8000, 0xffff), 6 (data offset), 7 (sport = 0, 1, 32767, 32768, 65535) and 8 (dport = 0, 1, 32767, 32768, 65535).

–6   Run IP test group #6. This test generates a large number of fragments in an attempt to exhaust the network buffers used for holding packets for later reassembly. WARNING: this may crash or cause serious performance degradation to the target host.

–7   Run IP test group #7. This test generates 1024 random IP packets with only the IP version, checksum, length and IP offset field correct.

–d <interface>
Set the interface name to be the name supplied.

–g <gateway>
Specify the hostname of the gateway through which to route packets. This is required whenever the destination host isn't directly attached to the same network as the host from which you're sending.

–m <MTU>
Specify the MTU to be used when sending out packets. This option allows you to set a fake MTU, allowing the simulation of network interfaces with small MTU's without setting them so.

–p <test>
Run a...

SEE ALSO

ipresend(1), ipsend(1), bpf(4), ipsend(5)

DIAGNOSTICS

Only one of the numeric test options may be given when *iptest* is run.

Needs to be run as root.

BUGS

If you find any, please send email to me at darrenr@pobox.com

NAME

ipwctl — configure Intel PRO/Wireless 2100 network adapter

SYNOPSIS

ipwctl [-i] *iface*
ipwctl [-i] *iface* -r

DESCRIPTION

The **ipwctl** utility controls the operation of Intel PRO/Wireless 2100 networking devices via ipw(4) driver.

You should not use this program to configure IEEE 802.11 parameters. Use ifconfig(8) instead.

OPTIONS

The options are as follows:

-i *iface*
        Display adapter's internal statistics.

-i *iface* -r
        Display the radio switch state (on or off).

FILES

The firmware, loaded automatically, is not shipped with NetBSD; install the pkgsrc/sysutils/ipw-firmware package. The original archive is available from Intel at: http://ipw2100.sourceforge.net/firmware.php?fid=3.

ipw2100-1.2.fw   BSS mode (connection to an access point) firmware
ipw2100-1.2-i.fw IBSS mode (point-to-point connection) firmware
ipw2100-1.2-p.fw Monitor mode firmware

SEE ALSO

ipw(4), ifconfig(8), pkgsrc/sysutils/ipw-firmware

AUTHORS

The **ipwctl** utility and this man page were written by Damien Bergamini ⟨damien.bergamini@free.fr⟩.

NAME
   irdaattach — attach serial lines to IrDA frame driver

SYNOPSIS
   irdaattach [**-d** *dongle*] [**-fHhlmnp**] *ttyname*

DESCRIPTION
   irdaattach is used to assign a tty line to an IrDA frame level driver. The following operands are supported by **irdaattach**:

   -d *dongle* Sets the dongle type. The following dongles are supported:

none	No dongle
tekram	Tekram IR-210B
jeteye	Extended Systems JetEye
actisys	ACTiSYS IR-220L
actisys+	ACTiSYS IR-220L+
litelink	Parallax LiteLink
girbil	Greenwich GIrBIL

   The default is none.

   -f   Print the name of the IrDA frame device that should be used to access the frames.

   -H   Turn on DTR/CTS flow control. By default, no flow control is done.

   -h   Turn on RTS/CTS flow control. By default, no flow control is done.

   -l   Turn on the CLOCAL flag, making it possible to run SLIP on a cable without modem control signals (e.g. DTR, DSR, DCD).

   -m   Maintain modem control signals after closing the line. Specifically, this disables HUPCL.

   -n   Do not detach from invoking tty.

   -p   Print process id to file.

   ttyname Specifies the name of the tty device. *Ttyname* should be a string of the form ttyXX, or /dev/ttyXX.

   Only the super-user may attach a network interface.

   The frame driver is detached by killing the **irdaattach** process.

EXAMPLES
```
irdaattach tty00
ircomm -Y -d 'irdaattach -p -f /dev/tty02'
```

DIAGNOSTICS
   Messages indicating that the specified interface does not exist, the requested address is unknown, or that the user is not privileged but tried to alter an interface's configuration.

SEE ALSO
   daemon(3), irframe(4), irframetty(4), slattach(8)

HISTORY
  The **irdaattach** command appeared in NetBSD 1.6.

NAME
iscsi-initiator — refuse-based iSCSI initiator

SYNOPSIS
iscsi-initiator [-46bcfVv] [-a *authentication-type*] [-d *digest-type*]
                [-h *target-hostname*] [-p *target-port-number*]
                [-t *target-number*] [-u *username*] mount_point

DESCRIPTION
The **iscsi-initiator** utility can be used to access an iSCSI target, such as iscsi-target(8), to access block storage which has been exported. Information pertaining to the target is displayed underneath the mount point, along with the device corresponding to the storage which the target exports.

The various arguments are as follows:

-4   Use an IPv4 connection to the target.

-6   Use an IPv6 connection to the target.

-a *authentication-type*
        Use the specified authentication type when communicating with the target. The possible values are chap, kerberos, srp or none. The default value is none.

-b   Show the storage as a block device.

-c   Show the storage as a character device.

-d *digest-type*
        Use the specified digest type when communicating with the target. The possible values are header, data, both, all or none. The default value is none.

-f   Show the storage as a regular file.

-h *hostname*
        Connect to the iSCSI target running on the host specified as the argument.

-p *port-number*
        Connect to the iSCSI target running on the port specified as the argument. The default value is 3260.

-t *target*
        Connect to the number of the iSCSI target running as the argument.

-u *username*
        Use the specified user's credentials when logging in to the iSCSI target. There is no default.

-V   Print out the version number and then exit.

-v   Be verbose in operation.

The refuse(3) library is used to provide the file system features.

The mandatory parameter is the local mount point.

This iSCSI initiator presents a view of the targets underneath the mount point. Firstly, it creates a directory tree with the hostname of the target, and, in that directory, a virtual directory is created for each target name exported by the iSCSI target program. Within that virtual target directory, symbolic links exist for the hostname (for convenience), a textual representation of the IP address, the iSCSI target product name, the iSCSI target IQN, the iSCSI target vendor and version number. One other directory entry is presented in the virtual target directory, relating to the storage presented by the iSCSI target. This can be in the form of a regular file, which is also the default, a block device or a character device.

Please note that the **iscsi-initiator** utility needs the "puffs" kernel module loaded via modload(8) to operate.

EXAMPLES

```
# ./iscsi-initiator -u agc iscsi-target0.alistaircrooks.co.uk /mnt
# ls -al /mnt/iscsi-target0.alistaircrooks.co.uk/target0
total 576
drwxr-xr-x  2 agc   agc          512 May 11 22:24 .
drwxr-xr-x  2 agc   agc          512 May 11 22:24 ..
lrw-r--r--  1 agc   agc           39 May 11 22:24 hostname -> iscsi-target0.alistairc:
lrw-r--r--  1 agc   agc           14 May 11 22:24 ip -> 172.16.135.130
lrw-r--r--  1 agc   agc           16 May 11 22:24 product -> NetBSD iSCSI
-rw-r--r--  1 agc   agc    104857600 May 11 22:24 storage
lrw-r--r--  1 agc   agc           43 May 11 22:24 targetname -> iqn.1994-04.org.netbs
lrw-r--r--  1 agc   agc            8 May 11 22:24 vendor -> NetBSD
lrw-r--r--  1 agc   agc            4 May 11 22:24 version -> 0
#
```

SEE ALSO

puffs(3), refuse(3), iscsi-target(8)

HISTORY

The **iscsi-initiator** utility first appeared in NetBSD 5.0.

AUTHORS

The **iscsi-initiator** utility was written by Alistair Crooks ⟨agc@NetBSD.org⟩.

NAME
   iscsi-target — service remote iSCSI requests

SYNOPSIS
   iscsi-target [**-46DV**] [**-b** *block length*] [**-f** *configuration file*]
                [**-p** *port number*] [**-s** *maximum number of sessions*]
                [**-t** *target name*] [**-v** *verbose arg*]

DESCRIPTION
   iscsi-target is the server for iSCSI requests from iSCSI initiators. **iscsi-target** listens for discovery and login requests on the required port, and responds to those requests appropriately.

   Options and operands available for **iscsi-target**:

   -4   **iscsi-target** will listen for IPv4 connections, and respond back using IPv4. This is the default address family.

   -6   **iscsi-target** will listen for IPv6 connections, and respond back using IPv6.

   -b *blocksize*
            Specify the underlying block size for iSCSI storage which will be served. The possible sizes are: 512, 1024, 2048, and 4096 bytes, with the default being 512 bytes.

   -D   When this option is specified, **iscsi-target** will not detach itself from the controlling tty, and will not become a daemon. This can be useful for debugging purposes.

   -f *configfile*
            Use the named file as the configuration file. The default file can be found in */etc/iscsi/targets*. See targets(5) for more information.

   -p *port number*
            Use the port number provided as the argument as the port on which to listen for iSCSI service requests from initiators.

   -s *maximum number of sessions*
            Allow the maximum number of sessions to be initiated when connecting to the target.

   -t *filename*
            The target name (as it appears to the iSCSI initiator) can be specified using this flag.

   -V   **iscsi-target** will print the utility name and version number, and the address for bug reports, and then exit.

   -v *argument*
            The amount of information shown can be varied by using this command. Possible values of *argument* are *net* to show network-related information, *iscsi* to show iSCSI protocol-related information, *scsi* to show SCSI protocol information, and *all* to show information from all of the above arguments.

FILES
   /etc/iscsi/targets   the list of exported storage
   /var/run/iscsi-target.pid the PID of the currently running **iscsi-target**

SEE ALSO
   targets(5)

HISTORY

The **iscsi-target** utility first appeared in NetBSD 4.0.

NAME

    isdnd — isdn4bsd ISDN connection management daemon

SYNOPSIS

    isdnd [**-c** *configfile*] [**-d** *debuglevel*] [**-f**] [**-F**] [**-l**] [**-L** *logfile*] [**-P**]
        [**-r** *device*] [**-s** *facility*] [**-t** *terminaltype*] [**-u** *charging unit length*]
        [**-m**]

DESCRIPTION

    isdnd is the isdn4bsd package demon which manages all ISDN related connection and disconnection of ISDN devices supported by the package.

    The options are as follows:

    -c   Use *configfile* as the name of the runtime configuration filename for **isdnd** instead of the default file /etc/isdn/isdnd.rc.

    -d   If debugging support is compiled into **isdnd** this option is used to specify the debugging level, or better which kind of debugging messages are displayed. The debugging level is the sum of the following values:

            0x001 general debugging.
            0x002 rates calculation.
            0x004 timing calculations.
            0x008 state transitions.
            0x010 retry handling.
            0x020 dialing.
            0x040 process handling.
            0x080 isdn4bsd kernel i/o calls.
            0x100 controller and channel busy/free messages.
            0x200 isdnd.rc configuration file processing.
            0x400 outgoing call budget handling.

    The value can be specified in any number base supported by the sscanf(3) library routine.

    In addition, this option accepts also the character 'n' as an argument to disable displaying debug messages on the full-screen display.

    -f   Specifying this option causes **isdnd** to enter the full-screen mode of operation. When operating in this mode, entering the control character *Control-L* causes the display to be refreshed and entering *Carriage-Return* or *Enter* will pop-up a command window. Because the **isdnd** daemon will not listen to messages while the command window is active, this command window will disappear automatically after 5 seconds without any command key press.

    While the command window is active, *Tab* or *Space* advances to the next menu item. To execute a command, press *Return* or *Enter* for the highlighted menu item, or enter the number corresponding to the item to be executed or enter the capitalized character in the menu item description.

    -l   If this option is set, logging is not done via the syslogd(8) facility but instead is appended to a file.

    -L   Specifies the name of the logfile which is used when the option **-l** is set. See also the keyword *rotatesuffix* in the system section of isdnd.rc(5).

    -P   This option prints out the parsed and verified isdnd configuration in the same format as the isdnd.rc file. This output can be used as an isdnd.rc file. This feature is especially useful when debugging an isdnd.rc file to see what the default settings of options are when they are not set in the isdnd.rc input file.

The **isdnd** exits after the printout is done.

−F This option prevents **isdnd** to detach from the controlling tty and become a daemon.

−r In conjunction with the **−t** option, *device* specifies a terminal device which becomes the controlling tty for **isdnd** and on which the full-screen mode output is displayed.

−s This option may be used to specify the logging facility in case syslog(3) logging is configured and another facility than the default LOCAL0 facility shall be used. The facility is to be specified as an integer in the range 0-11 or 16-23 (see the file /usr/include/syslog.h).

−t In conjunction with the **−f** and **−r** options, *terminaltype* specifies a terminal type or termcap entry name (such as vt220) for the device used for **isdnd** full-screen output. This is useful if an unused (no getty running) tty line is used for full-screen output for which no TERM environment variable exists.

−u Specifies the length of a charging unit in case the config file entry keyword *unitlengthsrc* is set to *cmdl*.

−m If the ISDN daemon is compiled with local or remote monitoring support, this option disables all monitoring access. It overrides the config file option *monitor-allowed*.

INTERACTION WITH THE KERNEL

isdnd communicates with the kernel part of isdn4bsd by receiving status and event messages (via read(2) from device /dev/isdn) and by transmitting commands and responses (via ioctl(2) on device /dev/isdn).

The messages and message parameters are documented in the include file */usr/include/machine/i4b_ioctl.h*.

Supported command and response messages (ioctl's) to the kernel are:

I4B_CDID_REQ
> Request a unique Call Description IDentifier (cdid) which identifies uniquely a single interaction of the local D channel with the exchange.

I4B_CONNECT_REQ
> Actively request a call setup to a remote ISDN subscriber.

I4B_CONNECT_RESP
> Respond to an incoming call, either accept, reject or ignore it.

I4B_DISCONNECT_REQ
> Actively terminate a connection.

I4B_CTRL_INFO_REQ
> Request information about an installed ISDN controller card.

I4B_DIALOUT_RESP
> Give information about call setup to driver who requested dialing out.

I4B_TIMEOUT_UPD
> Update the kernels timeout value(s) in case of dynamically calculated shorthold mode timing changes.

I4B_UPDOWN_IND
> Inform the kernel userland drivers about interface soft up/down status changes.

I4B_CTRL_DOWNLOAD
> Download firmware to active card(s).

I4B_ACTIVE_DIAGNOSTIC
> Return diagnostic information from active cards.

Supported status and event messages from the kernel are:

MSG_CONNECT_IND
> An incoming call from a remote ISDN user is indicated.

MSG_CONNECT_ACTIVE_IND
> After an incoming call has been accepted locally or an outgoing call has been accepted by a remote, the exchange signaled an active connection and the corresponding B-channel is switched through.

MSG_DISCONNECT_IND
> A call was terminated.

MSG_DIALOUT_IND
> A userland interface driver requests the daemon to dial out (typically a network interface when a packet arrives in its send queue).

MSG_IDLE_TIMEOUT_IND
> A call was terminated by the isdn4bsd kernel driver because a B-channel idle timeout occurred.

MSG_ACCT_IND
> Accounting information from a network driver.

MSG_CHARGING_IND
> Charging information from the kernel.

OUTGOING CALLS

Currently the only possibility to trigger an outgoing call is that an isdn4bsd network driver (*isdn<n>*) sends a *MSG_DIALOUT_IND* to the **isdnd** daemon.

The daemon requests a new CDID from the kernel by using the *I4B_CDID_REQ* ioctl message, this CDID is now used in all interactions with the kernel to identify this single call until a disconnect occurs.

After getting the CDID, the daemon looks up several additional information in its entry section of the configuration corresponding to that connection and issues a *I4B_CONNECT_REQ* ioctl message to the kernel. The kernel now dials the remote side and if the remote side accepts the call, the kernel sends a *MSG_CONNECT_ACTIVE_IND* to the daemon.

The call is terminated by either the local site timing out or the remote side hanging up the connection or the local side actively sending a *I4B_DISCONNECT_REQ* ioctl message, both events are signaled to the **isdnd** by the kernel sending the *I4B_DISCONNECT_IND* message and the CDID corresponding to the call is no longer valid.

INCOMING CALLS

Incoming calls are signaled to **isdnd** by the kernel transmitting the *MSG_CONNECT_IND* message to the daemon.

With the information contained in this message, **isdnd** searches the entry section of its configuration database and if a match is found, it accepts or rejects the call or, if no match is found, it ignores the call - all by issuing a *I4B_CONNECT_RESP* ioctl message with the appropriate parameters to the kernel.

In case the daemon decided to accept the call, the kernel signals this by sending a *MSG_CONNECT_ACTIVE_IND* message to the daemon.

The call is terminated by either the local site timing out or the remote side hanging up the connection or the local side actively sending a *I4B_DISCONNECT_REQ* ioctl message, both events are signaled to **isdnd** by the kernel sending the *I4B_DISCONNECT_IND* message and the CDID corresponding to the call is no longer valid.

SIGNALS

Sending a HUP signal to **isdnd** causes all open connections to be terminated and the configuration file is reread. In case aliasfile handling was enabled, the aliasfile is also reread.

Sending a USR1 signal to **isdnd** causes the accounting file and the logfile (if logging to a file is used instead of logging via the `syslog`(3) facility) to be closed and reopened to make logfile rotation possible.

ENVIRONMENT

The following environment variables affect the execution of **isdnd**:

TERM   The terminal type when running in full-screen display mode. See `environ`(7) for more information.

FILES

`/dev/isdn`	The device-file used to communicate with the kernel ISDN driver subsystem.
`/var/log/messages`	A record of the actions in case of syslogd logging support.
`/var/log/isdnd.acct`	The default accounting information filename (if accounting is configured).
`/var/log/isdnd.log`	The default logging filename (if logging to a file is configured).
`/var/run/isdnd.pid`	The process id of the ISDN daemon (also known as "lockfile" to isdnd, preventing multiple invocations of it).
`/etc/isdn`	The directory where isdnd expects some supplementary data files and programs for telephone answering support.
`/etc/isdn/isdnd.rc`	The default runtime configuration file.
`/etc/isdn/isdnd.rates`	The default unit charging rates specification file.
`/etc/isdn/isdntel.alias`	The default table (if aliasing is enabled) to convert phone number to caller's name.

EXAMPLES

For a first try, the following command should be used to start **isdnd** in foreground mode for better debugging the configuration setup:

```
isdnd -d0xf9 -F
```

This will start isdnd with reasonable debugging settings and produce output on the current terminal. **isdnd** can then be terminated by entering *Control-C*.

Another example, the command:

```
isdnd -d0xf9 -f -r /dev/ttyv3 -t vt100
```

will start **isdnd** with reasonable debugging messages enabled, full-screen mode of operation, full-screen display redirected to /dev/ttyv03 and using a termcap entry for vt100 on this display.

DIAGNOSTICS

Exit status is 0 on success, 1 on error.

SEE ALSO

`ippp`(4), `irip`(4), `isdnd.rates`(5), `isdnd.rc`(5), `isdntel`(8), `isdntrace`(8), `syslogd`(8)

AUTHORS

The **isdnd** daemon and this manual page were written by Hellmuth Michaelis ⟨hm@kts.org⟩.

NAME

    isdnmonitor — isdn4bsd / isdnd remote monitoring tool

SYNOPSIS

    isdnmonitor [**-c**] [**-d** *debuglevel*] [**-f** *filename*] [**-h** *hostspec*] [**-l** *pathname*]
            [**-p** *portspec*]

DESCRIPTION

    isdnmonitor is used to remotely monitor the operation of the ISDN demon, isdnd(8), which manages
    all ISDN related connection and disconnection of ISDN devices supported by the isdn4bsd package.

    The options are as follows:

    -c   Switch to (curses-) fullscreen mode of operation. In this mode, **isdnmonitor** behaves nearly
           exactly as isdnd(8) in fullscreen mode. In fullscreen mode, entering the control character
           Control-L causes the display to be refreshed and entering *Carriage-Return* or *Enter* will pop-up a
           command window. Because **isdnmonitor** will not listen to messages while the command win-
           dow is active, this command window will disappear automatically after 5 seconds without any com-
           mand key press.

           While the command window is active, *Tab* or *Space* advances to the next menu item. To execute a
           command, press *Return* or *Enter* for the highlighted menu item, or enter the number corresponding
           to the item to be executed or enter the capitalized character in the menu item description.

    -d   If debugging support is compiled into **isdnmonitor** this option is used to specify the debugging
           level.

           In addition, this option accepts also the character 'n' as an argument to disable displaying debug
           messages on the full-screen display.

    -f   Specifying this option causes **isdnmonitor** to write its normal output and - if enabled - debug-
           ging output to a file which name is specified as the argument.

    -l   is used to specify a Unix local domain socket name to be used for communication between
           isdnd(8) and **isdnmonitor**

    -h   is used to specify a hostname or a dotted-quad IP address of a machine where an isdnd(8) is run-
           ning which should be monitored.

    -p   This option may be used to specify a remote port number in conjunction with the **-h** option.

ENVIRONMENT

    The following environment variables affect the execution of **isdnmonitor**:

    TERM   The terminal type when running in full-screen display mode. See environ(7) for more informa-
           tion.

EXAMPLES

    For a first try, the following command should be used to start **isdnmonitor** to monitor a locally running
    isdnd:

```
isdnmonitor -h localhost
```

DIAGNOSTICS

    Exit status is 0 on success, 1 on error.

SEE ALSO
>   isdnd(8)

AUTHORS
>   The **isdnmonitor** utility was written by Martin Husemann and
>   Hellmuth Michaelis. This manual page was written by
>   Hellmuth Michaelis ⟨hm@kts.org⟩.

NAME

isdntel — isdn4bsd telephone answering management utility

SYNOPSIS

isdntel [**-a** *aliasfile*] [**-d** *spooldir*] [**-p** *playcommand*] [**-t** *timeout*]

DESCRIPTION

isdntel is used to provide an "answering machine" functionality for incoming telephone voice messages.

The following options are supported:

-a   Use *aliasfile* as the pathname for an aliasfile containing aliases for phone numbers. The default path is /etc/isdn/isdntel.alias. The format of an alias entry is the number string followed by one or more spaces or tabs. The rest of the line is taken as the alias string. Comments are introduced by a leading blank, tab or "#" character.

-d   Use *spooldir* as the directory where the incoming voice messages are stored by the "answ" script called by isdnd(8). This defaults to the directory /var/isdn. The format of a voice message filename is:

            YYMMDDhhmmss-dest_number-source_number-length_in_secs

-p   Use *playcommand* as the command string to execute for playing a voice message to some audio output facility. The characters *%s* are replaced by the currently selected filename. The default string is *cat %s | alaw2ulaw >/dev/audio*

-t   The value for *timeout* specifies the time in seconds the program rereads the spool directory when there is no keyboard activity.

The screen output should be obvious. If in doubt, consult the source.

SEE ALSO

isdntel(4), isdnd.rc(5), isdnd(8)

AUTHORS

The **isdntel** utility and this manual page were written by Hellmuth Michaelis ⟨hm@kts.org⟩.

NAME

    isdntelctl — control isdn4bsd telephone sound format conversion

SYNOPSIS

    isdntelctl [**-c**] [**-g**] [**-u** *unit*] [**-A**] [**-U**] [**-N**]

DESCRIPTION

    isdntelctl is part of the isdn4bsd package and is used to configure the sound format conversion facilities of the /dev/isdntel interfaces.

    The following options are available:

    -c   Clear the telephone input queue.

    -g   Get the sound format currently in use.

    -u   Set the `/dev/isdntel` unit number. The default value is zero to access device `/dev/isdntel0`.

    -A   Do A-law (ISDN line) -> mu-law (userland) conversion.

    -U   Do mu-law (ISDN line) -> A-law (userland) conversion.

    -N   Set sound conversion to do no format conversion.

    The telephony data stream comes out of the line in a bit-reversed format, so the isdntel(4) driver does the bit-reversion process in any case.

    Additionally, the user can specify to do A-law to mu-law, mu-law to A-law or no conversion at all in the isdntel driver by using the **isdntelctl** utility.

FILES

    /dev/isdntel<n>

EXAMPLES

    The command

        isdntelctl -g

    displays the currently used sound format for device /dev/isdntel0.

SEE ALSO

    isdntel(4), isdnd.rc(5), isdnd(8)

STANDARDS

    A-law and mu-law are specified in ITU Recommendation G.711.

AUTHORS

    The **isdntelctl** utility and this man page were written by Hellmuth Michaelis ⟨hm@kts.org⟩.

NAME

isdntrace — isdn4bsd ISDN protocol trace utility

SYNOPSIS

isdntrace [-a] [-b] [-d] [-f *filename*] [-h] [-i] [-l] [-n *number*] [-o]
            [-p *filename*] [-r] [-u *number*] [-x] [-B] [-F] [-P] [-R *unit*]
            [-T *unit*]

DESCRIPTION

isdntrace is part of the isdn4bsd package and is used to provide the user with a mnemonic display of the layers 1, 2 and 3 protocol activities on the D channel and hex dump of the B channel(s) activities.

Together with two passive supported cards and an easy to build cable it can also be used to monitor the complete traffic on a S0 bus providing S0 bus analyzer features.

The isdntrace utility is only available for passive supported cards.

Note

All filenames, user specified or default, get a date and time stamp string added in the form -yymmdd-hhmmss: a hyphen, two digits year, month, day, a hyphen and two digits hour, minutes and seconds. Trace files no longer get overwritten. In case a new filename is needed within a second, the filename-generating mechanism sleeps one second.

In case the program is sent a USR1 signal, a new user specified or default filename with a new date and time stamp is generated and opened.

The following options can be used:

-a   Run isdntrace in analyzer mode by using two passive cards and a custom cable which can be build as described in the file *cable.txt* in the isdn4bsd source distribution. One card acts as a receiver for the transmitting direction on the S0 bus while the other card acts as a receiver for the receiving direction on the S0 bus. Complete traffic monitoring is possible using this setup.

-b   switch B channel tracing on (default off).

-d   switch D channel tracing off (default on).

-f   Use *filename* as the name of a file into which to write tracing output (default filename is isdntrace<n> where n is the number of the unit to trace).

-h   switch display of header off (default on).

-i   print layer 1 (I.430) INFO signals to monitor layer 1 activity (default off).

-l   switch displaying of Layer 2 (Q.921) frames off (default on).

-n   This option takes a numeric argument specifying the minimum frame size in octets a frame must have to be displayed. (default 0)

-o   switch off writing trace output to a file (default on).

-p   Use *filename* as the name of a file used for the -B and -P options (default filename is isdntrace-bin<n> where n is the number of the unit to trace).

-r   Switch off printing a raw hexadecimal dump of the packets preceding the decoded protocol information (default on).

-u   Use *number* as the unit number of the controller card to trace (default 0).

-x   Switch on printing of packets with a non-Q.931 protocol discriminator. (default off.)

-B   Write undecoded binary trace data to a file for later or remote analyzing (default off.)

-F   This option can only be used when option -P (playback from binary data file) is used. The -F option causes playback not to stop at end of file but rather to wait for additional data to be available from the input file.

        This option is useful when trace data is accumulated in binary format (to save disk space) but a monitoring functionality is desired. (default off.)

-P   Read undecoded binary trace data from file instead from device (default off.)

-R   Use *unit* as the receiving interface unit number in analyze mode.

-T   Use *unit* as the transmitting interface unit number in analyze mode.

When the USR1 signal is sent to a **isdntrace** process, the currently used logfiles are reopened, so that logfile rotation becomes possible.

The trace output should be obvious. It is very handy to have the following standard texts available when tracing ISDN protocols:

I.430   ISDN BRI layer 1 protocol description.
Q.921   ISDN D-channel layer 2 protocol description.
Q.931   ISDN D-channel layer 3 protocol description.
1TR6   German-specific ISDN layer 3 protocol description. (NOTICE: decoding of the 1TR6 protocol is included but not supported since i dont have any longer access to a 1TR6 based ISDN installation.)

isdntrace automatically detects the layer 3 protocol being used by looking at the Protocol Discriminator (see: Q.931/1993 pp. 53).

FILES
/dev/isdntrc<n>
            The device file(s) used to get the trace messages for ISDN card unit <n> out of the kernel.

EXAMPLES
The command:

            isdntrace -f /var/tmp/isdn.trace

will start D channel tracing on passive controller 0 with all except B channel tracing enabled and logs everything into the output file /var/tmp/isdn.trace-yymmdd-hhmmss (where yymmdd and hhmmss are replaced by the current date and time values).

SEE ALSO
isdnd(8)

STANDARDS
ITU Recommendations I.430, Q.920, Q.921, Q.930, Q.931

FTZ Richtlinie 1TR3, Band III

ITU Recommendation Q.932 (03/93), Q.950 (03/93)

ETSI Recommendation ETS 300 179 (10/92), ETS 300 180 (10/92)

ETSI Recommendation ETS 300 181 (04/93), ETS 300 182 (04/93)

ITU Recommendation X.208, X.209

AUTHORS

The **isdntrace** utility was written by Gary Jennejohn and Hellmuth Michaelis.

This manual page was written by Hellmuth Michaelis ⟨hm@kts.org⟩.

NAME
   iteconfig — modify console attributes at run time

SYNOPSIS
   iteconfig [**-i**] [**-f** *file*] [**-v** *volume*] [**-p** *pitch*] [**-t** *msec*] [**-w** *width*]
               [**-h** *height*] [**-d** *depth*] [**-x** *offset*] [**-y** *offset*] [*color* ...]

DESCRIPTION
   iteconfig is used to modify or examine the attributes of the console bell and bitmapped console display.
   The console bell's volume, pitch, and count may be specified, as well as the bitmapped display's width,
   height, horizontal and vertical offset, pixel depth, and color map.

   The following flags are interpreted by **iteconfig**:

   -i   After processing all other arguments, print information about the console's state.

   -f   Open and use the terminal named by *file* rather than the default console /dev/ttye0.

   -v   Set the volume of the console bell to *volume*, which must be between 0 and 63, inclusive.

   -p   Set the pitch of the console bell to *pitch*, which must be between 10 and 1399.

   -t   Set the duration of the beep to *msec* milliseconds which must be between 1 and 5000 (5 seconds).

   -w   Set the width of the console display to *width* pixel columns. *Width* must be a positive integer.

   -h   Set the height of the console display to *height* pixel rows. *Height* must be a positive integer.

   -d   Set the number of bitplanes the console view should use to *depth*. For example, if *depth* is 3
            then 8 colors will be used.

   -x   Set the horizontal offset of the console view on the monitor to *offset* pixel columns. The hori-
            zontal offset may be a positive or a negative integer, positive being an offset to the right, negative
            to the left.

   -y   Set the vertical offset of the console view on the monitor to *offset* pixel rows. The vertical off-
            set may be a positive or a negative integer, positive being an offset down, negative up.

   Any additional arguments will be interpreted as colors and will be used to supply the color values for the
   console view's color map, starting with the first entry in the map. (See the **COLOR SPECIFICATION** section of this manual page for information on how to specify colors.) If more colors are supplied than are
   usable by the console view, a warning is printed and the extra colors are ignored.

COLOR SPECIFICATION
   Colors are hexadecimal numbers which have one of the following formats:

   0xRRGGBB *RR*, *GG*, and *BB* are taken to be eight-bit values specifying the intensities of the red, green and
            blue components, respectively, of the color to be used. For example, 0xff0000 is bright red,
            0xffffff is white, and 0x008080 is dark cyan.

   0xGG   *GG* is taken to be an eight-bit value specifying the intensity of grey to be used. A value of
            0x00 is black, a value of 0xff is white, and a value of 0x80 is a grey approximately half way
            in between.

   0xM   *M* is taken to be the one-bit monochrome value to be used. A value of 0x1 is black, and a value
            of 0x0 is white.

BUGS
    The **iteconfig** command is only available on the amiga and atari ports.

NAME

    iwictl — configure Intel(R) PRO/Wireless 2200BG/2915ABG network adapters

SYNOPSIS

    iwictl [−i] *iface*
    iwictl [−i] *iface* −r

DESCRIPTION

    The **iwictl** utility controls the operation of Intel(R) PRO/Wireless 2200BG/2915ABG networking devices
    via the iwi(4) driver.

    You should not use this program to configure IEEE 802.11 parameters. Use ifconfig(8) instead.

OPTIONS

    The options are as follows:

    −i *iface*
            Displays adapter's internal statistics.

    −i *iface* −r
            Displays the radio transmitter state (on or off).

FILES

    The firmware is shipped with NetBSD. See iwi(4) for details how to use it.

SEE ALSO

    iwi(4), ifconfig(8)

AUTHORS

    The **iwictl** utility and this man page were written by Damien Bergamini ⟨damien.bergamini@free.fr⟩.

NAME

kadmin — Kerberos administration utility

SYNOPSIS

kadmin [**-p** *string* | **--principal**=*string*] [**-K** *string* | **--keytab**=*string*]
       [**-c** *file* | **--config-file**=*file*] [**-k** *file* | **--key-file**=*file*]
       [**-r** *realm* | **--realm**=*realm*] [**-a** *host* | **--admin-server**=*host*]
       [**-s** *port number* | **--server-port**=*port number*] [**-l** | **--local**]
       [**-h** | **--help**] [**-v** | **--version**] [*command*]

DESCRIPTION

The **kadmin** program is used to make modifications to the Kerberos database, either remotely via the
kadmind(8) daemon, or locally (with the **-l** option).

Supported options:

-p *string*, **--principal**=*string*
    principal to authenticate as

-K *string*, **--keytab**=*string*
    keytab for authentication principal

-c *file*, **--config-file**=*file*
    location of config file

-k *file*, **--key-file**=*file*
    location of master key file

-r *realm*, **--realm**=*realm*
    realm to use

-a *host*, **--admin-server**=*host*
    server to contact

-s *port number*, **--server-port**=*port number*
    port to use

-l, **--local**
    local admin mode

If no *command* is given on the command line, **kadmin** will prompt for commands to process. Some of the
commands that take one or more principals as argument (**delete**, **ext_keytab**, **get**, **modify**, and
passwd) will accept a glob style wildcard, and perform the operation on all matching principals.

Commands include:

    add [**-r** | **--random-key**] [**--random-password**] [**-p** *string* |
    --password=*string*] [**--key**=*string*] [**--max-ticket-life**=*lifetime*]
    [**--max-renewable-life**=*lifetime*] [**--attributes**=*attributes*]
    [**--expiration-time**=*time*] [**--pw-expiration-time**=*time*] *principal...*

        Adds a new principal to the database. The options not passed on the command line will be
        promped for.

    add_enctype [**-r** | **--random-key**] *principal enctypes...*

        Adds a new encryption type to the principal, only random key are supported.

delete *principal...*

> Removes a principal.

del_enctype *principal enctypes...*

> Removes some enctypes from a principal; this can be useful if the service belonging to the principal is known to not handle certain enctypes.

ext_keytab [**-k** *string* | **--keytab**=*string*] *principal...*

> Creates a keytab with the keys of the specified principals.

get [**-l** | **--long**] [**-s** | **--short**] [**-t** | **--terse**] [**-o** *string* | **--column-info**=*string*] *principal...*

> Lists the matching principals, short prints the result as a table, while long format produces a more verbose output. Which columns to print can be selected with the **-o** option. The argument is a comma separated list of column names optionally appended with an equal sign ('=') and a column header. Which columns are printed by default differ slightly between short and long output.

> The default terse output format is similar to **-s** **-o** *principal*=, just printing the names of matched principals.

> Possible column names include: principal, princ_expire_time, pw_expiration, last_pwd_change, max_life, max_rlife, mod_time, mod_name, attributes, kvno, mkvno, last_success, last_failed, fail_auth_count, policy, and keytypes.

modify [**-a** *attributes* | **--attributes**=*attributes*] [**--max-ticket-life**=*lifetime*] [**--max-renewable-life**=*lifetime*] [**--expiration-time**=*time*] [**--pw-expiration-time**=*time*] [**--kvno**=*number*] *principal...*

> Modifies certain attributes of a principal. If run without command line options, you will be prompted. With command line options, it will only change the ones specified.

> Possible attributes are: new-princ, support-desmd5, pwchange-service, disallow-svr, requires-pw-change, requires-hw-auth, requires-pre-auth, disallow-all-tix, disallow-dup-skey, disallow-proxiable, disallow-renewable, disallow-tgt-based, disallow-forwardable, disallow-postdated

> Attributes may be negated with a "-", e.g.,

> kadmin -l modify -a -disallow-proxiable user

passwd [**-r** | **--random-key**] [**--random-password**] [**-p** *string* | **--password**=*string*] [**--key**=*string*] *principal...*

> Changes the password of an existing principal.

password-quality *principal password*

> Run the password quality check function locally. You can run this on the host that is configured to run the kadmind process to verify that your configuration file is correct. The verification is done locally, if kadmin is run in remote mode, no rpc call is done to the server.

privileges

> Lists the operations you are allowed to perform. These include add, add_enctype,
> change-password, delete, del_enctype, get, list, and modify.

rename *from to*

> Renames a principal. This is normally transparent, but since keys are salted with the principal
> name, they will have a non-standard salt, and clients which are unable to cope with this will
> fail. Kerberos 4 suffers from this.

check [*realm*]

> Check database for strange configurations on important principals. If no realm is given, the
> default realm is used.

When running in local mode, the following commands can also be used:

dump [**-d** | **--decrypt**] [*dump-file*]

> Writes the database in "human readable" form to the specified file, or standard out. If the data-
> base is encrypted, the dump will also have encrypted keys, unless **--decrypt** is used.

init   [**--realm-max-ticket-life=**string]
[**--realm-max-renewable-life=**string] *realm*

> Initializes the Kerberos database with entries for a new realm. It's possible to have more than
> one realm served by one server.

load *file*

> Reads a previously dumped database, and re-creates that database from scratch.

merge *file*

> Similar to **load** but just modifies the database with the entries in the dump file.

stash   [**-e**   *enctype* | **--enctype=**enctype]   [**-k**   *keyfile* |
--key-file=keyfile] [**--convert-file**] [**--master-key-fd=**fd]

> Writes the Kerberos master key to a file used by the KDC.

SEE ALSO
> kadmind(8), kdc(8)

NAME

kadmind — server for administrative access to Kerberos database

SYNOPSIS

kadmind [-c *file* | --config-file=*file*] [-k *file* | --key-file=*file*]
       [--keytab=*keytab*] [-r *realm* | --realm=*realm*] [-d | --debug] [-p *port*
       | --ports=*port*]

DESCRIPTION

kadmind listens for requests for changes to the Kerberos database and performs these, subject to permissions. When starting, if stdin is a socket it assumes that it has been started by inetd(8), otherwise it behaves as a daemon, forking processes for each new connection. The --debug option causes kadmind to accept exactly one connection, which is useful for debugging.

The kpasswdd(8) daemon is responsible for the Kerberos 5 password changing protocol (used by kpasswd(1))

This daemon should only be run on the master server, and not on any slaves.

Principals are always allowed to change their own password and list their own principal. Apart from that, doing any operation requires permission explicitly added in the ACL file /var/heimdal/kadmind.acl. The format of this file is:

principal rights [*principal-pattern*]

Where rights is any (comma separated) combination of:
* change-password or cpw
* list
* delete
* modify
* add
* get
* all

And the optional *principal-pattern* restricts the rights to operations on principals that match the glob-style pattern.

Supported options:

-c *file*, --config-file=*file*
       location of config file

-k *file*, --key-file=*file*
       location of master key file

--keytab=*keytab*
       what keytab to use

-r *realm*, --realm=*realm*
       realm to use

-d, --debug
       enable debugging

-p *port*, --ports=*port*
       ports to listen to. By default, if run as a daemon, it listens to port 749, but you can add any number of ports with this option. The port string is a whitespace separated list of port specifications, with the special string "+" representing the default port.

FILES
> /var/heimdal/kadmind.acl

EXAMPLES
> This will cause **kadmind** to listen to port 4711 in addition to any compiled in defaults:
>
> > **kadmind --ports**="+ 4711" &
>
> This acl file will grant Joe all rights, and allow Mallory to view and add host principals.
>
> > ```
> > joe/admin@EXAMPLE.COM        all
> > mallory/admin@EXAMPLE.COM  add,get  host/*@EXAMPLE.COM
> > ```

SEE ALSO
> kpasswd(1), kadmin(8), kdc(8), kpasswdd(8)

NAME
kcm — is a process based credential cache for Kerberos tickets.

SYNOPSIS
kcm [--cache-name=*cachename*] [-c *file* | --config-file=*file*] [-g *group* |
    --group=*group*] [--max-request=*size*] [--disallow-getting-krbtgt]
    [--detach] [-h | --help] [-k *principal* | --system-principal=*principal*]
    [-l *time* | --lifetime=*time*] [-m *mode* | --mode=*mode*]
    [-n | --no-name-constraints] [-r *time* | --renewable-life=*time*] [-s *path*
    | --socket-path=*path*] [--door-path=*path*] [-S *principal* |
    --server=*principal*] [-t *keytab* | --keytab=*keytab*] [-u *user* |
    --user=*user*] [-v | --version]

DESCRIPTION
kcm is a process based credential cache. To use it, set the KRB5CCNAME enviroment variable to KCM:*uid* or add the stanza

```
[libdefaults]
        default_cc_name = KCM:%{uid}
```

to the /etc/krb5.conf configuration file and make sure kcm is started in the system startup files.

The kcm daemon can hold the credentials for all users in the system. Access control is done with Unix-like permissions. The daemon checks the access on all operations based on the uid and gid of the user. The tickets are renewed as long as is permitted by the KDC's policy.

The kcm daemon can also keep a SYSTEM credential that server processes can use to access services. One example of usage might be an nss_ldap module that quickly needs to get credentials and doesn't want to renew the ticket itself.

Supported options:

--cache-name=*cachename*
    system cache name

-c *file*, --config-file=*file*
    location of config file

-g *group*, --group=*group*
    system cache group

--max-request=*size*
    max size for a kcm-request

--disallow-getting-krbtgt
    disallow extracting any krbtgt from the kcm daemon.

--detach
    detach from console

-h, --help

-k *principal*, --system-principal=*principal*
    system principal name

-l *time*, **--lifetime**=*time*
    lifetime of system tickets

-m *mode*, **--mode**=*mode*
    octal mode of system cache

-n, **--no-name-constraints**
    disable credentials cache name constraints

-r *time*, **--renewable-life**=*time*
    renewable lifetime of system tickets

-s *path*, **--socket-path**=*path*
    path to kcm domain socket

--door-path=*path*
    path to kcm door socket

-S *principal*, **--server**=*principal*
    server to get system ticket for

-t *keytab*, **--keytab**=*keytab*
    system keytab name

-u *user*, **--user**=*user*
    system cache owner

-v, **--version**

NAME
kdc — Kerberos 5 server

SYNOPSIS
kdc [-c *file* | --config-file=*file*] [-p | --no-require-preauth]
    [--max-request=*size*] [-H | --enable-http] [--no-524] [--kerberos4]
    [--kerberos4-cross-realm] [-r *string* | --v4-realm=*string*]
    [-K | --kaserver] [-P *portspec* | --ports=*portspec*] [--detach]
    [--disable-DES] [--addresses=*list of addresses*]

DESCRIPTION
kdc serves requests for tickets. When it starts, it first checks the flags passed, any options that are not specified with a command line flag are taken from a config file, or from a default compiled-in value.

Options supported:

-c *file*, --config-file=*file*
> Specifies the location of the config file, the default is /var/heimdal/kdc.conf. This is the only value that can't be specified in the config file.

-p, --no-require-preauth
> Turn off the requirement for pre-autentication in the initial AS-REQ for all principals. The use of pre-authentication makes it more difficult to do offline password attacks. You might want to turn it off if you have clients that don't support pre-authentication. Since the version 4 protocol doesn't support any pre-authentication, serving version 4 clients is just about the same as not requiring pre-athentication. The default is to require pre-authentication. Adding the require-preauth per principal is a more flexible way of handling this.

--max-request=*size*
> Gives an upper limit on the size of the requests that the kdc is willing to handle.

-H, --enable-http
> Makes the kdc listen on port 80 and handle requests encapsulated in HTTP.

--no-524
> don't respond to 524 requests

--kerberos4
> respond to Kerberos 4 requests

--kerberos4-cross-realm
> respond to Kerberos 4 requests from foreign realms. This is a known security hole and should not be enabled unless you understand the consequences and are willing to live with them.

-r *string*, --v4-realm=*string*
> What realm this server should act as when dealing with version 4 requests. The database can contain any number of realms, but since the version 4 protocol doesn't contain a realm for the server, it must be explicitly specified. The default is whatever is returned by **krb_get_lrealm**(). This option is only availabe if the KDC has been compiled with version 4 support.

-K, --kaserver
> Enable kaserver emulation (in case it's compiled in).

-P *portspec*, --ports=*portspec*
> Specifies the set of ports the KDC should listen on. It is given as a white-space separated list of services or port numbers.

--addresses=`list of addresses`
>   The list of addresses to listen for requests on. By default, the kdc will listen on all the locally con-
>   figured addresses. If only a subset is desired, or the automatic detection fails, this option might be
>   used.

--detach
>   detach from pty and run as a daemon.

--disable-DES
>   disable add des encryption types, makes the kdc not use them.

All activities are logged to one or more destinations, see `krb5.conf`(5), and `krb5_openlog`(3). The
entity used for logging is **kdc**.

CONFIGURATION FILE

The configuration file has the same syntax as `krb5.conf`(5), but will be read before `/etc/krb5.conf`,
so it may override settings found there. Options specific to the KDC only are found in the "[kdc]" section.
All the command-line options can preferably be added in the configuration file. The only difference is the
pre-authentication flag, which has to be specified as:

>   `require-preauth = no`

(in fact you can specify the option as **--require-preauth=no**).

And there are some configuration options which do not have command-line equivalents:

>   `enable-digest` = *boolean*
>>   turn on support for digest processing in the KDC. The default is FALSE.

>   `check-ticket-addresses` = *boolean*
>>   Check the addresses in the ticket when processing TGS requests. The default is TRUE.

>   `allow-null-ticket-addresses` = *boolean*
>>   Permit tickets with no addresses. This option is only relevant when check-ticket-addresses is
>>   TRUE.

>   `allow-anonymous` = *boolean*
>>   Permit anonymous tickets with no addresses.

>   `max-kdc-datagram-reply-length` = *number*
>>   Maximum packet size the UDP rely that the KDC will transmit, instead the KDC sends back a
>>   reply telling the client to use TCP instead.

>   `transited-policy`   =   `always-check` | `allow-per-principal` |
>   `always-honour-request`
>>   This controls how KDC requests with the `disable-transited-check` flag are handled. It
>>   can be one of:

>>>   `always-check`
>>>>   Always check transited encoding, this is the default.

>>>   `allow-per-principal`
>>>>   Currently this is identical to `always-check`. In a future release, it will be pos-
>>>>   sible to mark a principal as able to handle unchecked requests.

>>>   `always-honour-request`
>>>>   Always do what the client asked. In a future release, it will be possible to force a
>>>>   check per principal.

encode_as_rep_as_tgs_rep = *boolean*
> Encode AS-Rep as TGS-Rep to be bug-compatible with old DCE code. The Heimdal clients allow both.

kdc_warn_pwexpire = *time*
> How long before password/principal expiration the KDC should start sending out warning messages.

The configuration file is only read when the **kdc** is started. If changes made to the configuration file are to take effect, the **kdc** needs to be restarted.

An example of a config file:

```
[kdc]
        require-preauth = no
        v4-realm = FOO.SE
```

BUGS

If the machine running the KDC has new addresses added to it, the KDC will have to be restarted to listen to them. The reason it doesn't just listen to wildcarded (like INADDR_ANY) addresses, is that the replies has to come from the same address they were sent to, and most OS:es doesn't pass this information to the application. If your normal mode of operation require that you add and remove addresses, the best option is probably to listen to a wildcarded TCP socket, and make sure your clients use TCP to connect. For instance, this will listen to IPv4 TCP port 88 only:

```
kdc --addresses=0.0.0.0 --ports="88/tcp"
```

There should be a way to specify protocol, port, and address triplets, not just addresses and protocol, port tuples.

SEE ALSO

kinit(1), krb5.conf(5)

NAME
   kdigest — userland tool to access digest interface in the KDC

SYNOPSIS
   kdigest [**--ccache=**_string_] [**--version**] [**--help**] command [arguments]

DESCRIPTION
   Supported options:

   --ccache=_string_
        credential cache

   --version
        print version

   --help

   Available commands are:

   digest-probe [**--realm=**_string_] [**-h** | **--help**]

        --realm=_string_
             Kerberos realm to communicate with

   digest-server-init [**--type=**_string_] [**--kerberos-realm=**_realm_] [**--digest=**_digest-type_]
        [**--cb-type=**_type_]   [**--cb-value=**_value_]   [**--hostname=**_hostname_]
        [**--realm=**_string_]

        --type=_string_
             digest type

        --kerberos-realm=_realm_

        --digest=_digest-type_
             digest type to use in the algorithm

        --cb-type=_type_
             type of channel bindings

        --cb-value=_value_
             value of channel bindings

        --hostname=_hostname_
             hostname of the server

        --realm=_string_
             Kerberos realm to communicate with

   digest-server-request [**--type=**_string_] [**--kerberos-realm=**_realm_] [**--username=**_name_]
        [**--server-nonce=**_nonce_]   [**--server-identifier=**_nonce_]
        [**--client-nonce=**_nonce_]   [**--client-response=**_response_]
        [**--opaque=**_string_]   [**--authentication-name=**_name_]   [**--realm=**_realm_]
        [**--method=**_method_] [**--uri=**_uri_] [**--nounce-count=**_count_] [**--qop=**_qop_]
        [**--ccache=**_ccache_]

        --type=_string_
             digest type

--kerberos-realm=_realm_

--username=_name_
     digest type

--server-nonce=_nonce_

--server-identifier=_nonce_

--client-nonce=_nonce_

--client-response=_response_

--opaque=_string_

--authentication-name=_name_

--realm=_realm_

--method=_method_

--uri=_uri_

--nounce-count=_count_

--qop=_qop_

--ccache=_ccache_
     Where the the credential cache is created when the KDC returns tickets

digest-client-request [**--type=**_string_] [**--username=**_name_] [**--password=**_password_]
   [**--server-nonce=**_nonce_]   [**--server-identifier=**_nonce_]
   [**--client-nonce=**_nonce_]   [**--opaque=**_string_]   [**--realm=**_realm_]
   [**--method=**_method_] [**--uri=**_uri_] [**--nounce-count=**_count_] [**--qop=**_qop_]

--type=_string_
     digest type

--username=_name_
     digest type

--password=_password_

--server-nonce=_nonce_

--server-identifier=_nonce_

--client-nonce=_nonce_

--opaque=_string_

--realm=_realm_

--method=_method_

--uri=_uri_

--nounce-count=_count_

--qop=_qop_

ntlm-server-init [**--version=**_integer_] [**--kerberos-realm=**_string_]

--version=_integer_
     ntlm version

--kerberos-realm=_string_
    Kerberos realm to communicate with

NAME
kerberos — introduction to the Kerberos system

DESCRIPTION
Kerberos is a network authentication system. Its purpose is to securely authenticate users and services in an insecure network environment.

This is done with a Kerberos server acting as a trusted third party, keeping a database with secret keys for all users and services (collectively called *principals*).

Each principal belongs to exactly one *realm*, which is the administrative domain in Kerberos. A realm usually corresponds to an organisation, and the realm should normally be derived from that organisation's domain name. A realm is served by one or more Kerberos servers.

The authentication process involves exchange of 'tickets' and 'authenticators' which together prove the principal's identity.

When you login to the Kerberos system, either through the normal system login or with the kinit(1) program, you acquire a *ticket granting ticket* which allows you to get new tickets for other services, such as **telnet** or **ftp**, without giving your password.

For more information on how Kerberos works, and other general Kerberos questions see the Kerberos FAQ at http://www.nrl.navy.mil/CCS/people/kenh/kerberos-faq.html.

For setup instructions see the Heimdal Texinfo manual.

SEE ALSO
ftp(1), kdestroy(1), kinit(1), klist(1), kpasswd(1), telnet(1)

HISTORY
The Kerberos authentication system was developed in the late 1980's as part of the Athena Project at the Massachusetts Institute of Technology. Versions one through three never reached outside MIT, but version 4 was (and still is) quite popular, especially in the academic community, but is also used in commercial products like the AFS filesystem.

The problems with version 4 are that it has many limitations, the code was not too well written (since it had been developed over a long time), and it has a number of known security problems. To resolve many of these issues work on version five started, and resulted in IETF RFC 1510 in 1993. IETF RFC 1510 was obsoleted in 2005 with IETF RFC 4120, also known as Kerberos clarifications. With the arrival of IETF RFC 4120, the work on adding extensibility and internationalization have started (Kerberos extensions), and a new RFC will hopefully appear soon.

This manual page is part of the **Heimdal** Kerberos 5 distribution, which has been in development at the Royal Institute of Technology in Stockholm, Sweden, since about 1997.

NAME

kgmon — generate a dump of the operating system's profile buffers

SYNOPSIS

kgmon [**-bdhpr**] [**-M** *core*] [**-N** *system*]

DESCRIPTION

kgmon is a tool used when profiling the operating system. When no arguments are supplied, **kgmon** indicates the state of operating system profiling as running, off, or not configured (see config(1)). If the **-p** flag is specified, **kgmon** extracts profile data from the operating system and produces a gmon.out file suitable for later analysis by gprof(1).

The options are as follows:

-b Resume the collection of profile data.

-d Enable debug output.

-h Stop the collection of profile data.

-M Extract values associated with the name list from the specified core instead of the default /dev/kmem.

-N Extract the name list from the specified system instead of the default /netbsd.

-p Dump the contents of the profile buffers into a gmon.out file.

-r Reset all the profile buffers. If the **-p** flag is also specified, the gmon.out file is generated before the buffers are reset.

If neither **-b** nor **-h** is specified, the state of profiling collection remains unchanged. For example, if the **-p** flag is specified and profile data is being collected, profiling will be momentarily suspended, the operating system profile buffers will be dumped, and profiling will be immediately resumed.

FILES

/netbsd   the default system
/dev/kmem   the default memory

DIAGNOSTICS

Users with only read permission on /dev/kmem cannot change the state of profiling collection. They can get a gmon.out file with the warning that the data may be inconsistent if profiling is in progress.

SEE ALSO

config(1), gprof(1)

HISTORY

The **kgmon** command appeared in 4.2 BSD.

NAME

kimpersonate — impersonate a user when there exist a srvtab, keyfile or KeyFile

SYNOPSIS

kimpersonate [**-s** *string* | **--server=***string*] [**-c** *string* | **--client=***string*]
                [**-k** *string* | **--keytab=***string*] [**-5** | **--krb5**]
                [**-e** *integer* | **--expire-time=***integer*]
                [**-a** *string* | **--client-address=***string*]
                [**-t** *string* | **--enc-type=***string*]
                [**-f** *string* | **--ticket-flags=***string*] [**--verbose**] [**--version**]
                [**--help**]

DESCRIPTION

The **kimpersonate** program creates a "fake" ticket using the service-key of the service. The service key can be read from a Kerberos 5 keytab, AFS KeyFile or (if compiled with support for Kerberos 4) a Kerberos 4 srvtab. Supported options:

-s *string*, **--server=***string*
    name of server principal

-c *string*, **--client=***string*
    name of client principal

-k *string*, **--keytab=***string*
    name of keytab file

-5, **--krb5**
    create a Kerberos 5 ticket

-e *integer*, **--expire-time=***integer*
    lifetime of ticket in seconds

-a *string*, **--client-address=***string*
    address of client

-t *string*, **--enc-type=***string*
    encryption type

-f *string*, **--ticket-flags=***string*
    ticket flags for krb5 ticket

--verbose
    Verbose output

--version
    Print version

--help

FILES

Uses /etc/krb5.keytab, /etc/srvtab and /usr/afs/etc/KeyFile when avalible and the the **-k** is used with appropriate prefix.

EXAMPLES

kimpersonate can be used in **samba** root preexec option or for debugging. **kimpersonate** -s host/hummel.e.kth.se@E.KTH.SE -c lha@E.KTH.SE -5 will create a Kerberos 5 ticket for lha@E.KTH.SE for the host hummel.e.kth.se if there exists a keytab entry for it in /etc/krb5.keytab.

SEE ALSO
>   `kinit`(1), `klist`(1)

AUTHORS
>   Love Hornquist Astrand <lha@kth.se>

NAME
kpasswdd — Kerberos 5 password changing server

SYNOPSIS
kpasswdd [**--addresses**=*address*] [**--check-library**=*library*]
       [**--check-function**=*function*] [**-k** *kspec* | **--keytab**=*kspec*] [**-r** *realm* |
       --realm=*realm*] [**-p** *string* | **--port**=*string*] [**--version**] [**--help**]

DESCRIPTION
kpasswdd serves request for password changes. It listens on UDP port 464 (service kpasswd) and processes requests when they arrive. It changes the database directly and should thus only run on the master KDC.

Supported options:

--addresses=*address*
> For each till the argument is given, add the address to what kpasswdd should listen too.

--check-library=*library*
> If your system has support for dynamic loading of shared libraries, you can use an external function to check password quality. This option specifies which library to load.

--check-function=*function*
> This is the function to call in the loaded library. The function should look like this:

> const char * **passwd_check**(*krb5_context context, krb5_principal principal, krb5_data *password*)

> *context* is an initialized context; *principal* is the one who tries to change passwords, and *password* is the new password. Note that the password (in *password->data*) is not zero terminated.

-k *kspec*, **--keytab**=*kspec*
> Keytab to get authentication key from.

-r *realm*, **--realm**=*realm*
> Default realm.

-p *string*, **--port**=*string*
> Port to listen on (default service kpasswd - 464).

DIAGNOSTICS
If an error occurs, the error message is returned to the user and/or logged to syslog.

BUGS
The default password quality checks are too basic.

SEE ALSO
kpasswd(1), kdc(8)

NAME
kstash — store the KDC master password in a file

SYNOPSIS
kstash [-e *string* | --enctype=*string*] [-k *file* | --key-file=*file*]
        [--convert-file] [--random-key] [--master-key-fd=*fd*] [--random-key]
        [-h | --help] [--version]

DESCRIPTION
kstash reads the Kerberos master key and stores it in a file that will be used by the KDC.

Supported options:

-e *string*, --enctype=*string*
    the encryption type to use, defaults to DES3-CBC-SHA1.

-k *file*, --key-file=*file*
    the name of the master key file.

--convert-file
    don't ask for a new master key, just read an old master key file, and write it back in the new keyfile
    format.

--random-key
    generate a random master key.

--master-key-fd=*fd*
    filedescriptor to read passphrase from, if not specified the passphrase will be read from the terminal.

FILES
/var/heimdal/m-key is the default keyfile if no other keyfile is specified. The format of a Heimdal
master key is the same as a keytab, so ktutil list can be used to list the content of the file.

SEE ALSO
kdc(8)

NAME

ktutil — manage Kerberos keytabs

SYNOPSIS

ktutil [**-k** *keytab* | **--keytab**=*keytab*] [**-v** | **--verbose**] [**--version**]
[**-h** | **--help**] *command* [*args*]

DESCRIPTION

ktutil is a program for managing keytabs. Supported options:

-v, --verbose
    Verbose output.

command can be one of the following:

add [**-p** *principal*] [**--principal**=*principal*] [**-V** *kvno*] [**--kvno**=*kvno*] [**-e** *enctype*]
[**--enctype**=*enctype*] [**-w** *password*] [**--password**=*password*] [**-r**]
[**--random**] [**-s**] [**--no-salt**] [**-H**] [**--hex**]
    Adds a key to the keytab. Options that are not specified will be prompted for. This requires
    that you know the password or the hex key of the principal to add; if what you really want is
    to add a new principal to the keytab, you should consider the *get* command, which talks to
    the kadmin server.

change [**-r** *realm*] [**--realm**=*realm*] [**--a** *host*] [**--admin-server**=*host*] [**--s** *port*]
[**--server-port**=*port*]
    Update one or several keys to new versions. By default, use the admin server for the realm
    of a keytab entry. Otherwise it will use the values specified by the options.

    If no principals are given, all the ones in the keytab are updated.

copy *keytab-src keytab-dest*
    Copies all the entries from *keytab-src* to *keytab-dest*.

get [**-p** *admin principal*] [**--principal**=*admin principal*] [**-e** *enctype*]
[**--enctypes**=*enctype*] [**-r** *realm*] [**--realm**=*realm*] [**-a** *admin server*]
[**--admin-server**=*admin server*] [**-s** *server port*]
[**--server-port**=*server port*] *principal* . . .
    For each *principal*, generate a new key for it (creating it if it doesn't already exist), and
    put that key in the keytab.

    If no *realm* is specified, the realm to operate on is taken from the first principal.

list [**--keys**] [**--timestamp**]
    List the keys stored in the keytab.

remove [**-p** *principal*] [**--principal**=*principal*] [**-V** *-kvno*] [**--kvno**=*kvno*] [**-e**
-enctype] [**--enctype**=*enctype*]
    Removes the specified key or keys. Not specifying a *kvno* removes keys with any version
    number. Not specifying an *enctype* removes keys of any type.

rename *from-principal to-principal*
    Renames all entries in the keytab that match the *from-principal* to *to-principal*.

purge [**--age**=*age*]
    Removes all old versions of a key for which there is a newer version that is at least *age*
    (default one week) old.

srvconvert

srv2keytab [**-s** *srvtab*] [**--srvtab=***srvtab*]
> Converts the version 4 srvtab in *srvtab* to a version 5 keytab and stores it in *keytab*.
> Identical to:

```
ktutil copy krb4:srvtab keytab
```

srvcreate

key2srvtab [**-s** *srvtab*] [**--srvtab=***srvtab*]
> Converts the version 5 keytab in *keytab* to a version 4 srvtab and stores it in *srvtab*.
> Identical to:

```
ktutil copy keytab krb4:srvtab
```

SEE ALSO
> kadmin(8)

NAME
lastlogin — indicate last login time of users

SYNOPSIS
lastlogin [**-nrt**] [**-f** *filename*] [**-H** *hostsize*] [**-L** *linesize*] [**-N** *namesize*]
         [user ...]

DESCRIPTION
lastlogin will list the last login session of specified *users*, or for all users by default. Each line of output contains the user name, the tty from which the session was conducted, any hostname, and the start time for the session.

If multiple *users* are given, the session information for each user is printed in the order given on the command line. Otherwise, information for all users is printed, sorted by uid.

lastlogin differs from last(1) in that it only prints information regarding the very last login session. The last login database is never turned over or deleted in standard usage.

The following options are available:

-f *filename*
         Process input from *filename*. If the file ends with an "x", then it is assumed that it is a lastlogx(5) file, else it is assumed to be a lastlog(5) file.

-H *hostlen*
         Set the field width for host output to *hostlen* characters.

-L *linelen*
         Set the field width for line output to *linelen* characters.

-N *namelen*
         Set the field width for name output to *namelen* characters.

-n   Attempt to print numeric host addresses. This option is only supported with lastlogx(5) format files.

-r   Reverse the order of the sort.

-t   Sort by last login time (most recent first.)

FILES
/var/log/lastlogx default last login database
/var/log/lastlog   compatibility last login database

EXAMPLES
lastlogin looks by default to the /var/log/lastlogx database, where some old programs that are not utmpx(5) aware might only write to /var/log/lastlog. To look at the old database one can use:

         lastlogin -f /var/log/lastlog

SEE ALSO
last(1), lastlog(5), lastlogx(5), ac(8)

AUTHORS
John M. Vinopal wrote this program in January 1996 and contributed it to the NetBSD project.

NAME
ldconfig — configure the a.out shared library cache

SYNOPSIS
ldconfig [-cmrsSv] [*directory* ...]

DESCRIPTION
ldconfig is used to prepare a set of "hints" for use by the a.out run-time linker **ld.so** to facilitate quick lookup of shared libraries available in multiple directories. **ldconfig** is only available on systems that use the "a.out" format for executables and libraries – on ELF systems, all the work is done by **ld.elf_so**.

By default, it scans a set of built-in system directories, directories listed in /etc/ld.so.conf, and any *directories* specified on the command line (in the given order) looking for shared libraries and stores the results in the file /var/run/ld.so.hints to forestall the overhead that would otherwise result from the directory search operations **ld.so** would have to perform to load required shared libraries.

The shared libraries so found will be automatically available for loading if needed by the program being prepared for execution. This obviates the need for storing search paths within the executable.

The LD_LIBRARY_PATH environment variable can be used to override the use of directories (or the order thereof) from the cache or to specify additional directories where shared libraries might be found. LD_LIBRARY_PATH is a ':' separated list of directory paths that are searched by **ld.so** when it needs to load a shared library. It can be viewed as the run-time equivalent of the **−L** switch of **ld**.

ldconfig is typically run as part of the boot sequence.

The following options are recognized by **ldconfig**:

−c   Do not scan directories listed in /etc/ld.so.conf for shared libraries.

−m   Merge the result of the scan of the directories given as arguments into the existing hints file. The default action is to build the hints file afresh.

−r   Lists the current contents of ld.so.hints on the standard output. The hints file will not be modified.

−s   Do not scan the built-in system directory (/usr/lib), nor any directories listed in /etc/ld.so.conf for shared libraries.

−S   Do not scan the built-in system directory (/usr/lib), for shared libraries. (Directories listed in /etc/ld.so.conf are still scanned.)

−v   Switch on verbose mode.

FILES
/var/run/ld.so.hints, /etc/ld.so.conf

SEE ALSO
ld(1), ld.so(1), ld.so.conf(5), link(5)

HISTORY
A **ldconfig** utility first appeared in SunOS 4.0, it appeared in its current form in NetBSD 0.9A.

SECURITY CONSIDERATIONS
Special care must be taken when loading shared libraries into the address space of *set-user-ID* programs. Whenever such a program is run, **ld.so** will only load shared libraries from the ld.so.hints file. In particular, the LD_LIBRARY_PATH and LD_PRELOAD is not used to search for libraries. Thus, the role of

ldconfig is dual. In addition to building a set of hints for quick lookup, it also serves to specify the trusted collection of directories from which shared objects can be safely loaded. It is presumed that the set of directories specified to **ldconfig** is under control of the system's administrator. **ld.so** further assists set-user-ID programs by erasing the LD_LIBRARY_PATH and LD_PRELOAD from the environment.

NAME
lfs_cleanerd — garbage collect a log-structured file system

SYNOPSIS
lfs_cleanerd [**-bcDdfmqs**] [**-i** *segment-number*] [**-l** *load-threshhold*]
[**-n** *number-of-segments*] [**-r** *report-frequency*] [**-t** *timeout*]
node

DESCRIPTION
The **lfs_cleanerd** command starts a daemon process which garbage-collects the log-structured file system residing at the point named by *node* in the global file system namespace. This command is normally executed by mount_lfs(8) when the log-structured file system is mounted. The daemon will exit within a few minutes of when the file system it was cleaning is unmounted.

Garbage collection on a log-structured file system is done by scanning the file system's segments for active, i.e. referenced, data and copying it to new segments. When all of the active data in a given segment has been copied to a new segment that segment can be marked as empty, thus reclaiming the space taken by the inactive data which was in it.

The following options are available:

-b   Use bytes written, rather than segments read, when determining how many segments to clean at once.

-c   Coalescing mode. For each live inode, check to see if it has too many blocks that are not contiguous, and if it does, rewrite it. After a single pass through the filesystem the cleaner will exit. This option has been reported to corrupt file data; do not use it.

-D   Stay in the foreground, do not become a daemon process. Does not print additional debugging information (in contrast to **-d**).

-d   Run in debug mode. Do not become a daemon process, and print debugging information. More **-d** s give more detailed debugging information.

-f   Use filesystem idle time as the criterion for aggressive cleaning, instead of system load.

-i *segment-number*
Invalidate the segment with segment number *segment-number*. This option is used by resize_lfs(8), and should not be specified on the command line.

-l *load-threshhold*
Clean more aggressively when the system load is below the given threshhold. The default threshhold is 0.2.

-m   Does nothing. This option is present for historical compatibility.

-n *number-of-segments*
Clean this number of segments at a time: that is, pass this many segments' blocks through a single call to lfs_markv, or, if **-b** was also given, pass this many segments' worth of blocks through a single call to lfs_markv.

-q   Quit after cleaning once.

-r *report-frequency*
Give an efficiency report after every *report-frequency* times through the main loop.

-s   When cleaning the file system, send only a few blocks through lfs_markv at a time. Don't use this option.

−t *timeout*

      Poll the filesystem every *timeout* seconds, looking for opportunities to clean. The default is 300, that is, five minutes. Note that **lfs_cleanerd** will be automatically awakened when the filesystem is active, so it is not usually necessary to set *timeout* to a low value.

SEE ALSO

      lfs_bmapv(2), lfs_markv(2), lfs_segwait(2), mount_lfs(8)

HISTORY

      The **lfs_cleanerd** utility first appeared in 4.4BSD.

NAME
   link — call the **link**() function

SYNOPSIS
   link *file1 file2*

DESCRIPTION
   The **link** utility performs the function call **link**(*file1*, *file2*).

   file1 must be the pathname of an existing file, and *file2* is the pathname of the new link to *file1* to be created.

EXIT STATUS
   The **link** utility exits 0 on success, and >0 if an error occurs.

SEE ALSO
   ln(1), link(2), unlink(8)

STANDARDS
   The **link** utility conforms to X/Open Commands and Utilities Issue 5 ("XCU5").

NAME
lmcconfig — configuration program for LMC (and some SBE) wide-area network interface cards

SYNOPSIS
lmcconfig *interface* [**-abBcCdDeEfgGhiLmMpPsStTuUvVwxXyY?**]
lmcconfig *interface* **-1** [**-aABcdeEfFgiIlLpPstTuUxX**]
lmcconfig *interface* **-3** [**-aABcefFlLsSV**]

DESCRIPTION
The **lmcconfig** utility is the configuration program for the lmc(4) wide-area network device driver. It sets control values, such as T3 framing format, and it displays status, such as that of integrated modems, which are beyond the scope of ifconfig(8).

The **lmcconfig** utility displays the interface status when no parameters are specified; see the **EXAMPLES** section. For this case only, if no *interface* is specified, it defaults to "lmc0".

Only the super-user may modify the configuration of a network interface.

The following options are available:

interface This is the name of the interface; the default is "lmc0".

-1   All parameters after this apply to the T1E1 card.

-3   All parameters after this apply to the T3 card.

Parameters for all cards
The following parameters apply to more then one card type.

-a *number*   Set Transmitter clock source to *number*.

1	TxClk from modem	T1E1, HSSI	(default)
2	Internal source	T1E1, HSSI	
3	RxClk from modem	T1E1, HSSIc	(loop timed)
4	External connector	T1E1, HSSIc	

An HSSI card normally takes its Tx clock from the modem connector (it is a DTE) but can use the PCI bus clock (typically 33 MHz) for loopback and null modem testing; values 3 and 4 are only applicable to a few rare CompactPCI/HSSI cards.

A T1E1 card uses an on-board synthesized oscillator if the value is 1 or 2; it *loop times* (uses the clock recovered by the receiver as the transmitter clock) if the value is 3; and it uses a clock from a header connector on the card if the value is 4.

TxClk source is not applicable to other card types.

-b   Read BIOS ROM. Print the first 256 locations. The BIOS ROM is not used and not present on some cards.

-B   Write BIOS ROM. Write the first 256 locations with an address pattern.

-c   Use HDLC's 16-bit Cyclic Redundancy Checksum (CRC).

-C   Use HDLC's 32-bit Cyclic Redundancy Checksum (CRC).

-d   Clear the driver-level debug flag. Non-critical log messages are suppressed.

-D   Set the driver-level debug flag. The driver generates more log messages. The driver also generates more log messages if the interface-level debug flag is set by ifconfig(8).

-e   Set DTE (Data Terminal Equipment) mode (default). An SSI card transmitter uses the Tx clock signal from the modem connector and receives the Data Carrier Detect pin (DCD). DTE/DCE is not applicable to other card types except a few rare CompactPCI/HSSI cards.

-E   Set DCE (Data Communication Equipment) mode. An SSI card transmitter uses an on-board synthesized oscillator and drives the Data Carrier Detect pin (DCD).

-f *number*   Set the frequency of the built-in synthesized oscillator to *number* bits/second. The near-est frequency that the synthesizer can generate will be used. Only SSI cards and a few rare CompactPCI/HSSI cards have synthesizers.

-g   Load gate array microcode from on-board ROM; see also **-U**.

-G *filename*   Load gate array microcode from *filename*; see also **-U**.

-h   Print help (usage message).

-i   Set interface name (e.g. "lmc0").

-L *number*   Set loopback mode to *number*.

1	none	default	
2	payload	outward thru framer	T1E1. T3
3	line	outward thru line if	T1E1, T3
4	other	inward thru line if	T1E1, T3
5	inward	inward thru framer	T1E1, T3
6	dual	inward and outward	T1E1, T3
16	tulip	inward thru Tulip chip	all cards
17	pins	inward thru drvrs/rcvrs	SSI
18	LA/LL	assert LA/LL modem pin	HSSI, SSI
19	LB/RL	assert LB/RL modem pin	HSSI, SSI

-m   Read Tulip MII registers. Print the 32 16-bit registers in the Media Independent Interface.

-M *addr data*

                               Write Tulip MII register. Write *data* into register *addr*.

-p   Read Tulip PCI configuration registers. Print the first 16 32-bit registers in the PCI con-figuration space.

-P *addr data*

                               Write Tulip PCI configuration register. Write *data* into register *addr*.

-s   Read Tulip SROM. Print the 64 16-bit locations. The PCI subsystem vendor and device IDs are kept here.

-S *number*   Write Tulip SROM. Initializes the Tulip SROM to card type *number*.

                               3   HSSI
                               4   T3
                               5   SSI
                               6   T1E1
                               7   HSSIc
                               8   SDSL
                               0   auto-set from uCode type

                               If *number* is zero, then the card type is computed from the gate array microcode version field in the MII PHYID register. *CAUTION*: if the SROM is incorrect, the card will be unusable! This command is *so* dangerous that **lmcconfig** must be edited and recom-

	piled to enable it.
-t	Read Tulip CSRs. Print the 16 32-bit Control and Status Registers.
-T *addr data*	
	Write Tulip CSR. Write *data* into register *addr*. Note that *addr* is a CSR number (0-15) not a byte offset into CSR space.
-u	Reset event counters to zero. The driver counts events like packets in and out, errors, discards, etc. The time when the counters are reset is remembered.
-U	Reset gate array microcode.
-v	Set verbose mode: print more stuff.
-V	Print the card configuration; see the **EXAMPLES** section.
-x *number*	Set the line control protocol to *number*. Line control protocols are listed below along with the operating systems that implement them and the stacks that include them.

x	*Protocol*	*OpSys Stack*	
1	IPinHDLC	FNOBL	D--G-N
2	PPP	FNOBL	-SPGYN
3	CiscoHDLC	FNOBL	-SPGYN
4	FrameRelay	F--BL	-SPG-N
5	EthInHDLC	F---L	---G-N

OpSys: FreeBSD NetBSD OpenBSD BSD/OS Linux.
Stack: Driver SPPP P2P GenHDLC sYncPPP Netgraph.

-X *number*	Set the line control protocol stack to *number*. Line control protocol stacks are listed below along with the operating systems that include them and the protocols that they implement.

X	*Stack*	*OpSys Protocol*	
1	Driver	FNOBL	I----
2	SPPP	FNO--	-PCF-
3	P2P	---B-	-PCF-
4	GenHDLC	----L	IPCFE
5	SyncPPP	----L	-PC--
6	Netgraph	F----	IPCFE

OpSys: FreeBSD NetBSD OpenBSD BSD/OS Linux.
Protocol: IPinHDLC PPP CiscoHDLC FrmRly EthInHDLC.

-y	Disable SPPP/SyncPPP keep-alive packets,
-Y	Enable SPPP/SyncPPP keep-alive packets.
-?	Print help (usage message).

Parameters for T1E1 cards

The following parameters apply to the T1E1 card type:

-a y|a|b	Stop sending alarm signal (see table below).
-A y|a|b	Start sending alarm signal.

y	Yellow Alarm	varies with framing
a	Red Alarm	unframed all ones; aka AIS
b	Blue Alarm	unframed all ones

Red alarm, also known as AIS (Alarm Indication Signal), and Blue alarm are identical in T1.

-B *number*　　Send a Bit Oriented Protocol (BOP) message with code *number*. BOP codes are six bits.

-c *number*　　Set cable length to *number* meters (default: 10 meters). This is used to set receiver sensitivity and transmitter line build-out.

-d　　Print the status of the on-board T1 DSU/CSU; see the **EXAMPLES** section.

-e *number*　　Set the framing format to *number*.

9	T1-SF/AMI
27	T1-ESF/B8ZS (default)
0	E1-FAS
8	E1-FAS+CRC
16	E1-FAS+CAS
24	E1-FAS+CRC+CAS
32	E1-NO-framing

-E *number*　　Enable 64Kb time slots (TSs) for the T1E1 card. The *number* argument is a 32-bit hex number (default 0xFFFFFFFF). The LSB is TS0 and the MSB is TS31. TS0 and TS25-31 are ignored in T1 mode. TS0 and TS16 are determined by the framing format in E1 mode.

-f　　Read framer registers. Print the 512 8-bit registers in the framer chip.

-F *addr data*

　　Write framer register. Write *data* into register *addr*.

-g *number*　　Set receiver gain range to *number*.

0x24	Short	0 to 20 dB of equalized gain
0x2C	Medium	0 to 30 dB of equalized gain
0x34	Long	0 to 40 dB of equalized gain
0x3F	Extend	0 to 64 dB of equalized gain (wide open)
0xFF	Auto	auto-set based on cable length (default)

This sets the level at which *Loss-Of-Signal* is declared.

-i　　Send a *CSU loopback deactivate* inband command (T1 only).

-I　　Send a *CSU loopback activate* inband command (T1 only).

-l　　Send a *line loopback deactivate* BOP message (T1-ESF only).

-L　　Send a *line loopback activate* BOP message (T1-ESF only).

-p　　Send a *payload loopback deactivate* BOP message (T1-ESF only).

-P　　Send a *payload loopback activate* BOP message (T1-ESF only).

-s　　Print the status of the on-board DSU/CSU; see the **EXAMPLES** section.

-t　　Stop sending test pattern (see table below).

-**T** *number*   Start sending test pattern *number*.

0	unframed X^11+X^9+1
1	unframed X^15+X^14+1
2	unframed X^20+X^17+1
3	unframed X^23+X^18+1
4	unframed X^11+X^9+1 with 7ZS
5	unframed X^15+X^14+1 with 7ZS
6	unframed X^20+X^17+1 with 14ZS (QRSS)
7	unframed X^23+X^18+1 with 14ZS
8	framed X^11+X^9+1
9	framed X^15+X^14+1
10	framed X^20+X^17+1
11	framed X^23+X^18+1
12	framed X^11+X^9+1 with 7ZS
13	framed X^15+X^14+1 with 7ZS
14	framed X^20+X^17+1 with 14ZS (QRSS)
15	framed X^23+X^18+1 with 14ZS

-**u** *number*   Set transmit pulse shape to *number*.

0	T1 DSX 0 to 40 meters
2	T1 DSX 40 to 80 meters
4	T1 DSX 80 to 120 meters
6	T1 DSX 120 to 160 meters
8	T1 DSX 160 to 200 meters
10	E1 75-ohm coax pair
12	E1 120-ohm twisted pairs
14	T1 CSU 200 to 2000 meters; set LBO
255	auto-set based on cable length and framing format (default)

-**U** *number*   Set transmit line build-out to *number*.

0	0 dB	FCC option A
16	7.5 dB	FCC option B
32	15 dB	FCC option C
48	22.5 dB	final span
255	auto-set based on cable length (default)	

This is only applicable if the pulse shape is T1-CSU.

-**x**   Disable transmitter outputs.

-**X**   Enable transmitter outputs.

Parameters for T3 cards

The following parameters apply to the T3 card type:

-**a** y|a|b|i   Stop sending alarm signal (see table below).

-**A** y|a|b|i   Start sending alarm signal.

y	Yellow Alarm	X-bits set to 0
a	Red Alarm	framed 1010... aka AIS
b	Blue Alarm	unframed all-ones

	i Idle signal framed 11001100...
−B *number*	Send a Far End Alarm and Control (FEAC) message with code *number*. FEAC codes are six bits.
−c *number*	Set cable length to *number* meters (default: 10 meters). This is used to set receiver sensitivity and transmitter line build-out.
−d	Print the status of the on-board T3 DSU; see the **EXAMPLES** section.
−e *number*	Set the framing format to *number*.

100   T3-C-bit parity
101   T3-M13 format

−f	Read framer registers. Print the 22 8-bit registers in the framer chip.
−F *addr data*	
	Write framer register. Write *data* into register *addr*.
−l	Send a *line loopback deactivate* BOP message.
−L	Send a *line loopback activate* BOP message.
−s	Print the status of the on-board T3 DSU; see the **EXAMPLES** section.
−S *number*	Set payload scrambler polynominal to *number*.

1   payload scrambler disabled
2   X^43+1: DigitalLink and Kentrox
3   X^20+X^17+1 w/28ZS: Larscom

Payload scrambler polynomials are not standardized.

−V *number*	Set transmit frequency offset to *number*. Some T3 cards can offset the transmitter frequency from 44.736 MHz. *Number* is in the range (0..4095); 2048 is zero offset; step size is about 3 Hz. A *number* is written to a Digital-Analog Converter (DAC) which connects to a Voltage Controlled Crystal Oscillator (VCXO).

Event Counters

The device driver counts many interesting events such as packets in and out, errors and discards. The table below lists the event counters and describes what they count.

Rx bytes	Bytes received in packets with good ending status.
Tx bytes	Bytes transmitted in packets with good ending status.
Rx packets	Packets received with good ending status.
Tx packets	Packets transmitted with good ending status.
Rx errors	Packets received with bad ending status.
Tx errors	Packets transmitted with bad ending status.
Rx drops	Packets received but discarded by software because the input queue was full or the link was down.
Rx missed	Packets that were missed by hardware because the receiver was enabled but had no DMA descriptors.

Tx drops	Packets presented for transmission but discarded by software because the output queue was full or the link was down.
Rx fifo overruns	Packets that started to arrive, but were aborted because the card was unable to DMA data to memory fast enough to prevent the receiver fifo from overflowing. This is reported in the ending status of DMA descriptors.
Rx overruns	Rx Fifo overruns reported by the Tulip chip in the Status CSR. The driver stops the receiver and restarts it to work around a potential hardware hangup.
Tx fifo underruns	Packets that started to transmit but were aborted because the card was unable to DMA data from memory fast enough to prevent the transmitter fifo from under-flowing. This is reported in the ending status of DMA descriptors.
Tx underruns	Tx Fifo underruns reported by the Tulip chip in the Status CSR. The driver increases the transmitter threshold, requiring more bytes to be in the fifo before the transmitter is started.
Rx FDL pkts	Packets received on the T1 Facility Data Link.
Rx CRC	Cyclic Redundancy Checksum errors detected by the CRC-6 in T1 Extended SuperFrames (ESF) or the CRC-4 in E1 frames.
Rx line code	Line Coding Violation errors: Alternate Mark Inversion (AMI) errors for T1-SF, Bipolar 8-Zero Substitution (B8ZS) errors for T1-ESF, or High Density Bipolar with 3-Zero Substitution (HDB3) errors for E1 or Bipolar 3-Zero Substitution (B3ZS) errors for T3.
Rx F-bits	T1 or T3 bit errors in the frame alignment signal.
Rx FEBE	Far End Block Errors: T1 or T3 bit errors detected by the device at the far end of the link.
Rx P-parity	T3 bit errors detected by the hop-by-hop parity mechanism.
Rx C-parity	T3 bit errors detected by the end-to-end parity mechanism.
Rx M-bits	T3 bit errors in the multi-frame alignment signal.

If driver debug mode is enabled, more event counters are displayed.

Rx no bufs	Failure to allocate a replacement packet buffer for an incoming packet. The buffer allocation is retried later.
Tx no descs	Failure to allocate a DMA descriptor for an outgoing packet. The descriptor allocation is retried later.
Lock watch	The watchdog routine conflicted with an IOCTL syscall.
Lock intr	A CPU tried to enter the interrupt handler while another CPU was already inside. The second CPU simply walks away.
Spare1-4	Nameless events of interest to the device driver maintainer.

Transmit Speed

The hardware counts transmit clocks divided by 2048. The software computes "Tx speed" from this (see **EXAMPLES** below). The transmit clock is the bit rate of the circuit divided by two if the circuit is idle and divided by four if the circuit is carrying a packet. So an empty circuit reports a Tx speed equal to its bit rate, and a full circuit reports a Tx speed equal to half its bit rate.

This "bit rate" does not include circuit-level overhead bits (such as T1 or T3 frame bits) but does include HDLC stuff bits. An idle T1 circuit with a raw bit rate of 1544000 and a bit-rate-minus-overhead of 1536000 will report a "Tx speed" of ((1536000 bitand 4095) plus or minus 4096). Sometimes it will even get the correct answer of 1536000, and if the link is fully loaded it will report about 768000 bits/sec.

It is not a perfect bit rate meter (the circuit must be idle), but it is a useful circuit utilization meter if you know the circuit bit rate and do some arithmetic. Software recalculates Tx speed once a second; the measurement period has some jitter.

EXAMPLES

When "lmc0" is a T1E1 card, "lmcconfig lmc0" generates the following output:

```
Card name:           lmc0
Card type:           T1E1 (lmc1200)
Link status:         Up
Tx Speed:            1536000
Line Prot/Pkg:       PPP/P2P
CRC length:          16 bits
Tx Clk src:          Modem Rx Clk (loop timed)
Format-Frame/Code:   T1-ESF/B8ZS
TimeSlots [31-0]:    0x01FFFFFE
Cable length:        10 meters
Current time:        Wed Jan  4 05:35:10 2006
Cntrs reset:         Fri Dec 16 19:23:45 2005
Rx bytes:            176308259
Tx bytes:            35194717
Rx packets:          383162
Tx packets:          357792
```

When "lmc0" is a T1E1 card, "lmcconfig lmc0 -1 -d" generates the following output:

```
Format-Frame/Code:   T1-ESF/B8ZS
TimeSlots [31-0]:    0x01FFFFFE
Tx Clk src:          Modem Rx Clk (loop timed)
Tx Speed:            1536000
Tx pulse shape:      T1-DSX: 0 to 40 meters
Tx outputs:          Enabled
Line impedance:      100 ohms
Max line loss:       20.0 dB
Cur line loss:        0.0 dB
Invert data:         No
Line    loop:        No
Payload loop:        No
Framer  loop:        No
Analog  loop:        No
Tx AIS:              No
Rx AIS:              No
Tx BOP RAI:          No
Rx BOP RAI:          No
Rx LOS analog:       No
Rx LOS digital:      No
Rx LOF:              No
Tx QRS:              No
Rx QRS:              No
```

```
        LCV errors:             0
        CRC errors:             0
        Frame errors:           0
        Sev Err Frms:           0
        Change of Frm align:    0
        Loss of Frame events:   0
        SNMP Near-end performance data:
         LCV=0 LOS=0 FE=0 CRC=0 AIS=0 SEF=0 OOF=0  RAI=0
        ANSI Far-end performance reports:
         SEQ=0 CRC=0 SE=0 FE=0 LV=0 SL=0 LB=0
         SEQ=1 CRC=0 SE=0 FE=0 LV=0 SL=0 LB=0
         SEQ=2 CRC=0 SE=0 FE=0 LV=0 SL=0 LB=0
         SEQ=3 CRC=0 SE=0 FE=0 LV=0 SL=0 LB=0
```

DIAGNOSTICS

Messages indicating the specified interface does not exist, or the user is not privileged and tried to alter an interface's configuration.

SEE ALSO

ioctl(2), lmc(4), ifconfig(8), ifnet(9)

http://www.sbei.com/

HISTORY

This is a total rewrite of the program **lmcctl** by Michael Graff, Rob Braun and Andrew Stanley-Jones.

AUTHORS

David Boggs ⟨boggs@boggs.palo-alto.ca.us⟩

NAME
loadbsd — load and boot NetBSD/x68k kernel from Human68k

SYNOPSIS
loadbsd.x [**-hvV**] [**-abDs**] [**-r** *root_device*] *kernel_file*

DESCRIPTION
loadbsd is a program runs on Human68k. It loads and executes the specified NetBSD/x68k kernel.

The options (for **loadbsd** itself) are as follows:

-h   Show help and exit.

-v   Enable verbose mode.

-V   Print version of **loadbsd** and exit.

The options for NetBSD kernel are as follows:

-a   Auto (multi-user) boot. This disables **-s** flag.

-b   Ask boot device during boot. Pass RB_ASKNAME boot flag to the kernel.

-d   Use compiled-in rootdev. Pass RB_DFLTROOT boot flag to the kernel.

-D   Enter kernel debugger. Pass RB_KDB boot flag to the kernel.

-r *root_device*
          Specify boot device, which shall be mounted as root device. The default device is 'sd@0,0:a'.
          Note that the boot device name is *not* the same as that of NetBSD. See **BOOT DEVICE NAMES**
          below.

-s   Single user boot. Pass RB_SINGLE boot flag to the kernel. This disables **-a** flag. This flag is set by
          default.

Although listed separately, the options may be in any order.

BOOT DEVICE NAMES
The format of boot device names is:

          [/interface/]dev@unit[,lun][:partition]

interface   SCSI interface type. One of: 'spc@0', 'spc@1', 'mha@0'. If the dev is a SCSI device, and
             interface is omitted, the current boot interface is used.

dev   Device type. One of: 'fd' (floppy disk drive), 'sd' (SCSI disk), 'cd' (SCSI CD-ROM), 'md'
             (Memory disk).

unit   Device unit #. You must specify the target SCSI ID if dev is a SCSI device.

lun   SCSI LUN #. 0 is assumed if omitted.

partition   Partition letter of device. Partition 'a' is used if omitted.

FILES
/usr/mdec/loadbsd.x   You will find this program here.

SEE ALSO
reboot(2), boot(8)

LOADBSD (8)   NetBSD/x68k   LOADBSD (8)

HISTORY

The **loadbsd** utility first appeared in NetBSD 1.4.

BUGS

loadbsd reads the entire kernel image at once, and requires enough free area on the main memory.

NAME

local – Postfix local mail delivery

SYNOPSIS

local [generic Postfix daemon options]

DESCRIPTION

The **local**(8) daemon processes delivery requests from the Postfix queue manager to deliver mail to local recipients. Each delivery request specifies a queue file, a sender address, a domain or host to deliver to, and one or more recipients. This program expects to be run from the **master**(8) process manager.

The **local**(8) daemon updates queue files and marks recipients as finished, or it informs the queue manager that delivery should be tried again at a later time. Delivery status reports are sent to the **bounce**(8), **defer**(8) or **trace**(8) daemon as appropriate.

CASE FOLDING

All delivery decisions are made using the bare recipient name (i.e. the address localpart), folded to lower case. See also under ADDRESS EXTENSION below for a few exceptions.

SYSTEM-WIDE AND USER-LEVEL ALIASING

The system administrator can set up one or more system-wide **sendmail**-style alias databases. Users can have **sendmail**-style ˜/.**forward** files. Mail for *name* is delivered to the alias *name*, to destinations in ˜*name*/.**forward**, to the mailbox owned by the user *name*, or it is sent back as undeliverable.

The system administrator can specify a comma/space separated list of ˜/.**forward** like files through the **forward_path** configuration parameter. Upon delivery, the local delivery agent tries each pathname in the list until a file is found.

Delivery via ˜/.**forward** files is done with the privileges of the recipient. Thus, ˜/.**forward** like files must be readable by the recipient, and their parent directory needs to have "execute" permission for the recipient.

The **forward_path** parameter is subject to interpolation of **$user** (recipient username), **$home** (recipient home directory), **$shell** (recipient shell), **$recipient** (complete recipient address), **$extension** (recipient address extension), **$domain** (recipient domain), **$local** (entire recipient address localpart) and **$recipient_delimiter.** The forms *${name?value}* and *${name:value}* expand conditionally to *value* when *$name* is (is not) defined. Characters that may have special meaning to the shell or file system are replaced by underscores. The list of acceptable characters is specified with the **forward_expansion_filter** configuration parameter.

An alias or ˜/.**forward** file may list any combination of external commands, destination file names, **:include:** directives, or mail addresses. See **aliases**(5) for a precise description. Each line in a user's .**forward** file has the same syntax as the right-hand part of an alias.

When an address is found in its own alias expansion, delivery is made to the user instead. When a user is listed in the user's own ˜/.**forward** file, delivery is made to the user's mailbox instead. An empty ˜/.**forward** file means do not forward mail.

In order to prevent the mail system from using up unreasonable amounts of memory, input records read from **:include:** or from ˜/.**forward** files are broken up into chunks of length **line_length_limit**.

While expanding aliases, ˜/.**forward** files, and so on, the program attempts to avoid duplicate deliveries. The **duplicate_filter_limit** configuration parameter limits the number of remembered recipients.

MAIL FORWARDING

For the sake of reliability, forwarded mail is re-submitted as a new message, so that each recipient has a separate on-file delivery status record.

In order to stop mail forwarding loops early, the software adds an optional **Delivered-To:** header with the final envelope recipient address. If mail arrives for a recipient that is already listed in a **Delivered-To:** header, the message is bounced.

MAILBOX DELIVERY

The default per-user mailbox is a file in the UNIX mail spool directory (**/var/mail/***user* or **/var/spool/mail/***user*); the location can be specified with the **mail_spool_directory** configuration parameter. Specify a name ending in **/** for **qmail**-compatible **maildir** delivery.

Alternatively, the per-user mailbox can be a file in the user's home directory with a name specified via the **home_mailbox** configuration parameter. Specify a relative path name. Specify a name ending in **/** for **qmail**-compatible **maildir** delivery.

Mailbox delivery can be delegated to an external command specified with the **mailbox_command_maps** and **mailbox_command** configuration parameters. The command executes with the privileges of the recipient user (exceptions: secondary groups are not enabled; in case of delivery as root, the command executes with the privileges of **default_privs**).

Mailbox delivery can be delegated to alternative message transports specified in the **master.cf** file. The **mailbox_transport_maps** and **mailbox_transport** configuration parameters specify an optional message transport that is to be used for all local recipients, regardless of whether they are found in the UNIX passwd database. The **fallback_transport_maps** and **fallback_transport** parameters specify an optional message transport for recipients that are not found in the aliases(5) or UNIX passwd database.

In the case of UNIX-style mailbox delivery, the **local**(8) daemon prepends a "**From** *sender time_stamp*" envelope header to each message, prepends an **X-Original-To:** header with the recipient address as given to Postfix, prepends an optional **Delivered-To:** header with the final envelope recipient address, prepends a **Return-Path:** header with the envelope sender address, prepends a **>** character to lines beginning with "**From** ", and appends an empty line. The mailbox is locked for exclusive access while delivery is in progress. In case of problems, an attempt is made to truncate the mailbox to its original length.

In the case of **maildir** delivery, the local daemon prepends an optional **Delivered-To:** header with the final envelope recipient address, prepends an **X-Original-To:** header with the recipient address as given to Postfix, and prepends a **Return-Path:** header with the envelope sender address.

EXTERNAL COMMAND DELIVERY

The **allow_mail_to_commands** configuration parameter restricts delivery to external commands. The default setting (**alias, forward**) forbids command destinations in **:include:** files.

Optionally, the process working directory is changed to the path specified with **command_execution_directory** (Postfix 2.2 and later). Failure to change directory causes mail to be deferred.

The **command_execution_directory** parameter value is subject to interpolation of **$user** (recipient username), **$home** (recipient home directory), **$shell** (recipient shell), **$recipient** (complete recipient address), **$extension** (recipient address extension), **$domain** (recipient domain), **$local** (entire recipient address localpart) and **$recipient_delimiter.** The forms *${name?value}* and *${name:value}* expand conditionally to *value* when *$name* is (is not) defined. Characters that may have special meaning to the shell or file system are replaced by underscores. The list of acceptable characters is specified with the **execution_directory_expansion_filter** configuration parameter.

The command is executed directly where possible. Assistance by the shell (**/bin/sh** on UNIX systems) is used only when the command contains shell magic characters, or when the command invokes a shell built-in command.

A limited amount of command output (standard output and standard error) is captured for inclusion with non-delivery status reports. A command is forcibly terminated if it does not complete within

command_time_limit seconds. Command exit status codes are expected to follow the conventions defined in **<sysexits.h>**. Exit status 0 means normal successful completion.

Postfix version 2.3 and later support RFC 3463-style enhanced status codes. If a command terminates with a non-zero exit status, and the command output begins with an enhanced status code, this status code takes precedence over the non-zero exit status.

A limited amount of message context is exported via environment variables. Characters that may have special meaning to the shell are replaced by underscores. The list of acceptable characters is specified with the **command_expansion_filter** configuration parameter.

SHELL
> The recipient user's login shell.

HOME
> The recipient user's home directory.

USER   The bare recipient name.

EXTENSION
> The optional recipient address extension.

DOMAIN
> The recipient address domain part.

LOGNAME
> The bare recipient name.

LOCAL
> The entire recipient address localpart (text to the left of the rightmost @ character).

ORIGINAL_RECIPIENT
> The entire recipient address, before any address rewriting or aliasing (Postfix 2.5 and later).

RECIPIENT
> The entire recipient address.

SENDER
> The entire sender address.

Additional remote client information is made available via the following environment variables:

CLIENT_ADDRESS
> Remote client network address. Available as of Postfix 2.2.

CLIENT_HELO
> Remote client EHLO command parameter. Available as of Postfix 2.2.

CLIENT_HOSTNAME
> Remote client hostname. Available as of Postfix 2.2.

CLIENT_PROTOCOL
> Remote client protocol. Available as of Postfix 2.2.

SASL_METHOD
> SASL authentication method specified in the remote client AUTH command. Available as of Postfix 2.2.

SASL_SENDER
> SASL sender address specified in the remote client MAIL FROM command. Available as of Postfix 2.2.

SASL_USERNAME
> SASL username specified in the remote client AUTH command. Available as of Postfix 2.2.

The **PATH** environment variable is always reset to a system-dependent default path, and environment

3

variables whose names are blessed by the **export_environment** configuration parameter are exported unchanged.

The current working directory is the mail queue directory.

The **local**(8) daemon prepends a "**From** *sender time_stamp*" envelope header to each message, prepends an **X-Original-To:** header with the recipient address as given to Postfix, prepends an optional **Delivered-To:** header with the final recipient envelope address, prepends a **Return-Path:** header with the sender envelope address, and appends no empty line.

EXTERNAL FILE DELIVERY

The delivery format depends on the destination filename syntax. The default is to use UNIX-style mailbox format. Specify a name ending in **/** for **qmail**-compatible **maildir** delivery.

The **allow_mail_to_files** configuration parameter restricts delivery to external files. The default setting (**alias, forward**) forbids file destinations in **:include:** files.

In the case of UNIX-style mailbox delivery, the **local**(8) daemon prepends a "**From** *sender time_stamp*" envelope header to each message, prepends an **X-Original-To:** header with the recipient address as given to Postfix, prepends an optional **Delivered-To:** header with the final recipient envelope address, prepends a **>** character to lines beginning with "**From** ", and appends an empty line. The envelope sender address is available in the **Return-Path:** header. When the destination is a regular file, it is locked for exclusive access while delivery is in progress. In case of problems, an attempt is made to truncate a regular file to its original length.

In the case of **maildir** delivery, the local daemon prepends an optional **Delivered-To:** header with the final envelope recipient address, and prepends an **X-Original-To:** header with the recipient address as given to Postfix. The envelope sender address is available in the **Return-Path:** header.

ADDRESS EXTENSION

The optional **recipient_delimiter** configuration parameter specifies how to separate address extensions from local recipient names.

For example, with "**recipient_delimiter = +**", mail for *name+foo* is delivered to the alias *name+foo* or to the alias *name*, to the destinations listed in ˜*name*/**.forward**+*foo* or in ˜*name*/**.forward**, to the mailbox owned by the user *name*, or it is sent back as undeliverable.

DELIVERY RIGHTS

Deliveries to external files and external commands are made with the rights of the receiving user on whose behalf the delivery is made. In the absence of a user context, the **local**(8) daemon uses the owner rights of the **:include:** file or alias database. When those files are owned by the superuser, delivery is made with the rights specified with the **default_privs** configuration parameter.

STANDARDS

RFC 822 (ARPA Internet Text Messages)
RFC 3463 (Enhanced status codes)

DIAGNOSTICS

Problems and transactions are logged to **syslogd**(8). Corrupted message files are marked so that the queue manager can move them to the **corrupt** queue afterwards.

Depending on the setting of the **notify_classes** parameter, the postmaster is notified of bounces and of other trouble.

SECURITY

The **local**(8) delivery agent needs a dual personality 1) to access the private Postfix queue and IPC mechanisms, 2) to impersonate the recipient and deliver to recipient-specified files or commands. It is therefore security sensitive.

The **local**(8) delivery agent disallows regular expression substitution of $1 etc. in **alias_maps**, because that would open a security hole.

The **local**(8) delivery agent will silently ignore requests to use the **proxymap**(8) server within **alias_maps**. Instead it will open the table directly. Before Postfix version 2.2, the **local**(8) delivery agent will terminate with a fatal error.

BUGS

For security reasons, the message delivery status of external commands or of external files is never check-pointed to file. As a result, the program may occasionally deliver more than once to a command or external file. Better safe than sorry.

Mutually-recursive aliases or ~/.**forward** files are not detected early. The resulting mail forwarding loop is broken by the use of the **Delivered-To:** message header.

CONFIGURATION PARAMETERS

Changes to **main.cf** are picked up automatically, as **local**(8) processes run for only a limited amount of time. Use the command "**postfix reload**" to speed up a change.

The text below provides only a parameter summary. See **postconf**(5) for more details including examples.

COMPATIBILITY CONTROLS

biff (yes)

> Whether or not to use the local biff service.

expand_owner_alias (no)

> When delivering to an alias "aliasname" that has an "owner-aliasname" companion alias, set the envelope sender address to the expansion of the "owner-aliasname" alias.

owner_request_special (yes)

> Give special treatment to owner-listname and listname-request address localparts: don't split such addresses when the recipient_delimiter is set to "-".

sun_mailtool_compatibility (no)

> Obsolete SUN mailtool compatibility feature.

Available in Postfix version 2.3 and later:

frozen_delivered_to (yes)

> Update the **local**(8) delivery agent's idea of the Delivered-To: address (see prepend_delivered_header) only once, at the start of a delivery attempt; do not update the Delivered-To: address while expanding aliases or .forward files.

Available in Postfix version 2.5.3 and later:

strict_mailbox_ownership (yes)

> Defer delivery when a mailbox file is not owned by its recipient.

DELIVERY METHOD CONTROLS

The precedence of **local**(8) delivery methods from high to low is: aliases, .forward files, mailbox_transport_maps, mailbox_transport, mailbox_command_maps, mailbox_command, home_mailbox, mail_spool_directory, fallback_transport_maps, fallback_transport, and luser_relay.

alias_maps (see 'postconf -d' output)

> The alias databases that are used for **local**(8) delivery.

forward_path (see 'postconf -d' output)

> The **local**(8) delivery agent search list for finding a .forward file with user-specified delivery methods.

mailbox_transport_maps (empty)

> Optional lookup tables with per-recipient message delivery transports to use for **local**(8) mailbox delivery, whether or not the recipients are found in the UNIX passwd database.

mailbox_transport (empty)
>   Optional message delivery transport that the **local**(8) delivery agent should use for mailbox delivery to all local recipients, whether or not they are found in the UNIX passwd database.

mailbox_command_maps (empty)
>   Optional lookup tables with per-recipient external commands to use for **local**(8) mailbox delivery.

mailbox_command (empty)
>   Optional external command that the **local**(8) delivery agent should use for mailbox delivery.

home_mailbox (empty)
>   Optional pathname of a mailbox file relative to a **local**(8) user's home directory.

mail_spool_directory (see 'postconf -d' output)
>   The directory where **local**(8) UNIX-style mailboxes are kept.

fallback_transport_maps (empty)
>   Optional lookup tables with per-recipient message delivery transports for recipients that the **local**(8) delivery agent could not find in the **aliases**(5) or UNIX password database.

fallback_transport (empty)
>   Optional message delivery transport that the **local**(8) delivery agent should use for names that are not found in the **aliases**(5) or UNIX password database.

luser_relay (empty)
>   Optional catch-all destination for unknown **local**(8) recipients.

Available in Postfix version 2.2 and later:

command_execution_directory (empty)
>   The **local**(8) delivery agent working directory for delivery to external command.

MAILBOX LOCKING CONTROLS
deliver_lock_attempts (20)
>   The maximal number of attempts to acquire an exclusive lock on a mailbox file or **bounce**(8) logfile.

deliver_lock_delay (1s)
>   The time between attempts to acquire an exclusive lock on a mailbox file or **bounce**(8) logfile.

stale_lock_time (500s)
>   The time after which a stale exclusive mailbox lockfile is removed.

mailbox_delivery_lock (see 'postconf -d' output)
>   How to lock a UNIX-style **local**(8) mailbox before attempting delivery.

RESOURCE AND RATE CONTROLS
command_time_limit (1000s)
>   Time limit for delivery to external commands.

duplicate_filter_limit (1000)
>   The maximal number of addresses remembered by the address duplicate filter for **aliases**(5) or **virtual**(5) alias expansion, or for **showq**(8) queue displays.

local_destination_concurrency_limit (2)
>   The maximal number of parallel deliveries via the local mail delivery transport to the same recipient (when "local_destination_recipient_limit = 1") or the maximal number of parallel deliveries to the same local domain (when "local_destination_recipient_limit > 1").

local_destination_recipient_limit (1)
>   The maximal number of recipients per message delivery via the local mail delivery transport.

mailbox_size_limit (51200000)
>   The maximal size of any **local**(8) individual mailbox or maildir file, or zero (no limit).

SECURITY CONTROLS

allow_mail_to_commands (alias, forward)

Restrict **local**(8) mail delivery to external commands.

allow_mail_to_files (alias, forward)

Restrict **local**(8) mail delivery to external files.

command_expansion_filter (see 'postconf -d' output)

Restrict the characters that the **local**(8) delivery agent allows in $name expansions of $mailbox_command and $command_execution_directory.

default_privs (nobody)

The default rights used by the **local**(8) delivery agent for delivery to external file or command.

forward_expansion_filter (see 'postconf -d' output)

Restrict the characters that the **local**(8) delivery agent allows in $name expansions of $forward_path.

Available in Postfix version 2.2 and later:

execution_directory_expansion_filter (see 'postconf -d' output)

Restrict the characters that the **local**(8) delivery agent allows in $name expansions of $command_execution_directory.

Available in Postfix version 2.5.3 and later:

strict_mailbox_ownership (yes)

Defer delivery when a mailbox file is not owned by its recipient.

MISCELLANEOUS CONTROLS

config_directory (see 'postconf -d' output)

The default location of the Postfix main.cf and master.cf configuration files.

daemon_timeout (18000s)

How much time a Postfix daemon process may take to handle a request before it is terminated by a built-in watchdog timer.

delay_logging_resolution_limit (2)

The maximal number of digits after the decimal point when logging sub-second delay values.

export_environment (see 'postconf -d' output)

The list of environment variables that a Postfix process will export to non-Postfix processes.

ipc_timeout (3600s)

The time limit for sending or receiving information over an internal communication channel.

local_command_shell (empty)

Optional shell program for **local**(8) delivery to non-Postfix command.

max_idle (100s)

The maximum amount of time that an idle Postfix daemon process waits for an incoming connection before terminating voluntarily.

max_use (100)

The maximal number of incoming connections that a Postfix daemon process will service before terminating voluntarily.

prepend_delivered_header (command, file, forward)

The message delivery contexts where the Postfix **local**(8) delivery agent prepends a Delivered-To: message header with the address that the mail was delivered to.

process_id (read-only)

The process ID of a Postfix command or daemon process.

process_name (read-only)
> The process name of a Postfix command or daemon process.

propagate_unmatched_extensions (canonical, virtual)
> What address lookup tables copy an address extension from the lookup key to the lookup result.

queue_directory (see 'postconf -d' output)
> The location of the Postfix top-level queue directory.

recipient_delimiter (empty)
> The separator between user names and address extensions (user+foo).

require_home_directory (no)
> Whether or not a **local**(8) recipient's home directory must exist before mail delivery is attempted.

syslog_facility (mail)
> The syslog facility of Postfix logging.

syslog_name (see 'postconf -d' output)
> The mail system name that is prepended to the process name in syslog records, so that "smtpd" becomes, for example, "postfix/smtpd".

FILES
> The following are examples; details differ between systems.
> $HOME/.forward, per-user aliasing
> /etc/aliases, system-wide alias database
> /var/spool/mail, system mailboxes

SEE ALSO
> qmgr(8), queue manager
> bounce(8), delivery status reports
> newaliases(1), create/update alias database
> postalias(1), create/update alias database
> aliases(5), format of alias database
> postconf(5), configuration parameters
> master(5), generic daemon options
> syslogd(8), system logging

LICENSE
> The Secure Mailer license must be distributed with this software.

HISTORY
> The **Delivered-To:** message header appears in the **qmail** system by Daniel Bernstein.
>
> The *maildir* structure appears in the **qmail** system by Daniel Bernstein.

AUTHOR(S)
> Wietse Venema
> IBM T.J. Watson Research
> P.O. Box 704
> Yorktown Heights, NY 10598, USA

NAME
locate.updatedb — update locate database

SYNOPSIS
/usr/libexec/locate.updatedb

DESCRIPTION
The **locate.updatedb** program rebuilds the database used by the locate(1) program. It is usually run once per week, see weekly.conf(5).

The file systems and files (not) scanned can be configured in locate.conf(5).

FILES
/var/db/locate.database   Default database

SEE ALSO
find(1), locate(1), fnmatch(3), locate.conf(5), weekly.conf(5)

Woods, James A., "Finding Files Fast", *;login*, 8:1, pp. 8-10, 1983.

HISTORY
The **locate.updatedb** command appeared in 4.4 BSD.

NAME
   lockstat — display kernel locking statistics

SYNOPSIS
   lockstat [-ceflMmpstx] [-b nbuf] [-E event] [-F func] [-L lock] [-N nlist]
         [-o file] [-T type] command ...

DESCRIPTION
   The **lockstat** command enables system wide tracing of kernel lock events, executes the specified command, and when finished reports statistics to the user.

   Tracing may be ended early by sending SIGINT (Ctrl-C) to the process being executed by lockstat.

   The **lockstat** pseudo-device driver must be present in the kernel, and the **lockstat** command may only be used by the root user.

   The options are as follows:

   -b nbuf   Adjust the number of trace buffers allocated by the kernel to nbuf.

   -c   Report percentage of total events by count, and sort the output by number of events. The default is to key on event timings.

   -E event   Limit tracing to one type of event. Use the -e option to list valid events.

   -e   List valid event types for the -E option and exit.

   -F func   Limit tracing to locking operations performed within the specified function. func must be the name of a valid function in the kernel.

   -f   Trace only by calling functions; do not report on individual locks.

   -L lock   Limit tracing to one lock. lock may either be the name of a lock object in the kernel, or a kernel virtual address.

   -l   Trace only by lock; do not report on calling functions.

   -M   Merge lock addresses within unique objects.

   -m   Merge call sites within unique functions.

   -N nlist   Extract symbol information from the nlist file.

   -o file   Send output to the file named by file, instead of the standard output (the default).

   -p   Show the average number of events and time spent per CPU. The default is to show the total values. May be used in conjunction with the -s option.

   -s   Show the average number of events per second, and the average time spent per second. The default is to show the total values.

   -T type   Limit tracing to one type of lock. Use the -t option to list valid lock types.

   -t   List valid lock types for the -T option and exit.

   -x   Summarize events, and do not report on lock types.

FILES
   /dev/lockstat **lockstat** control device

```
/dev/ksyms      namelist
```

EXAMPLES
```
# lockstat -L uvm_pageqlock sleep 10
Elapsed time: 10.01 seconds.

-- Adaptive mutex spin

Total%  Count   Time/ms         Lock                        Caller
------  ------- ---------  --------------------  -----------------------------
100.00    1281       0.78  uvm_pageqlock         <all>
 39.81     385       0.31  uvm_pageqlock         uvm_fault_internal+11cc
 30.98     358       0.24  uvm_pageqlock         uvm_fault_internal+bb1
 28.06     522       0.22  uvm_pageqlock         uvm_anfree+132
  0.51       5       0.00  uvm_pageqlock         ubc_fault+28f
  0.20       4       0.00  uvm_pageqlock         uvm_fault_internal+12b6
  0.18       2       0.00  uvm_pageqlock         uao_detach_locked+58
  0.11       2       0.00  uvm_pageqlock         uvm_fault_internal+7d5
  0.08       2       0.00  uvm_pageqlock         ufs_balloc_range+160
  0.07       1       0.00  uvm_pageqlock         uvm_fault_internal+107b
```

DIAGNOSTICS

lockstat: incompatible lockstat interface version

The kernel device driver does not match the version of the **lockstat** command.

lockstat: overflowed available kernel trace buffers

Increase the number of buffers using the **−b** option.

lockstat: ioctl: Invalid argument

The number of trace buffers is outside the minimum and maximum bounds set by the kernel.

SEE ALSO

ps(1), systat(1), vmstat(1), iostat(8), pstat(8)

HISTORY

The **lockstat** command appeared in NetBSD 4.0.

NAME

lpc — line printer control program

SYNOPSIS

lpc [command [argument ...]]

DESCRIPTION

lpc is used by the system administrator to control the operation of the line printer system. For each line printer configured in /etc/printcap, lpc may be used to:

- disable or enable a printer,

- disable or enable a printer's spooling queue,

- rearrange the order of jobs in a spooling queue,

- find the status of printers, and their associated spooling queues and printer daemons.

Without any arguments, lpc will prompt for commands from the standard input. If arguments are supplied, lpc interprets the first argument as a command and the remaining arguments as parameters to the command. The standard input may be redirected causing lpc to read commands from file. Commands may be abbreviated; the following is the list of recognized commands.

? [command ...]
help [command ...]
> Print a short description of each command specified in the argument list, or, if no argument is given, a list of the recognized commands.

abort { all | printer }
> Terminate an active spooling daemon on the local host immediately and then disable printing (preventing new daemons from being started by lpr(1)) for the specified printers.

clean { all | printer }
> Remove any temporary files, data files, and control files that cannot be printed (i.e., do not form a complete printer job) from the specified printer queue(s) on the local machine.

disable { all | printer }
> Turn the specified printer queues off. This prevents new printer jobs from being entered into the queue by lpr(1).

down { all | printer } message ...
> Turn the specified printer queue off, disable printing and put *message* in the printer status file. The message doesn't need to be quoted, the remaining arguments are treated like echo(1). This is normally used to take a printer down and let others know why lpq(1) will indicate the printer is down and print the status message.

enable { all | printer }
> Enable spooling on the local queue for the listed printers. This will allow lpr(1) to put new jobs in the spool queue.

exit
quit Exit from lpc.

restart { all | printer }
> Attempt to start a new printer daemon. This is useful when some abnormal condition causes the daemon to die unexpectedly, leaving jobs in the queue. lpq(1) will report that there is no daemon present when this condition occurs. If the user is the super-user, try to abort the current daemon first (i.e., kill and restart a stuck daemon).

start { all | printer }
> Enable printing and start a spooling daemon for the listed printers.

status { all | printer }
> Display the status of daemons and queues on the local machine.

stop { all | printer }
> Stop a spooling daemon after the current job completes and disable printing.

topq printer [jobnum ...] [user ...]
> Place the jobs in the order listed at the top of the printer queue.

up { all | printer }
> Enable everything and start a new printer daemon. Undoes the effects of **down**.

FILES
```
/etc/printcap              printer description file
/var/spool/output/*        spool directories
/var/spool/output/*/lock   lock file for queue control
```

DIAGNOSTICS
?Ambiguous command
> abbreviation matches more than one command

?Invalid command
> no match was found

?Privileged command
> you must be a member of group "operator" or root to execute this command

SEE ALSO
lpq(1), lpr(1), lprm(1), printcap(5), lpd(8)

HISTORY
The **lpc** command appeared in 4.2 BSD.

NAME
lpd — line printer spooler daemon

SYNOPSIS
lpd [-dlsrW] [-b *bind-address*] [-n *maxchild*] [-w *maxwait*] [port]

DESCRIPTION
lpd is the line printer daemon (spool area handler) and is normally invoked at boot time from the rc(8) file. It makes a single pass through the printcap(5) file to find out about the existing printers and prints any files left after a crash. It then uses the system calls listen(2) and accept(2) to receive requests to print files in the queue, transfer files to the spooling area, display the queue, or remove jobs from the queue. In each case, it forks a child to handle the request so the parent can continue to listen for more requests.

Available options:

-b   Normally, if the −s option is not specified, lpd will listen on all network interfaces for incoming TCP connections. The −b option, followed by a *bind-address* specifies that lpd should listen on that address instead of INADDR_ANY. Multiple −b options are permitted, allowing a list of addresses to be specified. Use of this option silently overrides the −s option if it is also present on the command line. *bind-address* can be a numeric host name in IPv4 or IPv6 notation, or a symbolic host name which will be looked up in the normal way.

-d   The −d option turns on the SO_DEBUG socket(2) option. See setsockopt(2) for more details.

-l   The −l flag causes lpd to log valid requests received from the network. This can be useful for debugging purposes.

-n   The −n flag sets *maxchild* as the maximum number of child processes that lpd will spawn. The default is 32.

-r   The −r flag allows the "of" and "if" filters to be used if specified for a remote printer. Traditionally, lpd would not use filters for remote printers.

-s   The −s flag selects "secure" mode, in which lpd does not listen on a TCP socket but only takes commands from a UNIX domain socket. This is valuable when the machine on which lpd runs is subject to attack over the network and it is desired that the machine be protected from attempts to remotely fill spools and similar attacks.

-w   The −w flag sets *maxwait* as the wait time (in seconds) for dead remote server detection. If no response is returned from a connected server within this period, the connection is closed and a message logged. The default is 120 seconds.

-W   The −W option will instruct lpd not to verify a remote tcp connection comes from a reserved port (<1024).

If the [port] parameter is passed, lpd listens on this port instead of the usual "printer/tcp" port from /etc/services.

Access control is provided by three means. First, /etc/hosts.allow and /etc/hosts.deny are consulted as described in hosts_access(5) with daemon name lpd. Second, all requests must come from one of the machines listed in the file /etc/hosts.equiv or /etc/hosts.lpd. Lastly, if the rs capability is specified in the printcap(5) entry for the printer being accessed, *lpr* requests will only be honored for those users with accounts on the machine with the printer. Requests must pass all three tests.

The file *minfree* in each spool directory contains the number of disk blocks to leave free so that the line printer queue won't completely fill the disk. The *minfree* file can be edited with your favorite text editor.

The daemon begins processing files after it has successfully set the lock for exclusive access (described a bit later), and scans the spool directory for files beginning with *cf*. Lines in each *cf* file specify files to be printed or non-printing actions to be performed. Each such line begins with a key character to specify what to do with the remainder of the line.

J	Job Name. String to be used for the job name on the burst page.
C	Classification. String to be used for the classification line on the burst page.
L	Literal. The line contains identification info from the password file and causes the banner page to be printed.
T	Title. String to be used as the title for pr(1).
H	Host Name. Name of the machine where lpr(1) was invoked.
P	Person. Login name of the person who invoked lpr(1). This is used to verify ownership by lprm(1).
M	Send mail to the specified user when the current print job completes.
f	Formatted File. Name of a file to print which is already formatted.
l	Like "f" but passes control characters and does not make page breaks.
p	Name of a file to print using pr(1) as a filter.
t	Troff File. The file contains troff(1) output (cat phototypesetter commands).
n	Ditroff File. The file contains device independent troff output.
d	DVI File. The file contains Tex l output DVI format from Stanford.
g	Graph File. The file contains data produced by **plot**.
c	Cifplot File. The file contains data produced by **cifplot**.
v	The file contains a raster image.
o	The file contains PostScript data.
r	The file contains text data with FORTRAN carriage control characters.
1	Troff Font R. Name of the font file to use instead of the default.
2	Troff Font I. Name of the font file to use instead of the default.
3	Troff Font B. Name of the font file to use instead of the default.
4	Troff Font S. Name of the font file to use instead of the default.
W	Width. Changes the page width (in characters) used by pr(1) and the text filters.
I	Indent. The number of characters to indent the output by (in ascii).
U	Unlink. Name of file to remove upon completion of printing.
N	File name. The name of the file which is being printed, or a blank for the standard input (when lpr(1) is invoked in a pipeline).

If a file cannot be opened, a message will be logged via syslog(3) using the *LOG_LPR* facility. **lpd** will try up to 20 times to reopen a file it expects to be there, after which it will skip the file to be printed.

lpd uses flock(2) to provide exclusive access to the lock file and to prevent multiple daemons from becoming active simultaneously. If the daemon should be killed or die unexpectedly, the lock file need not be removed. The lock file is kept in a readable ASCII form and contains two lines. The first is the process id of the daemon and the second is the control file name of the current job being printed. The second line is updated to reflect the current status of **lpd** for the programs lpq(1) and lprm(1).

FILES

/etc/printcap	printer description file
/var/spool/output/*	spool directories
/var/spool/output/*/minfree	minimum free space to leave
/dev/lp*	line printer devices
/var/run/printer	socket for local requests
/etc/hosts.allow	explicit remote host access list.
/etc/hosts.deny	explicit remote host denial of service list.
/etc/hosts.equiv	lists machine names allowed printer access
/etc/hosts.lpd	lists machine names allowed printer access, but not under same administrative control.

SEE ALSO

lpq(1), lpr(1), lprm(1), setsockopt(2), syslog(3), hosts.equiv(5), hosts_access(5), hosts_options(5), printcap(5), lpc(8), pac(8)

4.3 BSD Line Printer Spooler Manual.

HISTORY

An **lpd** daemon appeared in Version 6 AT&T UNIX.

NAME

lptest — generate lineprinter ripple pattern

SYNOPSIS

lptest [*length* [*count*]]

DESCRIPTION

lptest writes the traditional "ripple test" pattern on standard output. In 96 lines, this pattern will print all 96 printable ASCII characters in each position. While originally created to test printers, it is quite useful for testing terminals, driving terminal ports for debugging purposes, or any other task where a quick supply of random data is needed.

The *length* argument specifies the output line length if the default length of 79 is inappropriate.

The *count* argument specifies the number of output lines to be generated if the default count of 200 is inappropriate. Note that if *count* is to be specified, *length* must be also be specified.

HISTORY

lptest appeared in 4.3 BSD.

NAME

lvchange – change attributes of a logical volume

SYNOPSIS

lvchange [--addtag Tag] [-A|--autobackup y|n] [-a|--available y|n|ey|en|ly|ln] [--alloc AllocationPolicy] [-C|--contiguous y|n] [-d|--debug] [--deltag Tag] [--resync] [-h|-?|--help] [--ignorelockingfailure] [--ignoremonitoring] [--monitor {y|n}] [-M|--persistent y|n] [--minor minor] [-P|--partial] [-p|--permission r|rw] [-r/--readahead ReadAheadSectors|auto|none] [--refresh] [-t|--test] [-v|--verbose] LogicalVolumePath [LogicalVolumePath...]

DESCRIPTION

lvchange allows you to change the attributes of a logical volume including making them known to the kernel ready for use.

OPTIONS

See **lvm** for common options.

-a, --available y|n|ey|en|ly|ln

Controls the availability of the logical volumes for use. Communicates with the kernel device-mapper driver via libdevmapper to activate (-ay) or deactivate (-an) the logical volumes.

If clustered locking is enabled, -aey will activate exclusively on one node and -aly will activate only on the local node. To deactivate only on the local node use -aln. Logical volumes with single-host snapshots are always activated exclusively because they can only be used on one node at once.

-C, --contiguous y|n

Tries to set or reset the contiguous allocation policy for logical volumes. It's only possible to change a non-contiguous logical volume's allocation policy to contiguous, if all of the allocated physical extents are already contiguous.

--resync

Forces the complete resynchronization of a mirror. In normal circumstances you should not need this option because synchronization happens automatically. Data is read from the primary mirror device and copied to the others, so this can take a considerable amount of time - and during this time you are without a complete redundant copy of your data.

--minor minor

Set the minor number.

--monitor y|n

Controls whether or not a mirrored logical volume is monitored by dmeventd, if it is installed. If a device used by a monitored mirror reports an I/O error, the failure is handled according to **mirror_image_fault_policy** and **mirror_log_fault_policy** set in **lvm.conf**.

--ignoremonitoring

Make no attempt to interact with dmeventd unless --monitor is specified. Do not use this if dmeventd is already monitoring a device.

-M, --persistent y|n

Set to y to make the minor number specified persistent.

-p, --permission r|rw

Change access permission to read-only or read/write.

-r, --readahead ReadAheadSectors|auto|none

Set read ahead sector count of this logical volume. For volume groups with metadata in lvm1 format, this must be a value between 2 and 120 sectors. The default value is "auto" which allows the kernel to choose a suitable value automatically. "None" is equivalent to specifying zero.

--refresh

If the logical volume is active, reload its metadata. This is not necessary in normal operation, but may be useful if something has gone wrong or if you're doing clustering manually without a clustered lock manager.

Examples
      "lvchange -pr vg00/lvol1" changes the permission on volume lvol1 in volume group vg00 to be read-only.

SEE ALSO
      lvm(8), **lvcreate**(8), **vgchange**(8)

NAME
lvconvert – convert a logical volume from linear to mirror or snapshot

SYNOPSIS
lvconvert −m|−−mirrors Mirrors [−−mirrorlog {disk|core}] [−−corelog] [−R|−−regionsize MirrorLogRegionSize] [−A|−−alloc AllocationPolicy] [−b|−−background] [−i|−−interval Seconds] [−h|−?|−−help] [−v|−−verbose] [−−version]
LogicalVolume[Path] [PhysicalVolume[Path]...]

lvconvert −s|−−snapshot [−c|−−chunksize ChunkSize] [−h|−?|−−help] [−v|−−verbose] [−Z|−−zero y|n] [−−version]
OriginalLogicalVolume[Path] SnapshotLogicalVolume[Path]

DESCRIPTION
lvconvert will change a linear logical volume to a mirror logical volume or to a snapshot of linear volume and vice versa. It is also used to add and remove disk logs from mirror devices.

OPTIONS
See **lvm** for common options.

Exactly one of −−mirrors or −−snapshot arguments required.

−m, −−mirrors Mirrors
> Specifies the degree of the mirror you wish to create. For example, "-m 1" would convert the original logical volume to a mirror volume with 2-sides; that is, a linear volume plus one copy.

−−mirrorlog {disk|core}
> Specifies the type of log to use. The default is disk, which is persistent and requires a small amount of storage space, usually on a separate device from the data being mirrored. Core may be useful for short-lived mirrors: It means the mirror is regenerated by copying the data from the first device again every time the device is activated - perhaps, for example, after every reboot.

−−corelog
> The optional argument "--corelog" is the same as specifying "--mirrorlog core".

−R, −−regionsize MirrorLogRegionSize
> A mirror is divided into regions of this size (in MB), and the mirror log uses this granularity to track which regions are in sync.

−b, −−background
> Run the daemon in the background.

−i, −−interval Seconds
> Report progress as a percentage at regular intervals.

−s, −−snapshot
> Create a snapshot from existing logical volume using another existing logical volume as its origin.

−c, −−chunksize ChunkSize
> Power of 2 chunk size for the snapshot logical volume between 4k and 512k.

−Z, −−zero y|n
> Controls zeroing of the first KB of data in the snapshot. If the volume is read-only the snapshot will not be zeroed.

Examples
"lvconvert -m1 vg00/lvol1"
converts the linear logical volume "vg00/lvol1" to a two-way mirror logical volume.

"lvconvert --mirrorlog core vg00/lvol1"
converts a mirror with a disk log to a mirror with an in-memory log.

"lvconvert --mirrorlog disk vg00/lvol1"

converts a mirror with an in-memory log to a mirror with a disk log.

"lvconvert -m0 vg00/lvol1"
converts a mirror logical volume to a linear logical volume.

"lvconvert -s vg00/lvol1 vg00/lvol2"
converts logical volume "vg00/lvol2" to snapshot of original volume "vg00/lvol1"

SEE ALSO
lvm(8), **vgcreate**(8), **lvremove**(8), **lvrename**(8), **lvextend**(8), **lvreduce**(8), **lvdisplay**(8), **lvscan**(8)

NAME

lvcreate – create a logical volume in an existing volume group

SYNOPSIS

lvcreate [--addtag Tag] [--alloc AllocationPolicy] [-A|--autobackup y|n] [-C|--contiguous y|n]
[-d|--debug] [-h|-?|--help] [-i|--stripes Stripes [-I|--stripesize StripeSize]] {-l|--extents LogicalExtentsNumber[%{VG|PVS|FREE}] |
 -L|--size LogicalVolumeSize[kKmMgGtT]} [-M|--persistent y|n] [--minor minor] [-m|--mirrors Mirrors [--nosync] [--mirrorlog {disk|core}] [--corelog] [-R|--regionsize MirrorLogRegionSize]]
[-n|--name LogicalVolumeName] [-p|--permission r|rw] [-r|--readahead ReadAheadSectors|auto|none]
[-t|--test] [-v|--verbose] [-Z|--zero y|n] VolumeGroupName [PhysicalVolumePath...]

lvcreate {-l|--extents LogicalExtentsNumber[%{VG|FREE}] |
 -L|--size LogicalVolumeSize[kKmMgGtT]} [-c|--chunksize ChunkSize] -s|--snapshot -n|--name
SnapshotLogicalVolumeName OriginalLogicalVolumePath

DESCRIPTION

lvcreate creates a new logical volume in a volume group (see **vgcreate(8), vgchange(8)**) by allocating logical extents from the free physical extent pool of that volume group. If there are not enough free physical extents then the volume group can be extended (see **vgextend(8)**) with other physical volumes or by reducing existing logical volumes of this volume group in size (see **lvreduce(8)**).

The second form supports the creation of snapshot logical volumes which keep the contents of the original logical volume for backup purposes.

OPTIONS

See **lvm** for common options.

-c, --chunksize ChunkSize
>   Power of 2 chunk size for the snapshot logical volume between 4k and 512k.

-C, --contiguous y|n
>   Sets or resets the contiguous allocation policy for logical volumes. Default is no contiguous allocation based on a next free principle.

-i, --stripes Stripes
>   Gives the number of stripes. This is equal to the number of physical volumes to scatter the logical volume.

-I, --stripesize StripeSize
>   Gives the number of kilobytes for the granularity of the stripes.
>   StripeSize must be 2^n (n = 2 to 9) for metadata in LVM1 format. For metadata in LVM2 format, the stripe size may be a larger power of 2 but must not exceed the physical extent size.

-l, --extents LogicalExtentsNumber[%{VG|PVS|FREE}]
>   Gives the number of logical extents to allocate for the new logical volume. This can also be expressed as a percentage of the total space in the Volume Group with the suffix %VG, of the remaining free space in the Volume Group with the suffix %FREE, or of the remaining free space for the specified PhysicalVolume(s) with the suffix %PVS,

-L, --size LogicalVolumeSize[kKmMgGtTpPeE]
>   Gives the size to allocate for the new logical volume. A size suffix of K for kilobytes, M for megabytes, G for gigabytes, T for terabytes, P for petabytes or E for exabytes is optional.
>   Default unit is megabytes.

--minor minor
>   Set the minor number.

-M, --persistent y|n
>   Set to y to make the minor number specified persistent.

−m, −−mirrors Mirrors
> Creates a mirrored logical volume with Mirrors copies. For example, specifying "-m 1" would result in a mirror with two-sides; that is, a linear volume plus one copy.
>
> Specifying the optional argument --nosync will cause the creation of the mirror to skip the initial resynchronization. Any data written afterwards will be mirrored, but the original contents will not be copied. This is useful for skipping a potentially long and resource intensive initial sync of an empty device.
>
> The optional argument --mirrorlog specifies the type of log to be used. The default is disk, which is persistent and requires a small amount of storage space, usually on a separate device from the data being mirrored. Using core means the mirror is regenerated by copying the data from the first device again each time the device is activated, for example, after every reboot.
>
> The optional argument --corelog is equivalent to --mirrorlog core.

−n, −−name LogicalVolumeName
> The name for the new logical volume.
> Without this option a default names of "lvol#" will be generated where # is the LVM internal number of the logical volume.

−p, −−permission r|rw
> Set access permissions to read only or read and write.
> Default is read and write.

−r, −−readahead ReadAheadSectors|auto|none
> Set read ahead sector count of this logical volume. For volume groups with metadata in lvm1 format, this must be a value between 2 and 120. The default value is "auto" which allows the kernel to choose a suitable value automatically. "None" is equivalent to specifying zero.

−R, −−regionsize MirrorLogRegionSize
> A mirror is divided into regions of this size (in MB), and the mirror log uses this granularity to track which regions are in sync.

−s, −−snapshot
> Create a snapshot logical volume (or snapshot) for an existing, so called original logical volume (or origin). Snapshots provide a 'frozen image' of the contents of the origin while the origin can still be updated. They enable consistent backups and online recovery of removed/overwritten data/files. The snapshot does not need the same amount of storage the origin has. In a typical scenario, 15-20% might be enough. In case the snapshot runs out of storage, use **lvextend(8)** to grow it. Shrinking a snapshot is supported by **lvreduce(8)** as well. Run **lvdisplay(8)** on the snapshot in order to check how much data is allocated to it.

−Z, −−zero y|n
> Controls zeroing of the first KB of data in the new logical volume.
> Default is yes.
> Volume will not be zeroed if read only flag is set.
> Snapshot volumes are zeroed always.
>
> Warning: trying to mount an unzeroed logical volume can cause the system to hang.

Examples

"lvcreate -i 3 -I 8 -L 100M vg00" tries to create a striped logical volume with 3 stripes, a stripesize of 8KB and a size of 100MB in the volume group named vg00. The logical volume name will be chosen by lvcreate.

"lvcreate -m1 -L 500M vg00" tries to create a mirror logical volume with 2 sides with a useable size of 500 MiB. This operation would require 3 devices - two for the mirror devices and one for the disk log.

"lvcreate -m1 --mirrorlog core -L 500M vg00" tries to create a mirror logical volume with 2 sides with a useable size of 500 MiB. This operation would require 2 devices - the log is "in-memory".

"lvcreate --size 100m --snapshot --name snap /dev/vg00/lvol1"
creates a snapshot logical volume named /dev/vg00/snap which has access to the contents of the original logical volume named /dev/vg00/lvol1 at snapshot logical volume creation time. If the original logical volume contains a file system, you can mount the snapshot logical volume on an arbitrary directory in order to access the contents of the filesystem to run a backup while the original filesystem continues to get updated.

SEE ALSO
lvm(8), vgcreate(8), lvremove(8), lvrename(8) lvextend(8), lvreduce(8), lvdisplay(8), lvscan(8)

NAME
lvdisplay – display attributes of a logical volume

SYNOPSIS
lvdisplay [–c|––colon] [–d|––debug] [–h|–?|––help] [––ignorelockingfailure] [––maps] [–P|––partial] [–v|––verbose] LogicalVolumePath [LogicalVolumePath...]

DESCRIPTION
lvdisplay allows you to see the attributes of a logical volume like size, read/write status, snapshot informa-tion etc.

lvs (8) is an alternative that provides the same information in the style of **ps** (1). **lvs** is recommended over **lvdisplay**.

OPTIONS
See **lvm** for common options.

–c, ––colon

Generate colon separated output for easier parsing in scripts or programs. N.B. **lvs** (8) provides considerably more control over the output.

The values are:

* logical volume name
* volume group name
* logical volume access
* logical volume status
* internal logical volume number
* open count of logical volume
* logical volume size in sectors
* current logical extents associated to logical volume
* allocated logical extents of logical volume
* allocation policy of logical volume
* read ahead sectors of logical volume
* major device number of logical volume
* minor device number of logical volume

–m, ––maps

Display the mapping of logical extents to physical volumes and physical extents.

Examples
"lvdisplay -v /dev/vg00/lvol2" shows attributes of that logical volume. If snapshot logical volumes have been created for this original logical volume, this command shows a list of all snapshot logical volumes and their status (active or inactive) as well.

"lvdisplay /dev/vg00/snapshot" shows the attributes of this snapshot logical volume and also which original logical volume it is associated with.

SEE ALSO
lvm(8), **lvcreate**(8), **lvscan**(8)

NAME

lvextend – extend the size of a logical volume

SYNOPSIS

lvextend [--alloc AllocationPolicy] [-Al--autobackup yln] [-dl--debug] [-hl-?l--help] [-il--stripes Stripes [-ll--stripesize StripeSize]] {-ll--extents [+]LogicalExtentsNumber[%{VGlLVlPVSlFREE}] l -Ll--size [+]LogicalVolumeSize[kKmMgGtT]} [-tl--test] [-vl--verbose] LogicalVolumePath [PhysicalVolumePath...]

DESCRIPTION

lvextend allows you to extend the size of a logical volume. Extension of snapshot logical volumes (see **lvcreate(8)** for information to create snapshots) is supported as well. But to change the number of copies in a mirrored logical volume use **lvconvert**(8).

OPTIONS

See **lvm** for common options.

-l, --extents [+]LogicalExtentsNumber[%{VGlLVlPVSlFREE}]

Extend or set the logical volume size in units of logical extents. With the + sign the value is added to the actual size of the logical volume and without it, the value is taken as an absolute one. The number can also be expressed as a percentage of the total space in the Volume Group with the suffix %VG, relative to the existing size of the Logical Volume with the suffix %LV, of the remaining free space for the specified PhysicalVolume(s) with the suffix %PVS, or as a percentage of the remaining free space in the Volume Group with the suffix %FREE.

-L, --size [+]LogicalVolumeSize[kKmMgGtTpPeE]

Extend or set the logical volume size in units of megabytes. A size suffix of M for megabytes, G for gigabytes, T for terabytes, P for petabytes or E for exabytes is optional. With the + sign the value is added to the actual size of the logical volume and without it, the value is taken as an absolute one.

-i, --stripes Stripes

Gives the number of stripes for the extension. Not applicable to LVs using the original metadata LVM format, which must use a single value throughout.

-I, --stripesize StripeSize

Gives the number of kilobytes for the granularity of the stripes. Not applicable to LVs using the original metadata LVM format, which must use a single value throughout.
StripeSize must be 2^n (n = 2 to 9).

Examples

"lvextend -L +54 /dev/vg01/lvol10 /dev/sdk3" tries to extend the size of that logical volume by 54MB on physical volume /dev/sdk3. This is only possible if /dev/sdk3 is a member of volume group vg01 and there are enough free physical extents in it.

"lvextend /dev/vg01/lvol01 /dev/sdk3" tries to extend the size of that logical volume by the amount of free space on physical volume /dev/sdk3. This is equivalent to specifying "-l +100%PVS" on the command line.

SEE ALSO

lvm(8), **lvcreate**(8), **lvconvert**(8), **lvreduce**(8), **lvresize**(8), **lvchange**(8)

NAME
lvm – LVM2 tools

SYNOPSIS
lvm [command | file]

DESCRIPTION
lvm provides the command-line tools for LVM2. A separate manual page describes each command in detail.

If **lvm** is invoked with no arguments it presents a readline prompt (assuming it was compiled with readline support). LVM commands may be entered interactively at this prompt with readline facilities including history and command name and option completion. Refer to **readline**(3) for details.

If **lvm** is invoked with argv[0] set to the name of a specific LVM command (for example by using a hard or soft link) it acts as that command.

Where commands take VG or LV names as arguments, the full path name is optional. An LV called "lvol0" in a VG called "vg0" can be specified as "vg0/lvol0". Where a list of VGs is required but is left empty, a list of all VGs will be substituted. Where a list of LVs is required but a VG is given, a list of all the LVs in that VG will be substituted. So "lvdisplay vg0" will display all the LVs in "vg0". Tags can also be used - see **addtag** below.

One advantage of using the built-in shell is that configuration information gets cached internally between commands.

A file containing a simple script with one command per line can also be given on the command line. The script can also be executed directly if the first line is #! followed by the absolute path of **lvm**.

BUILT-IN COMMANDS
The following commands are built into lvm without links normally being created in the filesystem for them.

dumpconfig — Display the configuration information after
loading **lvm.conf** (5) and any other configuration files.

formats — Display recognised metadata formats.

help — Display the help text.

pvdata — Not implemented in LVM2.

segtypes — Display recognised logical volume segment types.

version — Display version information.

COMMANDS
The following commands implement the core LVM functionality.

pvchange — Change attributes of a physical volume.

pvck — Check physical volume metadata.

pvcreate — Initialize a disk or partition for use by LVM.

pvdisplay — Display attributes of a physical volume.

pvmove — Move physical extents.

pvremove — Remove a physical volume.

pvresize — Resize a disk or partition in use by LVM2.

pvs — Report information about physical volumes.

pvscan — Scan all disks for physical volumes.

vgcfgbackup — Backup volume group descriptor area.

vgcfgrestore — Restore volume group descriptor area.

vgchange — Change attributes of a volume group.

vgck — Check volume group metadata.

vgconvert — Convert volume group metadata format.

vgcreate — Create a volume group.

vgdisplay — Display attributes of volume groups.

vgexport — Make volume groups unknown to the system.

vgextend — Add physical volumes to a volume group.

vgimport — Make exported volume groups known to the system.

vgmerge — Merge two volume groups.

vgmknodes — Recreate volume group directory and logical volume special files

vgreduce — Reduce a volume group by removing one or more physical volumes.

vgremove — Remove a volume group.

vgrename — Rename a volume group.

vgs — Report information about volume groups.

vgscan — Scan all disks for volume groups and rebuild caches.

vgsplit — Split a volume group into two, moving any logical volumes from one volume group to another by moving entire physical volumes.

lvchange — Change attributes of a logical volume.

lvconvert — Convert a logical volume from linear to mirror or snapshot.

lvcreate — Create a logical volume in an existing volume group.

lvdisplay — Display attributes of a logical volume.

lvextend — Extend the size of a logical volume.

lvmchange — Change attributes of the logical volume manager.

lvmdiskscan — Scan for all devices visible to LVM2.

lvmdump — Create lvm2 information dumps for diagnostic purposes.

lvreduce — Reduce the size of a logical volume.

lvremove — Remove a logical volume.

lvrename — Rename a logical volume.

lvresize — Resize a logical volume.

lvs — Report information about logical volumes.

lvscan — Scan (all disks) for logical volumes.

The following commands are not implemented in LVM2 but might be in the future: lvmsadc, lvmsar, pvdata.

OPTIONS

The following options are available for many of the commands. They are implemented generically and documented here rather than repeated on individual manual pages.

-h | --help — Display the help text.

--version — Display version information.

-v | --verbose — Set verbose level.
> Repeat from 1 to 3 times to increase the detail of messages sent to stdout and stderr. Overrides config file setting.

-d | --debug — Set debug level.
> Repeat from 1 to 6 times to increase the detail of messages sent to the log file and/or syslog (if configured). Overrides config file setting.

--quiet — Suppress output and log messages.
> Overrides -d and -v.

-t | --test — Run in test mode.
> Commands will not update metadata. This is implemented by disabling all metadata writing but nevertheless returning success to the calling function. This may lead to unusual error messages in multi-stage operations if a tool relies on reading back metadata it believes has changed but hasn't.

--driverloaded { y | n }
> Whether or not the device-mapper kernel driver is loaded. If you set this to **n**, no attempt will be made to contact the driver.

-A | --autobackup { y | n }
> Whether or not to metadata should be backed up automatically after a change. You are strongly advised not to disable this! See **vgcfgbackup (8).**

-P | --partial
> When set, the tools will do their best to provide access to volume groups that are only partially available. Where part of a logical volume is missing, **/dev/ioerror** will be substituted, and you could use **dmsetup (8)** to set this up to return I/O errors when accessed, or create it as a large block device of nulls. Metadata may not be changed with this option. To insert a replacement physical volume of the same or large size use **pvcreate -u** to set the uuid to match the original followed by **vgcfgrestore (8).**

-M | --metadatatype type
> Specifies which type of on-disk metadata to use, such as **lvm1** or **lvm2**, which can be abbreviated to **1** or **2** respectively. The default (lvm2) can be changed by setting **format** in the **global** section of the config file.

--ignorelockingfailure
> This lets you proceed with read-only metadata operations such as **lvchange -ay** and **vgchange -ay** even if the locking module fails. One use for this is in a system init script if the lock directory is mounted read-only when the script runs.

--addtag tag
> Add the tag **tag** to a PV, VG or LV. A tag is a word that can be used to group LVM2 objects of the same type together. Tags can be given on the command line in place of PV, VG or LV arguments. Tags should be prefixed with @ to avoid ambiguity. Each tag is expanded by replacing it with all objects possessing that tag which are of the type expected by its position on the command line. PVs can only possess tags while they are part of a Volume Group: PV tags are discarded if the PV is removed from the VG. As an example, you could tag some LVs as **database** and others as **userdata** and then activate the database ones with **lvchange -ay @database**. Objects can possess multiple tags simultaneously. Only the new LVM2 metadata format supports tagging: objects using the LVM1 metadata format cannot be tagged because the on-disk format does not support it. Snapshots cannot be tagged. Characters allowed in tags are: A-Z a-z 0-9 _ + . -

--deltag tag
> Delete the tag **tag** from a PV, VG or LV, if it's present.

--alloc AllocationPolicy
> The allocation policy to use: **contiguous**, **cling**, **normal**, **anywhere** or **inherit**. When a command needs to allocate physical extents from the volume group, the allocation policy controls how they are chosen. Each volume group and logical volume has an allocation policy. The default for a

volume group is **normal** which applies common-sense rules such as not placing parallel stripes on the same physical volume. The default for a logical volume is **inherit** which applies the same policy as for the volume group. These policies can be changed using **lvchange** (8) and **vgchange** (8) or over-ridden on the command line of any command that performs allocation. The **contiguous** policy requires that new extents be placed adjacent to existing extents. The **cling** policy places new extents on the same physical volume as existing extents in the same stripe of the Logical Volume. If there are sufficient free extents to satisfy an allocation request but **normal** doesn't use them, **anywhere** will - even if that reduces performance by placing two stripes on the same physical volume.

N.B. The policies described above are not implemented fully yet. In particular, contiguous free space cannot be broken up to satisfy allocation attempts.

ENVIRONMENT VARIABLES
LVM_SYSTEM_DIR
Directory containing lvm.conf and other LVM system files. Defaults to "/etc/lvm".

HOME
Directory containing .lvm_history if the internal readline shell is invoked.

LVM_VG_NAME
The volume group name that is assumed for any reference to a logical volume that doesn't specify a path. Not set by default.

VALID NAMES
The following characters are valid for VG and LV names: **a-z A-Z 0-9 + _ . -**

VG and LV names cannot begin with a hyphen. There are also various reserved names that are used internally by lvm that can not be used as LV or VG names. A VG cannot be called anything that exists in /dev/ at the time of creation, nor can it be called '.' or '..'. A LV cannot be called '.' '..' 'snapshot' or 'pvmove'. The LV name may also not contain the strings '_mlog' or '_mimage'

DIAGNOSTICS
All tools return a status code of zero on success or non-zero on failure.

FILES
/etc/lvm/lvm.conf
$HOME/.lvm_history

SEE ALSO
clvmd(8), **lvchange**(8), **lvcreate**(8), **lvdisplay**(8), **lvextend**(8), **lvmchange**(8), **lvmdiskscan**(8), **lvreduce**(8), **lvremove**(8), **lvrename**(8), **lvresize**(8), **lvs**(8), **lvscan**(8), **pvchange**(8), **pvck**(8), **pvcreate**(8), **pvdisplay**(8), **pvmove**(8), **pvremove**(8), **pvs**(8), **pvscan**(8), **vgcfgbackup**(8), **vgchange**(8), **vgck**(8), **vgconvert**(8), **vgcreate**(8), **vgdisplay**(8), **vgextend**(8), **vgimport**(8), **vgmerge**(8), **vgmknodes**(8), **vgreduce**(8), **vgremove**(8), **vgrename**(8), **vgs**(8), **vgscan**(8), **vgsplit**(8), **readline**(3), **lvm.conf**(5)

NAME
lvmchange – change attributes of the logical volume manager

SYNOPSIS
lvmchange

DESCRIPTION
lvmchange is not currently supported under LVM2, although **dmsetup (8)** has a **remove_all** command.

SEE ALSO
dmsetup(8)

NAME
>   lvmdiskscan − scan for all devices visible to LVM2

SYNOPSIS
>   **lvmdiskscan** [−d|−−debug] [−h|−?|−−help] [−l|−−lvmpartition] [−v|−−verbose]

DESCRIPTION
>   **lvmdiskscan** scans all SCSI, (E)IDE disks, multiple devices and a bunch of other block devices in the sys-
>   tem looking for LVM physical volumes. The size reported is the real device size. Define a filter in
>   **lvm.conf**(5) to restrict the scan to avoid a CD ROM, for example.

OPTIONS
>   See **lvm** for common options.
>
>   *−l, −−lvmpartition*
>   Only reports Physical Volumes.

SEE ALSO
>   **lvm**(8), **lvm.conf**(5), **pvscan**(8), **vgscan**(8)

NAME
lvmdump - create lvm2 information dumps for diagnostic purposes

SYNOPSIS
lvmdump [options] [-d directory]

DESCRIPTION
lvmdump is a tool to dump various information concerning LVM2. By default, it creates a tarball suitable for submission along with a problem report.

The content of the tarball is as follows:
- dmsetup info
- table of currently running processes
- recent entries from /var/log/messages (containing system messages)
- complete lvm configuration and cache
- list of device nodes present under /dev
- if enabled with -m, metadata dump will be also included
- if enabled with -a, debug output of vgscan, pvscan and list of all available volume groups, physical volumes and logical volumes will be included
- if enabled with -c, cluster status info

OPTIONS
−h — print help message

−a — advanced collection
> **WARNING**: if lvm is already hung, then this script may hang as well if **−a** is used

−m — gather LVM metadata from the PVs
> This option generates a 1:1 dump of the metadata area from all PVs visible to the system, which can cause the dump to increase in size considerably. However, the metadata dump may represent a valuable diagnostic resource.

−d directory — dump into a directory instead of tarball
> By default, lvmdump will produce a single compressed tarball containing all the information. Using this option, it can be instructed to only produce the raw dump tree, rooted in **directory**.

−c — if clvmd is running, gather cluster data as well

ENVIRONMENT VARIABLES
LVM_BINARY
> The LVM2 binary to use. Defaults to "lvm". Sometimes you might need to set this to "/sbin/lvm.static", for example.

DMSETUP_BINARY
> The dmsetup binary to use. Defaults to "dmsetup".

NAME
lvreduce – reduce the size of a logical volume

SYNOPSIS
lvreduce [–A|––autobackup y|n] [–d|––debug] [–f|––force] [–h|–?|––help] {–l|––extents [–]LogicalExtentsNumber[%{VG|LV|FREE}] | –L|––size [–]LogicalVolumeSize[kKmMgGtT]} [–t|––test] [–v|––verbose] LogicalVolume[Path]

DESCRIPTION
lvreduce allows you to reduce the size of a logical volume. Be careful when reducing a logical volume's size, because data in the reduced part is lost!!!

You should therefore ensure that any filesystem on the volume is resized *before* running lvreduce so that the extents that are to be removed are not in use.

Shrinking snapshot logical volumes (see **lvcreate(8)** for information to create snapshots) is supported as well. But to change the number of copies in a mirrored logical volume use **lvconvert (8).**

Sizes will be rounded if necessary - for example, the volume size must be an exact number of extents and the size of a striped segment must be a multiple of the number of stripes.

OPTIONS
See **lvm** for common options.

–f, ––force
> Force size reduction without any question.

–l, ––extents [–]LogicalExtentsNumber[%{VG|LV|FREE}]
> Reduce or set the logical volume size in units of logical extents. With the - sign the value will be subtracted from the logical volume's actual size and without it the will be taken as an absolute size. The number can also be expressed as a percentage of the total space in the Volume Group with the suffix %VG or relative to the existing size of the Logical Volume with the suffix %LV or as a percentage of the remaining free space in the Volume Group with the suffix %FREE.

–L, ––size [–]LogicalVolumeSize[kKmMgGtTpPeE]
> Reduce or set the logical volume size in units of megabyte by default. A size suffix of k for kilobyte, m for megabyte, g for gigabytes, t for terabytes, p for petabytes or e for exabytes is optional. With the - sign the value will be subtracted from the logical volume's actual size and without it it will be taken as an absolute size.

Example
"lvreduce -l -3 vg00/lvol1" reduces the size of logical volume lvol1 in volume group vg00 by 3 logical extents.

SEE ALSO
lvchange(8), **lvconvert**(8), **lvcreate**(8), **lvextend**(8), **lvm**(8), **lvresize**(8), **vgreduce**(8)

NAME
lvremove – remove a logical volume

SYNOPSIS
lvremove [–A|--autobackup y|n] [–d|--debug] [–f|--force] [–h|–?|--help] [–t|--test] [–v|--verbose]
LogicalVolumePath [LogicalVolumePath...]

DESCRIPTION
lvremove removes one or more logical volumes. Confirmation will be requested before deactivating any active logical volume prior to removal. Logical volumes cannot be deactivated or removed while they are open (e.g. if they contain a mounted filesystem). Removing an origin logical volume will also remove all dependent snapshots.

If the logical volume is clustered then it must be deactivated on all nodes in the cluster before it can be removed. A single lvchange command issued from one node can do this.

OPTIONS
See **lvm**(8) for common options.

–f, --force
> Remove active logical volumes without confirmation.

EXAMPLES
Remove the active logical volume lvol1 in volume group vg00 without asking for confirmation:

lvremove -f vg00/lvol1

Remove all logical volumes in volume group vg00:

lvremove vg00

SEE ALSO
lvcreate(8), **lvdisplay**(8), **lvchange**(8), **lvm**(8), **lvs**(8), **lvscan**(8), **vgremove**(8)

NAME

lvrename – rename a logical volume

SYNOPSIS

lvrename [–A|––**autobackup** {y|n}] [–d|––**debug**] [–f|––**force**] [–h|––**help**] [–t|––**test**] [–v|––**verbose**]
[––**version**]

OldLogicalVolumePath NewLogicalVolume{Path|Name}

VolumeGroupName OldLogicalVolumeName NewLogicalVolumeName

DESCRIPTION

lvrename renames an existing logical volume from *OldLogicalVolume{Name|Path}* to *NewLogicalVolume{Name|Path}*.

OPTIONS

See **lvm** for common options.

EXAMPLE

To rename **lvold** in volume group **vg02** to **lvnew**:

lvrename /dev/vg02/lvold /dev/vg02/lvnew

An alternate syntax to rename this logical volume is

lvrename vg02 lvold lvnew

SEE ALSO

lvm(8), **lvchange**(8), **vgcreate**(8), **vgrename**(8)

NAME

lvresize – resize a logical volume

SYNOPSIS

lvresize [−−alloc AllocationPolicy] [−A|−−autobackup y|n] [−d|−−debug] [−h|−?|−−help] [−i|−−stripes
Stripes [−I|−−stripesize StripeSize]] {−l|−−extents [+]LogicalExtentsNumber[%{VG|LV|PVS|FREE}] |
−L|−−size [+]LogicalVolumeSize[kKmMgGtT]} [−t|−−test] [−v|−−verbose] LogicalVolumePath [Physi-
calVolumePath...]

DESCRIPTION

lvresize allows you to resize a logical volume. Be careful when reducing a logical volume's size, because
data in the reduced part is lost!!! You should therefore ensure that any filesystem on the volume is shrunk
first so that the extents that are to be removed are not in use. Resizing snapshot logical volumes (see **lvcre-
ate(8)** for information about creating snapshots) is supported as well. But to change the number of copies
in a mirrored logical volume use **lvconvert**(8).

OPTIONS

See **lvm** for common options.

−l, −−extents [+|-]LogicalExtentsNumber[%{VG|LV|PVS|FREE}]

Change or set the logical volume size in units of logical extents. With the + or - sign the value is
added to or subtracted from the actual size of the logical volume and without it, the value is taken
as an absolute one. The number can also be expressed as a percentage of the total space in the
Volume Group with the suffix %VG, relative to the existing size of the Logical Volume with the
suffix %LV, as a percentage of the remaining free space of the PhysicalVolumes on the command
line with the suffix %PVS, or as a percentage of the remaining free space in the Volume Group
with the suffix %FREE.

−L, −−size [+|-]LogicalVolumeSize[kKmMgGtTpPeE]

Change or set the logical volume size in units of megabytes. A size suffix of M for megabytes, G
for gigabytes, T for terabytes, P for petabytes or E for exabytes is optional. With the + or - sign
the value is added to or subtracted from the actual size of the logical volume and without it, the
value is taken as an absolute one.

−i, −−stripes Stripes

Gives the number of stripes to use when extending a Logical Volume. Defaults to whatever the
last segment of the Logical Volume uses. Not applicable to LVs using the original metadata LVM
format, which must use a single value throughout.

−I, −−stripesize StripeSize

Gives the number of kilobytes for the granularity of the stripes. Defaults to whatever the last segment of the Logical Volume uses. Not applicable to LVs using the original metadata LVM format,
which must use a single value throughout.
StripeSize must be 2^n (n = 2 to 9)

SEE ALSO

lvm(8), **lvconvert**(8), **lvcreate**(8), **lvreduce**(8), **lvchange**(8)

NAME

lvs – report information about logical volumes

SYNOPSIS

lvs [--aligned] [-d|--debug] [-h|-?|--help] [--ignorelockingfailure] [--nameprefixes] [--noheadings]
[--nosuffix] [-o|--options [+]Field[,Field]] [-O|--sort [+|-]Key1[,[+|-]Key2[,...]]] [-P|--partial]
[--rows] [--segments] [--separator Separator] [--unbuffered] [--units hsbkmgtHKMGT] [--unquoted]
[-v|--verbose] [--version] [VolumeGroupName [VolumeGroupName...]]

DESCRIPTION

lvs produces formatted output about logical volumes.

OPTIONS

See **lvm** for common options.

--aligned

> Use with --separator to align the output columns.

--nameprefixes

> Add an "LVM2_" prefix plus the field name to the output. Useful with --noheadings to produce a
> list of field=value pairs that can be used to set environment variables (for example, in **udev (7)**
> rules).

--noheadings

> Suppress the headings line that is normally the first line of output. Useful if grepping the output.

--nosuffix

> Suppress the suffix on output sizes. Use with --units (except h and H) if processing the output.

-o, --options

> Comma-separated ordered list of columns. Precede the list with '+' to append to the default selec-
> tion of columns instead of replacing it. Column names are: lv_uuid, lv_name, lv_attr, lv_major,
> lv_minor, lv_kernel_major, lv_kernel_minor, lv_size, seg_count, origin, snap_percent, copy_per-
> cent, move_pv, lv_tags, segtype, stripes, stripesize, chunksize, seg_start, seg_size, seg_tags,
> devices, regionsize, mirror_log, modules.

> With --segments, any "seg_" prefixes are optional; otherwise any "lv_" prefixes are optional.
> Columns mentioned in **vgs (8)** can also be chosen. Use -o help to view the full list of fields avail-
> able.

> The lv_attr bits are:

> 1 Volume type: (m)irrored, (M)irrored without initial sync, (o)rigin, (p)vmove, (s)napshot,
>   invalid (S)napshot, (v)irtual, mirror (i)mage, mirror (I)mage out-of-sync, under (c)onversion

> 2 Permissions: (w)riteable, (r)ead-only

> 3 Allocation policy: (c)ontiguous, c(l)ing, (n)ormal, (a)nywhere, (i)nherited This is capitalised if
>   the volume is currently locked against allocation changes, for example during **pvmove (8)**.

> 4 fixed (m)inor

> 5 State: (a)ctive, (s)uspended, (I)nvalid snapshot, invalid (S)uspended snapshot, mapped (d)evice
>   present without tables, mapped device present with (i)nactive table

> 6 device (o)pen

--segments

> Use default columns that emphasize segment information.

-O, --sort

> Comma-separated ordered list of columns to sort by. Replaces the default selection. Precede any
> column with - for a reverse sort on that column.

    −−rows
        Output columns as rows.

    −−separator Separator
        String to use to separate each column. Useful if grepping the output.

    −−unbuffered
        Produce output immediately without sorting or aligning the columns properly.

    −−units hsbkmgtHKMGT
        All sizes are output in these units: (h)uman-readable, (s)ectors, (b)ytes, (k)ilobytes, (m)egabytes,
        (g)igabytes, (t)erabytes. Capitalise to use multiples of 1000 (S.I.) instead of 1024. Can also spec-
        ify custom (u)nits e.g. −−units 3M

    −−unquoted
        When used with --nameprefixes, output values in the field=value pairs are not quoted.

SEE ALSO
    lvm(8), **lvdisplay**(8), **pvs**(8), **vgs**(8)

NAME

lvscan – scan (all disks) for logical volumes

SYNOPSIS

lvscan [**–b**|**––blockdevice**] [**–d**|**––debug**] [**–h**|**––help**] [**––ignorelockingfailure**] [**–P**|**––partial**] [**–v**|**––verbose**]

DESCRIPTION

lvscan scans all known volume groups or all supported LVM block devices in the system for defined logical volumes.

OPTIONS

See **lvm** for common options.

–b, **––blockdevice**

Adds the device major and minor numbers to the display of each logical volume.

SEE ALSO

lvm(8), **lvcreate**(8), **lvdisplay**(8)

NAME

lwresd – lightweight resolver daemon

SYNOPSIS

lwresd [–**c** *config–file*] [–**C** *config–file*] [–**d** *debug–level*] [–**f**] [–**g**] [–**i** *pid–file*] [–**m** *flag*] [–**n** *#cpus*]
[–**P** *port*] [–**p** *port*] [–**s**] [–**t** *directory*] [–**u** *user*] [–**v**] [–**4**] [–**6**]

DESCRIPTION

lwresd is the daemon providing name lookup services to clients that use the BIND 9 lightweight resolver
library. It is essentially a stripped–down, caching–only name server that answers queries using the BIND 9
lightweight resolver protocol rather than the DNS protocol.

lwresd listens for resolver queries on a UDP port on the IPv4 loopback interface, 127.0.0.1. This means
that **lwresd** can only be used by processes running on the local machine. By default, UDP port number 921
is used for lightweight resolver requests and responses.

Incoming lightweight resolver requests are decoded by the server which then resolves them using the DNS
protocol. When the DNS lookup completes, **lwresd** encodes the answers in the lightweight resolver format
and returns them to the client that made the request.

If */etc/resolv.conf* contains any **nameserver** entries, **lwresd** sends recursive DNS queries to those servers.
This is similar to the use of forwarders in a caching name server. If no **nameserver** entries are present, or if
forwarding fails, **lwresd** resolves the queries autonomously starting at the root name servers, using a
built–in list of root server hints.

OPTIONS

–4

Use IPv4 only even if the host machine is capable of IPv6. –**4** and –**6** are mutually exclusive.

–6

Use IPv6 only even if the host machine is capable of IPv4. –**4** and –**6** are mutually exclusive.

–c *config–file*

Use *config–file* as the configuration file instead of the default, */etc/lwresd.conf*. –**c** can not be used
with –**C**.

–C *config–file*

Use *config–file* as the configuration file instead of the default, */etc/resolv.conf*. –**C** can not be used
with –**c**.

–d *debug–level*

Set the daemon's debug level to *debug–level*. Debugging traces from **lwresd** become more verbose as
the debug level increases.

–f

Run the server in the foreground (i.e. do not daemonize).

–g

Run the server in the foreground and force all logging to *stderr*.

–i *pid–file*

Use *pid–file* as the PID file instead of the default, */var/run/lwresd/lwresd.pid*.

–m *flag*

Turn on memory usage debugging flags. Possible flags are *usage*, *trace*, *record*, *size*, and *mctx*. These
correspond to the ISC_MEM_DEBUGXXXX flags described in <*isc/mem.h*>.

–n *#cpus*

Create *#cpus* worker threads to take advantage of multiple CPUs. If not specified, **lwresd** will try to
determine the number of CPUs present and create one thread per CPU. If it is unable to determine the
number of CPUs, a single worker thread will be created.

–P *port*

Listen for lightweight resolver queries on port *port*. If not specified, the default is port 921.

−p *port*
>   Send DNS lookups to port *port*. If not specified, the default is port 53. This provides a way of testing the lightweight resolver daemon with a name server that listens for queries on a non−standard port number.

−s
>   Write memory usage statistics to *stdout* on exit.
>   >   **Note:** This option is mainly of interest to BIND 9 developers and may be removed or changed in a future release.

−t *directory*
>   Chroot to *directory* after processing the command line arguments, but before reading the configuration file.
>   >   **Warning:** This option should be used in conjunction with the **−u** option, as chrooting a process running as root doesn't enhance security on most systems; the way **chroot(2)** is defined allows a process with root privileges to escape a chroot jail.

−u *user*
>   Setuid to *user* after completing privileged operations, such as creating sockets that listen on privileged ports.

−v
>   Report the version number and exit.

FILES
>   */etc/resolv.conf*
>   >   The default configuration file.
>
>   */var/run/lwresd.pid*
>   >   The default process−id file.

SEE ALSO
>   **named**(8), **lwres**(3), **resolver**(5).

AUTHOR
>   Internet Systems Consortium

COPYRIGHT
>   Copyright © 2004, 2005, 2007−2009 Internet Systems Consortium, Inc. ("ISC")
>   Copyright © 2000, 2001 Internet Software Consortium.

NAME
mail.local — store mail in a mailbox

SYNOPSIS
mail.local [**-l**] [**-f** *from*] *user* ...

DESCRIPTION
mail.local reads the standard input up to an end-of-file and appends it to each *user's* mail file. The *user* must be a valid user name.

The options are as follows:

-f *from*
    Specify the sender's name.

-l   Request that **username.lock** files be used for locking.

Individual mail messages in the mailbox are delimited by an empty line followed by a line beginning with the string "From ". A line containing the string "From ", the sender's name and a time stamp is prepended to each delivered mail message. A blank line is appended to each message. A greater-than character (">") is prepended to any line in the message which could be mistaken for a "From " delimiter line.

If the [**-l**] flag is specified mailbox locking is done with **username.lock** files. Otherwise, the mailbox is exclusively locked with flock(2) while mail is appended.

If the "biff" service is returned by getservbyname(3), the biff server is notified of delivered mail.

The **mail.local** utility exits 0 on success, and >0 if an error occurs.

ENVIRONMENT
TZ   Used to set the appropriate time zone on the timestamp.

FILES
/tmp/local.XXXXXX temporary files
/var/mail/user   user's mailbox directory

SEE ALSO
mail(1), flock(2), getservbyname(3), comsat(8), sendmail(8)

HISTORY
A superset of **mail.local** (handling mailbox reading as well as mail delivery) appeared in Version 7 AT&T UNIX as the program mail(1).

NAME

mailwrapper — invoke appropriate MTA software based on configuration file

SYNOPSIS

Special. See below.

DESCRIPTION

Once upon time, the only Mail Transfer Agent (MTA) software easily available was "sendmail". This famous MTA was written by Eric Allman and first appeared in 4.1BSD. The legacy of this MTA affected most Mail User Agents (MUAs) such as mail(1); the path and calling conventions expected by "sendmail" were compiled in.

But times changed. On a modern NetBSD system, the administrator may wish to use one of several available MTAs.

It would be difficult to modify all MUA software typically available on a system, so most of the authors of alternative MTAs have written their front end message submission programs that may appear in the place of /usr/sbin/sendmail, but still follow the same calling conventions as "sendmail".

The "sendmail" MTA also typically has aliases named mailq(1) and newaliases(1) linked to it. The program knows to behave differently when its *argv[0]* is "mailq" or "newaliases" and behaves appropriately. Typically, replacement MTAs provide similar functionality, either through a program that also switches behavior based on calling name, or through a set of programs that provide similar functionality.

Although having replacement programs that plug replace "sendmail" helps in installing alternative MTAs, it essentially makes the configuration of the system depend on hand installing new programs in /usr. This leads to configuration problems for many administrators, since they may wish to install a new MTA without altering the system provided /usr. (This may be, for example, to avoid having upgrade problems when a new version of the system is installed over the old.) They may also have a shared /usr among several machines, and may wish to avoid placing implicit configuration information in a read-only /usr.

The **mailwrapper** program is designed to replace /usr/sbin/sendmail and to invoke an appropriate MTA based on configuration information placed in /etc/mailer.conf. This permits the administrator to configure which MTA is to be invoked on the system at run time.

EXIT STATUS

mailwrapper exits 0 on success, and >0 if an error occurs.

FILES

Configuration for **mailwrapper** is kept in /etc/mailer.conf. /usr/sbin/sendmail is typically set up as a symlink to **mailwrapper** which is not usually invoked on its own.

DIAGNOSTICS

mailwrapper will print a diagnostic if its configuration file is missing or malformed, or does not contain a mapping for the name under which it was invoked.

SEE ALSO

mail(1), mailq(1), newaliases(1), postfix(1), mailer.conf(5)

HISTORY

The **mailwrapper** program appeared in NetBSD 1.4.

AUTHORS
> Perry E. Metzger ⟨perry@piermont.com⟩

BUGS
> The entire reason this program exists is a crock. Instead, a command for how to submit mail should be standardized, and all the "behave differently if invoked with a different name" behavior of things like `mailq(1)` should go away.

NAME
makedbm — create a NIS database

SYNOPSIS
makedbm **−u** *dbfile*
makedbm [**−bls**] [**−d** *yp_domain_name*] [**−i** *yp_input_file*] [**−m** *yp_master_name*]
        [**−o** *yp_output_file*] *infile outfile*

DESCRIPTION
makedbm is the utility in NIS that creates the db(3) database file containing the NIS map.

infile is the pathname of the source file (where "-" is standard input). Each line consists of the key and the value, with a space separating the items. Blank lines are ignored, and a "#" is a comment character and indicates that the rest of the line should be ignored.

outfile is the pathname of the generated database.

The options are as follows:

−b   Interdomain. Include an entry in the database informing a NIS server to use DNS to get information about unknown hosts. This option will only have effect on the maps hosts.byname and hosts.byaddr.

−l   Lowercase. Convert all keys to lower case before adding them to the NIS database.

−s   Secure map. Include an entry in the database informing ypxfr(8) and ypserv(8) that the NIS map is going to be handled as secure (i.e., not served to clients that don't connect from a reserved port).

−d *yp_domain_name*
        Include an entry in the map with 'YP_DOMAIN_NAME' as the key and *yp_domain_name* as the value.

−i *yp_input_file*
        Include an entry in the map with 'YP_INPUT_FILE' as the key and *yp_input_file* as the value.

−m *yp_master_name*
        Include an entry in the map with 'YP_MASTER_NAME' as the key and *yp_master_name* as the value.

−o *yp_output_file*
        Include an entry in the map with 'YP_OUTPUT_FILE' as the key and *yp_output_file* as the value.

−u *dbfile*
        Dump the contents of *dbfile* to standard output, in a format suitable to be passed back into **makedbm**. *dbfile* is the pathname to the database.

SEE ALSO
db(3), nis(8), ypserv(8), ypxfr(8)

AUTHORS
Mats O Jansson ⟨moj@stacken.kth.se⟩

NAME

    MAKEDEV — create system and device special files

SYNOPSIS

    MAKEDEV [**-fMs**] [**-m** *mknod*] [**-p** *pax*] [**-t** *mtree*] {*special* | *device*} [. . .]

DESCRIPTION

    MAKEDEV is used to create system and device special files. As arguments it takes the names of known devices, like *sd0*, or of special targets, like all or std, which create a collection of device special files, or local, which invokes MAKEDEV.local(8) with the all argument.

    The script is in /dev/MAKEDEV. Devices are created in the current working directory; in normal use, **MAKEDEV** should be invoked with /dev as the current working directory.

    Supported options are:

    -f   Force permissions to be updated on existing devices. This works only if **MAKEDEV** invokes mknod(8); it is not compatible with the **-p**, **-s**, or **-t** options.

    -M   Create a memory file system, union mounted over the current directory, to contain the device special files. The memory file system is created using mount_tmpfs(8) or mount_mfs(8), in that order of preference.

                If the **-M** flag is specified more than once, then **MAKEDEV** assumes that it is being invoked from init(8) to populate a memory file system for /dev. In this case, **MAKEDEV** will also redirect its output to the system console.

    -m *mknod*   Force the use of mknod(8), and specify the name or path to the mknod(8) program. [Usually, $TOOL_MKNOD or mknod.]

    -p *pax*   Force the use of pax(1), and specify the name or path to the pax(1) program. [Usually, $TOOL_PAX or pax.]

    -s   Generate an mtree(8) specfile instead of creating devices.

    -t *mtree*   Force the use of mtree(8), and specify the name or path to the mtree(8) program. [Usually, $TOOL_MTREE or mtree.]

    MAKEDEV has several possible methods of creating device nodes:

- By invoking the mknod(8) command once for each device node. This is the traditional method, but it is slow because each device node is created using a new process.

    The **-m** option forces **MAKEDEV** to use the mknod(8) method.

- By internally creating a specfile in a format usable by mtree(8), and providing the specfile on standard input to a pax(1) or mtree(8) command, invoked with options that request it to create the device nodes as well as any necessary subdirectories. This is much faster than creating device nodes with mknod(8), because it requires much fewer processes; however, it's not compatible with the **-f** option.

    The **-p** or **-t** options force **MAKEDEV** to use the pax(1) or mtree(8) methods.

- If the **-s** option is specified, then **MAKEDEV** will not create device nodes at all, but will output a specfile in a format usable by mtree(8).

    The **-m**, **-p**, **-s**, and **-t** flags are mutually exclusive. If none of these flags is specified, then **MAKEDEV** will use mtree(8), pax(1), or mknod(8), in that order of preference, depending on which commands appear to be available and usable. In normal use, it's expected that mtree(8) will be available, so it will be chosen. If **MAKEDEV** is invoked by init(8), it's expected that mtree(8) will not be available, but pax(1) may be available.

The special targets supported on NetBSD are:

all	Makes all known devices, including local devices. Tries to make the 'standard' number of each type.
init	A set of devices that is used for MFS /dev by init. May be equal to "all".
floppy	Devices to be put on install floppies
ramdisk	Devices to be put into INSTALL kernel ramdisks.
std	Standard devices
local	Configuration specific devices
wscons	Make wscons devices
usbs	Make USB devices
isdns	Make ISDN devices

Please note that any hash marks ("#") in the following list of supported device targets must be replaced by digits when calling **MAKEDEV**:

Tapes:

st #	SCSI tapes, see st(4)
wt #	QIC-interfaced (e.g. not SCSI) 3M cartridge tape, see wt(4)
ht #	MASSBUS TM03 and TU??, see vax/ht(4)
mt #	MSCP tapes (e.g. TU81, TK50), see vax/mt(4)
tm #	UNIBUS TM11 and TE10 emulations (e.g. Emulex TC-11), see vax/tm(4)
ts #	UNIBUS TS11, see vax/ts(4)
ut #	UNIBUS TU45 emulations (e.g. si 9700), see vax/ut(4)
uu #	TU58 cassettes on DL11 controller, see vax/uu(4)

Disks:

ccd#	Concatenated disk devices, see ccd(4)
cd#	SCSI or ATAPI CD-ROM, see cd(4)
cgd#	Cryptographic disk devices, see cgd(4)
raid#	RAIDframe disk devices, see raid(4)
sd#	SCSI disks, see sd(4)
wd#	"winchester" disk drives (ST506,IDE,ESDI,RLL,...), see wd(4)
bmd#	Nereid bank memory disks, see x68k/bmd(4)
ed#	IBM PS/2 ESDI disk devices, see edc(4)
fd#	"floppy" disk drives (3 1/2", 5 1/4"), see amiga/fdc(4), i386/fdc(4), sparc64/fdc(4)
fss#	Files system snapshot devices, see fss(4)
gdrom#	Dreamcast "gigadisc" CD-ROM drive, see dreamcast/gdrom(4)
hk #	UNIBUS RK06 and RK07, see vax/hk(4)
hp #	MASSBUS RM??, see vax/hp(4)
ld#	Logical disk devices (e.g., hardware RAID), see ld(4)
mcd#	Mitsumi CD-ROM, see mcd(4)
md#	Memory pseudo-disk devices, see md(4)
ofdisk#	OpenFirmware disk devices
ra#	MSCP disks (RA??, RD??)
rb#	730 IDC w/ RB80 and/or RB02
rd#	HDC9224 RD disks on VS2000, see hp300/rd(4)
rl#	UNIBUS RL02, see vax/rl(4)
rx#	MSCP floppy disk (RX33/50/...)
up#	Other UNIBUS devices (e.g. on Emulex SC-21V controller), see vax/up(4)

vnd#	"file" pseudo-disks, see vnd(4)
xbd#	Xen virtual disks
xd#	Xylogic 753/7053 disks, see sparc/xd(4)
xy#	Xylogic 450/451 disks, see sparc/xy(4)

Pointing devices:

wsmouse#	wscons mouse events, see wsmouse(4)
lms#	Logitech bus mouse, see i386/lms(4)
mms#	Microsoft bus mouse, see dreamcast/mms(4), i386/mms(4)
qms#	"quadrature mouse", see acorn32/qms(4)
pms#	PS/2 mouse
mouse	Mouse (provides events, for X11)

Keyboard devices:

wskbd#	wscons keyboard events, see wskbd(4)
kbd	Raw keyboard (provides events, for X11), see sparc/kbd(4), sun2/kbd(4), sun3/kbd(4)
kbdctl	Keyboard control

Terminals/Console ports:

tty[01]#	Standard serial ports, see tty(4)
tty0#	SB1250 ("sbscn") serial ports (sbmips), see tty(4)
ttyE#	wscons - Workstation console ("wscons") glass-tty emulators
ttyCZ?	Cyclades-Z multiport serial boards. Each "unit" makes 64 ports., see cz(4)
ttyCY?	Cyclom-Y multiport serial boards. Each "unit" makes 32 ports., see cy(4)
ttye#	ITE bitmapped consoles, see amiga/ite(4), hp300/ite(4)
ttyv0	pccons
ttyC?	NS16550 ("com") serial ports
ttyS#	SA1110 serial port (hpcarm)
ttyTX?	TX39 internal serial ports (hpcmips)
ttyB?	DEC 3000 ZS8530 ("scc") serial ports (alpha), see scc(4)
ttyA#	Mfc serial ports (amiga)
ttyB#	Msc serial ports (amiga)
ttyC#	Com style serial ports (DraCo, HyperCom) (amiga) On the DraCo, units 0 and 1 are the built-in "modem" and "mouse" ports, if configured.
ttyA0	8530 Channel A (formerly ser02) (atari)
ttyA1	8530 Channel B (formerly mdm02) (atari)
ttyB0	UART on first 68901 (formerly mdm01) (atari)
ixpcom	IXP12x0 COM ports
epcom	EP93xx COM ports
ttyM?	HP200/300 4 port serial mux interface (hp300)
ttya	"ttya" system console (luna68k)
ttyb	Second system serial port (luna68k)
tty#	Onboard serial ports (mvme68k) On the mvme147 these are: ttyZ1, ttyZ2 and ttyZ3. On the mvme167, and '177: ttyC1, ttyC2 and ttyC3. Note that tty[CZ]0 is grabbed by the console device so is not created by default, see tty(4)
dc#	PMAX 4 channel serial interface (kbd, mouse, modem, printer)
scc#	82530 serial interface (pmax), see scc(4)
ttyZ#	Zilog 8530 ("zstty") serial ports, see zstty(4)
tty[abcd]	Built-in serial ports (sparc)
tty#	Z88530 serial controllers (sparc64), see tty(4)

`ttyh#`	SAB82532 serial controllers (sparc64), see `sparc64/sab`(4)
`tty[a-j]`	Built-in serial ports (sun2, sun3)
`ttyC?`	pccons (arc)
`dz#`	UNIBUS DZ11 and DZ32 (vax), see `vax/dz`(4)
`dh#`	UNIBUS DH11 and emulations (e.g. Able DMAX, Emulex CS-11) (vax), see `vax/dh`(4)
`dmf#`	UNIBUS DMF32 (vax), see `vax/dmf`(4)
`dhu#`	UNIBUS DHU11 (vax), see `vax/dhu`(4)
`dmz#`	UNIBUS DMZ32 (vax), see `vax/dmz`(4)
`dl#`	UNIBUS DL11 (vax), see `vax/dl`(4)
`xencons`	Xen virtual console

Terminal multiplexors:

`dc#`	4 channel serial interface (keyboard, mouse, modem, printer)
`dh#`	UNIBUS DH11 and emulations (e.g. Able DMAX, Emulex CS-11), see `vax/dh`(4)
`dhu#`	UNIBUS DHU11, see `vax/dhu`(4)
`dl#`	UNIBUS DL11, see `vax/dl`(4)
`dmf#`	UNIBUS DMF32, see `vax/dmf`(4)
`dmz#`	UNIBUS DMZ32, see `vax/dmz`(4)
`dz#`	UNIBUS DZ11 and DZ32, see `vax/dz`(4)
`scc#`	82530 serial interface, see `scc`(4)

Call units:

`dn#`	UNIBUS DN11 and emulations (e.g. Able Quadracall), see `vax/dn`(4)

Pseudo terminals:

`ptm`	Pty multiplexor device, and pts directory, see `ptm`(4)
`pty#`	Set of 16 master and slave pseudo terminals, see `pty`(4)
`opty`	First 16 ptys, to save inodes on install media
`ipty`	First 2 ptys, for install media use only

Printers:

`arcpp#`	Archimedes parallel port
`lpt#`	Stock lp, see `lpt`(4), `acorn32/lpt`(4), `i386/lpt`(4), `mvme68k/lpt`(4)
`lpa#`	Interruptless lp
`par#`	Amiga motherboard parallel port
`cpi#`	Macintosh Nubus CSI parallel printer card, see `mac68k/cpi`(4)

USB devices:

`usb#`	USB control devices, see `usb`(4)
`uhid#`	USB generic HID devices, see `uhid`(4)
`ulpt#`	USB printer devices, see `ulpt`(4)
`ugen#`	USB generic devices, see `ugen`(4)
`urio#`	USB Diamond Rio 500 devices, see `urio`(4)
`uscanner#`	USB scanners, see `uscanner`(4)
`ttyHS#`	USB Option N.V. modems
`ttyU#`	USB modems, see `ucom`(4)
`ttyY#`	USB serial adapters

ISDN devices:

`isdn`	Communication between userland isdnd and kernel, see `isdn`(4)
`isdnctl`	Control device, see `isdnctl`(4)

`isdnbchan#`	Raw b-channel access, see `isdnbchan`(4)
`isdntel#`	Telephony device, see `isdntel`(4)
`isdnteld#`	Telephony dialout device
`isdntrc#`	Trace device, see `isdntrc`(4)

Video devices:

`bwtwo#`	Monochromatic frame buffer, see `sparc/bwtwo`(4), `sun2/bwtwo`(4), `sun3/bwtwo`(4)
`cgtwo#`	8-bit color frame buffer, see `sparc/cgtwo`(4), `sun3/cgtwo`(4)
`cgthree#`	8-bit color frame buffer, see `sparc/cgthree`(4)
`cgfour#`	8-bit color frame buffer, see `sparc/cgfour`(4), `sun3/cgfour`(4)
`cgsix#`	Accelerated 8-bit color frame buffer, see `sparc/cgsix`(4)
`cgeight#`	24-bit color frame buffer, see `sparc/cgeight`(4)
`etvme`	Tseng et-compatible cards on VME (atari)
`ik#`	UNIBUS interface to Ikonas frame buffer, see `vax/ik`(4)
`leo`	Circad Leonardo VME-bus true color (atari)
`ps#`	UNIBUS interface to Picture System 2, see `vax/ps`(4)
`qv#`	QVSS (MicroVAX) display
`tcx#`	Accelerated 8/24-bit color frame buffer, see `sparc/tcx`(4)

Maple bus devices:

`maple`	Maple bus control devices, see `dreamcast/maple`(4)
`mlcd#`	Maple bus LCD devices, see `dreamcast/mlcd`(4)
`mmem#`	Maple bus storage devices, see `dreamcast/mmem`(4)

IEEE1394 bus devices:

`fw#`	IEEE1394 bus generic node access devices
`fwmem#`	IEEE1394 bus physical memory of the remote node access devices

Special purpose devices:

`ad#`	UNIBUS interface to Data Translation A/D converter, see `vax/ad`(4)
`agp#`	AGP GART devices, see `agp`(4)
`altq`	ALTQ control interface
`amr#`	AMI MegaRaid control device, see `amr`(4)
`apm`	Power management device, see `i386/apm`(4)
`audio#`	Audio devices, see `audio`(4)
`bell#`	OPM bell device (x68k)
`bktr`	Brooktree 848/849/878/879 based TV cards, see `bktr`(4)
`bpf`	Packet filter, see `bpf`(4)
`bthub`	Bluetooth Device Hub control interface, see `bthub`(4)
`cfs#`	Coda file system device
`ch#`	SCSI media changer, see `ch`(4)
`cir#`	Consumer IR, see `cir`(4)
`clockctl`	Clock control for non root users, see `clockctl`(4)
`cpuctl`	CPU control
`crypto`	Hardware crypto access driver, see `crypto`(4)
`dmoverio`	Hardware-assisted data movers, see `dmoverio`(4)
`dpt#`	DPT/Adaptec EATA RAID management interface, see `dpt`(4)
`dpti#`	DPT/Adaptec I2O RAID management interface, see `dpti`(4)
`drm#`	Direct Rendering Manager interface, see `drm`(4)
`fb#`	PMAX generic framebuffer pseudo-device

`fd`	File descriptors
`grf#`	Graphics frame buffer device, see `amiga/grf`(4), `hp300/grf`(4)
`hdaudio#`	High Definition audio control device, see `hdaudio`(4)
`hil`	HP300 HIL input devices, see `hp300/hil`(4)
`icp`	ICP-Vortex/Intel RAID control interface, see `icp`(4)
`iic#`	IIC bus device, see `iic`(4)
`io`	X86 IOPL access for COMPAT_10, COMPAT_FREEBSD, see `hp700/io`(4), `i386/io`(4)
`iop#`	I2O IOP control interface, see `iop`(4)
`ipl`	IP Filter
`irframe#`	IrDA physical frame, see `irframe`(4)
`ite#`	Terminal emulator interface to HP300 graphics devices, see `amiga/ite`(4), `hp300/ite`(4)
`joy#`	Joystick device, see `joy`(4)
`kttcp`	Kernel ttcp helper device, see `kttcp`(4)
`lockstat`	Kernel locking statistics
`magma#`	Magma multiport serial/parallel cards, see `sparc/magma`(4)
`midi#`	MIDI, see `midi`(4)
`mlx#`	Mylex DAC960 control interface, see `mlx`(4)
`mly#`	Mylex AcceleRAID/eXtremeRAID control interface, see `mly`(4)
`np#`	UNIBUS Ethernet co-processor interface, for downloading., see `vax/np`(4)
`nsmb#`	SMB requester, see `nsmb`(4)
`openfirm`	OpenFirmware accessor
`pad#`	Pseudo-audio device driver, see `pad`(4)
`pci#`	PCI bus access devices, see `pci`(4)
`pf`	PF packet filter
`pow#`	Power management device (x68k), see `x68k/pow`(4)
`putter`	Pass-to-Userspace Transporter
`px#`	PixelStamp Xserver access, see `px`(4)
`radio#`	Radio devices, see `radio`(4)
`random`	Random number generator, see `rnd`(4)
`rtc#`	RealTimeClock, see `atari/rtc`(4), `evbppc/rtc`(4), `hp300/rtc`(4)
`satlink#`	PlanetConnect satellite receiver driver
`scsibus#`	SCSI busses, see `scsi`(4)
`se#`	SCSI Ethernet, see `se`(4)
`ses#`	SES/SAF-TE SCSI Devices, see `ses`(4)
`speaker`	PC speaker, see `speaker`(4)
`sram`	Battery backuped memory (x68k)
`ss#`	SCSI scanner, see `ss`(4)
`stic#`	PixelStamp interface chip
`sysmon`	System Monitoring hardware, see `envsys`(4)
`tap#`	Virtual Ethernet device, see `tap`(4)
`tun#`	Network tunnel driver, see `tun`(4)
`twa`	3ware Apache control interface, see `twa`(4)
`twe`	3ware Escalade control interface, see `twe`(4)
`uk#`	Unknown SCSI device, see `uk`(4)
`veriexec`	Veriexec fingerprint loader, see `veriexec`(4)
`video#`	Video capture devices, see `video`(4)
`view#`	Generic interface to graphic displays (Amiga)

vmegen#	Generic VME access
wsfont#	Console font control, see wsfont(4)
wsmux#	wscons event multiplexor, see wsmux(4)
xenevt	Xen event interface

ENVIRONMENT

The following environment variables affect the execution of **MAKEDEV**:

MAKEDEV_AS_LIBRARY

> If this is set, then **MAKEDEV** will define several shell functions and then return, ignoring all its command line options and arguments. This is used to enable MAKEDEV.local(8) to use the shell functions defined in **MAKEDEV**.

FILES

/dev	special device files directory
/dev/MAKEDEV	script described in this man page
/dev/MAKEDEV.local	script for site-specific devices

DIAGNOSTICS

If the script reports an error that is difficult to understand, you can get more debugging output by using
   sh -x *MAKEDEV argument*.

SEE ALSO

config(1), pax(1), intro(4), diskless(8), init(8), MAKEDEV.local(8), mknod(8), mount_mfs(8), mount_tmpfs(8), mtree(8)

HISTORY

The **MAKEDEV** command appeared in 4.2BSD. The **−f**, **−m**, and **−s** options were added in NetBSD 2.0. The **−p**, **−t**, and **−M** options were added in NetBSD 5.0. The ability to be used as a function library was added in NetBSD 5.0.

BUGS

The **−f** option is not compatible with the use of mtree(8) or pax(1).

NOTES

Not all devices listed in this manpage are supported on all platforms.

This man page is generated automatically from the same sources as /dev/MAKEDEV, in which the device files are not always sorted, which may result in an unusual (non-alphabetical) order.

In order to allow a diskless NetBSD client to obtain its /dev directory from a file server running a foreign operating system, one of the following techniques may be useful to populate a directory of device nodes on the foreign server:

- If the foreign server is sufficiently similar to NetBSD, run **MAKEDEV** in an appropriate directory of the foreign server, using the **−m** flag to refer to a script that converts from command line arguments that would be usable with the NetBSD mknod(8) command to the equivalent commands for the foreign server.

- Run **MAKEDEV** with the **−s** flag to generate an mtree(8) specification file; this can be done on any host with a POSIX-compliant shell and a few widely-available utilities. Use the pax(1) command with the **−w −M** flags to convert the mtree(8) specification file into an archive in a format that supports device nodes (such as *ustar* format); this can be done on a NetBSD host, or can be done in a cross-build environment using **TOOLDIR**/bin/nbpax. Finally, use apropriate tools on the foreign server to unpack the archive and create the device nodes.

NAME
    MAKEDEV.local — create site-specific device special files

SYNOPSIS
    MAKEDEV.local [**-fMs**] [**-m** *mknod*] [**-p** *pax*] [**-t** *mtree*] {all |
             site-specific-argument} [...]

DESCRIPTION
    MAKEDEV.local is used to create site-specific device special files. Each argument may be the word all
    or a site-specific argument. By default, there are no valid site-specific arguments, and the all argument has
    no effect; This may be changed by editing the script.

    The script is in /dev/MAKEDEV.local. Devices are created in the current working directory; in normal
    use, **MAKEDEV.local** should be invoked with /dev as the current working directory.

    Supported options for **MAKEDEV.local** are the same as for MAKEDEV(8).

FILES
    /dev   special device files directory
    /dev/MAKEDEV   script that invokes **MAKEDEV.local** with the all argument.
    /dev/MAKEDEV.local script described in this man page

SEE ALSO
    config(1), intro(4), MAKEDEV(8), mknod(8)

HISTORY
    The **MAKEDEV.local** command appeared in 4.2BSD. Handling of the same command line options as
    MAKEDEV(8), and the use of MAKEDEV(8) as a function library, was added in NetBSD 5.0.

NOTES
    The relationship between **MAKEDEV.local** and MAKEDEV(8) is complex:

    • If MAKEDEV(8) is invoked with the all or local argument, then it will invoke **MAKEDEV.local** as a
       child process, with options similar to those that were originally passed to MAKEDEV(8), and with the all
       argument.

    • **MAKEDEV.local** uses shell functions defined in MAKEDEV(8). This is done by loading MAKEDEV(8)
       using the shell "." command, with the MAKEDEV_AS_LIBRARY variable set (to inform MAKEDEV(8)
       that it should behave as a function library, not as an independent program).

NAME
   makefs — create a file system image from a directory tree

SYNOPSIS
   makefs [**-x**] [**-B** *byte-order*] [**-b** *free-blocks*] [**-d** *debug-mask*] [**-F** *specfile*]
           [**-f** *free-files*] [**-M** *minimum-size*] [**-m** *maximum-size*] [**-N** *userdb-dir*]
           [**-o** *fs-options*] [**-S** *sector-size*] [**-s** *image-size*] [**-t** *fs-type*]
           image-file directory

DESCRIPTION
   The utility **makefs** creates a file system image into *image-file* from the directory tree *directory*.
   No special devices or privileges are required to perform this task.

   The options are as follows:

   -B *byte-order*
         Set the byte order of the image to *byte-order*. Valid byte orders are 4321, big, or 'be' for big
         endian, and 1234, little, or 'le' for little endian. Some file systems may have a fixed byte order;
         in those cases this argument will be ignored.

   -b *free-blocks*
         Ensure that a minimum of *free-blocks* free blocks exist in the image. An optional '%' suffix may
         be provided to indicate that *free-blocks* indicates a percentage of the calculated image size.

   -d *debug-mask*
         Enable various levels of debugging, depending upon which bits are set in *debug-mask*. XXX: doc-
         ument these

   -F *specfile*
         Use *specfile* as an mtree(8) 'specfile' specification.

         If a specfile entry exists in the underlying file system, its permissions and modification time will be
         used unless specifically overridden by the specfile. An error will be raised if the type of entry in the
         specfile conflicts with that of an existing entry.

         In the opposite case (where a specfile entry does not have an entry in the underlying file system) the
         following occurs: If the specfile entry is marked **optional**, the specfile entry is ignored. Otherwise,
         the entry will be created in the image, and it is necessary to specify at least the following parameters
         in the specfile: **type**, **mode**, **gname**, or **gid**, and **uname** or **uid**, **device** (in the case of block or charac-
         ter devices), and **link** (in the case of symbolic links). If **time** isn't provided, the current time will be
         used. If **flags** isn't provided, the current file flags will be used. Missing regular file entries will be
         created as zero-length files.

   -f *free-files*
         Ensure that a minimum of *free-files* free files (inodes) exist in the image. An optional '%' suffix
         may be provided to indicate that *free-files* indicates a percentage of the calculated image size.

   -M *minimum-size*
         Set the minimum size of the file system image to *minimum-size*.

   -m *maximum-size*
         Set the maximum size of the file system image to *maximum-size*. An error will be raised if the tar-
         get file system needs to be larger than this to accommodate the provided directory tree.

   -N *dbdir*
         Use the user database text file master.passwd and group database text file group from *dbdir*,
         rather than using the results from the system's getpwnam(3) and getgrnam(3) (and related) library

calls.

-o *fs-options*
> Set file system specific options. *fs-options* is a comma separated list of options. Valid file system specific options are detailed below.

-S *sector-size*
> Set the file system sector size to *sector-size*. Defaults to 512.

-s *image-size*
> Set the size of the file system image to *image-size*.

-t *fs-type*
> Create an *fs-type* file system image. The following file system types are supported:

> > **ffs**   BSD fast file system (default).

> > **cd9660**   ISO 9660 file system.

-x   Exclude file system nodes not explicitly listed in the specfile.

Where sizes are specified, a decimal number of bytes is expected. Two or more numbers may be separated by an "x" to indicate a product. Each number may have one of the following optional suffixes:

> b   Block; multiply by 512
> k   Kibi; multiply by 1024 (1 KiB)
> m   Mebi; multiply by 1048576 (1 MiB)
> g   Gibi; multiply by 1073741824 (1 GiB)
> t   Tebi; multiply by 1099511627776 (1 TiB)
> w   Word; multiply by the number of bytes in an integer

FFS-specific options

ffs images have ffs-specific optional parameters that may be provided. Each of the options consists of a keyword, an equal sign ('='), and a value. The following keywords are supported:

avgfilesize	Expected average file size.
avgfpdir	Expected number of files per directory.
bsize	Block size.
density	Bytes per inode.
fsize	Fragment size.
maxbpg	Maximum blocks per file in a cylinder group.
minfree	Minimum % free.
optimization	Optimization preference; one of `space` or `time`.
extent	Maximum extent size.
maxbpcg	Maximum total number of blocks in a cylinder group.
version	UFS version. 1 for FFS (default), 2 for UFS2.

CD9660-specific options

cd9660 images have ISO9660-specific optional parameters that may be provided. The arguments consist of a keyword and, optionally, an equal sign ('='), and a value. The following keywords are supported:

allow-deep-trees	Allow the directory structure to exceed the maximum specified in the spec.
allow-max-name	Allow 37 instead of 33 characters for filenames by omitting the version id.

allow-multidot	Allow multiple dots in a filename.
applicationid	Application ID of the image.
archimedes	Use the ARCHIMEDES extension to encode RISC OS metadata.
boot-load-segment	Set load segment for the boot image.
bootimage	Filename of a boot image in the format "sysid;filename", where "sysid" is one of i386, mac68k, macppc, or powerpc.
generic-bootimage	Load a generic boot image into the first 32K of the cd9660 image.
hard-disk-boot	Boot image is a hard disk image.
keep-bad-images	Don't throw away images whose write was aborted due to an error. For debugging purposes.
label	Label name of the image.
no-boot	Boot image is not bootable.
no-emul-boot	Boot image is a "no emulation" ElTorito image.
no-trailing-padding	Do not pad the image (apparently Linux needs the padding).
preparer	Preparer ID of the image.
publisher	Publisher ID of the image.
rockridge	Use RockRidge extensions (for longer filenames, etc.).
volumeid	Volume set identifier of the image.

SEE ALSO
strsuftoll(3), installboot(8), mtree(8), newfs(8)

HISTORY
The **makefs** utility appeared in NetBSD 1.6.

AUTHORS
Luke Mewburn ⟨lukem@NetBSD.org⟩ (original program)
Daniel Watt,
Walter Deignan,
Ryan Gabrys,
Alan Perez-Rathke,
Ram Vedam (cd9660 support)

NAME
makekey — make encrypted keys or passwords

SYNOPSIS
makekey

DESCRIPTION
makekey encrypts a key and salt which it reads from the standard input and writes the result to the standard output. The key is expected to be eight bytes; the salt is expected to be two bytes. See `crypt`(3) for more information on what characters the key and salt can contain and how the encrypted value is calculated.

SEE ALSO
`login`(1), `crypt`(3)

HISTORY
A **makekey** command appeared in Version 7 AT&T UNIX.

NAME

makewhatis — create a whatis.db database

SYNOPSIS

/usr/libexec/makewhatis [**−fw**] [**−C** *file*] [*manpath* ...]

DESCRIPTION

makewhatis strips the NAME lines from compiled or raw man(1) pages and creates a whatis.db database for use in apropos(1), whatis(1), or with man(1)'s **−k** option. Man pages compressed with compress(1) and gzip(1) are uncompressed before processing.

When *manpath* is provided multiple times, the resulting database file is generated in the first directory specified, and contains entries for all the directories.

If *manpath* is not provided, **makewhatis** parses /etc/man.conf and regenerates the whatis database files specified there. Each database file is assumed to reside in the root of the appropriate man page hierarchy.

The options are as follows:

−C *file*   Use *file* (in man.conf(5) format) as configuration file instead of the default, /etc/man.conf.

−f   Don't spawn child processes to generate the individual database files, but do all the work synchronously in the foreground.

−w   Print warnings about input files we don't like.

FILES

whatis.db   name of the whatis database
/etc/man.conf man(1) configuration file, used to get the location of the whatis databases when **makewhatis** is called without arguments

SEE ALSO

apropos(1), man(1), whatis(1), man.conf(5)

HISTORY

makewhatis first appeared in NetBSD 1.0, as a shell script written by J.T. Conklin ⟨jtc@NetBSD.org⟩ and Thorsten Frueauf ⟨frueauf@ira.uka.de⟩. Further work was done by Matthew Green, Luke Mewburn, and Chris Demetriou.

Matthias Scheler has reimplemented **makewhatis** in C in NetBSD 1.5.

AUTHORS

Matthias Scheler ⟨tron@NetBSD.org⟩

NAME
map-mbone – Multicast connection mapper

SYNOPSIS
/usr/sbin/map-mbone [**–d** *debug_level*] [**–f**] [**–g**] [**–n**] [**–r** *retry_count*] [**–t** *timeout_count*] [**starting_router**]

DESCRIPTION
map-mbone attempts to display all multicast routers that are reachable from the multicast *starting_router*. If not specified on the command line, the default multicast *starting_router* is the localhost.

map-mbone traverses neighboring multicast routers by sending the ASK_NEIGHBORS IGMP message to the multicast starting_router. If this multicast router responds, the version number and a list of their neighboring multicast router addresses is part of that response. If the responding router has recent multicast version number, then *map-mbone* requests additional information such as metrics, thresholds, and flags from the multicast router. For each new occurrence of neighboring multicast router in the reply and provided the flooding option has been selected, then *map-mbone* asks each of this multicast router for a list of neighbors. This search for unique routers will continue until no new neighboring multicast routers are reported.

INVOCATION
"–d" option sets the debug level. When the debug level is greater than the default value of 0, addition debugging messages are printed. Regardless of the debug level, an error condition, will always write an error message and will cause *map-mbone* to terminate. Non-zero debug levels have the following effects:

level 1   packet warnings are printed to stderr.

level 2   all level 1 messages plus notifications down networks are printed to stderr.

level 3   all level 2 messages plus notifications of all packet timeouts are printed to stderr.

"–f" option sets flooding option. Flooding allows the recursive search of neighboring multicast routers and is enable by default when starting_router is not used.

"–g" option sets graphing in GraphEd format.

"–n" option disables the DNS lookup for the multicast routers names.

"–r retry_count" sets the neighbor query retry limit. Default is 1 retry.

"–t timeout_count" sets the number of seconds to wait for a neighbor query reply before retrying. Default timeout is 2 seconds.

IMPORTANT NOTE
map-mbone must be run as root.

SEE ALSO
mrouted(8), **mrinfo**(8), **mtrace**(8)

AUTHOR
Pavel Curtis

NAME
master – Postfix master process

SYNOPSIS
master [**-Ddtv**] [**-c** *config_dir*] [**-e** *exit_time*]

DESCRIPTION
The **master**(8) daemon is the resident process that runs Postfix daemons on demand: daemons to send or receive messages via the network, daemons to deliver mail locally, etc. These daemons are created on demand up to a configurable maximum number per service.

Postfix daemons terminate voluntarily, either after being idle for a configurable amount of time, or after having serviced a configurable number of requests. Exceptions to this rule are the resident queue manager, address verification server, and the TLS session cache and pseudo-random number server.

The behavior of the **master**(8) daemon is controlled by the **master.cf** configuration file, as described in **master**(5).

Options:

-c *config_dir*

Read the **main.cf** and **master.cf** configuration files in the named directory instead of the default configuration directory. This also overrides the configuration files for other Postfix daemon processes.

-D   After initialization, run a debugger on the master process. The debugging command is specified with the **debugger_command** in the **main.cf** global configuration file.

-d   Do not redirect stdin, stdout or stderr to /dev/null, and do not discard the controlling terminal. This must be used for debugging only.

-e *exit_time*

Terminate the master process after *exit_time* seconds. Child processes terminate at their convenience.

-t   Test mode. Return a zero exit status when the **master.pid** lock file does not exist or when that file is not locked. This is evidence that the **master**(8) daemon is not running.

-v   Enable verbose logging for debugging purposes. This option is passed on to child processes. Multiple **-v** options make the software increasingly verbose.

Signals:

SIGHUP

Upon receipt of a **HUP** signal (e.g., after "**postfix reload**"), the master process re-reads its configuration files. If a service has been removed from the **master.cf** file, its running processes are terminated immediately. Otherwise, running processes are allowed to terminate as soon as is convenient, so that changes in configuration settings affect only new service requests.

SIGTERM

Upon receipt of a **TERM** signal (e.g., after "**postfix abort**"), the master process passes the signal on to its child processes and terminates. This is useful for an emergency shutdown. Normally one would terminate only the master ("**postfix stop**") and allow running processes to finish what they are doing.

DIAGNOSTICS
Problems are reported to **syslogd**(8).

ENVIRONMENT
MAIL_DEBUG

After initialization, start a debugger as specified with the **debugger_command** configuration parameter in the **main.cf** configuration file.

MAIL_CONFIG
> Directory with Postfix configuration files.

CONFIGURATION PARAMETERS
> Unlike most Postfix daemon processes, the **master**(8) server does not automatically pick up changes to **main.cf**. Changes to **master.cf** are never picked up automatically. Use the "**postfix reload**" command after a configuration change.

RESOURCE AND RATE CONTROLS
default_process_limit (100)
> The default maximal number of Postfix child processes that provide a given service.

max_idle (100s)
> The maximum amount of time that an idle Postfix daemon process waits for an incoming connection before terminating voluntarily.

max_use (100)
> The maximal number of incoming connections that a Postfix daemon process will service before terminating voluntarily.

service_throttle_time (60s)
> How long the Postfix **master**(8) waits before forking a server that appears to be malfunctioning.

Available in Postfix version 2.6 and later:

master_service_disable (empty)
> Selectively disable **master**(8) listener ports by service type or by service name and type.

MISCELLANEOUS CONTROLS
config_directory (see 'postconf -d' output)
> The default location of the Postfix main.cf and master.cf configuration files.

daemon_directory (see 'postconf -d' output)
> The directory with Postfix support programs and daemon programs.

debugger_command (empty)
> The external command to execute when a Postfix daemon program is invoked with the -D option.

inet_interfaces (all)
> The network interface addresses that this mail system receives mail on.

inet_protocols (ipv4)
> The Internet protocols Postfix will attempt to use when making or accepting connections.

import_environment (see 'postconf -d' output)
> The list of environment parameters that a Postfix process will import from a non-Postfix parent process.

mail_owner (postfix)
> The UNIX system account that owns the Postfix queue and most Postfix daemon processes.

process_id (read-only)
> The process ID of a Postfix command or daemon process.

process_name (read-only)
> The process name of a Postfix command or daemon process.

queue_directory (see 'postconf -d' output)
> The location of the Postfix top-level queue directory.

syslog_facility (mail)
> The syslog facility of Postfix logging.

syslog_name (see 'postconf -d' output)
> The mail system name that is prepended to the process name in syslog records, so that "smtpd" becomes, for example, "postfix/smtpd".

2

FILES

To expand the directory names below into their actual values, use the command "**postconf config_directory**" etc.

$config_directory/main.cf, global configuration file.
$config_directory/master.cf, master server configuration file.
$queue_directory/pid/master.pid, master lock file.
$data_directory/master.lock, master lock file.

SEE ALSO

qmgr(8), queue manager
verify(8), address verification
master(5), master.cf configuration file syntax
postconf(5), main.cf configuration parameter syntax
syslogd(8), system logging

LICENSE

The Secure Mailer license must be distributed with this software.

AUTHOR(S)

Wietse Venema
IBM T.J. Watson Research
P.O. Box 704
Yorktown Heights, NY 10598, USA

NAME

mbr, **bootselect** — Master Boot Record bootcode

DESCRIPTION

An IBM PC boots from a disk by loading its first sector and executing the code in it. For a hard disk, this first sector usually contains a table of partitions present on the disk. The first sector of a disk containing such a table is called the Master Boot Record (MBR).

The code present in the MBR will typically examine the partition table, find the partition that is marked active, and boot from it. Booting from a partition simply means loading the first sector in that partition, and executing the code in it, as is done for the MBR itself.

NetBSD supplies serveral versions of the MBR bootcode:

Normal boot code /usr/mdec/mbr
> This version has the same functionality as that supplied by DOS/Windows and other operating systems: it picks the active partition and boots from it. Its advantage over other, older MBRs, is that it can detect and use extensions to the BIOS interface that will allow it to boot partitions that cross or start beyond the 8 Gigabyte boundary.

Bootselector /usr/mdec/mbr_bootsel
> The bootselecting MBR contains configurable code that will present the user with a simple menu, allowing a choice between partitions to boot from, and hard disks to boot from. The choices and default settings can be configured through fdisk(8).

Extended Bootselector /usr/mdec/mbr_ext
> The Extended Bootselecting MBR additionally allows NetBSD to be loaded from an Extended partition. It only supports systems whose BIOS supports the extensions to boot partitions beyond the 8 Gigabyte boundary.

Serial Bootselector /usr/mdec/mbr_com0
> This has the same features as mbr_ext but will read and write from the first serial port. It assumes that the BIOS has initialised the baud rate.

Serial Bootselector /usr/mdec/mbr_com0_9600
> This has the same features as mbr_com0. Additionally it initialises the serial port to 9600 baud.

The rest of this manual page will discuss the bootselecting versions of the MBR. The configurable items of the bootselector are:

timeout
> The number of seconds that the bootcode will wait for the user to press a key, selecting a menu item. Must be in the range 0-3600, or −1 when it will wait forever.

default
> The default partition or disk to boot from, should the timeout expire.

The bootselector will output a menu of the *bootmenu* names for each partition (as configured by fdisk(8)). The user can then select the partition or drive to boot from via the keyboard.

The numeric keys **1** upwards will initiate a startup from the corresponding partition.

Function keys **F1** through **F8** (keys **a** through **h** for the serial versions) will boot from harddisks 0 through 7 (BIOS numbers 0x80 through 0x87). Booting from a drive is simply done by reading the MBR of that drive and executing it, so the bootcode present in the MBR of the chosen drive determines which partition (if any) will be booted in the end.

The **Enter** key will cause the bootcode to find the active partition, and boot from it. If no key is pressed, the (configurable) default selection is picked.

DIAGNOSTICS

The following error are detected:

Code	Text message	Explanation
1	No active partition	The MBR has a partition table without an active partition.
2	Disk read error	There was an error reading the bootsector for the partition or drive selected.
3	No operating system	The bootsector was loaded successfully, but it was not valid (i.e., the magic number check failed, or it contained no code).
L	Invalid CHS read	The boot partition cannot be read using a CHS read and the system BIOS doesn't support LBA reads.
?		Unknown key.

The standard boot code will output the text message and stop. It may be necessary to reset to the system to continue.

The bootselect code will output 'Error <code>' and await further input.

SEE ALSO

boot(8), disklabel(8), fdisk(8), installboot(8), mbrlabel(8)

BUGS

The bootselect code has constraints because of the limited amount of space available. The only way to be absolutely sure that a bootselector will always fit on the disk when a partition table is used, is to make it small enough to fit into the first sector (512 bytes, 404 excluding the partition table and bootselect menu).

The error messages are necessarily terse.

NAME

mbrlabel — update disk label from MBR label(s)

SYNOPSIS

mbrlabel [-fqrw] [-s *sector*] *device*

DESCRIPTION

mbrlabel is used to update a NetBSD disk label from the Master Boot Record (MBR) label(s) found on disks that were previously used on DOS/Windows systems (or other MBR using systems).

mbrlabel scans the MBR contained in the very first block of the disk (or the block specified through the -s flag), then walks through every extended partition found and generates additional partition entries for the disk from the MBRs found in those extended partitions.

Each MBR partition which does not have an equivalent partition in the disk label (equivalent in having the same size and offset) is added to the first free partition slot in the disk label. A free partition slot is defined as one with an fstype of 'unused' and a size of zero ('0'). If there are not enough free slots in the disk label, a warning will be issued.

The raw partition (typically partition *c*, but *d* on i386 and some other platforms) is left alone during this process.

By default, the proposed changed disk label will be displayed and no disk label update will occur.

Available options:

-f   Force an update, even if there has been no change.

-q   Performs operations in a quiet fashion.

-r   In conjunction with -w, also update the on-disk label.

-s *sector*
            Specifies the logical sector number that has to be read from the disk in order to find the MBR. Useful if the disk has remapping drivers on it and the MBR is located in a non-standard place. Defaults to 0.

-w   Update the in-core label if it has been changed. See also -r.

SEE ALSO

disklabel(8), dkctl(8), fdisk(8), mbr(8)

HISTORY

The mbrlabel command appeared in NetBSD 1.4.

NAME
   mdconfig — configure MEMORY disks

SYNOPSIS
   mdconfig *special_file* *512-byte-blocks*

DESCRIPTION
   The **mdconfig** command configures memory disk devices. It will associate the special file *special_file* with a range of user-virtual memory allocated by the **mdconfig** process itself. The **mdconfig** command should be run in the background. If successful, the command will not return. Otherwise, an error message will be printed.

   To "unconfigure" the memory disk, just kill the background **mdconfig** process started earlier.

FILES
   /dev/rmd??
   /dev/md??

EXAMPLES
       mdconfig /dev/md0c 2048 &

   Configures the memory disk md0c with one megabyte of user-space memory.

SEE ALSO
   mount(8), swapon(8), umount(8)

BUGS
   The special device will become inoperative if the **mdconfig** process is killed while the special device is open.

NAME

    mDNSResponder — Multicast and Unicast DNS daemon

SYNOPSIS

    mDNSResponder

DESCRIPTION

    mDNSResponder (also known as **mdnsd** on some systems) is a daemon invoked at boot time to implement Multicast DNS and DNS Service Discovery. On Mac OS X 10.6 (Snow Leopard), **mDNSResponder** is also the system-wide Unicast DNS Resolver.

    mDNSResponder listens on UDP port 5353 for Multicast DNS Query packets. When it receives a query for which it knows an answer, **mDNSResponder** issues the appropriate Multicast DNS Reply packet.

    mDNSResponder also performs Unicast and Multicast DNS Queries on behalf of client processes, and maintains a cache of the replies.

    mDNSResponder has no user-specifiable command-line argument, and users should not run **mDNSResponder** manually.

LOGGING

    There are several methods with which to examine **mDNSResponder**'s internal state for debugging and diagnostic purposes. The syslog(1) logging levels map as follows:

```
Error - Error messages
Warning - Client-initiated operations
Notice - Sleep proxy operations
Info - Informational messages
```

By default, only log level Error is logged.

A SIGUSR1 signal toggles additional logging, with Warning and Notice enabled by default:

```
% sudo killall -USR1 mDNSResponder
```

Once this logging is enabled, users can additionally use syslog(1) to change the log filter for the process. For example, to enable log levels Emergency - Debug:

```
% sudo syslog -c mDNSResponder -d
```

A SIGUSR2 signal toggles packet logging:

```
% sudo killall -USR2 mDNSResponder
```

A SIGINFO signal will dump a snapshot summary of the internal state to /var/log/system.log:

```
% sudo killall -INFO mDNSResponder
```

FILES

    /usr/sbin/mDNSResponder

SEE ALSO

    mDNS(1)

For information on Multicast DNS, see http://www.multicastdns.org/

For information on DNS Service Discovery, see http://www.dns-sd.org/

For information on how to use the Multicast DNS and the DNS Service Discovery APIs on Mac OS X and other platforms, see http://developer.apple.com/bonjour/

For the source code to **mDNSResponder**, see
`http://developer.apple.com/darwin/projects/bonjour/`

BUGS

> **mDNSResponder** bugs are tracked in Apple Radar component "mDNSResponder".

HISTORY

> The **mDNSResponder** daemon first appeared in Mac OS X 10.2 (Jaguar).

> Also available from the Darwin open source repository (though not officially supported by Apple) are **mDNSResponder** daemons for other platforms, including Mac OS 9, Microsoft Windows, Linux, FreeBSD, NetBSD, Solaris, and other POSIX systems.

NAME

mdsetimage — set kernel RAM disk image

SYNOPSIS

mdsetimage [**-svx**] [**-b** *bfdname*] *kernel image*

DESCRIPTION

The **mdsetimage** command copies the disk image specified by *image* into the memory disk storage area in *kernel*. The file system present in *image* will typically be used by the kernel as the root file system.

To recognize kernel executable format, the **-b** flag specifies BFD name of kernel.

If the **-s** flags is given, **mdsetimage** will write back the actual disk image size back into *kernel*.

If the **-v** flag is given, **mdsetimage** will print out status information as it is copying the image.

If the **-x** flag is given, **mdsetimage** will extract the disk image from *kernel* into the file *image*. This is the opposite of the default behavior.

SEE ALSO

md(4), mdconfig(8)

NAME
   memswitch — get or set x68k memory switch

SYNOPSIS
   memswitch −a
   memswitch [**−h**] [**−n**] *variable* . . .
   memswitch −w *variable=value* . . .
   memswitch −r *filename*
   memswitch −s *filename*

DESCRIPTION
   The **memswitch** command gets or sets the x68k memory switch stored in the non-volatile static ram.

   The first form shows the current values of all the variables of the memory switch.

   The second form shows the current values of the specified variables. If the **−h** flag is specified, a brief descriptions of the variables are displayed. The **−n** flag suppresses printing of the variable name.

   The third form sets or modifies the specified variables to the given value.

   In the fourth and fifth form, the whole memory switch part of non-volatile SRAM is saved to, or restored from the specified file, respectively.

FILES
   /dev/sram non-volatile static memory control device

HISTORY
   The **memswitch** command first appeared in NetBSD 1.5.

NAME

mk-amd-map – create database maps for Amd

SYNOPSIS

mk-amd-map [**−p**] *mapname*

DESCRIPTION

mk-amd-map creates the database maps used by the keyed map lookups in amd(8). It reads input from the named file and outputs them to a correspondingly named hashed database.

−p This option prints the map on standard output instead of generating a database. This is usually used to merge continuation lines into one physical line.

SEE ALSO

amd(8).

"am-utils" **info**(1) entry.

Linux NFS and Automounter Administration by Erez Zadok, ISBN 0-7821-2739-8, (Sybex, 2001).

http://www.am-utils.org

Amd − The 4.4 BSD Automounter

AUTHORS

Jan-Simon Pendry <jsp@doc.ic.ac.uk>, Department of Computing, Imperial College, London, UK.

Erez Zadok <ezk@cs.sunysb.edu>, Computer Science Department, Stony Brook University, New York, USA.

Other authors and contributors to am-utils are listed in the **AUTHORS** file distributed with am-utils.

NAME
   mkalias — a NIS map conversion program

SYNOPSIS
   mkalias [**-deEnsuv**] *input* [*output*]

DESCRIPTION
   mkalias is used to convert a `mail.aliases` map to a `mail.byaddr` map. This is a inverse map of user@host (or user!host) back to alias.

   mkalias uses *input* as the input map, and if *output* is given, use that as the output map. If the output map isn't given don't create database. This can be useful when **-e** or **-E** is given.

   The options are as follows:

   -d   Assume domain names are OK. Only useful together with **-e** or **-E**.

   -e   Check host to verify that it exists.

   -E   Same as **-e**, but also check for any MX-record.

   -n   Capitalize name. E.g., mats.o.jansson becomes Mats.O.Jansson.

   -u   Assume UUCP names are OK. Only useful together with **-e** or **-E**.

   -s   Ignored (only provided for compatibility with SunOS 4.1.x).

   -v   Verbose mode.

SEE ALSO
   nis(8), ypserv(8)

AUTHORS
   Mats O Jansson ⟨moj@stacken.kth.se⟩

NAME

mkbootimage — turn Alpha bootstrap programs into bootable images

SYNOPSIS

/usr/mdec/mkbootimage [**-nv**] *infile* [*outfile*]

DESCRIPTION

The **mkbootimage** utility creates bootable image files from NetBSD/alpha bootstrap programs. Bootable image files can be placed directly on disk or tape to create bootable media which can be booted by the SRM console. This is primarily useful for creating bootable tapes or disk sets with the /usr/mdec/ustarboot bootstrap program, or for creating firmware upgrade media using firmware upgrade programs.

The bootstrap program *infile* is padded to a 512-byte boundary, has a properly formed Alpha Boot Block prepended, and is written to the output file *outfile*. If no output file is specified, the result is written to standard output.

The **mkbootimage** utility does not install bootstrap programs to make disks bootable. To do that, use installboot(8). Similarly, it is not necessary to use **mkbootimage** to create images to boot over the network; network-capable bootstrap programs are usable without modification.

The options recognized by **mkbootimage** are as follows:

-n   Do not actually write the result to the output file or standard output.

-v   Print information about what **mkbootimage** is doing.

The **mkbootimage** utility exits 0 on success, and >0 if an error occurs.

FILES

/usr/mdec/ustarboot "ustar" file system bootstrap program

EXAMPLES

```
mkbootimage as200_v5_8.exe as200_v5_8.exe.bootimage
```

Create a bootable image from the (firmware image) file as200_v5_8.exe. That bootable image could then be written to floppy, disk, CD-ROM, or tape to create bootable firmware update media.

```
(mkbootimage /usr/mdec/ustarboot; tar cvf - netbsd) | \
    dd of=/dev/rst0
```

Make a bootable image from the bootstrap program /usr/mdec/ustarboot, concatenate it with a tar file containing a kernel, and write the output to a tape. This is an example of how to create a tape which boots a kernel.

SEE ALSO

boot(8), installboot(8)

HISTORY

The NetBSD/alpha **mkbootimage** command first appeared in NetBSD 1.4.

AUTHORS

The **mkbootimage** utility was written by Chris Demetriou.

NAME

      mkbootimage — create a prep boot image

SYNOPSIS

      mkbootimage [**-lsv**] [**-m** *machine_arch*] [**-b** *bootfile*] [**-k** *kernel*] [**-r** *rawdev*]
              boot-image

DESCRIPTION

      mkbootimage is the utility used to create a bootable kernel image on NetBSD for prep, bebox or rs6000.

      The **mkbootimage** utility takes the boot-program, and the optional kernel, and creates a boot image from them. This image contains the boot code, kernel, and optionally an i386 partition table. The image can be written directly to a floppy or hard drive with the dd(1) command, or it can be directly netbooted via bootpd(8).

      The following options are available:

      -b   Specifies which bootloader to embed in the bootable image. Defaults to /usr/mdec/boot.

      -k   Specifies which kernel binary to embed in the bootable image. Defaults to /netbsd.

      -l   Creates a partition table for a 2.88MB floppy instead of a 1.44MB floppy. This is primarily used for El-Torrito style CD images.

      -m   Selects the machine architecture to build the image for. Currently supports prep, rs6000 and bebox. Defaults to the machine architecture you are currently running on. This option is required if you are building an image for another machine, such as building a prep boot image on i386.

      -r   Specifies the raw device to read to gather the current partition table. This is generally /dev/rsd0c.

      -s   Generates a standalone image with no partition table embedded.

      -v   Generates verbose output, useful for debugging.

      There are three primary ways to use **mkbootimage** to build a bootable image:

      The first method is to build an image suitable for a floppy or netboot. This will create an image with an embedded partition table with a single PReP boot partition of type 0x41(65). The image can be directly netbooted, or if it is small enough, written directly to a floppy with dd(1). **mkbootimage** will warn you if the generated image is too large to be written to a floppy.

      The second method is to build a standalone image with no partition table. This should be written to the PReP boot partition on your hard drive with dd(1).

      The third method is for use in upgrading older systems that have been built by writing the floppy image directly to the head of the hard drive. This method reads the existing partition table and embeds that in the image. This should prevent loss of your current partition layout. This image should be written directly to the head of the disk with dd(1).

      The recommended setup for a PReP machine is to build a partition table with fdisk(8) that contains a PReP boot partition (type 65) as partition 0, marked active, and a second partition for NetBSD encompassing the remainder of the disk. You should then create a disklabel on that disk with a partition (such as e) pointing to the PReP boot partition. Partition c should be the whole disk, and partition d can optionally be the NetBSD portion of the disk. You may then use the other partitions for your normal disk layout. The PReP boot partition can be placed anywhere on the disk, but it is recommended that it be placed at the beginning of the disk.

EXAMPLES
>   Create a floppy or netboot image for prep named 'boot.fs':
>
>   **mkbootimage −m prep −b /usr/mdec/boot −k /netbsd boot.fs**
>
>   Create a standalone bebox image for booting from a hard disk:
>
>   **mkbootimage −s −m bebox −b /usr/mdec/boot −k /netbsd boot.fs**
>
>   Use the partition information on 'sd0' to create a new bootable image with com0 as the console:
>
>   **mkbootimage −b /usr/mdec/boot_com0 −k /netbsd −r /dev/rsd0c boot.fs**

SEE ALSO
>   dd(1), boot(8), bootpd(8), disklabel(8), fdisk(8)

HISTORY
>   **mkbootimage** first appeared in NetBSD 1.5.

AUTHORS
>   **mkbootimage** was written by NONAKA Kimihiro.

NAME

mknetid — a NIS filter program

SYNOPSIS

mknetid [**-q**] [**-d** *domain*] [**-p** *passwdfile*] [**-g** *groupfile*] [**-h** *hostfile*]
[**-m** *netidfile*]

DESCRIPTION

mknetid is used to create a map named `netid.byname`. The map consists of information from
`passwd`(5), `group`(5) and `hosts`(5) eventually concatenated with a `netid`(5) file.

The options are as follows:

-d *domain*   NIS domain to use instead of the default domain.

-g *groupfile*   Alternate `group`(5) file. Default is `/etc/group`.

-h *hostfile*   Alternate `hosts`(5) file. Default is `/etc/hosts`.

-m *netidfile*   Alternate `netid`(5) file. Default is `/etc/netid`.

-p *passwdfile*
                     Alternate `passwd`(5) file. Default is `/etc/passwd`.

-q   Keep quiet about multiple occurrences of a uid; ignore all but the first.

FILES

```
/etc/group
/etc/hosts
/etc/netid
/etc/passwd
```

SEE ALSO

`domainname`(1), `group`(5), `hosts`(5), `netid`(5), `passwd`(5), `nis`(8)

AUTHORS

Mats O Jansson ⟨moj@stacken.kth.se⟩

NAME
   mknod — make device special file

SYNOPSIS
   mknod [**-rR**] [**-F** *fmt*] [**-g** *gid*] [**-m** *mode*] [**-u** *uid*] *name* [**c** | **b**] [*driver* | *major*]
         minor
   mknod [**-rR**] [**-F** *fmt*] [**-g** *gid*] [**-m** *mode*] [**-u** *uid*] *name* [**c** | **b**] *major unit*
         subunit
   mknod [**-rR**] [**-g** *gid*] [**-m** *mode*] [**-u** *uid*] *name* [**c** | **b**] *number*
   mknod [**-rR**] [**-g** *gid*] [**-m** *mode*] [**-u** *uid*] *name* **p**
   mknod **-l**

DESCRIPTION
   The **mknod** command creates device special files, or fifos. Normally the shell script /dev/MAKEDEV is
   used to create special files for commonly known devices; it executes **mknod** with the appropriate arguments
   and can make all the files required for the device.

   To make nodes manually, the arguments are:

   -r   Replace an existing file if its type is incorrect.

   -R   Replace an existing file if its type is incorrect. Correct the mode, user and group.

   -F *fmt*   Create device nodes that may be used by an operating system which uses device numbers packed
               in a different format than NetBSD uses. This is necessary when NetBSD is used as an NFS server
               for netbooted computers running other operating systems.

               The following values for the *fmt* are recognized: **native**, **386bsd**, **4bsd**, **bsdos**, **freebsd**, **hpux**,
               isc, **linux**, **netbsd**, **osf1**, **sco**, **solaris**, **sunos**, **svr3**, **svr4**, and **ultrix**.

   -g *gid*   Specify the group for the device node. The *gid* operand may be a numeric group ID or a group
               name. If a group name is also a numeric group ID, the operand is used as a group name. Precede
               a numeric group ID with a **#** to stop it being treated as a name.

   -m *mode*
               Specify the mode for the device node. The mode may be absolute or symbolic, see chmod(1).

   -u *uid*   Specify the user for the device node. The *uid* operand may be a numeric user ID or a user
               name. If a user name is also a numeric user ID, the operand is used as a user name. Precede a
               numeric user ID with a **#** to stop it being treated as a name.

   name   Device name, for example "sd" for a SCSI disk on an HP300 or a "pty" for pseudo-devices.

   b | **c** | **p**
               Type of device. If the device is a block type device such as a tape or disk drive which needs both
               cooked and raw special files, the type is **b**. All other devices are character type devices, such as
               terminal and pseudo devices, and are type **c**. Specifying **p** creates fifo files.

   driver | *major*
               The major device number is an integer number which tells the kernel which device driver entry
               point to use. If the device driver is configured into the current kernel it may be specified by
               driver name or major number. To find out which major device number to use for a particular
               device, use **mknod** **-l**, check the file /dev/MAKEDEV to see if the device is known, or check
               the system dependent device configuration file:

                     "/usr/src/sys/arch/<arch>/<arch>/conf.c"

(e.g. `/usr/src/sys/arch/vax/vax/conf.c`).

minor   The minor device number tells the kernel which one of several similar devices the node corresponds to; for example, it may be a specific serial port or pty.

unit and *subunit*
    The unit and subunit numbers select a subset of a device; for example, the unit may specify a particular SCSI disk, and the subunit a partition on that disk. (Currently this form of specification is only supported by the *bsdos* format, for compatibility with the BSD/OS **mknod**).

number   A single opaque device number. Useful for netbooted computers which require device numbers packed in a format that isn't supported by **-F**.

-l   List the device drivers configured into the current kernel together with their block and character major numbers.

SEE ALSO
    chmod(1), mkfifo(1), mkfifo(2), mknod(2), MAKEDEV(8)

HISTORY
    A **mknod** command appeared in Version 6 AT&T UNIX. The **-F** option appeared in NetBSD 1.4. The **-g**, **-l**, **-m**, **-r**, **-R**, and **-u** options, and the ability to specify a driver by name appeared in NetBSD 2.0.

NAME
    mld6query — send multicast listener query

SYNOPSIS
    mld6query [**-dr**] *intface* [*maddr*]

DESCRIPTION
    mld6query sends an IPv6 multicast listener discovery (MLD) query packet toward the specified multicast address, *maddr*, toward interface *intface*. If you omit *maddr*, linklocal all nodes multicast address(ff02::1) is used.

    After sending a query, **mld6query** waits for replies for at most 10 seconds. If a reply is returned, **mld6query** prints it with its type and then waits for another reply.

    This program is provided only for debugging. It is not necessary for normal use.

    With **-d**, **mld6query** will transmit MLD done packet instead of MLD query packet. With **-r**, similarly, MLD report packet will be transmitted. **-dr** options are for debugging purposes only.

EXIT STATUS
    The program exits 0 on success, and >0 on failures.

HISTORY
    The **mld6query** command first appeared in WIDE/KAME IPv6 protocol stack kit.

BUGS
    mld6query does not take care of multicast addresses which have non link-local scope.

NAME
mlxctl — Mylex DAC960 family management utility

SYNOPSIS
mlxctl [-f *dev*] [-v] [-a] status [*drive*] [. . .]
mlxctl [-f *dev*] [-a] detach [*drive*] [. . .]
mlxctl [-f *dev*] [-a] check [*drive*] [. . .]
mlxctl [-f *dev*] rebuild *channel:target*
mlxctl [-f *dev*] cstatus
mlxctl [-f *dev*] rescan
mlxctl [-f *dev*] config

DESCRIPTION
The **mlxctl** utility performs status monitoring and management functions for Mylex DAC960 RAID controllers and attached devices.

The following options are available:

-a   Apply the action to all drives attached to the controller.

-f *dev* Specify the control device to use. The default is /dev/mlx0.

-v   Increased verbosity.

The following commands are available:

cstatus   Display the controller's current status.

status   Display the status of the specified drives. This command returns 0 if all drives tested are online, 1 if one or more drives are critical and 2 if one or more are offline.

rescan   Re-scan the logical drive table, and attach or detach devices from the system as necessary.

detach   Detach the specified drives. Drives must be unmounted and unopened for this command to succeed.

check   Initiate a consistency check and repair pass on a drive that provides redundancy (e.g., RAID1 or RAID5). This command returns immediately. The *status* command can be used to monitor the progress of the check.

rebuild   Rebuild onto the specified physical drive. Note that there can be only one running rebuild operation per controller at any given time. This command returns immediately. The *cstatus* command can be used to monitor the progress of the rebuild.

config   Write the current system drive configuration to stdout.

EXAMPLES
Display the status of drive ld3 attached to the controller mlx1:

```
mlxctl -f /dev/mlx1 -v status ld3
```

SEE ALSO
ld(4), mlx(4)

HISTORY
The **mlxctl** command first appeared in NetBSD 1.5.3, and was based on the **mlxcontrol** utility found in FreeBSD.

BUGS

Modifying drive configuration is not yet supported.

Some commands do not work with older firmware revisions.

Error log extraction is not yet supported.

MMCFORMAT (8)   NetBSD   MMCFORMAT (8)

NAME

   mmcformat — format optical media

SYNOPSIS

   mmcformat [-BDFGHhIMOpRrSsw] [-b *blockingnr*] [-c *cert-num*] *special*

DESCRIPTION

   The **mmcformat** utility formats optical media conforming to the MMC standard. This includes CD, DVD, and Blu-Ray (BD) media.

   The options are as follows:

   -B   Blank media when possible before formatting it.

   -b *blockingnr*   Explicitly select packet size in sectors (for CD-RW only). It is not recommended to change this from its default of 32.

   -c *cert-num*   Certify media for DVD-RAM / DV-RE. The argument cert-num specifies:

                     0   no certification

                     1   full certification

                     2   quick certification

   -D   Debug mode. Print all SCSI/ATAPI command errors.

   -F   Format media.

   -G   Grow last CD-RW/DVD-RW session.

   -H   Show help and print formatting choices for the inserted media.

   -h   Show help and print formatting choices for the inserted media.

   -I   Show help and print formatting choices for the inserted media.

   -M   Select MRW (Mount Rainier) error correcting background format.

   -O   Old style CD-RW formatting; recommended for CD-RW.

   -p   Explicitly set packet format.

   -R   Restart previously stopped MCD-MRW or DVD+RW background format.

   -r   Recompile defect list for DVD-RAM.

   -S   Grow spare space DVD-RAM / BD-RE.

   -s   Format DVD+MRW / BD-RE with extra spare space.

   -w   Wait until completion of background format.

NOTES

   Due to the enormous varieties in optical media, **mmcformat** is made as generic as possible. This can result in confusion.

EXAMPLES

           mmcformat -B -O /dev/rcd0d

   Blanks and then formats a CD-RW disc using the "old style" format command. It is recommended to use this "old style" command unless your drive reports that it's not supported; in that case, resort to the default -F. Note that a CD-RW disc can be reformatted without being blanked. Blanking switches between sequential and fixed packet writing by erasing the disc. This can also help to revive old discs.

```
mmcformat -F -M /dev/rcd0d
```

Format a CD-RW or a DVD+RW to use MRW (Mount Rainier). This format tries to hide media flaws as much as possible by relocation.

SEE ALSO

scsictl(8)

HISTORY

The **mmcformat** command first appeared in NetBSD 5.0.

AUTHORS

Reinoud Zandijk ⟨reinoud@NetBSD.org⟩

BUGS

mmcformat could be merged with scsictl(8) but that tool is very hard disk oriented.

NAME
   modload — load a kernel module

SYNOPSIS
   modload [**-fP**] [**-b** *var=boolean*] [**-i** *var=integer*] [**-s** *var=string*] *module*
   modload -p [**-b** *var=boolean*] [**-d** *var*] [**-i** *var=integer*] [**-m** *plist*]
           [**-s** *var=string*]

DESCRIPTION
   The **modload** utility loads a kernel module specified by the *module* paramamter into the running system.

   The current working directory is first searched for the module object file. If not found there, the default system module areas are searched.

   The options to **modload** are as follows:

   -b *var=boolean*   Pass the module a boolean property with the name *var*. *boolean* may be either true or false.

   -d *var*   When used in conjuction with **-m**, delete *var* from the *plist* specified.

   -f   When a module is loaded, the kernel checks if the module is compatible with the running kernel and will refuse to load modules that are potentially incompatible. This option disables compatibility checks. *Note*: an incompatible module can cause system instability, including data loss or corruption.

                          This option is also required for re-enabling a builtin module that was disabled using modunload(8).

   -i *var=integer*   Pass the module an integer property with the name *var* and integral value *integer*.

   -m *plist*   When used in conjuction with **-p**, merge new options with an existing property list contained in *plist*.

   -P   This option tells the kernel not to load an associated property list.

   -p   Output a property list suitable for loading along with a module. When using this option, you do not need to specify a module. Use **-m** and **-d** to read and modify an existing property list.

   -s *var=string*   Pass the module a string property with the name *var* and string value *string*.

DIAGNOSTICS
   The **modload** utility exits with a status of 0 on success and with a nonzero status if an error occurs.

SEE ALSO
   modstat(8), modunload(8)

HISTORY
   The **modload** command was designed to be similar in functionality to the corresponding command in SunOS 4.1.3.

NAME

    modstat — display status of loaded kernel modules

SYNOPSIS

    modstat [**-n** *name*]

DESCRIPTION

    The **modstat** utility displays the status of any kernel modules present in the kernel.

    The options are as follows:

    -n *name*

        Display the status of only the module with this name.

    In addition to listing the currently loaded modules' name, the information reported by **modstat** includes:

    CLASS   Module class, such as "vfs", "driver", "exec", "misc" or "secmodel".

    SOURCE   Where the module was loaded from. "builtin" indicates that the module was built into the running kernel. "boot" indicates that the module was loaded during system bootstrap. "filesys" indicates that the module was loaded from the file system.

    SIZE   Size of the module in bytes.

    REFS   Number of references held on the module. Disabled builtin modules will show a count of -1 here.

    REQUIRES Additional modules that must be present.

EXIT STATUS

    The **modstat** utility exits with a status of 0 on success and with a nonzero status if an error occurs.

SEE ALSO

    modload(8), modunload(8)

HISTORY

    The **modstat** command was designed to be similar in functionality to the corresponding command in SunOS 4.1.3.

NAME

modunload — unload a kernel module

SYNOPSIS

modunload *name*

DESCRIPTION

The **modunload** utility unloads a loadable kernel module from a running system.

name is name of the module to be unloaded, as shown by modstat(8).

Builtin modules will not be unloaded from memory, but they will be disabled. They can be re-enabled using modload(8).

DIAGNOSTICS

The **modunload** utility exits with a status of 0 on success and with a nonzero status if an error occurs.

SEE ALSO

modload(8), modstat(8)

HISTORY

The **modunload** command was designed to be similar in functionality to the corresponding command in SunOS 4.1.3.

NAME
mopchk — MOP Check Utility

SYNOPSIS
mopchk [-a] [-v] [*filename*]

DESCRIPTION
mopchk shows information about which devices are known, version of mopd suite or information about a MOP-image.

If *filename* is given, information about the MOP-image is read from the header of the file.

OPTIONS
-a   Show all the Ethernets attached to the system.

-v   Show version of the mopd suite.

SEE ALSO
mopcopy(1), mopprobe(1), moptrace(1), mopd(8)

AUTHORS
Mats O Jansson ⟨moj@stacken.kth.se⟩

BUGS
In some implementations the same interface can occur more than once.

NAME
  mopcopy — Create MOP image from another executable format

SYNOPSIS
  mopcopy *infile outfile*

DESCRIPTION
  mopcopy is used to convert a file from another executable format to a MOP image.

  Elf32 and a.out VAX images are currently supported.

SEE ALSO
  mopchk(1), mopprobe(1), moptrace(1), a.out(5), elf(5), mopd(8)

AUTHORS
  Lloyd Parkes
  Jason R. Thorpe

NAME

mopd — Maintenance Operations Protocol (MOP) Loader Daemon

SYNOPSIS

mopd [**-adf**] [**-s** *mopdir*] [*interface*] [. . .]

DESCRIPTION

mopd services DEC Maintenance Operations Protocol (MOP) Load requests on the Ethernet connected to *interface* or all interfaces if **-a** option is given.

In a load request received by **mopd** a filename can be given by the client. This is the normal case for terminal servers. If a filename isn't in the client load request **mopd** must know what image to load.

Upon receiving a request, **mopd** checks if the requested file exists in /tftpboot/mop (unless the **-s** option is given, see below) the filename is normally uppercase and with an extension of .SYS. If the filename isn't given, the ethernet address of the target is used as filename, e.g. 08002b09f4de.SYS and it might be a soft link to another file.

mopd supports two kinds of files. The first type that is check is if the file is in a.out(5) format. If not, a couple of Digital's formats are checked.

In normal operation, **mopd** forks a copy of itself and runs in the background. Anomalies and errors are reported via syslog(3).

OPTIONS

-a   Listen on all the Ethernets attached to the system. If **-a** is omitted, an interface must be specified.

-d   Run in debug mode, with all the output to stdout. The process will run in the foreground.

-f   Run in the foreground.

-s   Change the directory to look for files in from /tftpboot/mop to *mopdir*.

FILES

/tftpboot/mop

NOTES

mopd automatically appends an upper case .SYS to the filename provided by the client. The typical client sends the requested file name in upper case.

SEE ALSO

mopchk(1), mopcopy(1), mopprobe(1), moptrace(1), bpf(4)

DECnet Digital Network Architecture Phase IV, Maintenance Operations Functional Specification V3.0.0, AA-X436A-TK.

DECnet Digital Network Architecture, Maintenance Operations Protocol Functional Specification V4.0.0, EK-DNA11-FS-001.

AUTHORS

Mats O Jansson ⟨moj@stacken.kth.se⟩

NAME

mopprobe — MOP Probe Utility

SYNOPSIS

mopprobe −a [**−3** | **−4**]
mopprobe [**−3** | **−4**] *interface*

DESCRIPTION

mopprobe prints the ethernet address and nodename of MOP SID message on the Ethernet connected to *interface* or all known interfaces if ' **−a**' is given.

OPTIONS

−a   Listen on all the Ethernets attached to the system. If ' **−a**' is omitted, an interface must be specified.

−3   Ignore MOP V3 messages (Ethernet II).

−4   Ignore MOP V4 messages (Ethernet 802.3).

SEE ALSO

mopchk(1), mopcopy(1), moptrace(1), mopd(8)

AUTHORS

Mats O Jansson ⟨moj@stacken.kth.se⟩

NAME
   moptrace — MOP Trace Utility

SYNOPSIS
   moptrace [**-a**] [**-d**] [**-3** | **-4**]
   moptrace [**-d**] [**-3** | **-4**] [*interface*]

DESCRIPTION
   moptrace prints the contents of MOP packages on the Ethernet connected to *interface* or all known interfaces if ' **-a**' is given.

OPTIONS
   -a   Listen on all the Ethernets attached to the system. If ' **-a**' is omitted, an interface must be specified.

   -d   Run in debug mode, with all the output to stderr.

   -3   Ignore MOP V3 messages (Ethernet II).

   -4   Ignore MOP V4 messages (Ethernet 802.3).

SEE ALSO
   mopchk(1), mopcopy(1), mopprobe(1), mopd(8)

   DECnet Digital Network Architecture Phase IV, Maintenance Operations Functional Specification V3.0.0, AA-X436A-TK.

   DECnet Digital Network Architecture, Maintenance Operations Protocol Functional Specification V4.0.0, EK-DNA11-FS-001.

AUTHORS
   Mats O Jansson ⟨moj@stacken.kth.se⟩

NAME
mount — mount file systems

SYNOPSIS
mount [**-Aadfruvw**] [**-t** *type*]
mount [**-dfruvw**] { *special* | *node* }
mount [**-dfruvw**] [**-o** *options*] [**-t** *type*] *special node*

DESCRIPTION
The **mount** command invokes a file system-specific program to prepare and graft the *special* device on to the file system tree at the point *node*, or to update options for an already-mounted file system.

The *node* argument is always interpreted as a directory in the name space of currently mounted file systems. The *special* argument is interpreted in different ways by the programs that handle different file system types; for example, mount_ffs(8) interprets it as a device node, mount_null(8) interprets it as a directory name, and mount_nfs(8) interprets it as reference to a remote host and a directory on that host.

The system maintains a list of currently mounted file systems. This list is printed if **mount** is invoked with no arguments, and with no options that require some other behaviour.

If exactly one of *special* or *node* is provided, then the missing information (including the file system type) is taken from the fstab(5) file. The provided argument is looked up first in the "fs_file", then in the "fs_spec" column. If the matching entry in fstab(5) has the string "from_mount" as its "fs_spec" field, the device or remote file system already mounted at the location specified by "fs_spec" will be used.

If both *special* and *node* are provided, then fstab(5) is not used. In this case, if the file system type is not specified via the **-t** flag, then **mount** may determine the type from the disk label (see disklabel(8)). In addition, if *special* contains a colon (':') or at sign ('@'), then the nfs type is inferred, but this behaviour is deprecated, and will be removed in a future version of **mount**.

In NetBSD, the file-system mounting policy is dictated by the running security models. The default security model may allow unprivileged mounting; see secmodel_suser(9) for details.

The options are as follows:

-A   Causes **mount** to try to mount all of the file systems listed in the fstab(5) file except those for which the "noauto" option is specified.

-a   Similar to the **-A** flag, except that if a file system (other than the root file system) appears to be already mounted, **mount** will not try to mount it again. **mount** assumes that a file system is already mounted if a file system with the same type is mounted on the given mount point. More stringent checks are not possible because some file system types report strange values for the mounted-from device for mounted file systems.

-d   Causes everything to be done except for the invocation of the file system-specific program. This option is useful in conjunction with the **-v** flag to determine what the **mount** command is trying to do.

-f   Forces the revocation of write access when trying to downgrade a file system mount status from read-write to read-only.

-o   Options are specified with a **-o** flag followed by a comma separated string of options. The following options are available:

      async   All I/O to the file system should be done asynchronously. In the event of a crash, *it is impossible for the system to verify the integrity of data on a file system mounted with this option.* You should only use this option if you have an application-specific data recovery mechanism, or are willing to recreate the file system from scratch.

noasync   Clear **async** mode.

force   The same as **−f**; forces the revocation of write access when trying to downgrade a
               file system mount status from read-write to read-only.

getargs   Retrieves the file system specific mount arguments for the given mounted file sys-
               tem and prints them.

hidden   By setting the MNT_IGNORE flag, causes the mount point to be excluded from the
               list of file systems shown by default with df(1).

noatime   Never update the access time field for files. This option is useful for optimizing
               read performance on file systems that are used as news spools.

noauto   This file system should be skipped when mount is run with the **−a** flag.

nocoredump Do not allow programs to create crash dumps (core files) on the file system. This
               option can be used to help protect sensitive data by keeping core files (which may
               contain sensitive data) from being created on insecure file systems. Only core files
               that would be created by program crashes are prevented by use of this flag; the
               behavior of savecore(8) is not affected.

nodev   Do not interpret character or block special devices on the file system. This option
               is useful for a server that has file systems containing special devices for architec-
               tures other than its own.

nodevmtime Do not update modification times on device special files. This option is useful on
               laptops or other systems that perform power management.

noexec   Do not allow execution of any binaries on the mounted file system. This option is
               useful for a server that has file systems containing binaries for architectures other
               than its own.

nosuid   Do not allow set-user-identifier or set-group-identifier bits to take effect.

port   (NFS only) Use the specified NFS port.

rdonly   The same as **−r**; mount the file system read-only (even the super-user may not
               write it).

reload   Reload all incore data for a file system. This is used mainly after running
               fsck(8) on the root file system and finding things to fix. The file system must be
               mounted read-only. All cached meta-data are invalidated, superblock and sum-
               mary information is re-read from disk, all cached inactive vnodes and file data are
               invalidated and all inode data are re-read for all active vnodes.

rump   Instead of running mount_type to mount the file system, run rump_type. This uses
               a userspace server to mount the file system and does not require kernel support for
               the specific file system type. See the **−t** flag and respective rump_type manual
               page for more information.

log   (FFS only with UFS2 superblock layout) Mount the file system with wapbl(4)
               meta-data journaling, also known simply as logging. It provides rapid metadata
               updates and eliminates the need to check file system consistency after a system
               outage. A file system mounted with **log** can not be mounted with **async**. It
               requires the WAPBL option to be enabled in the running kernel. See wapbl(4) for
               more information.

symperm   Recognize permission of symbolic link when reading or traversing link.

sync   All I/O to the file system should be done synchronously. This is not equivalent to the normal mode in which only metadata is written synchronously.

nosync   Clear **sync** mode.

union   Causes the namespace at the mount point to appear as the union of the mounted file system root and the existing directory. Lookups will be done in the mounted file system first. If those operations fail due to a non-existent file the underlying directory is then accessed. All creates are done in the mounted file system, except for the fdesc file system.

update   The same as **−u**; indicate that the status of an already mounted file system should be changed.

Any additional options specific to a given file system type (see the **−t** option) may be passed as a comma separated list; these options are distinguished by a leading "-" (dash). Options that take a value are specified using the syntax -option=value. For example, the mount command:

```
mount −t mfs −o nosuid,−N,−s=32m swap /tmp
```

causes **mount** to execute the equivalent of:

```
/sbin/mount_mfs −o nosuid −N −s 32m swap /tmp
```

−r   The file system is to be mounted read-only. Mount the file system read-only (even the super-user may not write it). The same as the "rdonly" argument to the **−o** option.

−t *type*
    The argument following the **−t** is used to indicate the file system type. The type *ffs* is the default. The **−t** option can be used to indicate that the actions should only be taken on file systems of the specified type. More than one type may be specified in a comma separated list. The list of file system types can be prefixed with "no" to specify the file system types for which action should *not* be taken. For example, the **mount** command:

```
mount −a −t nonfs,mfs
```

mounts all file systems except those of type NFS and MFS.

mount will attempt to execute a program in /sbin/mount_*XXX* where *XXX* is replaced by the type name. For example, nfs file systems are mounted by the program /sbin/mount_nfs.

−u   The **−u** flag indicates that the status of an already mounted file system should be changed. Any of the options discussed above (the **−o** option) may be changed; also a file system can be changed from read-only to read-write or vice versa. An attempt to change from read-write to read-only will fail if any files on the file system are currently open for writing unless the **−f** flag is also specified. The set of options is determined by first extracting the options for the file system from the fstab(5) file, then applying any options specified by the **−o** argument, and finally applying the **−r** or **−w** option.

−v   Verbose mode. If this flag is specified more than once, then the file system-specific mount arguments are printed for the given mounted file system.

−w   The file system object is to be read and write.

The options specific to the various file system types are described in the manual pages for those file systems' **mount_XXX** commands. For instance the options specific to Berkeley Fast File System (FFS) are described in the mount_ffs(8) manual page.

The particular type of file system in each partition of a disk can be found by examining the disk label with the disklabel(8) command.

FILES

/etc/fstab file system table

EXAMPLES

Some useful examples:

CD-ROM

mount -t cd9660 -r /dev/cd0a /cdrom

MS-DOS

mount -t msdos /dev/fd0a /floppy

NFS

mount -t nfs nfs-server-host:/directory/path /mount-point

MFS (32 megabyte)

mount -t mfs -o nosuid,-s=32m swap /tmp

The "noauto" directive in /etc/fstab can be used to make it easy to manually mount and unmount removable media using just the mountpoint filename, with an entry like this:

/dev/cd0a /cdrom cd9660 ro,noauto 0 0

That would allow a simple command like "mount /cdrom" or "umount /cdrom" for media using the ISO-9660 file system format in the first CD-ROM drive.

DIAGNOSTICS

The error "Operation not supported by device" indicates that the mount for the specified file-system type cannot be completed because the kernel lacks support for the said file-system. See options(4).

The error "Operation not permitted" may indicate that the mount options include privileged options and/or don't include options that exclude privileged options. One should try using at least "nodev" and "nosuid" in such cases:

mount -t cd9660 -o nodev,nosuid /dev/cd0a /mnt

SEE ALSO

df(1), mount(2), options(4), wapbl(4), fstab(5), disklabel(8), fsck(8), mount_ados(8), mount_cd9660(8), mount_ext2fs(8), mount_fdesc(8), mount_ffs(8), mount_filecore(8), mount_kernfs(8), mount_lfs(8), mount_mfs(8), mount_msdos(8), mount_nfs(8), mount_ntfs(8), mount_null(8), mount_overlay(8), mount_portal(8), mount_procfs(8), mount_tmpfs(8), mount_udf(8), mount_umap(8), mount_union(8), rump_cd9660(8), rump_efs(8), rump_ext2fs(8), rump_ffs(8), rump_hfs(8), rump_lfs(8), rump_msdos(8), rump_nfs(8), rump_ntfs(8), rump_sysvbfs(8), rump_tmpfs(8), rump_udf(8), umount(8)

HISTORY

A **mount** command appeared in Version 6 AT&T UNIX.

MOUNT_9P (8)   NetBSD   MOUNT_9P (8)

NAME

mount_9p — mount a file server using the 9P resource sharing protocol

SYNOPSIS

mount_9p [**-s**] [**-o** *mntopts*] [**-p** *port*] *[user@]host [:path] mount_point*

DESCRIPTION

The **mount_9p** program is used to mount a file hierarchy served with the Plan 9 file sharing protocol: 9P. After the file system is mounted, the files on the remote *host* will be accessed using the credentials of the user named *user* and whatever UID the user happens to have on the remote server. If *path* is supplied, it is used as the mount rootpath on the remote host. *path* must be an absolute path.

SEE ALSO

puffs(3), puffs(4), mount(8)

HISTORY

The **mount_9p** utility first appeared in NetBSD 5.0.

CAVEATS

Permissions are not handled well.

Authentication support is missing.

Error code handling is missing.

Under construction.

NAME

mount_ados — mount an AmigaDOS file system

SYNOPSIS

mount_ados [-o *options*] [-u *uid*] [-g *gid*] [-m *mask*] special node

DESCRIPTION

The **mount_ados** command attaches the AmigaDOS filesystem residing on the device special to the global filesystem namespace at the location indicated by node. Both *special* and *node* are converted to absolute paths before use. This command is normally executed by mount(8) at boot time, but can be used by any user to mount an AmigaDOS file system on any directory that they own (provided, of course, that they have appropriate access to the device that contains the file system).

The options are as follows:

-o *options*
Use the specified mount *options*, as described in mount(8).

-u *uid*
Set the owner of the files in the file system to *uid*. The default owner is the owner of the directory on which the file system is being mounted.

-g *gid*
Set the group of the files in the file system to *gid*. The default group is the group of the directory on which the file system is being mounted.

-m *mask*
Specify the maximum file permissions for files in the file system. (For example, a mask of 755 specifies that, by default, the owner should have read, write, and execute permissions for files, but others should only have read and execute permissions. See chmod(1) for more information about octal file modes.) Only the nine low-order bits of *mask* are used. The default mask is taken from the directory on which the file system is being mounted.

SEE ALSO

mount(2), unmount(2), fstab(5), mount(8)

HISTORY

The **mount_ados** utility first appeared in NetBSD 1.0.

BUGS

The 'ados' filesystem currently supports the Amiga fast file system.

The 'ados' filesystem implementation currently is read-only. The **mount_ados** utility silently retries the mount read-only, as if the ro option were specified, when it encounters the [EROFS] error.

NAME
mount_cd9660 — mount an ISO-9660 filesystem

SYNOPSIS
mount_cd9660 [**-o** *options*] *special node*

DESCRIPTION
The **mount_cd9660** command attaches the ISO-9660 filesystem residing on the device `special` to the global filesystem namespace at the location indicated by `node`. Both *special* and *node* are converted to absolute paths before use.

The options are as follows:

-o   Options are specified with a **-o** flag followed by a comma separated string of options. Besides options mentioned in `mount`(8) man page, following cd9660-specific options are supported:

extatt   Enable the use of extended attributes.

gens   Do not strip version numbers on files and leave the case of the filename alone. (By default, uppercase characters are translated to lowercase, and if there are files with different version numbers on the disk, only the last one will be listed.)

In either case, files may be opened without giving a version number, in which case you get the last one, or by explicitly stating a version number (albeit it's quite difficult to know it, if you are not using the **gens** option), in which case you get the specified version.

nocasetrans
A synonym for **nomaplcase**.

nojoliet
Do not make use of Joliet extensions for long filenames which may be present in the filesystem.

Interpretation of Joliet extensions is enabled by default, Unicode file names are encoded into UTF-8.

nomaplcase
File names on cd9660 cdrom without Rock Ridge extension present should be uppercase only. By default, cd9660 recodes file names read from a non-Rock Ridge disk to all lowercase characters. **nomaplcase** turns off this mapping.

norrip   Do not use any Rockridge extensions included in the filesystem.

nrr   Same as **norrip**. For compatibility with Solaris only.

rrcaseins
Makes all lookups case-insensitive even for CD-ROMs with Rock-Ridge extensions (for Rock-Ridge, default is case-sensitive lookup).

For compatibility with previous releases, following obsolete flags are still recognized:

-e   Same as **-o extatt**.

-j   Same as **-o nojoliet**.

-g   Same as **-o gens**.

    -r   Same as **-o norrip**.

SEE ALSO

mount(2), unmount(2), fstab(5), mount(8), mscdlabel(8)

HISTORY

The **mount_cd9660** utility first appeared 4.4BSD. Support for Joliet filesystem appeared in NetBSD 1.4. Options **nomaplcase** and **rrcaseins** were added in NetBSD 1.5. UTF-8 encoding of Unicode file names for Joliet filesystems was added in NetBSD 3.0.

NOTES

For Joliet filesystems, the Unicode file names used to be filtered to ISO-8859-1 character set. This changed in NetBSD 3.0, file names are encoded into UTF-8 now by default. The behaviour is controllable by the *vfs.cd9660.utf8_joliet* sysctl; the former behaviour is available by setting it to 0.

BUGS

For some cdroms the information in the Rock Ridge extension is wrong and the cdrom needs to be mounted with "norrip". A sign that something is wrong is that the stat(2) system call returns EBADF causing, e.g., "ls -l" to fail with "Bad file descriptor".

The cd9660 filesystem does not support the original "High Sierra" ("CDROM001") format.

POSIX device node mapping is currently not supported.

Version numbers are not stripped if Rockridge extensions are in use. In this case, you have to use the original name of the file as recorded on disk, i.e. use uppercase and append the version number to the file.

There is no ECMA support.

NAME
> **mount_efs** — Mount an SGI EFS file system

SYNOPSIS
> **mount_efs** [**-o** *options*] *special node*

DESCRIPTION
> The **mount_efs** command attaches an EFS file system *special* device on to the file system tree at the point *node*. Both *special* and *node* are converted to absolute paths before use.

> This command is normally executed by mount(8) at boot time.

> The options are as follows:

> **-o**   Options are specified with a **-o** flag followed by a comma-separated string of options. See the mount(8) man page for possible options and their meanings.

SEE ALSO
> mount(2), unmount(2), options(4), fstab(5), mount(8), svhlabel(8)

HISTORY
> The **mount_efs** utility first appeared in NetBSD 5.0.

BUGS
> Write support is not presently implemented.

> EFS file systems are limited to 8 gigabytes in size.

> Because of EFS limitations, an EFS file system can't be used with any UID or GID greater than 65535.

NAME

    mount_ext2fs — Mount an ext2 file system

SYNOPSIS

    mount_ext2fs [**-o** *options*] *special node*

DESCRIPTION

    The **mount_ext2fs** command attaches an ext2 file system *special* device on to the file system tree at the point *node*. Both *special* and *node* are converted to absolute paths before use.

    This command is normally executed by mount(8) at boot time.

    The options are as follows:

    -o   Options are specified with a **-o** flag followed by a comma-separated string of options. See the mount(8) man page for possible options and their meanings.

SEE ALSO

    mount(2), unmount(2), options(4), fstab(5), mount(8)

HISTORY

    The **mount_ext2fs** utility first appeared in FreeBSD 2.2.

BUGS

    Some ext2-specific options, features or file flags are not supported.

NAME
mount_fdesc — mount the file-descriptor file system

SYNOPSIS
mount_fdesc [**-o** *options*] *fdesc mount_point*

DESCRIPTION
The **mount_fdesc** command attaches an instance of the per-process file descriptor namespace to the global filesystem namespace. The conventional mount point is /dev and the filesystem should be union mounted in order to augment, rather than replace, the existing entries in /dev. The directory specified by *mount_point* is converted to an absolute path before use.

This command is normally executed by mount(8) at boot time.

The options are as follows:

-o   Options are specified with a **-o** flag followed by a comma separated string of options. See the mount(8) man page for possible options and their meanings.

The contents of the mount point are fd, stderr, stdin, stdout and tty.

fd is a directory whose contents appear as a list of numbered files which correspond to the open files of the process reading the directory. The files /dev/fd/0 through /dev/fd/# refer to file descriptors which can be accessed through the file system. If the file descriptor is open and the mode the file is being opened with is a subset of the mode of the existing descriptor, the call:

```
fd = open("/dev/fd/0", mode);
```

and the call:

```
fd = fcntl(0, F_DUPFD, 0);
```

are equivalent.

The files /dev/stdin, /dev/stdout and /dev/stderr appear as symlinks to the relevant entry in the /dev/fd sub-directory. Opening them is equivalent to the following calls:

```
fd = fcntl(STDIN_FILENO,  F_DUPFD, 0);
fd = fcntl(STDOUT_FILENO, F_DUPFD, 0);
fd = fcntl(STDERR_FILENO, F_DUPFD, 0);
```

Flags to the open(2) call other than O_RDONLY, O_WRONLY and O_RDWR are ignored.

The /dev/tty entry is an indirect reference to the current process's controlling terminal. It appears as a named pipe (FIFO) but behaves in exactly the same way as the real controlling terminal device.

FILES
```
/dev/fd/#
/dev/stdin
/dev/stdout
/dev/stderr
/dev/tty
```

SEE ALSO
mount(2), unmount(2), tty(4), fstab(5), mount(8)

HISTORY

The **mount_fdesc** utility first appeared in 4.4 BSD.

BUGS

This filesystem may not be NFS-exported.

NAME

mount_ffs, **mount_ufs** — mount a Berkeley Fast File System

SYNOPSIS

mount_ffs [**-o** *options*] *special node*

DESCRIPTION

The **mount_ffs** command attaches the Berkeley Fast File System on the *special* device on to the file system tree at point *node*. Both *special* and *node* are converted to absolute paths before use.

The **mount_ufs** form of the command is meant for backward compatibility only. Fast File Systems should no longer be listed as type "ufs" in fstab(5) and instead should be listed as type "ffs".

This command is normally executed by mount(8) at boot time. The options are as follows:

-o   Options are specified with a **-o** flag followed by a comma separated string of options. See the mount(8) man page for possible options and their meanings.

SEE ALSO

mount(2), unmount(2), fstab(5), mount(8)

M. McKusick and G. Ganger, "Soft Updates: A Technique for Eliminating Most Synchronous Writes in the Fast File System", *Proceedings of the FREENIX track: 1999 USENIX Annual Technical Conference*, pp. 1-17, June 1999.

HISTORY

A **mount_ffs** command appeared in NetBSD 1.1.

BUGS

It is possible for a corrupted file system to cause a crash.

NAME

mount_filecore — mount a FILECORE file system

SYNOPSIS

mount_filecore [**-afnR**] [**-g** *gid*] [**-o** *options*] [**-u** *uid*] special node

ORIGIN

The NetBSD FILECORE filesystem is a read only implementation of the filecore file system found in Acorn Computers RISC OS operating system. This operating system is the ROM based operating system found on their ARM 6, ARM7 and StrongARM 110 based RiscPC machines that are supported by the arm32 port. Under RISC OS, filecore will have multiple instantiations for file systems on different block devices such as floppies, IDE discs, SCSI discs etc. and these frequently are considered to be different filesystems e.g. ADFS, IDEFS, SCSIFS etc.

DESCRIPTION

The **mount_filecore** command attaches the FILECORE filesystem residing on the device special to the global filesystem namespace at the location indicated by node. Both *special* and *node* are converted to absolute paths before use. This command is normally executed by mount(8) at boot time, but can be used by any user to mount a FILECORE file system on any directory that they own (provided, of course, that they have appropriate access to the device that contains the file system).

The options are as follows:

-a   Give all files world access.

-f   Append the filetype to each filename. This option currently has no effect.

-g *gid*
          Set the group of the files in the file system to *gid*. The default group is the group of the directory on which the file system is being mounted.

-n   Give all files owner access.

-o *options*
          Use the specified mount *options*, as described in mount(8).

-R   Give all files owner read access.

-u *uid*
          Set the owner of the files in the file system to *uid*. The default owner is the owner of the directory on which the file system is being mounted.

SEE ALSO

mount(2), unmount(2), fstab(5), mount(8)

HISTORY

The **mount_filecore** utility first appeared in NetBSD 1.4.

CAVEATS

The 'filecore' filesystem currently supports the Acorn filecore file system found on Acorn Computers RiscPC desktop machines with versions of RISC OS up to 3.70.

NAME

mount_hfs — mount an Apple HFS+ File System

SYNOPSIS

mount_hfs [**−o** *options*] *special node*

DESCRIPTION

The **mount_hfs** command attaches the Apple HFS+ File System on the *special* device on to the file system tree at point *node*. Both *special* and *node* are converted to absolute paths before use.

This command is normally executed by mount(8) at boot time. The options are as follows:

−o   Options are specified with a **−o** flag followed by a comma separated string of options. See the mount(8) man page for possible options and their meanings.

NOTES

Apple disk images (.dmg files) and hybrid CD-ROMs contain multiple partitions with an HFS+ file system on one of them. Use apmlabel(8) to enter it into the disklabel and mount the resulting partition.

SEE ALSO

mount(2), unmount(2), fstab(5), apmlabel(8), mount(8)

HISTORY

The **mount_hfs** utility first appeared in NetBSD 5.0.

AUTHORS

mount_hfs was developed by Yevgeny Binder ⟨yevbee@comcast.net⟩ during the 2005 Google Summer of Code. It was improved and imported into NetBSD by Dieter Baron ⟨dillo@NetBSD.org⟩.

BUGS

HFS+ support is still experimental. Currently, no write support is present. Also, Unicode decomposition is not performed on file names prior to lookup.

NAME
  mount_kernfs — mount the /kern file system

SYNOPSIS
  mount_kernfs [**-o** *options*] */kern mount_point*

DESCRIPTION
  The **mount_kernfs** command attaches an instance of the kernel parameter namespace to the global filesystem namespace. The conventional mount point is /kern. The directory specified by *mount_point* is converted to an absolute path before use. This command is normally executed by mount(8) at boot time.

  The filesystem includes several regular files which can be read, some of which can also be written. The contents of the files is in a machine-independent format, either a string, or an integer in decimal ASCII. Where numbers are returned, a trailing newline character is also added.

  The options are as follows:

  -o   Options are specified with a **-o** flag followed by a comma separated string of options. See the mount(8) man page for possible options and their meanings.

FILES
  boottime   the time at which the system was last booted (decimal ASCII).
  copyright   kernel copyright message.
  hostname   the hostname, with a trailing newline. The hostname can be changed by writing to this file. A trailing newline will be stripped from the hostname being written.
  hz   the frequency of the system clock (decimal ASCII).
  ipsecsa   the directory that contains IPsec security associations (SA) in PF_KEY format. Filenames are SPI in decimal number. The content of files can be inspected by using setkey(8).
  ipsecsp   the directory that contains IPsec security policies in PF_KEY format. Filenames are security policy ID in decimal number. The content of files can be inspected by using setkey(8).
  loadavg   the 1, 5 and 15 minute load average in kernel fixed-point format. The final integer is the fix-point scaling factor. All numbers are in decimal ASCII.
  msgbuf   the kernel message buffer, also read by syslogd(8), through the log device, and by dmesg(8).
  pagesize   the machine pagesize (decimal ASCII).
  physmem   the number of pages of physical memory in the machine (decimal ASCII).
  rootdev   the root device.
  rrootdev   the raw root device.
  time   the second and microsecond value of the system clock. Both numbers are in decimal ASCII.
  version   the kernel version string. The head line for /etc/motd can be generated by running: "**sed 1q /kern/version**"

SEE ALSO
  mount(2), unmount(2), ipsec(4), fstab(5), dmesg(8), mount(8), setkey(8), syslogd(8)

HISTORY
  The **mount_kernfs** utility first appeared in 4.4BSD.

BUGS
  This filesystem may not be NFS-exported.

  lkm(4) version does not support IPsec-related files/directories.

NAME
mount_lfs — mount a log-structured file system

SYNOPSIS
mount_lfs [**-bdins**] [**-N** *nsegs*] [**-o** *options*] *special node*

DESCRIPTION
The **mount_lfs** command attaches a log-structured file system *special* device on to the file system tree at the point *node*. Both *special* and *node* are converted to absolute paths before use. In addition, the lfs_cleanerd(8) utility is invoked to clean the file system periodically.

This command is normally executed by mount(8) at boot time.

The options are as follows:

-b   Instruct the cleaner to count bytes written, rather than segments read, to determine how many segments to clean at once.

-d   Run lfs_cleanerd(8) in debug mode.

-i   Instruct the cleaner to use filesystem idle time as the criterion for aggressive cleaning, instead of system load.

-o   Options are specified with a **-o** flag followed by a comma separated string of options. See the mount(8) man page for possible options and their meanings.

-N *nsegs*
       Clean *nsegs* segments (or bytes' worth of segments if **-b** is also specified) at a time.

-n   Don't start lfs_cleanerd(8) on the file system.

-s   Cause lfs_cleanerd(8) to read data in small chunks when cleaning the file system.

SEE ALSO
mount(2), unmount(2), fstab(5), dump_lfs(8), lfs_cleanerd(8), mount(8), newfs_lfs(8)

Ousterhout and Douglis, "Beating the I/O Bottleneck: A Case for Log-structured File Systems", *Operating Systems Review*, No. 1, Vol. 23, pp. 11-27, 1989, also available as Technical Report UCB/CSD 88/467.

Rosenblum and Ousterhout, "The Design and Implementation of a Log-Structured File System", *ACM SIGOPS Operating Systems Review*, No. 5, Vol. 25, 1991.

Seltzer, "File System Performance and Transaction Support", *PhD Thesis, University of California, Berkeley*, 1992, also available as Technical Report UCB/ERL M92.

Seltzer, Bostic, McKusick and Staelin, "An Implementation of a Log-Structured File System for UNIX", *Proc. of the Winter 1993 USENIX Conf.*, pp. 315-331, 1993.

HISTORY
The **mount_lfs** function first appeared in 4.4BSD.

NAME
    mount_mfs — mount a memory based file system

SYNOPSIS
    mount_mfs [**-N**] [**-a** *maxcontig*] [**-b** *block-size*] [**-d** *rotdelay*] [**-e** *maxbpg*]
        [**-f** *frag-size*] [**-g** *groupname*] [**-i** *bytes-per-inode*]
        [**-m** *free-space*] [**-n** *inodes*] [**-o** *options*] [**-p** *permissions*]
        [**-s** *size*] [**-u** *username*] [**-V** *verbose*] *special node*

DESCRIPTION
    mount_mfs is used to build a file system in virtual memory and then mount it on a specified node.
mount_mfs exits and the contents of the file system are lost when the file system is unmounted. If
mount_mfs is sent a signal while running, for example during system shutdown, it will attempt to unmount
its corresponding file system. *special* is ignored.

    Options with numeric arguments may contain an optional (case-insensitive) suffix:
        b   Bytes; causes no modification. (Default)
        k   Kilo; multiply the argument by 1024
        m   Mega; multiply the argument by 1048576
        g   Giga; multiply the argument by 1073741824

    The following options define the general layout policies:

-N   Causes the memory file system parameters to be printed out without really mounting the memory file system.

-a *maxcontig*
          This specifies the maximum number of contiguous blocks that will be laid out before forcing a
rotational delay (see the **-d** option). The default value is 8. See tunefs(8) for more details
on how to set this option.

-b *block-size*
          The block size of the file system, in bytes. It must be a power of two. The smallest allowable
size is 4096 bytes. The default size depends upon the size of the file system:

file system size	block-size
< 20 MB	4 KB
< 1024 MB	8 KB
>= 1024 MB	16 KB

-d *rotdelay*
          This specifies the expected time (in milliseconds) to service a transfer completion interrupt and
initiate a new transfer on the same disk. The default is 0 milliseconds. See tunefs(8) for
more details on how to set this option.

-e *maxbpg*
          This indicates the maximum number of blocks any single file can allocate out of a cylinder
group before it is forced to begin allocating blocks from another cylinder group. The default is
about one quarter of the total blocks in a cylinder group. See tunefs(8) for more details on
how to set this option.

-f *frag-size*
          The fragment size of the file system in bytes. It must be a power of two ranging in value
between *block-size*/8 and *block-size*. The optimal *block-size*:*frag-size* ratio
is 8:1. Other ratios are possible, but are not recommended, and may produce unpredictable
results. The default size depends upon the size of the file system:

file system size	frag-size
< 20 MB	0.5 KB
< 1024 MB	1 KB
>= 1024 MB	2 KB

-g *groupname*
> This specifies the group name or group id of the root inode of the file system.

-i *bytes-per-inode*
> This specifies the density of inodes in the file system. If fewer inodes are desired, a larger number should be used; to create more inodes a smaller number should be given. The default is to create an inode for every (4 * *frag-size*) bytes of data space:

file system size	bytes-per-inode
< 20 MB	2 KB
< 1024 MB	4 KB
>= 1024 MB	8 KB

-m *free-space*
> The percentage of space reserved from normal users; the minimum free space threshold. The default value used is 5%. See tunefs(8) for more details on how to set this option.

-n *inodes*
> This specifies the number of inodes for the filesystem. If both **-i** and **-n** are specified then **-n** takes precedence.

-o
> Options are specified with a **-o** flag followed by a comma separated string of options. See the mount(8) man page for possible options and their meanings.

-p *permissions*
> This specifies the permissions of the root inode of the file system.

-s *size* The size of the file system in sectors. An 's' suffix will be interpreted as the number of sectors (the default). All other suffixes are interpreted as per other numeric arguments, except that the number is converted into sectors by dividing by the default sector size (which is 512 bytes) after suffix interpretation.

-u *username*
> This specifies the user name or user id of the root inode of the file system.

-V *verbose*
> This controls the amount of information written to stdout:
>
> | | |
> |---|---|
> | 0 | No output |
> | 1 | Overall size and cylinder group details. |
> | 2 | A progress bar (dots ending at right hand margin). |
> | 3 | The first few super-block backup sector numbers are displayed before the progress bar. |
> | 4 | All the super-block backup sector numbers are displayed (no progress bar). |
>
> The default is 0. If **-N** is specified **mount_mfs** stops before outputting the progress bar.

NOTES
The owner and group ids of the root node of the new file system are set to the effective uid and gid of the user mounting the file system.

EXAMPLES

Mount a 32 MB mfs on /tmp:

```
mount_mfs -s 32m swap /tmp
```

SEE ALSO

disktab(5), fs(5), disklabel(8), diskpart(8), dumpfs(8), fsck_ffs(8), fsirand(8), mount(8), newfs(8), tunefs(8)

M. McKusick, W. Joy, S. Leffler, and R. Fabry, "A Fast File System for UNIX,", *ACM Transactions on Computer Systems 2*, 3, pp 181-197, August 1984, (reprinted in the BSD System Manager's Manual).

HISTORY

The **mount_mfs** command appeared in 4.2BSD.

BUGS

The **async** mount(8) option is currently disabled in this file system because it causes hangs when writing lots of data. The problem is that MFS needs to allocate pages to clean pages, so if it waits until the last minute to clean pages then there may not be any of them available to do the cleaning.

NAME
mount_msdos — mount an MS-DOS file system

SYNOPSIS
mount_msdos [**-9Gls**] [**-g** *gid*] [**-M** *mask*] [**-m** *mask*] [**-o** *options*] [**-t** *gmtoff*]
            [**-u** *uid*] special node

DESCRIPTION
The **mount_msdos** command attaches the MS-DOS filesystem residing on the device special to the global filesystem namespace at the location indicated by node. Both *special* and *node* are converted to absolute paths before use. This command is normally executed by mount(8) at boot time, but can be used by any user to mount an MS-DOS file system on any directory that they own (provided, of course, that they have appropriate access to the device that contains the file system).

Support for FAT16 and VFAT32 as well as long file names is available.

The options are as follows:

-9   Ignore the special Win'95 directory entries even if deleting or renaming a file. This forces **-s**.

-G   This option causes the filesystem to be interpreted as an Atari-Gemdos filesystem. The differences to the MSDOS filesystem are minimal and limited to the boot block. This option enforces **-s**.

-g *gid*   Set the group of the files in the file system to *gid*. The default group is the group of the directory on which the file system is being mounted.

-l   Force listing and generation of Win'95 long filenames and separate creation/modification/access dates.

                 If neither **-s** nor **-l** are given, **mount_msdos** searches the root directory of the filesystem to be mounted for any existing Win'95 long filenames. If the filesystem is not empty and no such entries are found, **-s** is the default. Otherwise **-l** is assumed.

-M *mask*   Specify the maximum file permissions for directories in the file system. The value of **-m** is used if it is supplied and **-M** is omitted.

-m *mask*   Specify the maximum file permissions for files in the file system. (For example, a mask of 755 specifies that, by default, the owner should have read, write, and execute permissions for files, but others should only have read and execute permissions. See chmod(1) for more information about octal file modes.) Only the nine low-order bits of *mask* are used. The value of **-M** is used if it is supplied and **-m** is omitted. The default mask is taken from the directory on which the file system is being mounted.

-o *options*   Use the specified mount *options*, as described in mount(8).

-s   Force behaviour to ignore and not generate Win'95 long filenames. See also **-l**.

-t *gmtoff*   Set the time zone offset (in seconds) from UTC to *gmtoff*, with positive values indicating east of the Prime Meridian. If not set, the user's current time zone will be used.

-u *uid*   Set the owner of the files in the file system to *uid*. The default owner is the owner of the directory on which the file system is being mounted.

EXAMPLES
To remove the 'execute' permission bit for all files, but still keep directories searchable, use:

    mount_msdos -m 0644 -M 0755 /dev/wd0e /msdos

SEE ALSO
    mount(2), unmount(2), fstab(5), mount(8)

HISTORY
    The **mount_msdos** utility first appeared in NetBSD 0.9. Its predecessor, the **mount_pcfs** utility appeared in NetBSD 0.8, and was abandoned in favor of the more aptly-named **mount_msdos**.

BUGS
    Compressed partitions are not supported.

    The use of the **−9** flag could result in damaged filesystems, albeit the damage is in part taken care of by procedures similar to the ones used in Win'95.

    The default handling for **−s** and **−l** will result in empty filesystems to be populated with short filenames only. To generate long filenames on empty DOS filesystems use **−l**.

NAME
　　　　mount_nfs — mount NFS file systems

SYNOPSIS
　　　　mount_nfs [**-23bCcdilPpqsTUX**] [**-a** *maxreadahead*] [**-D** *deadthresh*]
　　　　　　　　[**-g** *maxgroups*] [**-I** *readdirsize*] [**-L** *leaseterm*] [**-o** *options*]
　　　　　　　　[**-R** *retrycnt*] [**-r** *readsize*] [**-t** *timeout*] [**-w** *writesize*]
　　　　　　　　[**-x** *retrans*] *rhost:path node*

DESCRIPTION
　　　　The **mount_nfs** command calls the mount(2) system call to prepare and graft a remote NFS file system
　　　　(rhost:path) on to the file system tree at the mount point *node*. The directory specified by *node* is con-
　　　　verted to an absolute path before use. This command is normally executed by mount(8). It implements the
　　　　mount protocol as described in RFC 1094, Appendix A and *NFS: Network File System Version 3 Protocol
　　　　Specification*, Appendix I.

　　　　The options are:

　　　　-2　　　Use the NFS Version 2 protocol.

　　　　-3　　　Use the NFS Version 3 protocol. The default is to try version 3 first, and fall back to version 2 if
　　　　　　　　the mount fails.

　　　　-a *maxreadahead*
　　　　　　　　Set the read-ahead count to the specified value. This may be in the range of 0 - 4, and determines
　　　　　　　　how many blocks will be read ahead when a large file is being read sequentially. Trying a value
　　　　　　　　greater than 1 for this is suggested for mounts with a large bandwidth * delay product.

　　　　-b　　　If an initial attempt to contact the server fails, fork off a child to keep trying the mount in the back-
　　　　　　　　ground. Useful for fstab(5), where the filesystem mount is not critical to multiuser operation.

　　　　-C　　　For UDP mount points, do a connect(2). Although this flag increases the efficiency of UDP
　　　　　　　　mounts it cannot be used for servers that do not reply to requests from the standard NFS port num-
　　　　　　　　ber 2049, or for servers with multiple network interfaces. In these cases if the socket is connected
　　　　　　　　and the server replies from a different port number or a different network interface the client will
　　　　　　　　get ICMP port unreachable and the mount will hang.

　　　　-c　　　For UDP mount points, do not do a connect(2). This flag is deprecated and connectionless UDP
　　　　　　　　mounts are the default.

　　　　-D *deadthresh*
　　　　　　　　Set the "dead server threshold" to the specified number of round trip timeout intervals. After a
　　　　　　　　"dead server threshold" of retransmit timeouts, "not responding" message is printed to a tty.

　　　　-d　　　Turn off the dynamic retransmit timeout estimator. This may be useful for UDP mounts that
　　　　　　　　exhibit high retry rates, since it is possible that the dynamically estimated timeout interval is too
　　　　　　　　short.

　　　　-g *maxgroups*
　　　　　　　　Set the maximum size of the group list for the credentials to the specified value. This should be
　　　　　　　　used for mounts on old servers that cannot handle a group list size of 16, as specified in RFC 1057.
　　　　　　　　Try 8, if users in a lot of groups cannot get response from the mount point.

　　　　-I *readdirsize*
　　　　　　　　Set the readdir read size to the specified value. The value should normally be a multiple of
　　　　　　　　DIRBLKSIZ that is ≤ the read size for the mount.

-i   Make the mount interruptible, which implies that file system calls that are delayed due to an unresponsive server will fail with `EINTR` when a termination signal is posted for the process.

-L *leaseterm*
Ignored. It used to be NQNFS lease term.

-l   Used with NFS Version 3 to specify that the **ReaddirPlus**() RPC should be used. This option
reduces RPC traffic for cases such as **ls -l**, but tends to flood the attribute and name caches with
prefetched entries. Try this option and see whether performance improves or degrades. Probably
most useful for client to server network interconnects with a large bandwidth times delay product.

-o *options*
Options are specified with a **-o** flag followed by a comma separated string of options. See the
`mount`(8) man page for possible options and their meanings.

The following NFS specific options are also available:

bg   Same as **-b**.

conn   Same as **-C**.

deadthresh=⟨*deadthresh*⟩
Same as **-D** *deadthresh*.

dumbtimer
Same as **-d**.

intr   Same as **-i**.

leaseterm=⟨*leaseterm*⟩
Same as **-L** *leaseterm*.

maxgrps=⟨*maxgroups*⟩
Same as **-g** *maxgroups*.

mntudp   Same as **-U**.

nfsv2   Same as **-2**.

nfsv3   Same as **-3**.

noresport
Same as **-p**.

nqnfs   Same as **-q**.

port=⟨*portnumber*⟩
Use the specified port number for NFS requests. The default is to query the portmapper
for the NFS port.

rdirplus
Same as **-l**.

readahead=⟨*maxreadahead*⟩
Same as **-a** *maxreadahead*.

rsize=⟨*readsize*⟩
Same as **--r** *readsize*.

soft   Same as **-s**.

tcp   Same as **−T**.

timeo=⟨*timeout*⟩
>   Same as **−t** *timeout*.

wsize=⟨*writesize*⟩
>   Same as **−w** *writesize*.

−P   Use a reserved socket port number. This is the default, and available for backwards compatibility purposes only.

−p   Do not use a reserved port number for RPCs. This option is provided only to be able to mimic the old default behavior of not using a reserved port, and should rarely be useful.

−q   A synonym of **−3**. It used to specify NQNFS.

−R *retrycnt*
>   Set the retry count for doing the mount to the specified value. The default is 10000.

−r *readsize*
>   Set the read data size to the specified value in bytes. It should normally be a power of 2 greater than or equal to 1024.
>
>   This should be used for UDP mounts when the "fragments dropped after timeout" value is getting large while actively using a mount point. Use netstat(1) with the **−s** option to see what the "fragments dropped after timeout" value is. See the **mount_nfs −w** option also.

−s   A soft mount, which implies that file system calls will fail after *retrans* round trip timeout intervals.

−T   Use TCP transport instead of UDP. This is recommended for servers that are not on the same physical network as the client. Not all NFS servers, especially not old ones, support this.

−t *timeout*
>   Set the initial retransmit timeout to the specified value in 0.1 seconds. May be useful for fine tuning UDP mounts over internetworks with high packet loss rates or an overloaded server. Try increasing the interval if nfsstat(1) shows high retransmit rates while the file system is active or reducing the value if there is a low retransmit rate but long response delay observed. Normally, the -d option should be specified when using this option to manually tune the timeout interval. The default is 3 seconds.

−U   Force the mount protocol to use UDP transport, even for TCP NFS mounts. This is necessary for some old BSD servers.

−w *writesize*
>   Set the write data size to the specified value in bytes.
>
>   The same logic applies for use of this option as with the **mount_nfs −r** option, but using the "fragments dropped after timeout" value on the NFS server instead of the client. Note that both the **−r** and **−w** options should only be used as a last ditch effort at improving performance when mounting servers that do not support TCP mounts.

−X   Perform 32 <-> 64 bit directory cookie translation for version 3 mounts. This may be need in the case of a server using the upper 32 bits of version 3 directory cookies, and when you are running emulated binaries that access such a filesystem. Native NetBSD binaries will never need this option. This option introduces some overhead.

−x *retrans*
>   Set the retransmit timeout count for soft mounts to the specified value. The default is 10.

EXAMPLES

The simplest way to invoke **mount_nfs** is with a command like:

```
mount -t nfs remotehost:/filesystem /localmountpoint
```

It is also possible to automatically mount filesystems at boot from your /etc/fstab by using a line like:

```
remotehost:/home /home nfs rw 0 0
```

PERFORMANCE

As can be derived from the comments accompanying the options, performance tuning of NFS can be a non-trivial task. Here are some common points to watch:

- Increasing the read and write size with the **-r** and **-w** options respectively will increase throughput if the network interface can handle the larger packet sizes.

  The default size for NFS version 2 is 8K when using UDP, 64K when using TCP.

  The default size for NFS version 3 is platform dependent: on NetBSD/i386, the default is 32K, for other platforms it is 8K. Values over 32K are only supported for TCP, where 64K is the maximum.

  Any value over 32K is unlikely to get you more performance, unless you have a very fast network.

- If the network interface cannot handle larger packet sizes or a long train of back to back packets, you may see low performance figures or even temporary hangups during NFS activity.

  This can especially happen with older Ethernet network interfaces. What happens is that either the receive buffer on the network interface on the client side is overflowing, or that similar events occur on the server, leading to a lot of dropped packets.

  In this case, decreasing the read and write size, using TCP, or a combination of both will usually lead to better throughput. Should you need to decrease the read and write size for all your NFS mounts because of a slow Ethernet network interface (e.g. a USB 1.1 to 10/100 Ethernet network interface), you can use

  ```
  options NFS_RSIZE=value
  options NFS_WSIZE=value
  ```

  in your kernel config(1) file to avoid having do specify the sizes for all mounts.

- For connections that are not on the same LAN, and/or may experience packet loss, using TCP is strongly recommended.

ERRORS

Some common problems with **mount_nfs** can be difficult for first time users to understand.

```
mount_nfs: can't access /foo: Permission denied
```

This message means that the remote host, is either not exporting the filesystem you requested, or is not exporting it to your host. If you believe the remote host is indeed exporting a filesystem to you, make sure the exports(5) file is exporting the proper directories.

A common mistake is that mountd(8) will not export a filesystem with the **-alldirs** option, unless it is a mount point on the exporting host. It is not possible to remotely mount a subdirectory of an exported mount, unless it is exported with the **-alldirs** option.

The following error:

```
NFS Portmap: RPC: Program not registered
```

means that the remote host is not running mountd(8). The program rpcinfo(8) can be used to determine if the remote host is running nfsd, and mountd by issuing the command:

```
rpcinfo -p remotehostname
```

If the remote host is running nfsd, and mountd, it would display:

```
100005   3   udp    719   mountd
100005   1   tcp    720   mountd
100005   3   tcp    720   mountd
100003   2   udp   2049   nfs
100003   3   udp   2049   nfs
100003   2   tcp   2049   nfs
100003   3   tcp   2049   nfs
```

The error:

```
mount_nfs: can't get net id for host
```

indicates that **mount_nfs** cannot resolve the name of the remote host.

SEE ALSO

nfsstat(1), mount(2), unmount(2), options(4), exports(5), fstab(5), mount(8), mountd(8), rpcinfo(8)

NFS: Network File System Protocol specification, RFC 1094, March 1989.

NFS Version 2 and Version 3 Security Issues and the NFS Protocol's Use of RPCSEC_GCC and Kerberos V5, RFC 2623, June 1999.

NFS Version 4 Design Considerations, RFC 2624, June 1999.

Authentication Mechanisms for ONC RPC, RFC 2695, September 1999.

CAVEATS

An NFS server shouldn't loopback-mount its own exported file systems because it's fundamentally prone to deadlock.

NAME
   mount_nilfs — mount a NILFS file system

SYNOPSIS
   mount_nilfs [**-c** *checkpoint*] [**-o** *options*] [**-t** *gmtoff*] *special node*

DESCRIPTION
   The **mount_nilfs** command attaches the NILFS file system residing on the specified *special* device node on the location indicated with *node*.

   -c *checkpoint*
              Select the checkpoint number *checkpoint* to be mounted instead of the default last one.

   -o *options*
              Use the specified mount *options* as specified in mount(8).

   -t *gmtoff*   Set the time zone offset (in seconds) from UTC to *gmtoff*, with positive values indicating east of the Prime Meridian. If not set, the user's current time zone will be used.

SEE ALSO
   mount(2), vnd(4), fstab(5), mount(8), umount(8), vnconfig(8)

NOTES
   NILFS is a file system developped by NTT and is currently in version 2.

NAME
mount_ntfs — mount an NTFS file system

SYNOPSIS
mount_ntfs [-a] [-i] [-u *uid*] [-g *gid*] [-m *mask*] special node

DESCRIPTION
The **mount_ntfs** command attaches the NTFS filesystem residing on the device special to the global filesystem namespace at the location indicated by node. Both *special* and *node* are converted to absolute paths before use. This command is normally executed by mount(8) at boot time, but can be used by any user to mount an NTFS file system on any directory that they own (provided, of course, that they have appropriate access to the device that contains the file system).

The supported NTFS versions include both NTFS4, as used by Microsoft Windows NT 4.0, and NTFS5, as used by Microsoft Windows 2000 and XP.

The options are as follows:

-a   Force behaviour to return MS-DOS 8.3 names also on **readdir**().

-i   Make name lookup case insensitive for all names except POSIX names.

-u *uid*
       Set the owner of the files in the file system to *uid*. The default owner is the owner of the directory on which the file system is being mounted.

-g *gid*
       Set the group of the files in the file system to *gid*. The default group is the group of the directory on which the file system is being mounted.

-m *mask*
       Specify the maximum file permissions for files in the file system.

FEATURES
NTFS file attributes
NTFS file attributes can be accessed in the following way:

```
foo[[:ATTRTYPE]:ATTRNAME]
```

'ATTRTYPE' is one of identifier listed in $AttrDef file of volume. Default is $DATA. 'ATTRNAME' is an attribute name. Default is none.

Examples:

To get volume name (in Unicode):

```
# cat /mnt/\$Volume:\$VOLUME_NAME
```

To read directory raw data:

```
# cat /mnt/foodir:\$INDEX_ROOT:\$I30
```

Limited support for writing
There is limited writing ability for files. Limitations:
- file must be non-resident
- file must *not* contain any holes (uninitialized areas)

- file can't be compressed

Note that it's not currently possible to create or remove files on NTFS filesystems.

Warning: do not mount NTFS filesystems read-write. The write support is not very useful and is not tested well. It's not safe to write to any file on NTFS; you might damage the filesystem. Unless you want to debug NTFS filesystem code, mount the NTFS filesystem read-only.

SEE ALSO

mount(2), unmount(2), fstab(5), disklabel(8), mbrlabel(8), mount(8)

HISTORY

Support for NTFS first appeared in FreeBSD 3.0. It was ported to NetBSD and first appeared in NetBSD 1.5.

AUTHORS

NTFS kernel implementation, **mount_ntfs** and this manual were originally written by Semen Ustimenko ⟨semenu@FreeBSD.org⟩.

The NetBSD port was done by
Christos Zoulas ⟨christos@NetBSD.org⟩ and
Jaromir Dolecek ⟨jdolecek@NetBSD.org⟩.

BUGS

The write support should be enhanced to actually be able to change file size, and to create and remove files and directories. It's not very useful right now.

If the attempt to mount NTFS gives you an error like this:

```
# mount -t ntfs /dev/wd0k /mnt
mount_ntfs: /dev/wd0k on /mnt: Invalid argument
```

make sure that appropriate partition has correct entry in the disk label, particularly that the partition offset is correct. If the NTFS partition is the first partition on the disk, the offset should be '63' on i386 (see disklabel(8)). mbrlabel(8) could help you to set up the disk label correctly.

If the NTFS partition is marked as dynamic under Microsoft Windows XP, it won't be possible to access it under NetBSD anymore.

NAME
mount_null — mount a loopback filesystem sub-tree; demonstrate the use of a null file system layer

SYNOPSIS
mount_null [**-o** *options*] *target mount-point*

DESCRIPTION
The **mount_null** command creates a null layer, duplicating a sub-tree of the file system name space under another part of the global file system namespace. This allows existing files and directories to be accessed using a different pathname.

The primary differences between a virtual copy of the filesystem and a symbolic link are that getcwd(3) functions correctly in the virtual copy, and that other filesystems may be mounted on the virtual copy without affecting the original. A different device number for the virtual copy is returned by stat(2), but in other respects it is indistinguishable from the original.

The **mount_null** filesystem differs from a traditional loopback file system in two respects: it is implemented using a stackable layers technique, and its "null-nodes" stack above all lower-layer vnodes (not just above directory vnodes).

Both *target* and *mount-point* are converted to absolute paths before use.

The options are as follows:

-o Options are specified with a **-o** flag followed by a comma separated string of options. See the mount(8) man page for possible options and their meanings.

The null layer has two purposes. First, it serves as a demonstration of layering by providing a layer which does nothing. Second, the null layer can serve as a prototype layer. Since it provides all necessary layer framework, new file system layers can be created very easily by starting with a null layer.

The remainder of this man page examines the null layer as a basis for constructing new layers.

INSTANTIATING NEW NULL LAYERS
New null layers are created with **mount_null**. **mount_null** takes two arguments, the pathname of the lower vfs (target-pn) and the pathname where the null layer will appear in the namespace (mount-point-pn). After the null layer is put into place, the contents of target-pn subtree will be aliased under mount-point-pn.

OPERATION OF A NULL LAYER
The null layer is the minimum file system layer, simply passing all possible operations to the lower layer for processing there. The majority of its activity centers on the bypass routine, through which nearly all vnode operations pass.

The bypass routine accepts arbitrary vnode operations for handling by the lower layer. It begins by examining vnode operation arguments and replacing any null-nodes by their lower-layer equivalents. It then invokes the operation on the lower layer. Finally, it replaces the null-nodes in the arguments and, if a vnode is returned by the operation, stacks a null-node on top of the returned vnode.

Although bypass handles most operations, *vop_getattr*, *vop_inactive*, *vop_reclaim*, and *vop_print* are not bypassed. *vop_getattr* must change the fsid being returned. *vop_inactive* and vop_reclaim are not bypassed so that they can handle freeing null-layer specific data. *vop_print* is not bypassed to avoid excessive debugging information.

INSTANTIATING VNODE STACKS
Mounting associates the null layer with a lower layer, in effect stacking two VFSes. Vnode stacks are instead created on demand as files are accessed.

The initial mount creates a single vnode stack for the root of the new null layer. All other vnode stacks are created as a result of vnode operations on this or other null vnode stacks.

New vnode stacks come into existence as a result of an operation which returns a vnode. The bypass routine stacks a null-node above the new vnode before returning it to the caller.

For example, imagine mounting a null layer with

```
mount_null /usr/include /dev/layer/null
```
Changing directory to `/dev/layer/null` will assign the root null-node (which was created when the null layer was mounted). Now consider opening `sys`. A vop_lookup would be done on the root null-node. This operation would bypass through to the lower layer which would return a vnode representing the UFS `sys`. null_bypass then builds a null-node aliasing the UFS `sys` and returns this to the caller. Later operations on the null-node `sys` will repeat this process when constructing other vnode stacks.

CREATING OTHER FILE SYSTEM LAYERS

One of the easiest ways to construct new file system layers is to make a copy of the null layer, rename all files and variables, and then begin modifying the copy. `sed`(1) can be used to easily rename all variables.

The umap layer is an example of a layer descended from the null layer.

INVOKING OPERATIONS ON LOWER LAYERS

There are two techniques to invoke operations on a lower layer when the operation cannot be completely bypassed. Each method is appropriate in different situations. In both cases, it is the responsibility of the aliasing layer to make the operation arguments "correct" for the lower layer by mapping any vnode arguments to the lower layer.

The first approach is to call the aliasing layer's bypass routine. This method is most suitable when you wish to invoke the operation currently being handled on the lower layer. It has the advantage that the bypass routine already must do argument mapping. An example of this is *null_getattrs* in the null layer.

A second approach is to directly invoke vnode operations on the lower layer with the *VOP_OPERATIONNAME* interface. The advantage of this method is that it is easy to invoke arbitrary operations on the lower layer. The disadvantage is that vnode arguments must be manually mapped.

SEE ALSO

mount(8)

UCLA Technical Report CSD-910056, *Stackable Layers: an Architecture for File System Development*.

HISTORY

The **mount_null** utility first appeared in 4.4 BSD.

NAME

mount_overlay — mount an overlay filesystem; demonstrate the use of an overlay file system layer

SYNOPSIS

mount_overlay [**-o** *options*] */overlay mount-point*

DESCRIPTION

The **mount_overlay** command creates an overlay layer, interposing the overlay filesystem between the over-mounted file store and future pathname lookups.

A different device number for the virtual copy is returned by stat(2), but in other respects it is indistinguishable from the original.

The **mount_overlay** filesystem differs from the null filesystem in that the **mount_overlay** filesystem does not replicate the sub-tree, it places itself between the sub-tree and all future access.

The overlay layer has two purposes. First, it serves as a demonstration of layering by providing a layer which does nothing other than insert itself over the over-mounted file system. Second, the overlay layer can serve as a prototype layer. Since it provides all necessary layer framework, new file system layers which need to block access to the overlayed file system can be created very easily by starting with an overlay layer.

The internal operation of the overlay layer is identical to that of the null layer. See its documentation for details.

SEE ALSO

mount(8), mount_null(8)

UCLA Technical Report CSD-910056, *Stackable Layers: an Architecture for File System Development*.

HISTORY

The **mount_overlay** utility first appeared in NetBSD 1.5.

NAME

mount_portal — mount the portal daemon

SYNOPSIS

mount_portal [**-o** *options*] */etc/portal.conf mount_point*

DESCRIPTION

The **mount_portal** command attaches an instance of the portal daemon to the global filesystem namespace. The conventional mount point is /p. The directory specified by *mount_point* is converted to an absolute path before use. This command is normally executed by mount(8) at boot time.

The options are as follows:

-o   Options are specified with a **-o** flag followed by a comma separated string of options. See the mount(8) man page for possible options and their meanings.

The portal daemon provides an *open* service. Objects opened under the portal mount point are dynamically created by the portal daemon according to rules specified in the named configuration file. Using this mechanism allows descriptors such as sockets to be made available in the filesystem namespace.

The portal daemon works by being passed the full pathname of the object being opened. The daemon creates an appropriate descriptor according to the rules in the configuration file, and then passes the descriptor back to the calling process as the result of the open system call.

NAMESPACE

By convention, the portal daemon divides the namespace into sub-namespaces, each of which handles objects of a particular type.

Currently, four sub-namespaces are implemented: tcp, fs, rfilter and wfilter. The tcp namespace takes a hostname and a port (slash separated) and creates an open TCP/IP connection. The fs namespace opens the named file, starting back at the root directory. This can be used to provide a controlled escape path from a chrooted environment.

The rfilter and wfilter namespaces open a pipe to a process, typically a data-filter such as compression or decompression programs. The rfilter namespace opens a read-only pipe, while the wfilter namespace opens a write-only pipe. See the **EXAMPLES** section below for more examples.

CONFIGURATION FILE

The configuration file contains a list of rules. Each rule takes one line and consists of two or more whitespace separated fields. A hash ("#") character causes the remainder of a line to be ignored. Blank lines are ignored.

The first field is a pathname prefix to match against the requested pathname. If a match is found, the second field tells the daemon what type of object to create. Subsequent fields are passed to the creation function.

The rfilter and wfilter namespaces have additional meanings for the remaining fields. The third field specifies a prefix that is to be stripped off of the passed name before passing it on to the pipe program. If the prefix does not match, no stripping is performed. The fourth argument specifies the program to use for the pipe. Any remaining fields are passed to the pipe program. If the string "%s" exists within these remaining fields, it will be replaced by the path after stripping is performed. If there is no field after the program name, "%s" will be assumed, to maintain similarity with the tcp and fs namespaces.

FILES

```
/p/*
```

EXAMPLES

A tutorial and several examples are provided in `/usr/share/examples/mount_portal`. The following is an example configuration file.

```
# @(#)portal.conf      5.1 (Berkeley) 7/13/92
tcp/            tcp tcp/
fs/             file fs/
echo/           rfilter echo/   echo %s
echo_nostrip/   rfilter nostrip echo %s
echo_noslash    rfilter echo_noslash    echo %s
gzcat/          rfilter gzcat/ gzcat %s
gzip/           wfilter gzip/   gzip > %s
gzip9/          wfilter gzip9/  gzip -9 > %s
ftp/            rfilter ftp/    ftp -Vo - %s
ftp://          rfilter nostrip ftp -Vo - %s
http://         rfilter nostrip ftp -Vo - %s
bzcat/          rfilter bzcat/  bzcat %s
nroff/          rfilter nroff/  nroff -man %s
```

As is true with many other filesystems, a weird sense of humor is handy.

Notice that after the keynames, like nroff/ and bzcat/, we typically use another slash. In reality, the **mount_portal** process changes directory to /, which makes the subsequent slash unnecessary. However, the extra slash provides a visual hint that we are not operating on an ordinary file. An alternative would be to change the configuration file to something like:

```
nroff% rfilter nroff% nroff -man
```

One might then use

```
less /p/nroff%/usr/share/man/man8/mount_portal.8
```

SEE ALSO

mount(2), unmount(2), fstab(5), mount(8)

HISTORY

The **mount_portal** utility first appeared in 4.4 BSD. The rfilter and wfilter capabilities first appeared in NetBSD 1.5. The portal kernel driver was removed and **mount_portal** was converted to use puffs(3) in NetBSD 6.0.

BUGS

This filesystem may not be NFS-exported.

NAME
   mount_procfs — mount the process file system

SYNOPSIS
   mount_procfs [**-o** *options*] /proc mount_point

DESCRIPTION
   The **mount_procfs** command attaches an instance of the process namespace to the global filesystem
   namespace. The conventional mount point is /proc. The directory specified by *mount_point* is converted to an absolute path before use. This command is normally executed by mount(8) at boot time.

   The options are as follows:

   -o nolinux
            Do not support nodes which are not part of the original procfs implementation but have been added
            for compatibility with the Linux procfs namespace. See **FILES** for more information.

   The root of the process filesystem contains an entry for each active process. These processes are visible as a
   directory whose name is the process' pid. In addition, the special entries curproc and self reference the
   current process. The self symlink appears for compatibility with the Linux procfs implementation.

   Each directory contains several files.

   cmdline
            This file is readonly and returns null-terminated strings corresponding to the process' command
            line arguments. For a system or zombie process, this file contains only a string with the name of
            the process.

   ctl   a writeonly file which supports a variety of control operations. Control commands are written as
            strings to the ctl file. The control commands are:
            attach   stops the target process and arranges for the sending process to become the debug con-
                     trol process.
            detach   continue execution of the target process and remove it from control by the debug
                     process.
            run   continue running the target process until a signal is delivered, a breakpoint is hit, or the
                     target process exits.
            step   single step the target process, with no signal delivery.
            wait   wait for the target process to stop. The target process must be stopped before any of the
                     run, step, or signal commands are allowed.

            The string can also be the name of a signal, lower case and without the SIG prefix, in which case
            that signal is delivered to the process (see sigaction(2)).

   cwd   A symbolic link that points to the current working directory of the process. If the target process's
            current working directory is not available or is not at or below the current process's root directory,
            this link will point to "/".

   fd/#   File descriptors which can be accessed through the file system. See fd(4) for more information.

   file   A reference to the vnode from which the process text was read. This can be used to gain access to
            the process' symbol table, or to start another copy of the process.

   map   A map of the process' virtual memory.

   maps   A map of the process' virtual memory in a form like the proc filesystem as implemented in Linux.
            Note that the paths corresponding to file backed mappings will not be present unless the kernel was
            built with the NAMECACHE_ENTER_REVERSE option.

mem   The complete virtual memory image of the process. Only those addresses which exist in the process can be accessed. Writes to this file modify the process. Writes to the text segment normally remain private to the process, since the text segment is mapped with MAP_PRIVATE; however, this is not guaranteed.

note   Not implemented.

notepg Not implemented.

regs   Allows read and write access to the process' register set. This file contains a binary data structure struct regs defined in <machine/reg.h>. regs can only be written when the process is stopped.

fpregs The floating point registers as defined by struct fpregs in <machine/reg.h>. fpregs is only implemented on machines which have distinct general purpose and floating point register sets.

root   A symbolic link that points to the root directory of the process. If the target process's root directory is not available or is not at or below the current process's root directory, this link will point to "/".

status The process status. This file is readonly and returns a single line containing multiple space-separated fields as follows:

- command name
- process id
- parent process id
- process group id
- session id
- $major, minor$ of the controlling terminal, or $-1, -1$ if there is no controlling terminal.
- a list of process flags: ctty if there is a controlling terminal, sldr if the process is a session leader, noflags if neither of the other two flags are set.
- the process start time in seconds and microseconds, comma separated.
- the user time in seconds and microseconds, comma separated.
- the system time in seconds and microseconds, comma separated.
- the wait channel message
- the process credentials consisting of the effective user id and the list of groups (whose first member is the effective group id) all comma separated.

In a normal debugging environment, where the target is fork/exec'd by the debugger, the debugger should fork and the child should stop itself (with a self-inflicted SIGSTOP for example). The parent should issue a wait and then an attach command via the appropriate ctl file. The child process will receive a SIGTRAP immediately after the call to exec (see execve(2)).

FILES
```
/proc/#
/proc/#/cmdline
/proc/#/ctl
/proc/#/cwd
/proc/#/exe
/proc/#/file
/proc/#/fpregs
/proc/#/map
```

```
/proc/#/maps
/proc/#/mem
/proc/#/note
/proc/#/notepg
/proc/#/regs
/proc/#/root
/proc/#/status
/proc/curproc
/proc/self
```

If the **linux** mount option is used, the following files are also available:

```
/proc/#/stat
/proc/cpuinfo
/proc/devices
/proc/meminfo
/proc/mounts
/proc/uptime
```

SEE ALSO

mount(2), sigaction(2), unmount(2)

HISTORY

The **mount_procfs** utility first appeared in 4.4 BSD.

BUGS

This filesystem may not be NFS-exported since most of the functionality of procfs requires that state be maintained.

NAME
    mount_psshfs — sshfs implementation for puffs

SYNOPSIS
    mount_psshfs [*options*] *user@host* [*:path*] *mount_point*

DESCRIPTION
The **mount_psshfs** utility can be used to mount a file system using the ssh sftp subprotocol, making a remote directory hierarchy appear in the local directory tree. This functionality is commonly known as *sshfs*.

The mandatory parameters are the target host name and local mount point. The target host parameter can optionally contain a username whose credentials will be used by the remote sshd, and a relative or absolute path for the remote mount point's root. If no user is given, the credentials of the user issuing the mount command are used. If no path is given, the user's home directory on the remote machine will be used.

The following command line options are available:

-c *nconnect*
> Opens *nconnect* connections to the server. Currently, the value has to be 1 or 2. If 2 is specified, a second connection is opened for the reading and writing of data, while directory operations are performed on their own connection. This can greatly increase directory operation performance (ls, mkdir, etc.) if **mount_psshfs** completely saturates the available bandwidth by doing bulk data copying. The default is 1.

-e
> Makes the mounted file system NFS exportable. If this option is used, it is very important to understand that **mount_psshfs** can not provide complete support for NFS due to the limitations in the backend. Files are valid only for the time that **mount_psshfs** is running and in the event of e.g. a server crash, all client retries to access files will fail.

-F *configfile*
> Pass a configuration file to ssh(1). This will make it ignore the system-wide /etc/ssh/ssh_config configuration file and use configfile instead of ~/.ssh/config.

-g *manglegid*
> Converts remote *manglegid* to the effective gid of the file server and vice versa. See **-u**.

-o *[no]option*
> This flag can be used to give standard mount options and options to puffs.

-O *sshopt=value*
> Pass an option to ssh(1), for example **-O** *Port=22*. For a list of valid options, see ssh_config(5).

-p
> Preserve connection. This option makes **mount_psshfs** to try to reconnect to the server if the connection fails. The option is very experimental and does not preserve open files or retry current requests and should generally only be used if the trade-offs are well understood.

-r *max_reads*
> Limits maximum outstanding read requests for each node to *max_reads*. This can be used to improve interactive performance on low-bandwidth links when also performing bulk data reads.

-s
> This flag can be used to make the program stay on top. The default is to detach from the terminal and run in the background.

-t *timeout*
> By default **mount_psshfs** caches directory contents and node attributes for 30 seconds before re-fetching from the server to check if anything has changed on the server. This option is used to adjust the timeout period to *timeout* seconds. A value 0 means the cache is never valid and −1 means it is

valid indefinitely. It is possible to force a re-read regardless of timeout status by sending SIGHUP to the **mount_psshfs** process.

Note: the file system will still free nodes when requested by the kernel and will lose all cached information in doing so. How frequently this happens depends on system activity and the total number of available vnodes in the system (kern.maxvnodes).

−u *mangleuid*

Converts remote *mangleuid* to the effective uid of the file server and vice versa. This is a simple special case of the functionality of mount_umap(8). For example: you mount remote me@darkmoon as the local user "me". If the uid of "me" on the local system is 101 and on darkmoon it is 202, you would use **−u** *202* to see files owned by 202 on darkmoon as owned by 101 when browsing the mount point. Apart from the cosmetic effect, this makes things like "chown me file" work. See **−g**.

EXAMPLES

The following example illustrates how to mount the directory */usr* on server *bigiron* as user *abc* on local directory */mnt* with ssh transport compression enabled:

```
mount_psshfs -O Compression=yes abc@bigiron:/usr /mnt
```

It is possible to use fstab(5) for psshfs mounts, with SSH public key authentication:

```
abc@bigiron:/usr                    /mnt                    psshfs
rw,noauto,-O=BatchMode=yes,-O=IdentityFile=/root/.ssh/id_rsa,-t=-1
```

SEE ALSO

sftp(1), puffs(3), puffs(4), fstab(5), ssh_config(5), mount(8), sshd(8)

HISTORY

The **mount_psshfs** utility first appeared in NetBSD 5.0. It was inspired by FUSE sshfs.

CAVEATS

Permissions are not handled. Do not expect the file system to behave except for a single user.

Depending on if the server supports the sftp(1) stavfs protocol extension, free disk space may be displayed for the mount by df(1). This information reflects the status at the server's mountpoint and may differ for subdiretories under the mount root.

NAME
    mount_ptyfs — mount the /dev/pts file system

SYNOPSIS
    mount_ptyfs [**-c**] [**-g** *group*|*gid*] [**-m** *mode*] [**-o** *options*] *ptyfs mount_point*

DESCRIPTION
    The **mount_ptyfs** command attaches an instance of the pseudo-terminal device filesystem to the global filesystem namespace. The conventional mount point is /dev/pts. The directory specified by *mount_point* is converted to an absolute path before use. This command is normally executed by mount(8) at boot time.

    The filesystem contains pseudo-terminal slave device nodes which are allocated dynamically via ptm(4), or they are already open via traditional BSD style ptys.

    The options are as follows:

    -c   Allows *ptyfs* to be mounted inside a chrooted environment.

    -g *group*|*gid*
            Specify the group ownership of the slave pseudo-tty.

    -m *mode*
            Specify the default *mode* of the slave pseudo-tty.

    -o   Options are specified with a **-o** flag followed by a comma separated string of options.

            mount_ptyfs specific options are chroot which corresponds to **-c**, group which corresponds to **-g**, and mode which corresponds to **-m**. See the mount(8) man page for possible options and their meanings.

FILES
   / n The nth pseudo-terminal device in use.

SEE ALSO
    mount(2), unmount(2), ptm(4), fstab(5), mount(8)

HISTORY
    The **mount_ptyfs** utility first appeared in NetBSD 3.0.

BUGS
    This filesystem may not be NFS-exported. This filesystem is experimental.

NAME

mount_puffs — print arguments to puffs mounts

SYNOPSIS

mount_puffs -o *getargs puffs mount_point*

DESCRIPTION

The **mount_puffs** program prints the kernel arguments for a puffs mount. It is typically executed by **mount -vv**.

SEE ALSO

puffs(4), mount(8)

HISTORY

The **mount_puffs** utility first appeared in NetBSD 6.0.

NAME
mount_smbfs — mount a shared resource from an SMB/CIFS file server

SYNOPSIS
mount_smbfs [-E cs1:cs2] [-I host] [-L locale] [-M crights:srights] [-N]
            [-O cowner:cgroup/sowner:sgroup] [-R retrycount] [-T timeout]
            [-W workgroup] [-c case] [-d mode] [-f mode] [-g gid] [-n opt]
            [-u uid] //user@server/share node

DESCRIPTION
The **mount_smbfs** command mounts a share from a remote server using SMB/CIFS protocol.

The options are as follows:

-E cs1:cs2
> Specifies local (cs1) and server's (cs2) character sets.

-I host
> Do not use NetBIOS name resolver and connect directly to host, which can be either a valid DNS name or an IP address.

-L locale
> Use locale for lower/upper case conversion routines. Set the locale for case conversion. By default, **mount_smbfs** tries to use an environment variable LC_* to determine it.

-M crights:srights
> Assign access rights to the newly created connection.

-N
> Do not ask for a password. At run time, **mount_smbfs** reads the ~/.nsmbrc file for additional configuration parameters and a password. If no password is found, **mount_smbfs** prompts for it.

-O cowner:cgroup/sowner:sgroup
> Assign owner/group attributes to the newly created connection.

-R retrycount
> How many retries should be done before the SMB requester decides to drop the connection.

-T timeout
> Timeout in seconds for each request.

-W workgroup
> This option specifies the workgroup to be used in the authentication request.

-c case
> Set a case option which affects name representation. case can be one of the following:

> *Value Meaning*

> l   All existing file names are converted to lower case. Newly created file gets a lower case.

> u   All existing file names are converted to upper case. Newly created file gets an upper case.

-f mode, -d mode
> Specify permissions that should be assigned to files and directories. The values must be specified as octal numbers. Default value for the file mode is taken from mount point, default value for the directory mode adds execute permission where the file mode gives read permission.

> Note that these permissions can differ from the rights granted by SMB server.

-u *uid*, **-g** *gid*
> User ID and group ID assigned to files. The default are owner and group IDs from the directory where the volume is mounted.

//user@server/share
> The **mount_smbfs** command will use *server* as the NetBIOS name of remote computer, *user* as the remote user name and *share* as the resource name on a remote server. If your connections are refused, try using the **-I** option and use a server name of '*SMBSERVER'.

node   Path to mount point.

FILES
`/etc/nsmb.conf`   System wide parameters for smbfs mounts.
`~/.nsmbrc`   Keeps static parameters for connections and other information. See `/usr/share/examples/smbfs/dot.nsmbrc` for details.

EXAMPLES
The following example illustrates how to connect to SMB server *SAMBA* as user *GUEST*, and mount shares *PUBLIC* and *TMP*:

```
mount_smbfs -I samba.mydomain.com //guest@samba/public /smb/public
mount_smbfs -I 192.168.20.3 -E koi8-r:cp866 //guest@samba/tmp /smb/tmp
```

If you keep on getting "Connection reset by peer" errors, try:

```
mount_smbfs -N -I 10.0.0.4 //'*SMBSERVER'/tmp /smb/tmp
```

It is possible to use `fstab`(5) for smbfs mounts:

```
//guest@samba/public    /smb/public    smbfs   rw,noauto 0    0
```

SEE ALSO
mount(8)

HISTORY
Support for SMBFS first appeared in FreeBSD 4.4. It has been ported to NetBSD and first appeared in NetBSD 2.0.

AUTHORS
Boris Popov ⟨bp@butya.kz⟩, ⟨bp@FreeBSD.org⟩. NetBSD port done by
Matt Debergalis ⟨deberg@NetBSD.org⟩, and
Jaromir Dolecek ⟨jdolecek@NetBSD.org⟩.

NAME

mount_sysctlfs — mount sysctl namespace as a directory hierarchy

SYNOPSIS

mount_sysctlfs [**-r**] [**-o** *mntopts*] *sysctlfs mount_point*

DESCRIPTION

The **mount_sysctlfs** program provides the sysctl(8) hierarchy through the file system namespace. It is possible to browse the tree, query node values and modify them. By default, the node contents are interpreted as ASCII. If the **-r** flag is given, the server uses raw mode and displays node contents as they are received from the kernel (binary).

SEE ALSO

puffs(3), puffs(4), mount(8), sysctl(8)

HISTORY

The **mount_sysctlfs** utility first appeared in NetBSD 5.0.

CAVEATS

Raw mode [**-r**] does not currently support node modification.

NAME

mount_sysvbfs — mount a System V Boot File System

SYNOPSIS

mount_sysvbfs [**-o** *options*] *special node*

DESCRIPTION

The **mount_sysvbfs** command attaches the System V Boot File System on the *special* device on to the file system tree at point *node*. Both *special* and *node* are converted to absolute paths before use.

This command is normally executed by mount(8) at boot time. The options are as follows:

-o   Options are specified with a **-o** flag followed by a comma separated string of options. See the mount(8) man page for possible options and their meanings.

SEE ALSO

mount(2), unmount(2), fstab(5), mount(8)

HISTORY

A **mount_sysvbfs** command first appeared in NetBSD 4.0.

BUGS

The sysvbfs support is still experimental and there are few sanity checks, so it is possible for a corrupted file system to cause a crash.

NAME
   mount_tmpfs — mount an efficient memory file system

SYNOPSIS
   mount_tmpfs [**-g** *group*] [**-m** *mode*] [**-n** *nodes*] [**-o** *options*] [**-s** *size*] [**-u** *user*]
         tmpfs mount_point

DESCRIPTION
   The **mount_tmpfs** command attaches an instance of the efficient memory file system to the global file system namespace. The *tmpfs* parameter only exists for compatibility with the other mount commands and is ignored. The directory specified by *mount_point* is converted to an absolute path before use and its attributes (owner, group and mode) are inherited unless explicitly overriden by the options described below.

   The following options are supported:

   -g *group*   Specifies the group name or GID of the root inode of the file system. Defaults to the mount point's GID.

   -m *mode*   Specifies the mode (in octal notation) of the root inode of the file system. Defaults to the mount point's mode.

   -n *nodes*   Specifies the maximum number of nodes available to the file system. If not specified, the file system chooses a reasonable maximum given its size at mount time, which can be limited with **-s**.

   -o *options*
                Options are specified with a **-o** flag followed by a comma-separated string of options. See the mount(8) man page for possible options and their meanings.

   -s *size*   Specifies the total file system size in bytes. If zero is given (the default), the available amount of memory (including main memory and swap space) will be used. Note that four megabytes are always reserved for the system and cannot be assigned to the file system.

   -u *user*   Specifies the user name or UID of the root inode of the file system. Defaults to the mount point's UID.

   Every option that accepts a numerical value as its argument can take a trailing 'b' to indicate bytes (the default), a trailing 'k' to indicate kilobytes, a trailing 'M' to indicate megabytes or a trailing 'G' to indicate gigabytes. Note that both lowercase and uppercase forms of these letters are allowed.

EXAMPLES
   The following command mounts a tmpfs instance over the /tmp directory, inheriting its owner, group and mode settings:

   mount -t tmpfs tmpfs /tmp

   The following command mounts a tmpfs instance over the /mnt directory, setting a 20 megabytes limit in space, owned by the 'joe' user and belonging to the 'users' group, with a restricted 0700 mode:

   mount -t tmpfs -o -s20M -o -ujoe -o -gusers -o -m0700 tmpfs /mnt

   See /usr/share/examples/fstab/fstab.ramdisk for some examples on how to add tmpfs entries to /etc/fstab.

SEE ALSO
   fstab(5), mount(8)

HISTORY

The **mount_tmpfs** utility first appeared in NetBSD 4.0.

BUGS

File system meta-data is not pageable. If there is not enough main memory to hold this information, the system may become unstable or very unresponsive because it will not be able to allocate required memory. A malicious user could trigger this condition if he could create lots of files inside a size-unbounded tmpfs file system. Limiting the number of nodes per file system (**−n**) will prevent this; the default value for this setting is also often adjusted to an adequate value to resolve this.

NAME

mount_udf — mount an UDF file system

SYNOPSIS

mount_udf [**-c**] [**-g** *gid*] [**-o** *options*] [**-t** *gmtoff*] [**-s** *session*] [**-u** *uid*] *special node*

DESCRIPTION

The **mount_udf** command attaches the UDF file system residing on the specified *special* device node on the location indicated with *node*.

Anonymous files stored on the UDF disc will be represented and saved in the specified uid:gid pair. If unspecified, it will default to nobody:nobody. Both uid and gid can be either specified with their names as with their numerical equivalents.

-c   Close the session after unmount creating remountable snapshots. Closing a session also allows -ROM devices to read the disc created. Note that this option only makes sense when mounting sequential recordable media like CD-R and DVD*R.

-g *gid*   Set the group of anonymous files on the file system. The default group is the nobody group.

-o *options*
                      Use the specified mount *options* as specified in mount(8).

-s *session*
                      Select the session *session* to be mounted instead of the default last one. Implements read-only snapshots on sequential media. Positive *session* values indicate an absolute session number. Negative *session* values are relative to the last session found on the disc. Note that this option only makes sense when mounting sequential recordable media like CD-R and DVD*R.

-t *gmtoff*   Set the time zone offset (in seconds) from UTC to *gmtoff*, with positive values indicating east of the Prime Meridian. If not set, the user's current time zone will be used.

-u *uid*   Set the owner of anonymous files on the file system. The default owner is the user nobody.

SEE ALSO

mount(2), vnd(4), fstab(5), mount(8), umount(8), vnconfig(8)

NOTES

UDF is a file system defined by the OSTA standardization group and is tailored for data interchange on optical discs (like CDs and DVDs) between different operating systems. Its also more and more common on other media like Compact Flash (CF) cards.

Read and write access is supported for all media types that CD/DVD type drives can recognise including DVD-RAM. BluRay support is preliminary; read-only access should work fine but write support is experimental.

Implemented and tested media types are CD-ROM, CD-R, CD-RW, CD-MRW, DVD-ROM, DVD*R, DVD*RW, DVD+MRW, DVD-RAM but the same code can also read HD-DVD and BluRay discs. Discs created and written by UDFclient, Nero's InCD, and Roxio's DirectCD/Drag2Disc can be read without problems. Both open and closed media are supported so there is no need to close discs or sessions.

All current UDF versions up to version 2.60 are supported.

Hard disk partitions and vnd(4) devices may also be mounted. Note when mounting a vnd(4) device it might be necessary to specify the file image sector size in the geomspec when creating the vnd(4) device or the disc sector size will be used.

BUGS

Write support for UDF version 2.50 is not completely mature and UDF version 2.01 should be used if possible; this is also the default format.

Due to lack of test media and recording devices, BluRay support and in particular BluRay-R is still preliminary as of writing.

NAME
    mount_umap — user and group ID remapping file system layer

SYNOPSIS
    mount_umap [**-o** *options*] **-g** *gid-mapfile* **-u** *uid-mapfile target mount-point*

DESCRIPTION
    The **mount_umap** command is used to mount a sub-tree of an existing file system that uses a different set of uids and gids than the local system. Such a file system could be mounted from a remote site via NFS, a local file system on removable media brought from some foreign location that uses a different user/group database, or could be a local file system for another operating system which does not support Unix-style user/group IDs, or which uses a different numbering scheme.

    Both *target* and *mount-point* are converted to absolute paths before use.

    The options are as follows:

-g *gid-mapfile*
        Use the group ID mapping specified in *gid-mapfile*. This flag is required.

-o   Options are specified with a **-o** flag followed by a comma separated string of options. See the mount(8) man page for possible options and their meanings.

-u *uid-mapfile*
        Use the user ID mapping specified in *uid-mapfile*. This flag is required.

    The **mount_umap** command uses a set of files provided by the user to make correspondences between uids and gids in the sub-tree's original environment and some other set of ids in the local environment. For instance, user smith might have uid 1000 in the original environment, while having uid 2000 in the local environment. The **mount_umap** command allows the subtree from smith's original environment to be mapped in such a way that all files with owning uid 1000 look like they are actually owned by uid 2000.

    target should be the current location of the sub-tree in the local system's name space. *mount-point* should be a directory where the mapped subtree is to be placed. *uid-mapfile* and *gid-mapfile* describe the mappings to be made between identifiers.

    The format of the user and group ID mapping files is very simple. The first line of the file is the total number of mappings present in the file. The remaining lines each consist of two numbers: the ID in the mapped sub-tree and the ID in the original subtree.

    For example, to map uid 1000 in the original subtree to uid 2000 in the mapped subtree:

       1
       2000 1000

    For user IDs in the original subtree for which no mapping exists, the user ID will be mapped to the user "nobody". For group IDs in the original subtree for which no mapping exists, the group ID will be mapped to the group "nobody".

    There is a limit of 64 user ID mappings and 16 group ID mappings.

    The mapfiles can be located anywhere in the file hierarchy, but they must be owned by root, and they must be writable only by root. **mount_umap** will refuse to map the sub-tree if the ownership or permissions on these files are improper. It will also report an error if the count of mappings in the first line of the map files is not correct.

SEE ALSO
> mount(8), mount_null(8)

HISTORY
> The **mount_umap** utility first appeared in 4.4 BSD.

BUGS
> The implementation is not very sophisticated.

NAME
mount_union — mount union filesystems

SYNOPSIS
mount_union [-b] [-o *options*] *directory uniondir*

DESCRIPTION
The **mount_union** command attaches *directory* above *uniondir* in such a way that the contents of both directory trees remain visible. By default, *directory* becomes the *upper* layer and *uniondir* becomes the *lower* layer.

Both *directory* and *uniondir* are converted to absolute paths before use.

The options are as follows:

-b   Invert the default position, so that *directory* becomes the lower layer and *uniondir* becomes the upper layer. However, *uniondir* remains the mount point.

-o   Options are specified with a -o flag followed by a comma separated string of options. See the mount(8) man page for possible options and their meanings.

Filenames are looked up in the upper layer and then in the lower layer. If a directory is found in the lower layer, and there is no entry in the upper layer, then a *shadow* directory will be created in the upper layer. It will be owned by the user who originally did the union mount, with mode "rwxrwxrwx" (0777) modified by the umask in effect at that time.

If a file exists in the upper layer then there is no way to access a file with the same name in the lower layer. If necessary, a combination of loopback and union mounts can be made which will still allow the lower files to be accessed by a different pathname.

Except in the case of a directory, access to an object is granted via the normal filesystem access checks. For directories, the current user must have access to both the upper and lower directories (should they both exist).

Requests to create or modify objects in *uniondir* are passed to the upper layer with the exception of a few special cases. An attempt to open for writing a file which exists in the lower layer causes a copy of the *entire* file to be made to the upper layer, and then for the upper layer copy to be opened. Similarly, an attempt to truncate a lower layer file to zero length causes an empty file to be created in the upper layer. Any other operation which would ultimately require modification to the lower layer fails with EROFS.

The union filesystem manipulates the namespace, rather than individual filesystems. The union operation applies recursively down the directory tree now rooted at *uniondir*. Thus any filesystems which are mounted under *uniondir* will take part in the union operation. This differs from the *union* option to mount(8) which only applies the union operation to the mount point itself, and then only for lookups.

EXAMPLES
The commands

```
mount -t cd9660 -o ro /dev/cd0a /usr/src
mount -t union /var/obj /usr/src
```

mount the CD-ROM drive /dev/cd0a on /usr/src and then attaches /var/obj on top. For most purposes the effect of this is to make the source tree appear writable even though it is stored on a CD-ROM.

The command

```
mount -t union -o -b /sys $HOME/sys
```

attaches the system source tree below the `sys` directory in the user's home directory. This allows individual users to make private changes to the source, and build new kernels, without those changes becoming visible to other users. Note that the files in the lower layer remain accessible via `/sys`.

SEE ALSO

`intro`(2), `mount`(2), `unmount`(2), `fstab`(5), `fsck_ffs`(8), `mount`(8), `mount_null`(8), `sysctl`(8)

HISTORY

The **mount_union** command first appeared in 4.4 BSD.

BUGS

Without whiteout support from the filesystem backing the upper layer, there is no way that delete and rename operations on lower layer objects can be done. An attempt to mount a union directory under one which does not have whiteout support will return `EOPNOTSUPP` ("Operation not supported"). Whiteout support can be added to an existing FFS filesystem by using the **-c** option of `fsck_ffs`(8).

Running `find`(1) over a union tree has the side-effect of creating a tree of shadow directories in the upper layer.

NAME
mountd — service remote NFS mount requests

SYNOPSIS
mountd [**-dNn**] [**-P** *policy*] [**-p** *port*] [*exportsfile*]

DESCRIPTION
mountd is the server for NFS mount requests from other client machines. **mountd** listens for service requests at the port indicated in the NFS server specification; see *Network File System Protocol Specification*, RFC 1094, Appendix A and *NFS: Network File System Version 3 Protocol Specification*, Appendix I.

Options and operands available for **mountd**:

-d   Enable debugging mode. **mountd** will not detach from the controlling terminal and will print debugging messages to stderr.

-N   Do not require privileged ports for mount or NFS RPC calls. This option is equivalent to specifying "-noresvport -noresvmnt" on every export. See exports(5) for more information.

-n   This flag used to indicate that clients were required to make requests from reserved ports, but it is now no longer functional. It is only provided for backwards compatibility. Requests are checked for reserved ports on a per-export basis, see exports(5).

-P *policy*
> IPsec *policy* string, as described in ipsec_set_policy(3). Multiple IPsec policy strings may be specified by using a semicolon as a separator. If conflicting policy strings are found in a single line, the last string will take effect. If an invalid IPsec policy string is used **mountd** logs an error message and terminates itself.

-p *port*
> Force **mountd** to bind to the given port. If this option is not given, **mountd** may bind to every anonymous port (in the range 600-1023) which causes trouble when trying to use NFS through a firewall.

exportsfile
> The *exportsfile* argument specifies an alternative location for the exports file.

When **mountd** is started, it loads the export host addresses and options into the kernel using the nfssvc(2) system call. After changing the exports file, a hangup signal should be sent to the **mountd** daemon to get it to reload the export information. After sending the SIGHUP (kill –s HUP `cat /var/run/mountd.pid`), check the syslog output to see if **mountd** logged any parsing errors in the exports file.

After receiving SIGTERM, **mountd** sends a broadcast request to remove the mount list from all the clients. This can take a long time, since the broadcast request waits for each client to respond.

FILES
/etc/exports	the list of exported filesystems
/var/run/mountd.pid	the pid of the currently running **mountd**
/var/db/mountdtab	the list of remotely mounted filesystems

SEE ALSO
nfsstat(1), nfssvc(2), exports(5), nfsd(8), rpcbind(8), showmount(8)

HISTORY
The **mountd** utility first appeared in 4.4BSD.

NAME
moused — pass mouse data to mouse mux

SYNOPSIS
moused [**-DPRacdfs**] [**-I** *file*] [**-F** *rate*] [**-r** *resolution*] [**-S** *baudrate*]
        [**-W** *devicename*] [**-a** *X*[,*Y*]] [**-m** *N=M*] [**-w** *N*] [**-z** *target*] [**-t** *mousetype*]
        [**-3** [**-E** *timeout*]] **-p** *port*

moused [**-Pd**] **-p** *port* **-i** *info*

DESCRIPTION
The mouse daemon **moused** and the console driver work together to support access to serial mice from user programs. They virtualize the mouse and provide user programs with mouse data in the standard format (see wsmouse(4)).

moused listens to the specified port for mouse data, interprets and then passes it via ioctls to the console driver. It reports translation movement, button press/release events and movement of the roller or the wheel if available. The roller/wheel movement is reported as "Z" axis movement.

If **moused** receives the signal SIGHUP, it will reopen the mouse port and reinitializes itself. Useful if the mouse is attached/detached while the system is suspended.

The following options are available:

-3   Emulate the third (middle) button for 2-button mice. It is emulated by pressing the left and right physical buttons simultaneously.

-D   Lower DTR on the serial port. This option is valid only if *mousesystems* is selected as the protocol type. The DTR line may need to be dropped for a 3-button mouse to operate in the *mousesystems* mode.

-E *timeout*
      When the third button emulation is enabled (see above), **moused** waits *timeout* milliseconds at most before deciding whether two buttons are being pressed simultaneously. The default timeout is 100 milliseconds.

-F *rate*
      Set the report rate (reports per second) of the device if supported.

-I *file*
      Write the process id of **moused** in the specified file. Without this option, the process id will be stored in /var/run/moused.pid.

-P   Do not start the Plug and Play COM device enumeration procedure when identifying the serial mouse. If this option is given together with the **-i** option, **moused** will not be able to print useful information for the serial mouse.

-R   Lower RTS on the serial port. This option is valid only if *mousesystems* is selected as the protocol type by the **-t** option below. It is often used with the **-D** option above. Both RTS and DTR lines may need to be dropped for a 3-button mouse to operate in the *mousesystems* mode.

-S *baudrate*
      Select the baudrate for the serial port (1200 to 9600). Not all serial mice support this option.

-W *devicename*
      Select the wsmux(4) control device. The default is /dev/wsmuxctl0.

-a *X*[,*Y*]

Accelerate or decelerate the mouse input. This is a linear acceleration only. Values less than 1.0 slow down movement, values greater than 1.0 speed it up. Specifying only one value sets the acceleration for both axes.

-c   Some mice report middle button down events as if the left and right buttons are being pressed. This option handles this.

-d   Enable debugging messages.

-f   Do not become a daemon and instead run as a foreground process. Useful for testing and debugging.

-i *info*

Print specified information and quit. Available pieces of information are:

port	Port (device file) name, e.g. /dev/tty00.
if	Interface type: serial, bus, inport or ps/2.
type	Protocol type. It is one of the types listed under the **-t** option below.
model	Mouse model. **moused** may not always be able to identify the model.
all	All of the above items. Print port, interface, type and model in this order in one line.

If **moused** cannot determine the requested information, it prints "unknown" or "generic".

-m *N=M*

Assign the physical button *M* to the logical button *N*. You may specify as many instances of this option as you like. More than one physical button may be assigned to a logical button at the same time. In this case the logical button will be down, if either of the assigned physical buttons is held down. Do not put space around '='.

-p *port*

Use *port* to communicate with the mouse.

-r *resolution*

Set the resolution of the device; in Dots Per Inch, or *low*, *medium-low*, *medium-high* or *high*. This option may not be supported by all the device.

-s   Select a baudrate of 9600 for the serial line. Not all serial mice support this option.

-t *type*

Specify the protocol type of the mouse attached to the port. You may explicitly specify a type listed below, or use *auto* to let **moused** automatically select an appropriate protocol for the given mouse. If you entirely omit this option on the command line, **-t** *auto* is assumed. Under normal circumstances, you need to use this option only if **moused** is not able to detect the protocol automatically.

Note that if a protocol type is specified with this option, the **-P** option above is implied and Plug and Play COM device enumeration procedure will be disabled.

Valid types for this option are listed below.

For the serial mouse:

microsoft	Microsoft serial mouse protocol. Most 2-button serial mice use this protocol.
intellimouse	Microsoft IntelliMouse protocol. Genius NetMouse, ASCII Mie Mouse, Logitech MouseMan+ and FirstMouse+ use this protocol too. Other mice with a roller/wheel may be compatible with this protocol.

mousesystems	MouseSystems 5-byte protocol. 3-button mice may use this protocol.
mmseries	MM Series mouse protocol.
logitech	Logitech mouse protocol. Note that this is for old Logitech models. *mouseman* or *intellimouse* should be specified for newer models.
mouseman	Logitech MouseMan and TrackMan protocol. Some 3-button mice may be compatible with this protocol. Note that MouseMan+ and FirstMouse+ use *intellimouse* protocol rather than this one.
glidepoint	ALPS GlidePoint protocol.
thinkingmouse	Kensington ThinkingMouse protocol.
mmhitab	Hitachi tablet protocol.
x10mouseremote	X10 MouseRemote.
kidspad	Genius Kidspad and Easypad protocol.
versapad	Interlink VersaPad protocol.

−w *N*   Make the physical button *N* act as the wheel mode button. While this button is pressed, X and Y axis movement is reported to be zero and the Y axis movement is mapped to Z axis. You may further map the Z axis movement to virtual buttons by the **−z** option below.

−z *target*

Map Z axis (roller/wheel) movement to another axis or to virtual buttons. Valid *target* maybe:

x

y   X or Y axis movement will be reported when the Z axis movement is detected.

N   Report down events for the virtual buttons *N* and *N+1* respectively when negative and positive Z axis movement is detected. There do not need to be physical buttons *N* and *N+1*. Note that mapping to logical buttons is carried out after mapping from the Z axis movement to the virtual buttons is done.

N1 N2

Report down events for the virtual buttons *N1* and *N2* respectively when negative and positive Z axis movement is detected.

N1 N2 N3 N4

This is useful for the mouse with two wheels of which the second wheel is used to generate horizontal scroll action, and for the mouse which has a knob or a stick which can detect the horizontal force applied by the user.

The motion of the second wheel will be mapped to the buttons *N3*, for the negative direction, and *N4*, for the positive direction. If the buttons *N3* and *N4* actually exist in this mouse, their actions will not be detected.

Note that horizontal movement or second roller/wheel movement may not always be detected, because there appears to be no accepted standard as to how it is encoded.

Note also that some mice think left is the negative horizontal direction, others may think otherwise. Moreover, there are some mice whose two wheels are both mounted vertically, and the direction of the second vertical wheel does not match the first one's.

Multiple Mice

As many instances of **moused** as the number of mice attached to the system may be run simultaneously; one instance for each serial mouse.

FILES

/dev/wsmuxctl0	default device to control mouse mux
/var/run/moused.pid	process id of the currently running **moused**

EXAMPLES

```
moused -p /dev/tty00 -i type
```

Let **moused** determine the protocol type of the mouse at the serial port /dev/tty00. If successful, **moused** will print the type, otherwise it will say "unknown".

```
moused -p /dev/tty00
```

If **moused** is able to identify the protocol type of the mouse at the specified port automatically, you can start the daemon without the **−t** option and enable the mouse pointer in the text console as above.

```
moused -p /dev/tty01 -t microsoft
```

Start **moused** on the serial port /dev/tty01. The protocol type *microsoft* is explicitly specified by the **−t** option.

```
moused -p /dev/tty01 -m 1=3 -m 3=1
```

Assign the physical button 3 (right button) to the logical button 1 (logical left) and the physical button 1 (left) to the logical button 3 (logical right). This will effectively swap the left and right buttons.

```
moused -p /dev/tty01 -t intellimouse -z 4
```

Report negative Z axis (roller) movement as the button 4 pressed and positive Z axis movement as the button 5 pressed.

The mouse daemon is normally enabled by setting moused=YES in /etc/rc.conf.

SEE ALSO

wsmouse(4), wsmux(4), rc.conf(5), wsmoused(8)

STANDARDS

moused partially supports "Plug and Play External COM Device Specification" in order to support PnP serial mice. However, due to various degrees of conformance to the specification by existing serial mice, it does not strictly follow version 1.0 of the standard. Even with this less strict approach, it may not always determine an appropriate protocol type for the given serial mouse.

HISTORY

The mouse daemon **moused** first appeared in FreeBSD 2.2 and NetBSD 1.6.

AUTHORS

moused was written by Michael Smith ⟨msmith@FreeBSD.org⟩. This manual page was written by Mike Pritchard ⟨mpp@FreeBSD.org⟩. The daemon and manual page have since been updated by Kazutaka Yokota ⟨yokota@FreeBSD.org⟩. The NetBSD port was done by Lennart Augustsson ⟨augustss@NetBSD.org⟩.

BUGS

Many pad devices behave as if the first (left) button were pressed if the user 'taps' the surface of the pad. In contrast, some ALPS GlidePoint and Interlink VersaPad models treat the tapping action as fourth button events. Use the option "-m 1=4" for these models to obtain the same effect as the other pad devices.

NAME
mrinfo – Displays configuration info from a multicast router

SYNOPSIS
/usr/sbin/mrinfo [**–d** *debug_level*] [**–r** *retry_count*] [**–t** *timeout_count*] **multicast_router**

DESCRIPTION
mrinfo attempts to display the configuration information from the multicast router *multicast_router.*

mrinfo uses the ASK_NEIGHBORS IGMP message to the specified multicast router. If this multicast router responds, the version number and a list of their neighboring multicast router addresses is part of that response. If the responding router has a recent multicast version number, then *mrinfo* requests additional information such as metrics, thresholds, and flags from the multicast router. Once the specified multicast router responds, the configuration is displayed to the standard output.

INVOCATION
"–d" option sets the debug level. When the debug level is greater than the default value of 0, addition debugging messages are printed. Regardless of the debug level, an error condition, will always write an error message and will cause *mrinfo* to terminate. Non-zero debug levels have the following effects:

level 1   packet warnings are printed to stderr.

level 2   all level 1 messages plus notifications down networks are printed to stderr.

level 3   all level 2 messages plus notifications of all packet timeouts are printed to stderr.

"–r retry_count" sets the neighbor query retry limit. Default is 3 retry.

"–t timeout_count" sets the number of seconds to wait for a neighbor query reply. Default timeout is 4 seconds.

SAMPLE OUTPUT
mrinfo mbone.phony.dom.net
127.148.176.10 (mbone.phony.dom.net) [version 3.3]:
127.148.176.10 -> 0.0.0.0 (?) [1/1/querier]
127.148.176.10 -> 127.0.8.4 (mbone2.phony.dom.net) [1/45/tunnel]
127.148.176.10 -> 105.1.41.9 (momoney.com) [1/32/tunnel/down]
127.148.176.10 -> 143.192.152.119 (mbone.dipu.edu) [1/32/tunnel]

For each neighbor of the queried multicast router, the IP of the queried router is displayed, followed by the IP and name of the neighbor. In square brackets the metric (cost of connection), the threshold (multicast ttl) is displayed. If the queried multicast router has a newer version number, the type (tunnel, srcrt) and status (disabled, down) of the connection is displayed.

IMPORTANT NOTE
mrinfo must be run as root.

SEE ALSO
mrouted(8), **map-mbone**(8), **mtrace**(8)

AUTHOR
Van Jacobson

NAME

mrouted — IP multicast routing daemon

SYNOPSIS

mrouted [-c *config_file*] [-d *debug_level*] [-p]

DESCRIPTION

mrouted is an implementation of the Distance-Vector Multicast Routing Protocol (DVMRP), an earlier version of which is specified in RFC 1075. It maintains topological knowledge via a distance-vector routing protocol (like RIP, described in RFC 1058), upon which it implements a multicast datagram forwarding algorithm called Reverse Path Multicasting.

mrouted forwards a multicast datagram along a shortest (reverse) path tree rooted at the subnet on which the datagram originates. The multicast delivery tree may be thought of as a broadcast delivery tree that has been pruned back so that it does not extend beyond those subnetworks that have members of the destination group. Hence, datagrams are not forwarded along those branches which have no listeners of the multicast group. The IP time-to-live of a multicast datagram can be used to limit the range of multicast datagrams.

In order to support multicasting among subnets that are separated by (unicast) routers that do not support IP multicasting, mrouted includes support for "tunnels", which are virtual point-to-point links between pairs of mrouted daemons located anywhere in an internet. IP multicast packets are encapsulated for transmission through tunnels, so that they look like normal unicast datagrams to intervening routers and subnets. The encapsulation is added on entry to a tunnel, and stripped off on exit from a tunnel. By default, the packets are encapsulated using the IP-in-IP protocol (IP protocol number 4). Older versions of mrouted tunnel using IP source routing, which puts a heavy load on some types of routers. This version does not support IP source route tunneling.

The tunneling mechanism allows mrouted to establish a virtual internet, for the purpose of multicasting only, which is independent of the physical internet, and which may span multiple Autonomous Systems. This capability is intended for experimental support of internet multicasting only, pending widespread support for multicast routing by the regular (unicast) routers. mrouted suffers from the well-known scaling problems of any distance-vector routing protocol, and does not (yet) support hierarchical multicast routing.

mrouted handles multicast routing only; there may or may not be unicast routing software running on the same machine as mrouted. With the use of tunnels, it is not necessary for mrouted to have access to more than one physical subnet in order to perform multicast forwarding.

INVOCATION

If no -d option is given, or if the debug level is specified as 0, mrouted detaches from the invoking terminal. Otherwise, it remains attached to the invoking terminal and responsive to signals from that terminal. If -d is given with no argument, the debug level defaults to 2. Regardless of the debug level, mrouted always writes warning and error messages to the system log daemon. Non-zero debug levels have the following effects:

    1   all syslog'ed messages are also printed to stderr.
    2   all level 1 messages plus notifications of "significant" events are printed to stderr.
    3   all level 2 messages plus notifications of all packet arrivals and departures are printed to stderr.

Upon startup, mrouted writes its pid to the file /var/run/mrouted.pid.

CONFIGURATION

mrouted automatically configures itself to forward on all multicast-capable interfaces, i.e., interfaces that have the IFF_MULTICAST flag set (excluding the loopback "interface"), and it finds other mrouted directly reachable via those interfaces. To override the default configuration, or to add tunnel links to other

mrouted configuration commands may be placed in /etc/mrouted.conf (or an alternative file, specified by the **-c** option). There are four types of configuration commands:

        phyint <local-addr> [disable] [metric <m>]
               [threshold <t>] [rate_limit <b>]
               [boundary (<boundary-name>|<scoped-addr>/<mask-len>)]
               [altnet <network>/<mask-len>]

        tunnel <local-addr> <remote-addr> [metric <m>]
               [threshold <t>] [rate_limit <b>]
               [boundary (<boundary-name>|<scoped-addr>/<mask-len>)]

    cache_lifetime <ct>

    pruning <off/on>

    name <boundary-name> <scoped-addr>/<mask-len>

The file format is free-form; whitespace (including newlines) is not significant. The *boundary* and
altnet options may be specified as many times as necessary.

The phyint command can be used to disable multicast routing on the physical interface identified by local IP
address *<local-addr>*, or to associate a non-default metric or threshold with the specified physical interface. The local IP address *<local-addr>* may be replaced by the interface name (e.g., le0). If a phyint is
attached to multiple IP subnets, describe each additional subnet with the altnet keyword. Phyint commands
must precede tunnel commands.

The tunnel command can be used to establish a tunnel link between local IP address *<local-addr>* and
remote IP address *<remote-addr>*, and to associate a non-default metric or threshold with that tunnel.
The local IP address *<local-addr>* may be replaced by the interface name (e.g., le0). The remote IP
address *<remote-addr>* may be replaced by a host name, if and only if the host name has a single IP
address associated with it. The tunnel must be set up in the mrouted.conf files of both routers before it can
be used.

The cache_lifetime is a value that determines the amount of time that a cached multicast route stays in kernel
before timing out. The value of this entry should lie between 300 (5 min) and 86400 (1 day). It defaults to
300.

The *pruning* option is provided for **mrouted** to act as a non-pruning router. It is also possible to start
mrouted in a non-pruning mode using the **-p** option on the command line. It is expected that a router
would be configured in this manner for test purposes only. The default mode is pruning enabled.

You may assign names to boundaries to make configuration easier with the name keyword. The boundary
option on phyint or tunnel commands can accept either a name or a boundary.

The metric is the "cost" associated with sending a datagram on the given interface or tunnel; it may be used
to influence the choice of routes. The metric defaults to 1. Metrics should be kept as small as possible,
because **mrouted** cannot route along paths with a sum of metrics greater than 31.

The threshold is the minimum IP time-to-live required for a multicast datagram to be forwarded to the given
interface or tunnel. It is used to control the scope of multicast datagrams. (The TTL of forwarded packets is
only compared to the threshold, it is not decremented by the threshold. Every multicast router decrements
the TTL by 1.) The default threshold is 1.

In general, all **mrouted** connected to a particular subnet or tunnel should use the same metric and threshold
for that subnet or tunnel.

The rate_limit option allows the network administrator to specify a certain bandwidth in Kbits/second which
would be allocated to multicast traffic. It defaults to 500Kbps on tunnels, and 0 (unlimited) on physical

interfaces.

The boundary option allows an interface to be configured as an administrative boundary for the specified scoped address. Packets belonging to this address will not be forwarded on a scoped interface. The boundary option accepts either a name or a boundary spec.

mrouted will not initiate execution if it has fewer than two enabled vifs, where a vif (virtual interface) is either a physical multicast-capable interface or a tunnel. It will log a warning if all of its vifs are tunnels; such an **mrouted** configuration would be better replaced by more direct tunnels (i.e., eliminate the middle man).

EXAMPLE CONFIGURATION
This is an example configuration for a mythical multicast router at a big school.
```
#
# mrouted.conf example
#
# Name our boundaries to make it easier.
name LOCAL 239.255.0.0/16
name EE 239.254.0.0/16
#
# le1 is our gateway to compsci, don't forward our
# local groups to them.
phyint le1 boundary EE
#
# le2 is our interface on the classroom net, it has four
# different length subnets on it.
# Note that you can use either an ip address or an
# interface name
phyint 172.16.12.38 boundary EE altnet 172.16.15.0/26
         altnet 172.16.15.128/26 altnet 172.16.48.0/24
#
# atm0 is our ATM interface, which doesn't properly
# support multicasting.
phyint atm0 disable
#
# This is an internal tunnel to another EE subnet.
# Remove the default tunnel rate limit, since this
# tunnel is over ethernets.
tunnel 192.168.5.4 192.168.55.101 metric 1 threshold 1
         rate_limit 0
#
# This is our tunnel to the outside world.
# Careful with those boundaries, Eugene.
tunnel 192.168.5.4 10.11.12.13 metric 1 threshold 32
         boundary LOCAL boundary EE
```

SIGNALS
mrouted responds to the following signals:

HUP   restarts **mrouted**. The configuration file is reread every time this signal is evoked.

INT   terminates execution gracefully (i.e., by sending good-bye messages to all neighboring routers).

TERM
   same as INT
USR1
   dumps the internal routing tables to `/var/tmp/mrouted.dump`.
USR2
   dumps the internal cache tables to `/var/tmp/mrouted.cache`.
QUIT dumps the internal routing tables to stderr (only if **mrouted** was invoked with a non-zero debug level).

For convenience in sending signals, **mrouted** writes its pid to `/var/run/mrouted.pid` upon startup.

FILES
   `/etc/mrouted.conf`
   `/var/run/mrouted.pid`
   `/var/tmp/mrouted.dump`
   `/var/tmp/mrouted.cache`

EXAMPLES
   The routing tables look like this:

```
Virtual Interface Table
 Vif   Local-Address                     Metric   Thresh   Flags
  0    36.2.0.8        subnet: 36.2         1        1      querier
                       groups: 224.0.2.1
                               224.0.0.4
                       pkts in: 3456
                       pkts out: 2322323

  1    36.11.0.1       subnet: 36.11        1        1      querier
                       groups: 224.0.2.1
                               224.0.1.0
                               224.0.0.4
                       pkts in: 345
                       pkts out: 3456

  2    36.2.0.8        tunnel: 36.8.0.77    3        1
                        peers: 36.8.0.77 (2.2)
                   boundaries: 239.0.1
                            : 239.1.2
                       pkts in: 34545433
                       pkts out: 234342

  3    36.2.0.8     tunnel: 36.6.8.23       3        16

Multicast Routing Table (1136 entries)
 Origin-Subnet   From-Gateway    Metric Tmr In-Vif   Out-Vifs
 36.2                              1     45    0      1* 2  3*
 36.8            36.8.0.77         4     15    2      0* 1* 3*
 36.11                            1     20    1      0* 2  3*
 .
 .
 .
```

In this example, there are four vifs connecting to two subnets and two tunnels. The vif 3 tunnel is not in use (no peer address). The vif 0 and vif 1 subnets have some groups present; tunnels never have any groups. This instance of **mrouted** is the one responsible for sending periodic group membership queries on the vif 0 and vif 1 subnets, as indicated by the "querier" flags. The list of boundaries indicate the scoped addresses on that interface. A count of the number of incoming and outgoing packets is also shown at each interface.

Associated with each subnet from which a multicast datagram can originate is the address of the previous hop router (unless the subnet is directly- connected), the metric of the path back to the origin, the amount of time since we last received an update for this subnet, the incoming vif for multicasts from that origin, and a list of outgoing vifs. "∗" means that the outgoing vif is connected to a leaf of the broadcast tree rooted at the origin, and a multicast datagram from that origin will be forwarded on that outgoing vif only if there are members of the destination group on that leaf.

mrouted also maintains a copy of the kernel forwarding cache table. Entries are created and deleted by **mrouted**.

The cache tables look like this:

```
Multicast Routing Cache Table (147 entries)
 Origin          Mcast-group   CTmr  Age Ptmr IVif Forwvifs
 13.2.116/22     224.2.127.255  3m   2m  -  0  1
>13.2.116.19
>13.2.116.196
 138.96.48/21    224.2.127.255  5m   2m  -  0  1
>138.96.48.108
 128.9.160/20    224.2.127.255  3m   2m  -  0  1
>128.9.160.45
 198.106.194/24  224.2.135.190  9m   28s 9m  0P
>198.106.194.22
```

Each entry is characterized by the origin subnet number and mask and the destination multicast group. The 'CTmr' field indicates the lifetime of the entry. The entry is deleted from the cache table when the timer decrements to zero. The 'Age' field is the time since this cache entry was originally created. Since cache entries get refreshed if traffic is flowing, routing entries can grow very old. The 'Ptmr' field is simply a dash if no prune was sent upstream, or the amount of time until the upstream prune will time out. The 'Ivif' field indicates the incoming vif for multicast packets from that origin. Each router also maintains a record of the number of prunes received from neighboring routers for a particular source and group. If there are no members of a multicast group on any downward link of the multicast tree for a subnet, a prune message is sent to the upstream router. They are indicated by a "P" after the vif number. The Forwvifs field shows the interfaces along which datagrams belonging to the source-group are forwarded. A "p" indicates that no datagrams are being forwarded along that interface. An unlisted interface is a leaf subnet with are no members of the particular group on that subnet. A "b" on an interface indicates that it is a boundary interface, i.e., traffic will not be forwarded on the scoped address on that interface. An additional line with a ">" as the first character is printed for each source on the subnet. Note that there can be many sources in one subnet.

SEE ALSO
map-mbone(8), mrinfo(8), mtrace(8)

DVMRP is described, along with other multicast routing algorithms, in the paper "Multicast Routing in Internetworks and Extended LANs" by S. Deering, in the Proceedings of the ACM SIGCOMM '88 Conference.

AUTHORS
Steve Deering, Ajit Thyagarajan, Bill Fenner

NAME

   mscdlabel — generate disk label from CD track information

SYNOPSIS

   mscdlabel [*device* | *file*]

DESCRIPTION

   mscdlabel is used to generate a NetBSD disk label from track information read from the CD. This way, data of previous sessions of a multi-session CD can be accessed.

   mscdlabel scans the CD's TOC, beginning with the last track. For each data track where an ISO9660 filesystem is identified, basic information (volume label, creation date) is printed and a partition entry added to the in-core disklabel.

   The raw partition (typically partition *c*, but *d* on i386 and some other platforms) is left alone during this process.

   The **mscdlabel** utility can also be used on files or non-CD devices. In this case a single track is assumed. If the device supports disk labels, a label will be written as described above. Otherwise, just the ISO volume label information will be printed.

SEE ALSO

   cdplay(1), disklabel(8), mbrlabel(8)

NAME

mtrace – print multicast path from a source to a receiver

SYNOPSIS

mtrace [**–g** *gateway*] [**–i** *if_addr*] [**–l**] [**–M**] [**–m** *max_hops*] [**–n**] [**–p**] [**–q** *nqueries*] [**–r** *resp_dest*] [**–s**] [**–S** *stat_int*] [**–t** *ttl*] [**–v**] [**–w** *waittime*] *source* [*receiver*] [*group*]

DESCRIPTION

Assessing problems in the distribution of IP multicast traffic can be difficult. **mtrace** uses a tracing feature implemented in multicast routers (**mrouted** version 3.3 and later) that is accessed via an extension to the IGMP protocol. A trace query is passed hop-by-hop along the reverse path from the *receiver* to the *source*, collecting hop addresses, packet counts, and routing error conditions along the path, and then the response is returned to the requestor.

The only required parameter is the *source* host name or address. The default *receiver* is the host running mtrace, and the default *group* is "MBone Audio" (224.2.0.1), which is sufficient if packet loss statistics for a particular multicast group are not needed. These two optional parameters may be specified to test the path to some other receiver in a particular group, subject to some constraints as detailed below. The two parameters can be distinguished because the *receiver* is a unicast address and the *group* is a multicast address.

NOTE: For Solaris 2.4/2.5, if the multicast interface is not the default interface, the -i option must be used to set the local address.

OPTIONS

–g *gwy* Send the trace query via unicast directly to the multicast router *gwy* rather than multicasting the query. This must be the last-hop router on the path from the intended *source* to the *receiver*.

        CAUTION!! Versions 3.3 and 3.5 of **mrouted** will crash if a trace query is received via a unicast packet and **mrouted** has no route for the *source* address. Therefore, do not use the **–g** option unless the target **mrouted** has been verified to be 3.4 or newer than 3.5.

–i *addr* Use *addr* as the local interface address (on a multi-homed host) for sending the trace query and as the default for the *receiver* and the response destination.

–l Loop indefinitely printing packet rate and loss statistics for the multicast path every 10 seconds (see **–S** *stat_int*).

–M Always send the response using multicast rather than attempting unicast first.

–m *n* Set to *n* the maximum number of hops that will be traced from the *receiver* back toward the *source*. The default is 32 hops (infinity for the DVMRP routing protocol).

–n Print hop addresses numerically rather than symbolically and numerically (saves a nameserver address-to-name lookup for each router found on the path).

–q *n* Set the maximum number of query attempts for any hop to *n*. The default is 3.

–p Listen passively for multicast responses from traces initiated by others. This works best when run on a multicast router.

–r *host* Send the trace response to *host* rather than to the host on which **mtrace** is being run, or to a multicast address other than the one registered for this purpose (224.0.1.32).

–s Print a short form output including only the multicast path and not the packet rate and loss statistics.

–S *n* Change the interval between statistics gathering traces to *n* seconds (default 10 seconds).

–t *ttl* Set the *ttl* (time-to-live, or number of hops) for multicast trace queries and responses. The default is 64, except for local queries to the "all routers" multicast group which use ttl 1.

–v Verbose mode; show hop times on the initial trace and statistics display.

$-$**w** *n*   Set the time to wait for a trace response to *n* seconds (default 3 seconds).

USAGE
How It Works
The technique used by the **traceroute** tool to trace unicast network paths will not work for IP multicast because ICMP responses are specifically forbidden for multicast traffic. Instead, a tracing feature has been built into the multicast routers. This technique has the advantage that additional information about packet rates and losses can be accumulated while the number of packets sent is minimized.

Since multicast uses reverse path forwarding, the trace is run backwards from the *receiver* to the *source*. A trace query packet is sent to the last hop multicast router (the leaf router for the desired *receiver* address). The last hop router builds a trace response packet, fills in a report for its hop, and forwards the trace packet using unicast to the router it believes is the previous hop for packets originating from the specified *source*. Each router along the path adds its report and forwards the packet. When the trace response packet reaches the first hop router (the router that is directly connected to the source's net), that router sends the completed response to the response destination address specified in the trace query.

If some multicast router along the path does not implement the multicast traceroute feature or if there is some outage, then no response will be returned. To solve this problem, the trace query includes a maximum hop count field to limit the number of hops traced before the response is returned. That allows a partial path to be traced.

The reports inserted by each router contain not only the address of the hop, but also the ttl required to forward and some flags to indicate routing errors, plus counts of the total number of packets on the incoming and outgoing interfaces and those forwarded for the specified *group*. Taking differences in these counts for two traces separated in time and comparing the output packet counts from one hop with the input packet counts of the next hop allows the calculation of packet rate and packet loss statistics for each hop to isolate congestion problems.

Finding the Last-Hop Router
The trace query must be sent to the multicast router which is the last hop on the path from the *source* to the *receiver*. If the receiver is on the local subnet (as determined using the subnet mask), then the default method is to multicast the trace query to all-routers.mcast.net (224.0.0.2) with a ttl of 1. Otherwise, the trace query is multicast to the *group* address since the last hop router will be a member of that group if the receiver is. Therefore it is necessary to specify a group that the intended receiver has joined. This multicast is sent with a default ttl of 64, which may not be sufficient for all cases (changed with the $-$**t** option). If the last hop router is known, it may also be addressed directly using the $-$**g** option. Alternatively, if it is desired to trace a group that the receiver has not joined, but it is known that the last-hop router is a member of another group, the $-$**g** option may also be used to specify a different multicast address for the trace query.

When tracing from a multihomed host or router, the default receiver address may not be the desired interface for the path from the source. In that case, the desired interface should be specified explicitly as the *receiver*.

Directing the Response
By default, **mtrace** first attempts to trace the full reverse path, unless the number of hops to trace is explicitly set with the $-$**m** option. If there is no response within a 3 second timeout interval (changed with the $-$**w** option), a "*" is printed and the probing switches to hop-by-hop mode. Trace queries are issued starting with a maximum hop count of one and increasing by one until the full path is traced or no response is received. At each hop, multiple probes are sent (default is three, changed with $-$**q** option). The first half of the attempts (default is one) are made with the unicast address of the host running **mtrace** as the destination for the response. Since the unicast route may be blocked, the remainder of attempts request that the response be multicast to mtrace.mcast.net (224.0.1.32) with the ttl set to 32 more than what's needed to pass the thresholds seen so far along the path to the receiver. For the last quarter of the attempts (default is one), the ttl is increased by another 32 each time up to a maximum of 192. Alternatively, the ttl may be set explicitly with the $-$**t** option and/or the initial unicast attempts can be forced to use multicast instead with the $-$**M** option. For each attempt, if no response is received within the timeout, a "*" is printed. After the specified number of attempts have failed, **mtrace** will try to query the next hop router with a DVMRP_ASK_NEIGHBORS2 request (as used by the **mrinfo** program) to see what kind of router it is.

EXAMPLES

The output of **mtrace** is in two sections. The first section is a short listing of the hops in the order they are queried, that is, in the reverse of the order from the *source* to the *receiver*. For each hop, a line is printed showing the hop number (counted negatively to indicate that this is the reverse path); the multicast routing protocol (DVMRP, MOSPF, PIM, etc.); the threshold required to forward data (to the previous hop in the listing as indicated by the up-arrow character); and the cumulative delay for the query to reach that hop (valid only if the clocks are synchronized). This first section ends with a line showing the round-trip time which measures the interval from when the query is issued until the response is received, both derived from the local system clock. A sample use and output might be:

```
oak.isi.edu 80# mtrace -l caraway.lcs.mit.edu 224.2.0.3
Mtrace from 18.26.0.170 to 128.9.160.100 via group 224.2.0.3
Querying full reverse path...
  0  oak.isi.edu (128.9.160.100)
 -1  cub.isi.edu (128.9.160.153)   DVMRP   thresh^ 1   3 ms
 -2  la.dart.net (140.173.128.1)   DVMRP   thresh^ 1   14 ms
 -3  dc.dart.net (140.173.64.1)    DVMRP   thresh^ 1   50 ms
 -4  bbn.dart.net (140.173.32.1)   DVMRP   thresh^ 1   63 ms
 -5  mit.dart.net (140.173.48.2)   DVMRP   thresh^ 1   71 ms
 -6  caraway.lcs.mit.edu (18.26.0.170)
Round trip time 124 ms
```

The second section provides a pictorial view of the path in the forward direction with data flow indicated by arrows pointing downward and the query path indicated by arrows pointing upward. For each hop, both the entry and exit addresses of the router are shown if different, along with the initial ttl required on the packet in order to be forwarded at this hop and the propagation delay across the hop assuming that the routers at both ends have synchronized clocks. The right half of this section is composed of several columns of statistics in two groups. Within each group, the columns are the number of packets lost, the number of packets sent, the percentage lost, and the average packet rate at each hop. These statistics are calculated from differences between traces and from hop to hop as explained above. The first group shows the statistics for all traffic flowing out the interface at one hop and in the interface at the next hop. The second group shows the statistics only for traffic forwarded from the specified *source* to the specified *group*.

These statistics are shown on one or two lines for each hop. Without any options, this second section of the output is printed only once, approximately 10 seconds after the initial trace. One line is shown for each hop showing the statistics over that 10-second period. If the **−l** option is given, the second section is repeated every 10 seconds and two lines are shown for each hop. The first line shows the statistics for the last 10 seconds, and the second line shows the cumulative statistics over the period since the initial trace, which is 101 seconds in the example below. The second section of the output is omitted if the **−s** option is set.

```
Waiting to accumulate statistics... Results after 101 seconds:

    Source          Response Dest   Packet Statistics For    Only For Traffic
    18.26.0.170     128.9.160.100   All Multicast Traffic    From 18.26.0.170
        |         __/ rtt   125 ms  Lost/Sent = Pct  Rate      To 224.2.0.3
        v        /   hop   65 ms    --------------------     ------------------
    18.26.0.144
    140.173.48.2    mit.dart.net
        |      ^       ttl   1       0/6    = --%   0 pps    0/2   = --%   0 pps
        v      |       hop   8 ms    1/52   = 2%    0 pps    0/18  = 0%    0 pps
    140.173.48.1
    140.173.32.1    bbn.dart.net
        |      ^       ttl   2       0/6    = --%   0 pps    0/2   = --%   0 pps
        v      |       hop   12 ms   1/52   = 2%    0 pps    0/18  = 0%    0 pps
    140.173.32.2
    140.173.64.1    dc.dart.net
        |      ^       ttl   3       0/271  = 0%    27 pps   0/2   = --%   0 pps
```

```
        v   |      hop   34 ms   -1/2652  =  0%   26 pps   0/18 =  0%   0 pps
140.173.64.2
140.173.128.1  la.dart.net
        |     ^     ttl    4     -2/831   =  0%   83 pps   0/2  = --%   0 pps
        v   |      hop   11 ms   -3/8072  =  0%   79 pps   0/18 =  0%   0 pps
140.173.128.2
128.9.160.153  cub.isi.edu
        |    \__    ttl    5      833           83 pps     2           0 pps
        v    \ hop  -8 ms         8075          79 pps    18           0 pps
128.9.160.100  128.9.160.100
   Receiver      Query Source
```

Because the packet counts may be changing as the trace query is propagating, there may be small errors (off by 1 or 2) in these statistics. However, those errors should not accumulate, so the cumulative statistics line should increase in accuracy as a new trace is run every 10 seconds. There are two sources of larger errors, both of which show up as negative losses:

- If the input to a node is from a multi-access network with more than one other node attached, then the input count will be (close to) the sum of the output counts from all the attached nodes, but the output count from the previous hop on the traced path will be only part of that. Hence the output count minus the input count will be negative.
- In release 3.3 of the DVMRP multicast forwarding software for SunOS and other systems, a multicast packet generated on a router will be counted as having come in an interface even though it did not. This creates the negative loss that can be seen in the example above.

Note that these negative losses may mask positive losses.

In the example, there is also one negative hop time. This simply indicates a lack of synchronization between the system clocks across that hop. This example also illustrates how the percentage loss is shown as two dashes when the number of packets sent is less than 10 because the percentage would not be statistically valid.

A second example shows a trace to a receiver that is not local; the query is sent to the last-hop router with the **-g** option. In this example, the trace of the full reverse path resulted in no response because there was a node running an old version of **mrouted** that did not implement the multicast traceroute function, so **mtrace** switched to hop-by-hop mode. The "Route pruned" error code indicates that traffic for group 224.2.143.24 would not be forwarded.

```
oak.isi.edu 108# mtrace -g 140.173.48.2 204.62.246.73 \
                       butter.lcs.mit.edu 224.2.143.24
Mtrace from 204.62.246.73 to 18.26.0.151 via group 224.2.143.24
Querying full reverse path... * switching to hop-by-hop:
  0  butter.lcs.mit.edu (18.26.0.151)
 -1  jam.lcs.mit.edu (18.26.0.144)  DVMRP  thresh^ 1  33 ms  Route pruned
 -2  bbn.dart.net (140.173.48.1)  DVMRP  thresh^ 1  36 ms
 -3  dc.dart.net (140.173.32.2)  DVMRP  thresh^ 1  44 ms
 -4  darpa.dart.net (140.173.240.2)  DVMRP  thresh^ 16  47 ms
 -5  * * * noc.hpc.org (192.187.8.2) [mrouted 2.2] didn't respond
Round trip time 95 ms
```

AUTHOR

Implemented by Steve Casner based on an initial prototype written by Ajit Thyagarajan. The multicast traceroute mechanism was designed by Van Jacobson with help from Steve Casner, Steve Deering, Dino Farinacci, and Deb Agrawal; it was implemented in **mrouted** by Ajit Thyagarajan and Bill Fenner. The option syntax and the output format of **mtrace** are modeled after the unicast **traceroute** program written by Van Jacobson.

SEE ALSO
     mrouted(8), **mrinfo**(8), **map-mbone**(8), **traceroute**(8)

NAME

mtree — map a directory hierarchy

SYNOPSIS

mtree [**-CcDdeLlMPrSUuWx**] [**-i** | **-m**] [**-E** *tags*] [**-f** *spec*] [**-I** *tags*] [**-K** *keywords*]
     [**-k** *keywords*] [**-N** *dbdir*] [**-p** *path*] [**-R** *keywords*] [**-s** *seed*]
     [**-X** *exclude-file*]

DESCRIPTION

The **mtree** utility compares a file hierarchy against a specification, creates a specification for a file hierarchy, or modifies a specification.

The default action, if not overridden by command line options, is to compare the file hierarchy rooted in the current directory against a specification read from the standard input. Messages are written to the standard output for any files whose characteristics do not match the specification, or which are missing from either the file hierarchy or the specification.

The options are as follows:

-C
Convert a specification into a format that's easier to parse with various tools. The input specification is read from standard input or from the file given by **-f** *spec*. In the output, each file or directory is represented using a single line (which might be very long). The full path name (beginning with "./") is always printed as the first field; **-k**, **-K**, and **-R** can be used to control which other keywords are printed; **-E** and **-I** can be used to control which files are printed; **-S** option can be used to sort the output.

-c
Print a specification for the file hierarchy originating at the current working directory (or the directory provided by **-p** *path*) to the standard output. The output is in a style using relative path names.

-D
As per **-C**, except that the path name is always printed as the last field instead of the first.

-d
Ignore everything except directory type files.

-E *tags*
Add the comma separated tags to the "exclusion" list. Non-directories with tags which are in the exclusion list are not printed with **-C** and **-D**.

-e
Don't complain about files that are in the file hierarchy, but not in the specification.

-f *spec*
Read the specification from *file*, instead of from the standard input.

-I *tags*
Add the comma separated tags to the "inclusion" list. Non-directories with tags which are in the inclusion list are printed with **-C** and **-D**. If no inclusion list is provided, the default is to display all files.

-i
If specified, set the schg and/or sappnd flags.

-K *keywords*
Add the specified (whitespace or comma separated) keywords to the current set of keywords. If all is specified, add all of the other keywords.

-k *keywords*
Use the **type** keyword plus the specified (whitespace or comma separated) keywords instead of the current set of keywords. If all is specified, use all of the other keywords. If the **type** keyword is not desired, suppress it with **-R** *type*.

-L	Follow all symbolic links in the file hierarchy.
-l	Do "loose" permissions checks, in which more stringent permissions will match less stringent ones. For example, a file marked mode 0444 will pass a check for mode 0644. "Loose" checks apply only to read, write and execute permissions -- in particular, if other bits like the sticky bit or suid/sgid bits are set either in the specification or the file, exact checking will be performed. This option may not be set at the same time as the **-u** or **-U** option.
-M	Permit merging of specification entries with different types, with the last entry take precedence.
-m	If the schg and/or sappnd flags are specified, reset these flags. Note that this is only possible with securelevel less than 1 (i.e., in single user mode or while the system is running in insecure mode). See init(8) for information on security levels.
-N *dbdir*	Use the user database text file master.passwd and group database text file group from *dbdir*, rather than using the results from the system's getpwnam(3) and getgrnam(3) (and related) library calls.
-P	Don't follow symbolic links in the file hierarchy, instead consider the symbolic link itself in any comparisons. This is the default.
-p *path*	Use the file hierarchy rooted in *path*, instead of the current directory.
-R *keywords*	Remove the specified (whitespace or comma separated) keywords from the current set of keywords. If all is specified, remove all of the other keywords.
-r	Remove any files in the file hierarchy that are not described in the specification.
-S	When reading a specification into an internal data structure, sort the entries. Sorting will affect the order of the output produced by the **-C** or **-D** options, and will also affect the order in which missing entries are created or reported when a directory tree is checked against a specification.
	The sort order is the same as that used by the **-c** option, which is that entries within the same directory are sorted in the order used by strcmp(3), except that entries for subdirectories sort after other entries. By default, if the **-S** option is not used, entries within the same directory are collected together (separated from entries for other directories), but not sorted.
-s *seed*	Display a single checksum to the standard error output that represents all of the files for which the keyword **cksum** was specified. The checksum is seeded with the specified value.
-t	Modify the modified time of existing files, the device type of devices, and symbolic link targets, to match the specification.
-U	Same as **-u** except that a mismatch is not considered to be an error if it was corrected.
-u	Modify the owner, group, permissions, and flags of existing files, the device type of devices, and symbolic link targets, to match the specification. Create any missing directories, devices or symbolic links. User, group, and permissions must all be specified for missing directories to be created. Note that unless the **-i** option is given, the schg and sappnd flags will not be set, even if specified. If **-m** is given, these flags will be reset. Exit with a status of 0 on success, 2 if the file hierarchy did not match the specification, and 1 if any other error occurred.

-w   Don't attempt to set various file attributes such as the ownership, mode, flags, or time when creating new directories or changing existing entries. This option will be most useful when used in conjunction with **-u** or **-U**.

-X *exclude-file* The specified file contains fnmatch(3) patterns matching files to be excluded from the specification, one to a line. If the pattern contains a '/' character, it will be matched against entire pathnames (relative to the starting directory); otherwise, it will be matched against basenames only. Comments are permitted in the *exclude-list* file.

-x   Don't descend below mount points in the file hierarchy.

Specifications are mostly composed of "keywords", i.e. strings that that specify values relating to files. No keywords have default values, and if a keyword has no value set, no checks based on it are performed.

Currently supported keywords are as follows:

cksum   The checksum of the file using the default algorithm specified by the cksum(1) utility.

device   The device number to use for **block** or **char** file types. The argument must be one of the following forms:

      format,major,minor
        A device with *major* and *minor* fields, for an operating system specified with *format*. See below for valid formats.

      format,major,unit,subunit
        A device with *major*, *unit*, and *subunit* fields, for an operating system specified with *format*. (Currently this is only supported by the **bsdos** format.)

      number
        Opaque number (as stored on the file system).

      The following values for *format* are recognized: **native**, **386bsd**, **4bsd**, **bsdos**, **freebsd**, **hpux**, **isc**, **linux**, **netbsd**, **osf1**, **sco**, **solaris**, **sunos**, **svr3**, **svr4**, and **ultrix**.

      See mknod(8) for more details.

flags   The file flags as a symbolic name. See chflags(1) for information on these names. If no flags are to be set the string none may be used to override the current default. Note that the schg and sappnd flags are treated specially (see the **-i** and **-m** options).

ignore   Ignore any file hierarchy below this file.

gid   The file group as a numeric value.

gname   The file group as a symbolic name.

link   The file the symbolic link is expected to reference.

md5   The MD5 cryptographic message digest of the file.

md5digest   Synonym for **md5**.

mode   The current file's permissions as a numeric (octal) or symbolic value.

nlink   The number of hard links the file is expected to have.

optional   The file is optional; don't complain about the file if it's not in the file hierarchy.

rmd160   The RMD-160 cryptographic message digest of the file.

rmd160digest	Synonym for **rmd160**.
sha1	The SHA-1 cryptographic message digest of the file.
sha1digest	Synonym for **sha1**.
sha256	The 256-bits SHA-2 cryptographic message digest of the file.
sha256digest	Synonym for **sha256**.
sha384	The 384-bits SHA-2 cryptographic message digest of the file.
sha384digest	Synonym for **sha384**.
sha512	The 512-bits SHA-2 cryptographic message digest of the file.
sha512digest	Synonym for **sha512**.
size	The size, in bytes, of the file.
tags	Comma delimited tags to be matched with **−E** and **−I**. These may be specified without leading or trailing commas, but will be stored internally with them.
time	The last modification time of the file.
type	The type of the file; may be set to any one of the following:

block	block special device
char	character special device
dir	directory
fifo	fifo
file	regular file
link	symbolic link
socket	socket

uid	The file owner as a numeric value.
uname	The file owner as a symbolic name.

The default set of keywords are **flags**, **gid**, **link**, **mode**, **nlink**, **size**, **time**, **type**, and **uid**.

There are four types of lines in a specification:

1. Set global values for a keyword. This consists of the string /set followed by whitespace, followed by sets of keyword/value pairs, separated by whitespace. Keyword/value pairs consist of a keyword, followed by an equals sign ('='), followed by a value, without whitespace characters. Once a keyword has been set, its value remains unchanged until either reset or unset.

2. Unset global values for a keyword. This consists of the string /unset, followed by whitespace, followed by one or more keywords, separated by whitespace. If all is specified, unset all of the keywords.

3. A file specification, consisting of a path name, followed by whitespace, followed by zero or more whitespace separated keyword/value pairs.

    The path name may be preceded by whitespace characters. The path name may contain any of the standard path name matching characters ('[', ']', '?' or '*'), in which case files in the hierarchy will be associated with the first pattern that they match. **mtree** uses strsvis(3) (in VIS_CSTYLE format) to encode path names containing non-printable characters. Whitespace characters are encoded as '\s' (space), '\t' (tab), and '\n' (new line). '#' characters in path names are escaped by a preceding backslash '\' to distinguish them from comments.

Each of the keyword/value pairs consist of a keyword, followed by an equals sign ('='), followed by the keyword's value, without whitespace characters. These values override, without changing, the global value of the corresponding keyword.

The first path name entry listed must be a directory named '.', as this ensures that intermixing full and relative path names will work consistently and correctly. Multiple entries for a directory named '.' are permitted; the settings for the last such entry override those of the existing entry.

A path name that contains a slash ('/') that is not the first character will be treated as a full path (relative to the root of the tree). All parent directories referenced in the path name must exist. The current directory path used by relative path names will be updated appropriately. Multiple entries for the same full path are permitted if the types are the same (unless **−M** is given, and then the types may differ); in this case the settings for the last entry take precedence.

A path name that does not contain a slash will be treated as a relative path. Specifying a directory will cause subsequent files to be searched for in that directory hierarchy.

4.   A line containing only the string '..' which causes the current directory path (used by relative paths) to ascend one level.

Empty lines and lines whose first non-whitespace character is a hash mark ('#') are ignored.

The **mtree** utility exits with a status of 0 on success, 1 if any error occurred, and 2 if the file hierarchy did not match the specification.

FILES
/etc/mtree system specification directory

EXAMPLES
To detect system binaries that have been "trojan horsed", it is recommended that **mtree** be run on the file systems, and a copy of the results stored on a different machine, or, at least, in encrypted form. The seed for the **−s** option should not be an obvious value and the final checksum should not be stored on-line under any circumstances! Then, periodically, **mtree** should be run against the on-line specifications and the final checksum compared with the previous value. While it is possible for the bad guys to change the on-line specifications to conform to their modified binaries, it shouldn't be possible for them to make it produce the same final checksum value. If the final checksum value changes, the off-line copies of the specification can be used to detect which of the binaries have actually been modified.

The **−d** and **−u** options can be used in combination to create directory hierarchies for distributions and other such things.

SEE ALSO
chflags(1), chgrp(1), chmod(1), cksum(1), stat(2), fnmatch(3), fts(3), strsvis(3), chown(8), mknod(8)

HISTORY
The **mtree** utility appeared in 4.3 BSD–Reno. The **optional** keyword appeared in NetBSD 1.2. The **−U** option appeared in NetBSD 1.3. The **flags** and **md5** keywords, and **−i** and **−m** options appeared in NetBSD 1.4. The **device**, **rmd160**, **sha1**, **tags**, and **all** keywords, **−D**, **−E**, **−I**, **−l**, **−L**, **−N**, **−P**, **−R**, **−W**, and **−X** options, and support for full paths appeared in NetBSD 1.6. The **sha256**, **sha384**, and **sha512** keywords appeared in NetBSD 3.0. The **−S** option appeared in NetBSD 6.0.

NAME

    multiboot — procedure for booting NetBSD/i386 from a Multiboot-compliant boot loader

DESCRIPTION

    Multiboot is a specification that defines a protocol between a boot loader and a kernel. This protocol allows passing boot information between the two in a standard way, allowing any Multiboot-compliant boot loader to boot any Multiboot-compliant kernel. The NetBSD kernel supports Multiboot if it was compiled with **options MULTIBOOT** (the default in the 'GENERIC' and 'GENERIC_LAPTOP' configurations).

    Unlike when using the native boot loader, the NetBSD kernel recognizes a set of command line arguments if booted through a Multiboot-compliant boot loader. This is because the Multiboot protocol is not complete enough to completely configure a NetBSD kernel.

    The following arguments are recognized:

console   Specifies the console device name. Can be one of 'com' or 'pc'. If the former, *console_addr* and *console_speed* should be given too.

console_addr   Specifies the serial port address for the console. Defaults to the value of **options CONADDR** or '0x3f8' if this was not given.

console_speed   Specifies the serial port speed for the console. Defaults to the value of **options CONSPEED** or '9600' if this was not given.

root   Specifies the name of the device to be mounted as the root partition. It should not be needed because the kernel tries its best to guess which is the root partition (basing the decision on the device from which the kernel was loaded from). In cases where the automatic detection fails, this flag comes useful. Example: 'root=wd0e'.

Booting with GRUB Legacy

    GRUB Legacy is the most popular bootloader that supports Multiboot. You can boot a NetBSD kernel (assuming it is compiled with Multiboot support) with a line similar to the following one:

```
kernel (fd0)/netbsd.gz -c console=pc root=wd0e
```

SEE ALSO

    options(4)

HISTORY

    multiboot support first appeared in NetBSD 4.0.

AUTHORS

    multiboot support was added by Julio M. Merino Vidal ⟨jmmv@NetBSD.org⟩.